# THE

# 100

## BEST

# STOCKS

# YOU CAN BUY

# 2006

*John Slatter, C.F.A.*

Adams Media
Avon, Massachusetts

## Dedication

To my best friend, Beverly G. Slatter, RN

## Acknowledgments

Writing a book is far easier than finding a publisher. My first book, *Safe Investing*, didn't find a home until I latched on to my dutiful agent, Edythea Ginis Selman. Edy knows how to find a publisher, and she knows how to convince the editor that I am worth paying a living wage.

My publisher, Adams Media, has treated me like a king. That could be because my editors are Jill Alexander and Larry Shea, easy people to do business with.

Also, a vote of thanks to George G. Morris, CFA, my broker with Wachovia Securities, who helped me gather research. If you need a full-service broker, George is your man in Cleveland at (800) 537-4105.

---

Published by Adams Media, an F+W Publications Company
57 Littlefield Street
Avon, MA 02322
*www.adamsmedia.com*

ISBN: 1-59337-378-3

Printed in the United States of America.
J I H G F E D C B A

Library of Congress Cataloging-in-Publication Data
available from publisher.

This publication is designed to provide accurate and authoritative information with regard to the subject matter covered. It is sold with the understanding that the publisher is not engaged in rendering legal, accounting, or other professional advice. If legal advice or other expert assistance is required, the services of a competent professional person should be sought.

—From a *Declaration of Principles* jointly adopted by a Committee of the American Bar Association and a Committee of Publishers and Associations

Many of the designations used by manufacturers and sellers to distinguish their product are claimed as trademarks. Where those designations appear in this book and Adams Media was aware of a trademark claim, the designations have been printed with initial capital letters.

This book is available at quantity discounts for bulk purchases.
For information, please call 1-800-872-5627.

# Contents

# Part I

# The Art and Science of Investing in Stocks

# Is This the Right Investment Book for You?

The last time I stopped by the investment section of my local bookstore, there was no shortage of books about investing in the stock market. Fortunately, several copies of the latest edition of *The 100 Best Stocks You Can Buy* were prominently displayed.

However, I saw only one lonely soul trying to find a book to his liking. I was tempted to suggest that mine was the best one on the shelf. But I refrained. I recalled that on my previous trip to the bookstore I made a similar suggestion and had been totally ignored. He didn't even look up to see who was offering him this sage advice. (I was tempted to report that recalcitrant cad to the manager but thought better of it.)

Since you have the book in your hands and are wondering whether this is the one for you, let me give you a song and dance that will convince you that your search has ended; you don't need to look any further.

To begin, let me congratulate you on making the decision to educate yourself on the intricacies of the stock market. Many people totally ignore the importance of saving money for the future. It could be that they believe their company 401(k), along with Social Security, will do the job. The odds are that you will need more, particularly if you work for a firm that insists your 401(k) should be stuffed with your employer's company stock.

If you want to build a solid portfolio, it makes better sense to buy stocks on a regular basis—at least once a year. I suggest setting aside at least 10 percent of your gross income every year for stock purchases. And don't skip a year because you don't like the antics of the stock market at that particular time. Forecasting the market is a no-no. You can't do it—nor can anyone else.

## Why People Don't Read about Investing

One reason that people don't read about investing is that they are overwhelmed by the complexity of the financial scene. I heartily concur—it *is* overwhelming. That's because there are thousands of mutual funds, common stocks, preferred stocks, certificates of deposit, options, bonds, annuities, and assorted investment products.

Even if you simply confined your search to the stocks listed on the New York Stock Exchange, the task would be daunting, since some 3,000 stocks are traded there. Or you might decide to "Let George do it," by investing in mutual funds. There, too, you will encounter infinite decisions, since there are more than 14,000 mutual funds—most of which underperform such market indexes as the Dow Jones Industrial Average (called the Dow, Dow Jones, or DJIA) or the Standard & Poor's 500 (S&P 500).

If you are like many buyers of my books, you are not a sophisticated investor. You have a good job, have an income that is well above average, and you are serious about your career. That means that you spend time improving yourself by reading trade journals and taking courses at a local college.

## Why Not Burn the Midnight Oil?

In other words, your day is already taken up with reading. How can you possibly start poring over annual reports, Standard & Poor's reports, *Fortune, Value Line Investment Survey,* the *Wall Street Journal, Forbes, BusinessWeek, Barron's,* and a half-dozen books on the stock market? Easy. Drink lots of coffee and stay up until two in the morning.

If you object to this routine, you will be better off with my book, since I try to make investing a lot simpler than you thought it would be. For one thing, my style of writing is easy to understand. At least that's what people tell me.

Incidentally, I am one of the few authors who take calls from readers. My address and phone number are on page 365. I assume you will confine your calls to regular business hours, based on Eastern Standard Time, since I live in Vermont.

Whenever I buy a book, I always check to see if the writer has good credentials. For my part, I have been on the investment scene for a good forty years. I started as a plain vanilla stockbroker, and then became editor of a publication devoted to mutual funds, followed by several years as a securities analyst for a brokerage firm. I spent a few years as a portfolio manager and started operating my own firm, managing portfolios on a fee basis for investors with assets of $150,000 or more.

During these years, I did a lot of writing, first for *Barron's Financial Weekly*, and later for such publications as *Physician's Management* and *Better Investing*. During the same period, I wrote tons of reports on stocks for the brokerage firms that paid my salary. In recent years, I have written a slew of books: *Safe Investing, Straight Talk About Stock Investing*, and nine previous editions of *The 100 Best Stocks You Can Buy*.

I also wrote two great novels, but no publisher seems to agree that they are great, so I am not currently getting royalties on those.

As I mentioned previously, the number of stocks and mutual funds out there is infinite. Besides the 3,000 stocks on the New York Stock Exchange, plus the thousands of mutual funds, there are also thousands of stocks listed on the Nasdaq and thousands more traded on markets in Europe, Asia, Latin America, and Canada.

The beauty of my book is that I whittle the number of stocks you need to know about down to 100. Among those 100 are four types of stocks, depending on your particular temperament: Income, Growth and Income, Conservative Growth, and Aggressive Growth.

## Diversification, the First Rule of Investing

Of course, there is no need to confine your investing exclusively to one category. A well-diversified portfolio could have half a dozen from each sector. Incidentally, diversity is the key to investing. Whenever you concentrate on one type of stock, such as technology, energy, banks, utilities, or pharmaceuticals, you expose yourself to extra risk. Don't do it. Let me emphasize that again—don't do it.

When I was a portfolio strategist in Cleveland a few years ago, I examined portfolios submitted to our firm for analysis. About 100 percent of them were not diversified. They were typically concentrated in only three industries: public utilities, banks, and oil.

Before you make up your mind about which stocks to buy, you will want to collect some information. If you have access to a brokerage house, you can easily get a copy of a report called *Value Line Investment Survey*. You can also subscribe yourself, but be prepared to spend over $500 a year for this service, which covers about 1,700 well-known stocks. A less expensive alternative is the same service limited to 600 stocks. Still another good source is Standard & Poor's tear sheets, which can be obtained from a broker or library. Finally, most brokerage houses have a staff of analysts that turn out reports on a multitude of stocks.

## My Sources of Information

A final source of information is this book, which is updated every year. I believe that my write-ups are valuable in ways that the other sources are not. When I first began writing this series of books, I obtained my information from each company's annual report, as well as from the two services mentioned.

Now, I go much further afield. On a daily basis, I collect information on these companies from such sources as *Barron's, Forbes, Better Investing, BusinessWeek,* and other monthly investment publications. In addition, I consult well-known newspapers across the country, including the *Boston Globe,* the *New York Times,* as well as papers in Chicago, Philadelphia, Atlanta, Denver, St. Louis, Houston, Milwaukee, Los Angeles, Detroit, San Francisco, Miami, and Dallas.

Whenever I see an article on one of my companies, I clip it out and file it for future reference and examine it again when I sit at my computer to prepare a report. Using this vast collection, I sift through the facts to find the reasons that this stock is attractive. I also look for factors that have a negative tone. In other words, I don't want to give you a purely one-sided view of this stock. By contrast, if you read the company's annual report, you will only hear about the attributes of the company and not about its problems and deficiencies.

Similarly, if you read a report from a brokerage house, it is rarely negative. The analyst normally tells you to buy—rarely to sell. One reason for this is the tie brokerage houses have to these companies that can lead to extremely lucrative underwriting and corporate finance deals. If the analyst tells investors to avoid the stock, the company may decide to avoid the brokerage house and give its business to someone else.

Obviously, I have no reason to be anything but unbiased.

## Forty Years of Experience Is the Key

Finally, the 100 stocks have to be selected. The publisher is not the one who picks the stocks. I do. My forty years of varied experience on the investment scene give me an edge in this regard. And, of course, I am intimately involved in stock selection from a personal perspective. I have a large portfolio of stocks, over fifty at present, which have made my wife and me millionaires.

If you would like to reach the same comfortable plateau, why not invest $14.95 and start reading?

Oh, and here's one more thing. If you read the rest of these introductory chapters, you will see that I have provided a helpful glossary that explains all the terms you need to know to understand the fundamentals of investing.

I also have a chapter on asset allocation that will tell you what percentage of your holdings should be in stocks and how much in such fixed-income vehicles as bonds and money-market funds. Finally, there also are chapters on how I select my stocks, an intriguing way to reduce risk, and still another on how to analyze stocks. There is also a short chapter that focuses on the four essentials of successful investing. You'll be surprised at how simple investing can be if you read this chapter.

# What's Wrong with Buying Mutual Funds?

When I picked up the phone, there seemed to be no one on the line, so I hung up. I was certain it was a telemarketer trying to sell me something I didn't want. Then the phone rang again, and the voice on the other end said, "Mr. Slatter, you hung up on me before I could get in a word in edgewise. I just finished reading your book, and I wanted to ask you a few questions. Is this a bad time?"

"I guess I goofed. I get so many marketing calls that I am quick to hang up—particularly when there is an empty pause, with no one speaking. That usually means I am about to be subjected to a sales pitch."

"Thank you for explaining, Mr. Slatter." she said. "My name is Rosario Santos, and I wanted to let you know that your 2005 edition was superb. Before I bought it, I looked at thirty or forty investment books. I am convinced that I made the right choice. Your book is insightful, readable, thorough, and full of useful bits of information. Besides, it was really fun to read. I intend to buy a few copies and give them as presents to my friends and relatives."

"I'm glad you called back Ms. Santos. After what the market did today, I needed someone to cheer me up. You said you had some questions . . ."

"Most people call me Rose. There is one thing about your book that disturbs me. I have been buying mutual funds, rather than individual stocks. Now I find out that maybe I should change my strategy. You seem to have some negative views of mutual funds."

"I hope it's okay to call you Rose," I said. "You can call me Slats."

"Yes, feel free to call me Rose."

"There was a time when I was a staunch defender of mutual funds, Rose, back when I was editor of a magazine called *Your Tomorrow.* I always stressed that mutual funds had two attributes: diversification and professional management. I still believe that diversification is important—in fact, critically important—but I am not sure that professional management is something to brag about. Most mutual funds perform worse than the market. In the period from 1984 through 2002, the Standard & Poor's index of 500 stocks climbed at an average annual rate of 12.2 percent. In that same span, equity mutual funds—those that invest in common stocks—performed much worse, averaging only 9.3 percent."

"How can that be? How can all these experts be so inept? Don't they have special training and advanced degrees?"

"Right on both counts. Most have such degrees as CFA (chartered financial analyst) or an MBA (a master's degree in business). Some may even have doctorates. In short, they are well educated and have high IQs."

"That's what I thought," said Rosario Santos. "Do you have any explanation of what's going on?"

"Absolutely," I said. "In today's market, a huge percentage of trades are made by these professionals, the people who manage endowment funds, mutual funds, closed-end funds, as well as those who work for banks or insurance companies or who manage accounts for individual investors.

"What it amounts to is this: you have professionals buying and selling to other professionals. In effect, one expert who thinks a stock is attractive is buying shares of a stock from another manager who is convinced it's time to sell."

"In other words, there are no dummies in the equation," said Rosario Santos. "Is there anything else?"

"Yes. The really big factor is the cost of running the fund, including the expense ratio, which is the fee you are paying for someone to handle your account. Let me quote you from an article by John C. Bogle for the *Wall Street Journal* on July 8, 2003. Mr. Bogle is pretty prominent in mutual fund circles and was the founder and former CEO of the Vanguard Group, one of the giants of the industry. He also served as chairman of the Board of Governors of the Investment Company Institute from 1968 to 1970. Here's what Jack Bogle had to say:

"The costs of playing the game are surprisingly large. They include mutual-fund expense ratios, which reached an all-time high of 1.6 percent of equity-fund assets last year (2002). Turnover costs, by conservative estimates, total another eight-tenths of 1 percent, as fund sales of portfolio securities now exceed 100 percent of equity-fund assets. Adding the impact of sales charges, out-of-pocket fees, and other expenses, 'all-in' costs for the average equity fund come to as much as 3 percent per year—not surprisingly, very close to the 2.9 percentage points by which the annual returns of mutual funds lagged the stock market during 1984–2002."

"What you are saying, Mr. Slatter, is that the managers who pick the stocks are not the culprits. It's the costs that make the difference."

"I think that's the answer, Rose. What that means for you is that if you can build your own portfolio—using my book, of course—you have a good chance of doing better than the average mutual fund, since you can avoid most of those costs."

"Thank you for all your help, Slats. I think I'll read your book again. I know you're a busy man, so I'll be on my way."

"Don't be in such a hurry, Rose. That's not the end of the story. There are a few other reasons to avoid mutual funds."

"I'm listening."

"To begin with, picking a mutual fund is not that easy. As Jack Bogle puts it, there is a 'bewildering array of choices among nearly 5,000 equity funds.' That number is even greater than the number of stocks listed on the New York Stock Exchange—about 3,000. If you decide to check the credentials of all 5,000 funds, it might take you a while. What's more, there are no criteria for making a selection."

"Why not use one of the recommended lists put out by the financial magazines?" asked Rosario Santos.

"Some people do, but I doubt that they end up very rich. Studies show that such recommendations often fail to do as well as funds in general—which, of course, is not that good. Many people use past performance as a guide in making their selections. If a fund was up 87 percent last year, they latch onto it, expecting it will continue to post extraordinary gains. Quite the opposite often happens. Such funds are usually at the bottom of the heap the following year."

"You're beginning to shake my confidence in mutual funds, Slats. But I assume you know what you are talking about. Do you have any more bad news?"

"One more thing. If your fund is not in a tax shelter, such as an IRA or 401(k), you will end up paying Uncle Sam quite a few dollars each year. The reason is turnover. Mutual fund managers are typically not content to buy and hold. They seem to be a nervous lot, and they often don't hold a stock more than one year. When they sell to buy something else, a capital gain has to be declared, assuming the stock has risen in price. That capital gain is passed along to you, the owner of the fund shares. Thus, even if the fund has gone down in price during the year, you will be saddled with a tax liability because of this excessive obsession with trading. It is one of the worst factors in owning a mutual fund."

"I've noticed that. It really galls me. My fund experience pretty much reflects what you have said. I assume that about wraps it up, Slats."

"Not quite. There is one thing more. Mutual fund buyers are not necessarily being duped. They tend to create some of their own problems by not sitting tight. When their fund has a disappointing year, they often dump it and try something else. According to a study by Dalbar, Inc., a research firm in Boston, the average time a mutual fund is held by a typical investor is less than thirty months. This lack of patience can be devastating. Here's another quote from Jack Bogle: 'The returns incurred by the average equity fund investor since 1984 have averaged just 2.7 percent per year, a shocking shortfall to the 9.3 percent return earned by the average fund. The result is that the average fund investor has earned less than one-quarter of the stock market's 12.2 percent annual return.' Need I say more?"

The phone went dead. Apparently, I had said something to irritate Rose, I said to myself. But I couldn't call her back, since I had no idea what state she was from.

A few days later, I received a letter from Rosario Santos. Enclosed was a check for $89.70 and an order for six autographed copies of *The 100 Best Stocks You Can Buy*. My faith in human nature was restored.

# How to Avoid Portfolio Blunders

When I first met Hans Gelderland, he had just finished an inspiring talk to a large group of Vermont's professional and aspiring freelance writers. As you are no doubt aware, he is the author of the highly acclaimed modern classic, *How to Make Up to $37,000 a Year As a Full-time Freelance Writer.*

Since Mr. Gelderland lives in nearby Colchester, I had no trouble getting in touch with him. "I haven't read your book, Mr. Slatter, but I certainly would like to talk shop with you some time."

"Super idea," I said. "How about dinner at my favorite restaurant, The Windjammer?"

After we filled our plates at the salad bar, we sat down at our booth. I started the ball rolling with a question. "What is your latest project, Mr. Gelderland?"

"Please, it's Hans. I've been struggling with a magazine article on the pre-Socratics. I assume you know something about philosophy."

"A smattering," I said. "As I recall, those were the philosophers who lived before Socrates, such as Anaximander, Thales, Heraclitus, and Parmenides."

"That's right. There was quite a stable of them, and I wanted to do a piece to educate people about this little-known group. But the editor said it was too big a project, and he suggested it would be better concentrate on just one. I chose Pythagoras and interviewed everybody in sight—I think I spent six solid weeks doing my research."

"Great. I can't wait to read it," I said.

"You'll have a long wait. It was rejected. 'Too sophisticated for our audience,' the editor told me."

"That happens, even to the best of us," I said.

"I had better luck on the one on beetles," Hans said. "But the editor told me it was too general. So I put more focus into it, and called it "The Veins in the Hind Wings of an Unborn Beetle." The editor told me to go ahead, but when I had finished a month of research and submitted my manuscript, he said it was perfect, except for one thing. He wanted a few quotes from the leading expert on the topic. So I called this professor in New Mexico, but he insisted I fly out for the interview—at my expense, of course."

"So you finally landed a good one, right?"

"I was hoping for at least $250, but the editor said his magazine was a small quarterly and could go no higher than $175. What's more, I won't get my money till the article appears, about nine months from now."

"That's how the ball bounces," I said, trying to be sympathetic to his plight. "I have an idea that might work, assuming you have an interest in the stock market."

"Always ready to tackle something new," said Hans. "What do you have in mind?"

"I have been dealing with investors for many years, and I see them doing some pretty stupid things. Maybe you could do a piece and call it "The 10 Most Heinous Goofs Made by Investors." How's that for a title?"

"Almost perfect," he said. "Just one change. Make it "Mistakes" instead of "Goofs." That's a little less intimidating. What's a good mistake to begin with, Mr. Slatter?"

"Since I put my phone number in my book, I get quite a few calls from readers. Not infrequently, they want my opinion on some obscure stock that is not in my book, and often not even in the *S&P Stock Guide.*

Really off-the-wall questions. My advice is to pick one of the 100 great stocks in my book, and forget about some stock they discovered under a rock."

"In other words, pick great companies, not ones that may not be here five years from now. What's else?"

"Next is diversification. Rarely do I come across a portfolio that is adequately diversified. Most people are aware that stocks have risk, and so they usually own several stocks. But they are often from a narrow sector of the market. For instance, they may have a penchant for medical stocks, such as Lilly, Abbott, Medtronic, Cardinal Health, Becton, Dickinson, or Varian Medical. All these stocks are fine, but they are not immune to the vagaries of the market. I would suggest that in a twenty-stock portfolio, investors should not own more than two from any one sector. And that includes tech stocks. In recent years, the biggest blunder made by unsophisticated investors was to own a portfolio stuffed with tech stocks. In the sagging market since early 2000, those stocks have been a total disaster."

"In other words, Mr. Slatter, what you are saying is that a good portfolio could have two oil stocks, a couple medical stocks, one or two real estate investment trusts, maybe a beverage stock, a couple machinery stocks, a utility or two, a food company, and so forth. How does that sound?"

"You're a quick study, Hans," I said.

"I guess that means I don't have to read your book."

"I intend to give you a copy, Hans, so I think someone in your family better read it. Which reminds me, another goof made by investors is not doing their homework. If you were going to buy a house, you would not buy the first one you looked at. You would go out with a realtor and look at a couple dozen before making your purchase. Why not spend as much time when you buy a stock?"

"You're trying to make investing sound time-consuming. Doesn't that take the fun out of it?"

"Investing is not fun, Hans. Not if you want to be successful. I would say you had better read the company's annual report, as well as the *Value Line* analysis and the Standard & Poor's tear sheet. Once you have the facts, you are ready to decide if the stock is priced right for immediate purchase."

"This interview is getting complicated, Mr. Slatter. I hope you will read my drivel after I finish my rough draft. Okay, what else shall we tell these people?"

"Once you start building a portfolio, you should keep yourself up to date by reading such periodicals as the *Wall Street Journal*, the *New York Times*, *Barron's*, *Forbes*, *BusinessWeek*, the *AAII Journal*, *Fortune*, *Better Investing*, or *Money*."

"I am beginning to wonder if I am qualified to write this article. It really sounds complicated. Maybe I had better read your book, after all. What's the next blunder?"

"If you can write an article on the veins in the hind wings of an unborn beetle, I think you have the ability to do one on the stock market. It's pretty simple stuff, once you get the hang of it.

"The most important part of investing is starting early in life. If you wait until you're fifty or fifty-five, you don't have enough years to build up a portfolio. I suggest starting in your thirties, if possible. If you start at thirty-five, for instance, and invest $10,000 a year and earn 12 percent a year, you'll have over $2.4 million when you reach sixty-five. If, however, you start at age fifty and invest the same $10,000 a year, you'll have only $373,000 when they hand you the proverbial gold timepiece."

"Where am I going to get $10,000?"

"You had better quit buying new cars, for one thing. That's one of the blunders that people make. They spend every cent they make, and even hit their credit card for a few thousand more. Being a spendthrift is the surest path to poverty at age sixty-five or seventy. If you are depending on Social Security to keep you afloat during retirement, you had better plan on eating a lot of hot dogs and hamburgers. And throw in a few bunches of celery and carrots, for good measure."

"You mean I have to give up the good life, Mr. Slatter?"

"I happen to be rich, Hans. My wife and I own well over fifty stocks, we own our home free and clear, and my bookshelves are loaded with hundreds of books I haven't yet read. And I drive a 1998 Cadillac, which I bought used. So, I'm not sure living a frugal life means you have to suffer."

"I assume you inherited your vast wealth."

"Not a penny came from my deceased relatives. My wife and I earned it all."

"You have convinced me I had better change a few things if I hope to be able retire in style. As soon as I get my check from my article on beetles, I will buy my first stock. Now, what else shall we tell these eager investors?"

"Whenever I meet someone new, the first question they ask me is what I think of the market. For example, one lady I met the other day at a garage sale said, 'This market has been really crazy. You're a professional, Mr. Slatter. Where do you think it's headed?' I told her I didn't have the faintest idea."

"I assume that didn't convince her to become one of your clients. She must really think you're stupid," said Hans Gelderland.

"I sold her a book, so maybe that will convince her otherwise. Most of my clients come from people who have read my book. But, getting back to predicting the market—it can't be done. I realize, of course, that everyone keeps trying, but I defy you to name one analyst or portfolio manager who has consistently predicted what the market will do. There ain't any. So quit trying. My best advice is to invest when you have the money—not when you think the market is poised for a big run. Forget about fore-

casting. If you buy stocks once or twice a year—and are patient—you'll end up a millionaire like me."

"Well, I think I've got enough for a solid article, Mr. Slatter. "Shall we flip to see who pays the tab?"

"I'm not through. One of the most important aspects of picking stocks is not to pay too much. The woods are filled with companies that are doing well and increasing their earnings like clockwork. The trouble is that everybody knows they're great, and you have to pay too much for them."

"What's too much?" asked Hans Gelderland.

"There's no good answer, but the gauge to use is the price/earnings ratio, or P/E ratio. Some people called it the multiple. It's calculated by dividing the annual earnings per share into the price. For instance, if Johnson Controls is priced at $85.60 (which it was at the end of June in 2003), you would divide their latest twelve-month earnings into that figure. That means dividing $6.75 into $85.60, and you get a P/E of 12.7. That was a remarkably low P/E for a company with an exceptional growth record. As it happens, I bought that stock at that time, and a month later it was up at the $95 level. Stocks with good records are rarely available at such a bargain price, but when you find one, latch onto it."

"No wonder you're rich. So I am to assume that 12.7 is a low multiple. But what would you consider a high one?"

"I prefer to buy stocks with a P/E of less than 30, and I certainly would never buy one above 40. On the other hand, you can find stocks with a low multiple that would not be worth pursuing. If their earnings are lackluster and going nowhere, they are not attractive, no matter how low the P/E ratio."

"My notebook is getting overloaded with your maxims, Mr. Slatter. And I'm wondering when the waiter will get fed up with us and toss us out on our ears. We are just taking up space."

"Relax, Hans. The Windjammer has never tossed me out yet. They know I'm a faithful customer, and I bring lots of new people here who later return. One more piece of advice for your notebook. Bear in mind that you can't buy stocks unless you have a broker. It pays to be a careful shopper. The one *not* to deal with is the one who calls you out of the blue to solicit your business. These brokers are often rookies who are still learning the business. *Never* do business with a stranger who calls you.

"The best way to find a broker is by word of mouth. Check with your friends and find out who has done a good job for one of them. And make sure that broker is not suggesting a lot of trades. Trading is the surest way to the poorhouse."

"Is that it?"

"Not quite. The most important rule of thumb is to be alert to when my book is published each year. Normally, it comes out around October 1. If you don't buy every edition and read it carefully, you are destined to suffer the consequences."

"Do you want to flip to see who pays?" asked Hans Gelderland.

"No, I'm rich. Let me handle it."

# The Essentials of Successful Investing

You don't have to be a brilliant stock-picker to become a successful investor. Here are a few factors that matter more.

## Start Early

Starting your program at an early age wins hands down. Let's say you want to reach age sixty-five with investments worth a million dollars. If you buy your first stock at age thirty-five and pick stocks that appreciate at a rate of 10 percent (dividends included), you will have to set aside $6,079 each year. But if you delay until age forty-five, the amount needed leaps to $17,460. Waiting until you're fifty-five boosts your annual contribution to a real back-breaker—$62,746.

## Don't Be a Spendthrift

Also important is your ability to set aside money out of your current income. You will have a lot of trouble if you buy a new car every two or three years. In fact, if you buy new cars at all, you will have trouble. I buy used cars, usually Buicks that are three years old but are in top condition. And don't buy the best house in town and saddle yourself with a huge mortgage. Buy an older home that has been well taken care of. And never fail to pay off your credit card balance before it includes interest charges. In short, don't be a spendthrift. If you need help, read *The Millionaire Mind*, by Thomas J. Stanley.

## Stocks Are the Answer

Next, make sure you invest mostly in common stocks. Over the years, stocks have provided 11 or 12 percent a year in total return. If you buy bonds, CDs, preferred stocks, or leave your cash in a money-market fund, you may not be able to pay your bills during retirement. On the other hand, you may want to have a portion of your investment money—let's say 30 percent—in short-term bonds, particularly if you are retired.

Still another alternative to be avoided are mutual funds. Why? Because the people who manage mutual funds scoop off about 1.5 percent of your holdings each year. They call it the "expense ratio." In addition, picking a good fund is made difficult because there are many thousands to choose from—and no effective way to separate the wheat from the chaff. In fact, there are not very many good ones. The average fund underperforms the market. Finally, mutual funds trade stocks as if they were going out of style, which means they distribute capital gains to you that are subject to income tax.

## The Keys to Picking Stocks

And now we come to the final factor: picking a good list of stocks.

The most important factor is diversification. I suggest owning at least twenty to thirty stocks. However, that doesn't mean you have to accomplish this objective on day one. Let's say you have $5,000 and will be able to save $5,000 each year. In the first year, you buy one or two stocks. That certainly is not a diversified portfolio—but don't let that worry you. If you start investing at age forty and buy one stock a year, you will have twenty-five stocks at age sixty-five.

The one thing you want to avoid is buying too many stocks that are similar. In 1998 and 1999, many investors were convinced that tech stocks were the wave of the future, so they loaded up on them, often to the exclusion of everything else—no oil stocks, no bank stocks, no drug stocks, no utilities, no REITs, no food stocks, and so forth—just tech stocks. Well, as you know, they crashed big time. Many were down 90 percent, and some didn't even survive the bear market of 2000–2002.

As far as picking stocks is concerned, don't fret over picking all winners. You can't do it. Don't worry about it. Just keep picking stocks from my book, *The 100 Best Stocks You Can Buy*, that appeal to you, and time will take care of the rest.

If you don't want to invest $14.95 in my book, you may find it helpful to use the Dow Jones Industrial Average to make your selections. That list contains thirty blue-chip stocks, such as Procter & Gamble, Merck, General Electric, Microsoft, Home Depot, Boeing, DuPont, Johnson & Johnson, United Technologies, and Coca-Cola. You can find this list on page C2 of the *Wall Street Journal*.

Incidentally, the list of thirty stocks, which remains relatively constant, does change from time to time. On average, about one stock each year is dropped and a new one inserted. Quite often, these changes are not made singly. For instance, on April 8, 2004, three stocks were cast aside: Eastman Kodak, AT&T, and International Paper, which were replaced with Pfizer, American International Group, and Verizon. Before these latest changes, the last time new stocks were added was November 1, 1999, when four stocks were booted out: Goodyear Tire, Chevron, Union Carbide (now part of Dow Chemical), and Sears, Roebuck. Those added in 1999 were Home Depot, SBC Communications, Microsoft, and Intel.

If you are a busy person, this short list may appeal to you, since it reduces the number of stocks you might like to keep track of. By contrast, there are about 3,000 stocks listed on the New York Stock Exchange.

### A Few Guidelines

But whichever route you care to traverse, you still have to make up your mind which stock or stocks you will purchase. Ideally, a stock should have these characteristics:

- A rising trend of earnings, dividends and book value
- A balance sheet with less debt than other companies in its particular industry
- A Standard & Poor's Rating of B+ or better
- A price/earnings ratio no higher than average
- A dividend yield that suits your particular needs
- A below-average dividend payout patio. (For instance, if a company has annual earnings per share of $4.00, I would prefer that it pays out $2.00 or less in the form of dividends.)
- Company's return on shareholders' equity is 15 percent or higher

### Sources of Information

You can obtain this information from *Value Line Investment Survey*, which is available at most brokerage offices and some libraries. *Value Line* covers about 1700 stocks with one page devoted to each stock; these are revised every three months. What's more, all the stocks in a given industry are presented together.

An equally helpful source of information is Standard & Poor's, which publishes a two-page report on nearly any stock you can think of. You can also find these sheets online. For instance, I have an account at Charles Schwab, so I merely bring up my portfolio and click on News/Chart, then scroll down Select a Report until I see S&P Stock Report. I click Go, and the report appears on the screen, which I can print out.

Finally, there's no law against calling the company and ordering the latest annual report. Or, if you are computer literate, you can find a wealth of information on the company's Web site. The easiest way to get to the Web site is to bring up the financial section of the *New York Times* and enter the ticker symbol where it offers to give you a quote. When that comes on your screen, you will see a place to click on the company's Web site. Then click Investor Relations, and the rest is easy.

Once you sink your hard-earned cash into a stock, you will immediately start wondering when to sell. This is not an easy decision, but I think you should use the list of characteristics that I discussed above, such as the trend of earnings, the P/E ratio, and the return on equity. If your stock no longer measures up, it may be time to sell. Even so, the more you tinker with your holdings, the worse your performance will be. Buy and hold is the best strategy.

# Twenty-One Ways to Reduce Investment Risk

No matter where you invest your money, there is always risk. Even bonds are not safe from inflation and rising interest rates. CDs also suffer from inflation. Stocks, as everyone knows, are regarded as the riskiest investments. However, they are also the most profitable—at least in the long run. In the short run, who knows what they will do.

Based on my long experience in the stock market, I have figured out twenty-one ways you can reduce this risk. Since I use most of them myself and for my clients, I have emerged from the recent bear market relatively intact. Since more bear markets are not out of the question, here are my thoughts on ways to mitigate your discomfort.

You will find some of these same ideas discussed in greater detail in other chapters of this book. This may seem repetitive, but sometimes repetition is one of the best ways to cram new knowledge into your gray matter. Here are the twenty-one ways to reduce your risk, presented for the first time:

**1.** The first rule of investing is *diversification.* Although most investors are aware of this concept, most do not know how to implement it. Of course, the most grievous blunder is to invest your whole portfolio in one stock. I have seen what this can do.

A few years ago, I met an architect after delivering a lecture. He had more than a million dollars invested in an obscure stock called Comdisco, which was selling around $30 a share. I convinced him to sell $300,000 worth and have me manage that portfolio, which is now worth about $500,000. Meanwhile, Comdisco climbed to $57 a share, which made the architect happy. However, by the end of 2001 it was worth only fifty-two cents a share, and my client had failed to sell it.

Still another investor came to me with all his money invested in WorldCom. He had bought the shares much lower and was well ahead of the game. He agreed to sell it all and have me manage his portfolio by buying twenty-five stocks. It's no secret what has happened to WorldCom.

When I was in Cleveland, I had the task of evaluating portfolios for a firm's clients. Almost without exception, these customers had some diversification. They often had twenty, thirty, or forty stocks, which is considered adequate. But most of these stocks were in three industries: oil, utilities, and banks. That's certainly a far cry from prudent diversification.

**2.** Not to be forgotten is asset allocation. This concept is similar to diversification, but it goes one step further. Instead of investing all your money in stocks, you should spread it around in such assets as bonds, foreign stocks, and money-market funds. No one knows what the market is going to do, so it makes sense to hedge your bets with prudent asset allocation. In the past three years, bonds have far outperformed stocks. That doesn't mean you should sell all your stocks and concentrate in bonds. Who knows? Now may be the time to be in stocks. Still, it pays to have some money in fixed-income assets, even if you think a new bull market is just ahead.

**3.** One way to measure whether a stock is overpriced is to calculate its price-earnings ratio (known as the P/E ratio). Simply divide the stock price by the company's most recent twelve-month earnings per share. P/E ratios can vary all the way from 10 to 100 or more.

In most instances, a high ratio indicates a company with good prospects for the future. A low P/E ratio often means the company has a lackluster future. Although I am not suggesting that you stuff your portfolio with low P/E stocks, I am suggesting that you avoid stocks that are selling at very high P/E ratios. I would avoid any stock with a ratio of 40 or higher. In the long run, they don't do well. Many studies prove this point.

**4.** Many investors ignore real estate investment trusts, usually known as REITs. They look stodgy and dull and typically have a dividend yield of 5 percent or higher. In the past two years, REITs have not only avoided the debacle that has engulfed most other stocks, but they have also actually risen in value. That's because REITs act counter to the market. In a rising market, for instance, they would not do as well as growth stocks.

For my own part, I own several of them, such as Washington Real Estate Investment Trust and Equity Office Properties. REITs are not all alike. Some invest in apartment buildings, some in office buildings, and some in shopping malls. And there are others, as well. Most REITs are well diversified geographically.

**5.** In recent years, dividends have largely been ignored. Historically, however, dividends have played a prominent role in investing. Approximately half of the 11- or 12-percent annual return that investors enjoy can be attributed to dividends. Lately this has not been the case, as companies have tended to buy back their own shares, rather than pay out profits to shareholders. Even so, when I pick stocks, I look for a dividend and a history of regular increases. Stocks that pay a dividend are less likely to plunge in value than those that prefer to reinvest their profits in growth.

**6.** A strong balance sheet is an essential for a company that you want to consider. It's simply a relationship between the amount of debt as a percentage of capitalization. My preference is for 75 percent in equity (the book value of the common stock). A strong balance sheet makes it easier for the company to finance an acquisition. If you have access to *Value Line Investment Survey*, it's easy to find out this percentage.

**7.** If you elect to buy bonds, don't look for the highest yield. For one thing, a high yield is often characteristic of a weak company. When the yield gets too large, the bonds are referred to as "junk bonds." The safest bonds are those issued by the federal government. In today's market, you can't get much more of a return than 4 percent, and that's for bonds that mature in twenty or thirty years. Shorter maturities are as low as 3 percent or less. It's best to stick to maturities of five years or less. The reason is that the bond will sink like a stone if interest rates start climbing. This does not happen for bonds due in less than five years, since all you have to do is wait and you'll get the face value of the bond. A bond due in thirty years, by contrast, will drop, and you may not live long enough to get the face value.

**8.** In an effort to avoid the risk of owning stocks, some people think it pays to buy preferred stocks, convertible bonds, annuities, or commodities, or to sell short. None of these vehicles are recommended—at least not by me. Here's why:

• **Preferred stocks sound safe and sound?** Not necessarily. A preferred stock is somewhat like a bond, in that the dividend is paid regularly and never changes. But a preferred stock—unlike a bond—never matures. In other words, you can't get your money back by waiting for the maturity date. Unlike a common stock, the dividend will never be increased. But if the company has problems, the dividend can be cut. If interest rates go up, the value of a preferred stock will decline.

• **Convertible bonds** appeal to some investors because they have a higher yield than the same company's common stock. They can also be converted into the company's common stock. On the other hand, unless you really know what you are doing, you may find that the company calls in the convertible when it suits their purposes. If you are bound and determined to buy convertibles, I advise you to do it by investing in a mutual fund that is managed by professionals. Even so, I'm not so sure you will be a happy camper.

• **Annuities** are issued by insurance companies. There are two main types. The more conservative is invested in such things as bonds and mortgages. When you are ready to retire, the insurance company will set up a monthly payment plan that will assure you of the same amount each month until you die. Assuming you leave behind a husband or wife, the income will not continue to that survivor. However, if you are willing to take a smaller monthly payment, the company will continue paying that amount to your survivor until his or her death, too. Finally, insurance companies charge a pretty penny for their products, since they have to pay the agent for talking you into it.

• **Variable annuities** are another version of annuity, called "variable" since it is invested in common stocks and other assets of your choosing. Here again, the cost of these products is high. You would be better off buying a conventional mutual fund. The costs are usually about 1.5 percent a year.

• **If you are a speculator, you may find an interest in options, such as puts and calls, and many variations.** A call enables you to buy a particular common stock some weeks or months in the future at today's price. If the stock goes up substantially, this works out fine. But if it drops or advances only modestly, you lose the price of the option. "Puts" work for stocks that are expected to decline. But if they don't decline, you lose. In short, options are best avoided.

• **Commodities** have to do with speculating in such agricultural items as corn, wheat, soybeans, and pork bellies. It is possible to make a lot of money quickly in commodities. But very few people actually do because Mother Nature has a hand in your results. If you think a drought will help the price of your commodity, you might get rich—unless it starts raining, which can lead to a surplus and too much of that commodity, thus reducing prices drastically. This is no game for amateurs.

• **Selling short is similar to calls and puts.** If you think a stock is likely to decline in price, you can make money by selling short. You simply instruct your broker to borrow the shares from one of the firm's accounts. You then sell those shares at today's price. Let's say the stock is selling for $50 a share. Then, when the price drops to $30, you buy shares in the market and give them back to the investor who loaned them to you. Thus, you make a tidy profit of $20 a share. The catch is that the price may very well shoot up to $75, and what do you do then? If you buy back at this level, you lose $25 a share. There is no limit to the amount you can lose when you sell short. If you wait until the price goes to $150, you lose $100 a share. This is not my idea of having fun.

**9.** The biggest problem with investing is its vast scope. There are thousands of mutual funds and tens of thousands of stocks, both domestic and foreign. A simple way to get rid of the clutter is to concentrate your investing on a small universe, the thirty stocks that make up the Dow Jones Industrial Average. They include such blue chips as General Electric, Johnson & Johnson, Procter & Gamble, ExxonMobil, and Coca-Cola. Over the years, the Dow has performed well, so why not buy all thirty stocks, rather than hunt under every rock looking for the stock that will make you a millionaire? Another advantage is knowing when to sell. My strategy is sell only when a stock is removed from the Index, about one stock a year. This cuts down on your capital gains taxes, since most of the stocks you remove from your portfolio are losers, not winners.

**10.** Some investors can't stand inaction. Instead of buying and holding, they insist on selling winners and holding losers. All you do that way is end up with a portfolio of losers. It's better to let your winners run. The more you buy and sell, the more taxes you will have to pay.

**11.** Be careful in selecting a stockbroker. Most people start with a traditional full-service firm, since their salespeople are aggressively seeking new clients. Brokerage firms can supply you with research material, but these firms rely heavily for their profits on investment banking and their analysts may not be impartial. For their part, the salespeople make their money from commissions, which are much higher than such discount firms as Schwab or Scottrade. Even worse, they tend to recommend products that have a high commission and limited prospects.

**12.** If you invest in stocks, avoid companies that are losing money. Instead, look for companies with a long history of profitable operation, with a rising trend in earnings per share. If you buy stocks that are losing money, you are a speculator, not an investor.

**13.** Stocks are traded on the New York Stock Exchange, the American Stock Exchange, and NASDAQ. The leading companies are usually listed on the New York Stock Exchange. Those traded elsewhere are less mature and often of lower quality.

**14.** If you buy mutual funds, make sure you examine the "expense ratio." Even no-load funds are not free. To pay the salary of analysts and other employees, along with expenses like advertising, rent, and travel, mutual funds subtract these costs from your profits. The average expense ratio is about 1.5 percent per year. Studies show that funds with the highest expense ratios perform worst, while those with the lowest perform the best.

**15.** Although I am not a fan of mutual funds, if advising on how to invest in them, I would say avoid those with new management. Before you invest, call the company and ask the age of the manager and how long he has been in charge. I would prefer a manager at least forty years of age and a tenure of at least five years.

**16.** Avoid stocks with excessively high yields, at least in relation to other companies in that industry. Those with high yields are often in trouble and are likely to cut their dividend.

**17.** Seek companies that are financially strong. This can be determined in two ways. Standard & Poor's rates stocks by letter. The highest rating is A+. An average rating is B+. Avoid those with a rating below B+. *Value Line* uses a similar rating, but its highest rating is A++, and an average one is B++. Again, don't go below B++.

**18.** Examine the dividend payout ratio. It's calculated by dividing the annual dividend by the annual earnings per share for the past twelve months. If the dividend is $1, and the earnings per share are $4, the payout ratio would be 25 percent. That signifies a company that is plowing back earnings into research, new products, stock repurchase, debt reduction, or acquisitions. If the payout ratio is high, let's say 75 percent, this is an indication that that the company has limited growth potential.

**19.** The economy has an impact on most companies, but there are some industries that are considered cyclical, such as chemicals, autos, appliances, machinery, metals and mining, paper, and railroads. Most of these have limited long-term growth. The only way to make money is by buying them when they are in trouble and selling them when money is rolling in. It's not that easy to be able to jump in and out with any consistency. Instead of cyclical stocks, concentrate on industries that are more stable, such as food processors, banks, REITs, utilities, food supermarkets, life insurance, medical supplies, and household products.

**20.** When a major company buys another major company, avoid the buyer. A good case in point is the purchase of Compaq by Hewlett-Packard. Rarely is there an exception to this rule.

**21.** Most investors are busy people, such as doctors, accountants, executives, and business owners. That means their time is limited. Even so, some time must be allotted for reading annual reports, the *Wall Street Journal, BusinessWeek,* and *Value Line.* To be a successful investor, you have to know how the game is played. This should also include reading at least one book on investing every year. I'll send you a list of good books if you call me or send me an e-mail (for contact information, see "About the Author" on page 365). I will also include a list of great books on other topics, such as biographies.

# Basic Terminology

If you are new to the investment arena, you may have difficulty understanding parts of this book. To get you over the rough spots, I have listed some common expressions that appear frequently in books on investing. You will also encounter them in the *Wall Street Journal, Forbes, BusinessWeek, Barron's*, and other periodicals devoted to investing.

This is not a glossary but merely a brief list of terms essential to understanding this book. If you would like a more complete glossary, refer to either of my previous books: *Safe Investing* (Simon & Schuster, 1991) or *Straight Talk About Stock Investing* (McGraw-Hill, 1995).

## Analyst

In nearly every one of the 100 articles, you will note that I refer to "analysts" and what they think about the prospects for a particular stock. Analysts are individuals who have special training in analyzing stocks. Typically, they have such advanced degrees as M.B.A. or C.F.A. Many of them work for brokerage houses, but they may work for banks, insurance companies, mutual funds, pension plans, or other institutions. Most analysts specialize in one or two industries. A good analyst can tell you nearly everything there is to know about a particular stock or the industry it's part of.

However, analysts can be dead wrong about the future action of a stock. The reason: surprises. Companies are constantly changing, which means they are acquiring, divesting, developing new products, restructuring, buying back their shares, and so forth. When they make a change and announce this change to Wall Street, the surprise can change the course of the stock.

In short, analysts can be helpful, but don't bet the store on what they tell you.

As you can see, analysts are usually intelligent, hardworking, and conscientious. Even so, they don't always succeed in guiding you to riches. Perhaps the biggest beef most people have is the tie that analysts have to the companies they follow. They know these companies well and may be reluctant to say anything negative.

One reason for this is economic. Most brokerage firms make a ton of money from their investment banking division. If the analyst antagonizes the company, that company may give its investment banking business to a firm that says nice things rather than pointing out its warts and all.

This reluctance to see no evil and speak no evil can be seen when you examine the number of times that analysts advise investors to sell. According to the research firm First Call, more than 70 percent of the 27,000 recommendations outstanding in November 2000 were strong buys or buys. Fewer than 1 percent were sells or strong sells. To recap: Of the 27,000 recommendations, 26.6 percent were holds, 36.8 percent were buys, 35.7 percent were strong buys, and a mere 0.9 percent were sells or strong sells. I rest my case.

## Annual Report

If you own a common stock, you can be certain that you will receive a fancy annual report a couple of months after the close of the year. If the year ends December 31, look for your annual report in March or April. If the fiscal year ends some other time of the year, such as September 30, the annual report will appear in your mailbox two or three months later.

Not all investors read annual reports, but they might be better off if they did. Although most companies will not list their problems, you can usually get a pretty good idea how things are going. In particular, read the report by the president or CEO. It's usually one, two, or three pages long and is written in language you can understand.

If you want detailed information on the company's various businesses, the annual report will often overwhelm you with details that may be difficult to fathom. If you are really curious about what they are trying to say, feel free to call the investor contact. I have provided the phone number of this person for all 100 stocks listed. Have a list of questions ready, and call during the person's lunch hour, leaving your name and phone number. This sneaky little strategy means the cost of the call back will be paid by the company, not you. By the way, don't assume you will be intimidated by the investor contact. Investor contacts are usually quite personable and helpful.

## Argus Research Company

Argus is an independent research organization that provides information on stocks to institutions, such as brokerage houses, banks, mutual funds, and banks. It is normally not available to individual investors. However, you may be able to obtain Argus reports through your broker. You will note that I have quoted liberally from Argus in the analysis of my 100 stocks. You should be able to obtain this information from a brokerage house, such as Charles Schwab & Company. Analysts with Argus typically revise their reports quite often, depending on changes in earnings and important developments.

## Asset Allocation

This is not the same as diversification. Rather, it refers to the strategy of allocating your investment funds among different types of investments, such as stocks, bonds, or money-market funds. In the long run, you will be better off with all of your assets concentrated in common stocks. In the short run, this may not be true, since the market occasionally has a sinking spell. A severe one, such as that of 2000–2002, can cause your holdings to decline in value by 20 percent or more. To protect against this, most investors spread their money around. They may, for instance, allocate 50 percent to stocks, 40 percent to bonds, and 10 percent to a money-market fund. A more realistic breakdown might be 70 percent in stocks, 25 percent in bonds, and 5 percent in a money-market fund.

## Balance Sheet

All corporations issue at least two financial statements: the balance sheet and the income statement. Both are important. The balance sheet is a financial picture of the company on a specific date, such as December 31 or at the end of a quarter.

On the left side of the balance sheet are the company's assets, such as cash, current assets, inventories, accounts receivable, and buildings. On the right side are its liabilities, including accounts payable and long-term debt. Also on the right side is shareholders' equity. The right side of the balance sheet adds up to the same value as the left side, which is why it is called a balance sheet.

In most instances, corporations give you figures for the current year and the prior year. By examining the changes, you can get an idea of whether the company's finances are improving or deteriorating.

## Bonds

Entire books have been written on the various kinds of bonds. A bond, unlike a stock, is not a form of ownership. A bond is a contractual agreement that means you have loaned money to some entity and that entity has agreed to pay you a certain sum of money (interest) every six months until that bond matures. At that time, you will also get back the money you originally invested—no more, no less. Most bonds are issued in $1,000 denominations. The safest bonds are those issued by the U.S. government. The two advantages of bonds are safety and income. If you wait until the maturity date, you will be assured of getting the face value of the bond. In the meantime, however, the bond will fluctuate, because of changes in interest rates or the creditworthiness of the corporation. Long-term bonds, moreover, fluctuate far more than short-term bonds. But enough about bonds. This book is about stocks.

## Capital Gains

When you buy common stocks, you expect to make money in two ways: capital gains and dividends. Over an extended period of time, about half of your total return will come from each sector. If the stock rises in value and you sell it above your cost, you are enjoying a capital gain. The tax on long-term capital gains is a maximum of 15 percent if the stock is held for twelve months.

## Chief Executive Officer (CEO)

This is the executive of a company who reports to the board of directors. That corporate body can terminate the CEO if he or she fails to do an effective job of managing the company. In some instances, the CEO may also have the title of either president or chairman of the board, or both.

## Closed-End Investment Company

A managed investment portfolio, similar to a mutual fund, a closed-end investment company is generally traded on a stock exchange. The price fluctuates with supply and demand, not because of changes in the assets within the trust. An open-end investment trust, or mutual fund changes in size as investors buy new shares or surrender their shares for cash. A closed-end trust, by contrast, does not permit new money to be invested, nor can shares be redeemed by the company. Thus, the number of shares

remains the same once the trust begins trading. One feature of the closed-end trust is worth mentioning: They often sell at a discount to their asset value. An open-end trust always sells at precisely its asset value.

## Common Stocks

We might as well define what a common stock is, since this whole book is devoted to them. All publicly owned companies—those that trade their shares outside of a small group of executives or the founding family—are based on common stocks. A common stock is evidence of partial ownership in a corporation. Most of the stocks described in this book have millions of shares of their stock outstanding, and the really large ones may have in excess of 100 million shares. When you own common stock, there are no guarantees. If the company is successful, it will probably pay a dividend four times a year. These dividends may be raised periodically, perhaps once a year. If, however, the company has problems, it may cut or eliminate its dividend. This can happen even to a major company, such as IBM, Goodyear, or General Motors. As I said, there are no guarantees.

Investors who own common stock can sell their shares at any time. All you do is call your broker, and the trade is executed a few minutes later at the prevailing price—which fluctuates nearly every day, sometimes by a few cents or sometimes two or three points.

## Current Ratio

The current ratio is calculated by dividing current assets by current liabilities. Current assets include any assets that will become cash within one year, including cash itself. Current liabilities are those that will be paid off within a year. A current ratio of 2 is considered ideal. Most companies these days have a current ratio of less than 2.

## Diversification

Since investments are inherently risky, it pays to spread the risk by diversifying. If you don't, you may be too heavily invested in a stock or bond that turns sour. Even well-known stocks such as Alcoa, International Paper, Eastman Kodak, and American Express can experience occasional sinking spells.

To be on the safe side, don't invest more than 5 percent of your portfolio in any one stock. In addition, don't invest too heavily in any one sector of the economy. A good strategy is to divide stocks among ten sectors: drugs and health care, industrials, materials, energy, telecommunications, utilities, consumer staples, consumer discretionary, financials, and information technology.

Here's a rule of thumb that will keep you out of trouble: Invest at least 4 percent in each sector but not more than 12 percent. That means that you should own at least ten stocks so that you have representation in all ten sectors.

## Dividends

Unlike bonds, which pay interest, common stocks may pay a dividend. Most dividends are paid quarterly, but there is no set date that all corporations use. Some, for instance, may pay on January 1, March 1, July 1, and September 1. Another company may pay on February 10, May 10, August 10, and November 10. If you want to receive checks every month, you will have to make sure you buy stocks that pay dividends at different times of the year. The Standard & Poor's *Stock Guide* is a source for this information, as is the *Value Line Investment Survey*. Most companies like to pay the same dividend every quarter until they can afford to increase it. Above all, they don't like to cut their dividends, since investors who depend on this income will sell their shares, and the stock will decline in price. If you use good judgment in selecting your stocks, you can expect that your companies will increase their dividends nearly every year.

## Dividend Payout

If a company earns $4 a share in a twelve-month period and pays out $3 to shareholders in the form of dividends, it has a payout ratio of 75 percent. However, if it pays only $1, the payout ratio is 25 percent. In the past, many investors looked favorably on a low payout ratio. The thinking was that such a company was plowing back its earnings into such projects as research, new facilities, acquisitions, and new equipment. It sounds logical.

Now, there is evidence that you are better off buying a company with a higher payout ratio. Mark Hulbert, who writes frequently for the Sunday *New York Times*, has come up with some studies that focus on this concept. According to work done by Michael C. Jensen, currently an emeritus professor of business administration at the Harvard Business School, "The more cash that companies have now (beyond what is needed for current projects), the less efficient they will be in the future."

Two other scholars concur that a higher payout ratio serves investors better than a low one. They are Robert D. Arnott of First Quadrant and Clifford S. Asness of AQR Capital Management. For one thing, they found that "For the overall stock market between 1871 and 2001, corporate profits grew fastest in the ten years following the calendar year in which companies had the highest average dividend payout ratio." What's more, their study showed that in the period from 1946 to 1991, there was a strong correlation that demonstrates conclusively that companies with a high payout ratio performed far better than the ones who were stingy with their dividend distributions.

Mr. Hulbert concludes that "The common theme that emerges from these various studies is a very unflattering portrait of corporate management: give executives lots of rope and they too often end up hanging themselves. It would appear that a high dividend payout ratio is an effective way to reduce the length of that rope."

## Dividend Reinvestment Plans

Unless you are retired, you might like to reinvest your dividends in more shares.

Many companies have a dividend reinvestment plan (also known as a DRIP) that will allow you to do this, and the charge for this service is often minimal. Most of these companies also allow you to mail in additional cash, which will be used to purchase new shares, again at minimal cost.

In recent years, a few companies have created "direct" dividend reinvestment plans. Unlike most plans, direct plans enable you to buy your initial shares directly from the company. To alert you to which companies have direct plans, I have inserted the word *direct*. Companies with such plans include ExxonMobil, McDonald's, Procter & Gamble, Merck, and Lilly. Incidentally, you can rarely buy just one share. Many companies have a minimum purchase amount, such as $500.

This may sound like a good way to avoid paying brokerage commissions, but there are some drawbacks to bear in mind. For one thing, you can't time your purchases, since it may be a week or more before your purchase is made.

Even worse is calculating your cost basis for tax purposes. By the time you sell, you may have made scores of small investments in the same stock, each with a different cost basis. Make sure you keep a file for each company so that you can make these calculations when the time comes. Or, better still, don't sell.

## Dollar-Cost Averaging

Dollar-cost averaging is a systematic way to invest money over a long period, such as ten, fifteen, or twenty years. It entails investing the same amount of money regularly, such as each month or each quarter. If you do this faithfully, you will be buying more stock when the price is lower and less stock when the price is higher. This tends to smooth out the gyrations of the market. Dollar-cost averaging is often used with a mutual fund, but it can just as easily be done with a company that has a dividend reinvestment plan (DRIP).

## Income Statement

Most investors are more interested in the income statement than they are in the balance sheet. They are particularly interested in the progress (or lack of it) in earnings per share (EPS). The income statement lists such items as net sales, cost of sales, interest expense, and gross profit. As with the balance sheet, it makes sense to compare this year's numbers with those of the prior year.

## Inflation-Indexed Treasury Bonds

Conventional bonds—those that pay a fixed rate of return, such as 5 percent—have one big drawback: They are vulnerable to rising interest rates. For example, if you buy a bond that promises to pay you 5 percent for the next fifteen or twenty years, you will lose principal if interest rates climb to 7 percent. The reason is that new bonds being issued give investors a much better return. Thus, those that pay only 5 percent will sag in price until they hit a level that equates them to the new bonds that pay 7 percent. The loss of principal, moreover, is much greater with long-term bonds, such as those due in fifteen, twenty, or thirty years.

By contrast, short-term bonds, those coming due in three or four years, are much less volatile because you can often hold the bonds until the maturity date. Thus, you are certain to receive the full face value. Of course, you can do the same thing with a twenty-year bond, but twenty years is a long time.

The way to beat this disadvantage is to buy the relatively new bonds being issued by the U.S. government, since they are indexed to inflation. For this reason, you are unlikely to lose principal. To be sure, they pay less initially, currently 3.8 percent. But the ultimate return may be much better if inflation continues to impact the economy.

Suppose you invested $1,000 in inflation bonds at the current yield of 3.8 percent. If consumer prices rose 2.5 percent over the next year, your principal would climb to $1,025, and you would earn interest equal to 3.8 percent on this growing sum. Thus, if you spent the interest but didn't cash in any bonds, you would enjoy a rising stream of income while keeping your principal's spending power intact.

One thing to bear in mind is that with inflation-indexed treasury bonds, you have to pay federal income taxes each year on both the interest you earn and also the increase in the bonds' principal value. One way to take the sting out of this tax is to use these bonds in a tax-deferred account, such as an IRA.

Despite the tax implications, inflation bonds may be useful outside an IRA. Because these bonds don't perform as erratically as conventional bonds, they can be a good place to park money you may need if something unexpected comes along, such as a medical bill not fully covered by insurance. If inflation-indexed bonds ring a bell, ask the teller at your bank to get you started. She won't charge you a fee, and there is no red tape.

## Investment Advisor

Investors who do not have the time or inclination to manage their own portfolios may elect to employ an investment advisor. Most advisors charge 1 percent a year. Thus, if you own stocks worth $300,000, your annual fee would be $3,000. Advisors differ from brokers, since they do not profit from changes. Brokers, by contrast, charge a commission on each transaction, which means they profit from changes in your portfolio. Advisors profit only when the value of your holdings increases. For instance, if the value of your portfolio increases to $500,000, the annual fee will be $5,000. You, of course, will be $200,000 richer.

## Moving Average

Some investors use the moving average to time the market. The strategy is to buy a stock when it is selling above its moving average and sell when it falls below. A popular moving

average is the 200-day version. A dotted line is drawn, taking the average price of the stock over the previous 200 days. The actual price of the stock is plotted on the same graph. Studies show that this method of timing the market does not work on a consistent basis.

## PEG Ratio

The PEG ratio is supposed to be helpful in determining if a stock is too expensive. It is calculated by dividing the price-earnings ratio by the expected earnings growth rate. Let's say the P/E ratio of American International Group is 34.39, which is calculated by dividing the price ($98) by the expected EPS in 2001 of $2.85. Meanwhile, the earnings per share in the 1989–1999 period expanded from $0.67 to $2.18, a compound annual growth rate of 12.52 percent. When you divide 34.39 by 12.52, the PEG ratio is 2.75. According to Michael Sivy, a writer for *Money* magazine, "Stocks with a PEG ratio of 1.5 or less are often the best buys."

By that rule, you would avoid American International Group. Curiously, Mr. Sivy includes AIG on his list of "100 Stocks for Long-Term Investors," published in January 2001. By his calculation, AIG had a PEG ratio at that time of 2.5.

Once again, I am a doubting Thomas. Who is to say what a company's future growth rate will be? You can easily determine what it has been in the past. And that may give you some indication of the future, but it is far from reliable. The P/E ratio is also a slippery number, since you are expected to base it on the EPS for the year ahead. I prefer to base it on the most recent twelve months, since that is a figure that does not depend on a crystal ball.

## Preferred Stock

The name sounds impressive. In actual practice, owning preferred stocks is about as exciting as watching your cat take a bath. A preferred stock is much like a bond. It pays the same dividend year in and year out.

The yield is usually higher than a common stock. If the company issuing the preferred stock does well, you do not benefit. If it does poorly, however, you may suffer, since the dividend could be cut or eliminated.

## Price-Earnings Ratio (P/E)

This is a term that is extremely important. Don't make the mistake of overlooking it. Whole books have been written on the importance of the P/E ratio, which is sometimes referred to as "the P/E" or "the multiple."

The P/E ratio tells you whether a stock is cheap or expensive. It is calculated by dividing the price of the stock by the company's earnings per share over the most recent twelve months. For instance, if you refer to the *Stock Guide,* you will see that Leggett and Platt had earnings of $2.23. At the time, the stock was selling for $52. Divide that figure by $2.23, and you get a P/E of 23.32.

A high P/E ratio tends to indicate a stock with good prospects for the future. However, this evaluation tends to be overdone. In an article written by Mark Hulbert for the *New York Times* on January 25, 2004, Mr. Hulbert said, "Although the stock market is not as expensive as it was in 2000, it has many 'pockets of craziness,' in the view of Josef Lakonishok, a finance professor at the University of Illinois at Urbana-Champaign.

"Professor Lakonishok bases his assessment on a historical study that found that companies trading at high price-to-earnings ratios almost never grow as quickly as they need to justify their valuations."

The study was conducted by the above professor and two other academics. Mr. Hulbert went on to say, "The professors concluded that very high P/E ratios were hardly ever justified."

## Profit Margins

Profit margins fall into two categories: Net Profit Margin and Operating Profit Margin.

*Net Profit Margin* is simply net income divided by sales. It measures profitability after all expenses and taxes have been paid—and after all accounting adjustments have been made.

*Operating Profit Margin* is operating income divided by sales. It measures profitability after only those expenses related to current operations have been paid.

## Reverse Stock Split

Stock splits are normally a happy occasion. If you have 100 shares of a stock selling for $80 a share, the company may announced a two-for-one stock split. In due course, you will have 200 shares, each worth $40. You are no richer, but you may be happier.

A reverse stock split, however, is *not* good news. If you have 200 shares of a stock selling for $1.25, the company may be contemplating upgrading your shares by announcing a reverse stock split. They will issue new shares worth, say, ten times as much. Now you have only twenty shares, each one worth $12.50. Again, you are no richer. But you may be unhappy. You should be. Studies show that a reverse stock split is a bad omen.

In July 1997, the *Journal of Business* measured all reverse stock splits from 1926 to 1991. The authors were two professors of accounting, Hemang A. Desai of Southern Methodist University and Prem C. Jain of Georgetown. According to an article in the *New York Times* by Mark Hulbert (dated November 3, 2002), "They found that, over the year after the announcement, the average stock undergoing a reverse stock split performed 8.5 percent worse than the stock market."

Mr. Hulbert explained why some companies resort to this device. "David L. Ikenberry, a finance professor at the University of Illinois at Urbana-Champaign, and Sundaresh Ramnath, an accounting professor at Georgetown, have developed a theory that does explain it. They believe that when management lacks confidence in its company's stock, it is more likely to use a reverse split. By contrast, they say, if management believes that the low price is just temporary, it will be more likely to leave the stock alone."

## Standard & Poor's Stock Reports

S&P is a major provider of financial information, primarily to institutions, such as stock brokers, mutual funds, and banks. However, individuals can tap into this information by requesting a "tear sheet" on almost any stock. You will note that I have quoted liberally from Standard & Poor's in the analysis of my 100 stocks. S&P stock tear sheets are revised quite frequently, depending on earnings changes and important developments.

## Stock Split

Corporations know that investors like to invest in lower-priced stocks. Thus, when the price of the stock gets to a certain level, which varies with the company, they will split the stock. For instance, if the stock is $75, they might split it three-for-one. Your original 100 shares now become 300 shares. Unfortunately, your 300 shares are worth exactly the same as your original 100 shares. What it amounts to is this: Splits please small investors, but they don't make them any richer. One company, Berkshire Hathaway, has never been split. It is now worth a huge amount per share: over $70,000. It also pays no dividend. The company is run by the legendary Warren Buffett, and has made a lot of people very wealthy without a stock split or dividend.

## Technician

There are two basic ways to analyze stocks. One is *fundamental*; the other is *technical*.

Fundamental analysts examine a stock's management, sales and earnings potential, research capabilities, new products, competitive strength, balance sheet strength, dividend growth, political developments, and industry conditions.

Technicians, by contrast, rarely consider any of these fundamental factors. They rely on charts and graphs and a host of other arcane statistical factors, such as point-and-figure charts, breadth indicators, head-and-shoulders formations, relative strength ratings, and the 200-day-moving average. This technical jargon is often difficult for the average investor to fathom. The fundamental approach predominates among professional portfolio managers, although some institutions may also employ a technician.

The question is, Do technicians have the key to stock picking or predicting the trend of the market? Frankly, I am a skeptic, as are most academic analysts. Among the nonbelievers is Kenneth L. Fisher, the longtime columnist for *Forbes* magazine whom I mentioned earlier. His columns are among my favorites. Here is what Mr. Fisher says about technicians: "One of the questions I hear most often is, 'Can charts really predict stock prices?' Naturally, there is only one answer: a flat 'No.'"

Mr. Fisher goes on to say, "There is virtually nothing in theory or empiricism to indicate anyone can predict stock prices based solely on prior stock price action. Nevertheless, a big world of chartists continues to exist, amplified by recent Internet day trading. Yet the world of investors with long-lasting success is devoid of them."

Such eminently successful portfolio managers as Peter Lynch and Warren Buffett, for instance, don't resort to charts and other technical mumbo jumbo.

## Value Line Investment Survey

Value Line provides one-page reports on about seventeen hundred stocks. It is normally available in brokerage houses and libraries. You will note that I have quoted liberally from Value Line in the analysis of my 100 stocks. Although Value Line is too expensive for most individual investors, the company does have a much less expensive version that covers 600 major corporations. Stocks are revised by Value Line every three months.

## Yield

If your company pays a dividend, you can relate this dividend to the price of the stock in order to calculate the yield. A $50 stock that pays a $2 annual dividend (which amounts to 50 cents per quarter) will have a yield of 4 percent. You arrive at this figure by dividing $2 by $50. Actually, you don't have to make this calculation, since the yield is given to you in the stock tables of the *Wall Street Journal*. Here are some typical yields: Coca-Cola, 1.5 percent; ExxonMobil, 2.0 percent; General Electric, 1.3 percent; Illinois Tool Works, 1.2 percent; Kimberly-Clark, 1.8 percent; and 3M Company, 2.0 percent. Although the yield is of some importance, you should not judge a stock by its yield without looking at many other factors.

# How to Arrange Your Portfolio for Retirement

If you would like to kill some time on a Friday or Saturday morning, why not try attending a few garage sales. To get a good selection of merchandise, it's best to be on hand early—when the owner opens the garage door, normally 8 a.m. If you wait until the afternoon, all the good stuff will be gone. Usually, I take my own advice, but one day in August, I was on the way back from cashing a check at the Chittenden Bank, and I spotted a sign for a garage sale. Although it was after three in the afternoon, I couldn't resist and stopped to see what they had that I might need—at a bargain price, of course. I was particularly tempted because the garage sale was on Oliver Cromwell Terrace.

Since it was late in the day, I was the only customer. I spotted some books and proceeded to examine them to see if there was something I might need. The prices were right: 25 cents and 50 cents. One volume caught my eye: *The 100 Best Stocks You Can Buy*, the 2002 edition—for a mere 50 cents. I asked the proprietor if she knew the author. When I informed her that I was the guilty party, she nearly fell out of her chair. It turned out that she had purchased this out-of-date copy from The Book Rack, a well-known independent bookstore. She had several other investment books on sale, as well, but all at least ten years old, so I was not tempted to invest in one.

"Are you the one who reads these books?" I asked.

"Most of them. My husband is a fisherman, not a reader. All he reads are books and magazines on fishing and baseball. He's also a rabid Boston Red Sox fan. While he's watching baseball, I am huddled in my favorite chair reading a book. I blot out the game completely—after years of practice."

"As you know, I'm John Slatter, but I don't know your name. Anyone who reads books on investing must have a few stocks hidden away somewhere."

"I'm glad to meet you Mr. Slatter. I'm Orlinda Adams. I've been investing for the past thirty years or more. Now, my husband and I are looking forward to retirement. You can see by my shock of gray hair that I'm no longer a teenager. We have a good portfolio, but we're not sure what to do with it."

"That's an interesting question, Mrs. Adams. My latest book does not address this issue, nor do I have a chapter in any of my previous editions. So, I guess I can't direct you to one of my books for the answer. But I do have some ideas that might be of help. Maybe, sometime I could arrange to meet with you and the fisherman, and we could discuss some alternatives."

"I'm afraid my illustrious husband hasn't a clue about investing. He does the fishing; I do the investing. I'm about to close up shop here, Mr. Slatter. Would this be a good time to have a cup of coffee and discuss my plight?"

"I'm a total stranger, Mrs. Adams. Are you sure you want to divulge your financial situation to someone you have only known for ten or fifteen minutes?"

"If you can write books, you can't be a total dunce. I have read three of your books, so I know you wouldn't lead me astray."

"If you have Green Mountain coffee, I'll take you up on your offer."

"I can see we have something in common. Let me shut the garage door, and we'll see what's in the kitchen. By the way, please call me Orlinda. And I'll call you Mr. Slatter."

"Call me Slats. In fact, as long as you don't call me Mr. Slater, Mr. Slattery, or Mr. Slaughter, I'm at your service."

When we were seated at the kitchen table and had gulped down some reheated Green Mountain coffee, Orlinda Adams told me her portfolio was worth $680,000, mostly in stocks, a few mutual funds and more than $200,000 in money-market funds. She brought out her latest brokerage statement, and here's what it contained:

## Common Stocks in IRAs

| Symbol | Name | Shares | Market Value |
|--------|------|--------|--------------|
| BBBY | Bed Bath & Beyond | 320 | $11,990 |
| BXP | Boston Properties | 96 | 5,252 |
| EAT | Brinker Int'l | 300 | 9,188 |
| BDK | Black & Decker | 200 | 13,928 |
| COST | Costco | 400 | 6,820 |
| DOV | Dover | 400 | 15,508 |
| EOP | Equity Office Properties | 200 | 5,608 |
| GD | General Dynamics | 116 | 11,414 |
| GIS | General Mills | 200 | 9,440 |
| HD | Home Depot | 74 | 2,708 |
| ITW | Illinois Tool Works | 70 | 6,442 |

## Common Stocks Outside the IRAs

| Symbol | Name | Shares | Market Value |
|--------|------|--------|--------------|
| A | Agilent Technologies | 20 | $432 |
| AA | Alcoa | 176 | 5,782 |
| BN | Banta | 300 | 11,568 |
| BKS | Barnes & Noble | 400 | 13,804 |
| CNI | Canadian National Railway | 300 | 13,698 |
| CAT | Caterpillar | 200 | 14,740 |
| C | Citigroup | 112 | 5,232 |
| IBM | Int'l Business Machines | 44 | 3,738 |
| JNJ | Johnson & Johnson | 80 | 4,616 |
| JCI | Johnson Controls | 400 | 22,456 |
| JPM | JPMorgan Chase | 118 | 4,686 |
| MKC | McCormick | 400 | 13,392 |
| MSFT | Microsoft | 600 | 16,476 |
| PG | Procter & Gamble | 80 | 4,478 |
| RARE | RARE Hospitality | 400 | 11,064 |
| SOTR | SouthTrust | 400 | 16,412 |
| SPLS | Staples | 400 | 11,760 |
| TEVA | Teva Pharmaceutical | 400 | 11,356 |
| UPS | United Parcel | 94 | 6,840 |
| UNH | UnitedHealth Group | 302 | 19,954 |
| UTX | United Technologies | 60 | 5,604 |
| WMT | Wal-Mart Stores | 84 | 4,500 |
| WFC | Wells Fargo | 200 | 11,732 |

## Mutual Funds

| Name | Shares | Market Value |
|------|-------:|-------------:|
| Mutual Shares Fund | 2,758.144 | $59,576 |
| FBR American Gas Index Fund | 609.415 | 8,258 |
| DIAMONDS Trust | 100 | 10,175 |
| Nuveen Quality Preferred | 1685 | 24,618 |
| Invest. Co. of America | 263.799 | 7,542 |
| Money-market funds | | 237,652 |
| Total | | $680,439 |

After examining this long list of holdings, I said, "I have reviewed scores of portfolios, and I must congratulate you on yours. It's extremely well diversified, and I like your stocks picks. For some reason, many of your holdings are ones that I have used in my books."

"That's because I read your books, Slats—and I take your advice. But now, what do I do next? Bud—that's the fisherman—and I need income, not pure riches. An insurance man called me on the telephone the other day, and he said the best way to achieve income is with an annuity. I didn't fall for his line, but maybe he's right."

"In a way, he has a good case. Stocks don't provide much income, perhaps about two or three percent. And quite a few have no dividend at all. If you invested $100,000 in an annuity, you would receive something like 7 percent a year, depending on which options you selected. Let's assume you're about fifty-eight . . ."

"Thanks for the compliment, Slats, but I'm actually a little more ancient than that. I'm sixty-seven, and Bud is seventy-one. You were saying . . ."

"I thought women were not supposed to reveal their age. But as long as you have given me this information, I can give you an idea how an annuity would work in your situation. But first, I will need to consult an insurance rate book. A good buddy of mine, Ned Hyskool, is an insurance agent. Let me see if the rate book is still on the back seat of my 1998 Cadillac—purchased used, of course."

With Ned's rate book in hand, I was able to provide Orlinda Adams with some figures. I said, "One way to set up an annuity is to tell the representative that you want the highest possible income. The agent will then tell you that has one serious disadvantage. As soon as you start receiving this income—in this instance, $612.76 per month—you are depriving your husband and children of the principal in the event of your death. If you had no husband and no offspring, that might be a good option. But I assume you have both."

"Bud and three grown children—I can assure you that I don't want to take that option, since my family could use that money in the event of my untimely demise. So, let's forget that idea—which I am sure you expected."

"I suppose a few people might prefer that option, but most people are like you—they have relatives that they don't want to disinherit. A more popular option will give you a smaller income—in this instance, $597.12—but it will be guaranteed for at least ten years. In that instance, you might draw on your annuity for a few years before dying, but the income would continue for the balance of the ten years. I suspect that would not suit you, since at the time of your death, Bud might still be hale and hearty, and he would not be entitled to any income if you died at the end of the ten-year period. Am I right?"

"I'm beginning to think that insurance man didn't have our best interests in mind when he suggested we invest in an annuity. Are there any other options you haven't mentioned?"

"One more. If you are willing to take an even smaller annual payout, you can get a joint-and-survivor plan that will pay you and Bud as long as either of you is still living. Such a plan would pay $563.72 per month. But even this plan has a shortcoming. If you both die unexpectedly—let's say in a car accident—there would be nothing left for your three children. However, if you elect the 10-years certain feature, the monthly payment is nearly as good, $561.7 (that amounts to an annual return of 6.7 percent). Here again, if you both live beyond that 10-year period, there would be nothing for your children."

"I see what you mean. On the other hand, if we invested only a portion of our holdings, let's say $100,000, with the insurance company, that wouldn't affect the rest of our assets in stocks and mutual funds. In other words, we wouldn't be completely disinheriting them. Maybe we shouldn't discard the annuity option out of hand. In fact, I think it might work for us."

"You have a point, Orlinda. Now, let's get back to your stock portfolio. These days, most stocks have rather skimpy dividends. In years past, you could obtain five or six percent from a solid common stock portfolio, particularly if you included some public utilities. Not anymore. To be sure, you can invest in preferred stocks for a higher yield, but that limits your growth potential. Preferred stocks are not like common stocks. They pay the same dividend year after year, whereas common stocks often raise their payout—some nearly every year. You can also invest some of your money in real estate investment trusts, or REITs. As I recall, you already own Boston Properties and Equity Office Properties, but both are tiny holdings. I would suggest bolstering this segment of your portfolio, with additional shares in those two REITs and perhaps Washington Real Estate or Kimco."

"That sounds fine to me. I like the higher income and the stability of real estate. But I assume that you wouldn't advise investing more than 10 percent in REITs. Am I correct?"

"I can see you have been reading my chapter on diversification. Many investors have found themselves in hot water concentrating on their favorite sector. You are clearly not guilty of that blunder.

"Next, we should look at asset allocation. As your portfolio now stands, you are mostly invested in common stocks and mutual funds, with only a moderate amount in fixed-income, such as bonds, preferred stocks, and cash. You might prefer to cushion your holdings with more in that sector. I like to use a person's age to make that determination. As you may recall, a person who is sixty-five should have 65 percent in common stocks, with the rest in fixed-income. That way, if the market heads south and takes the Dow Jones Average down ten or fifteen percent, you won't end up bleeding at the mouth. As you get older, the fixed-income holdings should be increased by 1 percent each year. By age eighty, you would be fifty-fifty. Right now, you have 38 percent in money-market funds, plus preferred stock. That's close to my guidelines. Actually, if we average your age (sixty-seven) and Bud's age (seventy-one), that comes to sixty-nine. Based on my formula, you should have fifty-nine percent in common stocks and thirty-nine percent in money-market funds, and so forth. So, you're very close to that now. I see no reason to make an adjustment at the moment."

"I think I can see your reasoning. What's next?"

"Since you need income, now that you are retired, we have to put together a plan that will supplement your Social Security and any pensions."

"We both have Social Security, but Bud was in business for himself, and I am a nurse, but I did mostly private duty, so I don't have a pension either. That's why we have to rely on our holdings. What worries me is taking money out of principal. If dividends are not sufficient, and we dip into the principal, we might end up dead broke at the age of eighty-five. We certainly can't eat much steak on that. And no more new cars. And what if we need a new roof on the house, or the cellar starts leaking and we have to dig up the whole yard to keep from drowning? I hope you can come up with some solution to our situation."

"I can't make you rich, Orlinda, but I think I can suggest a plan that will keep you solvent—although not exactly able to take an annual trip to Paris, Calcutta, Istanbul, or Rome. You are right that dipping into principal can get a bit scary. In the old days, this wasn't necessary, since dividends were much higher. But today, a sensible plan for using principal can be set up. For instance, you can get a good income from your mutual funds. Nearly all have a systematic withdrawal plan. They will agree to send you a monthly check that will gradually dip into principal, but won't deplete the principal, unless you elect a ridiculously high payout, such as 10 percent. If you elect to take out only 5 percent each year, normal growth, coupled with dividends, will normally maintain the value of your holdings. To be sure, some years, your principal may decline, but it will be offset by other years when the market has been rising. So, I think you should call each of your mutual fund companies and ask them to send you a history of how a 5 percent withdrawal has worked historically, let's say over the past ten or fifteen years. Then, you can decide whether 5 percent is okay, or whether you should settle for 4 percent."

"So far, I think you've given me some good ideas. I hope your fee won't damage my pocketbook beyond repair."

"I'm glad you brought that up. It's true that I make my living by managing portfolios for people like you and Bud. In most instances, our fee is 1 percent a year. On larger portfolios, that can be reduced somewhat below 1 percent. However, I don't charge for my initial interview. But if you and your husband need further guidance, then you would be expected to become a client of the firm I'm associated with, Klopp Investment Management."

"What a relief! I was certain you were going to present me a bill. Since this is still the first interview, can I assume that I can ask you a few more questions?"

"As long as the Green Mountain coffee holds out."

"A few minutes ago, you mentioned setting up a monthly income with our mutual funds. I like that. And, if we do something with an annuity, that would also enhance our regular income. But so far, you haven't mentioned how we should deal with our huge stock portfolio. We certainly can't buy much caviar on the meager dividends most of them pay."

"Exactly. But I do have a solution. Suppose we set up a plan that would pay you 5 percent of the value each year?"

"But that would be invading the principal, wouldn't it? That's pretty risky."

"Right. Most people don't want to invade principal. But what I am suggesting is taking only 5 percent of the current principal each year. So, if the total value of your holdings drops 10 percent in a given year, you will be taking out only 5 percent of this reduced value, rather than 5 percent of the value it had at the beginning of the period. You can never use up your total principal if you always restrict your withdrawal to 5 percent of the value of the portfolio at the beginning of each period."

"I see what you mean. But what happens to our income if the portfolio sags a couple years in a row, like it did in 2000, 2001, and 2002?"

"Admittedly, that was a really bad stretch. In fact, it was just about the worst period I can ever remember, with the possible exception of 1973–1974. On the other hand, the stock market typically goes up a lot more than it declines. In those years, you will still be deducting your usual 5 percent. Let's say the portfolio increases by 20 percent in a really good year. You are still way ahead of the game if you only remove 5 percent. That makes it a lot easier for your holdings to withstand a dip in a bad year."

"You are beginning to make a lot of sense, Slats. On the other hand, we would have to get by on a smaller amount during those declining years. Right?

"It's not as bad as you might think, Orlinda. Bear in mind that your Social Security is not likely to decline merely because the stock market takes a hit. In fact, it is likely to keep increasing to keep up with inflation. Then, too, your mutual fund withdrawal won't change, regardless of what the market does. It is based on taking out a fixed amount based on the beginning value this year, such as 5 percent, or a fixed dollar amount. What's more, if you buy an annuity, that too will keep paying you the same amount each year. All in all, a 10 percent decline in the stock market will not mean a 10 percent drop in your total income. In fact, I doubt that it will even mean a 5 percent drop in your total income."

"I can see why you write such great books, Slats. You have really solved my problem. Except for one thing: If I am going to adopt your 5 percent stock plan, I still have to decide which stock to sell each year. That might not be easy, since I like my current portfolio."

"That's where I come into the picture. If you can't decide, then you need an investment adviser. That could be me and Klopp Investment Management. Why don't you give it some thought and call me in a few days if you decide I might be of service to you and the fisherman."

The next day, I wrote Orlinda a thank you letter and pointed out why I was the ideal adviser to handle her account. I guess I didn't present my case very effectively. She hasn't called yet. I wonder if I should send her another thank you letter. It's now been eight months since I attended her garage sale. Of course, she could be peeved that I didn't buy anything.

# A Novel Approach to Asset Allocation

I'm not sure whether my neighborhood is characteristic of Vermont as a whole, but Beech Street in Essex Junction seems to teem with dog-walkers. One dog-walker, in particular, is a real puzzle. The lady who leads this little canine is an attractive widow who looks younger than her fifty-eight years.

But Brutus Kutch III, her little over-wrought monster, is about as big as an *Alley Cat Felis domestica*. I am convinced this diminutive wretch is bent on having me for lunch. As soon as he sees me—even from a block away—he starts to yap with ferocity and petulance. Apparently, he is convinced that I am guilty of some heinous crime. Fortunately, the other dogs in the area are unaware of my crimes against the family Canidae, since rarely do any of them bare their fangs or utter a word of discontent when I encounter them on my daily walk through the streets of Essex Junction.

I have not tried petting Brutus (I value my hands), but I have offered him some delicious morsels of fancy dog food. But to no avail—I am still his mortal enemy. It's too bad, because I enjoy chatting with Alice Hardleigh, the lady at the other end of the leash who lives nearby on Taffeta Trail. She tells me that Brutus is the only Mongolian toy mastiff in Chittenden County. That's certainly good news!

One day, when Brutus had finally calmed down after Ms. Hardleigh held the little cuss in her arms, she said, "Mr. Slatter, I have been reading your book, but I'm not sure how I should set up my portfolio. I wonder whether you could have lunch with me at the Lincoln Inn sometime and get me headed in the right direction."

"I assume you'll bring Brutus with you," I said.

"Only if you insist. He's never liked the Lincoln Inn."

Once the waiter had taken our orders for Diet Cokes, Alice opened the conversation about her situation. (She doesn't like me to call her Ms. Hardleigh, but persists in addressing me as Mr. Slatter. It must be my gray hair. Hers is auburn, with no trace of old age.)

"I know you have a chapter in your book on asset allocation, but somehow I thought I would feel more comfortable getting your thoughts on my particular situation. Does that make sense?"

"Everyone is different, Alice. I assume that your late husband left you with adequate finances. Can you give me an idea of what your holdings are?"

"Yes, you're right, Mr. Slatter, I'm not exactly a pauper. Besides a pension, Fillmore left me an insurance policy worth $300,000. Right now, I don't have to touch the principal, since I manage to keep the bills paid from my piano lessons. I have a waiting list, so I guess it has paid to keep my fingers limber over the years. Fillmore and I used to entertain our friends with my playing and his singing."

"I get the feeling that your $300,000 is still in cash," I said.

"In a money market, which is yielding practically nothing. I know I should put this money to work, but I think I need a little nudge."

"Unfortunately, there is no secret formula for asset allocation," I said. "A few people invest entirely in stocks or mutual funds, with no bonds and very little cash. If you start investing young enough, let's say in your twenties or thirties, stocks are the best way to go. Over the years, stocks (including dividends) have returned about 11 percent a year, compounded. By contrast, bonds, CDs, and other fixed-income vehicles have rarely done much better than 6 percent. That's quite a difference. Let's say you were thirty-five years of age and had $300,000 to invest, and you put it all in stocks. By age sixty-five, your nest egg would be worth more than $8.8 million. On the other hand, if you invested the same $300,000 at 6 percent, you would have only $2.5 million when you reached retirement age."

"Are you suggesting that I invest all my money in common stocks, Mr. Slatter? That sounds a little scary to me. I think Fillmore would turn over in his grave."

"I'm not surprised. Most people know that stocks involve risk—sometimes a lot of risk—and they simply can't stand the worry that it may involve. Of course, diversification can help some. If you own twenty or thirty stocks, you are spreading the risk of owning only a half dozen. However, the risk of stock ownership is still there.

"There are a number of formulas that have been devised. A simple rule of thumb is to invest 70 percent in stocks and the rest in fixed income, such as bonds. This percentage might be suitable for an average investor. But for someone who tends to be conservative, a more suitable breakdown might be 60 percent stocks, with the rest in bonds and money-market funds. Finally, for those who are ultraconservative, the best formula would be to balance stocks and fixed income fifty-fifty."

"I'm not sure which camp I might fall into. Do you have any other magic formulas?" asked Alice, as she munched on her caesar salad.

"Another one that I devised is based on age. My thinking is that younger people should be more aggressive than older people. At fifty-eight, you're kind of in the middle."

"How does it work?"

"It's quite simple and revolves around the investor who is sixty-five years old.

At that age, I suggest having 65 percent in stocks and the rest in bonds and other fixed-income vehicles. But if you are older than sixty-five, you should edge toward the fixed-income sector. My formula says to deduct 1 percent each year from the common stock sector, so that when you reach seventy, you will have 60-percent invested in stocks. Going a step further, when you reach eighty, you'll be fifty-fifty."

"I can't see how that works for me. I'm only fifty-eight." said Alice, as she broke her club sandwich into small portions.

"I was just getting to that. For those younger than sixty-five, the strategy is to add to the percentage invested in common stocks. For each year younger, add 1 percent. That means that for you we would add 7 percent, bringing the total of 72 percent. How does that sound?"

"I can see the logic of your formula, but somehow I don't think I would sleep at night knowing I had more than $200,000 in stocks. How could I afford food for Brutus if the stock market went into a tailspin? I think we had better go to plan C. Do you have any more strategies?"

"Just one more. If you don't like this one, I'm afraid there is no plan D."

"I see you have finished off your prime rib," she said. "Why don't we get another cup of coffee before you start?"

When the coffee arrived, I began my explanation of plan C. "Incidentally, this strategy is not in any of my other books. So, pay close attention."

"I guess I had better takes notes. Okay, my pen is ready to record your words of wisdom. If I like this one, I will give specific orders to Brutus Kutch III to stop barking at you."

"Thanks. Now I won't have to carry a gun when I walk by 36 Taffeta Trail. I think you'll like this one—it's got a little bit of everything. Let's take your $300,000. We divide it into three equal segments, with $100,000 in each. The first $100,000 is invested in twenty blue-chip stocks, with $5,000 in each. These are all huge companies, most of them in the Dow Jones Industrial Average—stocks like General Electric, United Technologies, Coca-Cola, Citigroup, ExxonMobil, Home Depot, IBM, Johnson & Johnson, Merck, 3M Company, Procter & Gamble, Wal-Mart, Anheuser-Busch, Colgate-Palmolive, Costco, FedEx, United Parcel, Lowe's, and Walgreen. How does that sound so far?"

"Great. I think we're onto something. I will alert Brutus that you are not all bad."

"On to the second part. There are those who think that index funds are the best way to invest. They contend that actively managed mutual funds can't compete against them because of the high cost of management, usually about 1.5 percent a year. I agree. A good index fund is the Standard & Poor's 500. You can buy it on the American Stock Exchange. It trades there as an exchange-traded fund with a ticker symbol of IVV. In effect, you are buying all 500 stocks, so diversification is outstanding. One big advantage of an index fund is the low cost. Those managed by Vanguard have an expense ratio of less than 0.25 percent, compared with 1.5 percent for a typical managed mutual fund. I suggest putting $33,000 in IVV.

"The next $33,000 should go into another index fund. This one is called DIAMONDS, or DIA. It invests in the thirty stocks that make up the Dow Jones Industrial Average.

"The third $33,000 goes into a very broad group of stocks that are not in the S&P 500. In other words, they are stocks that are smaller. Many smaller companies may not be familiar, but they are nonetheless worth owning for their future growth. If past history is any indication of the future, small stocks are somewhat more volatile (or more risky), but they tend to perform better than industry giants over the long haul. This index fund is called the Vanguard Extended Market Index, and has a symbol of VXF.

"According to my friend Don Dempsey, an investment advisor in Burlington, Vermont, the Extended Market Index is designed to track the performance of the Wilshire 4500 Completion Index, a broadly diversified index of small- and medium-size U.S. companies. The Wilshire 4500 Index contains all of the U.S. common stocks regularly traded on the New York and American Exchanges and the NASDAQ over-the-counter market, except those stocks included in the S&P 500.

"By investing in these three market indexes, Alice, you should do well—assuming the stock market does well."

"I'm beginning to like your idea," said Alice Hardleigh. "That still leaves $100,000. So far, we have lots of stocks."

"Right. The rest is left in a money-market fund or in U.S. treasury bonds that mature in less than five years. Bonds that mature within a few years, as opposed to those that mature twenty or thirty years from now, are much less volatile, and are far better to hold when interest rates start back up.

"Thus, if stocks have a temporary sinking spell, you will still have an anchor to the windward to preserve a good part of your holdings. To be sure, this is a conservative strategy, but I think it fits the bill for you and Brutus. But before we go ahead with it, you will want to consult with him. After all, he's the one that wants to have me for lunch."

"I still can't understand why he has such a loathing for you, Mr. Slatter. He's normally such a mild-mannered pooch—like all the other Mongolian toy mastiffs. They're a wonderful breed."

The next day I walked by her house on Taffeta Trail and heard the familiar yapping of Brutus Kutch III. It was coming from inside the house, so I knew I was safe from attack.

# A Word about My Record

I was working out in my exercise room when the phone rang. It was J. Dirndl Smith, calling from upstate New York. He said his wife had purchased a copy of my book for his birthday, and he had read it cover to cover. Apparently, he really liked it; he asked me to reserve a copy of my next edition—and to "make sure you autograph it."

"I've never understood why some people ignore their first name and prefer to be called by their middle name," I said. "Or, am I being too personal?"

"I got sick and tired of seeing half the phone book devoted to guys named John Smith. I wanted to be different. My first name happens to be John—like yours. I notice that you prefer to be called Slats."

"I see what you mean. There are definitely far too many Johns in this world. I assume that you have some questions. I thought my book explained everything that an investor would want to know. But I guess I left out a few things."

"Nothing is perfect, Mr. Slatter. But your book comes pretty close. For one thing, your manner of writing appeals to me. No big words or fancy lingo. Every chapter is understandable, even for a novice like me. Still, there is one thing that I wanted to clear up, and your willingness to let me call you is appreciated. I hope this is not a bad time."

"Well, I was just finishing up with my seven torture machines. I am a fiend for daily exercise. Most of my seven machines were purchased at garage sales for no more than $25—two of them for a paltry $5. And they're not cheap machines. Bought new, they probably cost several hundred each. Apparently, a lot of people have good intentions, but then give it up and want to get rid

of the beast for a song. Normally, I prefer that people call during business hours, but the Red Sox game was rained out tonight, so I guess I'll make an exception."

"I'm a Yankee fan, so I suppose we're enemies," said J. Dirndl Smith, but I didn't denote any evidence of a smile.

"Not anymore, Mr. Smith."

"Just call me Dirndl, Slats. My question is why don't you publish your record? I assume it isn't very good, or you would be bragging about it."

"I've been asked that question many times, Dirndl. There are several reasons why I don't brag about how well my 100 stocks have performed over the past nine or ten years. For one thing, I am never sure when I should begin counting. Normally, the book hits the bookstores in early October. Should I assume that this is when everyone buys the book and then calculate how each stock performed a year later, or should I start counting on January 1 and end with January 1 the following year? On the other hand, why should I confine my calculation to one year? Most investors don't buy my stocks for a few months or a year. They often hold them for several years, which is fine—that's what they *should* do. So, one year is not necessarily indicative of how my stocks are performing."

"I see what you mean," said Dirndl Smith. "Any other reasons?"

"One reason is time. I have better things to do than make a zillion calculations. Then, too, my 100 stocks are not the same from one year to another. In a typical year, I delete twenty-five or thirty stocks and replace them with a similar number that look attractive to me. Some people ask me if they should sell the deleted stocks, and I usually tell them that my stocks are long-term recommendations and that there is not necessarily any reason to make wholesale switches every year."

"I see what you mean; anything else?"

"Most of the people who buy my book seem happy as clams with their results. And they keep buying more copies, year after year. It is one of the strongest selling books published by Adams Media. Here's what one satisfied customer told me in an e-mail on August 2004:

"'I have purchased many copies of your 2003 and 2004 *100 Best Stocks You Can Buy* book. I have used your book myself to significantly diversify my stock portfolio. I have also given many copies to friends, advising them to use the book as a guide as how to get into the market. I look forward to the 2005 edition!'"

"That sounds like a satisfied customer, Slats, but he doesn't say it has made him rich. Frankly, I am beginning to have my doubts."

"From time to time, I have made spot checks on my stocks, just to satisfy my own curiosity. In many instances, my record outperforms the market, but not always. What it tells me is this: In all likelihood, my record would not outperform the Dow Jones Industrial Average or the Standard & Poor's 500 every year. By the same token, if you examined a random list of mutual funds, you would find the same pattern. Every portfolio manager has a particular method of picking stocks. Some prefer growth stocks, for instance; some like value stocks; while still others look for momentum. There are plenty of other strategies, as well. None of those strategies is a consistent winner. To give you an idea how difficult it is to outperform the market (such as the Dow Jones Average or the Standard & Poor's 500), I selected five major funds and calculated their total return (growth plus dividends) for the years 1999 through the most recent year. Not one of these funds outperformed the S&P 500 in all of these years. And four of them failed to equal or exceed the market twice during this brief span of time. Let me e-mail you these results. I have marked with an asterisk the years in which those funds failed to equal the S&P 500:

| | 2003 | 2002 | 2001 | 2000 | 1999 |
|---|---|---|---|---|---|
| Fidelity Magellan | +24.7* | -23.3* | -11.6 | -9.1 | +23.5 |
| Inv. Co. of America | +24.8* | -14.3 | -6.2 | +3.6 | +15.9* |
| Washington Mutual | +26.2* | -14.9 | -1.3 | +7.1 | +1.0* |
| Fidelity Contrafund | +28.1 | -9.1 | -12.6* | -6.7 | +14.7* |
| Dodge & Cox Stock Fund | +30.6 | -8.9 | +9.2 | +1.9 | +13.4* |
| S&P 500 Index | +27.0 | -21.7 | -12.1 | -9.2 | +20.0 |

"Then, I picked five more common stock mutual funds—essentially at random—that had been in business at least ten years. Only one of them had a perfect record during the same five-year period: Gabelli Value Fund outperformed the S&P 500 throughout. The other four each had at least two years of failure, and three of them failed to do as well as the Index on three or four separate occasions:

| | 2003 | 2002 | 2001 | 2000 | 1999 |
|---|---|---|---|---|---|
| AIM Aggressive Growth | +27.4 | -22.6* | -26.0* | +2.7 | +43.5 |
| Burnham Fund Class A | +21.4* | -24.8* | -20.8* | +2.1 | +25.5 |
| Fidelity Blue Chip | +24.7 | -25.3* | -16.6* | -14.3* | +23.8 |
| Gabelli Value Fund | +31.9 | -15.6 | +5.1 | +0.9 | +31.7 |
| MassMutual Inv. Trust | +21.8* | -22.4* | -16.2* | -0.3 | +4.3* |
| S&P 500 Index | +27.0 | -21.7 | -12.1 | -9.2 | +20.0 |

"I am certain that my stocks won't be world beaters every year," I told Mr. Smith, "so why go to the trouble of advertising it?"

"Thanks for your thoughts, Mr. Slatter," said J. Dirndl Smith. "I think I can understand your position. Please cancel my order for your next book."

The phone went dead. I wasted no time in hopping back on my rowing machine. I switched on my headset and began listening to *Eisenhower*, written by Geoffrey Perret and narrated by Nelson Runger, my absolute favorite *Recorded Books* reader.

# When to Sell

Deciding when to sell is often a wrenching experience. Not long ago, I was fretting over whether to sell Eli Lilly. For one thing, it was not acting well, often sagging when the rest of the market was moving ahead. For another, I was concerned that Lilly was hurting my overall performance, since it was my largest holding. Those are two good reasons to sell a stock—or at least part of it. I ended up selling 300 shares.

Over the years, I have read a number of articles on when to sell, such as one written by Manuel Schiffres for *Kiplinger's Personal Finance Magazine* in February of 1994. He said, "There are some general rules for when to sell a stock—such as when it reaches preposterous valuation levels or when the reason you bought it no longer applies. For example, if you bought a stock because you had high hopes for a new product, you should sell if the product is a lemon. Or, if you owned a stock for its high dividends—as many IBM investors did—and the company slashes the payout, that is also a strong signal to sell.

"Consider selling if your goals change, you desire a more defensive investment posture or you want to establish a gain or loss for tax reasons. Also consider selling if a more attractive opportunity comes along. Always ask yourself, 'What's my potential for this stock over the next twelve months?'" says Michael DiCarlo, who runs the John Hancock Special Equities fund. "If it's 15 percent, and you have something you think can make 50 percent, that's an easy swap to make."

## Advice from *Better Investing*

To be sure, there are any number of reasons to sell one of your holdings. Here are seven that are enumerated by the National Association of Investors Corporation (NAIC), which gives assistance and advice to the nation's investment clubs. NAIC also publishes an outstanding monthly magazine, *Better Investing*—I am a faithful subscriber. Here are the sell signals featured by NAIC:

- Sell because an issue of equal or better quality offers the potential for higher returns.
- Sell because of an adverse management change.
- Sell because of declining profit margins or a deteriorating financial structure.
- Sell because direct or indirect competition is affecting the prosperity of the company.
- Sell because a company has great dependence on a single product whose cycle is running out.
- Sell to increase quality or decrease quality as circumstances dictate.
- Sell companies that have become cyclical and have low-growth-rate issues because prosperity is about to succumb to recession.

## Helpful Criteria to Use When Judging a Stock

If those reasons for selling don't cover all the bases, perhaps you should consider some of my own ideas on the subject. In an earlier chapter, I discussed what to look for when you are buying a stock. If you examine that list of factors—a version of which is given below—and find that the stock in question does not measure up, that could be a signal to sell:

- A rising trend in earnings, dividends, and book value per share. This information can be obtained from such publications as

*Value Line Investment Survey* or Standard & Poor's tear sheets. You'll find them at most brokerage offices and some libraries.

- A balance sheet with less debt—compared with equity—than other companies in its particular industry. In most instances, I look for 75 percent or more in shareholders' equity, and the rest in long-term debt.

- An S&P quality rating of B+ (which is average) or better. If you refer to Value Line, their average financial strength rating is B++.

- A P/E ratio (defined below) no higher than average for that industry.

- A dividend yield—such as 2 percent or 3 percent—that suits your particular needs. If a $30 stock has an annual dividend of $.75, that's a yield of 2.5 percent ($.75 divided by $30).

- A stock that insiders—such as officers and board members—are not selling in significant quantities.

- A below-average dividend payout ratio. For instance, if a company earns $4 a share and pays out $3 in dividends, it doesn't have much left to invest in new facilities, acquisitions, research, or marketing. A payout ratio of 25 percent would be far better.

- A history of earnings and dividends not pockmarked by erratic ups and downs.

- Companies whose return on equity is 15 or better.

- A ratio of price to cash flow that is not too high when compared to other stocks in the same industry. Here again, you can obtain this information from Value Line or Standard & Poor's.

To be sure, you are not likely to find a company that fits all of those criteria precisely. But if the stock you are worried about misses the mark on the majority of those benchmarks, perhaps the time has come to make a switch. What's more, if you already have a stock in mind that *does* fit the above criteria, you have a good reason to sell the one that doesn't.

## Is the Stock Priced Too High?

One good reason to sell a stock is price. Even though the company has most of the other features, if it has climbed to a level that doesn't make sense, it may be prudent to unload it. One of the best gauges to determine price level is the price/earnings ratio. If you bought the stock when it had a P/E of 22, for example, and it is now in the high 30s, it may be a good time to find something that's more reasonably priced, assuming it also fits the pattern described above. The P/E is calculated by dividing the price by the annual earnings per share. If a stock sells for $40 and earned $1.32 in the past twelve months, that works out to a P/E of 30.3—which is much higher than stocks in general. But if the earnings were $2.75, that would be a multiple of 14.6, which is below the market, and might be a bargain if it has the features described above.

## Don't Fall in Love with a Stock

You may recall that one reason I sold 300 shares of Eli Lilly was because I owned too much of the stock. A good rule of thumb is to invest no more than 5 percent of your portfolio in any single stock. That means that you should own at least twenty stocks. I own more than 50 stocks.

I can appreciate you may be reluctant to pare back one of your large holdings, since the price has risen appreciably, and you would have to cough up a chunk of cash for the tax collector. That used to make sense, but no more. The maximum capital gains tax is now a mere 15 percent.

One thing to bear in mind when you are giving thought to selling a stock is portfolio turnover. Most conservative investors should avoid too much trading. Buy and hold is a good strategy. Most mutual funds, however, don't adhere to this dictum. They often hold their stocks for no more than twelve months. According to an article in *Fortune* magazine on August 23, 2004: "As it turns out, most of that activity is not paying off for investors. Quite the opposite, in fact," says the author Janice Revell. "A recent Morningstar study shows that managers who adhere to a buy-and-hold strategy—and stifle the impulse to react to short-term market gyrations—tend to outperform their faster-fingered rivals.

"Morningstar analyst Kerry O'Boyle first screened the universe of actively managed equity funds for 1992–98 to find those that fell into the lowest quartile for both portfolio turnover and the number of stocks held. He then went back and tracked the five-year performance for each fund, year by year, from 1992 through 2003. The result: Among all style categories, the concentrated low-turnover funds overwhelmingly beat their peers."

My thought is to make occasional changes, but don't get carried away with change. If your annual turnover is 10 or 20 percent, that should be sufficient. On the other hand, if you *never* bother to update your portfolio, you will end up with too many dogs that should have been sold long ago.

# Part II

# 100 Best Stocks You Can Buy

The following table lists the 100 stocks discussed in this book, with a brief description of each.

The ticker symbol is given so that you can easily look up the stock on the Internet or use the quote machine in your broker's office. This also makes it easier to get a quote over the phone from your broker, since brokers don't know every ticker symbol.

In the table, the heading "Industry" refers to one of the company's main businesses. This is not always easy to express in one or two words.

For instance, United Technologies is involved in such industries as aircraft engines, elevators, and air-conditioning equipment. To describe the company succinctly, I arbitrarily picked the designation "aircraft engines."

General Electric presents an even more daunting problem since it owns NBC and makes appliances, aircraft engines, medical devices, and a host of other things.

"Sector" indicates the broad economic industry group that the company operates in. In this book, I specify the following ten sectors: Energy, Financial, Drug and Health Care, Consumer Staples, Consumer Discretion, Information Technology, Industrials, Materials, Telecommunications, and Utilities. A properly diversified portfolio should include at least one stock from each of the ten sectors.

The heading "Category" describes the type of investment the stock represents, as follows: Income is for income stocks; Gro Inc stands for growth and income; Con Grow means conservative growth; and Aggr Gro signifies aggressive growth. As with the sectors your stocks represent, it might make sense to have some stocks from each category, even if you have a strong preference for only one.

I have not included the page numbers because of space limitations. In any event, it is easy enough to find a particular stock, since they appear alphabetically in the book.

| Company | Symbol | Industry | Sector | Category |
|---|---|---|---|---|
| –A– | | | | |
| Abbott Laboratories | ABT | Med. supplies | Drugs Health | Con Grow |
| Air Products | APD | Gases | Materials | Con Grow |
| Alberto-Culver | ACV | Cosmetics | Cons. Staples | Con Grow |
| Alcoa | AA | Aluminum | Materials | Aggr Gro |
| Alltel Corporation | AT | Telephone | Telecommunications | Gro Inc |
| American Standard * | ASD | Plumbing | Cons. Discret. | Con Grow |
| AutoZone | AZO | Auto parts | Cons .Discret. | Aggr Gro |
| AvalonBay * | AVB | Apartments | Financial | Gro Inc |
| Avon Products | AVP | Beauty prod. | Cons. Staples | Con Grow |
| | | | | |
| –B– | | | | |
| Bank of America | BAC | Money center bank | Financial | Gro Inc |
| Banta | BN | Printing | Industrials | Gro Inc |
| Bard, C. R. | BCR | Hosp. prod. | Drugs Health | Con Grow |
| Barnes & Noble | BKS | Bookstores | Cons. Discret. | Aggr Gro |
| Becton, Dickinson | BDX | Med. supplies | Drugs Health | Con Grow |
| Bemis Company | BMS | Packaging | Materials | Gro Inc |
| Biomet, Inc. | BMET | Orthopedic | Drugs Health | Aggr Gro |
| Black & Decker | BDK | Power tools | Cons. Discret. | Gro Inc |
| Brinker Internat'l | EAT | Restaurants | Cons. Discret. | Aggr Gro |

| Company | Symbol | Industry | Sector | Category |
| --- | --- | --- | --- | --- |
| –C– | | | | |
| Canadian Nat'l Railway * | CNI | Railway | Industrials | Con Grow |
| Carnival Corp. * | CCL | Cruise line | Cons. Discret. | Aggr Gro |
| Caterpillar | CAT | Machinery | Industrials | Aggr Gro |
| Chevron | CVX | Gas and oil | Energy | Income |
| Cintas | CTAS | Uniforms | Industrials | Aggr Gro |
| Colgate-Palmolive | CL | Household pd. | Cons. Staples | Con Grow |
| ConAgra | CAG | Food | Cons. Staples | Income |
| ConocoPhillips * | COP | Petroleum | Energy | Gro Inc |
| Costco Wholesale | COST | Wholesale | Cons. Discret. | Aggr Gro |
| CVS Corporation | CVS | Pharmacy | Cons. Staples | Con Gro |
| | | | | |
| –D– | | | | |
| Darden Restaurants | DRI | Restaurants | Cons. Discret. | Con Gro |
| Deere & Company * | DE | Agric. equip. | Industrials | Aggr Gro |
| Dell * | DELL | Computers | Inform. Tech. | Aggr Gro |
| Denstply * | XRAY | Dental supplies | Drugs Health | Con Gro |
| Devon Energy * | DVN | Petroleum | Energy | Aggr Gro |
| Dollar General | DG | Retail | Cons. Discret. | Aggr Gro |
| Donaldson | DCI | Filtration | Industrials | Con Grow |
| Dover Corp. * | DOV | Indust. equip. | Industrials | Aggr Gro |
| Dow Chemical * | DOW | Chemicals | Materials | Gro Inc |
| | | | | |
| –E– | | | | |
| Eaton Corp. * | ETN | Engine parts | Industrials | Gro Inc |
| Ecolab | ECL | Cleaning | Materials | Aggr Gro |
| Emerson Electric | EMR | Elect. equip. | Industrials | Gro Inc |
| Energen * | EGN | Petroleum | Energy | Con Gro |
| Estée Lauder | EL | Skin care | Cons. Staples | Con Gro |
| Ethan Allen | ETH | Furniture | Cons. Discret. | Aggr Gro |
| ExxonMobil | XOM | Petroleum | Energy | Gro Inc |
| | | | | |
| –F– | | | | |
| Family Dollar Stores | FDO | Retail | Cons. Discret. | Aggr Gro |
| FedEx Corporation | FDX | Air freight | Industrials | Aggr Gro |
| Fortune Brands | FO | Consumer prod. | Cons. Discret. | Gro Inc |
| | | | | |
| –G– | | | | |
| Gannett | GCI | Media | Cons. Discret. | Con Grow |
| General Dynamics * | GD | Military vehic. | Industrials | Con Gro |
| General Electric | GE | Elect. equip. | Industrials | Gro Inc |
| General Mills | GIS | Packaged foods | Cons. Staples | Gro Inc |
| | | | | |
| –H– | | | | |
| Home Depot | HD | Retail | Cons. Discret. | Con Gro |
| Hormel Foods | HRL | Food | Cons. Staples | Con Grow |
| | | | | |
| –I– | | | | |
| Illinois Tool Works | ITW | Machinery | Industrials | Con Grow |
| Intel | INTC | Computers | Inform. Tech. | Aggr Gro |

| Company | Symbol | Industry | Sector | Category |
|---|---|---|---|---|
| –I– | | | | |
| Int'l Business Mach. | IBM | Computer | Inform. Tech. | Aggr Gro |
| Int'l Flavors & Fragr. * | IFF | Flavors | Cons Staples | Con Gro |
| | | | | |
| –J– | | | | |
| Johnson & Johnson | JNJ | Med. supplies | Drugs Health | Con Grow |
| Johnson Controls | JCI | Elect. Equip. | Cons Discret. | Con Grow |
| | | | | |
| –K– | | | | |
| Kellogg * | K | Cereals | Cons Staples | Con Grow |
| Kimco Realty | KIM | REIT | Financial | Gro Inc |
| Kinder Morgan Energy * | KMP | Pipelines | Energy | Gro Inc |
| | | | | |
| –L– | | | | |
| Lilly, Eli | LLY | Drugs | Drugs Health | Aggr Gro |
| Lowe's Companies | LOW | Retail | Cons. Discret. | Con Grow |
| | | | | |
| –M– | | | | |
| McCormick & Co. | MKC | Spices | Cons. Staples | Con Grow |
| McGraw-Hill | MHP | Publishing | Cons. Discret. | Con Grow |
| MDU Resources | MDU | G&E Utility | Utilities | Gro Inc |
| Medtronic | MDT | Med. devices | Drugs Health. | Aggr Gro |
| Meredith | MDP | Publishing | Cons Discret. | Con Gro |
| Microsoft | MSFT | Comp. soft. | Inform. Tech. | Con Gro |
| | | | | |
| –O– | | | | |
| Oshkosh Truck | OSK | Trucks | Industrials | Aggr Gro |
| | | | | |
| –P– | | | | |
| Patterson Companies | PDCO | Dental | Drugs Health | Aggr Gro |
| PepsiCo | PEP | Beverages | Cons. Staples | Con Grow |
| Pfizer | PFE | Drugs | Drugs Health | Aggr Gro |
| Piedmont Nat'l Gas | PNY | Nat'l gas | Utilities | Income |
| Pitney Bowes * | PBI | Mail systems | Inform. tech. | Gro Inc |
| Praxair | PX | Indust. gases | Materials | Con Grow |
| Procter & Gamble | PG | Household pd. | Cons Staples | Con Grow |
| Progressive Corp. * | PGR | Auto ins. | Financial | Aggr Gro |
| | | | | |
| –R– | | | | |
| RPM Int'l * | RPM | Coatings | Cons Staples | Gro Inc |
| Ruby Tuesday | RI | Restaurants | Cons Discret. | Con Grow |
| | | | | |
| –S– | | | | |
| St. Jude Medical * | STJ | Med. devices | Drugs Health | Aggr Gro |
| Sherwin-Williams * | SHW | Paints | Cons Staples | Aggr Gro |
| J. M. Smucker * | SJM | Jams | Cons Staples | Gro Inc |
| Staples | SPLS | Office prod. | Cons Discret. | Aggr Gro |
| Stryker | SYK | Med. supplies | Drugs Health | Con Grow |
| Sysco Corp. | SYY | Food distrib. | Cons Staples | Aggr Gro |

| Company | Symbol | Industry | Sector | Category |
|---|---|---|---|---|
| –T– | | | | |
| T. Rowe Price * | TROW | Investments | Financial | Con Grow |
| Teva Pharmaceutical | TEVA | Pharmaceuticals | Drugs Health | Aggr Gro |
| Textron * | TXT | Aircraft | Industrials | Gro Inc |
| 3M Company | MMM | Diversified | Industrials | Con Grow |
| –U– | | | | |
| UnitedHealth | UNH | Health care | Drugs Health | Con Grow |
| United Parcel | UPS | Expr. carrier | Industrials | Aggr Gro |
| United Technologies | UTX | Aircraft eng. | Industrials | Con Grow |
| –V– | | | | |
| Valspar Corp. * | VAL | Coatings | Materials | Con Grow |
| Varian Medical | VAR | Med. devices | Drugs Health | Aggr Gro |
| –W– | | | | |
| Walgreen | WAG | Drugstores | Cons. Staples | Con Grow |
| Wal-Mart | WMT | Retail | Cons. Discret. | Aggr Gro |
| Washington Real Est. | WRE | REIT | Financial | Income |
| Wells Fargo * | WFC | Banks | Financial | Gro Inc |

*New in this edition.

Conservative Growth

# Abbott Laboratories

100 Abbott Park Road ❑ Abbott Park, IL 60064–3500 ❑ (847) 938–4475 ❑ Dividend reinvestment plan available: (847) 937–7300 ❑ Web site: www.abbott.com ❑ Ticker symbol: ABT ❑ Listed: NYSE ❑ S&P rating: A ❑ Value Line financial strength rating: A++

"Two of Abbott's drugs are getting a boost, thanks to the withdrawal of Merck's Vioxx arthritis drug and concerns surrounding Pfizer's Celebrex arthritis drug," said an article from the *Dow Jones News Service* by Daniel Rosenberg on December 23, 2004. "Mobic—a pain drug that Abbott co-markets with Boehringer Ingelheim Pharmaceuticals—is getting new prescriptions from former Vioxx and Celebrex users. Celebrex and Vioxx can cause cardiovascular problems, according to studies. Mobic's main ingredient is Meloxicam. Meloxicam is in the class of medicine called nonsteroidal anti-inflammatory medications; ibuprofen is also in this class."

The *Dow Jones* article went on to say, "Prevacid—a stomach drug sold by Tap Pharmaceutical Products, a joint venture between Abbott and Takeda Pharmaceutical Company Ltd—is also benefiting from the Vioxx/Celebrex situation. Dr. Scott Zashin, a rheumatologist in Dallas, said when he switches patients to traditional pain medications from Vioxx or Celebrex, he often prescribes a proton pump inhibitor like Prevacid or Prilosec, to counter possible stomach problems."

## Company Profile

Abbott Laboratories is one of the largest diversified healthcare manufacturers in the world. The company's products are sold in more than 130 countries, with about 40 percent of sales derived from international operations. ABT has paid consecutive quarterly dividends since 1924.

Abbott's major business segments include Pharmaceuticals & Nutritionals (prescription drugs, medical nutritionals and infant formulas) and Hospital & Laboratory Products (intravenous solutions, administrative sets, drug-delivery devices, and diagnostic equipment and reagents).

The company's leading brands are:

• AxSym systems and reagents (immunodiagnostics)

• Biaxin/Biaxin XL/Klalcid/Klaricid (macrolide antibiotic)

• Depakote (bipolar disorder, epilepsy, migraine prevention)

• Depakote ER (migraine prevention)

• Ensure (adult nutritionals)

• Humira (rheumatoid arthritis)

• Isomil (soy-based infant formula)

• Kaletra (HIV infection)

• MediSense glucose monitoring products

• Mobic (to control pain)

• Similac (infant formula)

• Synthroid (hypothyroidism)

• Tricor (a lipid-control agent)

• Ultane/Sevorane (anesthetic)

Although revenue growth in Abbott's infant formula and diagnostics businesses has slowed in recent years, new drugs (such as the antibiotic clarithromycin), new indications (including the BPH claim for Hytrin), the launch of disease-specific medical nutritionals and cost-cutting (diagnostics and hospital supplies) continue to boost the company's profits.

## Shortcomings to Bear in Mind

■ Sarah A. Klein, writing for *Crain's Chicago Business* on March 22, 2004, had these negative observations, "Some of Abbott's best sellers are up for replacement. Biaxin, an antibiotic that accounted for $539 million, or 10.3 percent, of the company's U.S. drug sales last year (2003) loses its patent in 2005. Depakote, used to combat seizures, migraines, and bipolar disorder, was responsible for $886 million, or 16.9 percent of 2003 U.S. drug sales; it loses its patent in 2008. Abbott's license to sell Flomax, Micardis and Mobic, which combined made up another 21.6 percent of 2003 U.S. sales, ends in 2008, as well.

"And if that weren't enough, companies with substitutes for Abbott's Synthroid and Tricor—treatments for thyroid disorder and high cholesterol that together made up more than $1 billion in U.S. drug sales last year—are nipping at Abbott's heels."

## Reasons to Buy

■ "Abbott has one of the most robust pipelines in the pharmaceutical industry," according to a research report issued by the prestigious brokerage firm, Morgan Stanley, on December 6, 2004. "The pipeline includes 1) Humira for Psoriasis and Crohn's disease, 2) oral Zemplar for pre-dialysis patients, 3) Xinlay for prostate cancer, and 4) ABT 874 for Crohn's. This pipeline certainly creates an environment that, at minimum, should allow for Abbott to weather potential 'storms.'

"As a result of a robust pipeline and a significant reduction in risk regarding generic threats, we are maintaining our OVERWEIGHT rating on ABT."

■ Abbott is the leader in rapid testing, in both hospitals and doctors' offices, with tests for strep, pregnancy and a microbe that causes ulcers. The company's Determine line of tests is self-contained, low cost, and easy to use. Since its acquisition of MediSense, Inc. in 1996, the company's blood glucose monitoring systems have been well received by diabetic patients.

- In 2004, Abbott paid $1.2 billion for TheraSense Inc., a fast-growing and innovative maker of blood glucose-monitoring test and equipment for people with diabetes. This move made Abbott a strong number three player in the glucose-monitoring market, behind Roche Holding AG and Johnson & Johnson.

- "Abbott's pipeline of new drugs is strong, and it hopes to file ten new drug applications in 2005," said William C. Lewittes, an analyst with *Value Line Investment Survey,* on December 3, 2004. "The company is most excited about the prospects of Xinlay, a novel prostate cancer chemotherapy treatment. Abbott expects to file a new drug application by year-end (2004), which would imply a launch in early 2006. The company also expects to file for approval of heart disease drug Sindax next year (2005), as well as launch Zemplar for dialysis patients with hyperparathyroidism. Abbott's Medical Products group (20 percent of sales) also has several promising products in development, including a user-friendly glucose-monitoring device for diabetics and additions to its Zomaxx vascular stent line."

- *Standard & Poor's Stock Reports* also had some interesting comments on December 17, 2004. Frank DiLorenzo, CFA, said, "Following recent company guidance for 2005, we maintain our BUY recommendation on our view that ABT's valuation is reasonable and growth prospects are intact."

  Mr. DiLorenzo went on to say, "We also have increased confidence that generic threats will be more than offset by ABT's pipeline and current product offerings."

- The Argus Research Company also gave a BUY rating to Abbott on December 30, 2004. Its analyst, John Watkins, said, "We anticipate that sales and earnings growth for Abbott will pick up into 2005, based on the label expansion of the Humira. We also like the diversity of Abbott into the medical device and testing fields. We believe that the portion of Abbott that remains after the spring spin-off of Hospira will be stronger, as overall margins and growth rates improve."

- On August 23, 2004, an article in *Barron's* referred to Abbott Laboratories and some comments made by twenty-nine-year-old Christopher Tsai, who runs a small investment firm, Tsai Capital, in New York, with $17 million under management in pooled separate accounts. The author of the *Barron's* article was Neil A. Martin, who said, "He is particularly high on Abbott Labs, believing an aging global society will spur sales of the company's anti-arthritis drug Humira. He also foresees strong demand for Abbott's anti-AIDS drug Kaletra. Management gave a big lift to the company's bottom line a few months ago, Tsai says, by shedding its slow-growing hospital-products operation, Hospira. 'I think that the Street will start to re-evaluate Abbott Labs and give it a higher multiple,' Tsai says."

- On December 16, 2004, Banc of America Securities analyzed several key Abbott drugs, three of which are described below by analyst, Glenn J. Novarro:

  • "Humira is a fully human anti-TNF antibody administered every other week by a pre-filled, subcutaneous self-injection for the treatment of rheumatoid arthritis (the most severe type of the disease). It works by blocking the ability of tumor necrosis factor alpha to cause painful joint inflammation. We forecast worldwide Humira sales of $1.28 billion. We expect U.S. sales of $480 billion in 2005, driven by aggressive sales and marketing efforts by Abbott, and international sales of $440 million.

  • "Depakote is used to treat seizures, migraine headaches and mania associated with bipolar disorder. We forecast worldwide

Depakote sales of about $1.05 billion, up 3 percent. We expect U.S. sales of Depakote to grow 3 percent, to $995 million, as it faces increasing competition in the epilepsy category. We also project international sales of $52 million, up 6 percent.

• "Kaletra is a protease inhibitor used to treat HIV infection. We forecast worldwide sales of $1.01 billion, up 13 percent. Kaletra should post $418 million in U.S. sales, up 4 percent from 2004, and $595 million in international sales, up 20 percent."

Total assets: $26,155 million
Current ratio: 1.29
Common shares outstanding: 1,570 million
Return on 2004 shareholders' equity: 24%

|                      | 2004   | 2003   | 2002   | 2001   | 2000   | 1999   | 1998   | 1997   |
|----------------------|--------|--------|--------|--------|--------|--------|--------|--------|
| Revenues (millions)  | 19,680 | 19,681 | 17,685 | 16,285 | 13,746 | 13,178 | 12,513 | 11,889 |
| Net income (millions)| 3,566  | 3,479  | 3,243  | 1,550  | 2,786  | 2,446  | 2,334  | 2,079  |
| Earnings per share   | 2.27   | 2.21   | 2.06   | .99    | 1.78   | 1.57   | 1.50   | 1.32   |
| Dividends per share  | 1.03   | .97    | .92    | .82    | .76    | .68    | .60    | .54    |
| Price        high    | 47.6   | 47.2   | 58.0   | 57.2   | 56.2   | 53.3   | 50.1   | 34.9   |
|              low     | 38.3   | 33.8   | 29.8   | 42.0   | 29.4   | 27.9   | 32.5   | 24.9   |

Conservative Growth

# Air Products and Chemicals, Inc.

7201 Hamilton Boulevard □ Allentown, PA 18195–1501 □ (610) 481–7461 □ Direct dividend reinvestment plan available: (877) 322–4941 □ Web site: *www.airproducts.com* □ Listed: NYSE □ Fiscal years end September 30 □ Ticker symbol: APD □ S&P rating: B+ □ Value Line financial strength rating: B++

"If you've ever pounded a PC, watched a flat-screen TV or filled up at the gas pump, chances are Air Products & Chemicals in Allentown, PA, had something to do with it. This generic giant, with $7 billion in sales and the unsexiest of names, is fast becoming a crucial player in some sexy businesses," said Brett Nelson, writing for *Forbes* magazine on February 14, 2005.

"Makers of computer chips and flat-panel televisions need its chemical molecules and gases to build better chips and snazzy screens. Oil refineries and automakers count on it for the hydrogen needed to make gasoline (and, someday, to power fuel cells). The elderly breathe easier with its portable, lightweight oxygen canisters. It even has a hand in the budding field of nanotechnology.

"The company made its name in the industrial gas business, supplying oxygen, nitrogen, and argon gases at customer factories. But today Air Products gets half its sales from three faster-growing arenas—energy, electronics, and health care—up from 30 percent in 1999."

## Company Profile

Air Products and Chemicals, Inc. is a leading supplier of industrial gases and related equipment, specialty and intermediate chemicals, as well as environmental and energy systems. It has operations in thirty countries.

Air Products' industrial gas and chemical products are used by a diverse base of customers in manufacturing, process and service industries.

In the environmental and energy businesses, Air Products and its affiliates own and operate facilities to reduce air and water pollution, dispose of solid waste, and generate electric power.

## Industrial Gases
• APD is a world leader.
• Its products are essential in many manufacturing processes.
• Gases are produced by cryogenic, adsorption, and membrane technologies.
• They are supplied by tankers, on-site plants, pipelines, and cylinders.
• International sales, including the company's share of joint ventures, represent more than half of Air Products' gas revenues.

The markets served by Industrial Gases include chemical processing, metals, oil, and gas production, electronics, research, food, glass, health care, and pulp and paper. Principal products are industrial gases, such as nitrogen, oxygen, hydrogen, argon, and helium, and various specialty, cutting, and welding gases.

## Chemicals
• APD has a leadership position in over 80 percent of the markets served.
• Markets include a wide range of attractive, diversified end uses that reduce overall exposure to economic cycles.
• World-scale, state-of-the-art production facilities and process technology skills ensure consistent, low-cost products while enhancing long-term customer relationships.
• International sales, including exports to more than 100 countries, represent about 40 percent of APD's business.

The markets served by the Chemicals operation include adhesives, agriculture, furniture, automotive products, paints and coatings, textiles, paper and building products. Its principal products are emulsions, polyvinyl alcohol, polyurethane and epoxy additives, surfactants, amines, and polyurethane intermediaries.

## Environmental and Energy Systems
• Facilities, owned and operated with partners, dispose of solid waste, reduce air pollution, and generate electrical power.
• Strong positions are built by extending core skills developed in the industrial gas business.
• Forces driving this market are environmental regulations, demand for efficient sources of electrical power, utility deregulation, and privatization. Principal products are waste-to-energy plants, electric power services, and air pollution-control systems.

The markets served by Environmental and Energy Systems include solid waste disposal, electrical power generation, and air pollution reduction.

## Equipment and Services
• Cryogenic and noncryogenic equipment is designed and manufactured for various gas-processing applications.
• Equipment is sold worldwide or manufactured for Air Products industrial gas business and its international network of joint ventures.

The markets served by Equipment and Services include chemicals, steel, oil and gas recovery, and power generation.

## Shortcomings to Bear in Mind
■ Air Products has a somewhat leveraged balance sheet. Its common stock represents only 67 percent of capitalization. My preference is for common stock to represent 75 percent of capitalization.

## Reasons to Buy
■ In fiscal 2004 (ended September 30, 2004), Air Products bounced back from an off-year in 2003. Sales climbed to $7.4 billion, a hefty gain of 18 percent. About

half of that increase came from acquisitions and favorable currency effects. Net income, moreover, was up an impressive 22 percent, and Earnings per share came in at $2.64, up 19 percent (excluding the prior year's global cost-reduction charge).

Reflecting on the year, CEO John P. Jones III said, "We built our position serving growth markets and geographics, further improved our portfolio, strengthened our customer relationships and drove up return on capital."

Mr. Jones goes on to say, "We anticipate another solid year of improvement in 2005, driven by a step-change in productivity and modest global economic growth, which will help us load our existing asset base and further improve our return on capital. In Gases, we expect continued growth in our electronics, refinery hydrogen, health care, and Asian businesses. We know we must fix our Chemicals business, and we are committed to delivering significant margin improvements through pricing actions and managing our raw material costs."

- In the 1994–2004 period, earnings per share expanded from $1.03 to $2.64, a solid—although not spectacular—compound annual growth rate of 9.9 percent. In the same ten-year span, dividends increased from $.48 to $1.04, a somewhat lower growth rate of 8 percent. However, the dividend has been raised for twenty-two consecutive years.

- Lehman Brothers rated the stock OVERWEIGHT on January 27, 2005. The analyst said, "As we argued in our recent report, we believe the company's future growth prospects and low volatility deserve multiples in line with other leading industrial companies, such as 3M, Emerson Electric, and Honeywell."

- On February 7, 2005, the Argus Research Company had good things to say about Air Products. Bill Selesky said, "Our rating on Air Products & Chemicals Inc. remains a BUY, and the stock remains in the *Argus Focus List*. We still believe the potential exists for solid revenues, better earnings, and better margins going forward, as the company benefits from its cost reduction program started in the third quarter of 2003. In addition, the company is benefiting from better price realizations."

- APD's CPI division is the world's leading supplier of HyCO products (hydrogen, carbon monoxide, and syngas, a mix of hydrogen and carbon monoxide). The company has increased its capacity tenfold in the last ten years, and about 75 percent of its volume is delivered to major global refining and chemical centers via APD's pipelines.

  Air Products's technical leadership, operational expertise, and established franchises make the company the first choice of customers in the petrochemical, refining, specialty chemical, and life sciences industries. Air Products is also NASA's sole supplier of liquid hydrogen for space shuttle launches.

- Air Products got its start in helium in the 1950s, when the federal government hired the company to extract this "noble gas" from natural gas deposits in the midwestern United States—currently the world's main source of helium. Nearly 50 years later, Air Products is the world's leading helium producer.

  Helium has the lowest melting and boiling points of any element. It is colorless, odorless, and noninflammable. Helium is used in light-air balloons, to make artificial "air" (with oxygen) for deep-sea divers. It is also used in welding, semiconductors, and lasers. In addition, liquid helium is used in cryogenics, a branch of physics that studies materials and effects at temperatures approaching absolute zero.

The helium market is expected to expand by at least 6 percent per year, a rate that suggests another expansion in the Kansas complex will be needed about every two years. And by supplying helium to high-growth markets such as laser welding, semiconductor manufacturing, and fiber optics manufacturing, Air Products is growing faster than the market. The company's KeepCOLD Cryogen Fill Services Program supplies more than 4,500 MRI customer sites around the world. Finally, Air Products owns Gardner Cryogenics, a world leader in manufacturing liquid helium and liquid hydrogen distribution and storage equipment.

- On February 18, 2005, *Value Line Investment Survey* had some favorable thoughts on Air Products, according to Mario Ferro. He said: "Air Products and Chemicals appears to be headed for another good year. The first fiscal quarter (year ends September 30), got off to a fly-ing start, with share net up 24 percent on an 18 percent increase in revenues. The Gases segment continues to provide the bulk of the gains, but we expect results in Chemicals to pick up in the quarters ahead."

- In 2004, Air Products had its share of customer awards and recognitions:
  - Samsung Electronics Company Ltd.'s 2004 Excellent Supplier award
  - Intel Corporation's Preferred Quality Supplier award
  - Taiwan Semiconductor Manufacturing Company's Electronic Gas Supplier of the Year award
  - Siemens Medical Systems' Best Practices—Logistics award for Keep-COLD MRI services
  - The Queen's Award for Enterprise: Innovation 2004 for BIP cylinder technology
  - Home Medical Equipment Excellence award for respiratory therapy

Total assets: $9,992 million
Current ratio: 1.38
Common shares outstanding: 229 million
Return on 2004 shareholders' equity: 14.7%

| | 2004 | 2003 | 2002 | 2001 | 2000 | 1999 | 1998 | 1997 |
|---|---|---|---|---|---|---|---|---|
| Revenues (millions) | 7,411 | 6,297 | 5,401 | 5,858 | 5,467 | 5,020 | 4,919 | 4,638 |
| Net income (millions) | 604 | 397 | 525 | 466 | 533 | 451 | 489 | 429 |
| Earnings per share | 2.64 | 1.78 | 2.42 | 2.12 | 2.46 | 2.09 | 2.22 | 1.95 |
| Dividends per share | 1.04 | .88 | .82 | .78 | .74 | .70 | .64 | .58 |
| Price        high | 59.2 | 53.1 | 53.5 | 49.0 | 42.2 | 49.3 | 45.3 | 44.8 |
|                  low | 46.7 | 37.0 | 40.0 | 32.2 | 23.0 | 25.7 | 33.2 | 25.2 |

# Alberto-Culver Company

2525 Armitage Avenue ❑ Melrose Park, IL 60160 ❑ (708) 450–3145 ❑ Web site: *www.alberto.com* ❑ Dividend reinvestment plan not available ❑ Fiscal years end September 30 ❑ Listed: NYSE ❑ Ticker symbol: ACV ❑ Standard & Poor's rating: A+ ❑ Value Line financial strength rating: A+

"In the early 1950s, entrepreneur and beauty-supply distributor, Blaine Culver, found a chemist named Alberto to formulate a hair treatment that helped motion picture starlets contend with the drying effects of harsh film studio Klieg lights," says a brokerage-house report prepared by UBS Warburg.

The report goes on to say, "The product, a combination of five vital oils, was labeled Alberto V05. In 1955, the year Leonard Lavin purchased Alberto-Culver, the company reported sales of $500,000. From such improbable niche beginnings and through more than 40 years of brand and trade consolidation, Alberto-Culver has somehow managed to navigate a global personal care landscape dominated by the likes of Procter & Gamble, Unilever, and L'Oreal."

In fiscal 2004, Alberto-Culver's had seen its revenues climb to $3.26 billion, and had also seen its sales and earnings increase during good times and bad, including the recession and turmoil that has affected the country during the past few years.

## Company Profile

Alberto-Culver Company, a pioneer on the global package goods stage, has carried the flag from country to country, continent to continent. Today, the company sells its products, such as Alberto V05 and St. Ives Swiss Formula, in 120 countries, with manufacturing facilities in Sweden, the United Kingdom, Australia, Argentina, Mexico, Puerto Rico, and Canada, as well as here at home.

Alberto-Culver is a leading developer, manufacturer of personal-care products, primarily for hair care, retail food products, household items, and health and hygiene products.

Alberto-Culver is comprised of three strong businesses built around potent brands and trademarks:

• Alberto-Culver USA develops innovative brand name products for the retail, professional beauty and institutional markets. Personal-use products include: hair fixatives, shampoos, hair dressings, and conditioners sold under such trademarks as Alberto V05, Bold Hold, Alberto, Alberto Balsam, Consort, TRESemme, and FDS (feminine deodorant spray).

Retail food product labels include: SugarTwin, Mrs. Dash, Molly McButter, Baker's Joy, and Village Saucerie.

Household products include: Static Guard (anti-static spray) and Kleen Guard (furniture polish).

• Alberto-Culver International has carried the Alberto V05 flag into more than 120 countries, and from that solid base has built products, new brands, and businesses focused on the needs of each market.

• Sally Beauty Company is the engine that drives Alberto-Culver. With 2,355 outlets (at the end of 2004) in the United States, the United Kingdom, Canada, Puerto Rico, Japan, and Germany, Sally is the largest cash-and-carry supplier of professional beauty products in the world.

The typical Sally Beauty store averages 1,800 square feet and is situated in a strip shopping center. It carries more than 3,000 items. About three-quarters of Sally Beauty's sales are to small beauty salons and barber shops, with the rest to retail customers.

Sally is the only national player in the United States in cash-and-carry beauty supplies sold primarily to professionals. It is the market leader by a wide margin. Sally capitalizes on its dominance in that niche, which provides beauty professionals the opportunity to purchase products from a wide selection of vendors at wholesale prices without having to manage and carry inventory in their stores.

The company's products do not have a common origin. They have come to Alberto-Culver in diverse ways. For instance, the original Alberto V05 Hairdressing was a small regional brand that the company acquired because it felt it had national sales potential.

In another instance, the FDS products and its mousse products had counterparts in the marketplace in Europe. ACV brought the ideas to the United States and introduced its products to an American audience.

In another realm, Mrs. Dash, Static Guard and Consort were all developed internally by the company's research and development team because its customers identified a need that these products met.

In yet another instance, SugarTwin and TRESemme were acquired by the company as tiny brands and grown to the strong positions they hold today.

Perhaps the company's most important acquisition—after the original purchase of Alberto V05 Conditioning Hairdressing—was the purchase of the Sally Beauty Company, originally a chain of twelve stores, many of which were franchised.

BSG (Beauty Systems Group) network of exclusive professional distributorships has 1,201 sales consultants calling directly on salons in the United States and Canada, and 692 stores at the end of 2004 for the convenience of the salon professional.

## Shortcomings to Bear in Mind

- Sally Beauty Company experiences domestic and international competition from a wide range of retail outlets, including mass merchandisers, drug stores, and supermarkets, carrying a full line of health and beauty products. In addition, Sally Beauty competes with thousands of local and regional beauty supply stores and full-service dealers selling directly to salons through both professional and distributor sales consultants as well as cash-and-carry outlets open only to salon professionals. Sally also faces competition from certain manufacturers that employ their own sales forces to distribute professional beauty products directly to salons.

## Reasons to Buy

- In North America, Alberto-Culver's three largest brands—Alberto V05, TRESemme, and St. Ives—constitute more than 30 percent of the domestic value-priced shampoo/general conditioner market.
- Alberto V05 Hot Oil Conditioning Treatments and Alberto V05 hairdressing, along with St. Ives Facial Scrubs, Consort, and Motions are all number one in their respective domestic categories.
- ACV has increased its dividend for twenty-one consecutive years.
- BSG (Beauty Systems Group), which distributes products to top professional salons for resale to customers, is growing explosively, and is presently in 80 percent of the country as well as parts of Canada and Mexico. Alberto-Culver expects to continue to consolidate this fragmented industry. As it goes national, BSG's sale are projected to surpass the $1 billion level from almost $800 million today—through acquisitions of private companies, synergies, and attractive comparable same-store sales growth.
- *Standard & Poor's Stock Reports* had a favorable view of ACV on February 9, 2005. It analyst, Howard Choe, said: "We have a BUY recommendation on the shares, reflecting what we view as ACV's solid, consistent performance, and attractive valuation."

Despite the high level of industry competition, we believe ACV can continue to execute well, given its experience at the value end of the price spectrum, new products, and what we see as the ability to raise prices in its specialty distribution segment."

■ Alberto V05 Conditioning Hairdressing remains by far the number one brand in its category and the bestselling hairdressing in the world. V05 is among the market leaders in the United States, Great Britain, Scandinavia, Canada, Mexico, Australia, and Japan.

■ In more than 120 countries, Alberto-Culver International markets or manufactures many of the consumer brands that it markets in the United States, including Alberto V05 and St. Ives Swiss Formula brands.

In addition, some of the company's international units offer products unique to their markets. In the Scandinavian countries, for example, ACV is the market leader in a wide range of toiletries and household products. In the United Kingdom, the company is a market leader in hairstyling products. What's more, it has introduced several items in the hair-coloring segment. Finally, in Canada, Alberto-Culver produces the top-selling Alberto-European styling line; and its SugarTwin artificial sweetener is number one in its category.

■ In the 1994–2004 period, Earnings per share advanced impressively, from $.52 to $2.13, for a compound annual growth rate of 15.1 percent. What's more, there were no declines along the way. In the same ten-year stretch, Dividends per share climbed from $.09 to $.37, a growth rate of 15.2 percent.

Total assets: $2,057 million
Current ratio: 2.11
Common shares outstanding: 91 million
Return on 2004 shareholders' equity: 16.4%

|  | 2004 | 2003 | 2002 | 2001 | 2000 | 1999 | 1998 | 1997 |
|---|---|---|---|---|---|---|---|---|
| Revenues (millions) | 3,258 | 2,891 | 2,651 | 2,494 | 2,247 | 1,976 | 1,835 | 1,775 |
| Net income (millions) | 195.4 | 162.1 | 137.7 | 110.4 | 97.2 | 86.3 | 83.1 | 75.6 |
| Earnings per share | 2.13 | 1.80 | 1.55 | 1.27 | 1.22 | 1.01 | 0.91 | 0.83 |
| Dividends per share | .37 | .27 | .23 | .21 | .19 | .17 | .16 | .13 |
| Price          high | 52.3 | 42.9 | 38.6 | 30.8 | 29.0 | 18.6 | 21.6 | 21.7 |
|                low | 39.5 | 31.4 | 27.7 | 24.6 | 12.9 | 14.4 | 13.2 | 15.7 |

---

Aggressive Growth

# Alcoa Inc.

201 Isabella Street at 7th Street Bridge □ Pittsburgh, PA 15212–5858 □ (212) 836–2674 □ Dividend reinvestment plan available: (800) 317–4445 □ Web site: *www.alcoa.com* □ Listed: NYSE □ Ticker symbol: AA □ S&P rating: B+ □ Value Line financial strength rating: A

"The company's revenue growth is being driven by increasing prices of aluminum, reflecting strong demand worldwide for the metal, which is used to make manufactured

goods, airplanes, cars and beverage cans," said Paul Glader, writing for the *Wall Street Journal* on July 8, 2004. "Aluminum prices have risen more than 20 percent in the past year, averaging 76 cents a pound on the London Metal Exchange in the second quarter. That is up from both the first quarter, when the average price was 71.7 cents a pound, and the year-ago quarter, when aluminum was selling at an average of 64.1 cents a pound."

Mr. Glader also said, "Alcoa expects the aerospace industry, one of the company's key markets, generating $2 billion in revenue last year, to improve as Boeing Co. and Airbus prepare to launch new models. Alcoa is adding two hundred and fifty new jobs in Southern California and another one hundred at its Davenport facility in Iowa, immediately for production of fastening systems for use on the new Airbus A-380 airliners that are expected to begin flying in 2006."

## Company Profile

Alcoa (formerly Aluminum Company of America), founded in 1888, is the world's leading integrated producer of aluminum products. The company is active in all major aspects of the industry—technology, mining, refining, smelting, fabricating, and recycling.

Alcoa's aluminum products and components are used worldwide in aircraft, automobiles, beverage cans, buildings, chemicals, sports and recreation, and a wide variety of industrial and consumer applications, including such Alcoa consumer brands as Alcoa wheels, Reynolds Wrap aluminum foil, and Baco household wraps.

Related businesses include packaging machinery, precision castings, vinyl siding, plastic bottles and closures, fiber optic cables, and electrical distribution systems for cars and trucks.

Since aluminum is expensive and has difficulty competing against steel—even though it has some admirable qualities—it might appear to be a rare element. Not so.

Aluminum is an abundant metal and, in fact, is the most abundant metal in the earth's crust. Of all the elements, only oxygen and silicon are more plentiful. Aluminum makes up 8 percent of the crust. It is found in the minerals of bauxite, mica and cryolite, as well as in clay.

Until about 100 years ago, aluminum was virtually a precious metal. Despite its abundance, it was very rare as a pure metal. The reason: it was so difficult to extract from its ore.

This is because aluminum is a reactive metal, and it cannot be extracted by smelting with carbon. To solve the enigma, displacement reactions were tried, but metals such as sodium or potassium had to be used, making the cost prohibitive.

Electrolysis of the molten ore was tried, but the most plentiful ore, bauxite, contains aluminum oxide, which does not melt until it reaches 2050 degrees centigrade.

The solution to the problem of extracting aluminum from its ore was discovered by Charles Hall in the United States and by Paul Heroult in France—both working independently. The method now used to extract aluminum from its ore is called the Hall-Heroult process.

I won't bore you with the steps taken to effect this process. The important fact to remember is that it is far from cheap. Even so, it can be done economically enough to make aluminum the second most widely used metal. However, it is not likely to replace iron and steel any time soon. Iron makes up more than 90 percent of the metals used in the world.

The main cost in the Hall-Heroult process is electricity. So much energy is required that aluminum smelters have to be situated near a cheap source of power, normally hydro-electric.

The price of entry into the business is so high that it discourages most upstarts from taking the plunge.

On the other hand, this frustrating effort to produce commercial aluminum is worth the cost, since the white metal has a number of valuable attributes:

It has a low density.

It is highly resistant to corrosion.

It is light weight—one-third the weight of steel.

It is an excellent reflector of heat and light.

It is nonmagnetic.

It is easy to assemble.

It is nontoxic.

It can be made strong with alloys.

It can be easily rolled into thin sheets.

It has good electrical conductivity.

It has good thermal conductivity.

Aluminum doesn't rust.

## Shortcomings to Bear in Mind

- Alcoa is not a classic growth company. Rather, it is a cyclical company, and earnings fluctuate with the economy. What's more, its beta coefficient is 1.35, which means that the stock rises and falls 35 percent more than the market. That's why I have classified the stock as aggressive growth.
- In the fourth quarter of 2004, net income fell 8 percent, as stronger aluminum prices failed to offset higher energy and labor costs. Profits also suffered from foreign-currency swings.

## Reasons to Buy

- Commenting on results in 2004, Mr. Belda said, "This year, we achieved the highest revenue in Alcoa's history and the second highest profitability. Strong cash flows allowed us to reduce debt by more than $1 billion and invest in the company's future. While we are benefiting from strong aluminum fundamentals and improving end use markets, U.S. dollar weakness and higher input costs continue to pressure margins. We will continue to attack costs, streamline our organization, and take advantage of the strong market environment."
- Alcoa makes a very sustainable product: almost 70 percent of the aluminum ever produced is still in use, equaling 480 million metric tons (529 million tons) of a total 690 million metric tons (761 million tons) manufactured since 1886.

- "Over the years, we have improved productivity, managed capital, and worked every lever in our control to offset cost increases for raw materials, energy, benefits, and the impact of a weakened dollar," said CEO Alain Belda in 2004. "The result was consistently improving profitability, a considerably stronger balance sheet, and a company that is well positioned for future growth as world markets continue to strengthen. That is what we promised last year, and our team delivered."
- The company is seeking to bolster its production capacity overseas. In addition to building a 322,000-metric-ton smelter in Eastern Iceland, Alcoa is investigating the possibility of building additional smelters in Brunei and the Kingdom of Bahrain. Sites such as these fit into Alcoa's long-term plan of shifting its smelting capacity to lower-cost regions.
- During periods when the aluminum industry suffers through a protracted slump in aluminum prices, Alcoa has seen its profits rise. Part of that is due to the effects of recent acquisitions. But much of the improvement can be traced to a new corporate philosophy, called the "Alcoa Business System." Essentially, it calls for plants to produce more, produce it faster, and not let it sit on the docks for too long. The new production processes are "deceptively simple and seemingly obvious," says one analyst. But, on top of other cost-cutting efforts already in the works, they are helping Alcoa weather what otherwise might be a dismal year. As aluminum prices recover—either because of growing demand or because excess capacity is shuttered—Alcoa stands to see earnings jump dramatically. Analysts say that each penny increase in the LME

price of aluminum boosts Alcoa's per-share earnings by about 12 cents. LME refers to the spot price of aluminum ingots on the London Metals Exchange. Normally, the prevailing world price of aluminum is an important determinant of aluminum companies' profits. From 1982 through 1995, Alcoa's earnings and the LME price moved in lock step. Since then, however, the LME price has dropped while Alcoa's earnings have held steady or drifted up. According to the company's chief financial officer, Richard Kelson, "We are breaking away from the LME pricing."

- In 2004, Alcoa Advanced Transportation Systems (AATS) said that it had been selected by Ferrari as the sole provider for the next generation aluminum space frame for its new 12-cylinder front-engine 2+2 sports car, the 612 Scaglietti.

"Alcoa is pleased to have been chosen to collaborate with Ferrari once again to help meet the design, interior space and performance challenges of what is destined to become one of the world's most exciting automobiles," said Rick Milner, President of AATS. "The Ferrari 360 Modena has successfully demonstrated the capability of a highly engineered aluminum structure to significantly increase interior space and occupant comfort while not only maintaining, but improving, driving performance. We also believe that the demonstrated safety performance of Alcoa's aluminum structures will be very important in helping Ferrari satisfy Europe's demanding safety requirements."

Alcoa's revenues in the automotive sector come from a range of products, from chassis, suspension, and drive-train components to body structures and wheels, and electrical distribution systems.

Since 1990 in the United States, the use of aluminum has doubled in cars and has tripled in sport-utility vehicles, light trucks, and vans. Aluminum use in automobiles is forecast to increase in North America from 258 pounds per vehicle in 2000 to 318 pounds by 2010; in Europe from 196 pounds to 268; and in Japan from 196 to 263.

- *Value Line Investment Survey* rated Alcoa a below-average 4 for Timeliness on January 21, 2005. However, its analyst, Stuart Plesser, had this positive comment: "The company has a slew of new projects in the works. It's in the process of adding 1.1 million metric tons of capacity at three facilities it jointly owns with Alcoa World Aluminas and Chemicals. It also recently broke ground at its new Icelandic smelter (a 320,000-metric ton facility). We note that capital spending is apt to rise significantly this year in order to fund these projects."

- "We rate Alcoa OVERWEIGHT as we expect Alcoa to participate in the benefits from a higher aluminum price," said John C. Tumazos, CFA, writing for Prudential Equity Group, LLC, on January 11, 2005.

- "We have felt for some time that the cyclical rebound in Alcoa's earnings was likely to be fairly subdued," said an analyst with Lehman Brothers (a major brokerage house), on March 7, 2005. "We believe this subdued earnings outlook is largely factored into the stock. In our opinion, the stock is near a bottom of what is likely to be a narrow short-term trading range." The firm rated the stock OVERWEIGHT (similar to BUY).

- *Standard & Poor's Stock Reports* viewed Alcoa more positively on January 14, 2005, rating the stock a BUY. Here's what the S&P analyst, Leo Larkin, had to say: "We view AA as a solid vehicle for capitalizing on a cyclical upturn in aluminum. We believe aluminum prices hit a cyclical bottom in 2002, and will move higher at least through 2005. In our view, a higher aluminum price will occur as a result of rising global consumption and a reduction in production from China, stemming from higher costs for power and alumina. In recent years, China's output has been a drag on the aluminum price."

Total assets: $32,609 million
Current ratio: 1.32
Common shares outstanding: 870 million
Return on 2004 shareholders' equity: 10%

|  | 2004 | 2003 | 2002 | 2001 | 2000 | 1999 | 1998 | 1997 |
|---|---|---|---|---|---|---|---|---|
| Revenues (millions) | 23,478 | 21,504 | 20,351 | 22,859 | 22,936 | 16,323 | 15,340 | 13,319 |
| Net income (millions) | 1,310 | 938 | 420 | 908 | 1,484 | 1,054 | 859 | 759 |
| Earnings per share | 1.49 | 1.08 | .49 | 1.05 | 1.80 | 1.41 | 1.22 | 1.09 |
| Dividends per share | .60 | .60 | .60 | .60 | .50 | .40 | .38 | .25 |
| Price    high | 39.4 | 38.9 | 39.8 | 45.7 | 43.6 | 41.7 | 20.3 | 22.4 |
|          low | 28.5 | 18.4 | 17.6 | 27.4 | 23.1 | 18.0 | 14.5 | 16.1 |

Growth and Income

# Alltel Corporation

One Allied Drive ❑ Little Rock, AR 72202 ❑ (501) 905–8991 ❑ Dividend reinvestment plan available: (877) 446–3628 ❑ Web site: *www.alltel.com* ❑ Listed: NYSE ❑ Ticker symbol: AT ❑ S&P rating: B+ ❑ Value Line financial strength rating: A

Alltel, a regional telephone company that provides wireless, local telephone, long distance, Internet, and high-speed data services to residential and business customers in twenty-six states—mainly in small towns and rural markets—had another solid year in 2004. Here are some highlights:

• Total revenues were $8.2 billion, a 3 percent increase over the prior year. Total operating income was $1.9 billion, a 1 percent gain over 2003. Net income from current businesses reached $1 billion, a 9 percent increase.

• The company's net new wireless customer additions reached nearly 511,000, an 86 percent jump over 2003 and the largest annual gain since 1998. Average revenue per customer was $48.13, the highest annual rate in four years.

• Alltel now has more than 243,000 broadband customers, a 59 percent increase

from year-end 2003. Average revenue per wireless customer was $65.87, a 2 percent increase over the prior year.

• Equity free cash flow from current businesses was $1.2 billion, a 17 percent gain over a year earlier. Net cash from operations remained level, at $2.5 billion.

• Alltel returned more than $1 billion in capital to shareholders by paying more than $450 million in dividends and repurchasing 11.2 million share of stock for $600 million. *When a company repurchases its own stock, it reduces the number of outstanding shares and thus increases Earnings per share.*

• In 2004, the company expanded its footprint by acquiring the wireless assets of Mobile Tel in Louisiana and certain wireless assets from U.S. Cellular and TDS Telecom in Georgia, Florida, Mississippi, North Carolina, Ohio, and Wisconsin. Alltel also announced in 2004 that it would acquire

Cingular assets in Oklahoma, Texas, Kentucky, Connecticut, Mississippi, and Kansas. The transaction closed in the second quarter of 2005.

## Company Profile

Alltel is a customer-focused communications company with more than 13 million customers and $8 billion in annual revenues. Alltel provides wireless, local telephone, long-distance, Internet and high-speed data services to residential and business customers in twenty-six states, largely those situated in the Southeast, the South, Midwest, and Southwest. The company does not serve New England, the West Coast, or the northern states west of Wisconsin.

Alltel is:

• The nation's seventh largest wireless company, with 8 million customers. This segment of the company accounts for close to 60 percent of operating profits.

• It is the nation's sixth largest local telephone company, with more than 3 million customers.

• The company has strong and growing cash flows.

• Alltel has paid its stockholders a dividend for forty-three consecutive years. In the 1994–2004 period, the dividend per share advanced from $0.90 to $1.49, a compound annual growth rate of 5.2 percent, or well ahead of inflation. In the same 10-year span, Earnings per share performed even better, advancing from $1.60 to $3.37, a growth rate of 7.7 percent.

• Alltel's customer base has grown from 2.5 million communications customers in 1996 to 13 million customers today.

• Revenues over the same period advanced from $2.4 billion to $8 billion.

• What's more, total assets are up from $4.6 billion to $16.7 billion.

• Operating income during these years nearly tripled, from $644 million to $1.9 billion.

## Shortcomings to Bear in Mind

■ Alltel operates in an industry with more than its share of competition. Most of the Baby Bells, among others, have seen its customers leave to join the scores of upstarts that pervade the industry. To be sure, Alltel has suffered less than most. In other words, it's the best of a bad lot.

■ *Standard & Poor's Stock Reports* had some doubts about Alltel on January 31, 2005, according to analyst Todd Rosenbluth, "We continue to view positively the company's growing rural wireless base and the stability in its wireline operations. Unlike Baby Bell peers, AT's wireline access lines held relatively steady in 2004. However, we are somewhat skeptical about the benefits of the proposed purchase of WWCA at a 30 percent premium to our initial net asset value calculation, as we view WWCA's prospects as largely derived from international operations with limited synergies. If the deal is completed as planned, about 70 percent of AT's revenues would be derived from higher growth wireless operations, including retail and roaming."

## Reasons to Buy

■ In January 2005, Alltel reached an agreement to merge with Western Wireless Corporation in a $6 billion stock-and-cash transaction that closed in mid-2005. In this move, Alltel gained about 1.4 million domestic wireless customers in nineteen Midwestern and Western states that are contiguous to existing properties.

As a result of the Western Wireless move, Alltel is now the nation's fifth-largest wireless carrier with 10 million domestic wireless customers serving a population of 72 million in thirty-three states, covering about 25 percent of the U.S. population and 56 percent of the land mass in the contiguous United States; 1.6 million international wireless customers in six countries, serving a population of more than 50 million; and 3 million wireless customers in fifteen states.

- "The company recently penned a deal to purchase additional wireless assets," said David M. Reimer, writing for *Value Line Investment Survey* on December 31, 2004. "In late November, Cingular Wireless (a BellSouth/SBC Comm. venture) agreed to sell A&T Wireless properties, licenses, equipment, and subscribers in seven states to Alltel for $170 million in cash. This deal will help Alltel to expand and better focus its market coverage and consolidate partnership interests. We look for the transaction to be finalized early next year (*2005*). It follows a just-completed $140 million purchase from Telephone and Data Systems Inc. of wireless assets across several U.S. markets. Given strong cash flow, rich cash balances, a solid capital structure, and the conversion of $1.4 billion in equity unit notes next May, Alltel will likely make more wireless acquisitions, even after share buybacks and dividend hikes."
- Alltel derives about 60 percent of its revenues from the growing wireless business, a far greater share than any of the larger Bell telephone companies—and even larger than Sprint before its deal with Nextel.
- "The stock, now at $58.25, is worth $70 in a buyout, says Tavis McCourt of investment firm Morgan Keegan," according to an article in *BusinessWeek* on December 27, 2004. The writer was Gene G. Martial, who went on to say, "David Barden of Banc of America Securities, who rates Alltel a BUY, figures it will earn $3.31 a share in 2004 and $3.55 in 2005, vs. $3.05 in 2003."
- In January 2004, Alltel said that it began offering Touch2Talk, an instant walkie-talkie service, across the company's digital and analog networks. With Touch2Talk, customers are able to talk instantly to

each other and switch to a wireless call at the touch of a button.

"Touch2Talk will provide instant communication on the broadest footprint of any provider in many of Alltel's markets, as well as the best features and functionality," said Kevin Beebe, Alltel's group president of communications.

Touch2Talk's innovative features will enable customers to see on their phones the availability of other Touch2Talk customers, while also giving all customers the option of using a "do not disturb" feature.

"Touch2Talk will deliver clear benefits for our customers and fill an important niche in the markets we serve," Mr. Beebe said. "Businesses will enhance productivity by using this more effective and convenient walkie-talkie service. Families and friends will be connected at the touch of a button."

Customers will be able to use their existing phone numbers with Touch2Talk. Customers will also be able to use their phones to set up individual contacts of a group list with up to ten participants. A maximum of thirty groups can be created.

Touch2Talk became available in January 2004 in markets covering about 50 percent of Alltel's POPs (points of presence), including Little Rock, Cleveland, Phoenix, Charlotte, New Orleans, and Tampa, and became available in all markets on March 31, 2004.

- In recent years, the company has picked up a host of new customers through the acquisition route. In 2003, Alltel acquired wireless properties in southern Mississippi from Cellular XL Associates, adding about 50,000 customers. In 2002, the company agreed to acquire the wireless operation of Century Tel. This transaction boosted AT's customer base by about 762,000. This move enabled Alltel to expand into new markets in Arkansas, Louisiana, Michigan, Mississippi, Texas, and Wisconsin.

Total assets: $16,604 million
Current ratio: 1.11
Common shares outstanding: 304 million
Return on 2004 shareholders' equity: 14.8%

|  | 2004 | 2003 | 2002 | 2001 | 2000 | 1999 | 1998 | 1997 |
|---|---|---|---|---|---|---|---|---|
| Revenues (millions) | 8,246 | 7,980 | 7,983 | 7,599 | 7,067 | 6,302 | 5,194 | 3,264 |
| Net income (millions) | 1,046 | 954 | 912 | 838 | 857 | 756 | 580 | 400 |
| Earnings per share | 3.37 | 3.05 | 2.96 | 2.67 | 2.70 | 2.39 | 2.09 | 2.12 |
| Dividends per share | 1.49 | 1.42 | 1.37 | 1.33 | 1.29 | 1.24 | 1.18 | 1.10 |
| Price      high | 60.6 | 56.2 | 63.3 | 68.7 | 82.9 | 91.8 | 61.4 | 41.6 |
|               low | 46.6 | 40.7 | 35.3 | 49.4 | 47.8 | 56.3 | 38.3 | 29.8 |

Conservative Growth

# American Standard Companies

One Centennial Avenue ❑ P. O. Box 6820 ❑ Piscataway, NJ 08854–3996 ❑ (732) 980–6000 ❑ Dividend reinvestment plan not available ❑ Web site: *www.americanstandard.com* ❑ Ticker symbol: ASD ❑ S&P rating: B- ❑ Value Line financial strength rating: B+

"Maker of everything from toilets to air conditioners to brakes, American Standard has shown how to make a collection of mature industries hum," said Christopher Steiner, writing for *Forbes* magazine on September 20, 2004.

"During the worst of the recession, it continued to increase profits and sales," said Mr. Steiner. "In 2004's first half, earnings rose 24 percent, to $244 million, on revenues up 13 percent, to $4.8 billion. Still better times seem in the offing. The company's biggest line, air conditioning (58 percent of revenues), should benefit because many commercial buildings are due to replace old systems. An undaunted housing sector is stoking demand for its plumbing and other household fixtures. And the division making brakes for trucks and buses has huge orders from North America and China, says Credit Suisse First Boston analyst Nicole Parent."

## Company Profile

American Standard is the world's largest global manufacturer of bath and kitchen products. ASD has the industry's most diverse range of products. It makes faucets, fixtures, whirlpools, accessories, showers—and even the kitchen sink!

Not only does American Standard make the widest range of products, it has been making plumbing products longer than just about anyone else. In fact, the company can trace its history back to 1875 when The Standard Sanitary Manufacturing Company made cast-iron bathtubs, washstands, and water closets in Pittsburgh, Pennsylvania.

Today, ASD makes products to serve customers around the world. Its global brands include: American Standard, Ideal Standard, Ceramica Dolomite, Porcher, Børma, Sottini, JADO, and Absolute.

American Standard's roots and its name are American, but its business is global. The company is part of people's lives in more than 40 countries, from the air they breathe to the water they drink to their level of safety on the highway. The company does that through three businesses: Air Conditioning Systems and Services, Bath & Kitchen Products, and Vehicle Control Systems. Each business is a market leader.

In air conditioning, sold under the Trane and American Standard brands, the company is number one globally in chiller equipment and number one in the U.S. for commercial systems. Its residential systems are the premium brand in the United States.

American Standard is the world's leading producer of bathroom and kitchen fixtures and faucets, sold under such brands as American Standard and Ideal Standard, for consumer and commercial markets.

And the company leads the world in electronic braking, stability, suspension, and transmission control systems, sold under the WABCO name, for heavy commercial vehicles.

## Bath & Kitchen Business at-a-Glance:

- The number one maker of bath and kitchen products worldwide.*
- Number one in Europe.*
- Number one in the U.S. commercial market.*
- A strong number two in the U.S. fixtures (sinks, bathtubs, toilets) market.*
- "We are the only company that truly competes in both fixtures and fittings (faucets, shower heads) or, as our customers see it, in the Total Bathroom and Kitchen."
- In terms of annual sales.

## Heating & Air Conditioning Business at-a-Glance:

- On average, one of our air conditioning units is installed every minute of every day.
- Trane is a global market leader in chiller equipment.
- Trane is a leading supplier of equipment and services to customers in industry, retail, health care, and government markets.
- Satisfaction rate among residential customers: 95 percent.

## Vehicle Controls Business at-a-Glance

- WABCO products are in two out of three commercial vehicles with advanced braking systems.

- First Heavy Truck Anti-Lock Braking System (1981)
- First CV Suspension (1986)
- First CV Auto Transmission Controls (1988)
- First Heavy Truck Electronic Braking System (1996)
- First Car "Air Glide" Suspension System (1986)

## Shortcomings to Bear in Mind

- *Value Line Investment Survey* had a mixed view of the company on January 28, 2005, according to its analyst, John Marrin, "A rising interest-rate environment here in the U.S. may take some of the steam out of the housing market, which would likely pressure results at Bath & Kitchen and the residential air-conditioning business. High commodity prices, meanwhile, promise to lean on customers' profits much the same way they are affecting ASD.

  "On the flip side, though, there are growth avenues overseas (which already account for a little less than half of total sales), and any weakness in the U.S. dollar may make it easier to capitalize on those opportunities. Still, the clouds on the horizon should make investors uneasy."

- On November 11, 2004, American Standard announced that it has been contacted by the European Commission as part of an industry-wide investigation into alleged infringement of EU competition regulations relating to bath and kitchen fixtures and fittings in certain European countries. The company said that it would be cooperating fully with the investigation.

## Reasons to Buy

- *Standard & Poor's Stock Reports* gave American Standard five stars, its best rating, on February 8, 2005. Michael W. Jaffe said, "We expect ASD's primary commercial air conditioning segment to stage a slightly more robust revival over the coming year. What we view as strong brand names and a well-run business also leave us positive about ASD's long-term outlook. Based on those views and valuation considerations, we recommend buying ASD shares."

In this same report, the S&P analyst also said, "Net margins should widen in 2005. We see this forecasted improvement driven by the better demand we see, the likely benefits of productivity and materials purchasing initiatives, and our view of a calming of materials costs after a big run-up that was seen in 2004. Those factors should outweigh the likely costs of the implementation of new streamlining activities, plus expected outlays for ongoing new product development and marketing programs."

■ A typical toilet made before 1980 uses 4.5 to 7 gallons of water per flush. However, a toilet made between 1980 and 1992 uses 3.5 gallons. Today's low-consumption toilets (such as the Champion with America's Best Flushing System) use only 1.6 gallons per flush. Designed to conserve water, American Standard's new flushing technology—with its proprietary Flush Tower—forcefully directs toilet contents down the drain in less than a second, using no more than 1.6 gallons of water.

■ From 1994 to 1997, New York City offered a rebate to people who replaced old toilets with newer, low-consumption toilets. The city's Department of Environmental Protection estimates that the city saves between 70 and 90 million gallons of water each day, thanks to the new toilets. That's enough water to fill 6,700 Olympic-size swimming pools. (Source: *Scientific American,* February 2001).

■ Famous buildings that use Trane for heating/cooling:

● The new Busch (baseball) Stadium in St. Louis, Missouri.

● The High Museum and the Woodruff Arts Center in Atlanta, Georgia.

● Sea World in Orlando, Florida.

● Monticello (former home of Thomas Jefferson) in Charlottesville, Virginia.

● The Washington Monument in Washington, D.C.

● Grand Hyatt Hotel in Jakarta, Indonesia.

● Suwannabhumi International Airport in Bangkok, Thailand.

■ The company's WABCO, its vehicle controls business, is the world's leading producer of electronic braking, stability, suspension, and transmission control systems for heavy commercial vehicles. WABCO's products are also increasingly used in luxury cars and sport utility vehicles (SUVs).

ASD is a global leader in vehicle control systems—a position built on strong customer relationships and leading technologies. WABCO is also a leader in improving highway safety—its products help drivers avoid accidents by improving vehicle responsiveness and stability.

For example, its stability control system for trucks constantly monitors the vehicle's speed, steering angle, and motion. If it detects danger—such as the driver swerving to avoid another vehicle—it responds by downshifting the transmission, applying the brakes at specific wheels, or taking other actions to prevent a rollover. WABCO is the only company in the world that offers this system today.

■ Another advanced product is the company's "Air Glide" suspension system. It uses compressed air instead of steel springs to deliver improved handling, comfort, and fuel efficiency. It's now being used in automobiles and SUVs by DaimlerChrysler, Renault, BMW, Audi, Land Rover, GM, Porsche, Volkswagen, and Ford.

This segment's name, WABCO, originally stood for Westinghouse Air Brake Company. Today, the company is applying its expertise with air and brakes to improve cars, trucks, and other vehicles—and to make the nation's roads safer.

**Total assets: $6,842 billion**
**Current ratio: 1.23**
**Common shares outstanding: 215 million**
**Return on 2004 shareholders' equity: 38.1%**

|                     | 2004  | 2003  | 2002  | 2001  | 2000  | 1999  | 1998  | 1997  |
|---------------------|-------|-------|-------|-------|-------|-------|-------|-------|
| Revenues (millions) | 9,509 | 8,568 | 7,795 | 7,465 | 7,598 | 7,189 | 6,654 | 6,007 |
| Net income (millions)| 313  | 405   | 371   | 331   | 316   | 260   | 219   | 210   |
| Earnings per share  | 1.42  | 1.83  | 1.68  | 1.51  | 1.45  | 1.20  | 0.99  | 0.92  |
| Dividends per share | Nil   | —     | —     | —     | —     | —     | —     | —     |
| Price        high   | 41.8  | 34.0  | 26.3  | 23.6  | 16.6  | 16.5  | 16.4  | 17.2  |
|              low    | 33.1  | 21.3  | 19.4  | 15.6  | 11.4  | 10.4  | 7.2   | 11.5  |

---

Aggressive Growth

# AutoZone, Inc.

123 South Front Street ❏ Memphis, TN 38103–3607 ❏ (901) 495–7005 ❏ Dividend reinvestment plan not available ❏ Fiscal years end last Saturday in August ❏ Listed: NYSE ❏ Web site: *www.autozone.com* ❏ Ticker symbol: AZO ❏ S&P rating: B+ ❏ Value Line financial strength rating: B

"This is an exciting industry with incredible growth potential," said Steve Odland, CEO of AutoZone, Inc., the nation's largest retailer of auto parts and accessories in the United States.

"According to the Federal Highway Administration, Americans are driving over 2.5 trillion miles per year. The number of older vehicles on the road is increasing. SUVs, mini-vans and light trucks are aging and becoming 'our-kind-of-vehicles,' or OKVs. The number of people engaged in do-it-yourself (DIY) automotive activities is growing. Today, almost half of all U.S. households engage in DIY automotive maintenance and repairs.

"An estimated $60 billion in automotive maintenance goes unperformed each year, and an estimated 25 million cars are driven with the check-engine lights on. Tapping these opportunities has the potential to significantly increase the size of our industry."

## Company Profile
Founded in 1979, AutoZone sells auto and light truck replacement parts, from additives to motor oil, from accessories to detailing kits. The stores are, according to the company, "designed to inspire the do-it-yourselfer." However, the company also, provides "state-of-the-art diagnostics, technical advice and easy on-line ordering," as well as "reaching out to the professional technician, through our commercial business."

AutoZone sells auto and light truck parts, chemicals, and accessories through 3,420 AutoZone stores in forty-eight states and the District of Columbia, sixty-three AutoZone stores in Mexico, and online at AutoZone.com. AutoZone also sells automotive diagnostic and repair software through ALLDATA, and alldatadiy.com. The company's stores are highly concentrated in such states as California (about 400 stores), Texas (about 350), Ohio, Florida, Illinois, Tennessee, Michigan, Indiana, Georgia, and North Carolina, with at least 100 outlets in each. Some 1,300 stores are spread out over the other states.

The company's stores are generally in high-visibility locations and range in size from 4,000 square feet to just over 8,000, with newer stores tending toward the larger size. AZO offers low everyday prices and endeavors to be the price leader in hard parts. Stores typically carry between 19,000 and 22,000 stock-keeping units.

## Shortcomings to Bear in Mind

- The company has a very leveraged balance sheet, with far more debt than common equity.
- In mid-March 2005, the company announced that its CEO Steve Odland, has accepted the CEO post with Office Depot.
- *Value Line Investment Survey,* in a report issued February 11, 2005, was somewhat negative, in the words of analyst Damon Churchwell: "Long-term earnings growth prospects continue to be decent. Out to 2007–2009, we look for roughly 10 percent annual share-earnings growth, on modestly wider margins. AutoZone will continue to target 15 percent returns-on-invested capital for new units. The debt level should remain lofty, supporting ongoing share buybacks. Though timely, AutoZone stock's long-term appreciation potential is limited."
- "AutoZone is the most profitable auto parts retailer by almost every measure," said John Tomlinson, writing for Prudential Equity Group, LLC, on March 15, 2005. "The company has the highest

margins and returns on invested capital, the most productive stores, the most efficient distribution system, a business model that generates substantial free cash flow and a management team with a track record for creating shareholder value. However, AutoZone appears to have hit a pothole on the road to future growth. We believe that management's focus on free cash flow may have led to an underinvestment in its stores over the past few years, which may be impacting its comps, relative to its peers." The analyst gave AutoZone a NEUTRAL rating.

## Reasons to Buy

- *Standard & Poor's Stock Reports,* however, was more positive in its report issued March 8, 2005. Analyst Michael Sauers said, "We have a BUY recommendation on the shares. We believe that AZO and its peers have been restricted in 2004 by relatively mild summer weather and high gas prices. For the longer term, we see the company poised to benefit from what we see as favorable vehicle demographic trends, including a rising number of cars older than seven years (the point after which vehicles tend to require more post-warranty repairs) and increasing vehicle usage."
- The *Argus Analyst Report* of March 3, 2005 was also positive. Analyst Kevin P. Tynan had this comment: "We are maintaining our BUY rating on AutoZone Inc. We continue to believe that the fundamentals of the business and the aftermarket parts industry are intact. Strong retail auto sales, driven by aggressive manufacturer rebates, have put the number of registered vehicles at an all-time high. All those vehicles will eventually need parts. Though a good percentage of those parts will be from the OE (original manufacturer), there is still enough retail DIY and

commercial business to justify the retail stores. There are obviously near-term concerns, such as consumer spending in face of rising gas prices, but longer-term trends should become more favorable."

- In the past ten years (1994–2004), AutoZone carved out an impressive record of growth. During that span, Earnings per share mushroomed from $.78 to $6.56, for a compound annual growth rate of 23.7 percent. This is nothing short of phenomenal.

- AutoZone is active in promoting its assets. "Our upbeat ads communicate—in English and in Spanish—the importance of automotive safety and reliability," said Mr. Odland. "Owning a car is a significant investment. We explain the role that routine maintenance, cleaning, waxing, and tuning play in preserving vehicle longevity and value.

  "Inside our stores, we create attention-getting product displays—'Zones'—that encourage maintenance and enhancement.

  Zones feature filters, waxes, polishes and products that upgrade aging vehicles, such as car mats and seat covers. Our stores also offer products that personalize vehicles and that improve the driving experience, such as hands-free-phone and other driving accessories."

- One key to the success of AutoZone is its well-trained sales people. The company says, "We're trouble-shooters simplifying repairs, demystifying technology, enhancing reliability and providing solutions.

  "We keep making it easier to diagnose automotive problems. On-line, at *www.autozone.com,* we help troubleshoot problems through a series of questions about vehicles' symptoms. In-store and curbside, we have ASE certified parts professionals, diagnostic specialists and equipment to decode the on-board computer systems in cars today.

  "Through our Loan-a-Tool program, we take the cost and complexity out of repairs by putting specialty tools in the hands of the do-it-yourselfer. Ultimately, our goal is to help folks keep their vehicles in good repair, making them safer, longer lasting and reliable."

- In fiscal 2004, Mr. Odland said, "Automotive trends bode well for continued growth. The number and age of cars on the road are increasing, as is the number of miles being driven. SUVs, vans and light trucks, which have dominated new car sales the past five years, are beginning to move out of warranty cycles and into repair cycles–becoming 'our-kind-of-vehicles.' Almost half of all U.S. households are engaging in do-it-yourself automotive maintenance and repairs. Embedded within each of these statistics are opportunities for us to bring in new customers and drive future growth."

- To be sure, the do-it-yourself market is not the whole story. Many motorists prefer to have a professional patch up their ailing vehicles. With millions of vehicles on the road today and more than 400,000 professional technicians to serve them, the need for one-stop parts ordering and delivery is clear. Yet, the market supplying repair and replacement parts is highly fragmented. Company-owned and operated, full-assortment, national suppliers are virtually nonexistent, leaving most commercial technicians reliant on a myriad of supply sources to fulfill parts orders.

  Sensing a unique opportunity, said a company spokesman, "We began establishing a commercial delivery business. Today, we are a leading national player and full-assortment provider to professional technicians. With the full-assortment inventories and extensive reach of our AutoZone stores, we put brand name parts in the hands of 'do-it-for-me' technicians faster and more cost effectively than ever before."

Total assets: $3,913 million
Current ratio: 0.97
Return on 2004 shareholders' equity: 207.7%

|  | 2004 | 2003 | 2002 | 2001 | 2000 | 1999 | 1998 | 1997 |
|---|---|---|---|---|---|---|---|---|
| Revenues (millions) | 5,637 | 5,457 | 5,326 | 4,818 | 4,483 | 4,116 | 3,243 | 2,691 |
| Net income (millions) | 566 | 518 | 428 | 176 | 268 | 245 | 228 | 195 |
| Earnings per share | 6.56 | 5.34 | 4.00 | 1.54 | 2.00 | 1.63 | 1.48 | 1.48 |
| Dividends per share | Nil | — | — | — | — | — | — | — |
| Price    high | 91.6 | 103.5 | 89.3 | 80.0 | 31.6 | 37.3 | 38.0 | 32.8 |
| low | 70.4 | 58.2 | 59.2 | 24.4 | 21.0 | 22.6 | 20.5 | 19.5 |

Growth and Income

# AvalonBay Communities, Inc.

2900 Eisenhower Avenue ❑ Suite 300 ❑ Alexandria, VA 22314 ❑ Listed: NYSE ❑ (703) 329–6300 ❑ Dividend reinvestment plan not available ❑ Web site: *www.avalonbay.com* ❑ Ticker symbol: AVB ❑ S&P rating: A ❑ Value Line financial strength rating: B+

"We have a long-established presence in our markets, providing a significant advantage over competitors seeking market entry," said a company official in 2004. "These high barrier-to-entry markets are characterized by supply constraints due to a lack of zoned land and difficult and lengthy processes. Over the last ten years, the rate of new products in our markets compared to existing stock, has been 60 percent of the national average.

"Our markets are also characterized by high single-family prices that have increased at double-digit rates over the past several years. Lower housing affordability results in a higher propensity to rent. Our markets require less job growth to generate equivalent demand when compared to other markets. More favorable long-term demand/supply fundamentals and lower housing affordability have contributed to our relative outperformance over the past decade."

The official went on to say, "Proof is in the results. Our markets generated revenue growth that was 16 percent higher than provided by other domestic markets between 1993 and 2003. We will continue to capitalize on these favorable market attributes through in-house expertise in development, redevelopment, acquisitions, dispositions, and property operations to provide outsized returns to investors.

"Avalon Darien, a community we recently completed in Darien, Connecticut, is a case study in how we will continue shaping our future through hard-to-replicate, ground-up development in our high barrier-to-entry markets. Darien is an affluent submarket in Fairfield County benefited by the larger metro New York market. With a per-capita income of $85,000, a median home price of $735,000 and little new supply, rental apartments in this market will provide excellent long-term returns. AvalonBay began pursuing the entitlements to this site in 1991, and after more than ten years, construction began in late 2002, demonstrating the embedded value we create through our in-house expertise and market knowledge."

## Company Profile

AvalonBay Communities, Inc. is in the business of developing, redeveloping, acquiring and managing high-quality apartment communities in the high barrier-to-entry markets of the United States. These markets are located in the Northeast, Mid-Atlantic, Midwest, Pacific Northwest, and Northern and Southern California regions of the country.

As of December 31, 2004, AvalonBay owned or held interest in 148 apartment communities containing 42,810 apartment homes in ten states and the District of Columbia, of which ten communities were under construction and four communities were under reconstruction. In addition, the company held future development rights for 49 communities.

The company elected to be taxed as a REIT for federal income tax purposes for the year ending December 31, 1994, and it has not revoked that election. AvalonBay was incorporated under the laws of the State of California in 1978 and was reincorporated in the State of Maryland in June 1995. Management's principal executive offices are located at 2900 Eisenhower Avenue, Suite 300, Alexandria, Virginia 22314. AvalonBay also maintain regional offices and administrative or specialty offices in or near the following cities: San Jose, California; New Canaan, Connecticut; Boston, Massachusetts; Chicago, Illinois; Newport Beach, California; New York, New York; Woodbridge, New Jersey; and Seattle, Washington.

## Some Historical Dates

August 24, 1993, Avalon Properties, Inc. is incorporated in the State of Maryland to continue and expand the multifamily apartment community acquisition, construction, development, and management operations of the Trammel Crow Residential Mid-Atlantic and Northeast Groups.

November 18, 1993, Avalon Properties, Inc. completes its Initial Public Offering (IPO) at $20.50 per share on the New York

Stock Exchange. At the IPO, Avalon Properties had a portfolio of 22 communities containing 7,044 apartment homes in the Mid-Atlantic and Northeast.

March 17, 1994, Bay Apartment Communities, the successor apartment business of Greenbriar Homes, completes its Initial Public Offering at $20 per share on the New York Stock Exchange. At the IPO, Bay Apartment Communities had a portfolio of 14 communities containing 3,481 apartment homes in Northern California.

June 4, 1998, AvalonBay Communities, Inc. is formed by the merger of Avalon Properties, Inc. with and into Bay Apartment Communities, Inc.

December 31, 2000, AvalonBay Communities, Inc. achieves its best operating performance in the history of the company with $3.70 Funds from Operations per share (14.9 percent growth), 8.9 percent same store rental revenue growth, and 10.7 percent same store net operating income.

December 31, 2001, AvalonBay Communities, Inc. has another successful year achieving $4.06 Funds from Operations per share (9.7 percent growth), 6.6 percent rental revenue growth, and 7.5 percent same store net operating income.

December 31, 2002, AvalonBay Communities, Inc. reports Funds from Operations of $3.65 per share due to the difficult economic operating environment. Despite the challenging times, the company successfully completed ten communities with a total capitalization of approximately $470 million; completed $140 million in acquisitions; and issued $450 million of long-term debt at an average interest rate of 5.8 percent.

December 31, 2003, AvalonBay Communities, Inc. celebrates its 10-year anniversary by ringing the closing bell on the NYSE and generates total shareholder return in 2003 of 30 percent, outperforming the S&P 500 and the apartment sector.

## Shortcomings to Bear in Mind

- On February 2, 2005, *Standard & Poor's Stock Reports* was less than enthusiastic about AvalonBay, giving it only two stars, which is one notch below HOLD. This is what Raymond Mathis had to say, "The shares have been resilient over the past year, despite the soft industry fundamentals. We think historically low interest rates made AVB attractive, as lower interest rates spurred private market demand for rental properties, primarily for condominium conversion. This increase in demand boosted multifamily residential property prices and raised our estimate of net asset value (NAV) per share. However, with a current yield of 45 basis points (*there are 100 basis points in one percent*) below that of the ten-year Treasury note, we view the shares as overvalued."

- On January 28, 2005, Lehman Brothers, a leading brokerage firm, had a similar comment: "AVB is optimistic for 2005, both for operations and for development properties. They expect to expand developments to $700–$850 million, from the present $550 million program during 2005. AVB currently has a $3 billion development pipeline, up from $2 billion a year ago. We continue to have concerns about residential demand in high-cost locations. Though we regard AVB as a quality company, it is overpriced."

## Reasons to Buy

- "We continue to expect earnings and funds from operations (FFO) to strengthen in 2005," said Adam Rosner, writing for *Value Line Investment Survey* on January 21, 2005. "Results should benefit from a healthier apartment sector. Rising interest rates may eventually make purchasing single-family housing more difficult. In addition, as the economy continues to strengthen and unemployment levels decline, demand for apartment rentals should pick up."

- AvalonBay Communities, Inc. has been recognized by the National Association of Home Builders (NAHB) in several prestigious categories. These awards include:
  - 1996 Property Management Firm of the Year
  - 1998 Best Mid- or High-Rise Development of the Year
  - 1998 Development Firm of the Year
  - 1999 Development Firm of the Year
  - 1999 Best Rehabilitation of a Multifamily Property
  - 1999 Best Mid- or High-Rise Apartment Community
  - 1999 Best Mid- or High-Rise Development of the Year
  - 2000 Best Multifamily Community by a REIT
  - 2001 Best Luxury Multifamily Development
  - 2003 Best Corporate Web site
  - 2004 Best Luxury Rental Apartment, Avalon at Newton Highlands, Newton, Massachusetts
  - AvalonBay Communities was the recipient of the 2004 *Multifamily Executive* magazine's prestigious "Builder of the Year" award. The company also received the award for "Project of the Year, Resort/Luxury category" for Avalon at Mission Bay in San Francisco, California.

- In 2004, CEO Bryce Blair said, "Since 1994, our FFO per share has grown at a compound annual rate that has exceeded the sector average by more than 400 basis points. During the same time period, estimated Net Asset Value (NAV) per share increased at a compound annual rate of 8.1 percent per year—while our compound Total Shareholder Return was 16.6 percent per year. These performance measures have exceeded both our peer group and the broader equity markets over the past decade."

Total assets: $5,130 million
Return on 2004 equity: 9%
Common shares outstanding: 73 million

|  | 2004 | 2003 | 2002 | 2001 | 2000 | 1999 | 1998 | 1997 |
|---|---|---|---|---|---|---|---|---|
| Revenues (millions) | 648 | 610 | 632 | 639 | 573 | 504 | 371 | 170 |
| Net income (millions) | 211 | 88 | 132 | 186 | 170 | 142 | 98 | 65 |
| Earnings per share | 2.92 | 1.10 | 1.62 | 2.22 | 1.93 | 1.55 | 1.35 | 1.59 |
| Funds from operations | 3.38 | 3.27 | 3.65 | 4.06 | 3.70 | 3.22 | 2.87 | 2.77 |
| Dividends per share | 2.80 | 2.80 | 2.80 | 2.56 | 2.24 | 2.06 | 2.00 | 1.94 |
| Price      high | 75.9 | 49.7 | 52.7 | 51.9 | 50.6 | 37.0 | 39.3 | 40.6 |
|              low | 46.7 | 35.2 | 36.4 | 42.4 | 32.6 | 30.8 | 30.5 | 32.1 |

Conservative Growth

# Avon Products, Inc.

1345 Avenue of the Americas ❑ New York, NY 10105 ❑ Listed: NYSE ❑ (212) 282–5623 ❑ Dividend reinvestment plan available: (781) 575–2723 ❑ Web site: *www.avon.com* ❑ Ticker symbol: AVP ❑ S&P rating: A ❑ Value Line financial strength rating: B++

"In the nearly five years since Andrea Jung took over as CEO at Avon, she's given the venerable cosmetics peddler quite a make-over," said Kate Bonamici, writing for *Fortune* magazine in August 2004. "Sales have risen 28.5 percent—from $5.29 billion in 1999 to $6.8 billion in 2003—and the stock is up 251 percent. And with a roster of new products and big opportunities abroad, Jung may be just getting started.

"Avon is no longer merely your mother's source of inexpensive perfume. The bulk of Avon's sales *do* still come from independent sales reps, who work on commission using catalogs and parties, but Jung has repositioned the company as a supplier of advanced skin treatments and trendy, high-quality makeup. Last fall Avon launched Mark, a division aimed at younger women, complete with a new generation of Avon ladies. There are already 20,000 Mark reps (average age twenty-one), and Avon says Mark is on target to hit $35 million to $40 million in sales this year."

## Company Profile

Dating back to 1886, Avon Products is a global manufacturer of beauty and related products. The company has four product categories: Beauty, which consists of cosmetics, fragrances, and toiletries; Beauty Plus, which includes jewelry, watches, apparel, and accessories; Beyond Beauty, which is made up of home products, gift and decorative candles; and Health and Wellness, which consists of vitamins, an aromatherapy line, exercise equipment, as well as stress relief and weight-management products.

The company specializes in direct selling and does business in North America, Latin America, the Pacific, and Europe. Avon has operations in fifty-eight countries, and sells its products in eighty-five additional countries, for a total of 143 markets.

Avon distributes its products through nearly 4 million sales representatives who are independent contractors or independent dealers. They are not agents or employees of the company. These representatives purchase their products directly from Avon Products and sell them to their customers.

Although Avon has been doing business abroad for decades, it is now emphasizing expansion into countries with emerging or developing economies. The company has set up shop in thirty new markets since 1990, including Russia, China, as well as rapidly emerging nations throughout Central and Eastern Europe.

## Manufacturing

Avon manufactures and packages almost of its cosmetic, fragrance, and toiletries (CFT) products. Raw materials, consisting chiefly of essential oils, chemicals, containers, and packaging components, are purchased from various suppliers. Additionally, Avon produces brochures that are used by the representatives to sell Avon products. The loss of any one supplier would not have a material impact on Avon's ability to source raw materials or paper from the brochures. Packages, consisting of containers and packaging components, are designed by its staff of artists and designers.

Avon has seventeen manufacturing facilities around the world.

## Shortcomings to Bear in Mind

- "We maintain our HOLD opinion on the shares," said Howard Choe, an analyst with *Standard & Poor's Stock Reports,* on February 8, 2005. "We believe AVP's prospects in international markets will remain strong for at least several years. The U.S. market, however, remains a challenge for AVP, given intense competition at mass and drug retail channels, as well as other direct sellers, in our opinion. We expect weakness in the U.S. market to continue for the near term, in light of what we see as a lack of significant catalysts. We believe weakness in the U.S. Market has added risk to earnings growth and consistency."

- According the company's 10-K, "The cosmetic, fragrance and toiletries (CFT), gift and decorative, apparel, and fashion jewelry industries are highly competitive. Avon's principal competitors in the CFT industry are large, and well-known cosmetics and fragrances companies that manufacture and sell broad product lines through various types of retail establishments. There are many other companies that compete in particular CFT products or product lines sold through retail establishments.

  "Avon has many competitors in the gift and decorative products and apparel industries in the United States, including retail establishments, principally department stores, gift shops, and specialty retailers, and direct-mail companies specializing in these products."

## Reasons to Buy

- "Avon is becoming more of an emerging-market story," said Jerome H. Kaplan, writing for *Value Line Investment Survey* on December 31, 2004. "Roughly half of Avon's 2004 sales came from markets such as China, Russia, and Turkey. These fast-growing markets are targeted to reach 68 percent of corporate sales in 2015 (compared with 39 percent in 1990).

  "Currently, sales to China are projected to grow from $220 million in 2004 to $600 million in 2007. The goals for Russia and Turkey are $410 million to $800 million, and $100 million to $200 million, respectively. Additionally, Turkey is likely to serve as a hub for expansion into the Middle East and North Africa. We expect overseas activities to more than offset domestic woes and higher tax rates in 2005 and to permit full-year share earnings to expand 10 percent to 15 percent."

- On December 7, 2004, Andrea Jung said, "The past three years have given us an extraordinary foundation on which to continue the transformation of Avon. While we have delivered top-line (sales) growth, earnings growth and operating margin expansion at or near the top of our peer group, we continue to have tremendous future prospects in all these measures.

"Over the next three years, we intend to further penetrate and expand in rapidly growing geographies in which our direct selling model excels. Our increased scale in the fast-growth and highly profitable developing international markets, combined with a repositioned U.S. business, should enable us to generate continuing growth in sales and earnings as we evolve to the next generation of Avon's transformation."

■ Sales promotion and sales development activities are directed at assisting representatives, through sales aids such as brochures, product samples, and demonstration products. In order to support the efforts of representatives to reach new customers, specially designed sales aides, promotional pieces, customer flyers, television, and print advertising are used. In addition, Avon seeks to motivate its representatives through the use of special incentive programs that reward superior sales performance. Periodic sales meetings with representatives are conducted by the District Sales Managers. The meetings are designed to keep sales people abreast of product line changes, explain sales techniques, and provide recognition for sales performance.

A number of merchandise techniques are used, including the introduction of new products, the use of combination offers, the use of trial sizes, and samples, and the promotion of products packaged as gift items. In general, for each sales campaign, a distinctive brochure is published, in which new products are introduced, and selected items are offered at special prices, or are given particular prominence in the brochure.

Avon has furthered its image through increased advertising, introduction of the Health and Wellness business, creation of a corporate slogan "the company for women," and the launching of "Mark."

■ In the fall of 2003, Avon Products was named as the only beauty company selected by *Working Mother* magazine in its annual survey of the "100 Best Companies for Working Mothers." This annual list recognizes companies that accommodate the needs of employees through a variety of family friendly benefits and initiatives. In 2003, *Working Mother* gave particular weight to three issues: flexible scheduling, advancement of women, and childcare options.

■ In the fall of 2003, Avon launched a new global cosmetics brand called Mark. It focuses on the fast-growing market for young women in the sixteen-to-twenty-four age bracket. The new Mark line is sold by the company's core direct-selling representatives and a separate Mark sales force. With employment opportunities at the lowest level in thirty years—and experts nationwide estimating that 60 percent of recent college graduates will have difficulty finding jobs—the launch of Mark provides an important and timely earnings opportunity. "With Mark, a new generation of young women will enjoy selling great beauty products, as well as an unprecedented earnings opportunity," said Deborah I. Fine, President of Avon Future, the business unit responsible for the new venture.

The Mark beauty product collection consists of some 300 diverse, first-to-market, makeup, skin care, fragrance, and accessory items, with a focus on innovative beauty products and accessories. According to Ms. Fine, "Mark was inspired by and developed with the lifestyle of young women in mind. The Mark product collection will benefit from Avon's world-renowned research and development. Prices range from $5 to $35."

Total assets: $4,148 million
Current ratio: 1.64
Common shares outstanding: 473 million
Return on 2004 shareholders' equity: NMF *

| | 2004 | 2003 | 2002 | 2001 | 2000 | 1999 | 1998 | 1997 |
|---|---|---|---|---|---|---|---|---|
| Revenues (millions) | 7,748 | 6,805 | 6,171 | 5,952 | 5,674 | 5,289 | 5,213 | 5,079 |
| Net income (millions) | 846 | 665 | 535 | 497 | 451 | 424 | 393 | 322 |
| Earnings per share | 1.77 | 1.39 | 1.11 | 1.05 | 0.92 | 0.82 | 0.74 | 0.61 |
| Dividends per share | .70 | .42 | .40 | .38 | .37 | .36 | .34 | .32 |
| Price      high | 46.6 | 34.9 | 28.6 | 25.1 | 24.9 | 29.6 | 23.2 | 19.5 |
| low | 30.5 | 24.5 | 21.8 | 17.8 | 12.7 | 11.7 | 12.5 | 12.7 |

* No meaningful figure.

Growth and Income

# Bank of America Corporation

Bank of America Corporate Center ❑ Charlotte, NC 28255 ❑ (704) 388–6780 ❑ Direct dividend reinvestment plan available: (800) 642–9855 ❑ Web site: *www.bankofamerica.com* ❑ Listed: NYSE ❑ Ticker symbol: BAC ❑ S&P rating: A- ❑ Value Line financial strength rating: A+

"This remains one of the most attractive U.S. bank franchises," said Michael Mayo, an analyst with Prudential Equity Group, LLC, on January 18, 2005. "As the third-largest U.S. bank, Bank of America has number one national deposit market share, and number one market share in some of the most important states, including Florida, Texas, and California. The breadth of the customer base is favorable. It does business with one in four households in the United States and has relationships with 90 percent of the *Fortune* 500 customers through offices in thirty countries around the world."

The Prudential report also said, "The acquisition of FleetBoston increases Bank of America's dominant U.S. Deposit market share to 9.8 percent ($542 billion), up from 7.4 percent . . . and more than double the market share of the nation's second-largest bank."

Finally, Mr. Mayo said, "We believe that the banking industry is transitioning from recovery to growth, but that revenue growth is difficult to find. In the context of our cautious view of the group, one way to invest is to purchase a bank with earnings driven by an expense-related theme. At BAC, we believe expense savings can drive earnings for the next couple of years. Thanks to expense savings from the Fleet merger and continued restructuring, Bank of America is one of the few major banks that doesn't have negative operating leverage."

## Company Profile

Bank of America is one of the world's largest financial institutions, serving individual consumers, small businesses, and large corporations with a full range of banking, investing, asset management, and other financial and risk-management products and services.

The company provides unmatched convenience for consumers in the United States, serving one in four American households with 5,885 banking centers, more than 16,770 ATMs, and an award-winning Internet site, with more than 12.4 million active online users.

Bank of America is rated the number one Small Business Administration Lender in the United States by the SBA. The company serves clients in 150 countries and has relationships with 94 percent of the U.S. *Fortune* 500 companies and 76 percent of the Global *Fortune* 500.

The seventh most profitable company in the United States, Bank of America had $1,045 billion in assets, $6,275 billion in deposits, and a market capitalization of $190 billion at the end of 2004.

## Highlights of 2004

• Number of net new checking accounts grew by 2.1 million.

• Number of net new savings accounts grew by 2.6 million.

• Opened 5.6 million new credit card accounts.

• Active online banking users increased to 12.4 million, while bill payers reached 5.8 million, and volume increased to more than $25 billion in 2004.

• Core deposits continued to grow, climbing to $527 billion and have increased by $44 billion, or 9 percent, over 2003.

• Loans grew 6 percent, to $505 billion.

• Assets under management ended the year at $451 billion.

How a bank makes money (excerpted from *Better Investing* in June of 2004, by Ann Cuneaz). "To understand the banking industry, it's helpful to understand how a bank makes money. The banking industry uses a somewhat different language from that of manufacturing or industrial companies, so it's necessary to learn a few new terms.

"When you think about it, a bank's main product really is money. Banks borrow money from their depositors, paying them the lowest possible interest rate that competition and current market conditions will allow. This payment is an example of what banking companies call interest expense.

"Banks also loan money to customers, charging them the highest possible interest rate that competition and current market conditions will allow. This is an example of interest income. Interest income minus interest expense is known as the net interest income, and this tends to make up the majority of new earnings for most banks.

"The difference between the interest rates a bank charges to its loan customers and the interest rates a bank pays its depositors is known as the interest rate spread, or net interest margin. It's the spread that generates much of a bank's income, and banks with the highest spread are generally the most profitable.

"Banks also make money from collecting all kinds of fees from customers. As banks offer more and more services, they have more opportunities to charge fees, such as for ATM usage, online bill payment, and trust and brokerage services. Any income not related to lending is known as noninterest income."

## Shortcomings to Bear in Mind

▪ The Argus Research Company was less than enthusiastic about the company on February 15, 2005. David Ritter gave the stock a HOLD rating. He said:

"Bank of America Corp. turned in a solid fourth quarter with sequential revenue growth of about 4 percent and expense growth of about 2 percent (ex merger charges).

• We are maintaining our 6.5 percent growth forecast for 2005, a bit below the growth rate we expect from other large-cap banks (8 percent to 10 percent range), but in line with the average forecast.

• We reiterate our HOLD rating on the shares.

• Last week, BAC finalized an agreement to settle allegations of wrongdoing in its mutual fund units."

- An article in *Forbes* magazine on September 20, 2004, was also negative. Bernard Condon said, "Bank of America chief executive Kenneth Lewis has spent more than $200 million over one and a half years for media ads touting the bank's 'higher standards.'

  But lately the Charlotte, N.C. bank has been caught up in a series of embarrassing acts that don't quite fit that spin: illegal trades, the stonewalling of regulators and lousy due diligence."

## Reasons to Buy

- *Standard & Poor's Stock Reports* had a solid BUY recommendation on Bank of America on February 24, 2005, awarding the big bank five stars, its highest rating. Evan M. Momios, CFA, said, "Over the year ahead, we expect strong economic conditions to support revenue growth in consumer and small business lending, offsetting comparatively weak large corporate lending results we foresee. We see productivity and efficiency improvements increasing the contribution of the FleetBoston franchise, which was acquired on April 1, 2004."

- In its November 2004 issue, *Better Investing* magazine (which is the voice of the investment club community) had the stock as its Featured Company. It said, "With its acquisition of FleetBoston Financial Corporation, Bank of America Corporation has achieved several top rankings within its industry. Based in Charlotte, North Carolina, the bank holding company now is the largest as measured by earnings. It's number three in assets and has more service centers nationwide than any of its competitors." The author was Associate Editor Kevin Lamiman.

- On October 18, 2004, Bank of America closed its $1.4 billion acquisition of National Processing, Inc., creating the nation's second-largest bank card merchant acquirer, representing about one of every five VISA and MasterCard transactions processed nationally. Bank of America believes that with the acquisition of National Processing, it is strongly positioned to innovate and create efficiencies in electronic payments. Bank of America is the number one check processor, the number one debit card issuer and the number four credit issuer in the United States.

  National Processing, through its wholly owned subsidiary National Processing Company, LLC (NPC), is a leading provider of merchant credit and debt card processing. NPC supports more than 700,000 merchant locations, representing one of every six MasterCard and VISA transactions processed nationally.

- The company's Global Corporate and Investment Banking group has offices in 30 countries, serving clients in more than 150 countries, with associates in major business centers in the Americas, Europe, and Asia.

- More than 175,000 Bank of America associates provide financial products, services, ideas and solutions to customers and clients in fifty states and the District of Columbia.

- A pioneer in debit-card transactions, Bank of America is the number one debit card issuer in the United States, with some 17 million cards outstanding. Debit cards enable people an alternative to checks or cash at the point of sale for goods and services, and their popularity is growing dramatically.

- Bank of America was recently named one of the nation's top ten companies for corporate diversity and opportunity by *Minority MBA* magazine for the second straight year.

- Bank of America was rated the Best Derivatives Dealer across all product categories in a *Treasury and Risk Management Magazine* survey of CFOs and treasurers at U.S. companies.

- *Forbes* magazine named Bank of America among the "Best of the Web," and *Global Finance* magazine ranked the company as the world's best consumer Internet bank.
- Bank of America is the number one financial institution in number of relationships, investment banking, treasury management, syndications, secured and unsecured credit, and leasing.
- "When Bank of America announced its $47 billion deal for FleetBoston Financial in October 2003, Wall Street groaned," according to an article that appeared in *BusinessWeek* on April 4, 2005. "Bank of America's stock plunged 10 percent that day. But in its first year with Fleet, Bank of America wrung out $909 million in cost savings even while making a hard push to bring in new customers. The result: . . . Bank of America added 184,000 new consumer checking accounts and 196,000 new savings accounts last year in Fleet's Northeast stronghold. Bank of America's profits rose 31 percent last year. Its shares have returned 61.9 percent over the past three years—not bad for what was once considered a terrible deal."

Total assets: $1,011 billion
Return on average Assets in 2004: 1.39%
Common shares outstanding: 4,049 million
Return on 2004 shareholders' equity: 17.3%

|  | 2004 | 2003 | 2002 | 2001 | 2000 | 1999 | 1998 | 1997 |
|---|---|---|---|---|---|---|---|---|
| Loans (millions) | 515,463 | 371,463 | 342,755 | 322,278 | 385,355 | 363,834 | 350,206 | 141,010 |
| Net income (millions) | 14,143 | 10,810 | 9,249 | 8,042 | 7,863 | 8,240 | 6,490 | 3,077 |
| Earnings per share | 3.67 | 3.57 | 2.96 | 2.48 | 2.36 | 2.34 | 1.82 | 2.09 |
| Dividends per share | 1.70 | 1.44 | 1.22 | 1.14 | 1.03 | 0.93 | 0.80 | 0.69 |
| Price high | 47.5 | 42.4 | 38.5 | 32.8 | 30.5 | 38.2 | 44.2 | 35.8 |
| low | 38.5 | 32.1 | 27.0 | 22.5 | 18.2 | 23.8 | 22.0 | 24.0 |

Growth and Income

# Banta Corporation

225 Main Street ❑ P. O. Box 8003 ❑ Menasha, WI 54952–8003 ❑ (920) 751–7713 ❑ Dividend reinvestment program is available: (800) 278–4353 ❑ Web site: *www.banta.com* ❑ Listed: NYSE ❑ Ticker symbol: BN ❑ S&P rating: B ❑ Value Line financial strength rating: B++

Banta Corporation, a technology and market leader in printing and supply chain management, has a solid foundation for growth:
- Superior business mix
- Strong, predictable cash and earnings generation in the print sector
- Higher-growth potential supply-chain management sector to drive top-line growth
- Strong balance sheet
- 18 percent debt to total capital
- Unrelenting cost reduction and continuous improvement
- Technology and systems integration capabilities in both print and supply-chain management
- Blue-chip customer base
- Customer-focused value chains differentiate Banta
- Multiple layers of diversification

- Strong leadership team
- 103-year history of superior performance and values-based management

## Company Profile

Banta is much more than a leading provider of printing and digital imaging services. The supply-chain management business, the fastest-growing segment of Banta's operations, offers important value-added products and services to support the growth of Banta's core printing businesses.

Although you probably never gave it much thought, the last time you opened a carton containing a new computer, VCR, or other piece of electronic gear, there was good chance that Banta printed the instruction booklet, installation guide, warranty cards, and other printed matter inside; provided how-to video or audio tape; supplied the software kit, including diskettes; and provided all of the packaging, whether plastic, cardboard, or paper.

Banta Corporation is a market leader in two primary businesses: printing and supply-chain management. The company has more than 35 operations in North America, Europe, and the Far East. Founded in 1901, Banta became a public company in 1971.

Business, trade and special-interest magazine publishers turn to Banta for the production of nearly 800 titles. Three modern facilities provide a focused production environment for printing and mailing short- to medium-run publications.

Its publishing market products include:
- Educational, trade, juvenile, professional, and religious books
- Business, trade, association, and consumer special-interest magazines
- Journals and newsletters
- Technical manuals
- Calendars
- Directories
- Multimedia kits
- Instructional games
- CD-ROMs

- Video and audio cassettes
- Web sites

Banta provides a full spectrum of direct marketing materials and personalization technologies that maximize the effectiveness of direct-response print. The company is the leader in the production and distribution of specialty and retail catalogues.

Finally, Banta holds a leadership position in each of its market segments.

Banta Healthcare products extend the company's reach beyond the traditional printing and digital-imagine segments. Three manufacturing facilities produce sterile and nonsterile products used in hospitals, outpatient clinics and dental offices. These specialized products are composed of paper, nonwoven materials and polyethylene film. The product line also extends to related applications in the foodservice industry, such as disposable bibs, tablecloths and gloves.

The healthcare assets were sold to Fidelity Strategic Investments on February 14, 2005 for $67 million. The proceeds will be used to buy back some of its own shares, so as to increase Earnings per share.

## Shortcomings to Bear in Mind

- All businesses have their risks. I have excerpted the following risks and caveats from a report issued by Robert W. Baird & Company, Inc., a brokerage firm based in Milwaukee, Wisconsin, on October 28, 2004:
  - Cyclical. Sales fluctuate approximately in-step with broader economic changes. For example, Banta's operations are exposed to cyclical changes in advertising, technology, and education, in addition to most other economic sectors.
  - Seasonal. Educational book activity tends to be strongest in the first half of the year, while catalog, direct marketing and certain technology outsourcing activity tend to be strongest in the

second half. Banta also prints a large bi-annual catalog every other year (even years).

- Raw materials. Banta buys and resells the vast majority of the paper it uses in its printing operation. Weakness in the paper market would depress sales, all else being equal. Banta often passes raw material price increases along to customers.
- Acquisitions. Strategic acquisitions are a core element in Banta's growth strategy. Failure to make suitable acquisitions or the inability to adequately integrate a target company into Banta's operations could affect the company's operating performance.

## Reasons to Buy

- "We are optimistic about business prospects for the remainder of this year and next year," said CEO Stephanie A. Streeter on October 26, 2004. "The solid economy is supporting an active direct mail and catalog environment; we're realizing our planned cost savings from last year's restructuring activities; and we are accelerating our productivity efforts, which should help increase Print Sector margins."

    Ms. Street went on to say, "Supporting next year's growth is an active schedule of states adopting new curriculum programs, which drives educational print activity and should produce additional opportunities for our book division. Expectations for our literature management business remain strong as we've realigned the business and expanded its capacity to provide print-related supply-chain solutions for our customers' marketing collateral and program enrollment materials.

    "In our Supply-Chain Management Sector, we're continuing to gain additional opportunities with our existing

customers and aggressively pursuing expansion into new markets. We also have several productivity initiatives underway, which should help us maintain solid profitability in this attractive growth business."

- "We view the company as among the leaders in its industry and believe it should continue to do well, despite challenges facing it," said William H. Donald, an analyst with *Standard & Poor's Stock Reports*, on December 13, 2004. "We believe BN has widened its reach in Europe, and has boosted U.S. growth opportunities."
- Donald D. Belcher, Banta's just-retired chairman of the board, explained why his company favors working with special-interest magazines. "These magazines are attractive to advertisers because the specialized readerships allows them to target their messages to their best prospects. As a result, special-interest magazines are less prone to advertising cycles.

    "This has been one of our fastest-growing print markets, and we see that growth continuing for us through both market growth and by taking market share, which we have effectively done over the years. Our customers realize that we really specialize in producing short- to medium-run monthly magazines and, as a result, provide the value-added services and print schedule fidelity that are essential to their businesses."

- He went on to explain why Banta does well in direct marketing. "Direct marketing is the fastest-growing print category. The material that shows up in your mailbox seems to increase instead of reduce, and that's an area which is projected to continue growing in the 6 percent to 7 percent annual range over the next several years."
- Supply-chain management has been a key factor in Banta's growth. Commenting on

this business, Mr. Belcher said, "Supply-chain management is our global growth engine. This is a business where the underlying trends for outsourcing services, which are really what we provide in supply-chain management, are very strong. More and more companies, particularly in technology—but other industries as well, are looking for companies to help take over all or part of their manufacturing and distribution processes, so that they can concentrate on their own core competencies. Industry forecasts indicate that the demand for these services will expand at a more than 30 percent compound annual growth rate over the next several years."

- Mr. Belcher went on to say, "In the supply-chain management area, I would say we are extremely well positioned with technology companies. One of the things that we are working on very hard right now is looking to find other related industries where we can bring this same outsourcing solution to capitalize on our particular strengths.

   "One very good product example is medical devices. A company we are working with right now manufactures diabetic testing kits. We source the various materials for the kit, assemble and test the devices and then provide the packaging, distribution and fulfillment

requirements for our customer. Those are the same type of services that we are providing for companies like Compaq, Microsoft, Dell, Cisco, IBM, and several other key players in the technology arena."

- Sidoti & Company, LLC, a brokerage firm with offices in New York City, had these comments on November 30, 2004:
  - We think the macro environment for the printing industry is improving. Since it is difficult for printers to add new capacity quickly, we expect the industry leaders to benefit most from a rebound in the print market. We suggest that the print market has stabilized during the last three months and could begin to show traction in 2005. We expect Banta's print business to benefit from new schoolbook-adoption cycles, while an improving economy helps the company's direct mail, catalog and specialty magazine print divisions.
  - Banta's supply-chain management business offers diversification and better growth prospects than its printing services operation. We think Banta's supply-chain division revenue can expand at a low- to mid-double-digit rate, versus the low-single-digits for the print business.

Total assets: $906 million
Current ratio: 2.35
Common shares outstanding: 25 million
Return on 2004 shareholders' equity: 12.9%

| | 2004 | 2003 | 2002 | 2001 | 2000 | 1999 | 1998 | 1997 |
|---|---|---|---|---|---|---|---|---|
| Revenues (millions) | 1,523 | 1,418 | 1,366 | 1,453 | 1,538 | 1,278 | 1,336 | 1,202 |
| Net income (millions) | 68 | 47 | 44 | 50 | 59 | 54 | 53 | 52 |
| Earnings per share | 2.67 | 2.34 | 2.35 | 2.31 | 2.35 | 2.02 | 1.80 | 1.73 |
| Dividends per share | .68 | .68 | .64 | .62 | .60 | .52 | .51 | .47 |
| Price high | 47.5 | 41.0 | 39.1 | 31.0 | 25.7 | 27.4 | 35.3 | 29.9 |
| low | 36.7 | 27.0 | 29.0 | 22.5 | 17.2 | 16.8 | 21.8 | 21.6 |

Conservative Growth

# C. R. Bard, Inc.

730 Central Avenue ❑ Murray Hill, NJ 07974 ❑ (908) 277–8413 ❑ Direct dividend reinvestment plan available: (800) 828–1639 ❑ Web site: *www.crbard.com* ❑ Listed: NYSE ❑ Ticker symbol: BCR ❑ S&P rating: B+ ❑ Value Line Financial Rating: A

On January 12, 2005, C. R. Bard announced that it had acquired certain assets of Genyx Medical, Inc., of Aliso Viejo, California, related to the Uryx implantable bulking agent for the treatment of stress urinary incontinence. The Uryx product has received pre-market approval from the U.S. Food and Drug Administration, and Bard launched it in the first half of 2005. The company's Urological division, located in Covington, Georgia, markets the product.

Stress urinary incontinence is an often debilitating condition that affects an estimated 50 million people globally, 85 percent of whom are women. Minimally invasive bulking agent therapy can be a first line treatment choice and is often used for patients who are not candidates for surgery. The Uryx product is a proprietary polymer implanted into the tissue surrounding the urethra to reduce or eliminate this form of urinary incontinence.

CEO Timothy M. Ring commented, "With the aging population and the increasing demand for more effective, minimally invasive therapies for stress urinary incontinence, we view this acquisition as an important opportunity for Bard. We believe that the addition of the Uryx device will further strengthen our broad product line and enhance our position in the incontinence market."

## Company Profile
Founded in 1907 by Charles Russell Bard, the company initially sold urethral catheters and other urinary products.

One of its first medical products was the silk urethral catheter imported from France.

Today, C. R. Bard markets a wide range of medical, surgical, diagnostic and patient-care devices. It does business worldwide to hospitals, individual health care professionals, extended care facilities, and alternate site facilities. In general, Bard's products are intended to be used once and then discarded.

The company offers a complete line of urological diagnosis and intervention products (about one-third of annual sales), including the well-known Foley catheters, procedure kits and trays, and related urine monitoring and collection systems; urethral stents; and specialty devices for incontinence.

### Urology
The Foley catheter, introduced by Bard in 1934, remains one of the most important products in the urological field. Foley catheters are marketed in individual sterile packages, but, more importantly, they are included in sterile procedural kits and trays, a concept pioneered by Bard. The company is the market leader in Foley catheters, which currently are Bard's largest-selling urological product.

Newer products include the Infection Control Foley catheter, which reduces the rate of urinary tract infections; an innovative collagen implant and sling materials used to treat urinary incontinence, and brachytherapy services, devices, and radioactive seeds to treat prostate cancer.

### Oncology
In the realm of oncology (nearly a quarter of revenues), C. R. Bard's products are designed for the detection and treatment of various types of cancer. Products include specialty access catheters, and ports; gastroenterological products (endoscopic accessories,

percutaneous feeding devices and stents); biopsy devices; and a suturing system for gastroesophageal reflux disease. The company's chemotherapy products serve a well-established market in which Bard holds a major market position.

## Vascular Products

The company's line of vascular diagnosis and intervention products (more than 20 percent) includes peripheral angioplasty stents, catheters, guide wires, introducers and accessories, vena cava filters and biopsy devices; electro physiology products such as cardiac mapping and laboratory systems, and diagnostic and temporary pacing electrode catheters; fabrics and meshes; and implantable blood vessel replacements.

Bard's memotherm nitinol stent technology from the company's Angiomed subsidiary established the company as a major player in this peripheral growth market. With the acquisition of Impra, Inc. in 1996, Bard has the broadest line available of vascular grafts.

## Surgical Products

Surgical specialties products (close to 20 percent of annual revenues) include meshes for vessel and hernia repair; irrigation devices for orthopedic and laparoscopic procedures; and topical hemostatic devices.

The innovation of Bard's PerFix plug and Composix sheet has significantly improved the way hernias are repaired and has reduced the time needed for repair from hours to minutes. Hernia operations can now be done in an outpatient setting in about 20 minutes. What's more, the patient generally can return to normal activity with little or no recovery time.

The balance of sales (about 5 percent) fall into the "other" category.

## International

Bard markets its products through twenty-two subsidiaries and a joint venture in ninety-two countries outside the United States.

Principal markets are Japan, Canada, the United Kingdom, and continental Europe.

## Shortcomings to Bear in Mind

- Robert M. Gold, an analyst with *Standard & Poor's Stock Reports,* gave Bard a HOLD rating on October 25, 2004. Here are his comments—which aren't that negative: "We believe investments in R&D will drive double-digit EPS (Earnings per share) growth over the next three years. We view positively newly launched products and those nearing commercialization, such as a dialysis catheter, a diagnostic electrophysiology catheter, and a constant-flow pain pump. In the interim, we see continued strength for products such as peripheral angioplasty, stents for grafts, implantable drug ports, and specialty catheters."

Mr. Gold also had some reservations, "The stock has performed strongly in 2004, reducing the valuation gap versus device peers. We see further valuation expansion as difficult in the absence of material upside earnings surprises."

## Reasons to Buy

- "We have raised our earnings estimate for this year," said *Value Line* analyst George Rho on March 4, 2005. "Bard has consistently topped bottom-line expectations of late, including last year's closing quarter when share net was four pennies above our figure and 23 percent above the year-earlier tally.

"Recently launched products are gaining traction, supported by an expanding sales force. As well, the medical devices maker is poised to introduce a host of new products in 2005 and 2006."

- C. R. Bard has an acquisition strategy that targets small research or developing companies as well as larger established companies with market leadership positions. In addition to acquiring companies, Bard has expanded its business in the medical field by acquiring product lines, entering into licensing agreements and joint ventures, and making equity investments in companies with emerging technologies.

- In 2003, Bard acquired assets related to the manufacture and distribution of a new biopsy device from PIP Biomedical Instruments and Products GmbH, located in Turkenfeld, Germany.

  The new minimally invasive device has a proprietary vacuum-assisted design. It is initially targeted at breast biopsies, for which there are an estimated 2.3 million procedures performed each year around the world. About half of these procedures are performed using less invasive biopsy devices with the balance being done surgically.

  Bard's new biopsy product is a self-contained, portable unit that fits into the physician's hand, providing optimal control, accuracy and flexibility for biopsy procedures. The device is suitable for use with a range of imaging technologies, including stereotactic x-ray and ultrasound. In the words of the company's CEO, "This acquisition leverages our market leadership position in core needle biopsy, enabling us to enter the larger and faster growing vacuum-assisted segment."

- In 2003, Bard announced that its wholly owned subsidiary, Bard Peripheral Vascular, Inc., had received FDA (Food and Drug Administration) clearance to market the Recovery vena cava filter as a removable device. Vena cava filters are designed to prevent emboli from traveling to the lungs and are placed primarily in patients who have failed, or are contraindicated for, anticoagulation therapy. For the vast majority of people, the duration of risk of pulmonary embolism is finite but unknown at the time the filter is placed.

Removable filters are currently available only outside the United States, but must be removed within two weeks of placement. Bard's Recovery filter does not have an indicated time limit for removal, but rather gives doctors the flexibility to assess patient's risk and determine the appropriate time of removal.

Patients with various types of disease, especially forms of cancer or those undergoing surgery, including orthopedic and neurological procedures, risk developing venous thrombosis, and pulmonary embolism. In the U.S., an estimated 600,000 hospitalizations and as many as 150,000 deaths each year result from pulmonary emboli.

"We are very excited to have the first vena cava filter on the market in the United States with a removable option," said CEO Timothy M. Ring. "We believe that the addition of the removable indication to the Recovery filter provides us an opportunity to gain market share and expand the market. This is yet another example of Bard's ability to enhance our core product portfolio and market position with innovative new technology."

Total assets: $2,009 million
Current ratio: 2.70
Common shares outstanding: 210 million
Return on 2004 equity: 25.2%

|  | 2004 | 2003 | 2002 | 2001 | 2000 | 1999 | 1998 | 1997 |
|---|---|---|---|---|---|---|---|---|
| Revenues (millions) | 1,656 | 1,433 | 1,274 | 1,181 | 1,099 | 1,037 | 1,165 | 1,214 |
| Net income (millions) | 303 | 169 | 155 | 143 | 125 | 118 | 96 | 96 |
| Earnings per share | 1.41 | 0.80 | 0.74 | 0.69 | 0.62 | 0.57 | 0.43 | 0.42 |
| Dividends per share | .24 | .23 | .22 | .21 | .20 | .20 | .19 | .18 |
| Price    high | 32.6 | 20.4 | 16.0 | 16.3 | 13.8 | 15.0 | 12.6 | 9.8 |
|          low | 20.1 | 13.5 | 11.1 | 10.3 | 8.8 | 10.5 | 7.2 | 6.6 |

# Barnes & Noble, Inc.

122 Fifth Avenue ❑ New York, NY 10011 ❑ (212) 633–3489 ❑ Dividend reinvestment plan not available ❑ Web site: *www.barnesandnobleinc.com* ❑ Fiscal years end January 31 ❑ Listed: NYSE ❑ Ticker symbol: BKS ❑ S&P rating: B ❑ Value Line financial strength rating: B++

"Borders and Barnes & Noble have been different from the get-go, which is obvious to many customers," says Sarah Fister Gale, a freelance writer in Minneapolis in an article in *Workforce Management*. "Borders focuses on offering the widest assortment of titles, whereas Barnes & Noble draws customers with low prices on the most popular books. The result is that while both companies say 'passion' is the most important quality in an applicant, what they are passionate about, and how they express that passion, varies dramatically with each store.

"Barnes & Noble hires people with a passion for customer service, a 'love of books' and a scholarly background, says Mitchell Klipper, chief operating officer. 'Our booksellers are nice, educated people. They wear collared shirts and have a cleaner look, as opposed to tattoos and T-shirts.' They're also committed to providing excellent customer service, he says. 'Putting the book in the customer's hand and fast cashiering are the two principles the company was founded on.'"

According to Ms. Gale, "There's an ample pool of potential employees to choose from in almost every market they enter. It's not uncommon for Barnes & Noble to receive 2,000 applications at a job fair, Klipper said. Borders receives up to 150 inquiries for each job opening. This wealth of potential employees means there's little competition for talent between the two companies."

Ms. Gale also said, "Despite their differences, both companies continue to rule the book-selling industry, creeping steadily into every corner of America. In an industry where profits increase in direct proportion to expansion, its ability to open and staff a new location efficiently determines the success of both businesses, says John Beaulieu, financial analyst for Morningstar.

"Both stores sell an average of about $240 per square foot of retail space, with a total inventory turnover about twice a year. 'It's hard to get big returns when your inventory is so massive,' Beaulieu says, noting both companies grow primarily through store openings. Barnes & Noble opens an average of fifty new stores a year."

## Company Profile

Barnes & Noble is the largest domestic bookseller, with 868 outlets. Through its 75 percent interest in Barnes & Noble.com, Inc., the company is also one of the largest online booksellers.

The majority of the company's bookstores (634), operate under the Barnes & Noble Booksellers, Bookshop, and Bookstar trade names. Management believes it leads book retailing with the "community store" concept. The company seeks to make each superstore an active part of its community by offering customers a diverse title selection that reflects in part local interests; a café; a children's section; a music department; a magazine section; and a calendar of ongoing events. BKS also emphasizes books published by small and independent publishers as well as university presses.

The company operates the balance of its bookstores (234) under the B. Dalton Bookseller, Doubleday Book Shops, and Scribner's Bookstore trade names. These mainly mall-based stores focus on the mainstream consumer book market, with a wide selection of bestsellers and general-interest titles. Because of superstore competition,

BKS is continuing to close underperforming units. It has shuttered between thirty-five and ninety outlets each year since 1989.

Barnes & Noble.com, Inc., through its Web site, has access to about 1 million titles, supplemented by more than 30 million listings from a nationwide network of out-of-print, rare and used book dealers. This venture was put together in 1998 by Barnes & Noble and Bertelsmann AG. In 2003, the company acquired Bertelsmann's 36.8 percent interest for $164 million.

In another sector, Barnes & Noble publishes books under the Barnes & Noble Books imprint, for exclusive sale through its retail stores and mail order catalogs. In 2003, the company acquired Sterling Publishing Company, Inc., a leading publisher of how-to books, for $126 million. Sterling has an active list of more than 4,500 owned and distributed titles. Each year, it publishes and distributes more than 1,000 titles. With the addition of Sterling, Barnes & Noble has publishing or distribution rights to nearly 10,000 titles.

On October 4, 2004, the company announced that it would spin off to its shareholders its stake in GameStop, the nation's largest video-game and entertainment software specialty retailer. Commenting on the move, chairman Leonard Riggio said, "By all measures, Barnes & Noble's acquisition of GameStop has been a huge success. Though both companies are doing extremely well and are each industry leaders, we believe they will be more valuable trading separately than together."

## Shortcomings to Bear in Mind

- *Standard & Poor's Stock Reports* was not too enthusiastic about Barnes & Noble on February 24, 2005. Jason N. Asaeda said, "Our recommendation is HOLD. We see BKS's recent divestiture of its stake in GME (GameStop) as a possible profit-taking move. The company had said that its $400 million investment had appreciated to over $850 million.

In becoming a pure-play bookseller and publisher, BKS has lost about 25 percent of its annual earnings stream, and in our view, has less downside protection against weakness in the book trade.

"Balancing this concern against what we see as easier historical sales comparisons in fiscal 2006, our expectation of strong sales of J. K. Rowling's long-awaited *Harry Potter and the Half Blood Prince,* which the company is offering at an attractive 40 percent discount to the publisher's listed price of $29.99, and our favorable opinion of BKS's longer-term prospects as a multichannel bookseller, we would hold the shares."

## Reasons to Buy

- "Within the bookselling segment, we're very pleased with the emergence of 'big' books, several of which had a significant direct impact on sales as well as on store traffic," said chairman Leonard Riggio in 2004. "While we believe that many more blockbusters are in the offing, our own publishing program has clearly begun to even out some of the bumps in the publishing cycle, in terms of sales and, more importantly, margins. Led by the phenomenally successful launch of Barnes & Noble Classics, and Spark Notes, our publishing program has a total of more than 1,600 titles in print. All sell for much less than comparable publisher titles and deliver much greater margins. And, while sure-fire backlist titles are our mainstay, our re-issue of Dow Mossman's novel, *The Stones of Summer,* and the amazing *Weird N.J.* (80,000 copies sold in New Jersey alone!) demonstrated our ability to place self-published titles at the top of the bestseller lists. In all, self-published titles have now reached 5 percent of total bookstore sales, well on the way to our target of 10 percent."

- In response to the ever-increasing interest in the science of forensics, Barnes &

Noble.com, Inc. announced in the fall of 2003 that it would offer a new online course at Barnes & Noble University, created in partnership with Court TV–The Investigation Channel, dedicated to the techniques and history of forensics. "Learn Forensics with Court TV" costs $14.95 and began in October 2003. The reference book, *The Forensics Casebook: the Science of Crime Scene Investigation,* complements the course and is only $11.86. The course offers a high level of instructor participation via message boards and e-mail, hands-on forensics experiments and interactive activities using online and reference book material.

Barnes & Noble University (BNU) is home to some of the best and most varied educational content on the Internet. Each month, dozens of courses are offered, each taught by an expert in the field, often a bestselling author. The courses cover everything from technology and computer skills to literature, writing, business, foreign language, and self-help.

Many of the course are free, and BNU's reasonably priced Premier courses enhance the level of learning with such features as Certificates of Completion, interactive activities, available Continuing Education Units (CEUs), Learning Paths, and more. Barnes & Noble University is not an accredited program or institution.

■ In the fall of 2003, BKS announced that it was significantly expanding its selection of books in Spanish, in order to meet their customers' growing demand. Starting in September, 488 Barnes & Noble stores across the country began to add thousands of Spanish-language titles to the Libros en Espanol section of each bookstore. The company's Web site, *www.BarnesandNoble.com,* launched a new line featuring thousands of Spanish-language books, CDs, and movies that can be accessed directly at *www.bn.com/espanol* as well as from the homepage at *www.bn.com.*

Spanish-language titles in thousands of categories are now available, including works originally written in Spanish by such popular authors as Laura Esquivel, Isabel Allende, Carlos Fuentes, and Gabriel Garcia Marquez. In addition, the section now offers Spanish-language translations of bestselling books in English.

"Up until now, books in Spanish have been tremendously difficult to buy in the United States, even though so many people in this country prefer reading books in Spanish," said Jorge Ramos, Emmy Award-winning journalist and author of *No Borders: A Journalist's Search for Home* and *The Other Face of America.* "It's wonderful to see major booksellers stepping up to meet the demand of the millions of Latinos in the United States who love to read."

Total assets: $3, 351 million
Current ratio: 1.48
Common shares outstanding: 76 million
Return on 2004 shareholders' equity: 11.9%

| | 2004 | 2003 | 2002 | 2001 | 2000 | 1999 | 1998 | 1997 |
|---|---|---|---|---|---|---|---|---|
| Revenues (millions) | 4,874 | 5,951 | 5,269 | 4,870 | 4,376 | 3,486 | 3,006 | 2,797 |
| Net income (millions) | 143 | 152 | 100 | 64 | -52 | 129 | 92 | 65 |
| Earnings per share | 1.93 | 2.07 | 1.39 | 1.28 | -.81 | 1.81 | 1.29 | .93 |
| Dividends per share | Nil | — | — | — | — | — | — | — |
| Price      high | 32.6 | 34.0 | 35.0 | 44.0 | 29.9 | 44.4 | 48.0 | 33.9 |
|            low | 20.0 | 15.9 | 16.8 | 21.6 | 16.3 | 20.1 | 22.2 | 12.9 |

# Becton, Dickinson and Company

1 Becton Drive ❑ Franklin Lakes, NJ 07417–1880 ❑ (201) 847–5453 ❑ Direct dividend reinvestment plan available: (800) 955–4743 ❑ Web site: *www.bd.com* ❑ Fiscal years end September 30th ❑ Ticker symbol: BDX ❑ S&P rating: A ❑ Value Line financial strength rating: A+

Domestic sales of insulin needles and syringes are expected to increase in the high-single digits during the next few years, fueled by the estimated five percent annual growth in the number of Americans suffering from diabetes, plus the trend toward multiple insulin injections. Recent scientific studies have shown that the use of multiple daily injections of insulin reduces the severity of the disease's longer-term deleterious effects.

Becton Dickinson, which accounts for about 90 percent of the domestic insulin syringe market, has entered into an arrangement with Eli Lilly, the largest domestic producer of insulin products, and Boehringer Mannheim, a major manufacturer of glucose monitoring devices, to provide information to diabetics regarding the best manner in which to control their disease. Over time, this program should accelerate the trend toward multiple daily insulin injections.

The company is also reviewing a number of noninvasive techniques to monitor glucose levels in diabetics. This device could reach the market before the end of the decade and further enhance the company's overall position in the diabetic sector.

## Company Profile

Becton, Dickinson is a medical technology company that serves healthcare institutions, life science researchers, clinical laboratories, industry, and the general public. BD manufactures and sells a broad range of medical supplies, devices, laboratory equipment, and diagnostic products.

Becton, Dickinson focuses strategically on achieving growth in three worldwide business segments—BD Medical (formerly BD Medical Systems), BD Biosciences, and BD Diagnostics (formerly BD Clinical Laboratory Solutions). BD products are marketed in the United States both through independent distribution channels and directly to end-users. Outside the United States, BD products are marketed through independent distribution channels and sales representatives and, in some markets, directly to end-users.

BDX generates close to 50 percent of its revenues outside the United States. Worldwide demand for healthcare products and services continues to be strong, despite the ongoing focus on cost containment. The health care environment favors continued growth in medical delivery systems due to the growing awareness of the need to protect health care workers from accidental needlesticks and legislative/regulatory activity favoring conversion to safety-engineered devices.

BD Biosciences, one of the world's largest businesses serving the life sciences, provides research tools and reagents to study life—from normal processes to disease states—and accelerate the pace of biomedical discovery. Throughout the world, clinicians and researchers use BD Biosciences' tools to study genes, proteins, and cells to better understand disease, improve technologies for diagnosis and disease management, and facilitate the discovery and development of novel therapeutics.

BD Diagnostics (formerly BD Clinical Laboratory Solutions) offers system solutions for collecting, identifying, and transporting specimens, as well as advanced instrumentation for quickly and accurately analyzing specimens. The business also provides services that focus on customers' process flow, supply chain management, and training and education.

BD Medical (formerly BD Medical Systems) holds leadership positions in hypodermic needles and syringes, infusion therapy devices, insulin injection systems, and pre-fillable drug-delivery systems for pharmaceutical companies. It offers the industry's broadest, deepest line of safety-engineered sharps products, as well as surgical and regional anesthesia, ophthalmology, critical care, and sharps disposal products.

BDX is dedicated to producing solutions—and the best solution of all is helping all people live healthy lives. Their vision is to become a great company, defined by great performance, great contributions made to society, and being a great place to work.

## Shortcomings to Bear in Mind

- Nearly half of the company's sales come from abroad. This exposes Becton to the risks associated with foreign currency rates which could create increased volatility in reported earnings. On the other hand, BDX has done a good job of managing foreign currency exposure, and the impact on earnings has typically been limited to only 1 or 2 percent.

## Reasons to Buy

- Argus Research Company had an upbeat view of BDX on February 8, 2005, according to analyst David H. Toung. "We are reiterating our BUY-rating for Becton ,Dickinson & Company and boosting our target price to $74. The company reported solid results for its recent first quarter of 2005. These results are another demonstration of the company's long-term track record of consistent and profitable growth. With its products as staples in disease management and healthcare safety, we believe that BDX is a good defensive play in the healthcare sector."

- "We believe BDX should benefit from improved revenue visibility amid signs of recovering end user demand in the life sciences industry and momentum in the diagnostics and diabetes management areas," said Robert M. Gold, writing for *Standard & Poor's Stock Reports* on January 31, 2005. "The company boosted its quarterly cash dividend by 20 percent in November 2004, and the stock's 1.3 percent dividend yield is among the highest in our medical equipment coverage universe. We think this dividend payment will provide added support to the stock in a generally more defensive environment."

- On March 4, 2005, *Value Line Investment Survey* had an upbeat view of Becton, Dickinson. Erik Antonson said, "BD's strong balance sheet and cash flow continue to enable it to aggressively repurchase stock. The company is expected to spend another $400 million to $500 million on buybacks this year, although the number of shares outstanding should only decrease slightly.

  "This timely equity should merit the consideration of many. It appears poised for above-average, year-ahead performance and offers three- to five-year capital gains potential that is on par with the *Value Line* median. Too, due to a Safety rank of 1 (Highest) and a dividend that should continue growing, the stock offers alluring total-return potential out to 2008–2010 on a risk-adjusted basis."

- According to a company spokesman, "We are a leader in a number of platforms in the Biosciences segment. In the last few years, we made key acquisitions in the areas of immunology, cell biology, and molecular biology. Growth in research products is driven by the expansion in genomic research and increased pharmaceutical and government spending in this area.

  "In the Clinical Laboratory Solutions' segment, we have strong marketing positions. We also have opportunities for further growth in this segment. For example, nearly half of the world's population lives in medical markets that do not currently use evacuated blood collection systems, one of our principal products in this segment."

- "Looking further into the future," said CEO E. J. Ludwig, "we have a range of genuinely exciting technologies and product platforms under development, particularly in the area of advanced drug delivery. This opportunity is especially compelling because these drug delivery systems are coming of age at the dawn of the biotechnology era. Large molecule biotechnology-based drugs today most often must be injected, as opposed to ingested. Early tests indicate that the delivery systems we have under development could significantly increase the effectiveness of such drugs. When added to the drug discovery role played by BD Biosciences and the diagnostics performed by BD Clinical Laboratory Solutions, BD is poised to participate in every phase of the biotechnology revolution, from drug discovery through diagnostics to drug delivery."

- The company's use of computer-aided design and manufacturing technology enables Becton to bring quality products to market faster and at a lower cost. One such technology is stereo lithography, which uses a laser system to quickly create a three-dimensional physical object from a computer-aided design model. Engineers can use this extremely accurate model as a prototype, improving both the quality of the product design and the speed of the product development process.

Becton, Dickinson has the technology to help reduce the medical errors that have received attention of late. A U.S. government scientific panel found that about 75,000 hospital patients die each year from medical mistakes. Yet, only 9 percent of the facilities have invested in equipment to address the problem.

For its part, BDX is offering two hand-held devices, based on 3Com's Palm Computing technology. One tracks drugs from the initial order through their administration. The other serves a similar purpose for specimen collection, testing, and patient file management.

Total assets: $5,753 million
Current ratio: 2.52
Common shares outstanding: 250 million
Return on 2004 shareholders' equity: 19.7%

| | 2004 | 2003 | 2002 | 2001 | 2000 | 1999 | 1998 | 1997 |
|---|---|---|---|---|---|---|---|---|
| Revenues (millions) | 4,935 | 4,528 | 4,033 | 3,746 | 3,618 | 3,418 | 3,117 | 2,810 |
| Net income (millions) | 582 | 547 | 480 | 402 | 393 | 386 | 360 | 315 |
| Earnings per share | 2.21 | 2.07 | 1.79 | 1.63 | 1.49 | 1.46 | 1.37 | 1.21 |
| Dividends per share | .60 | .40 | .39 | .38 | .37 | .34 | .29 | .26 |
| Price        high | 58.2 | 41.8 | 38.6 | 39.3 | 35.3 | 44.2 | 49.6 | 27.8 |
|                 low | 40.2 | 28.8 | 24.7 | 30.0 | 21.8 | 22.4 | 24.4 | 20.9 |

Growth and Income

# Bemis Company, Inc.

222 South Ninth Street, Suite 2300 ❑ Minneapolis, MN 55402–4099 ❑ (612) 376–3030 ❑ Dividend reinvestment plan is available: (800) 551–6161 ❑ Listed: NYSE ❑ Web site: www.bemis.com ❑ Ticker symbol: BMS ❑ S&P rating: A ❑ Value Line financial strength rating: A+

On January 5, 2005, Bemis announced that it had acquired majority ownership of Dixie Toga, one of the largest packaging companies in South America. Headquartered in Sao Paolo, Brazil, Dixie Toga recorded annual sales in excess of $300 million in 2004.

"The Dixie Toga business is an exciting addition to Bemis Company and further strengthens our position as the leading flexible packaging supplier in North America and South America," said CEO Jeff Curler. "The Dixie Toga operations are well managed, growing businesses with leading market positions and strong customer relationships. This business is achieving strong revenue growth and profit margins through a combination of new product introductions, focused cost control and improved production efficiencies."

According to a report issued by the brokerage firm of Lehman Brothers on January 17, 2005, "In our view, the Dixie Toga acquisition should add to the long-term secular growth rate of Bemis, given their increased exposure to the faster-growing Brazilian market, combined with a pickup in their core flexible packaging business more recently."

## Company Profile

Dating back to 1858, Bemis is a leading manufacturer of flexible packaging and pressure-sensitive materials. More than 75 percent of the company's sales are packaging-related.

Flexible packaging refers to product packaging that can be easily bent, twisted or folded. The opposite is rigid packaging which includes things like glass and plastic bottles, metal cans and cardboard boxes. Examples of flexible packaging include candy bar wrappers, pouches for shredded cheese, bread bags, and dog food bags.

Flexible packaging (about 80 percent of company revenue in 2004) is an attractive means of packaging a wide variety of products because of its light weight, strength, and the ability to use small amounts of material in most applications. That results in lower costs for the package itself and less material to be disposed of after the package is used.

The primary market for the company's products is the food industry. Other markets include medical, pharmaceutical, chemical, agribusiness, printing and graphic arts, as well as a variety of other industrial end uses. Bemis holds a strong position in many of its markets and actively seeks new market segments where its technical skill and other capabilities provide a competitive advantage.

Bemis has a strong technical base in polymer chemistry, film extrusion coating and laminating, printing and converting, and pressure-sensitive adhesive technologies. These capabilities are being integrated to provide greater innovation and accelerated growth in the company's core businesses.

## Business Segments

### Flexible Packaging

Bemis is the leading manufacturer of flexible packaging in North America. The company provides multinational and North American food and consumer products companies with packaging solutions that protect contents during shipment, extend shelf life, and offer attractive, consumer-friendly designs. Over 60 percent of Flexible Packaging sales are printed film materials. The balance are sold as plain film for retail and institutional food as well as a variety of other markets.

This segment breaks down into three smaller pieces:

• High Barrier Products includes controlled and modified atmosphere packaging for food, medical, personal care, and non-food applications consisting of complex barrier, multilayer polymer film structures and laminates. Primary markets are processed and fresh meat, liquids, snacks, cheese, coffee, condiments, candy, pet food, personal care, and medical packaging.

• Polyethylene Products include mono-layer and co-extruded polymer films that have been converted to bags, roll stock, or shrink wrap. Primary markets are bakery products, seed, retail, lawn and garden, ice, fresh produce, frozen vegetables, shrink wrap, tissue, and sanitary products.

• Paper products include multiwall and single-ply paper bags, balers, printed paper roll stock, and bag closing materials. Primary markets are pet products, seed, chemicals, dairy products, fertilizers, feed, minerals, flour, rice, and sugar.

### Pressure-Sensitive Materials

Bemis is a major world-wide manufacturer of pressure-sensitive adhesive-coated materials for a variety of markets. Under the brand name of MACtac, Bemis delivers advanced product performance to the pressure-sensitive industry. Examples include labeling for cold temperature food packaging, harsh environment conditions, wet manufacturing processes, miniature electronic components, tamper-evident packaging, and technologically advanced fastener applications.

This segment is divided up as follows:

• Roll Label Products include unprinted rolls of pressure-sensitive adhesive-coated papers and film. These products are sold to converters who print labels for bar coding, product decoration, identification, safety marking, and product instructions. Primary markets are food packaging, personal care product packaging, inventory control labeling, and laser/ink jet printed labels.

• Graphics and Distribution Products include unprinted rolls or sheets of pressure-sensitive adhesive coated papers and films. Offset printers, sign makers, and photo labs use these products on short-run and/or digital printing technology to create labels, sign, or vehicle graphics. Primary markets are sheet printers, shipping labels, indoor and outdoor signs, photograph and digital print over-laminates, and vehicle graphics.

• Technical and Industrial products include pressure-sensitive adhesive-coated tapes used for mounting, bonding, and fastening. Tapes sold to medical markets feature medical-grade adhesives suitable for direct skin contact. Primary markets are batteries, electronics, medical, and pharmaceuticals.

### Shortcomings to Bear in Mind

■ "Prices of resin, a key raw material in plastic manufacturing, continue to weigh heavily on margins," said Eric M. Gottlieb, writing for *Value Line* on January 7, 2005. "Although Bemis has been able to pass off most of the increased costs to its customers, this can take several months to implement due to contractual agreements. Resin prices may in fact fall during 2005 (contingent on oil/gas prices), allowing margins to improve and earnings to advance at levels consistent with historical growth." At the time of this writing, *Value Line* had a somewhat negative Timeliness rating of 4 (3 is average).

### Reasons to Buy

■ On January 26, 2005, Mr. Curler said, "The market for our flexible packaging products is expanding. Our customers have a growing appetite for innovative film structures that perform well on their packaging lines and for graphics and convenience features that capture consumers' attention on store shelves.

"During 2004, our flexible packaging business segment successfully managed significant increases in raw material costs and achieved solid growth in unit sales volume. Our expanded flexible packaging capabilities in Europe and Mexico will continue to transition into their regional markets during 2005. Our North American business is healthy and growing at a steady pace. This year, we will be making substantial investments in new capacity to meet expected customer demand in 2006 and beyond."

■ "We have a BUY recommendation on the shares of BMS, based on our valuation models and favorable global markets," said Stewart Scharf, writing for Standard & Poor's on February 2, 2005. "We expect the company to boost its capital expenditure budget to nearly $200 million, targeting a minimum return on invested capital of 15 percent, as it focuses on its higher-margin businesses and leading products on a global basis. We think free cash flow will be used mainly for further debt pay-downs and, possibly, acquisitions."

- Bemis has a solid record of growth. In the 1994–2004 period, Earnings per share expanded from $0.70 to $1.67, a compound annual growth rate of 9.1 percent. The dividend in the same ten-year span advanced from $0.27 to $0.64, a growth rate of 9 percent—and was raised every year during that period.

- "Our attention to maintaining a world-class manufacturing organization has rewarded our customers with competitive edge and flexibility in packaging options," said a company spokesman. "Over the past five years, Bemis has devoted substantial resources to improving capacity and expanding world-class operating facilities to meet the increasing demand for sophisticated barrier films.

"Since the majority of the packages we sell in the Flexible Packaging business are printed, graphics capabilities are a significant source of expertise and competitive edge for Bemis. We are vertically integrated, offering customers our graphic design and color separation expertise. Bemis manufacturing operators work directly with graphic designers to create the highest quality printed package. Our state-of-the-art printing presses significantly improve our manufacturing efficiencies with robotics to reduce press idle-time during change over to new colors."

- At Bemis's Flexible Packaging operations, differing grades of polymers, such as polyethylene, polystyrene, polypropylene, nylon, and polyester, are combined in a variety of ways to create films that are stronger, shinier, clearer, abuse-resistant, peelable, easier to print, sterilizable, and easier to process on machinery.

What's more, the company's recent acquisition of a shrink-packaging business introduced a patented technology that was not previously available to Bemis. The combination of this shrink film technology and "our material science expertise creates sizable opportunities for a variety of new innovations for our Flexible Packaging operations," said a company spokesman.

"Our research and development efforts go beyond the laboratory to the manufacturing floor, designing films that work better on even the newest high-speed machinery. We go into customer plants to design innovative solutions for their packaging and marketing needs. Bemis consistently devotes a significant effort to the development of new products and processes that will keep us at the forefront of the industry and keep our customers anticipating the next generation of packing innovation."

Total assets: $2,487 million
Current ratio: 2.33
Common shares outstanding: 107 million
Return on 2004 shareholders' equity: 14.7%

|  |  | 2004 | 2003 | 2002 | 2001 | 2000 | 1999 | 1998 | 1997 |
|---|---|---|---|---|---|---|---|---|---|
| Revenues (millions) |  | 2,834 | 2,635 | 2,369 | 2,293 | 2,165 | 1,918 | 1,848 | 1,877 |
| Net income (millions) |  | 180 | 147 | 166 | 140 | 131 | 115 | 111 | 108 |
| Earnings per share |  | 1.67 | 1.36 | 1.54 | 1.32 | 1.22 | 1.09 | 1.04 | 1.00 |
| Dividends per share |  | .64 | .62 | .52 | .50 | .48 | .46 | .44 | .40 |
| Price | high | 29.5 | 25.6 | 29.1 | 26.2 | 19.6 | 20.2 | 23.4 | 24.0 |
|  | low | 23.2 | 19.6 | 19.7 | 14.3 | 11.4 | 15.1 | 16.7 | 16.8 |

# Biomet, Incorporated

56 East Bell Drive □ Warsaw, IN 46582–0587 □ (574) 267–6639 □ Dividend reinvestment plan not available □ Fiscal years end May 31 □ Listed: NASDAQ □ Web site: *www.biomet.com* □ Ticker symbol: BMET □ S&P rating: A- □ Value Line financial strength rating: A+

In its first year of operation (1977), Biomet recorded sales of $17,000—and a net loss of $63,000. Today, the company is a leader in the musculoskeletal marketplace, with sales not far from $1.8 billion. Its products include the design and manufacture of four major product groups: reconstructive devices, fixation products, spinal products, and other products.

Favorable demographics and a shift to technologically advanced products are fueling the estimated 12 percent growth in the $7.62 billion domestic musculoskeletal market. The demand for musculoskeletal products continues to grow with the aging of the baby boomer generation. According to the U.S. Census Bureau projections, the fifty-five-to-seventy-five-year-old population group is expected to grow about 70 percent in the next twenty years, to 74.7 million people. What's more, the traditional fifty-five-to-seventy-five-year-old orthopedic implant population continues to expand below age fifty-five and above age seventy-five.

Procedures are now being recommended for patients at younger ages, as skilled engineering of new products and increasingly effective technology directly contribute to the greater probability of successful implant performance and longevity. In addition, the elderly are leading more active lifestyles than past generations, resulting in stronger, healthier individuals who are excellent candidates for reconstructive implant procedures, creating a greater need for products and services to treat musculoskeletal disorders.

## Company Profile

Biomet ranks among the world's largest orthopedic manufacturers. The company offers a wide variety of products that are used primarily by orthopedic medical specialists in the surgical replacement of hip and knee joints and in fracture fixation procedures as an aid in healing. They include reconstructive implants, electrical bone stimulators, and related products.

Reconstructive devices, which accounted for 65 percent of sales in fiscal 2004, are employed to replace joints that have deteriorated because of such diseases as osteoarthritis or injury. These include implants for replacement of hips, knees, shoulders, ankles, and elbows.

Fixation products accounted for 15 percent of revenues in 2004. These devices are used to treat stubborn bone fractures that have not healed with conventional surgical or nonsurgical therapy. In addition, some external fixation devices are used for complicated trauma, limb-lengthening, and deformity correction uses and fracture repair. Internal fixation devices include nails, plates, screws, pins, and wires to stabilize bone injuries.

Spinal products made up 11 percent of sales in 2004. These include implantable, direct-current electrical-stimulation devices that provide an adjunct to surgical intervention in the treatment of nonunions and spinal fusions.

Other products (10 percent of 2004 revenues) include orthopedic support devices, arthroscopy products, operating room supplies, casting materials, general surgical instruments, and related items.

Biomet now operates more than fifty facilities, including eighteen manufacturing centers, with a marketing arm of about 1,850 sales representatives. The company's products are distributed in more than 100 countries.

## Shortcomings to Bear in Mind

- Because of its outstanding record, Biomet is rarely on the bargain table. Its P/E ratio is usually far above the market.
- The analyst for the *Standard & Poor's Stock Report*, Robert M. Gold, had this mixed observation on December 21, 2004: "We believe Biomet remains one of the most consistent generators of revenues, cash flow, and EPS (Earnings per share) in our device universe. We see the company capturing share in the knee implant and spine segments. However, we think that the company is currently at a competitive disadvantage in the hip implant market, due to the absence of ceramic-on-ceramic and minimally invasive product offerings." (See the company's response to this assertion in the first item under Reasons to Buy.)

  Mr. Gold also said, "Risks to our opinion and target price include unfavorable Medicare reimbursement proposals, rising competition in some key orthopedic markets, and adverse outcomes in patent liability lawsuits."
- On February 23, 2005, Prudential Equity Group (a well-known brokerage firm) had a negative (UNDERWEIGHT) view of Biomet. Robert Faulkner said, "At this point, the company's growth relies almost entirely on its knee line. Knees are currently undergoing a growth spurt, but will face competition at the hands of new products from Stryker primarily, and Zimmer secondarily. Most other businesses are under pressure from either competition, market deceleration, or integration difficulties."

## Reasons to Buy

- Lehman Brothers (a major brokerage firm) had a more encouraging view of Biomet on January 14, 2005. "While we would argue that BMET should trade at a discount, and the stock is not cheap relative to historical average forward P/E, we believe that many are overlooking its strong new pipeline of hip and knee implants, which is arguably the best in the group."
- On July 13, 2004, the company announced the signing of a definitive agreement with Diamicron, Inc. of Orem, Utah, to develop and distribute, on a worldwide basis, diamond articulation technology for total hip arthroplasty. Based on Diamicron's proprietary polycrystalline diamond composite technology, diamond wear couples offer an alternative to conventional wear couples with both structural integrity and superior wear properties.

  Under terms of the agreement, Biomet has been granted semi-exclusive rights to distribute initial hip products, along with Exactech, Inc. In addition, the agreement provides Biomet with option rights to develop and market other extremity joint replacement products, including knee replacements, based on Diamicron's proprietary polycrystalline diamond composite technology.

  Dane A. Miller, Ph.D., President and CEO of Biomet, said "This strategic partnership with Diamicron strengthens Biomet's development pipeline for alternative bearing technology. Diamond-on-diamond technology will be complementary to Biomet's existing programs in metal-on-metal articulation and ceramic-on-ceramic articulation bearing technologies. We believe that Biomet's development efforts in alternative bearing technologies comprise the most comprehensive product pipeline in the industry."
- During fiscal 2004, Biomet continued to expand its presence in the estimated $20-billion worldwide musculoskeletal products market. Particularly effective in driving sales growth were products and services in the fastest-growing segments of the musculoskeletal market, including orthopedic reconstructive devices

and dental reconstructive implants, as well as spinal hardware and orthobiologics. During fiscal 2004, reconstructive device sales advanced more than 21 percent, from $867.6 million to about $1.1 billion; fixation sales increased 5 percent, from $237.1 million to $248.8 million; spinal product sales experienced 11 percent growth, from $143.6 million to $159.9 million; and "other products" sales advanced 8 percent, from $142 million to $153.6 million.

- In the most recent ten years (1994–2004), Earnings per share climbed from $0.27 to $1.27—without interruption—for a compound annual growth rate of 16.7 percent.
- On June 18, 2004, the company announced the completion of the acquisition of Interpore International, Inc. for $280 million. Interpore's three major product groups include spinal implants, orthobiologics, and minimally invasive surgery products used by surgeons in a wide range of applications.
- According to Mr. Miller, "We intend to introduce several new products during fiscal 2005, which should meaningfully contribute to our revenue growth, such as the larger head M2a Magnum Metal-on-Metal System, as well as the bone-conserving ReCap Femoral and Total Resurfacing Systems. Subject to regulatory approvals, we also plan to introduce

a ceramic-on-ceramic hip system during calendar 2005 and ArCom XL, Biomet's highly crosslinked polyethylene.

"A burgeoning portfolio of spinal products, expected to increase sales growth during fiscal year 2005, includes the company's first product addressing the spinal deformity market segment, the Array Top-Loading Rod System, as well as key products from Interpore, such as the Synergy Spinal System, the ACCESS Generation II AGF (Autologous Growth Factors) System and Pro Osteon coral-derived synthetic bone graft substitute. As evidenced by the company's more than 14,000 product offerings, we believe the breadth and depth of our products and technologies, augmented by new product introductions, should position Biomet for escalating growth opportunities during fiscal year 2005 and beyond."

- Biomet was one of the first companies to use and promote the use of titanium alloy for its orthopedic implants. Titanium alloy is now the material of choice because of its high bio-compatibility, strength, durability, and its elasticity, which is more similar to that of natural bone than other metals. Biomet also pioneered the utilization of a proprietary titanium porous coating, known as plasma spray, to encourage bone growth onto the implant for stability.

Total assets: $1,788 million
Current ratio: 3.57
Common shares outstanding: 254 million
Return on 2004 shareholders' equity: 23.3%

|  | 2004 | 2003 | 2002 | 2001 | 2000 | 1999 | 1998 | 1997 |
|---|---|---|---|---|---|---|---|---|
| Revenues (millions) | 1,615 | 1,390 | 1,192 | 1,031 | 921 | 757 | 651 | 580 |
| Net income (millions) | 326 | 287 | 240 | 198 | 174 | 116 | 125 | 106 |
| Earnings per share | 1.27 | 1.10 | .88 | .73 | .65 | .46 | .49 | .42 |
| Dividends per share | .15 | .10 | .09 | .07 | .06 | .05 | .05 | .04 |
| Price     high | 49.6 | 38.0 | 33.3 | 34.4 | 27.8 | 20.3 | 18.3 | 12.0 |
|            low | 35.0 | 26.7 | 21.8 | 20.5 | 12.1 | 10.9 | 10.5 | 6.3 |

# The Black & Decker Corporation

701 East Joppa Road □ Towson, MD 21286 □ (410) 716–3979 □ Dividend reinvestment plan is available: (800) 432–0140 □ Web site: *www.bdk.com* □ Listed: NYSE □ Ticker symbol: BDK □ S&P rating: B+ □ Value Line financial strength rating: B+

On October 4, 2004, The Black & Decker Corporation announced that it had completed the purchase of the Tools Group from Pentair, Inc. for about $775 million in cash. The Tools Group, which includes the Porter-Cable, Delta, DeVilbiss Air Power, Oldham Saw, and FLEX businesses, had sales of $1.08 billion and operating profit of $82 million in 2003.

Black & Decker is a leading global manufacturer and marketer of power tools and accessories, hardware and home improvement products, and technology-based fastening systems.

Nolan D. Archibald, Chairman and Chief Executive Officer, commented, "We are pleased to have received regulatory clearance. By adding the Tools Group's well-respected brands and products, we expand our offerings where we have relatively low market share. Further, we are enhancing our distribution network, particularly in the industrial and construction channel. The acquisition of Pentair's Tools Group is a great strategic fit with our DEWALT division and will nearly double our North American professional business.

"From a strategic and financial perspective, this is an ideal bolt-on acquisition. We will leverage our proven strengths in product innovation, brand management, strong customer relationships, end-user focus, and cost reduction to add value to the acquired businesses. We anticipate that we will realize $65 million of annual cost savings by the end of 2007.

"The acquisition should be slightly accretive to earnings per share in 2004, and as we previously announced, we expect accretion of approximately $0.50 per share

in 2005 and an incremental $0.25 per share in both 2006 and 2007, for a total annual accretion of $1.00 per share by the end of 2007. The acquisition has a very positive net present value and should be accretive to our return on capital employed by 2007."

## Company Profile

In 1910, Duncan Black and Alonzo Decker launched the company on a shoestring in Baltimore, initially producing candy dippers and milk-bottle capping machines. In 1916, they brought out the company's first major power tool, a portable electric drill.

Black & Decker is a global manufacturer of quality power tools and accessories, hardware, and home-improvement products. BDK also has a stake in technology-based fastening systems. The company's products and services are marketed in more than 100 countries, and it has thirty-nine manufacturing operations, including ten outside the U.S.

Black & Decker has established a reputation for product innovation, quality, end-user focus, design, and value. Its strong brand names and new product development capabilities enjoy worldwide recognition, and the company's global distribution is unsurpassed in its industries. Black & Decker operates three business segments:

### Power Tools and Accessories

This segment manufactures and markets products under three brand names: Black & Decker, Momentum Laser, and DeWalt. They include consumer power tools, accessories, electric lawn and garden tools, as well as electric cleaning and lighting products. In addition, this segment produces high-performance power tools, accessories, and industrial equipment, laser products, and air compressors.

## Hardware and Home Improvement

This segment consists of Kwikset security hardware, Price Pfister plumbing products and three security hardware companies in Europe. Kwikset, a world leader in the manufacturing of residential door hardware, markets products in North America, Australia, and Asia under the brand names Kwikset Security, Kwikset Maximum Security, Kwikset UltraMax Security, Black & Decker, and Geo. Price Pfister is a major competitor in the North American faucet and plumbing products market with products sold under the Price Pfister and Bach brands.

## Fastening and Assembly Systems

Serving the global automotive and industrial markets, the Fastening and Assembly Systems segment, known as Emhart Teknologies, is the originator of several highly recognizable brands, including Pop blind rivets, Parker-Kalon screws, Gripco locknuts, HeliCoil wire inserts, Dodge inserts, Tucker stud welding equipment, and Warren plastic and metal fasteners.

## Shortcomings to Bear in Mind

- On February 11, 2005 *Standard & Poor's Stock Reports* gave a HOLD rating on Black & Decker. Here is what Amy Glynn, CFA, said, "In light of recent restructuring and productivity initiatives, we believe BDK is better positioned than most tool manufacturing peers for an industry sales recovery. Margins have widened as a result of these initiatives, but we see limited additional margin upside, as we think cost savings from the restructuring will taper off in 2005. We think the company will continue to execute well on integrating acquisitions,

which we think should aid EPS (Earnings per share) over the next few years."

- Here is what *Callard Research* had to say on January 7, 2005: "We decided on B&D's HOLD rating by incorporating several factors, which our experience has shown to be powerful indicators of future price performance. Our decision was based on (1) valuation, which compares the firm's intrinsic value against the price of its stock, (2) intermediate and long-term price momentum, (3) other measures of fundamental trend, and (4) qualitative analysis."

## Reasons to Buy

- "A year ago, it was fair to ask whether Black & Decker Corp. and its shares had much power left following a 60 percent rise in less than a year," said Peter Loftus, writing for the *Wall Street Journal* on March 9, 2005. "But the company appears to have power to spare. Not only has the stock price gained another 60 percent, but the power-tools maker increased its dividend payout by one third."

  The article went on to say, "Drilling beneath the stock's solid performance, investors have found a company that has made its manufacturing leaner, ridden the wave of a construction boom, and unveiled innovative products. Also, the Towson, Md. company has made several acquisitions that are adding to earnings."

- On February 10, 2005, the company declared a quarterly dividend of $0.28 per share, a hefty increase of 33 percent over the previous dividend. Mr. Archibald said, "Black & Decker generated $526 million of free cash flow in 2004, setting a record for the third year in a row. Our outstanding cash flow enables us to return cash to our shareholders as well as grow the business internally and through compelling bolt-on acquisitions."

- *Thomas White International* had this favorable comment on January 7, 2005: "Our team of analysts decided to make B&D a BUY after addressing the factors below that they feel are important within this particular industry. Conclusions in each of the areas are shown to document the firm's decision-making process."

  Here is a summary of those valuations; however, I have not included the discussion of each.
  - Valuation: Net income: Neutral
  - Valuation: Net income (fiscal year 1): Positive
  - Valuation: Net income (fiscal year 2): Positive
  - Valuation: Analyst Adjustments: Very Positive
  - Business Momentum: Earnings Growth: Positive
- On March 4, 2005, *Value Line Investment Survey* gave Black & Decker a Timeliness rating of 2 (Above average). Kenneth A. Nugent said, "We look for Black & Decker to continue its string of hefty double-digit earnings advances in 2005. The company finished off 2004 with record top- and bottom-line performance. Factors responsible for the good news are myriad. First, the ongoing strength of the United States economy, a number of recent acquisitions, and a favorable foreign exchange environment all helped boost BDK's sales across its three product lines. In addition, the company's margins have widened as a result of the continued success of its restructuring program and strong sales."
- In October 2003, Masco Corporation and Black & Decker announced that they had finalized the purchase of Baldwin Hardware Corporation and Weiser Lock Corporation by Black & Decker from Masco. The cash purchase price was about $275 million.

  Baldwin Hardware, headquartered in Reading, Pennsylvania, is a leading provider of architectural and decorative products for the home. Weiser, based in Tucson, Arizona, manufactures a wide range of locksets and decorative exterior hardware and accessories. Combined Baldwin and Weiser 2002 net sales were about $250 million.

  "The addition of Baldwin and Weiser to our leading Kwikset brand will enable Black & Decker to offer our customers the broadest range of styles and price points available from any manufacturer, and attests to our long-term commitment to the security hardware business," said Mr. Archibald. "We expect that the acquisition will not materially affect our 2003 results and will be accretive in 2004."

Total assets: $5,531 million
Current ratio: 1.63
Common shares outstanding: 82 million
Return on 2004 shareholders' equity: 36.7%

| | 2004 | 2003 | 2002 | 2001 | 2000 | 1999 | 1998 | 1997 |
|---|---|---|---|---|---|---|---|---|
| Revenues (millions) | 5,398 | 4,483 | 4,394 | 4,333 | 4,561 | 4,520 | 4,560 | 4,940 |
| Net income (millions) | 441 | 287 | 261 | 179 | 296 | 300 | 246 | 227 |
| Earnings per share | 5.40 | 3.68 | 3.23 | 2.20 | 3.51 | 3.40 | 2.63 | 2.35 |
| Dividends per share | .84 | .57 | .48 | .48 | .48 | .48 | .48 | .48 |
| Price high | 87.5 | 49.9 | 50.5 | 46.9 | 50.2 | 64.6 | 65.5 | 43.4 |
| low | 48.1 | 33.2 | 35.0 | 28.3 | 27.6 | 41.0 | 37.9 | 29.6 |

Aggressive Growth

# Brinker International, Inc.

6820 LBJ Freeway □ Dallas, TX 75240 □ (972) 770–7228 □ Dividend reinvestment plan not available □ Web site: *www. brinker.com* □ Listed: NYSE □ Fiscal years end last Wednesday in June □ Ticker symbol: EAT □ S&P rating: B+ □ Value Line financial strength rating: A

"Brinker is a $3.7-billion company that is consistently recognized by *Fortune* magazine as one of America's Most Admired Companies," said CEO Douglas H. Brooks in fiscal 2005. "In keeping with our long tradition of success, Brinker's performance remained very strong is fiscal 2004, with many of our restaurants breaking all-time sales records."

Mr. Brooks went on to say, "We continued to bring new choices to our guests across the nation and around the world this year, with the addition of 103 company-owned facilities and 31 franchise restaurants, including our one hundredth international location and our first Chili's restaurants at international military bases at U.S. Army Forces Central Command in Qatar and Kadena Air Force Base in Japan. And on August 3, 2004, we celebrated the opening our one thousandth Chili's with a special ribbon-cutting ceremony at our Pinnacle Park restaurant in the Dallas area.

"In addition to our growing number of locations, Brinker's seven distinctive dining concepts continue to satisfy a wide range of tastes: Chili's Grill & Bar, Romano's Macaroni Grill, On The Border Mexican Grill & Cantina, Maggiano's Little Italy, Corner Bakery Café, Big Bowl Asian Kitchen, and Rockfish Seafood Grill. No matter what you're hungry for, chances are you'll find it at a Brinker restaurant. Our menus include proven favorites that guests expect to see, along with fresh new additions to our legendary lineups. By constantly reviewing and strategically updating our offerings, we're able to keep our brands relevant and popular while preserving the essence of the restaurants that our guests have grown to love."

Mr. Brooks also said, "One example of our ongoing food innovation is the introduction of more healthful items on our menus in response to guests' requests for low-fat and low-carbohydrate options. As these and other dietary trends continues to evolve, our newly appointed Nutrition Advisory Council, formed in January 2004, will be on hand to help us evaluate current menu initiatives and develop a long-term nutrition strategy."

## Company Profile

In little more than two decades, Brinker International (formerly Chili's) has grown from a single restaurant in Dallas to multiple casual dining concepts. The company provides dining experiences for nearly 500,000 people every day. Its strategy is to aggressively expand concepts that exceed its high expectations for return on invested capital, and to reposition or divest those concepts that fail to measure up. As a result, the company continues to develop new concepts. What's more, over the years, Brinker International has acquired restaurant concepts, using shares of its own stock in payment.

Among the company's concept restaurant chains are Chili's Grill & Bar (1000 units), Romano's Macaroni Grill (215), On The Border's (129), Maggiano's Little Italy (28), the Corner Bakery Café (86), Big Bowl Asian Kitchen (18), and Rockfish Seafood Grill (25).

Chili's is committed to "providing our guests with new and exciting menu items," said management, "while keeping the sizzle of our *Famous and Favorites,* such as Big Mouth Burgers, Baby Back Ribs, Fajitas, and the Presidente Margarita."

Romano's Macaroni Grill has a "distinctive chef-driven menu," according to the company's annual report. It features imported Italian ingredients such as olive oil, sun-baked tomatoes, balsamic vinegar, prosciutto, and Parmesan buffalo mozzarella cheese. "A newly redesigned menu showcases favorites like the Mama's Trio and Spaghettini and Meatballs, while featuring signature dishes like Chicken Portobello and Filet Firenza."

The company's On The Border Mexican Grill & Cantina has a menu that features such items as Quesadillas, Enchiladas, Fajitas, and "our famous Border Sampler." These dishes have been augmented recently by such items as Salmon Mexicano, Blackened Chicken Salad, and Carnitas.

At the Big Bowl Asian Kitchen, "distinctive and flavorful noodle and rice dishes, prepared in our open display kitchens, blend centuries-old Asian cuisine with contemporary, lighthearted fun," said management. "We're brought together the best Asian culinary traditions in our menu favorites such as Kung Pao and Lemon Chicken, Pad Thai, the Ultimate Combo appetizer, and our *You Choose* interactive stir-fry bar."

The company's Rockfish Seafood Grill features such menu items as "our generous Shrimp Basket, Fish Tacos, Stuffed Fish, Rock-a-Rita Margarita, 18-ounce beer schooner, and award-winning Mexican Shrimp Martini."

## Shortcomings to Bear in Mind

- The company has never paid a cash dividend, which prompted me to classify EAT as aggressive growth.
- According to a company publication, "The restaurant business is highly competitive with respect to price, service, restaurant location, and food quality. What's more, it is often affected by changes in consumer tastes, economic conditions, population and traffic patterns."

The publication went on to say, "The company competes with each market with locally owned restaurants as well as national and regional restaurant chains, some of which operate more restaurants and have greater financial resources and longer operating histories than the company.

"There is active competition for management personnel and for attractive commercial real estate sites suitable for restaurants. In addition, factors such as inflation, increased food, labor and benefit costs, and difficulty in attracting hourly employees may adversely affect the restaurant industry in general and the company's restaurants in particular."

- A large number of insiders, such as officers and board members, were selling their shares in a recent nine-month stretch. There were sixteen separate sells and no buys.

## Reasons to Buy

- Dennis P. Milton, an analyst with the *Standard & Poor's Company Reports,* had this observation on February 18, 2005, "We expect favorable long-term demographic trends in the U.S. to continue to boost customer traffic in the casual dining sector. We see the company continuing to benefit from the expansion of its restaurant concepts, particularly the Chili's brand, which we view as well positioned in what we regard as the attractive bar and grill sector."
- A recent "Hot Concept of the Year" award winner, Big Bowl has also been recognized for its child-friendly menu and atmosphere.

According to management, "The kids' menu comes tucked inside a Chinese carry-out carton containing a fortune cookie, toy, and children's chopsticks, designed for young fingers."

- Over the past twenty years, the company has had explosive growth. In 1983, Chili's had twenty-three outlets in six states, with 1,800 employees and annual sales of $30 million. Today, Brinker International has grown to more than 1,475 restaurants in forty-nine states and twenty-two countries, with 90,000 employees and annual sales approaching $4 billion. Industry analysts have dubbed the EAT portfolio "the mutual fund of casual dining."

- This growth has been reflected in earnings per share over the past ten years (1994–2004). In that span earnings per share advanced from $0.57 to $1.57, a compound annual growth rate of 10.7 percent.

- According to a Brinker spokesman, "The company purchases certain commodities such as beef, chicken, flour, and cooking oil. These commodities are generally purchased based upon market prices established with vendors. These purchase arrangements may contain contractual features that limit the price paid by establishing certain price floors or caps. The company dose not use financial instruments to hedge commodity prices because these purchase arrangements help control the ultimate cost paid, and any commodity price aberrations are generally short term in nature."

- "Eating away from home has become such an important part of everyday life.

Currently, close to half the dollars spent on food are spent on meals away from home. This is a dramatic shift over the last three or four decades." said Joseph Buckley in an interview conducted by Kenneth N. Gilpin for the *New York Times*. Mr. Buckley is a restaurant analyst with Bear Stearns, a major brokerage firm.

He went on to say, "The move to two-wage-earner families, and the fact that baby boomers have grown up with chains, many of which are about to celebrate their 50th birthdays, are other reasons. In short, dining out has become so ingrained in the American lifestyle that it is cut back very grudgingly, if at all."

In answer to another question, the Bear Stearns analyst said, "In the casual dining sector, which is defined as an average check of $10 to $20 with full service and having alcohol as an option, growth has been great. As America has shifted its food budget to spending more and more away from home, they have become more sophisticated in their spending."

Total assets: $2,212 million
Current ratio: 1.06
Common shares outstanding: 96 million
Return on 2004 shareholders' equity: 14.2%

| | 2004 | 2003 | 2002 | 2001 | 2000 | 1999 | 1998 | 1997 |
|---|---|---|---|---|---|---|---|---|
| Revenues (millions) | 3,707 | 3,285 | 2,887 | 2,407 | 2,100 | 1,818 | 1,529 | 1,335 |
| Net income (millions) | 154 | 169 | 153 | 145 | 118 | 79 | 69 | 61 |
| Earnings per share | 1.57 | 1.70 | 1.52 | 1.46 | 1.20 | .80 | .70 | .54 |
| Dividends per share | Nil | — | — | — | — | — | — | — |
| Price          high | 39.8 | 37.2 | 36.0 | 41.3 | 28.9 | 20.4 | 19.5 | 11.9 |
| low | 28.9 | 26.3 | 24.1 | 21.3 | 13.8 | 13.3 | 10.0 | 7.1 |

Conservative Growth

# Canadian National Railway Company

935 de la Gauchetiere Street West □ Montreal, Quebec, Canada H3B 2M9 □ (514) 399–7212 □ Dividend reinvestment plan not available □ Web site: *www.cn.ca* □ Ticker symbol: CNI □ Listed: NYSE □ S&P rating: B+ □ Value Line financial strength rating: B

Commenting on results in the fourth quarter of 2004 and the full year, CEO E. Hunter Harrison said, "I am delighted to report these record results. Our railroaders delivered the best quarterly and full-year operating ratio in company history, along with record annual operating income, net income and free cash flow."

Here are the highlights of those results:

• Fourth-quarter net income of $376 million, or $1.29 per diluted share. Net income for the fourth quarter of 2003 was $224 million, or $0.78 per diluted share.

• Quarterly revenue of $1,736 million, an increase of 15 percent.

• Fourth quarter operating income of $607 million, up 19 percent, compared with the same period the prior year.

• Quarterly operating ratio of 65.0 percent, a 1.1 percentage point improvement over the final quarter of 2003.

• Full-year 2004 free cash flow of $1,025 million, compared with $578 million for 2003.

Mr. Harrison went on to say, "CN's outstanding performance resulted from strong core business growth at low incremental cost, the early benefits of two acquisitions and the discipline of precision railroading.

"This winning combination allowed CN to generate free cash flow of more than $1 billion, an exceptional achievement that underscores the quality of our earnings. CN's proven ability to produce strong free cash flow gives management the flexibility to reward investors: it will support a 28 percent increase in our 2005 dividend—the ninth consecutive increase since CN's privatization in 1995."

Business levels benefited from the acquisition of BC Rail and the railroad and related holdings of Great Lakes Transportation, which added $145 million to the company's revenue in the final quarter in 2004. Central to Canadian National's performance in 2004 was strong demand for lumber, chemicals, iron ore, coal, consumer goods from Asia, as well as Canadian wheat and barley.

## Company Profile

Canadian National Railway, which was controlled by the Canadian government until 1995, operates the largest Canadian railroad. The acquisition of Illinois Central in 1999 enables CNI to cross the continent both east-west and north-south, linking customers in Canada, the United States, and Mexico.

Since late 1998, the company has offered scheduled train service. Railroads typically hold trains until enough cars accumulate. With a time schedule, CNI runs shorter trains, but has realized greater operating efficiency and timeliness, with service peaks and valleys smoothed out. Its operating ratio is among the best in the industry.

Canadian National Railway is a leader in the North American rail industry. Following its acquisition of Illinois Central in 1999, WC in 2001, and GLT in 2004, as well as its partnership agreement with BC Rail in 2004, CNI provides shippers with more options and greater reach in the rapidly expanding market for north-south trade.

CNI has one of the best operating ratios in this industry and is committed to moving more freight, more quickly, and with fewer assets.

Canadian National is the only railroad that crosses the continent east-west and north-south, serving ports on the Atlantic, Pacific, and Gulf coasts while linking customers to all three NAFTA nations.

CNI is a more diverse railroad. The company's revenues derive from the movement of a diversified and balanced portfolio of goods, including petroleum and chemicals, grain and fertilizers, coal, metals and minerals, forest products, intermodal, and automotive.

### Quick Facts about Canadian National Railway

• Operates the largest rail network in Canada and the only transcontinental network in North America. The company operates in eight Canadian provinces and sixteen U.S. states.

- Spans Canada and mid-America from the Atlantic and Pacific oceans to the Gulf of Mexico, serving the ports of Vancouver; Prince Rupert, British Columbia; Montreal; Halifax; New Orleans; and Mobile, Alabama; and the key cities of Toronto; Buffalo; Chicago; Detroit; Duluth, Minn./Superior, Wisconsin; Green Bay, Wisconsin; Minneapolis/St. Paul; Memphis; St. Louis; Jackson, Mississippi; with connections to all points in North America.

- Has the shortest route from the Atlantic coast to the U.S. Midwest through the St. Clair Tunnel between Sarnia, Ontario, and Port Huron, Michigan.

- Originates approximately 85 percent of traffic, allowing the company to capitalize on service advantages, efficient asset utilization, and negotiations with other carriers on revenue division arrangements

## Shortcomings to Bear in Mind

- "We believe the shares have limited upside potential from current levels," said Andrew West, CFA, writing for the *Standard & Poor's Stock Reports,* on November 1, 2004. "We think CNI, as the most efficiently run railroad we cover, has less room for long-term operating margin improvements. We believe low expense levels are due, in part, to past charges, long assumed depreciable asset lives, and relatively strong pensions."

## Reasons to Buy

- "Canadian National is on a roll," said Craig Sirois, writing for *Value Line Investment Survey* on March 11, 2005. "The railroad achieved record quarterly revenues and operating income in the December quarter. The operating ratio improved 110 basis points, year over year, to 65 percent, also the best in company history. CN is setting the pace for rail efficiency in North America." There are 100 basis points in each percent.

- Canadian National has a strong stake in intermodal transportation, which involves a combination of shipping companies, typically utilizing a railroad, as well as a trucking company or a seagoing vessel. For instance, a shipment of goods that starts out from Asia on a ship could be loaded onto to a railroad flatcar—still in its original container—for several hundred miles, and then be transferred to a trucking company for its final destination.

Intermodal is by far the company's most complex businesses, with a high degree of randomness, uneven flow of traffic, and numerous points in the chain for delays to occur. CNI launched Intermodal Excellence, called IMX, in 2003 to smooth traffic flows, increase speed and reliability, as well as to improve asset utilization and margins.

At the heart of IMX is the application of scheduled railroading's discipline and precision to intermodal transportation. IMX requires shippers to make reservations to get on trains, while pricing encourages the shift to traffic to off-peak days. This, along with required gate reservations at the company's largest terminals, enables Canadian National to align traffic with equipment and gate capacity and improve speed and asset utilization. Even though implementation throughout the entire CNI system wasn't complete until year-end, the company had already seen improvements in profit margins. What's more, customers were aware of the benefits: better speed and reliability of service.

- "Merchandise traffic—forest products, petroleum, and chemicals, metals and minerals, and automotive—is the heart of our franchise," said a company official in 2004. "The strength of CN's merchandise business distinguishes us from other Class 1 railroads. No other major rail carrier has as high a percentage of its business in merchandise, and with our scheduled railroad concept, no one does it better than CN. Our greatest potential for profitable growth lies in our merchandise business. The key to realizing that potential is taking share from trucks. Improvements in our speed and reliability over the past several years removed the first barrier to market share gain. Investment in new, high-quality equipment and our improved eBusiness capability, Velocity (*see below*), is removing still others. CN's well-trained and highly focused sales force is converting these improvements into growth and market share gains, one carload at a time."

- In another context, the company official went on to say, "Velocity, powered by CN—that's the name of our industry-leading eBusiness service offering. Velocity instantly delivers critical business information to help customers make faster and better decisions across the entire order cycle.

"CN's full suite of eBusiness tools delivers major benefits. Car Order enables customers to optimize car supply, and Shipping Instructions allows them to send their bills of lading and release their railcars in one easy step. My Shipments provides access to diagnostic tools for tracking the progress of shipments on CN and other connecting railroads, and eBill provides our customers with secure online access to their complete CN account. CN also offers industry-specific solutions such as Intermodal Direct, developed and enhanced based on our in-depth knowledge of our customers' processes.

"These advanced tools—combined with CN's expertise in transportation and customs requirements, and our more than twenty years of experience working electronically with our customers—make it easy to see why customers increasingly trust Velocity."

**Total assets: $22,365 million**
**Current ratio: 0.76**
**Common shares outstanding: 286 million**
**Return on 2004 shareholders' equity: 14.2%**

|  | 2004 | 2003 | 2002 | 2001 | 2000 | 1999 | 1998 | 1997 |
|---|---|---|---|---|---|---|---|---|
| Revenues (millions) | 6,548 | 4,531 | 3,874 | 3,555 | 3,637 | 3,613 | 2,651 | 3,025 |
| Net income (millions) | 1,258 | 782 | 667 | 615 | 590 | 531 | 359 | 328 |
| Earnings per share | 4.34 | 2.70 | 2.21 | 2.06 | 1.96 | 1.68 | 1.33 | 1.27 |
| Dividends per share | .78 | .51 | .36 | .33 | .31 | .28 | .23 | .21 |
| Price      high | 61.9 | 42.6 | 35.8 | 33.0 | 22.0 | 24.4 | 22.4 | 19.0 |
|            low | 36.5 | 26.3 | 24.0 | 19.2 | 15.0 | 13.8 | 11.3 | 11.6 |

Aggressive Growth

# Carnival Corporation

3655 N.W. 87th Avenue ❑ Miami, FL 33178–2428 ❑ (305) 406–4832 ❑ Dividend reinvestment plan available: (800) 568–3476 ❑ Fiscal years end November 30 ❑ Web site: *www.carnivalcorp.com* ❑ Listed: NYSE ❑ Ticker symbol: CCL ❑ S&P rating: A+ ❑ Value Line financial strength rating: B+

"Maneuverability is one of Carnival's greatest assets," said Christopher Palmeri in an article that appeared in *BusinessWeek* on November 15, 2004. "And that means much more than just dodging storms. When the travel industry slumped after the September 11 terrorist attacks, CEO Micky Arison shifted boats to closer-in ports such as New York and Galveston, Tex. He also cut fares and offered shorter cruises to attract increasingly budget-conscious travelers.

"Then, when rival Royal Caribbean Cruises Ltd. inked a deal to buy P&O Princess Cruises in late 2001, Arison countered with a higher bid and ultimately won the company for $8 billion. With that deal and a bevy of previous acquisitions, Carnival now owns twelve cruise brands, a fleet of seventy-eight vessels, and nearly half of worldwide industry revenues. Thanks in part to its penchant for deal-making, Carnival has racked up 18 percent average annual revenue growth over the past three years."

## Company Profile

Carnival Corporation and its British affiliate is a global cruise company with a portfolio of twelve distinct brands, comprised of the leading cruise operators in North America, Europe, and Australia. Included in this group are: Carnival Cruise Lines (twenty ships), Holland America Line (thirteen), Princess Cruises (fourteen), AIDA (four), Costa Cruises (ten), Cunard Line (three), P&O Cruises (four), Windstar Cruises (three), Seabourn Cruise Line (three), Ocean Village (one), Swan Hellenic (one). All told, these seventy-six vessels have more than 128,000 lower berths.

The company has eight new ships scheduled for delivery between November 2004 and December 2006. With the additional tonnage, Carnival Corporation & PLC's fleet will consist of eighty-four vessels with more than 145,000 lower berths by December 2006.

Carnival also operates two tour companies, which include seventeen hotels or lodges in Alaska and the Canadian Yukon, more than 500 motor coaches, and twenty domed rail cars; and two day boats.

Although the name Carnival Corporation didn't come into existence until 1993, the foundation for the company was laid when its flagship brand, Carnival Cruise Lines, was formed in 1972 by cruise industry pioneer, the late Ted Arison.

On April 17, 2003, agreements were finalized to combine Carnival Corporation with P&O Princess Cruises, PLC, creating a global vacation leader with twelve brands, making it one of the largest leisure travel companies in the world.

## Shortcomings to Bear in Mind

- Insiders, such as officers and board members, have been net sellers of their own stock in recent months. In one nine-month stretch, there were fifty-seven sales and not a single purchase. On the other hand, CEO Micky Arison (son of the company's founder, Ted Arison) has a 34 percent stake in the company, so he apparently is a great believer in what happens to Carnival stock in the years ahead.

- For investors looking for a conservative stock, you may decide that Carnival is not for you. It has a beta coefficient of 1.30, which means that its stock price is 30 percent more volatile than the general market. However, if you have a yen for speculation, this might be an ideal stock.
- *Value Line Investment Survey* had a few negative comments on February 18, 2005, when its analyst, Marina Livson, said, "The company's capacity growth over the next few years should be much slower. This fiscal year, CCL will add a total of seven ships. This number includes the largest vessel in the world, The Queen Mary 2, which is already in service. Carnival plans to reduce the introduction rate to two to four ships a year. We think that a slowdown is needed for the company to digest recent additions and for demand to catch up with supply. This should also allow CCL to pay down some debt."

## Reasons to Buy

- On April 4, 2005, *BusinessWeek* said, "Cruise queen Carnival last year put to rest the dark memories of September 11 and its profit-crushing aftermath. Buoyed by rising ticket prices and fatter passenger spending, the Miami cruise line saw net income surge 55 percent. Net revenue yield, the amount of profit that Carnival receives from each passenger per day, rose 9.8 percent. Those advances were driven largely by a sharp increase in cash ponied up by passengers for food, drinks, entertainment, and other onboard frills. Outlays on tickets jumped 48 percent, to $7.4 billion, while nonticket revenue soared 50 percent, to $2.1 billion."
- *Standard & Poor's Stock Reports* was more optimistic on December 16, 2004. Its analyst, Tom Graves, CFA, said, "Our BUY opinion on the shares reflects our view that the stock will benefit from expectations of year-ahead profit growth and from investor focus on prospective benefits to the company from what we expect to be slowing growth in industry capacity and rising free cash flow beyond fiscal 2004."
- On March 1, 2005, Argus Research Company was also upbeat. John Staszak said, "We are maintaining our BUY rating on *Focus List* selection Carnival Corp. Our opinion is based on the company's ability to raise ticket prices higher than increases in fuel prices and operating expenses. We think Carnival will be able to raise prices 12 percent within the next twelve to eighteen months, surpassing previous peaks. From 1990 to 2003, the number of Carnival passengers increased 12 percent annually, a trend we see continuing as a result of the successful acquisition of Princess P&O Cruises."
- On February 15, 2005, a Lehman Brothers analyst said the stock was an OVERWEIGHT or BUY. "We remain buyers of CCL. Our bullish stance is predicated on the fact that higher pricing will benefit the company even in a rising cost environment."
- With an array of brands, Carnival can offer something for every breed of cruise fanatic. There's the high-end Yachts of Seabourn, which feature onboard lectures by Ivy League professors. At the other end of the spectrum are the Carnival "Fun Ships," which offer midnight buffets and dancing until 4 a.m.
- On September 23, 2004, the company said that it had signed a "historic" multibillion-dollar cooperation agreement with Italian shipyard Fincantieri to construct four new cruise ships as well as significantly redesign the Queen Victoria for its Cunard Line brand.

    Mr. Arison said that this unique alliance with Fincantieri lays the foundation for its new building program in 2007 and 2008 and enables the company to simultaneously execute its two-pronged growth strategy. "For our U.S. brands, it is important for us to build vessels at reasonable U.S. dollar costs, especially under the favorable U.S. dollar/euro currency environment that exists today. At the same time, we must continue to reinvest in our European brands to develop the cruise business there and maintain the leadership position of those brands in their respective markets."

The U.S. dollar agreement calls for the construction of a 110,000-ton "Conquest-class" ship for Carnival Cruise Lines at Fincantieri's Sestri yard and a 116,000-ton "Caribbean Princess-class" ship for the Princess Cruises at Fincantieri's Monfalcone yard. Both ships are expected to be delivered in the spring of 2007.

Mr. Arison said that the cost for these two vessels compares favorably to the $165,000-$175,000 per berth price that Carnival has historically paid for new ships for those brands and should allow the company to achieve the financial targets it sets for it shipbuilding projects. "These two classes of ships presently have some of the highest returns in the cruise industry," said Mr. Arison.

- On October 19, 2004, Carnival's management said it had ordered two new 68,500-ton cruise ships for its AIDA brand, which caters exclusively to the German-speaking market. To be built at Germany's Meyer Werft shipyard, the vessels have a cost of about 315 million euro each and are expected to be delivered in April 2007 and April 2009. Each vessel, which will operate under AIDA's informal "club resort" cruise concept aimed at younger, more active passengers, will carry about 2,030 berths—roughly 22 percent more than the largest vessel in the German cruise operator's current fleet.

"Part of our European strategy is to aggressively grow the German market," said Micky Arison. "Exciting new ships like these are needed, and they must be specifically designed to meet the demands of German travelers who are increasingly discovering the value and convenience of cruise holidays."

Total assets: $24,491 million
Current ratio: 0.64
Common shares outstanding: 633 million
Return on 2004 shareholders' equity: 12%

| | 2004 | 2003 | 2002 | 2001 | 2000 | 1999 | 1998 | 1997 |
|---|---|---|---|---|---|---|---|---|
| Revenues (millions) | 9,727 | 6,717 | 4,368 | 4,536 | 3,778 | 3,497 | 3,009 | 2,447 |
| Net income (millions) | 1,854 | 1,194 | 1,016 | 926 | 965 | 1,027 | 836 | 666 |
| Earnings per share | 2.24 | 1.66 | 1.73 | 1.58 | 1.60 | 1.66 | 1.40 | 1.12 |
| Dividends per share | .52 | .44 | .42 | .42 | .42 | .36 | .32 | .24 |
| Price　high | 58.3 | 39.8 | 34.6 | 34.9 | 51.3 | 53.5 | 48.5 | 27.9 |
| 　　　low | 39.0 | 20.3 | 22.1 | 17.0 | 18.3 | 38.1 | 19.0 | 15.7 |

Aggressive Growth

# Caterpillar, Inc.

100 N. E. Adams Street □ Peoria, IL 61629–5310 □ (309) 675–4549 □ Direct dividend reinvestment plan is available: (800) 842–7629 □ Web site: *www.cat.com* □ Listed: NYSE □ Ticker symbol: CAT □ S&P rating: B+ □ Value Line financial strength rating: A

"Cat has enriched its dividend eleven times, by nearly 1,000 percent on a split-adjusted basis, since 1993. (In June 1994, the quarterly was increased for the first time since having been halved in December 1991, because of labor woes and a weak global economy.)" said an article in *Barron's* on June 14, 2004. The author was Shirley A. Lazo. "The company most recently boosted its payout in October. Dividends have been paid without interruption since Cat's formation in 1925 via a merger of a pair of companies dating back to 1890.

"Chief executive James W. Owens said the new payout reinforces management's confidence in the company's future. It's 'just one example of our ongoing commitment to improve shareholder value and deliver attractive returns on an investment in Caterpillar,' he noted. Owens called Cat a 'dynamic, profitable company,' and added that 'our strong financial position and cash flow, along with solid operational performance, should result in continued shareholder satisfaction.'"

## Company Profile

Caterpillar's distinctive yellow machines are in service in nearly every country in the world. About 48 percent of the company's revenues is derived from outside North America. Europe/Africa/Middle East contributes 27 percent, Asia/Pacific, 13 percent and Latin America, 8 percent. What's more, about 71 percent of Cat's 220 independent dealers are based outside the United States.

Headquartered in Peoria, Illinois, Caterpillar is the world's largest manufacturer of construction and mining equipment, diesel and natural gas engines and industrial gas turbines. It is a *Fortune* 50 industrial company with more than $37 billion in assets.

Caterpillar's broad product line ranges from the company's new line of compact construction equipment to hydraulic excavators, backhoe loaders, track-type tractors, forest products, off-highway trucks, agricultural tractors, diesel and natural gas engines, and industrial gas turbines. Cat products are used in the construction, road-building, mining, forestry, energy, transportation, and material-handling industries.

Caterpillar products are sold in more than 200 countries—and rental services are offered through more than 1,200 outlets worldwide. The company delivers superior service through its extensive worldwide network of 220 dealers. Many of these dealers have relationships with their customers that have spanned at least two generations. More than 80 percent of Cat's sales are to repeat customers.

Caterpillar products and components are manufactured in forty-one plants in the United States and forty-three plants in Australia, Brazil, Canada, England, France, Germany, Hungary, India, Indonesia, Italy, Japan, Mexico, The Netherlands, Northern Ireland, China, Poland, Russia, South Africa, and Sweden.

The company conducts business through three operating segments: Machinery, Engines, and Financial Products.

### Machinery

Caterpillar's largest segment, the Machinery unit (60 percent of revenues, and 74 percent of operating profits) makes the company's well-known earthmoving equipment. Machinery's end-markets include heavy construction, general construction, and mining quarry and aggregate, industrial, waste, forestry, and agriculture.

End markets are very cyclical and competitive. Demand for Caterpillar's earthmoving equipment is driven by many volatile factors, including the health of global economies, commodity prices, and interest rates.

### Engines

For decades, the Engine segment (32 percent of sales and 11 percent of operating profits) made diesel engines solely for the company's own earthmoving equipment.

Now, Engine derives about 90 percent of sales from third-party customers, such as Paccar, Inc., the maker of well-known Kenworth and Peterbilt brand tractor/trailer trucks. Engine's major end markets are electric power generation, on-highway truck, oil and gas, industrial/OEM and marine.

## Financial Products

The Financial Products segment (7.6 percent of revenues and 20 percent of operating profits) primarily provides financing to Caterpillar dealers and customers. Financing plans include operating and finance leases, installment sales contracts, working capital loans, and wholesale financing plans.

## Shortcomings to Bear in Mind

- Caterpillar has an extremely leveraged balance sheet—only 31 percent of its capitalization is in common equity. I prefer 75 percent. What's more, coverage of bond interest is not impressive, at five times. I prefer six times.
- On February 4, 2005, *Standard & Poor's Stock Reports* was lukewarm about Caterpillar. Anthony M. Fiore, CFA, said, "We have a HOLD recommendation on the shares. While we expect favorable end market conditions to continue over the next twelve months, we believe that our outlook is largely reflected in the price of the stock." The price at the time was $99.96.

## Reasons to Buy

- "The world's hunger for raw materials has paid off hugely for Caterpillar," according to an April 4, 2005 article in *BusinessWeek*. "Orders for its earth-moving equipment and heavy-duty engines poured in faster than Cat could build them, especially in the U.S. After years of struggling with minimal price hikes, the . . . manufacturer finally gained leverage with its customers. It was able to raise prices three times in a year."

- Jim Owens joined Caterpillar in 1972 as a corporate economist and held management positions worldwide before becoming chief financial officer in 1993 and group president in 1995. According to former CEO Glen Barton, "Jim has a broad understanding of Caterpillar's business strategy, having served as group president for a diverse set of business units—human services, component manufacturing, product support, logistics, information technology and Latin American operations."
- On January 27, 2005, Jim Owens said, "2004 was a great year to be a member of the worldwide Caterpillar family. We celebrated a series of impressive milestones—100 years since the invention of the track-type tractor, seventy-five years on the New York Stock Exchange and fifty years of operation in Brazil, as well as the introduction of ACERT Technology into the earthmoving machine business—and set all-time sales and revenues and profit per share records.

  "In a year of explosive growth and largely unanticipated global demand, our sales increased by more than $7 billion, as we surpassed our $30 billion sales and revenue goal a full two years ahead of schedule. Through it all, we maintained product quality and grew our global leadership position. We ended the year with a record order backlog for our larger machines—indicating continuing market strength for 2005."
- Over the years, Caterpillar has earned a reputation for rugged machines that typically set industry standards for performance, durability, quality, and value. The company's goal is to remain the technological leader in its product lines. Today, thanks to accelerated design and testing, computer-based diagnostics and operations, and greatly improved materials, the company can

deliver to customers new and better products sooner.

- Caterpillar is an innovator and spends heavily on research and development. Historically, the company invests about 3.1 percent of annual revenues on R&D. In 2003, the company allocated $669 million; in 2002 it was $656 million; and the year before it was $696 million.

- Caterpillar's commitment to customer service is demonstrated by the fastest parts delivery system in its industry. Caterpillar's customers can obtain replacement parts from their dealers usually upon request. If not, Caterpillar ships them anywhere in the world within twelve hours, often much sooner.

- In 2004, Caterpillar acquired Turbomach S.A., a Swiss packager of industrial gas turbines and related systems. Turbomach's power-generation packages incorporate gas turbines manufactured by San Diego-based Solar Turbines Incorporated, a wholly owned subsidiary of Caterpillar.

Solar Turbines is a world leader in the design, manufacture, and service of industrial gas turbine engines in its size range. More than 11,000 Solar gas turbine engines and turbo machinery systems are used on land and offshore in ninety nations for the production and transmission of crude oil, petroleum products and natural gas, and for generating electricity and thermal energy for a wide variety of industrial applications.

"Turbomach has distributed Solar brand turbines and equipment to the industrial power-generation market for almost 20 years," said Caterpillar Group President Rich Thompson. "This acquisition will benefit both Caterpillar and its customers by assuring the continuity of this relationship and enhancing our ability to sell and support such systems, particularly in the expanding markets in Europe, Africa, and Asia."

- Caterpillar is not noted for good labor relations. However, its latest tussle with the union turned out okay. Here's what the *Associated Press* had to say on September 8, 2004. Jan Dennis said, "During more than a half-century of bargaining, heavy-equipment maker Caterpillar, Inc. and the United Auto Workers have forged only two labor contracts without a strike. But there's been only a fleeting whiff of a walkout this year, as more than 9,000 members have stayed on the job without a contract even after turning down two take-it-or-leave-it offers over the past nine months. Labor experts say the standoff signals a shift in bargaining power that has given the Peoria-based Caterpillar the upper hand and left union leaders wary of playing their traditional trump card."

Total assets: $43,091 million
Current ratio: 1.29
Common shares outstanding: 684 million
Return on 2004 shareholders' equity: 30%

|  | 2004 | 2003 | 2002 | 2001 | 2000 | 1999 | 1998 | 1997 |
|---|---|---|---|---|---|---|---|---|
| Revenue (millions) | 30,251 | 22,763 | 20,152 | 20,450 | 20,175 | 19,702 | 20,977 | 18,925 |
| Net income (millions) | 2,035 | 1,099 | 798 | 805 | 1,051 | 946 | 1,513 | 1,665 |
| Earnings per share | 2.88 | 1.57 | 1.15 | 1.16 | 1.51 | 1.32 | 2.06 | 2.19 |
| Dividends per share | .78 | .72 | .70 | .70 | .67 | .63 | .58 | .48 |
| Price        high | 49.4 | 42.5 | 30.0 | 28.4 | 27.6 | 33.2 | 30.4 | 30.8 |
|              low | 34.3 | 20.6 | 16.9 | 19.9 | 14.8 | 21.0 | 19.6 | 18.3 |

# Chevron Corporation

6001 Bollinger Canyon Road ❑ San Ramon, CA 94583–2324 ❑ (415) 894–9376 ❑ Direct dividend reinvestment plan is available: (800) 368–8357 ❑ Web site: *www.chevrontexaco.com* ❑ Listed: NYSE ❑ Ticker symbol: CVX ❑ S&P rating: B+ ❑ Value Line financial strength rating: A++

"China is said to be emerging as a global power in energy," said Peter Robertson, vice chairman of Chevron, on October 13, 2004. "That's no surprise to Chevron, which has long been a true believer in China, its people and its economy.

"And when I say 'long,' I mean long—at least by Western standards:

• "Our kerosene sign appeared on Shanghai's Great White Way almost 100 years ago."

• "Junks, camels, and pony carts delivered our products."

• "Our Caltex colors have for many years flown over Indonesia, Thailand, Korea, Singapore, India, Malaysia, and the Philippines as well as China."

"In this, our 125th year, we are active in twenty-seven Asian nations, and our work here accounts for more than 20 percent of our global oil and gas production. We have more than 7,000 Caltex service stations and three major refineries in Asia. One in five of our employees works in this region."

Finally, Mr. Robertson said, "We are approaching an era of unprecedented opportunity in what is often called the coming 'Asian Century'—an era in which economic globalization, the rapid growth of heavily energy-dependent industries and the increasing capabilities of the region's population have created favorable conditions for Asian economies in general and China in particular."

## Company Profile

Chevron (formerly ChevronTexaco) is the world's fourth-largest publicly traded, integrated energy company based on oil-equivalent reserves and production. It is engaged in every aspect of the oil and gas industry, including exploration and production; refining, marketing and transportation; chemicals manufacturing and sales; and power generation.

The corporation traces its roots to an 1879 oil discovery at Pico Canyon, north of Los Angeles. This find led to the formation, in the same year, of the Pacific Coast Oil Company. Active in more than 180 countries, Chevron has reserves of 11.9 billion barrels of oil and gas equivalent and daily production of 2.6 million barrels.

In addition, it has global refining capacity of more than 2.3 million barrels a day and operates more than 24,000 retail outlets (including affiliates) around the world. The company also has interests in thirty power projects now operating or being developed.

Chevron's upstream success includes:

• The number one oil and gas producer in the U.S. Gulf of Mexico Shelf and number two in the Permian Basin.

• The number one oil producer in the San Joaquin Valley in California.

• The number one oil and natural gas producer in Kazakhstan.

• The number one oil producer in Indonesia and Angola.

• The number one natural gas resource holder in Australia.

• The number one deepwater leaseholder and number three oil and gas producer in Nigeria.

• One of the top producers and leaseholders in the deepwater Gulf of Mexico.

Its downstream business includes:

• Four refining and marketing units, which operate in North America; Europe and West Africa; Latin America; and Asia, the Middle East, and southern Africa. Downstream also has five global businesses: aviation, lubricants, trading, shipping, and fuel and marine marketing.

• The company's global refining network comprises twenty-three wholly owned and joint-venture facilities, which process more than 2 million barrels of oil per day.

• Chevron sells more than 2 million barrels of gasoline and diesel per day through more than 24,000 retail outlets under three well-known consumer brands: Chevron in North America; Texaco in Latin America, Europe, and West Africa; and Caltex in Asia, the Middle East, and southern Africa.

• CVX is the number one jet fuel marketer in the United States and third worldwide, marketing 550,000 barrels per day in eighty countries.

• The company's industrial and consumer lubricants business operates in more than 180 countries and sells more than 3,500 products, from specialized hydraulic fluids to leading branded products, such as Delo, Havoline, Revtex, and Ursa.

• Chevron's global trading business buys and sells more than 6 million barrels of hydrocarbons per day in some sixty-five countries.

• The company's fuel and marine marketing business is a leading global supplier and marketer of fuels, lubricants, and coolants to the marine and power markets, with about 500,000 barrels of sales per day.

• CVX's shipping company manages a fleet of thirty-one vessels and annually transports more than a billion barrels of crude oil and petroleum products.

## Shortcomings to Bear in Mind

■ Although *Value Line* rated Chevron a 2 (an above-average rating) for Timeliness, its analyst was less than enthusiastic on

December 17, 2004. Jeremy J. Butler said, "Earnings in 2005 should retreat from the high expected this year. We look for oil and gas prices to pull back somewhat, although the high price of energy will exert inflationary pressures on Chevron's cost of goods sold in the refining area. Elsewhere, the ongoing expense of ramping up production at developing fields in Nigeria, Angola, Kazakhstan, and Australia will probably raise capital spending needs."

He went on to say, "Income-oriented investors may be attracted to the hefty and dependable dividend, but the timely stock's capital gains potential is modest."

## Reasons to Buy

■ On April 4, 2005, Chevron announced that it had acquired Unocal is a deal worth about $18 billion, including net debt. To finance the deal, Chevron issued about 210 million shares of its own stock and paid $4.4 billion in cash. Some industry analysts say Chevron was wise to buy the company mostly with its own stock, since it reduces the risk of overpaying in a high-price environment.

Unocal is based in El Segundo, California. Acquiring Unocal gives Chevron a portfolio of attractive fields in Azerbaijan, Bangladesh, Thailand, and Indonesia, as well as in the Gulf of Mexico, all of which are to begin producing in 2005. These projects, if successful, could increase Unocal's production as much as 10 percent a year through 2010, making it one of the industry's best performers.

■ On January 5, 2005, Chevron announced that its Angolan subsidiary, Cabinda Gulf Oil Company Ltd. (CABGOC) had achieved first oil from the Bombocco Field in its operated Block O concession, offshore Malongo, Cabinda province. Bombocco is expected to reach an average daily production of 30,000 barrels of oil within the next year and is an integral component of CABGOC's Sanha Condensate project.

Commenting on the announcement, John Watson, president of Chevron Overseas Petroleum, said, "Bombocco's first oil is an important milestone in the broader Sanha Condensate project, which will give a boost to Chevron's production in Africa—a continent where we continue to make strong progress toward achieving our strategic growth objectives."

■ Chevron's upstream business, encompassing exploration and production activities, is the company's primary source of value growth. Its upstream portfolio is rich and broadly based, with premier resource, reserves, and production positions in many of the world's largest and most abundant oil and natural gas regions, including Angola, Australia, Indonesia, Kazakhstan, Nigeria, the United States, and Venezuela.

■ Chevron is one of the world's largest producers of heavy crude oil, which represents about one-third of the world's hydrocarbon reserves. Industry production of heavy oil is projected to grow by 30 percent by the end of this decade. Because the company is committed to extracting greater value from its extensive heavy-oil resource base, it is implementing improved technologies and processes for producing, transporting, refining, and marketing this challenging resource.

Meanwhile, Chevron has made significant advances in using steam to enhance recovery as well as in upgrading heavy oil to lighter crude and crude products. Its heavy-oil assets include fields in California's Joaquin Valley, where Chevron is the largest heavy-oil operator; the Duri Field in Indonesia, the world's largest steam-flood project; the Hamaca project in Venezuela, which alone contains nearly 2 billion barrels of recoverable oil; and the Athabasca Oil Sands in Canada, where bitumen is extracted for upgrading into synthetic crude oil.

■ "We are upgrading our rating on Chevron Corp. From HOLD to BUY with a target price of $66," said Jeb Armstrong, writing for Argus Research Company on January 31, 2005. "The upgrade is based on the stock's value relative to its peers rather than on any change in the company's growth plan, which is good, but not exceptional. We believe our outlook for energy price in 2005 will generate stronger earnings than is generally expected. Much depends on refining margins in California and Southeast Asia."

**Total assets: $93,208 million**
**Current ratio: 1.52**
**Common shares outstanding: 2128 million**
**Return on 2004 shareholders' equity: 29.4%**

|  |  | 2004 | 2003 | 2002 | 2001 | 2000 | 1999 | 1998 | 1997 |
|---|---|---|---|---|---|---|---|---|---|
| Revenue (millions) |  | 150,865 | 121,761 | 98,913 | 106,245 | 52,129 | 36,586 | 30,557 | 35,009 |
| Net income (millions) |  | 13,034 | 7,230 | 1,132 | 3,288 | 5,185 | 2,070 | 1,339 | 3,180 |
| Earnings per share |  | 6.14 | 3.48 | .54 | 1.55 | 3.99 | 1.57 | 1.02 | 2.43 |
| Dividends per share |  | 1.53 | 1.43 | 1.40 | 1.33 | 1.30 | 1.24 | 1.22 | 1.14 |
| Price | high | 56.1 | 43.5 | 45.8 | 49.2 | 47.4 | 57.0 | 45.1 | 44.6 |
|  | low | 41.6 | 30.7 | 32.7 | 39.2 | 35.0 | 36.6 | 33.9 | 30.9 |

# Cintas Corporation

P. O. Box 625737 ❑ Cincinnati, OH 45262–5737 ❑ (513) 459–1200 ❑ Dividend reinvestment plan not available ❑ Web site: *www.cintas.com* ❑ Fiscal years end May 31 ❑ Listed: NASDAQ ❑ Ticker symbol: CTAS ❑ S&P rating: A+ ❑ Value Line financial strength rating: B++

Cintas, the nation's leading manufacturer of corporate identity uniforms, had another impressive year of accomplishments in fiscal 2004:

## Financial:

• Achieved thirty-fifth consecutive year of uninterrupted growth in sales and profits. Wal-Mart is the only public company that has achieved a longer record.

• Revenue was a record $2.81 billion, up 5 percent.

• Achieved record profits of $272 million, a gain of 9 percent.

• Increased dividends by 7 percent.

## Expansion:

• Expanded uniform rental presence into four new cities.

• Opened four new state-of-the-art uniform rental plants.

• Expanded First Aid and Safety expertise to include fire services.

• More than half of all new uniform rental business was from first-time users.

• Cintas has nearly 5,000 uniform rental facility service routes and more than 700 first aid and safety routes, covering 296 of the top 315 cities in the United States and Canada.

## Achievements:

• Ranked according to *Fortune* magazine as the nation's "America's Most Admired Company" in the diversified outsourcing industry—the second time in the past four years that the company has topped the industry list.

• Highlighted by *Fortune* magazine as one of "America's Most Admired Companies"

across all industries, marking the fourth consecutive year Cintas has made the overall list.

• Named as one of "America's Best Managed Companies" by *Forbes* magazine.

• Received the Consumer's Choice Award in the category of Uniform Supply Service.

• Two years straight, Cintas named "Best in Business" by *Food Processing* magazine.

## Company Profile

Cintas is North America's leading provider of corporate identity uniforms through rental and sales programs, as well as related business services, including entrance mats, hygiene products, cleanroom services, and first aid and safety supplies.

Cintas serves businesses of all sizes, from small shops to large national companies employing thousands of people. Today, more than 5 million people go to work wearing a Cintas uniform every day. That is well over 3 percent of the nonfarm, civilian work force in the United States and Canada.

Cintas provides its award-winning design capability and top quality craftsmanship to the high end of the market—hotels, airlines, cruise ships, and the like. The company delivers the proper uniform to anyone in any job classification from the doorman to the cocktail waitress in a hotel; from the mechanic to the pilot at the airlines; and even people working in the retail sector.

According to a Cintas spokesman, "Companies use Cintas uniforms to identify their employees to their customers. An employee who wears a clean, crisp, and attractive uniform is always viewed as more professional than someone in ordinary work clothes. Uniforms also complement a company's esprit de corps by building camaraderie and loyalty. Bottom line—we don't just sell uniforms—we sell image, identification, teamwork, morale, pride and professionalism." Put another way, Cintas believes that when people *look* good, they *feel* good. And when they feel good, they work better. What's more, their improved attitude results in a decline in absenteeism and turnover.

## Shortcomings to Bear in Mind

- To be sure, Cintas is a superior company with an outstanding record. But it is rarely available at a low price/earnings ratio. It often sells for more than thirty times earnings.

## Reasons to Buy

- On December 21, 2004, Standard & Poor's analyst, Bryan J. Korutz, said, "We have a BUY opinion on the shares. S&P projects that read GDP (*Gross Domestic Product*) will grow 3.4 percent in calendar 2005. We see this eventually supporting improved uniform rentals, and purchases, as we believe that a firming economy will boost employment levels and subsequently stimulate demand for uniforms, mainly in the gaming, and lodging industries."

- "The company continues to increase free cash flow, affording it leeway in conducting its business," said Scott Mintz, writing for *Value Line Investment Survey* on December 10, 2004. "It will likely use excess funds to expand. Management anticipates making acquisitions both to enhance existing businesses and to move into new areas. The company expects acquisitions to not only bolster the top line (*sales*) through cross selling, but through increases to its customer base as well. All told, acquisitions have already contributed to its growth, and we expect this trend to continue."

- According to an analytical report issued by Robert W. Baird & Co. (a brokerage firm, with offices in the United States, France, Spain, Germany, and The United Kingdom), "In addition to the current market served, there are another roughly 25 million employees (according to *American Apparel Manufacturer*) that currently purchase work apparel specific for their occupation through retail outlets, which we believe could potentially be served by the industry.

  "Furthermore, we believe that there are another 20–25 million employees in occupations that could be conducive to a uniform program, but that do not currently utilize one. If the industry penetrated these two potential markets, we estimate that the direct sales market could potentially reach $11 billion."

- Many large corporations are re-engineering all aspects of their business, and they are consolidating their source of supply of products and services. They prefer to deal with fewer suppliers to reduce purchasing and administrative costs. They often prefer to do business with Cintas because the company is a complete uniform service, whether the customer wants to rent, lease, or buy their uniforms. In addition, Cintas also provides online ordering, inventory control, and paperless systems.

- According to the company, "When on-the-job injuries occur, business need to handle them. Cintas can help by delivering our Xpect line of first aid and safety products and services.

  "Cintas regularly and reliably stocks first aid cabinets, provides safety and emergency products and conducts training to ensure that work places are safer and more prepared. Our products and services run the gamut—everything from pain relievers to defibrillators, from back injury prevention to emergency oxygen, from ergonomics to OSHA compliance."

- "If you are considering an investment in Cintas, here some facts you should know," said William C. Gale, Senior Vice President–Finance & CFO.

- "We are the largest company in our industry.
- "We have grown 35 consecutive years, through all economic cycles.
- "We are a market leader with an excellent reputation.
- "We have an outstanding management team, most of whom have been with the company for many years.
- "We are ownership-driven. Most of the executives have a majority of their net worth invested in Cintas stock. We are motivated more by the long-term value of Cintas than by salaries, bonuses or perks."
- Over the past ten years (1994–2004), Cintas achieved an enviable record of consistent growth. In that span, revenue growth compounded at a 13.4 percent rate; net income 15 percent; diluted earning per share, 13.9 percent; Dividends per share, 17.1 percent; total assets, 14.9 percent; shareholders' equity, 16.5 percent.

- During this same ten-year stretch, return on equity was never less than 15.4 percent, and was as high as 20.2 percent. Return on equity is a good measure of management's skill in running the company. A return of 15 percent or better is seen as a solid indication that the company is doing well.

Total assets: $2,810 million
Current ratio: 3.17
Common shares outstanding: 171 million
Return on 2004 shareholders' equity: 15.4%

| | 2004 | 2003 | 2002 | 2001 | 2000 | 1999 | 1998 | 1997 |
|---|---|---|---|---|---|---|---|---|
| Revenues (millions) | 2,814 | 2,687 | 2,271 | 2,161 | 1,902 | 1,752 | 1,198 | 840 |
| Net income (millions) | 272 | 249 | 234 | 222 | 193 | 139 | 123 | 91 |
| Earnings per share | 1.58 | 1.45 | 1.36 | 1.30 | 1.14 | .82 | .79 | .64 |
| Dividends per share | .29 | .27 | .25 | .22 | .19 | .15 | .10 | .08 |
| Price     high | 50.5 | 50.7 | 56.2 | 53.3 | 54.0 | 52.3 | 47.5 | 28.3 |
|      low | 39.5 | 30.6 | 39.2 | 33.8 | 23.2 | 26.0 | 26.0 | 17.0 |

Conservative Growth

# Colgate-Palmolive Company

300 Park Avenue ❏ New York, NY 10022–7499 ❏ Listed: NYSE ❏ (212) 310–2575 ❏ Dividend reinvestment plan available: (800) 756–8700 ❏ Web site: *www.colgate.com* ❏ Ticker symbol: CL ❏ S&P rating: A+ ❏ Value Line financial strength rating: A++

"Our aggressive commercial spending in key countries around the world is showing results," said Colgate's CEO Reuben Mark on October 20, 2004. He went on to say, "Market shares are high and getting higher worldwide. Toothpaste share is at an all-time record high in the United States, and our leadership in this core category is increasing in other competitive markets around the world. Underlying these share gains are large media increases here and abroad."

Mr. Mark also said, "In the United States and overseas, Colgate's marketing and financial fundamentals are very solid. Top-line growth is excellent and is expected to remain so, although it has come at a cost to short-term profits. Looking forward, Colgate has always been very good at methodically improving profitability, and we fully expect our current investment in key countries, combined with accelerated 'Funding the Growth' programs, will lead to higher profits in 2005 and beyond."

## Company Profile

Colgate-Palmolive is a leading global consumer products company, marketing its products in over 200 countries and territories under such internationally recognized brand names as Colgate toothpaste and brushes, Palmolive, Mennen Speed Stick deodorants, Ajax, Murphy Oil Soap, Fab and Soupline/Suavitel, as well as Hill's Science Diet and Hill's Prescription Diet.

With two-thirds of its sales and earnings coming from abroad, Colgate is making its greatest gains in overseas markets.

Travelers, for instance, can find Colgate brands in a host of countries:

- They'll find Total toothpaste, with its proprietary antibacterial formula that fights plaque, tartar and cavities, in more than seventy countries.
- The Care brand of baby products is popular in Asia.
- Colgate Plax makes Colgate No. 1 in mouth rinse outside the U.S.
- The Colgate Zig Zag toothbrush, popular in all major world regions outside the United States, helps make Colgate the No. 1 toothbrush company in the world.
- Axion is an economical dishwashing paste popular in Asia, Africa, and Latin America.

## Shortcomings to Bear in Mind

- "Over the past two decades, Colgate's Reuben Mark built up one of the most

enviable records of any big-company CEO—year after year of dependable profit growth, with stock price gains to match," said Nelson D. Schwartz on October 18, 2004, in an article in *Fortune* magazine.

The article went on to say, "But now, as the 65-year-old Mark prepares to hand over the reins, it looks as if Colgate's winning streak could be coming to an end. In late September the company shocked Wall Street with a major earnings disappointment that knocked the shares down 11 percent in a single day. Now some observers are wondering if Mark, who took over in 1984, has overstayed his welcome in the top job. While archrival Procter & Gamble has returned 28 percent over the past five years, Colgate has risen by just over 1 percent. And in the past two years, Colgate shares are down 14 percent, while the S&P 500 is up 44 percent. In July, Colgate named Ian Cook, who previously ran North American and European operations, as chief operating officer, setting the stage for him to take over in the next year or two."

## Reasons to Buy

- *Barron's* financial weekly had a different opinion of Colgate on September 27, 2004, in an article written by Jacqueline Doherty. She said, "Investors should take a second look at Colgate-Palmolive shares—now that its cavities are visible. While Colgate has had to slash it earnings outlook and step up spending on marketing because of the intensely competitive retail environment, it retains strong market shares for its most important products, and has an enviable presence in some of the world's fastest-growing markets."
- Technology-based new products and veterinary endorsements are driving growth at Hill's, the world's leader in specialty pet food. Hill's markets pet foods mainly under two trademarks: Science

Diet, which is sold through pet supply retailers, breeders and veterinarians; and Prescription Diet for dogs and cats with disease conditions. Hill's sells its products in eighty-five countries.

Recent introductions gaining wide acceptance are Science Diet Canine and Feline Oral Care, Science Diet Canine Light Small Bites, and new Prescription Diet Canine b/d, a clinically proven product that reduces the effect of canine aging.

- Colgate concentrates research expenditures on priority segments that have been identified for maximum growth and profitability. For example, the fast-growing liquid body-cleansing category has benefited from continuous innovation. The result: European sales of Palmolive shower gel have nearly tripled during the past four years. The latest innovation, Palmolive Vitamins, uses unique technology to deliver two types of Vitamin E to the skin, thus providing both immediate and long-lasting protection.

In another sector, focused R&D at Colgate's Hills subsidiary has resulted in a superior antioxidant formula that helps protect pets from oxidative damage, including to the immune system. This discovery led to a significant nutritional advance of Hill's Science Diet dry pet foods, introduced in the U.S. in 2000. The product has gained excellent reception from vets, retailers, and their customers, aided by national media advertising. Hill's scientists have also developed a new Prescription Diet brand formulation that nutritionally helps avoid food-related allergies.

- Adding to region-specific initiatives is the company's vast consumer intelligence. Colgate interviews more than 500,000 consumers in more than thirty countries annually to learn more about their habits and usage of the company's product.

- Colgate's global reach lets the company conduct consumer research in countries with diverse economies and cultures to create product ideas with global appeal. The new product development process begins with the company's Global Technology and Business Development groups analyzing consumer insights from various countries to create products that can be sold in the greatest possible number of countries. Creating "universal" products saves time and money by maximizing the return on R&D, manufacturing, and purchasing. To assure the widest possible global appeal, potential new products are test-marketed in lead countries that represent both developing and mature economies.

- To best serve its geographic markets, Colgate has set up regional new product innovation centers. From these centers, in-market insight from thousands of consumer contacts is married with R&D, technology, and marketing expertise to capitalize on the best opportunities. Early on, the consumer appeal, size, and profitability of each opportunity are assessed. Once a new product concept is identified, it is simultaneously tested in different countries to assure acceptance across areas. Then, commercialization on a global scale takes place rapidly.

A prime example is Colgate Fresh Confidence, a translucent gel toothpaste aimed at young people seeking the social benefits of fresh breath and oral health reassurance. The process from product concept to product introduction in Venezuela took only one year. Within another six months, Colgate Fresh Confidence had been expanded throughout Latin America and began entering Asia and Europe. Today, less than a year after its first sale, Colgate Fresh Confidence is available in thirty-nine countries and is gaining new Colgate users among the targeted age group. Colgate Fresh Confidence, moreover, has expanded even faster than Colgate Total, the most successful toothpaste introduction ever.

The U.S. Surgeon General recently cited oral disease as a "silent epidemic," of which the primary victims are inner city children. Initially designed to improve the oral health of urban youngsters in the United States, Colgate's Bright Smiles, Bright Futures program has expanded to address oral care needs in eighty countries.

In the midst of expanding the company's reach, Colgate dental vans are stopping in cities across the country. New York, Houston, Atlanta, Chicago, and Los Angeles are examples of the many cities where children benefit from the expertise of volunteer dental professionals. Colgate's partnership with retail giants such as Wal-Mart and Kmart reaches children and their families outside stores across the U.S. Each year, this campaign reaches 5 million children in the United States as well as another 49 million around the world.

On February 23, 2005, *Standard & Poor's Stock Reports* had some positive comments on Colgate-Palmolive. Howard Choe said, "We are maintaining our STRONG BUY recommendation on the shares, reflecting our belief that CL's recently announced restructuring program is likely to drive improved profitability, and that the shares will likely trade close to peer levels. We believe savings derived from the restructuring program will be reinvested in R&D and marketing in an effort to drive product sales. The program will also allocate more resources to faster-growing markets, in our view. In addition, the company anticipates a greater gross margin expansion, and sees EPS (*Earnings per share*) growth in the low double digits from 2006 on."

- On February 3, 2005, the Argus Research Company gave Colgate a BUY rating. Analyst Erin Ashley Smith said, "We continue to think that the restructuring program that the company announced toward the end of fiscal 2004 is a step in the right direction. The charges from the restructuring program negatively influenced earnings and accounted for the drop in ESP for the quarter and the year; however, we think the improvements currently being made at the company will help to drive long-term growth."

Total assets: $8,673 million
Current ratio: 1.00
Common shares outstanding: 530 million
Return on 2004 shareholders' equity: NMF*

|  | 2004 | 2003 | 2002 | 2001 | 2000 | 1999 | 1998 | 1997 |
|---|---|---|---|---|---|---|---|---|
| Revenues (millions) | 10,584 | 9,903 | 9,294 | 9,084 | 9,358 | 9,118 | 8,972 | 9,057 |
| Net income (millions) | 1,327 | 1,421 | 1,288 | 1,147 | 1,064 | 937 | 849 | 740 |
| Earnings per share | 2.33 | 2.46 | 2.19 | 1.89 | 1.70 | 1.47 | 1.31 | 1.14 |
| Dividends per share | .96 | .90 | .72 | .68 | .63 | .59 | .55 | .53 |
| Price    high | 59.0 | 61.0 | 58.9 | 64.8 | 66.8 | 58.9 | 49.4 | 39.3 |
| low | 42.9 | 48.6 | 44.1 | 48.5 | 40.5 | 36.6 | 32.5 | 22.5 |

\* NMF means no meaningful figure.

Income

# ConAgra Foods, Inc.

One ConAgra Drive ❑ Omaha, NE 68102–5001 ❑ (402) 595–4154 ❑ Dividend reinvestment plan available: (800) 214–0349 ❑ Web site: *www.conagra.com* ❑ Listed: NYSE ❑ Fiscal years end last Sunday in May ❑ Ticker symbol: CAG ❑ S&P rating: A ❑ Value Line financial strength rating: A

"ConAgra Foods is in the food business like no other food company," said CEO Bruce Rohde in mid-2004. "We have significant presence with retail, foodservice, and ingredients customers, creating growth opportunities across a variety of consumers, occasions, and locations. Our business model puts us where we think the growth will be and allows us to use assets efficiently to better serve customers and consumers.

"Let me explain:

"In general terms, consumers spend a little more than half of their food dollars on products sold in supermarkets, club stores, mass merchandise stores, convenience stores, dollar stores, and other retail outlets. There are well over 150,000 such outlets in North America, all of them needing to continually improve the products and services they offer consumers, which means there's plenty of room for us to grow.

Mr. Rohde went on to say, "The corollary is that consumers spend a little less than half of their food dollars eating away from home, in casual dining, fine dining, quick service, hotels, workplace cafeterias, vending machines, amusement parks, entertainment locales, kiosks, and other foodservice venues that number close to 1 million—again, plenty of room for us to grow, especially when you take into account that our trade customers need to continually improve what they offer consumers. And, of course, all food, regardless of channel, requires quality ingredients that are often blended, mixed, milled, sized or specified to order.

"We're in great shape because we have a variety of foods that are on trend with today's customers and consumers, and are well-known favorites across America. So, whether it's with retail, foodservice or ingredient customers, we have what it takes to satisfy consumers, and we have a portfolio of selections to be the supplier of choice for our trade customers. Every day people eat, and this gives us unlimited potential."

## Company Profile

ConAgra Foods, Inc. is one of the world's most successful food companies. As North America's largest foodservice manufacturer and second-largest retail food supplier, ConAgra is a leader in several segments of the food business.

ConAgra has uniquely positioned its assets to take advantage of meals prepared at home as well as in such foodservice institutions as schools, hospitals, and restaurants. As a result of a constantly improving business mix, more than 75 percent of the company's profits are generated from sales of branded and value-added products. Less than 25 percent of the company's food profits come from commodity operations.

ConAgra's operations broke down as follows in fiscal 2004 (in millions of dollars):

| | Sales | Operating Profit |
|---|---|---|
| Retail Products | $8,434.1 | $1,206.8 |
| Food Ingredients | 2,373.6 | 196.6 |
| Foodservice Products | 3,714.4 | 321.4 |
| Total | $14,522.1 | $1,724.8 |

### Retail Products

This includes branded packaged foods, which are sold through various retail channels and include products in frozen, refrigerated, and shelf-stable classes. Retail brands include: Andy Capp's, Banquet Dessert Bakes, Banquet Homestyle Bakes, Banquet Crock-Pot Classics, Cook's, Decker, Del Maestro, Dennison's, Hershey's Portable Pudding, Inland Valley, Jiffy Pop, Jolly Rancher Gel Snacks, Kid Cuisine, Life Choice, Lightlife, Lunch Makers, Mama Rosa's, Marie Callender's, Move Over Butter, Patio, Penrose, Ready Crisp, and Wolfgang Puck.

### Food Ingredients Products

This includes branded and commodity food ingredients, including milled grain ingredients, seasonings, blends, and flavorings, which are sold to food processors, as well as certain commodity sourcing and merchandising operations. Specialty Ingredients products include: wheat; oat and barley products; dehydrated, controlled moisture and fresh vegetable ingredients as well as processed seasonings, seasoning blends, and flavorings. Basic Ingredient products include: grains, oilseeds, feed ingredients, edible beans, livestock, natural gas, crude oil, and refined products. Food Ingredient brands include: Controlled Moisture Vegetables, Garden Frost, Gilroy, J. M. Swank, SpiceTec, Sustagrain, and Ultragrain.

## Foodservice Products

This includes branded and customized food products, including meals, entrees, prepared potatoes, meats, seafood, sauces, and a variety of custom-manufactured culinary products packaged for sale to restaurants and other foodservice establishments. Foodservice brands include: Andale Gourmet, Award, Break O Morn, Canola Quick, CrissCut, Critters, El Extremo, Ever Fresh, Fernando's Florida Sea, Generation 7 Fries, Holly Ridge Bakery, J. Hungerford Smith, Lamb Weston, Lamb's Supreme, Longmont, LW Private Reserve, MaxSnax, MaxStix, Munchers, Starz, Stealth, Stuffed Spud, Sweet Things, Tantalizers, Texas Signature Foods, The Max, The Max Meals, Touch of Butter, and Twister.

## Shortcomings to Bear in Mind

- In recent years, ConAgra has pursued an aggressive acquisition policy. To be sure, this strategy has helped the company to enhance its profit margins. However, it has left it highly leveraged. At the end of 2004, common equity represented only 48 percent of ConAgra's balance sheet.
- On February 22, 2005, Prudential Equity Group gave ConAgra a NEUTRAL rating. John McMillin said, "Our main concern regarding CAG was whether higher costs were going to take a bigger bite out of margins in the remaining quarters of fiscal (May) 2005. But CAG was implementing pricing moves, and we

wondered how much was being realized after promotional spending.

"We remain concerned about the promotional dependency of CAG's marketing mix. As we have detailed in past reports, CAG has cut advertising in both of the last two calendar years. Efforts going forward to improve brand strength may have some up-front costs, leading us to believe that margin improvement in retail products is well down the road."

## Reasons to Buy

- Following the end of the second quarter of fiscal 2005 (which ended November 28 2004), Mr. Rohde said, "As we mark the midpoint of our fiscal year, we're making progress with the marketing, operating, and information systems initiatives that are key to improving profit margins and strengthening returns on capital over time.

  "Our second-quarter financial performance reflects progress in many respects.
  - Overall sales rose 8 percent, to $4.1 billion, driven by strong 7 percent volume growth for retail brands.
  - All segments posted operating profit growth.
  - Diluted EPS (Earnings per share) from continuing operations increased to $0.47, from $0.45 a year ago.
  - We strengthened our balance sheet by retiring $300 million of debt; shortly after the end of the quarter, we retired another $600 million of debt, reflecting our commitment to prudent capital allocation."
- ConAgra is the most diversified food company in the world, with more than 70 brands, along with meat processing, grain milling, and trading operations across major sectors.
- In recent years, income stocks have been difficult to find. For its part, ConAgra is an ideal dividend stock, with a generous yield and a dividend that has been boosted on a regular basis, with annual

increases dating back before 1985. In the past ten years (1994–2004), the per-share dividend climbed from $0.35 to $1.02, an impressive compound annual growth rate of 11.3 percent.

- "Some say the flour—milled very finely from a special white wheat that ConAgra bred—could help improve the fortunes of the deeply troubled bread industry and, perhaps, improve the health of many Americans," according to an August 9, 2004, article in the *Gannett News Service,* written by Bruce Horovitz.

  "ConAgra has spent millions of dollars over the past five years to develop the flour, which can be used in everything from pizzas to tortillas. The flour's made in a patent-pending milling process that uses the whole grain but makes the particle sizes uniform."

  Mr. Horovitz went on to point out that "The flour has 352 percent more dietary fiber than refined, unenriched wheat flour and has 1,100 percent more Vitamin E, 392 percent more niacin and 527 percent more magnesium."

- ConAgra has a solid business with restaurants, schools, college cafeterias, fairs, vending machines, movie theaters, sports arenas, hotel dining rooms, hospitals, and cruise ships. This group of customers is referred to as "foodservice."

  One of the reasons so many foodservice customers choose ConAgra Foods is basically, "because we work every day to make their jobs easier and their businesses more profitable," according to a company spokesman. "Many of our products arrive at restaurants pre-seasoned or pre-cooked, which reduces labor costs and improves consistency and quality of the product served to patrons. Our understanding of consumer wants and needs allows our research and development teams to offer their expertise to chain customers who continually revamp or update their menus. Our R&D teams routinely partner with customer R&D teams to develop new items to increase customers' sales and profits. By helping our customers grow their businesses, we grow ours."

Total assets: $14,230 million
Current ratio: 1.71
Common shares outstanding: 520 million
Return on 2004 shareholders' equity: 16.8%

|  | 2004 | 2003 | 2002 | 2001 | 2000 | 1999 | 1998 | 1997 |
|---|---|---|---|---|---|---|---|---|
| Revenues (millions) | 14,522 | 19,839 | 27,630 | 27,194 | 25,386 | 24,594 | 23,841 | 24,002 |
| Net income (millions) | 796 | 840 | 783 | 683 | 801 | 696 | 628 | 615 |
| Earnings per share | 1.50 | 1.58 | 1.47 | 1.33 | 1.67 | 1.46 | 1.36 | 1.34 |
| Dividends per share | 1.02 | .98 | .92 | .88 | .79 | .69 | .61 | .53 |
| Price high | 29.5 | 26.4 | 27.6 | 26.2 | 24.4 | 34.4 | 33.6 | 38.8 |
| low | 25.4 | 17.8 | 20.9 | 17.5 | 15.1 | 20.6 | 22.6 | 24.5 |

# ConocoPhillips

600 North Dairy Ashford ❑ Houston, TX 77252–2197 ❑ (281) 293–1000 ❑ Direct dividend reinvestment plan available: (888) 887–2968 ❑ Web site: *www.conocophillips.com* ❑ Listed: NYSE ❑ Ticker symbol: COP ❑ S&P rating: B ❑ Value Line financial strength rating: B++

"When Conoco and Phillips Petroleum announced plans to merge in late 2001, it looked to some like a desperate move to survive in a business squeezed by falling oil and gas prices and increasingly dominated by such giants as ExxonMobil and Chevron," said Wendy Zellner, writing for *BusinessWeek* on December 13, 2004. But more than two years after the marriage was completed, ConocoPhillips is proving that it's nimble enough to play with the big boys as it takes larger risks around the globe.

Ms. Zellner goes on to say, "Hefty cost cutting helped vault the company to number eight on last spring's *BusinessWeek* 50 ranking of top-performing companies. More important for future growth, though, ConocoPhillips has assembled a promising pipeline of oil and gas projects—including its recent $2.6 billion stake in Russia's biggest oil company, Lukoil.

## Company Profile

ConocoPhillips is an international, integrated energy company. It is the third-largest integrated energy company in the United States, based on market capitalization, oil and gas proved reserves, and production. The company is the largest refiner in the United States. Worldwide, of nongovernment controlled companies, ConocoPhillips has the eighth-largest total of proved reserves and is the fourth-largest refiner in the world.

ConocoPhillips is known worldwide for its technological expertise in deepwater exploration and production, reservoir management and exploitation, 3-D seismic technology, high-grade petroleum coke upgrading, and sulfur removal.

Headquartered in Houston, Texas, ConocoPhillips operates in more than forty countries. The company has about 35,800 employees worldwide and assets of $86 billion. The company has four core activities worldwide:

- Petroleum exploration and production.
- Petroleum refining, marketing, supply, and transportation.
- Natural gas gathering, processing and marketing, including a 30.3 percent interest in Duke Energy Field Services, LLC.
- Chemicals and plastics production and distribution through a 50 percent interest in Chevron Phillips Chemical Company LLC.

In addition, the company is investing in several emerging businesses—fuels technology, gas-to-liquids, power generation and emerging technologies—that provide current and potential future growth opportunities.

### Exploration and Production (E&P)

ConocoPhillips explores for and produces crude oil, natural gas, and natural gas liquids on a worldwide basis. The company also mines oil sands to produce Syncrude. A key strategy is to accelerate growth by developing legacy assets—very large oil and gas developments that can provide strong financial returns over long periods of time—through exploration, exploitation, redevelopments, and acquisitions; and by focusing exploration on larger, lower-risk areas.

At year-end 2003, ConocoPhillips held a combined 52.6 million net developed and undeveloped acres in 25 countries and produced hydrocarbons in 13. Crude oil production in 2003 averaged 934,000 barrels per day (BPD), gas production averaged

3.5 billion cubic feet per day, and natural gas liquids production averaged 69,000 BPD.

## Refining & Marketing (R&M)
R&M refines crude oil and markets and transports petroleum products. ConocoPhillips is the largest refiner in the United States and, of nongovernment-controlled companies, is the fourth-largest refiner in the world.

ConocoPhillips owns twelve U.S. refineries, owns or has an interest in five European refineries and has an interest in one refinery in Malaysia. At year-end 2003, ConocoPhillips refineries had a combined net crude oil refining capacity of 2.6 million barrels of oil per day.

ConocoPhillips' gasoline and distillates are sold through about 17,300 branded outlets in the United States, Europe, and Southeast Asia. In the United States, products are primarily marketed under the Phillips 66, 76, and Conoco brands. ConocoPhillips also markets lubricants, commercial fuels, aviation fuels, and liquid petroleum gas. R&M owns or has an interest in about 32,800 miles of pipeline systems in the United States.

## Midstream
Midstream consists of ConocoPhillips' 30.3 percent interest in Duke Energy Field Services (DEFS), as well as certain ConocoPhillips assets in the United States, Canada, and Trinidad. Midstream gathers natural gas, extracts and sells the natural gas liquids (NGL), and sells the remaining (residue) gas. Headquartered in Denver, Colorado, DEFS is one of the largest natural gas gatherers, natural gas liquids (NGL) producers, and NGL marketers in the United States.

DEFS' gathering and transmission systems include some 58,000 miles of pipelines, mainly in six of the major U.S. gas regions, plus western Canada. DEFS also owns and operates, or owns an equity interest in sixty-six NGL extraction plants. Raw natural gas

throughput averaged 6.7 billion cubic feet per day, and NGL extraction averaged 365,000 BPD in 2003. In addition to its interest in DEFS, ConocoPhillips owns or has an interest in an additional eleven gas processing plants and six NGL fractionators.

DEFS' strengths include assets in major gas-producing regions; efficient, reliable low-cost operations; and critical mass for growth transactions.

DEFS' customers are primarily major and independent natural gas producers, local gas distribution companies, electrical utilities, industrial users, and marketing companies. Among DEFS' customers for NGL are Chevron Phillips Chemical Company and ConocoPhillips' R&M operations.

## Chemicals
ConocoPhillips participates in the chemicals sector through its 50 percent ownership of Chevron Phillips Chemical Company (CPChem), a joint-venture with Chevron. Headquartered in The Woodlands, Texas, its major product lines include: olefins and polyolefins, including ethylene, polyethylene, normal alpha olefins, and plastic pipe; aromatics and styrenics, including styrene, polystyrene, benzene, cyclohexane, paraxylene and K-Resin styrene-butadiene copolymer; and specialty chemicals and plastics.

CPChem's major facilities in the United States are at Baytown, Borger, Conroe, La Porte, Orange, Pasadena, Port Arthur and Old Ocean, Texas; St. James, Louisiana; Pascagoula, Mississippi; and Marietta, Ohio. The company also has nine plastic pipe plants and one pipefittings plant in eight states, and a petrochemical complex in Puerto Rico. Major international facilities are in Belgium, China, Saudi Arabia, Singapore, South Korea, and Qatar. CPChem also has a plastic pipe plant in Mexico.

CPChem is one of the world's largest producers of ethylene, polyethylene, styrene,

alpha olefins, and one of the largest marketers of cyclohexane.

CPChem's customers are primarily
companies that produce industrial products
and consumer goods.

## Shortcomings to Bear in Mind

- ConocoPhillips's fortunes are closely tied
to the price of oil, which in 2005 was in
the stratosphere. In the event of a recession, demand for energy would suffer,
and the price of oil would sink back—far
below the $50-a-barrel level.

## Reasons to Buy

- "We recently upgraded our recommendation on the shares to BUY, from HOLD,"
said T. J. Vital, writing for *Standard &
Poor's Stock Reports* on February 24, 2005.
"The company has been reshaping its
portfolio to focus on higher-growth assets:
A divestiture program was completed in
the 2004 first half. We calculate COP's
2003 organic reserve replacement at 132
percent, but the company estimates that
its 2004 rate dropped to 60 to 65 percent,
due to a negative revision of proved crude
oil reserves for the Surmont project."

- On April 4, 2005, *BusinessWeek* had this
comment: "Nearly three years after the
merger that created it, ConocoPhillips is
proving a nimble competitor. It's built an
enviable portfolio of oil and gas projects,
including a 10 percent stake in Russia's
Lukoil. Properties like that should keep
production growing at a healthy clip.
The Houston-based company is also
investing in refining projects that let it
benefit from lower prices for heavier,
lower-quality oils."

- On November 24, 2004, the Argus
Research Company rated ConocoPhillips
as a BUY, for these reasons:
  - "We are raising our 2004 estimate by
  $1, to $11, and our 2005 estimate by
  $2.25, to $10.50, based on our higher
  outlook for energy prices in 2005 and

the company's acquisition of up to 10
percent of Russian oil giant Lukoil.
  - The Argus financial strength rating
  for ConocoPhillips is High, our best
  rating.
  - The company recently acquired 7.5
  percent of Lukoil from the Russian
  Government. ConocoPhillips is on
  track to raise that stake to 10 percent
  through open-market purchases by
  the end of the year."

- "CEO James J. Mulva, age 58, is well on
his way to fulfilling a longtime goal: creating a truly integrated oil giant," said Ms.
Zellner, in her article for *BusinessWeek*.
"'He wanted membership in the exclusive club,' with the likes of ExxonMobil,
BP, and Total, says Oppenheimer & Co.
senior oil analyst Fadel Gheit. Mulva's
dealmaking streak began with the acquisitions of Atlantic Richfield Co.'s Alaska
production assets in 2000, followed by
independent refiner Tosco Corp. in 2001.
Then came the $16-billion Conoco deal,
for which the hard-charging Mulva paid
no premium."

- In 2004, Mr. Mulva said, "ConocoPhillips is exercising the same capital and cost
discipline in emerging businesses that we
are elsewhere in the company. We have
several technologies with both long-term
and short-term potential. Our immediate
goal is to apply technologies to our existing businesses, but we also want to ensure
the company is positioned for the future.

  "One example is our gas-to-liquids
(GTL) technology, which converts
natural gas into transportable liquids,
creating an opportunity to develop some
of the world's remote, large natural gas
fields. Our new GTL semi-works facility
in Ponca City, Okla., completed in 2003,
is meeting the technical and commercial
milestones set for the project. In late
2003, we signed a Statement of Intent
with Qatar Petroleum to build a full-scale
GTL plant in Ras Laffan, Qatar."

Total assets: $92,861 billion
Current ratio: 0.96
Common shares outstanding: 1,378 million
Return on 2004 shareholders' equity: 21%

|  | 2004 | 2003 | 2002 | 2001 | 2000 | 1999 | 1998 | 1997 |
|---|---|---|---|---|---|---|---|---|
| Revenues (millions) | 135,076 | 104,196 | 56,748 | 26,729 | 20,835 | 13,571 | 11,545 | 15,210 |
| Net income (millions) | 8,107 | 4,591 | 1,511 | 1,709 | 1,916 | 548 | 389 | 911 |
| Earnings per share | 5.79 | 3.35 | 1.56 | 2.90 | 3.74 | 1.08 | 0.75 | 1.72 |
| Dividends per share | 0.90 | 0.82 | 0.74 | 0.70 | 0.68 | 0.68 | 0.68 | 0.67 |
| Price    high | 45.6 | 33.0 | 32.1 | 34.0 | 35.0 | 28.7 | 26.7 | 26.2 |
| low | 32.2 | 22.6 | 22.0 | 25.0 | 18.0 | 18.9 | 20.1 | 18.7 |

Aggressive Growth

# Costco Wholesale Corporation

999 Lake Drive ❑ Issaquah, WA 98027 ❑ (425) 313–8203 ❑ No dividend reinvestment plan available ❑ Web site: *www. costco.com* ❑ Listed: NASDAQ ❑ Fiscal years end Sunday nearest August 31 ❑ Ticker symbol: COST ❑ S&P rating: B+ ❑ Value Line financial strength rating: B++

The CEO of Costco is sixty-eight-year-old James D. Sinegal. "A lifelong retailer, Sinegal opened the first Costco warehouse in 1983 in Seattle, with Jeffrey H. Brotman, who is chairman," according to an article in *BusinessWeek*. "Their strategy was to offer lower prices and better value by stripping away everything they deemed unnecessary, including deluxe store fixtures, salespeople, even delivery and backup inventory. And it works. Over the past five years, sales have grown 11.7 percent annually, as earnings climbed 13.2 percent a year.

"Their original concept has led to some revolutionary behavior. One of Sinegal's rules, for example, is to strictly limit markups to 12 percent on national brand items and 14 percent for private-label, Kirkland Signature, goods."

Costco's strategy of retailing has grown in popularity among consumers and small-business owners in recent years. As a consequence, it has taken market share from such traditional retailers as supermarkets and drugstores. As the leader in its field, Costco should be able to strengthen its position further by broadening its line of products and services, coupled with further penetration into new markets, both at home and abroad.

A reputation for merchandising excellence and quality are a hallmark of Costco operations. These attributes have not gone unnoticed. The American Customer Satisfaction Index survey conducted by the University of Michigan Business School showed that Costco had the highest customer satisfaction rating of any domestic traditional national retailer.

## Company Profile

Costco is the largest wholesale club operator in the United States (ahead of Wal-Mart's Sam's Club). Costco operates a chain of membership warehouses that sell high quality, nationally branded and selected private label merchandise at low prices.

Costco is open only to members; it offers three types of membership: Business, Gold Star (individual), and Executive membership. Business members qualify by owning or operating a business, and pay an annual fee ($45 in the U.S.) to shop for resale, business or personal use. This fee includes a spouse card. Business members may purchase up to six additional membership cards ($35 each) for partners or associates in the business. Gold Star members pay a $45 fee (in the U.S.), and is available to those individuals that do not own a business. This fee includes a spouse membership. Finally, the company has a third membership level, called the Executive Membership. In addition to offering all the usual membership benefits, it enables members to purchase a wide variety of discounted consumer services.

Costco's business is based on achieving high sales volumes and rapid inventory turnover by offering a limited assortment of merchandise in a wide variety of product categories at very competitive prices.

As of October 7, 2004, the company operated a chain of 442 warehouses, including 327 in the United States, 63 in Canada, 15 in the United Kingdom, five in Korea, three in Taiwan, four in Japan, and 24 in Mexico. The company also operates Costco Online, an electronic commerce web site, at *www.costco.com*. The company plans to open ten additional new warehouses (including the relocation of two existing warehouses to larger and better-located facilities) prior to the end of the 2004 calendar year.

Costco units offer discount prices on nearly 4,000 products, ranging from alcoholic beverages and computer software to pharmaceuticals, meat, vegetables, books, clothing, and tires. Food and sundries account for 60 percent of sales. Certain club memberships also offer products and services, such as car and home insurance, mortgage services, and small-business loans.

A typical warehouse format averages about 132,000 square feet. Floor plans are designed for economy and efficiency in the use of selling space, in the handling of merchandise and in the control of inventory.

Merchandise is generally stored on racks above the sales floor and is displayed on pallets containing large quantities of each item, reducing labor required for handling and stocking.

Specific items in each product line are limited to fast-selling models, sizes and colors. Costco carries only an average of about 3,500 to 4,500 stock keeping units (SKUs) per warehouse. Typically, a discount retailer or supermarket stocks 40,000 to 60,000 SKUs. Many products are offered for sale in case, carton, or multiple-pack quantities only.

Low prices on a limited selection of national brand merchandise and selected private-label products in a wide range of merchandise categories produce high sales volume and rapid inventory turnover. Rapid inventory turnover, combined with operating efficiencies achieved by volume purchasing in a no-frills self-service warehouse facility, enables the company to operate profitably at significantly lower gross margins than traditional retailers, discounters, or supermarkets.

The company buys virtually all of its merchandise from manufacturers for shipment either directly to the warehouse clubs or to a consolidation point (depot) where shipments are combined so as to minimize freight and handling costs.

Additionally, Costco Wholesale Industries, a division of the company, operates manufacturing businesses, including special food packaging, optical laboratories, meat processing, and jewelry distribution.

## Shortcomings to Bear in Mind

- "We are maintaining our HOLD rating on Costco Wholesale Corp.," said Christopher Graja, CFA, writing for Argus Research Company on March 14, 2005. "We are still weighing the company's solid growth prospects and financial strength against a valuation that seems to be full. This is a company we would like to add to our BUY list at a lower valuation."

The analyst also said, "There are two other factors that we find attractive about Costco. The first is its operation of self-service gasoline stations. While higher gasoline prices hurt the economy and consumer spending, higher revenue from the pumps offsets some of that for Costco. The company's lower-than-average gas prices may also entice people to become members. We also believe that Costco is in a good position because it sells value-priced merchandise and because its customers are probably in better financial shape than the average American."

- "Shares of Costco, the nation's largest members-only warehouse club retailer in terms of sales, have jumped more than 30 percent over the past year," said Kortney Stringer, writing for the *Wall Street Journal* on February 22, 2005. The author also said, "Now, some investors and analysts say increased competition from supermarkets, discounters, and Wal-Mart Stores Inc.'s Sam's Club—the number two warehouse club—may slow Costco's momentum. Indeed, Costco may represent a classic Wall Street/Main Street split. The company continues to perform well, but its shares have become too expensive to entice buyers."

## Reasons to Buy

- "One problem for Wall Street is that Costco pays its workers much better than archrival Wal-Mart Stores Inc. does, and analysts worry that Costco's operating expenses could get out of hand," said Stanley Holmes and Wendy Zellner, in an article in *BusinessWeek* on April 12, 2004. The two *BusinessWeek* writers also said, "Surprisingly, however, Costco's high-wage approach actually beats Wal-

Mart at its own game on many measures. *BusinessWeek* ran through the numbers from each company to compare Costco and Sam's Club, the Wal-Mart warehouse unit that competes directly with Costco. We found that by compensating employees generously to motivate and retain good workers, one fifth of whom are unionized, Costco gets lower turnover and higher productivity. Combined with a smart business strategy that sells a mix of higher-margin products to more affluent customers, Costco actually keeps its labor costs lower than Wal-Mart's as a percentage of sales, and its 68,000 hourly workers in the U.S. sell more per square foot."

The article went on to say, "Bottom line: Costco pulled in $13,647 in U.S. operating profits per hourly employee last year, vs. $11,039 at Sam's. Over the past five years, Costco's operating income grew at an average of 10.1 percent annually, slightly besting Sam's 9.8 percent."

- *Value Line Investment Survey* had a favorable view of Costco on February 11, 2005. Its analyst, Deborah Y. Fung, said: "Costco ought to benefit from the stocking of more luxury goods, and the introduction of new products and services. We also look for profitability to continue to improve moderately, as the company realizes further efficiencies in warehouse operations and as changes in workers' compensation legislation take hold." The analyst also said, "This neutrally ranked stock is a good choice for the three- to five-year pull, given its above-average appreciation potential over that period."

- Costco warehouses generally operate on a seven-day, sixty-eight-hour week, and are open somewhat longer during the holiday season. Generally, warehouses are open between 10 a.m. and 8:30 p.m., with earlier closing hours on the weekend. Because these hours of operation are shorter than those of traditional discount grocery stores and supermarkets, labor costs are lower relative to the volume of sales.

- Costco's policy generally is to limit advertising and promotional expenses to new warehouse openings and occasional direct mail marketing to prospective new members. These practices result in lower marketing expenses as compared to typical discount retailers and supermarkets.

  In connection with new warehouse openings, Costco's marketing teams personally contact businesses in the region that are potential wholesale members. These contacts are supported by direct mailings during the period immediately prior to opening.

- "Costco Wholesale is one of the few retailers that can lay claim to besting mighty Wal-Mart, whose Sam's Clubs is second to Costco in the warehouse club business," said Andrew Bary, writing for *Barron's* on March 28, 2005. "Under Jim Senegal, who co-founded the discounter in 1983, and became its CEO in 1988, Costco has attracted affluent shoppers who like its quality wine, meat and vegetables—even its diamonds. Big-spending business customers appreciate the stores, too. In all, more than 23 million members pay $45 or more a year to shop there. Senegal, 69, has resisted suggestions from Wall Street to boost prices and squeeze employees. Partly as a result, Costco doesn't encounter the kind of labor-union and activist opposition that Wal-Mart does opening new stores. Sales are surging and likely will top $50 billion this year."

Total assets: $15,093 million
Current ratio: 1.18
Common shares outstanding: 461 million
Return on 2004 shareholders' equity: 12.4%

|  |  | 2004 | 2003 | 2002 | 2001 | 2000 | 1999 | 1998 | 1997 |
|---|---|---|---|---|---|---|---|---|---|
| Revenues (millions) |  | 48,107 | 41,693 | 37,993 | 34,797 | 32,164 | 27,456 | 24,269 | 21,874 |
| Net income (millions) |  | 882 | 721 | 700 | 602 | 631 | 545 | 460 | 351 |
| Earnings per share |  | 1.85 | 1.53 | 1.48 | 1.29 | 1.35 | 1.18 | 1.02 | .82 |
| Dividends per share |  | .40 | Nil | — | — | — | — | — | — |
| Price | high | 50.5 | 39.0 | 46.9 | 46.4 | 60.5 | 46.9 | 38.1 | 22.6 |
|  | low | 35.0 | 27.0 | 27.1 | 29.8 | 25.9 | 32.7 | 20.7 | 11.9 |

Conservative Growth

# CVS Corporation

One CVS Drive ❑ Woonsocket, RI 02895 ❑ (914) 722–4704 ❑ Direct dividend reinvestment plan is available: (877) 287–7526 ❑ Web site: *www.cvs.com* ❑ Listed: NYSE ❑ Ticker symbol: CVS ❑ S&P rating: B ❑ Value Line financial strength rating: A+

"With more than forty years of dynamic growth in the retail pharmacy industry, CVS/pharmacy is committed to providing superior customer service—to bring the easiest pharmacy retailer for customers to use," said an official of the company in 2004.

"With more than 5,000 stores, CVS fills one of every eight retail prescriptions in America. What's more, our ExtraCare program boasts 50 million cardholders, making it the largest and most successful retail loyalty program in the country.

"CVS has created innovative approaches to serve the healthcare needs of all customers through its CVS/pharmacy stores; its online pharmacy, CVS.com; and its pharmacy benefit management and specialty pharmacy subsidiary, PharmaCare Management Services.

"We're making investments in new stores and technology to drive strong future growth—both organically and through acquisition. Recently, we completed the acquisition of more than 1,200 Eckerd drugstores, primarily in the higher-growth Sunbelt markets of Florida and Texas, making us the largest drugstore chain and providing us with the opportunity for higher growth off a higher base.

"The demographics in the Sunbelt states are very favorable; these states are experiencing rapid population growth, particularly among seniors, resulting in pharmaceutical utilization rates among the highest in the nation. With the acquisition, CVS now holds number one or number two market shares in 75 percent of the markets we serve."

## Company Profile
Stanley and Sid Goldstein were distributing health and beauty products in the early 1960s when they decided to branch out into retailing. The brothers then opened their first Consumer Value Store in Lowell, Massachusetts, in 1963. The CVS chain had grown to 40 outlets by 1969, the year they sold the business to Melville Shoes. Melville underwent a restructuring in the mid-1990s, spinning off CVS and other retail units.

CVS Corporation is now the largest domestic drug store chain, based on store count. As of January 1, 2005, CVS operated 5,375 retail and specialty pharmacy stores in thirty-two states and the District of Columbia. The company holds the leading market share in thirty-two of the 100 largest U.S. drug store markets, or more than any other retail drug store chain.

Stores are situated primarily in strip shopping centers or free-standing locations, with a typical store ranging in size from 8,000 square feet to 12,000. Most new units being built are based on either a 10,000 square foot or 12,000 square foot prototype building that typically includes a drive-thru pharmacy. The company says that about one-half of its stores were opened or remodeled over the past five years.

Celebrating more than forty years of dynamic growth in the pharmacy retail industry, CVS is committed to being the easiest pharmacy retailer for customers to use. CVS has created innovative approaches to serve the healthcare needs of all customers through nearly 4,200 CVS/pharmacy stores; its online pharmacy, CVS.com; and its pharmacy benefit management and specialty pharmacy subsidiary, PharmaCare Management Services. The pharmacy industry has some of the best long-term growth dynamics in all of retail, and CVS is extremely well positioned to seize further growth opportunities

## Some Recent History:
2004: In April 2004, J. C. Penney sold its Eckerd drug store chain of 2,800 units to two purchasers: Canada's Jean Coutu Group Inc. and CVS. Of the 1,260 stores allocated to CVS, 622 are in Florida, a favorite home of retirees, and 437 are in Texas, a large, fast-growing state. The rest are also situated in the South. CVS also received Eckerd's pharmacy benefits management and mail order businesses. CVS paid $2.15 billion for its share of the Eckerd stores. Coutu was awarded the remaining 1,540 outlets, situated mainly in thirteen Northeast and Mid-Atlantic states.

2002: CVS continues to enter and open new stores in new, high population growth markets such as Dallas, Houston, Phoenix, and Las Vegas.

2001: CVS has sales that exceed $22 billion and operates over 4,000 stores in thirty-two states and the District of Columbia. CVS is a leading pharmacy retailer in many markets in the Northeast, Mid-Atlantic, Midwest, and Southeast regions. The company also begins its expansion into high-growth markets, including Central and South Florida.

1999: CVS launches CVS.com, the first fully integrated online pharmacy in the US.

1998: CVS acquires Arbor Drugs, Inc., of Michigan. Tom Ryan is named President and CEO of CVS. Ryan began working for CVS in 1978 as a pharmacist and is only the third CEO in the history of the company.

1997: CVS completes its acquisition of the Revco pharmacy chain—the largest and most successful acquisition in the history of the U.S. retail pharmacy industry. The acquisition of Revco gives CVS new key store locations in the Midwest, Southeast, and other parts of the country.

1994: CVS launches PharmaCare, a pharmacy benefit management company providing a wide range of pharmacy management benefit services to employers and insurers.

1990: CVS acquires Peoples Drug, which put CVS into new markets, including Washington, D.C., Pennsylvania, Maryland, and Virginia.

1985: CVS hits the $1 billion in sales milestone.

1980: CVS becomes the 15th largest pharmacy chain in the U.S. with 408 stores and $414 million in sales.

1974: CVS hits the $100 million in sales milestone.

## Shortcomings to Bear in Mind

- Drugstores face growing competition from major retailers. Wal-Mart, Target, and Costco, for instance, are among the big chains that have added pharmacies.

- Mail-order prescriptions are still a small segment of all drug sales. On the other hand, consumers who need maintenance drugs to treat chronic health ailments, such as hypertension, diabetes and arthritis, may find that their health plans now require that they use mail-order suppliers.

## Reasons to Buy

- "We have a STRONG BUY recommendation on CVS shares, based on our view of the potential for significant earnings benefits following the acquisition of 1,268 Eckerd drug stores in July," said Joseph Agnese, writing for *Standard & Poor's Stock Reports* on February 3, 2005. He also said, "We believe the integration of Eckerd stores provides a significant opportunity to accelerate earnings growth. Potential synergies are expected to be generated initially through the elimination of corporate personnel and purchasing efficiencies and then from improved customer counts due to increased service levels."

- *Value Line Investment Survey* also had good things to say about CVS on December 31, 2004. Andre J. Costanza said, "We think that CVS is poised for strong growth out to late decade. The recent purchase makes it the largest drug chain in the United States and increases its footprint in the fast-growing and profitable southern region, which is host to the rapidly growing retirement community. Although the Eckerd deal limits near-term appeal, the stock holds wide three- to five-year appreciation potential, given the growth we envision out to 2007–2009."

- Lehman Brothers (a major brokerage house) gave CVS an OVERWEIGHT (the same as a BUY) rating on March 3, 2005. Its analyst said, "CVS has improved its operations markedly over the last two years and is now taking the steps to achieve higher levels of service and efficiency. In addition, the company has been expanding successfully at a manageable pace into new, high-growth geographies, including Florida, Arizona, Nevada, and California, while continuing to relocate, remodel and add stores in its current markets."

▪ Since the company was spun off by Melville in 1995, it has compiled an enviable record of growth. In the 1995–2004 period, Earnings per share advanced from $0.40 to $2.15, a compound annual growth rate of 20.6 percent. Dividends, however, have not done as well. In the

1997–2004 stretch, Dividends per share barely inched ahead from $0.22 to $0.26.

▪ David B. Rickard, executive vice president and chief financial officer of CVS was named by in the August 2004 issue of *Corporate Finance Magazine* (U.K.) as one of the twenty most influential CFOs of the last twenty years. Rickard was recognized for his role in establishing CVS as the industry leader in sales performance, productivity and earnings growth, as well as his role in the successful restructuring of RJR Nabisco in the 1990s.

Total assets: $14,492 million
Current ratio: 1.66
Common shares outstanding: 800 million
Return on 2004 shareholders' equity: 14.7%

|  |  | 2004 | 2003 | 2002 | 2001 | 2000 | 1999 | 1998 | 1997 |
|---|---|---|---|---|---|---|---|---|---|
| Revenues (millions) | | 30,594 | 26,588 | 24,182 | 22,241 | 20,088 | 18,098 | 15,274 | 12,738 |
| Net income (millions) | | 959 | 847 | 719 | 638 | 734 | 635 | 510 | 380 |
| Earnings per share | | 1.15 | 1.03 | .88 | .78 | .90 | .78 | .63 | .54 |
| Dividends per share | | .13 | .12 | .12 | .12 | .12 | .12 | .12 | .11 |
| Price | high | 23.7 | 18.8 | 17.9 | 31.9 | 30.2 | 29.2 | 28.0 | 17.5 |
| | low | 16.9 | 10.9 | 11.5 | 11.5 | 13.9 | 15.0 | 15.2 | 9.8 |

Conservative Growth

# Darden Restaurants, Inc.

P. O. Box 593330 ❏ Orlando, FL 32859–3330 ❏ (800) 832–7336 ❏ Web site: *www.darden.com* ❏ Dividend reinvestment plan available: (800) 829–8432 ❏ Fiscal years end last Sunday in May ❏ Listed: NYSE ❏ Ticker symbol: DRI ❏ Standard & Poor's rating: A- ❏ Value Line financial strength rating: A

In the heart of Tuscany is Riserva di Fizzano, a captivating, restored eleventh century village, complete with a winery and restaurant. This faraway Italian town is a key reason why Olive Garden—one of Darden's restaurant chains—dominates the fiercely competitive segment of the casual dining market.

Each year, culinary managers from more than 100 different Olive Garden

restaurants travel to this Tuscan village to immerse themselves in Italian cuisine and culture at the Olive Garden Riserva di Fizzano restaurant and adjoining Culinary Institute of Tuscany. Here they take courses from Executive Chef Romana Neri on Italian cooking essentials, such as the importance of the freshest of ingredients, the art of cooking pasta, the layering of flavors, and the marriage of Italian food and wine.

This represents an unprecedented partnership Olive Gardens established with the Zingarelli family, owners of the property and the Rocca della Macie winery. It has helped Olive Garden's talented culinary development team create award-winning dishes, such as Pork Filettino, Mixed Grill, Tortelloni di Fizzano, Spaghetti delle Rocca, and Lobster Spaghetti.

What's more, in recent years, according to the company, "We have focused on making wine an integral part of the Olive Garden dining experience. We created the Olive Garden Wine Institute of Napa Valley to train managers on how to make wine approachable and enjoyable for their guests, and expanded our offerings to include 38 award-winning wines. *The Wall Street Journal* took notice and honored Olive Garden for having the best wine program in casual dining, as did the *Monterey Wine Festival.*"

## Company Profile

Darden Restaurants dates back to 1968 when William Darden launched the first Red Lobster restaurant in Lakeland, Florida. In 1970, the company was sold to General Mills. In May of 1995, the company became independent when General Mills distributed all Darden shares to its shareholders.

Darden Restaurants, Inc. is the largest publicly traded casual dining company in the world, serving more than 300 million meals a year at 1,325 restaurants in forty-nine states across the United States and Canada. The company, which operates four distinct restaurant concepts, had sales in 2004 of $5 billion.

The flagship brands, Red Lobster (649 units) and Olive Garden (537 units) are the market leaders in their segments of casual dining, making Darden the only company in the industry to operate more than one restaurant company with sales exceeding $2 billion.

Bahama Breeze (thirty-two units) and Smokey Bones BBQ Sports Bar (sixty-nine units) are Darden's two newest concepts, and both were developed internally.

### Red Lobster

Founded in 1968, Red Lobster is America's most successful casual dining seafood restaurant company. It has led this segment of the industry since its inception. It had sales of $2.4 billion in fiscal 2004. Its average restaurant sales were $3.6 million.

### Olive Garden

Founded twenty-two years ago, Olive Garden, a family of local restaurants, is the leader in the highly competitive Italian segment of casual dining. As of the end of fiscal 2004, Olive Garden could boast a record of consecutive thirty-nine quarters of same-restaurant sales growth. Total sales in 2004 for Olive Garden were $2.2 billion, with average unit sales of $4.1 million.

### Bahama Breeze

After eight years of operation, Bahama Breeze, according to management, "has built an exciting brand based on its promise of memorable Island vacation experience, with delicious Caribbean cuisine, handcrafted drinks, live music, and a relaxed atmosphere." In fiscal 2004, this concept had total sales of $176 million.

### Smokey Bones

Darden's newest concept, Smokey Bones BBQ Sports Bar, was introduced in September 1999 and began a national expansion in fiscal 2002. The company says, "The restaurant mixes great-tasting barbecue with mountain lodge comfort and exciting sports action." It had sales of $174 million in 2004—nearly double the level of the prior year. Average annual sales per restaurant were $3.2 million.

## Shortcomings to Bear in Mind

- Red Lobster's total sales in fiscal 2004 were a record $2.44 billion. However, the gain was a minuscule 0.1 percent. Average annual sales per restaurant were $3.6 million (on a 52-week basis), and Red Lobster built seven net new restaurants. On the plus side, a new leadership team for this operation "is in place and working to improve operating efficiency and sharpen the positioning of the brand, while achieving sustainable and profitable growth," according to CEO Joe R. Lee.

## Reasons to Buy

- Highlights of fiscal 2004:

    Sales increased 7.5 percent, to $5 billion, driven primarily by new restaurant growth at Olive Garden and Smokey Bones, same-restaurant sales growth at Olive Garden, and an additional operating week in the fourth quarter. Net earnings were $231.5 million, or $1.36 per diluted share.

    Oliver Garden's total sales were a record $2.21 billion, up 11.1 percent over 2003. Operating profits also reached new record levels, with a double-digit increase over the prior year. Average annual sales per restaurant were a record $4.1 million (on a fifty-two-week basis), and Olive Garden built nineteen new restaurants. Olive Garden's domestic same-restaurant sales growth for the year was 4.6 percent, and the chain ended the year with thirty-nine consecutive quarters of same-restaurant sales growth. Commenting on this performance, Mr. Lee said, "Olive Garden continues to demonstrate how strong brand positioning, brilliance with basics of in-restaurant operations, compelling food news, and great advertising combine to drive excellent guest satisfaction, as well as strong growth in sales, traffic, and operating profits."

    Bahama Breeze's total sales of $176 million were up 28 percent from 2003. In May 2004, Bahama Breeze closed six underperforming restaurants "as part of our plan to improve overall profitability,

leaving thirty-two restaurants in operation at the end of the fiscal year," said Mr. Lee. Average annual sales per restaurant, excluding the closed restaurants, were $5.2 million in fiscal 2004 (on a fifty-two-week basis).

Smokey Bones' total sales were $174 million, an 87 percent increase from 2003, as the company nearly doubled in size in 2004 by adding thirty new restaurants to its base of thirty-nine. According to Mr. Lee, "Smokey Bones continued to drive strong consumer acceptance through its unique combination of slow-smoked barbeque and a variety of other grilled favorites, served in a lively, yet comfortable, mountain lodge atmosphere, where guests can watch their favorite sports. Annual sales averaged $3.2 million per restaurant (on a 52-week basis), and expansion will continue in fiscal 2005, as it seeks to take advantage of a compelling opportunity."

Finally, "Seasons 52, the casually sophisticated fresh grill and wine bar we're testing in Orlando, continued to post impressive results. Plans are in place to open two to three more test restaurants in fiscal 2005 to further explore the concept's viability," said Mr. Lee.

- "Americans are dining out again, putting an end to the worse downturn in the restaurant business in a decade," said Katy McLaughlin, in the *Wall Street Journal* on March 30, 2004. "After a sharp downturn in sales growth that lasted three years, customers are returning to the table as a result of a healthier economy and an uptick in consumer confidence. The largest chains are reporting 5 percent to 6 percent sales growth in January and February compared with the year-earlier period, says market research firm NPD Group." She went on to say, "Fast-food establishments and major chains like Olive Garden, a unit of Darden Restaurants, are rebounding the fastest."

- "Higher volumes and lower costs should combine to lift profits" said Warren Thorpe, an analyst with *Value Line Investment Survey*, on March 11, 2005. "Growth prospects to 2008–2010 are good. Red Lobster and Olive Garden are proven brands within the casual dining sector. . . . Darden stock is timely. With

heavy marketing, the restaurateur should remain competitive. Consumers are likely to dine out with greater frequency as the economy further expands."

- In the 1995–2004 period, Earnings per share climbed from $.45 to $1.36, a compound annual growth rate of 13.1 percent.

Total assets: $2,780 million
Current ratio: 0.51
Common shares outstanding: 161 million
Return on 2004 shareholders' equity: 19%

|  | 2004 | 2003 | 2002 | 2001 | 2000 | 1999 | 1998 | 1997 |
|---|---|---|---|---|---|---|---|---|
| Revenues (millions) | 5,003 | 4,655 | 4,369 | 4,021 | 3,701 | 3,458 | 3,287 | 3,172 |
| Net income (millions) | 231 | 232 | 236 | 197 | 173 | 135 | 102 | 54 |
| Earnings per share | 1.36 | 1.31 | 1.30 | 1.06 | .87 | .64 | .46 | .23 |
| Dividends per share | .08 | .07 | .05 | .05 | .05 | .05 | .05 | .05 |
| Price        high | 28.5 | 23.0 | 29.8 | 25.0 | 18.0 | 15.6 | 12.6 | 8.3 |
|               low | 18.5 | 16.5 | 18.0 | 12.7 | 8.3 | 10.4 | 7.8 | 4.5 |

Aggressive Growth

# Deere & Company

One John Deere Place □ Moline, IL 61265 □ (309) 765–4491 □ Direct dividend reinvestment plan available: (309) 765–4539 □ Web site: *www.deere.com* □ Listed: NYSE □ Fiscal years end October 31 □ Ticker symbol: DE □ S&P rating: B □ Value Line financial strength rating: B++

"Today John Deere and iRobot unveiled the Military R-Gator, an intelligent unmanned ground vehicle that will use off-the-shelf technology to autonomously perform dangerous and taxing missions," said Greg Doherty, Director, Product and Market Development, John Deere Worldwide Commercial & Consumer Equipment Division of Deere & Company, on October 25, 2004. "Until now, autonomous ground vehicles have been developed and built using custom technology on an individual basis, which can be a time-consuming and costly process. Using available systems, John Deere and iRobot plan to begin production of the R-Gator by mid-2005, with full production slated to begin by 2006."

Mr. Doherty goes on to say, "This joint effort between John Deere and iRobot combines our legacy of rugged reliability and excellent performance in the field with iRobot's extensive, proven military robotics expertise. Moreover, the fact that it will be available off-the-shelf will allow the R-Gator to be swiftly deployed to help keep soldiers out of harm's way."

The Robotic Gator, or R-Gator as it is called, is built on the combat-proven John Deere M-Gator military utility vehicle platform, and enhanced with proven iRobot military robotic controls and navigation and obstacle avoidance systems. The intelligent, durable and flexible R-Gator is designed to serve numerous important roles, including acting as an unmanned scout, point man, perimeter guard, pack/ammo/supply carrier, and more for soldiers, marines, and airmen. What's more, the R-Gator can relay real-time video, sounds, and sensor readings from a potentially hostile area without putting soldiers at risk.

## Company Profile

Deere & Company, founded in 1837, grew from a one-man blacksmith shop into a worldwide corporation that today does business in more than 160 countries and employs more than 40,000 people around the globe. Deere consists of three equipment operations, credit operations, and four support operations:

### Equipment Operations

Agricultural Equipment: John Deere has been the world's premier producer of agricultural equipment since 1963. Products include tractors; combines, cotton and sugar cane harvesters; tillage, seeding and soil-preparation machinery; hay and forage equipment; materials-handling equipment; and integrated agricultural management systems technology for the global farming industry.

Construction & Forestry Equipment: The world's leading manufacturer of forestry equipment, and a major manufacturer of construction equipment, whose key products are backhoes, four-wheel-drive loaders, graders, excavators, crawler dozers, log skidders, skid steer loaders, wheeled and tracked harvesters, forwarders, and log loaders.

Commercial & Consumer Equipment: Deere is the world leader in premium turf-care equipment and world vehicles. The company produces a broad range of outdoor power products for both homeowners and commercial users, including tractors, mowers, utility vehicles, golf and turf equipment, and hand-held products.

### Credit Operations

John Deere Credit is one of the largest equipment finance companies in the United States, with more than 1.8 million accounts and a managed asset portfolio of nearly $16 billion. It provides retail, wholesale, and lease financing for agricultural, construction, forestry, commercial, and consumer equipment, including lawn and ground care—and revolving credit for agricultural inputs and services. John Deere Credit also provides financing in Argentina, Australia, Brazil, Canada, Finland, France, Germany, Italy, Luxembourg, Spain, and the United Kingdom.

### Support Operations

Parts: John Deere is a major supplier of service parts for its own products as well as those of other manufacturers.

Power Systems: A world leader in the production of off-highway diesel engines in the 50- to 600-horsepower range, supplying heavy-duty engines and drive train systems for OEM (original equipment) markets in addition to John Deere Equipment Operations.

Technology Services: Offers a wide range of electronic, wireless-communication, information system, and Internet-related products and services to Deere and outside customers.

Health Care: John Deere Health Care subsidiaries provide health care management services to about 4,400 employer groups and covers more than 515,000 members.

## Shortcomings to Bear in Mind

- Deere is not a typical growth stock with steady gains in Earnings per share and dividends that follow along. Rather, Deere is a cyclical company with earnings that can vary from year to year. For instance, EPS dropped sharply in 1999 to $1.02, compared with $4.16 the prior year. Similarly, Earnings per share fell from $2.06 in 2000, to $0.65 in 2001. Nor were dividends anything to boast about. In the six-year span from 1998 through 2003, the annual dividend remained at $0.88.

- "We have a HOLD recommendation on the shares," said Anthony M. Fiore, CFA, writing for *Standard & Poor's Stock Reports* on February 17, 2005. "We anticipate that favorable conditions will continue over the next twelve months for many of the end markets that DE serves, but we believe that our outlook is fairly reflected in the current price."

## Reasons to Buy

- Prudential Equity Group gave Deere an OVERWEIGHT (similar to BUY) on February 24, 2005. Andrew Casey said, "We believe the combination of very good current fundamental conditions, likely continued increases to consensus expectations, and cash allocation back to shareholders should provide a strong set of catalysts to move the stock higher. While cycle duration of North American agricultural equipment still remains uncertain, we believe that the stock is discounting this and more. We believe that the valuation is attractive when viewed in the context of likely increased earnings power on relatively flat volume growth."
- "We believe the recent sell-off in shares of BUY-rated Deere & Company offers a good buying opportunity," said Dana Richardson, writing for the Argus Research Company on February 17, 2005. "We believe that DE is an under-valued stock, based on its historical multiples and the projected surge in 2005 free cash flow to $1.5 billion, from $799 million in 2004."
- "The company recently noted that its order book was in better shape than it was last year," said Morton L. Siegel, writing for *Value Line Investment Survey* on January 28, 2005. "In addition, Deere now expects domestic farm income to be close to last year's record, instead of the modest falloff we had earlier estimated."

- Writing for *Barron's*—Harlan S. Byrne had this comment on November 1, 2004: "As the fall harvest season gets under way, the bright tractors of Deere & Co. are rumbling across America's farmlands like never before.

  "These are heady times down on the farm, thanks to an improving economy here and abroad. And that has given a nice lift to sales and profits at the 167-year-old Deere. Earnings have nearly doubled in the fiscal year ended October 31, to about $5.15 a share, and they could rise another 20 percent in the coming year."

  Mr. Byrne goes on to say, "Investors may finally get their own harvest time. The environment for equipment makers like Deere is likely to stay strong for at least the next year or so, some top farming experts say. Deere, meanwhile, is cutting costs, rolling out new products, strengthening ties to dealers—and building a nice hoard of cash.

  "The company now has about $3 billion in its coffers, roughly double the level a year ago. With a $1 billion stock-buyback program nearing completion, another such effort could soon follow. In all, veteran analyst John E. McGinty of Credit Suisse First Boston sees the stock hitting 85 within a couple of years, up nearly 45 percent from the current level."
- "Satellite-assisted guidance systems are the latest technological revolution in agriculture," said Gordon Culp, division manager marketing, John Deere Ag Management Solutions on November 1, 2004. "These systems have brought more efficiency to planting, spraying, tillage, and harvesting by reducing overlap, saving fuel and chemicals, and reducing operator fatigue. John Deere has been a leader with guidance systems on tractors, sprayers, and combines; and has helped to introduce this technology to select producers throughout the world.

"In order to bring this technology to an even larger number of growers, John Deere introduced StarFire iTC and the next generation of Parallel Tracking. The new Parallel system will be a more economical system to help producers get started with guidance technology. The basic package includes the three common GreenStar components and a Parallel Tracking KeyCard, providing a manual guidance system at a very economical price. This system can be used on any tractor, sprayer, combine, or any other machine with a twelve-volt power source.

"The three common components include a StarFire iTC receiver, Green-Star display, and mobile processor. Parallel Tracking guides the operator through the field, and while the operator steers the tractor, the display keeps him on a straight or curved path. New or used equipment, any make or model, can use the system.

"We've currently priced the entire Parallel Tracking system for a GreenStar-ready vehicle at $4,495. This will help growers who never considered using a guidance system to try this new technology. Some will be able to get into the new Parallel Tracking system for less money because they already own a GreenStar display for yield monitoring, SeedStar display for population monitoring or SprayStar display for sprayer controls."

■ "After a downturn that stretches back to the 1990s, the U.S. Agriculture sector is back—and so is Deere," according to an article in *BusinessWeek* dated April 4, 2005. "With farm incomes at record highs in 2004, Deere's earnings nearly doubled from the 2005 bottom line. Its three-year average annual growth was 85.2 percent, easily placing Deere in the top 10 percent of S&P 500 companies by that measure. The company owes its record to more than farmers. Sales of heavy equipment for construction and forestry soared by more than 50 percent."

Total assets: $28,754 million
Current ratio: 1.85
Common shares outstanding: 247 million
Return on 2004 shareholders' equity: 30.6%

|  | 2004 | 2003 | 2002 | 2001 | 2000 | 1999 | 1998 | 1997 |
|---|---|---|---|---|---|---|---|---|
| Revenues (millions) | 19,635 | 13,349 | 11,703 | 11,077 | 11,169 | 9,701 | 11,926 | 11,082 |
| Net income (millions) | 1,406 | 643 | 319 | 153 | 486 | 239 | 1,021 | 960 |
| Earnings per share | 5.56 | 2.64 | 1.33 | .64 | 2.06 | 1.02 | 4.16 | 3.78 |
| Dividends per share | 1.06 | .88 | .88 | .88 | .88 | .88 | .88 | .80 |
| Price high | 74.9 | 67.4 | 51.6 | 46.1 | 49.6 | 45.9 | 64.1 | 60.5 |
| low | 56.7 | 37.6 | 37.5 | 33.5 | 30.3 | 30.2 | 28.4 | 39.9 |

# Dell, Inc.

One Dell Way ❑ Round Rock, TX 78682 ❑ (512) 728–7800 ❑ Dividend reinvestment plan not available ❑ Web site: www.dell.com ❑ Listed: NASDAQ ❑ Ticker symbol: DELL ❑ S&P rating: B+ ❑ Value Line financial strength rating: A++

"Dell has outfoxed Hewlett-Packard before, but this time it's using different tactics," said Andrew Park, with Lauren Young, writing for *BusinessWeek* on September 6, 2004. "After three years of slashing prices to grab PC market share, Dell is backing away from the industry's bloodiest price wars in a bid to goose its profits. Since July (2004), the company has raised prices as much as 13 percent on some desktops, including its low-end ones, and held pricing firm on most others, according to researcher *Current Analysis Inc.*

"If Dell stays the course, could this mark a significant shift in PC pricing after years of downward pressure? Most experts say that's unlikely since Dell's rivals are locked in a brutal battle at the bottom of the market and are in no position to raise prices."

The *BusinessWeek* article went on to say, "But whatever its rivals do, Dell's shift is already helping the bottom line (*profits*). While raising prices has slowed sales growth—second-quarter unit shipments were up just 19 percent, the slowest rate in more than a year—revenues rose 20 percent, to $11.7 billion, while net income soared to $799 million."

## Company Profile

Dell Inc. is a trusted and diversified information-technology supplier and partner, and sells a comprehensive portfolio of products and services directly to customers worldwide. Revenue for the last four quarters totaled $49.2 billion and the company employs approximately 55,200 team members around the globe.

Dell was founded in 1984 by Michael Dell, the computer industry's longest-tenured chief executive officer, on a simple concept: that by selling computer systems directly to customers, Dell could best understand their needs and efficiently provide the most effective computing solutions to meet those needs. This direct business model eliminates retailers that add unnecessary time and cost, or can diminish Dell's understanding of customer expectations.

### Harnessing the Internet

Dell led commercial migration to the Internet, launching *www.dell.com* in 1994 and adding e-commerce capability in 1996. The following year, Dell became the first company to record $1 million in daily online sales. Today, Dell operates one of the highest volume Internet commerce sites in the world based on Microsoft Corp.'s Windows operating systems. The company's Web site, which runs entirely on Dell PowerEdge servers, receives more than 2 billion page requests per quarter at eighty-one country sites in twenty-eight languages/dialects and twenty-six currencies.

The company is increasingly realizing Internet-associated efficiencies throughout its business, including procurement, customer support, and relationship management. At *www.dell.com,* customers may review, configure, and price systems within Dell's entire product line; order systems online; and track orders from manufacturing through shipping. At *https://valuechain. dell.com,* Dell shares information with its suppliers on a range of topics, including product quality and inventory. Dell also uses the Internet to deliver industry-leading customer services. For instance, thousands of business and institutional customers worldwide use Dell's Premier.Dell.com Web pages to do business with the company online.

Dell's high return to shareholders has been the result of a focused effort over time to balance growth with profitability and liquidity. Dell has consistently led its largest competitors in each of those categories.

## Shortcomings to Bear in Mind

- Everyone knows that Dell is a great company, and most people these days buy their computers from Dell. My last two are Dell models. Consequently, Dell has a high P/E ratio, up near forty. At one time, I decided not to include Dell in this edition, since I don't like high-multiple stocks. Most of the time they are poor investments. However, I decided not to "fight city hall." So, here it is, for better or worse.
- I found it difficult to find any brokerage house or research organization that had an unkind word about Dell. But the Argus Research Company came through on February 11, 2005. The company's analyst, Wendy Abramowitz, dubbed the stock a HOLD. She pointed out that the fourth quarter was disappointing, since Dell's revenues "did not beat forecasts—causing investors to take profits."

## Reasons to Buy

- "Dell continues to mint money where others fear to tread: the cutthroat personal-computer market," said *BusinessWeek* on April 4, 2005. "Almost 80 percent of Dell's revenue last year came from desktops and notebooks, but that didn't stop the Round Rock (Tex.) giant from increasing sales by 19 percent and profits by 15 percent. Dell is expanding even faster overseas, and its nascent printer line topped $1 billion in sales in 2004. Little wonder Dell is gunning for $80 billion in annual revenue in the next several years."
- Dell finished fiscal 2005 (ended January 31, 2005) with a flourish. Strong growth throughout Dell's range of products in the fiscal fourth-quarter

2005 led to the company's best-ever operating period. The company achieved quarterly records for revenue, unit shipments, operating income and cash flow from operations.

Sales increased 22 percent in Europe, the Middle East, and Africa and 21 percent in Asia-Pacific and Japan. Worldwide revenue growth from servers and storage systems accelerated from the previous quarter, increasing 20 percent year-over-year. In the United States, sales to business customers grew 19 percent year-over-year. Full-year pro-forma earnings were $1.29 per share, up 28 percent; fiscal 2005 reported earnings, including a special one-time charge, were $1.18 per share. Full-year revenue was $49.2 billion, up a hefty 19 percent.

- "We have a STRONG BUY recommendation on the shares," said Megan Graham-Hackett, writing for *Standard & Poor's* on February 17, 2005. "In our view, Dell sets the standard for the computer industry, reflecting the strength of its direct sales model and what we see as its superior cash flow management. We believe the company has an opportunity to boost its PC market share in 2005 more than we originally anticipated, due to the potential sale of IBM's PC business."
- On February 11, 2005, Steven M. Fortuna and his colleagues, writing for *Prudential Equity Group, LLC,* had this comment: "We would recommend investors use this opportunity to buy Dell shares aggressively near the $40 level, while selling HPQ (*Hewlett-Packard*) which we believe is likely to underperform in the near term. We strongly reiterate our OVERWEIGHT rating on Dell."
- "The stock is still ranked 1 (Highest) for Timeliness. And if our long-term projections are on the mark, the issue should be a rewarding selection for the pull to 2007–2009," said Theresa Brophy,

writing for *Value Line Investment Survey* on January 14, 2005. "Dell has been gaining market share in the European region (which includes the Middle East and Africa) and the Asia/Pacific area, and may increase its market penetration in those parts of the world. Sales should also get some help from new products, including Dell's eighth-generation of server products, color printers for business customers, and two new printers with advanced digital photography features for consumer use."

■ "Of all the cards dealt to Carly Fiorina, the now-departed HP diva, there was one that just couldn't be played. Dell." said Steven Levy, writing for *Newsweek* on February 21, 2005. "She fought like a tiger to merge her company with Compaq, hoping the two of the more

innovative-minded computer makers might bring on some *agita* for Michael Dell and his CEO Kevin Rollins. But last spring at an industry confab, Rollins was boasting that Dell reaps *more than 100 percent* of the profits of the entire industry. Sounds weird, but think of it this way: Dell is making big money while everybody else combined is operating at a loss. Sorry, Carly."

Mr. Levy went on to say, "In Dell's view, only one big player has a right to exist in the business of selling Windows-based PCs—the firm Michael Dell founded in his college dorm room. Profitless rivals should take up something with a better chance of putting change in their pockets."

Total assets: $23,215 million
Current ratio: 1.20
Common shares outstanding: 2,484 million
Return on 2004 shareholders' equity: 47.7%

|                      | 2004   | 2003   | 2002   | 2001   | 2000   | 1999   | 1998   | 1997   |
|----------------------|--------|--------|--------|--------|--------|--------|--------|--------|
| Revenues (millions)  | 49,205 | 41,444 | 35,404 | 31,168 | 31,888 | 25,265 | 18,243 | 12,327 |
| Net income (millions)| 3,043  | 2,645  | 2,122  | 1,780  | 2,310  | 1,860  | 1,460  | 944    |
| Earnings per share   | 1.18   | 1.01   | .80    | .65    | .84    | .68    | .53    | .32    |
| Dividends per share  | Nil    | —      | —      | —      | —      | —      | —      | —      |
| Price      high      | 42.6   | 37.2   | 31.1   | 31.3   | 59.7   | 55.0   | 37.9   | 13.0   |
|            low       | 31.1   | 22.6   | 21.9   | 16.0   | 16.3   | 31.4   | 9.9    | 3.1    |

Conservative Growth

# Dentsply International, Inc.

221 W. Philadelphia Street ❑ P. O. Box 872 ❑ York, PA 17405 ❑ (717) 849–4718 ❑ Dividend reinvestment plan not available ❑ Web site: *www.dentsply.com* ❑ Listed: NASDAQ ❑ Ticker symbol: XRAY ❑ S&P rating: A- ❑ Value Line financial strength rating: B++

"Dentsply, a leading manufacturer of dental supplies, has been cashing in on the graying of both America and Europe," according to an article written by Harlan S. Byrne

for *Barron's* on January 10, 2005. "Thanks to several savvy acquisitions both here and abroad in the past five years, the York, Pa.-based company has expanded its product lineup to include new materials for bridges, crowns, and artificial teeth; new anesthetics, and prosthetic and endodontic devices."

Barron's also commented on the stock on August 30, 2004: "'We like the stock very much and have given it our highest rating, which happens to be a Buy,' Frank H. Pinkerton of Banc of America Securities tells *Barron's*. He feels Dentsply is ready for another acquisition, which could give an added push to company prospects and the stock.

"Overall, could the company ask for much better prospects?

"Hardly, given the graying of America. Baby boomers were on the cusp of those who had the advantage of fluoridization in water supplies—but many still have fallen victim to tooth decay. Boomers also are more apt to avail themselves of dental services than previous generations, given greater insurance coverage by employers. And even if they don't succumb to the cavities and deterioration of previous generations, they aren't about to forego cosmetic dental procedures while they get hair implants and tummy tucks."

## Company Profile

Dentsply designs, develops, manufactures, and markets a broad range of products for the dental market. The company believes that it is the world's leading manufacturer and distributor of dental prosthetics, precious metal dental alloys, dental ceramics, endodontic instruments and materials, prophylaxis paste, dental sealants, ultrasonic scalers, and crown and bridge materials; the leading United States manufacturer and distributor of dental x-ray equipment, dental handpieces, intraoral cameras, dental x-ray film holders, film mounts, and bone substitute/grafting materials; and a leading worldwide manufacturer or distributor of dental injectable anesthetics, impression materials, orthodontic appliances, dental cutting instruments, and dental implants.

Dentsply International Inc. is among the largest manufacturers of dental products in the world. The company has a presence in more than 120 countries, though its main operations take place in Canada, Germany, Switzerland, Italy, the UK, Japan, and Italy. The company markets its products under the following brand names: Caulk, Cavitron, Ceramco, Dentsply, Detrey, and Gende.

Dentsply International is a major company involved in the manufacture of dental products. Many of the company's products are best sellers in the domestic dental market. The company's operations encompass the design, manufacture, and marketing of a variety of dental products.

The company has an extensive sales network of around 1,800 sales representatives, distributors, and importers. Its products are manufactured both domestically and internationally, and have some of the most well established brand names in the industry, such as Caulk, Cavitron, Ceramco, Dentsply, Detrey, Midwest, R&R Rinn, and Trubyte.

The company operates under the following segments: US dental consumables; UK dental consumables, endodontics/professional division dental consumables; Africa/European dental laboratory business; Australia/Canada/Latin America/US pharmaceutical; US dental laboratory business/implants/orthodontics; and all others.

### The dental consumables

US and Europe/Japan/nondental segment produces small equipment, chair-side consumable products, and laboratory products. The segment is also engaged in design in the nondental business of the company. The operations of this segment are concentrated in Germany, Scandinavia, the United States, Iberia, Eastern Europe, and Japan.

### The endodontics/professional division

The Dental consumables/Asia segment designs and manufactures endodontic products for the Switzerland, Germany, and US markets. The segment also produces small equipment and chair-side consumable products for the domestic market. For the Chinese market, the segment produces laboratory products. The segment's operations also encompass sale and distribution of all products of the company to the Asian market and sale of endodontic products to countries that include Canada, Switzerland, Scandinavia, Benelux, and the United States.

The Australia/Canada/Latin America/U.S. pharmaceutical segment focuses largely on the design, production, sale, and distribution of the company's dental anesthetics.

This segment caters for the dental anesthetics demand of U.S. and Brazil markets. Furthermore, the segment also handles the selling and distribution of all products of the company to Canada, Australia, Mexico, and Latin America.

The U.S. dental laboratory business/implants/orthodontics segment caters to the U.S. market's demand for laboratory products. The segment is primarily focused on the design, manufacture, sale, and distribution of laboratory products. It also handles the global sale and distribution of the dental implant, bone generation, and orthodontic products of the company.

## Shortcomings to Bear in Mind

- "There is no rush to make new commitments to this equity," said George Rho, writing for *Value Line* on March 4, 2005. "Dentsply has an impressive track record, with consistent earnings growth supporting solid share-price appreciation. Moreover, given prevailing demographic trends, there's no reason that earnings won't keep ascending. The stock is only neutrally ranked for the year ahead, though, and valuations suggest that it won't shine out to 2008–2010. Thus, we would find the issue more appealing at moderately lower levels."

## Reasons to Buy

- On January 4, 2005, the company announced that it had acquired rights to a unique compound called Satif from the Sanofi-Aventis Group for an undisclosed amount. Gary Kunkle, Dentsply's CEO stated, "Satif is another excellent example of the progress our Office of Advanced Technology has made in their efforts to locate and acquire new technologies with potential applications in dentistry. Satif is a unique Titanium-Fluoride derivative, which has demonstrated in studies the ability to protect the tooth surface, which could be of particular value in preventive and aesthetic dentistry. We believe that the potential applications from this technology could be seen as a significant innovation in oral healthcare, similar to the discovery of the benefits of fluorides."

- *Standard & Poor's Stock Reports* gave Dentsply its highest rating, five stars, on November 1, 2004. Massimo Santicchia said, "In October 2004, XRAY launched its new dental anesthetic, Oraquix. In addition, it has introduced eighteen new products over the past three quarters, and plans to launch seven more during the 2004 fourth quarter. We project 2005 revenue of $1.78 billion, and expect the introduction of several new value-added products and productivity gains to incrementally boost margins and asset turnover."

  The S&P report went on to say, "Free cash grew at a compound annual rate of 29 percent over the past five years. We believe a return to long-term organic growth of 4 percent to 6 percent and the introduction of new value-added products should boost operating margins, return on capital and free cash flow. We would buy the stock."

- "While the company in recent times has been able to add twenty to twenty-five new products a year, it's beginning to look well beyond its current product markets," said Mr. Byrne in his *Barron's* article of August 30, 2004. "As a starter, it has a deal with Georgia Tech for the development of some radically new products. Mr. Kunkle doesn't spell it out, but predicts that at least one new prod-

uct will come from the joint work with Georgia Tech and avers that deals with other college labs are in the making. In any event, Dentsply said recently it had a 'full pipeline' of new products set for introduction in this year's second half."

Total assets: $2,801 million
Current ratio: 2.61
Common shares outstanding: 80 million
Return on 2004 shareholders' equity: 19.7%

|  |  | 2004 | 2003 | 2002 | 2001 | 2000 | 1999 | 1998 | 1997 |
|---|---|---|---|---|---|---|---|---|---|
| Revenues (millions) | | 1,694 | 1,571 | 1,514 | 1,129 | 890 | 831 | 795 | 721 |
| Net income (millions) | | 253.2 | 172.6 | 146.1 | 109.9 | 101.0 | 89.9 | 80.2 | 74.6 |
| Earnings per share | | 2.56 | 2.14 | 1.83 | 1.39 | 1.29 | 1.13 | 1.00 | .92 |
| Dividends per share | | .22 | .19 | .18 | .18 | .17 | .15 | .14 | .13 |
| Price | high | 56.8 | 47.4 | 43.5 | 34.7 | 28.9 | 19.5 | 23.4 | 21.2 |
| | low | 41.8 | 32.1 | 31.3 | 21.7 | 15.4 | 13.7 | 13.3 | 14.9 |

Aggressive Growth

# Devon Energy Corporation

20 North Broadway, Suite 1500 ❑ Oklahoma City, OK 73102–8260 ❑ (405) 552–4526 ❑ Dividend reinvestment plan not available ❑ Web site: *www.devonenergy.com* ❑ Ticker symbol: DVN ❑ Listed: NYSE ❑ S&P rating: B+ ❑ Value Line financial strength rating: B+

On January 20, 2005, Devon Energy Corporation announced that it had completed a multiyear program to divest noncore midstream assets. The midstream divestiture program was launched in 2002 and has involved nine separate transactions. The final transaction took place in mid-2005. Aggregate proceeds from these transactions are about $330 million.

"Devon's midstream operations continue to perform exceptionally well," said Darryl G. Smette, senior vice president of marketing and midstream. "These divestitures, which are in addition to the divestitures of producing oil and gas properties we announced in September, have allowed us to bring increased focus to our core midstream assets."

The divested assets include six gas processing plants and about 7,000 miles of gas gathering pipelines. The assets are situated in Oklahoma, Texas, Louisiana, Kansas, and Wyoming. The midstream assets sold in 2004 and expected to be sold in 2005 contributed about $48 million to Devon's marketing and midstream operating margin in 2004.

Following the divestitures, Devon is still one of the largest independent gas processors in North America. The company retains ownership in sixty-four gas processing plants in the United States and Canada, with aggregate net processing capacity of nearly 2.1 trillion cubic feet of natural gas per day. The company also owns an interest in 11,320 miles of gas gathering pipelines.

## Company Profile

Devon Energy Corporation is the largest U.S.-based independent oil and gas producer and one of the largest independent processors of natural gas and natural gas liquids in North America.

The company's portfolio of oil and gas properties provides stable, environmentally responsible production and a platform for future growth. About 86 percent of Devon's production is from North America. The company also operates in selected international areas, including Brazil, West Africa, the Middle East, and China. The company's production mix is about 60 percent natural gas and 40 percent oil and natural gas liquids, such as propane, butane, and ethane. Devon produces over 2.4 billion cubic feet of natural gas each day, about 4 percent of all the gas consumed in North America.

Headquartered in Oklahoma City, Devon has about 4,000 employees worldwide. Devon is a *Fortune* 500 company and is included in the S&P 500 index.

The company's primary goal is to build value per share by:

- Exploring for undiscovered oil and gas reserves.
- Purchasing and exploiting producing oil and gas properties.
- Enhancing the value of its production through marketing and midstream activities.
- Optimizing production operations to control costs.
- Maintaining a strong balance sheet.

## Shortcomings to Bear in Mind

- "We are downgrading DVN from Overweight to Equal-weight, said the analyst writing for Lehman Brothers—a leading brokerage firm—on February 4, 2005. "Strong share price appreciation since late 2003, combined with the c/flow reductions that we have built into the model as a result of planned assets sales, lower realized oil and gas prices and cash

cost creep have left DVN at about a 10 percent premium to broad peer group."

## Reasons to Buy

- "Devon is swimming in cash," said *BusinessWeek* on April 4, 2005. "Thanks to a 10 percent increase in production and rising oil and gas prices, profits jumped 26 percent last year. It's spending heavily to drill in areas such as the Barnett Shale in north Texas, the Gulf of Mexico, and offshore Brazil. But Devon is also hiking dividends and buying back shares—reflected in its 65.8 percent stock return in the past year. Criticized in the past for its spending to find new deposits, the Oklahoma City company now wins praise for the savings it has wrung from a string of acquisitions. No wonder some consider it a takeover target."

- Devon Energy Corporation reported record net earnings for the year ended December 31, 2004, of $2.2 billion, or $4.51 per common share ($4.38 per diluted common share). This was a 25 percent increase over Devon's 2003 net earnings of $1.7 billion, or $4.16 per common share ($4.04 per diluted common share). Per-share amounts reflect a two-for-one stock split completed in November 2004. A 10 percent increase in oil, gas, and natural gas liquids production and higher realized prices for these products led to the record results.

  "Devon delivered record-breaking performance in 2004, from nearly every perspective," said CEO J. Larry Nichols early in 2005. "Record production of 251 million barrels of oil equivalent and rising oil and gas prices led to record net earnings and Earnings per share. Furthermore, with drill-bit capital of $2.8 billion we added 313 million barrels of proved reserves, before price revisions. Simultaneously, the company reduced net debt by $1.8 billion with free cash flow. Devon is clearly performing at a very high level and we couldn't be more enthusiastic about our future."

- Devon's operating strategy balances lower-risk, near-term investment in the company's gas-weighted, North American asset base with longer-term investment in high-impact exploration projects. Notable operational achievements during 2004 include:

  - Devon completed its 100th horizontal natural gas well in the Barnett Shale field in north Texas in June, and at year-end had 144 horizontal wells on production. Horizontal wells account for about 22 percent of Devon's total Barnett Shale production of approximately 556 million cubic feet of gas equivalent per day.

  - A discovery on the Jack prospect in the deepwater Gulf of Mexico marked Devon's third discovery in the emerging lower Tertiary trend. The Jack prospect on Walker Ridge block 759 encountered more than 350 feet of oil pay. Devon has a 25 percent working interest in Jack.

  - The company drilled a successful delineation well on the St. Malo lower Tertiary prospect. Devon plans further drilling at St. Malo, Jack, and Cascade in 2005. Cascade was the company's initial lower Tertiary discovery in 2002.

  - A discovery on the BM-C-8 block, offshore Brazil, encountered more than 150 feet of oil pay. Devon has a 60 percent working interest in the block and will conduct additional drilling in 2005.

  - Production from Devon's 50 percent-owned deepwater Red Hawk field commenced in July. In total, Red Hawk is producing in excess of 120 million cubic feet of gas per day.

  - The first well in the Magnolia deepwater field was brought online in December. Two wells are now on stream. These wells are now producing a combined seven thousand barrels of oil equivalent (BOE) per day, net to Devon. Devon has a 25 percent working interest in Magnolia.

  - Devon received final governmental approvals for its wholly-owned Jackfish Canadian oil sands project in December. Jackfish is designed to produce 35,000 barrels of oil per day when fully operational in 2008.

- On December 2, 2004, *Standard & Poor's Stock Reports* awarded Devon Energy five stars, its highest rating. Charles LaPorta, CFA, said, "We believe DVN's recently announced divestiture of noncore acreage will help drive its relatively high finding and development costs down to more reasonable levels; significant high-impact exploration programs in the deepwater Gulf of Mexico and international geographies should meaningfully add to production in the 2006–2008 time frame. Meanwhile, the substantial excess cash generated from operations as well as divestiture proceeds are expected to be used to accelerate balance sheet improvements and repurchase up to 10 percent of the shares outstanding over the next eighteen months."

- Devon's Bridgeport Gas Processing Plant in north Texas has gas processing capacity of 650 million cubic feet per day and natural gas liquids production capacity of 54,000 barrels per day. It serves the largest gas field in Texas, the Barnett Shale field. Devon produces about 550 million cubic feet of gas equivalent per day from the Barnett Shale field.

A decade ago the Barnett Shale formation in north Texas represented a geological puzzle that had gone unsolved for more than forty years. Geoscientists knew vast energy reserves were sealed inside the tight, black rock formed from organic deposits 325 million years ago. The challenge was recovering them.

The Barnett is not particularly deep or impervious to the drill bit, but it would take more than conventional thinking to recover the gas locked inside the stingy shale known for its low porosity and high complexity.

Devon Energy is a pioneer in the Barnett, using innovations in technology to literally crack open the shale to release the natural gas sealed inside. Engineers are using a method known as fracturing to foster permeability in the rock. Crews inject fresh water and a little sand into the shale at a very high pressure to shatter the surrounding formation and release gas trapped inside. The technology has given Devon access to vast reserves, transforming this challenging play northwest of Fort Worth into one of the nation's most important natural gas producing zones.

Devon has drilled about 800 wells into the Barnett Shale since 2001. Use of fracturing technology has helped Devon increase its Barnett production from 345 million cubic feet of natural gas equivalent per day to nearly 600 million today.

In all, Devon is operating more than 1,700 wells in what is known as the Barnett's core area, where dense layers of limestone separate the shale's gas deposits from the watery Ellenberger formation which lies below. Today, Devon is continuing to confront the most challenging questions in the Barnett. It ventured outside the core with horizontal drilling projects where geological complexities have impeded development in the past. Those projects have shown promise, and Devon geoscientists continue to explore the Barnett's noncore area, where it is a major lease holder with 390,000 net acres of land.

Through Devon's pioneering effort, the Barnett Shale formation has emerged as the largest natural gas field in Texas and one of the most important gas fields in the nation. With recent inroads into the vast noncore area, the Barnett has potential to remain one of the country's most vital energy resources for years to come.

Total assets: $29,736 million
Current ratio: 1.16
Common shares outstanding: 486 million
Return on 2004 shareholders' equity: 17.6%

|  |  | 2004 | 2003 | 2002 | 2001 | 2000 | 1999 | 1998 | 1997 |
|---|---|---|---|---|---|---|---|---|---|
| Revenues (millions) |  | 9,189 | 7,352 | 4,316 | 3,075 | 2,784 | 734 | 388 | 313 |
| Net income (millions) |  | 2,176 | 1,731 | 549 | 674 | 715 | 87 | 48 | 75 |
| Earnings per share |  | 4.38 | 4.04 | 1.71 | 2.52 | 2.73 | .67 | .50 | 1.09 |
| Dividends per share |  | .20 | .10 | .10 | .10 | .10 | .10 | .10 | .10 |
| Price | high | 41.6 | 29.4 | 26.5 | 33.4 | 32.4 | 22.5 | 20.6 | 24.6 |
|  | low | 25.9 | 21.2 | 16.9 | 15.3 | 15.7 | 10.1 | 13.1 | 9.9 |

Aggressive Growth

# Dollar General Corporation

100 Mission Ridge ❑ Goodlettsville, TN 37072–2170 ❑ (615) 855–5525 ❑ Direct dividend reinvestment program is available: (800) 368–5948 ❑ Fiscal years end on Saturday nearest to January 31 ❑ Web site: *www.dollargeneral.com* ❑ Listed: NYSE ❑ Ticker symbol: DG ❑ S&P rating: A+ ❑ Value Line financial strength rating: B

In 1939, with only a third grade education, J.L. Turner formed his own company in Scottsville, Kentucky, with his son, Cal. Each invested $5,000 in the new venture—J.L. Turner & Son—and began work as wholesalers of basic dry goods.

In 1945, the Turners switched from wholesale to retail in order to get rid of an oversupply of ladies' lingerie. They opened their first retail store in Albany, Kentucky, in May 1946. By 1955, J.L. Turner & Son owned and operated thirty-five self-service dry goods stores with annual sales reaching $2 million.

The Turners' dollar store concept, (no item above $1), was adopted on an experimental basis in 1955, and the first Dollar General Store opened in Springfield, Kentucky, in May of that year. The new concept was extremely successful, and in ten years the company had grown to 255 stores with annual sales of $25.8 million.

Third generation Cal Turner, Jr. joined the company in 1965 and became a director one year later. In 1968, the company changed its name to Dollar General Corporation and went public. By the end of 1976, retail sales had reached $109 million.

In 1977, Cal Turner, Jr. was named president of Dollar General. Later that year, the company acquired United Dollar Stores, an Arkansas-based retail chain. Dollar General saw great success in the early 1980s averaging a 23 percent increase in total revenues and 33 percent increase in net income between 1981 and 1984.

Dollar General continued its growth pattern in 1983 when it bought the 280-store P.N. Hirsch chain, a division of Interco, Inc. Two years later, the company increased its presence in the Florida market by acquiring the 203-store Eagle Family Discount chain, also an Interco, Inc., property. Growth through acquisition, however, did not prove to be successful. Financial results for 1986 gave news of a 3 percent decline in sales and a 76 percent decline in earnings.

In 1988, Cal Jr. succeeded his father as Chairman of the Board. Determined to set a solid strategy for long-term growth, the company saw a turnaround that led to an average 16.5 percent increase in total revenues and a 40.7 percent increase in net income between 1990 and 1993. These results gave Dollar General the confidence to pursue store growth again. In 1995, with a newly articulated strategy of being a "customer-driven distributor of consumable basics," the company began to grow its distribution center capacity to support additional stores and its merchandising strategy.

Today, the company has distribution centers in Scottsville, Kentucky; Ardmore, Oklahoma; South Boston, Virginia; Indianola, Mississippi; Fulton, Missouri; Alachua, Florida; and Zanesville, Ohio. In January 2005, the company began hiring 525 workers for still another distribution center, this one in Jonesville, SC, which opened in the spring of that year.

## Company Profile

Dollar General is a *Fortune* 500 discount retailer with 7,321 neighborhood stores in twenty-seven states (with a few in three new states), as of December 31, 2004. Dollar General stores offer convenience and value to customers, by offering consumable basics, items that are frequently used and replenished, such as food, snacks, health and beauty aids, and cleaning supplies, as well as an appealing selection of basic apparel, housewares, and seasonal items at everyday low prices. The typical Dollar General store has 6,750 square feet of selling space and is situated within five miles of its target customers. The average Dollar General store is staffed by six to ten employees, including the manager. Many of the stores' customers earn a small paycheck or depend on monthly government assistance. A considerable number are retired.

Although the company does business mostly in twenty-seven states, the largest concentration are in such states as Alabama (350 stores), Florida (397), North Carolina (371), Ohio (355), Pennsylvania (364), Tennessee (340) and Texas (814). Among the states with fewest stores are Maryland (sixty-two stores), Nebraska (seventy-nine), New Jersey (twenty-four), and Delaware (twenty-four).

## Shortcomings to Bear in Mind

- Retail businesses rarely lack for competitors. New ideas in merchandising come along periodically and give fits to companies that are unable to adjust to a new environment. The "big boxes," for instance (such as Wal-Mart, Staples, Bed Bath & Beyond, Home Depot, and Lowe's) have punched holes in such companies as Montgomery Ward, Sears, J. C. Penney, and the thousands of mom-and-pop operations.

## Reasons to Buy

- In recent years, store expansion has been aggressive, with store count increasing from 2,059 on January 31, 1995, to 6,192 on February 28, 2003. The company opened 622 outlets in fiscal 2003 and 673 stores in the year ended January 30, 2004. In the year beginning January 31, 2004, DG plans to add 675 new stores. What's more, new store openings are likely to continue at its current pace in 2005 and 2006. In fiscal 2003, about one-half of new units were situated in small towns, with the rest in more densely populated areas.

  While most new units are slated to open in the company's existing twenty-seven-state market area, Dollar General opened stores in three new states in 2004: Wisconsin, Arizona, and New Mexico.

  In addition to the 675 new conventional Dollar General stores opened in 2004, the company says it plans to continue testing its Dollar General Market concept by adding twenty Dollar General Market stores in 2004. The Dollar General Market is a larger format store that offers an expanded selection of Dollar General's core mix of consumable basic merchandise, apparel, seasonal merchandise, home entertainment items, including DVDs, videos, and magazines, as well as a selection of fresh produce and a broad assortment of refrigerated, frozen, and nonperishable food items.

- To support store growth, Dollar General opened a new distribution center in the Southeastern United States in 2005, and to add another distribution center in 2006. The company also plans to expand its distribution facilities in Ardmore, Oklahoma; South Boston, Virginia; and Indianola, Mississippi and to convert these facilities to a dual sortation system, which the company believes will significantly increase operating capacity.

- Dollar General doesn't try to compete with Wal-Mart's broad range of goods. "When you're in a 'big box' retail environment, you're obligated to compete on assortment," said CEO David Perdue. "In our 'small box' environment, we don't have that luxury. So the merchandise mix we put in our stores has to be much more productive."

  While Wal-Mart has moved into big cities, competing with major supermarket chains, Dollar General had concentrated on small towns, opening stores in cities with a population below 25,000, and rarely more than 75,000. Its major competitors are Family Dollar, Dollar Tree, 99 Cents Only, and Fred's.

- "This stock's long-term potential is appealing," said Jerome H. Kaplan, writing for *Value Line Investment Survey* on February 11, 2005. "We like Dollar General's merchandise strategy that combines value, convenience, and a consumable product mix, which is even starting to appeal to higher-income customers. Moreover, 10 percent annual square-footage growth, along with mid-single-digit comp growth, should translate into meaningful share-earnings increases through 2007–2009."

- "We recently raised our recommendation to BUY, from HOLD, based on valuation," said Jason N. Asaeda, writing for *Standard & Poor's Stock Reports* on December 9, 2004. "Despite difficult industry conditions, DG posted a 3.2 percent same-store sales increase in its recent third quarter, well ahead of its closest dollar store peers. This achievement, in our view, reflects favorable customer response to changes made to store operations in fiscal 2005 that were aimed at improving merchandise flow and raising sales productivity."

- "Dollar General Corporation is one of several rapidly growing chains of self-service stores that are giving giant retailers like Wal-Mart a run for their money," said Kevin Lamiman, writing for *Better Investing* in July 2004. "The company locates its stores mostly in small cities, generally sticking to communities with populations below 75,000. When Dollar General opens stores in larger cities, it chooses neighborhoods inhabited by lower-income consumers, its core customers. It therefore can compete not only by offering low prices, but also by providing convenience in the form of shorter trips, easier parking and quicker shopping than is possible at 'big box' stores."

- On December 2, 2004, Lehman Brothers, a major brokerage house, had this comment, "Dollar General's return on assets, lease-adjusted, has been rising steadily since 2001, and though it slipped slightly in the latest quarter, it is still one of the best returns of the sector, at 9.7 percent. Yet we see more room for improvement, as the company benefits from the significant investments in technology made recently and the steps being taken by the new management team to improve operations, especially store-level execution. Three specific potential opportunities include 1) better in-stocks and higher inventory turns from the roll-out of automatic replenishment and new in-store procedures; 2) lower shrink, which the company believes could decline by 50 basis points (*there are 100 basis points in one percent*) over the next several years from current levels; and 3) improved procurement, including from increased importing of high-margin merchandise and more 'opportunistic' buys."

Total assets: $2,842 million
Current ratio: 2.10
Common shares outstanding: 332 million
Return on 2004 shareholders' equity: 21.2%

| | 2004 | 2003 | 2002 | 2001 | 2000 | 1999 | 1998 | 1997 |
|---|---|---|---|---|---|---|---|---|
| Revenues (millions) | 7,661 | 6,872 | 6,100 | 5,323 | 4,551 | 3,888 | 3,221 | 2,627 |
| Net income (millions) | 344 | 301 | 265 | 208 | 170 | 219 | 182 | 145 |
| Earnings per share | 1.04 | .92 | .75 | .62 | .51 | .65 | .54 | .43 |
| Dividends per share | .16 | .14 | .13 | .13 | .13 | .10 | .08 | .09 |
| Price    high | 23.2 | 23.4 | 20.0 | 24.0 | 23.2 | 26.1 | 24.2 | 16.4 |
| low | 16.9 | 9.5 | 11.7 | 10.5 | 13.4 | 14.9 | 12.8 | 7.8 |

# Donaldson Company, Inc.

P. O. Box 1299 ❑ Minneapolis, MN 55440 ❑ (952) 887–3753 ❑ Dividend reinvestment plan available: Wells Fargo Bank Minnesota, N.A., Shareholder Services, P. O. Box 64854, St. Paul, MN 55164–0854 ❑ Web site: *www.donaldson. com* ❑ Fiscal years end July 31 ❑ Listed: NYSE ❑ Ticker symbol: DCI ❑ S&P rating: A+ ❑ Value Line financial strength rating: B++

You expect to see Donaldson Company's filtration products on the heavy-duty truck traveling the interstate highway, or on the construction equipment on the side of the road. "After all, that's where our company began," said William G. Van Dyke, the company's chairman of the board.

"But you aren't as likely to expect our filters in the camera that captures memories of your daughter's birthday party. Or in the backup generator providing electricity to your computer center or office.

"Donaldson filters and related products are in many unexpected places—in products you see, touch and use every day. Our long-term, focused investment in filtration technology has created the leverage to carry us into new product lines, new markets and new geography. This diversification in end markets, linked by a common technology base, has enabled us to smooth out the ups and downs of the various market segments and to achieve our 12th consecutive year of double-digit earnings growth—no small feat in these turbulent economic times.

"Donaldson holds more than 450 U.S. patents and related patents filed around the world, and our employees are constantly developing new ways to utilize superior filtration and acoustic technology for products that are still years away from market."

## Company Profile

Donaldson Company is a leading worldwide provider of filtration systems and replacement parts. Founded in 1915, Donaldson is a technology-driven company committed to satisfying customers' needs

for filtration solutions through innovative research and development.

The company's product mix includes air and liquid filters, as well as exhaust and emission-control products for mobile equipment; in-plant air-cleaning systems; air intake systems for industrial gas turbines; and specialized filters for such diverse applications as computer disk drives, aircraft passenger cabins, and semiconductor processing.

Donaldson operates plants throughout the world. Of these, fourteen facilities are in the United States, three in the United Kingdom, two each in Germany, Japan, China, South Africa, and Mexico. Finally, the company has one plant in each of the following countries: Australia, France, Hong Kong, Italy, Belgium, and India.

The company has two reporting segments engaged in the design, manufacture and sale of systems to filter air and liquid and other complementary products:

The Engine Products segment makes air intake systems, exhaust systems, and liquid filtration systems. The company sells to original-equipment manufacturers (OEMs) in the construction, industrial, mining, agriculture, and transportation markets, independent distributors, OEM dealer networks, private-label account, and large private fleets. This segment is further subdivided as follows:

Off-Road Equipment includes products sold to industrial equipment and defense contractor OEMs (original equipment manufacturers) for agriculture, construction, mining, and military applications.

The company's Truck operation produces products sold to manufacturers of light-, medium-, and heavy-duty trucks.

In the Aftermarket sector, Donaldson sells a broad line of replacement filters and hard parts for all of the equipment applications noted above.

Industrial Products consist of dust, fume, and mist collectors, static and pulse-clean air filter systems of industrial gas turbines, computer disk drive filter products, and other specialized air-filtration systems. DCI sells to various industrial end-users, OEMs of gas-fired turbines, and OEMs and users requiring highly purified air. This segment is further broken down, as follows:

Under Industrial Air Filtration, the company sells under such trade names as Donaldson Torit and Donaldson Torit DCE. It provides equipment to control and capture process dust, fumes and mist in manufacturing and industrial processing plants.

Under Gas Turbine Systems, Donaldson provides complete systems to deliver clean air to gas-fired turbines. Products include self-cleaning filter units, static air filter units, inlet ducting and silencing, evaporative coolers, chiller coils, inlet heating, and anti-icing systems.

Under Ultrafilter, the company provides a complete line of compressed air filters and a wide assortment of replacement filters, a complete offering of refrigeration and desiccant dryers, condensate management devices, and after-sale services.

Under Special Applications, the company provides a wide range of high-efficiency media, filters, and filtration systems for various commercial, industrial, and product applications.

Key Investment Characteristics:

• Fifteen consecutive years of record earnings growth.

• Average annual Earnings per share (EPS) for the fifteen-year period: 16 percent.

• Revenue for fiscal 2004: $1.415 billion.

• Consistent growth drivers: diversified portfolio of filtration businesses, global marketplace coverage and aggressive cost management.

• Targeting double-digit annual earnings growth.

• Strong balance sheet.

• At the end of fiscal 2004, total backlog climbed to $376 million, up twenty percent from a year earlier.

• Forty-nine consecutive years of quarterly dividends.

• An active share-repurchase program: The company has reduced shares outstanding for fifteen consecutive years. (When shares are repurchased, Earnings per share tend to increase—even when earnings remain level.)

## Shortcomings to Bear in Mind

■ Some analysts point out the risk factors for Donaldson because of greater shortages of steel and an inability of the company to recover these higher costs, along with unrest in parts of the world, most notably Iraq.

■ The *Standard & Poor's Stock Report's* analyst, Stewart Scharf, had these observations on March 2, 2005: "We maintain our HOLD recommendation, as we believe the shares are fairly priced, based on our valuation models, and in light of volatile steel and other commodity prices, along with, in our view, some difficult comparisons ahead."

## Reasons to Buy

■ "Donaldson continues to build on its outstanding track record," said Eric M. Gottlieb, writing for *Value Line Investment Survey* on January 28, 2005. "For fiscal 2005 (ends July 31, 2005), we look for revenues to rise about 13 percent, as Donaldson stands to benefit from recovering world economies, highlighted by the Middle East and Asia. Entering the year, the order backlog was roughly

$215 million, about 20 percent higher than at the end of fiscal 2003. Looking further out, acquisitions, an increasing international presence, and new products should help support steady revenue gains through the late decade."

- Donaldson has an enviable record of growth. In the past ten years (1994–2004), Earnings per share advanced from $0.30 to $1.18, (with no dips along the way), a compound annual growth rate of 14.7 percent. In the same span, dividends climbed from $0.06 to $0.22, a compound annual growth rate 13.9 percent.

  Despite this fine record of growth, the stock sells at a very reasonable price/earnings multiple.

- In fiscal 2004, a company official said, "Fluid dynamics has played a vital role in positioning Donaldson's Torit Down-Flo Oval dust collector product as the pace-setter for its industry. The proprietary oval design, introduced in 2000, delivers longer life and better perfor-

mance. More than 1.4 million pounds of dust and 16,000 hours of laboratory and job testing went into developing the DownFlo Oval. The DFO won the 2002 'Product of the Year' recognition from *Filtration and Separation* magazine, the leading trade publication for the industry."

- The spokesman went on to say, "Today's demanding tolerances on moving mechanical parts require finer filtration to prevent particle wear and eventual failure. At the same time, higher pressures and flow rates require robust and reliable filters. Our Donaldson engineers factored in the intense pressures of hydraulic circuits and transmissions when designing Duramax filters. We also recognized the economic pressures on manufacturers and equipment owners to extend their maintenance cycles. With the optimum balance of performance and cost, the Duramax brand offers the highest-rated, medium pressure spin-on filter in its category."

Total assets: $1,001.6 million
Current ratio: 2.02
Common shares outstanding: 86 million
Return on 2004 shareholders' equity: 21.3%

| | 2004 | 2003 | 2002 | 2001 | 2000 | 1999 | 1998 | 1997 |
|---|---|---|---|---|---|---|---|---|
| Revenues (millions) | 1,415 | 1,218 | 1,126 | 1,137 | 1,092 | 944 | 940 | 833 |
| Net income (millions) | 106.3 | 95.3 | 86.9 | 75.5 | 70.2 | 62.4 | 57.1 | 50.6 |
| Earnings per share | 1.18 | 1.05 | .95 | .83 | .76 | .66 | .57 | .50 |
| Dividends per share | .22 | .18 | .16 | .15 | .14 | .12 | .10 | .09 |
| Price      high | 34.4 | 30.8 | 22.5 | 20.2 | 14.4 | 13.0 | 13.4 | 13.8 |
| low | 25.0 | 16.1 | 15.0 | 12.2 | 9.4 | 8.5 | 6.8 | 7.7 |

Aggressive Growth

# Dover Corporation

280 Park Avenue ❑ New York, NY 10017–1292 ❑ (212) 922–1640 ❑ Direct dividend reinvestment plan available: (800) 842–7629 ❑ Web site: *www.dovercorporation.com* ❑ Ticker symbol: DOV ❑ S&P rating: A- ❑ Value Line financial strength rating: A

Dover Corporation announced on September 1, 2004, that its Dover Technologies subsidiary had completed the acquisition of Corning Frequency Control (CFC), a division of Corning Incorporated. CFC is a leading supplier of quartz crystals, oscillators, and filters to the communications, test and instrumentation, position location, automotive, and military/aerospace electronic markets.

CFC will be integrated into Dover Technologies' Vectron International division. "This acquisition is in keeping with Vectron International's strategy to be a leader in the precision frequency generation and control industry," said Rick Hajec, President, Vectron International. "We believe the strengths of this combination offer a great deal of value to our customers. The expanded product offerings, dynamic corporate culture and dedication to innovation and customer service of the new Vectron give us a strong industry position and one of the most comprehensive lines of custom engineered solutions in the industry. We have a world-class staff to support these products, as well as global manufacturing and services to satisfy the needs of our customers throughout the world."

Vectron International is a world leader in the design, manufacturing, and marketing of frequency generation and frequency control products. With ten development and manufacturing centers in the United States, Europe, and China, the company supplies products that fulfill critical functions in the telecommunications, data communications, wireless, military, satellite communications, and multimedia markets in both consumer and industrial applications worldwide.

## Company Profile

Dover Corporation is a diversified industrial manufacturer with over $5 billion in annual revenues and is comprised of about fifty operating companies that manufacture specialized industrial products and manufacturing equipment.

Dover's overall strategy is to acquire and develop platform businesses, marked by growth, innovation, and higher-than-average profits margins. Traditionally, the company has focused on purchasing entities that could operate independently (stand-alones). However, over the past ten years, Dover has put increased emphasis on also acquiring businesses that can be added to existing operations (add-ons).

On October 1, 2003, Dover completed its largest-ever acquisition with the $326-million purchase of WARN Industries, the world's most recognized brand in winches and wheel hubs for off-road vehicles. WARN makes equipment and accessories to enhance the performance of four-wheel-drive and all-terrain vehicles. The Oregon-based company, founded in 1948 to manufacture locking hubs to convert World War II Jeeps into on-road vehicles, developed the first recreational winch in 1959. In addition to specialized wheel hubs, WARN makes self-recovery, towing, and utility winches.

### A New Breakdown of Operations

In the fall of 2004, Dover announced that it would expand its existing subsidiary structure from four to six reporting market segments and concurrently realigned its forty-nine operating businesses in thirteen more focused business groupings. Management believes that this realignment will better-position Dover for "enhanced growth by providing increased management oversight of its operating businesses by expanding the company's acquisition capacity and by supporting the development of future executive management talent."

Effective January 1, 2005, the six subsidiaries and their respective operating company groups were:

### Dover Diversified

• Industrial Equipment: Crenlo, Performance Motorsports, and Sargent

• Process Equipment: Graphics Microsystems, Hydratight Sweeney, SWEP, Tranter PHE, and Waukesha Bearings

### Dover Electronics

• Components: Dielectric, Dow-Key, K&L Microwave, Kurz-Kasch, Novacap, and Vectron

• Commercial Equipment: Hydro Systems, and Triton

### Dover Industries

• Mobile Equipment: Heil Environmental, Heil Trailer, Marathon, and Somero

• Service Equipment: Chief Automotive, Koolant Koolers, PDQ, and Rotary Lift

### Dover Resources

• Petroleum Equipment: C. Lee Cook, Energy Products Group

• Fluid Solutions: Blackmer, OPW Fluid Transfer Group, OPW Fueling Components, RPA Technologies, and Wilden

• Materials Handling: De-Sta-Co Industries, Texas Hydraulics, Tulsa Winch, and WARN Industries

### Dover Systems

• Food Equipment: DI Foodservice, and Hill Phoenix

• Packaging: Belvac, SWF, and Tipper Tie

### Dover Technologies

• Circuit Assembly and Test: Alphasem, DEK, Everett Charles, Hover-Davis, OK International, Universal, Vitronics, and Soltec

• Product Identification: Imaje, and Mark Andy

## Shortcomings to Bear in Mind

■ Some analysts point out such risks as:
  • Reduced industrial capital spending in a rising interest rate environment
  • Deterioration in demand for technology products, should the semiconductor cycle peak
  • Rising raw material costs

■ Dover does not have the typical pattern of a growth company. Earnings per share have fluctuated widely over the years. For instance, EPS hit a peak in 2000 of $2.57, but retreated to $0.82 the following year.

■ *Standard & Poor's Stock Reports* viewed Dover somewhat unfavorably on February 1, 2005. John F. Hingher, CFA, said, "We have a HOLD recommendation on the shares, given our positive view of management's ability to generate strong free cash flow, expected continuing solid growth in the industrial economy, inherent operating leverage of DOV's businesses, and consistent dividend payments. In our opinion, these factors are adequately discounted in the current price, particularly taking into account an expected slowdown in the Technologies segment."

## Reasons to Buy

■ Dover announced on August 31, 2004, that its Dover Resources subsidiary had completed the acquisition of US Synthetic Corporation, a leading supplier of polycrystalline diamond cutters (PDCs) used in drill bits for oil and gas exploration. Based in Orem, Utah, US Synthetic joined the Energy Products Group of companies in the Dover Resources subsidiary.

"We are very excited about our future with Dover," said Louis Pope, President and Chief Executive Officer of US Synthetic. "We believe joining Dover will allow US Synthetic to continue to grow, while retaining our character as a company. We see this transaction as beneficial to all the stakeholders in our organization."

"US Synthetic is a fine example of the kind of company that makes up the Energy Products Group, Dover Resources and Dover," said Vernon Pontes, President of Dover's Energy Products Group. "It is a company with a strong management team, a culture of innovation, industry leading R&D capabilities, strong customer relationships and a focus on improving its customer economics."

The companies in Dover's Energy Products Group, which include Norris, Alberta Oil Tool, Quartzdyne, Ferguson Beauregard, Norriseal, and now US Synthetic, provide a variety of products which facilitate the drilling, completion, and production of oil and gas wells.

- On January 28, 2005, *Value Line Investment Survey* had some favorable comments to make on Dover. Its analyst, David M. Reimer, said, "Sales growth and improved returns on investment remain the two most important objectives. Dover has a good track record of increasing sales through product development, geographic expansion, and market-share gains. Add-on acquisitions have, and will continue to, play a key role in raising the top line (*sales*). Management is careful to ensure that purchased businesses are leaders within their respective sectors, well run, a good fit with existing operations, and additive to sales and operating income."

- Dover has built its group of companies largely through acquisitions. However, management is extremely careful when considering which companies to bring into the fold. Management has these strict rules to guide its decisions:

  - We seek manufacturers of high value-added, engineered products.
  - Our focus is on equipment and machinery sold to a broad customer base of industrial and/or commercial users.
  - We prefer companies that are niche-oriented market leaders with either a number one or a strong number two market position.
  - Candidates should have strong national distribution (if not international, which is preferred).
  - Dover is decentralized—we will only buy businesses which have strong management teams in place. We expect management of each operating company to behave as the emotional owners of that business and we have longer term financial incentives designed to encourage continued growth of the business.
  - Our judgment on the skill, energy, ethics, and compatibility of the top executives at each acquisition candidate is one of the most critical factors in our decision making.
  - We expect that operating companies will continue to be run by the management team in place upon acquisition. This reflects our decentralized structure and the fact that Dover buys companies for the long-term; we do not have a 'portfolio' mentality.
  - Since we seek market leaders, we expect outstanding operating financial performance that can be built upon. EBIT's above 15 percent are the norm in Dover operating companies. We also expect that any business we own will generate significant real growth over time.

Total assets: $5,488 million
Current ratio: 1.59
Common shares outstanding: 203 million
Return on 2004 shareholders' equity: 14.1%

| | 2004 | 2003 | 2002 | 2001 | 2000 | 1999 | 1998 | 1997 |
|---|---|---|---|---|---|---|---|---|
| Revenues (millions) | 5,488 | 4,413 | 4,184 | 4,460 | 5,401 | 4,446 | 3,978 | 4,548 |
| Net income (millions) | 413 | 285 | 211 | 167 | 525 | 395 | 326 | 393 |
| Earnings per share | 2.00 | 1.40 | 1.04 | .82 | 2.57 | 1.87 | 1.45 | 1.74 |
| Dividends per share | .62 | .57 | .54 | .52 | .48 | .44 | .40 | .36 |
| Price    high | 44.1 | 40.4 | 43.6 | 43.6 | 54.4 | 47.9 | 39.9 | 36.7 |
| low | 35.1 | 22.8 | 23.5 | 26.45 | 34.1 | 29.3 | 25.5 | 24.1 |

# Dow Chemical Company

2030 Dow Center ❑ Midland, MI 48674 ❑ (969) 636–2876 ❑ Dividend reinvestment plan available: (800) 369–5606 ❑ Web site: *www.dow.com* ❑ Ticker symbol: DOW ❑ Listed: NYSE ❑ S&P rating: B ❑ Value Line financial strength rating: B++

"Four years ago, William S. Stavropoulos stepped aside as chief executive of Dow Chemical Company, turning the job over to his handpicked successor, Michael D. Parker, a thirty-four-year veteran. Parker lasted two years," according to an article in *BusinessWeek* on January 31, 2005. "As losses deepened and Dow's share price melted down, Stavropoulos who had stayed on as chairman, reclaimed the CEO post in December 2002. Last November, the baton was passed to then-COO Andrew N. Liveris. And this time, it looks as if the new guy—a Dow lifer—will stick.

"What's different? For one, Dow is much leaner. Over the past two years, Dow has gone through a deep restructuring, or as Liveris terms it, 'an intervention.' The Midland (Mich.) Company has closed or sold off dozens of plants and cut 7,000 jobs, or 14 percent of its global payroll.

"Another difference is rising global demand for Dow's chemicals and plastics, especially from China. Indeed, Dow's upswing comes as the chemicals sector is emerging from a punishing slowdown. After five years of little-to-no change in total output and meager revenue growth, industry-wide sales surged nearly 9 percent last year and are expected to grow another 6 percent in 2005, to $531 billion, according to *American Chemistry Council,* an industry group."

The *BusinessWeek* article went on to say, "Now fifty, Liveris joined Dow in 1976 just after getting his bachelor's degree in chemical engineering. But he has preserved something of an outsider's perspective, having been born and raised in Darwin, Australia."

## Company Profile

Dow is a leader in science and technology, providing innovative chemical, plastic, and agricultural products and services to many essential consumer markets. With annual sales of $40 billion, Dow serves customers in 175 countries and a wide range of markets that are vital to human progress, including food, transportation, health and medicine, personal and home care, and building and construction, among others.

The Dow Chemical Company is a multinational corporation, the second-largest chemical company in the world—DuPont is number one.

Dow is the world's largest producer of plastics, including polystyrene, polyurethanes, polyethylene terephthalate, polypropylene, and synthetic rubbers. It is also a major producer of the chemicals calcium chloride, and ethylene oxide, as well as various acrylates, surfactants, and cellulose resins. It produces many agricultural chemicals, perhaps being most famous for its pesticide Lorsban. At the consumer level, the company's best-known products include Saran wrap, Ziploc bags (which now have been sold to SC Johnson), and Styrofoam.

Dow Chemical Company dates back to 1897. At that time, its founder, Herbert Henry Dow, set out to extract chlorides and bromides from brine deposits which were found underground at Midland, Michigan. Its initial products included bromine and bleach. During these early years, the company established a tradition of rapidly diversifying its product line. Within twenty years, Dow had become a major producer of agricultural chemicals, elemental chlorine, phenol and other dyestuffs, and magnesium metal.

During the Great Depression, Dow began production of plastic resins, which would grow to become one of the corporation's major businesses. Its first plastic products were ethylcellulose which was made in 1935 and polystyrene made in 1937.

In 1930, Dow built its first plant to produce magnesium extracted from seawater rather than underground brine. Growth of this business made Dow a strategically important business during World War II, as magnesium became important in fabricating lightweight parts for airplanes. Also during the war, Dow and Corning began their joint venture, Dow Corning, to produce silicones for military and later civilian use.

Following World War II, Dow began expanding abroad, founding its first foreign subsidiary in Japan in 1952, with several other nations following rapidly thereafter. Based largely on its burgeoning plastics business, Dow opened a consumer products division beginning with Saran wrap in 1953. Based on its growing chemicals and plastics businesses, Dow's sales exceeded $1 billion in 1964, $2 billion in 1971, and $10 billion in 1980.

In September 2004, Dow obtained the naming rights of the Saginaw County Event Center in nearby Saginaw, Michigan, and the facility's new name is now The Dow Event Center. The deal is worth $10 million, and is said to last until 2014. The center houses the OHL ice hockey team, Saginaw Spirit.

Today, Dow is the world's largest producer of plastics, and with its 1999 acquisition of Union Carbide has become a major player in the petrochemical industry as well.

Dow is also a world leader in the production of olefins and styrene, hydrocarbons and energy. Other businesses include advanced electronic materials and industrial biotechnology.

More than 60 percent of Dow's revenues come from abroad. In fact, most of the company's basic chemicals expansion is being directed at Asia and the Mideast.

## Shortcomings to Bear in Mind

- Stuart Plesser, writing for *Value Line Investment Survey* on January 21, 2005, had this comment: "These neutrally ranked shares offer limited long-term appreciation potential. We expect earnings to peak sometime in 2006–2007 (at about $5.50 per share) and to decline significantly by 2008. We note that Dow is a cyclical stock and that, historically, the best time to sell such issues is sometime before earnings start to peak."

- Although this is a Growth and Income stock, you should be aware that dividends have not been raised every year. In fact, in the past ten years (1994–2004), the dividend increased from $0.87 to $1.34, a compound annual growth rate of only 4.4 percent. On the plus side, there is no indication that the company is likely to cut the dividend—even during years when earnings were depressed, as they were in 2001 and 2002.

## Reasons to Buy

- Dow reported annual 2004 sales of $40.2 billion, compared with $32.6 billion the prior year—a 23 percent increase. Net income, moreover, was $2.8 billion, up from $1.7 billion in 2003. Overall volume increased 6 percent, compared with the prior year. Price was up 17 percent, more than offsetting a $3.4 billion increase in feedstock and energy costs compared with 2003. As a result, the company achieved significant additional margin expansion and has now recovered about one third of the margin lost between 1995 and 2002.

Commenting on the company's results, Mr. Liveris said, "We began 2004 determined to maintain the momentum of our drive for financial fitness, to sustain the gains of 2003 and to further develop the foundation for long-term strategic growth. Supported by improving chemical industry fundamentals, we achieved success on all fronts."

- On March 11, 2005, *Standard & Poor's Stock Reports* was gung ho on Dow Chemical, giving it a five-star rating, its best.

  Richard O'Reilly said, "We have a strong BUY recommendation on the shares. We believe the commodity chemical industry's supply/demand fundamentals will continue to show cyclical improvement over the next two years. DOW plans additional overhead cost reductions and a continued focus on capital discipline, as capital spending in 2005 should remain well below depreciation. We view the dividend, which provides a yield well above the market average, as secure."

- "We are reiterating our Favorable rating for the chemical companies and our Overweight ratings for commodity players," said analyst Andrew Rosenfeld writing for Prudential Equity Group, LLC, on January 28, 2005. "We forecast that demand for commodity chemicals (i.e., volume) will continue to improve in 2005, as the result of: 1) a continuing economic recovery, although at slightly lower rates; 2) low inventories leading to an attempt by customers to replenish

low stocks (inventory restocking) and; 3) lower energy and raw material prices."

Mr. Rosenfeld also said, "We believe that the tide has changed for the chemical industry as the global economy continues to grow. This broad economic growth is leading to sustained demand growth for the industry as well."

- The Argus Research Company had some upbeat comments on February 8, 2005, according to Bill Selesky, "Our rating on Dow Chemical Company remains a BUY. When we upgraded several chemical stocks in early December, including Dow, we did so with the belief that these stocks had significant upside potential. We believe that DOW offers an attractive valuation, with the potential to deliver better-than-expected earnings growth, margin growth, and top-line (*sales*) growth."

- Dow says it has high hopes for a diesel engine emission filtration system that is currently under development. The system reduces particulate matter by more than 90 percent and has fast regeneration at low exhaust temperature, with minimum fuel consumption. Dow also says that further out on the horizon are products that include animal health vaccines and more products based on alternative feedstocks, such as corn sugar and soybean oil.

Total assets: $45,885 million
Current ratio: 1.51
Common shares outstanding: 943 million
Return on 2004 shareholders' equity: 26.1%

|  | 2004 | 2003 | 2002 | 2001 | 2000 | 1999 | 1998 | 1997 |
|---|---|---|---|---|---|---|---|---|
| Revenues (millions) | 40,161 | 32,632 | 27,609 | 27,805 | 23,008 | 18,929 | 18,441 | 20,018 |
| Net income (millions) | 2,797 | 1,278 | 299 | 438 | 1,513 | 1,396 | 1,374 | 1,808 |
| Earnings per share | 2.93 | 1.38 | .33 | .52 | 2.22 | 2.07 | 2.04 | 2.60 |
| Dividends per share | 1.34 | 1.34 | 1.34 | 1.30 | 1.16 | 1.16 | 1.16 | 1.12 |
| Price    high | 51.3 | 42.0 | 37.0 | 39.7 | 47.2 | 46.0 | 33.8 | 34.2 |
|          low | 36.4 | 24.8 | 23.7 | 25.1 | 23.0 | 28.5 | 24.9 | 25.5 |

Growth and Income

# Eaton Corporation

Eaton Center ❑ 1111 Superior Avenue ❑ Cleveland, OH 44114 ❑ (216) 523–4501 ❑ Dividend reinvestment plan is available: (800) 446–2617 ❑ Listed: NYSE ❑ Web site: *www.eaton.com* ❑ Ticker symbol: ETN ❑ S&P rating: B+ ❑ Value Line financial strength rating: A+

Andrew Casey, writing for the Prudential Equity Group, LLC on January 24, 2005, had this comment, "Eaton appears to have successfully transformed itself from reliance on automotive and truck markets to a more diversified, cohesive business that has more consistent earnings growth and lower volatility in total business returns. The company is achieving double-digit revenue and earnings growth and is strengthening its balance sheet and increasing dividends."

The report also said, "In each of its four business groups, ETN has developed products that should enable the business to grow at faster than end-market rates over the next five years. There are three trends that should drive ETN's growth above market. They are as follows: 1) the need to increase fuel economy is already helping ETN, 2) the need to reduce vehicle emissions is bolstering ETN's growth prospects, and 3) continued outsourcing will likely drive the company's ability to grow."

For its part, Eaton Corporation had solid results in 2004, according to CEO Alexander M. Cutler. "We are pleased with our performance in the fourth quarter," he said on January 24, 2005. "Sales growth in the fourth quarter of 26 percent consisted of 12 percent organic growth, 12 percent from acquisitions and 2 percent from higher exchange rates. Our organic growth was made up of 8 percent growth in our end markets and 4 percent growth from out-growing our end markets Looking at 2004 as a whole, we had an outstanding year. Our sales grew 22 percent, net income grew 68 percent, and return on equity was 20 percent."

*Organic growth refers to internal growth, that is, without taking into account acquisitions.*

## Company Profile

Eaton Corporation is a globally diversified industrial manufacturer engaged in the design and manufacture of fluid power systems; electrical power quality, distribution and control; automotive engine air management and power train controls for fuel economy; and intelligent drive train systems for fuel economy and safety in trucks. The principal markets for the company's Fluid Power, Automotive, and Truck segments are original equipment manufacturers (OEMs) and after-market customers of aerospace products and systems; off-highway agricultural and construction vehicles; industrial equipment; passenger cars; and heavy-, medium-, and light-duty trucks. The principal markets for the Electrical segment are industrial, construction, commercial, automotive, and government customers.

Here is a breakdown of the company's segments:

### Automotive

Eaton's automotive business segment is a partner to the passenger car and light truck industry. The company makes superchargers, engine valves, cylinder heads, locking and limited slip differentials, sensors, actuators, intelligent cruise control systems, tire valves, fluid connectors, and decorative body moldings and spoilers.

The automotive industry faces an ever-increasing list of challenges—from design and aesthetic choices to demands for power and performance. The industry's two main challenges are clear: fuel economy and emissions. Eaton products bridge the gap. With the company's "green machine" focus, its innovative and industry-leading technologies help manufacturers meet tough environmental standards and consumer preferences.

Eaton's vision has been recognized by top manufacturers. It will supply Ford and General Motors with "Smart Transmission" controls, and superchargers for Mercedes and Nissan. Both of these Eaton products increase engine power and performance by helping engines to work more efficiently.

Eaton, a partner to seventy of the world's premier vehicle OEMs, operates plants in Brazil, Canada, China, France, Germany, India, Indonesia, Italy, Japan, Korea, Mexico, Monaco, the Netherlands, Poland, Spain, Taiwan, Turkey, the United Kingdom, and the United States.

## Fluid Power

Eaton is a worldwide leader in the design, manufacture, and marketing of a comprehensive line of reliable, high-efficiency hydraulic systems and components. ETN's full line of powerful hydraulic component brand names, which include Aeroquip, Char-Lynn, Eaton, Hydro-Line, and Vickers, provide customers with a quality selection of Eaton-engineered products. From a single product to complete systems, Eaton supplies products that keep its customers moving.

Eaton's innovations meet the specific needs of its customers—reducing noise, increasing operating pressure, integrating electromechanical controls, and creating complex integrated solutions. Eaton's fluid power systems are found in earthmoving, agriculture, construction, mining, forestry, utility, and material handling applications.

## Mobile Hydraulics

Mobile hydraulics applications demand speed, reliability, and durability under harsh environmental conditions. Mining equipment performs rigorous cycles at Chilean copper pits 16,000 feet above sea level and South African gold mines 11,000 feet underground. Agriculture machinery works the vast American plains. In coastal cities, earthmoving equipment creates land from sea.

## Industrial Hydraulics

Eaton hydraulics provide heavy lifting power in static uses, such as baggage handling and factory equipment. Eaton is also found in leading entertainment venues, creating the motion in virtual reality experiences and bringing inanimate objects to life. Eaton fluid power systems provide the control, quiet operation, and sheer power needed to fuel the most creative minds.

## Aerospace

Eaton's aerospace business is a leading designer and manufacturer of hydraulic power generation and fuel fluid management components and systems; hydraulic and electro-mechanical motion control components and systems; fluid conveyance components and systems; electrical power and load management subsystems; cockpit controls and displays; pressure sensors; and fluid monitoring systems for a global group of diverse customers. For more than eighty years, the company has been the innovator and pioneering leader in the development of hydraulic and electronic technology for the aerospace industry.

## Electrical

Eaton brings power control and distribution solutions to the utility, industrial, commercial, and residential segments. The company is a global manufacturer of switches, circuit breakers, and power controls that are designed to enhance factory performance. Its control and automation equipment include contactors and motor starters, variable speed drives, photoelectric and proximity sensors, video control panels, microprocessor-based control and protection devices, as well as pushbuttons and switches. Eaton is well positioned to respond to emerging requirements for power quality and availability that have joined the traditional focus on AC distribution and automation.

ETN's power distribution equipment includes the most complete family of circuit breakers in the industry, ranging from miniature breakers rated from 120 volts to world-class vacuum breakers rated up to 38 kilovolts.

## Truck Components

Eaton is the leader in the design, manufacturing and marketing of drivetrain systems and components for medium-duty and heavy-duty commercial vehicles on the American continents. In concert with the company's manufacturing and marketing partners, principally Dana Corporation, Eaton markets the "Roadranger System"—a complete line of drivetrain components and truck systems, including manual and automatic transmissions, clutches, driveshafts, steer and drive axles, trailer axles and suspensions, brakes, anti-lock braking systems, tire pressure management systems, and collision warning systems.

## Shortcomings to Bear in Mind

- "We are maintaining our SELL recommendation on ETN, as the stock is trading at a material premium to our discounted-cash-flow twelve-month target price," said Robert E. Friedman, CPA, writing for *Standard & Poor's* on January 27, 2005.
- The Argus Research Company had some negative thoughts, as well, on January 26, 2005. Here's what Dana Richardson said, "With Street EPS (*Earnings per share*) estimates for 2005 substantially above company guidance (consensus of $5.27 versus guidance of $4.90–$5.10), we believe that Eaton Corp. is at risk to underperform expectations." *In this instance, Dana Richardson is comparing*

*estimates from Eaton management to estimates made by Wall Street analysts.*

## Reasons to Buy

- "We expect Eaton Corp. to post strong financial results in 2005," said Jason Dalavagas, writing for *Value Line Investment Survey* on April 1, 2005. "The company is coming off an impressive year, where sales increased by roughly 22 percent, and earnings rose by 58 percent. Acquisitions during the year contributed about 12 percent of the sales growth, with most of the remainder coming from organic growth. Management has decided to use some of the excess cash flow that it has generated in the past year to increase its quarterly dividend to $0.31 per share."
- Eaton's electrical products are sold throughout the world and supported by a worldwide distribution and service network. Eaton product lines are renowned for their ingenuity, reliability, and quality. Eaton's fast-growing Electrical Services & Systems offers an exciting mix of products, services, and expertise to help companies and facilities improve operations, ensure integrity of power, and utilize capital resources efficiently. Eaton is advanced product development, world-class manufacturing, and global engineering services and support.
- ETN currently supplies more than 80 percent of all of the new commercial aircraft platform hydraulic engine-driven pumps. Its power generation systems' success includes the Raytheon Hawker Horizon, the Airbus A380, the Lockheed Martin F-35, and CargoLifter. Eaton is the leader in higher pressure hydraulic systems development including the Bell/Boeing MV-22 and the Boeing F-18 E/F. Eaton supplies the rudder and aileron flight controls on the Boeing C-17 and they supply the electrical power and load management subsystem on the Apache

Longbow attack helicopter. In addition, Eaton is the leader in aftermarket fluid power and motion control customer support around the world.

- Eaton is committed to ongoing research and development efforts to address the compelling needs of the truck industry: fuel economy, safety, ease of operation, reliability, and uptime.

The Eaton Fuller AutoShift combines the economy and dependable performance of a manual with the easy-to-drive convenience and fuel efficiency of an automatic. AutoShift transmissions completely eliminate lever shifts and respond to performance requirements by providing perfect, hands-free shifting every time.

Total assets: $9,075 million
Current ratio: 1.41
Common shares outstanding: 152 million
Return on 2004 shareholders' equity: 19.3%

|                      | 2004  | 2003  | 2002  | 2001  | 2000  | 1999  | 1998  | 1997  |
|----------------------|-------|-------|-------|-------|-------|-------|-------|-------|
| Revenues (millions)  | 9,817 | 8,061 | 7,209 | 7,299 | 8,309 | 8,402 | 6,625 | 7,563 |
| Net income (millions)| 675   | 402   | 315   | 233   | 383   | 439   | 349   | 464   |
| Earnings per share   | 4.13  | 2.67  | 2.20  | 1.65  | 3.26  | 2.98  | 2.40  | 3.03  |
| Dividends per share  | 1.08  | .92   | .88   | .88   | .88   | .88   | .88   | .86   |
| Price        high    | 72.6  | 54.7  | 44.3  | 40.7  | 43.3  | 51.8  | 49.8  | 51.7  |
|              low     | 52.7  | 33.0  | 29.5  | 27.6  | 28.8  | 31.0  | 28.8  | 33.6  |

---

Aggressive Growth

# Ecolab, Inc.

Ecolab Center ❑ 370 Wabasha Street North ❑ St. Paul, MN 55102 ❑ (651) 293–2809 ❑ Dividend reinvestment program available: (800) 322–8325 ❑ Web site: *www.ecolab.com* ❑ Listed: NYSE ❑ Ticker symbol: ECL ❑ S&P rating: A ❑ Value Line financial strength rating: B++

"If you eat out more than you used to, Douglas Baker thanks you. The forty-six-year-old Ecolab chief executive's glasses fog over when he looks at the increasing concern over food safety and industrial cleanliness in general. No wonder. Ecolab makes counter-top sanitizers, floor cleaners, and degreasers, selling them complete with dispensers, installation and service to outfits like McDonald's, Wal-Mart, and Coors. That's a $36 billion market, of which Ecolab has the largest share, 12 percent."

That comment (one of the publication's *Best Managed Companies in America*) was made by Chana R. Schoenberger in an article in *Forbes* magazine on January 10, 2005. The author goes on to say, "Baker knows his customers can't afford a hygiene breakdown. 'They have other things to focus on,' he says. To that end, last year (2004), he spent $150 million to buy up six smaller competitors. Ecolab is also giving its field technicians hand-held PCs and laptops to feed info back to headquarters quickly. It has also expanded into equipment repair and 'food-safety auditing' (in other words, making sure employees wash their hands.) 'All these guys are doing is selling soap to a thousand

Marriotts around the country—and with a high degree of reliability,' says Deutsche Bank analyst David Begleiter, CFA."

## Company Profile

According to the company's former CEO, Allan Schuman, "When it comes to delivering premium commercial cleaning and sanitizing solutions on a truly global basis, Ecolab is the one. No other company comes close to rivaling our world-wide reach or the extraordinary breadth of products, systems and services we offer.

"We meet the varied and specialized needs of thousands of diverse businesses and institutions in North America, Europe, Asia, Latin America, Africa, the Middle East—the list of countries in which we do business reads like an atlas. In 2001, we took decisive actions to ensure that Ecolab remains number one in the world for many years to come."

Founded in 1923, Ecolab is the leading global developer and marketer of premium cleaning, sanitizing, pest elimination, maintenance, and repair products and services for the world's hospitality, institutional, and industrial markets.

In the early years, Ecolab served the restaurant and lodging industries and has since broadened its scope to include hospitals, laundries, schools, retail and commercial property, among others.

The company conducts its domestic business under these segments:

The Institutional Division is the leading provider of cleaners and sanitizers for warewashing, laundry, kitchen cleaning and general housecleaning, product-dispensing equipment and dishwashing racks and related kitchen sundries to the foodservice, lodging, and healthcare industries. It also provides products and services for pool and spa treatment.

The Food & Beverage division offers cleaning and sanitizing products and services to farms, dairy plants, food and beverage processors, and pharmaceutical plants.

The Kay Division is the largest supplier of cleaning and sanitizing products for the quick-service restaurant, convenience store, and flood retail markets.

Ecolab also sells janitorial and healthcare products (detergents, floor care, disinfectants, odor control, and hand care under the Airkem and Huntington brand names; textile care products for large institutional and commercial laundries; vehicle care products for rental, fleet and retail car washes; and water-treatment products for commercial, institutional, and industrial markets.

Other domestic services include institutional and commercial pest elimination and prevention; and the GCS commercial kitchen equipment repair services.

Around the world, the company operates directly in nearly seventy countries. International sales account for 22 percent of sales. In addition, the company reaches customers in more then 100 countries through distributors, licensees, and export operations. To meet the global demands for its products, Ecolab operates more than fifty state-of-the-art manufacturing and distribution facilities worldwide.

## Shortcomings to Bear in Mind

- Wall Street seems well aware that Ecolab has a bright future, since it has tagged it with a lofty multiple, close to thirty times earnings.
- *Standard & Poor's Stock Reports* had some reservations about owning Ecolab. On March 3, 2005, Richard O'Reilly, CFA, said, "We have lowered our opinion on the shares to a HOLD from a BUY, based on valuation. The shares were selling at what we viewed as an historical high P/E premium to the S&P 500. While we view a premium as justified, based on what we regard as the company's attractive EPS

(*Earnings per share*) record and outlook, the premium widened in 2004, as the stock's appreciation year to date strongly outpaced that of the S&P 500. We view ECL as a strong company, with attractive longer-term growth prospects and cash flow, and believe the travel and hotel sectors will continue to show improved trends."

- "The stock has lost some ground in recent months, arising partly, it seems, from investors' anticipation of slower earnings growth this year," said Frederick L. Harris, III, writing for *Value Line Investment Survey* on March 18, 2005. "This lackluster recent price action is part of the reason why the equity holds a 3 (Average) rank for Timeliness. Also, long-term capital appreciation potential is subpar at the current quotation (*it was $32.57*)."

## Reasons to Buy

- Ecolab is the fourth-best manufacturing company in the United States to sell for, according to *Selling Power Magazine*. *Selling Power Magazine,* a monthly sales management publication, annually lists the fifty best companies to sell for in the United States. It ranks the top twenty-five manufacturing companies and the top twenty-five service companies with more than 500 sales people, based on three key categories: compensation, training, and career mobility for their sales people.

    "Ecolab's most important asset is our sales-and-service team," said Mr. Baker. "Clearly, this is a terrific recognition for us. Our investments to carefully select, train, compensate, and develop our associates are critical to our company's growth and future."

- "Ecolab was proud to once again be named to *Business Ethics* magazine's list of the '100 Best Corporate Citizens in America,' said former CEO, Allan L. Schuman in 2004, just before he turned

the reins over to Douglas Baker on July 1, 2004. "This recognition, our fourth in as many years, is a reaffirmation of our company's commitment to corporate integrity and good citizenship."

- Despite the company's high P/E ratio, the shares of Ecolab have a low Beta Coefficient of only 0.90, compared with an average of 1.00 for the S&P 500. This means that it fluctuates less than the general market.

- Over the past ten years (1994–2004) Earnings per share advanced from $.34 to $1.19, a compound annual growth rate of 13.4 percent. During that stretch, EPS declined only once, and then only modestly, from $0.75 in 2000 to $0.73 in 2001. In the same 10-year period, dividends climbed from $0.12 to $0.33, a growth rate of 10.3 percent. What's more, the dividend has been boosted every year since 1992.

- Ecolab has a highly skilled research and development team, which continues to turn out innovative new products. According to a company spokesman, "Never content with the status quo, we strive for constant improvement, so far earning nearly 2,600 patents worldwide. And we boast the industry's most sophisticated R&D facilities—where breakthroughs happen every day."

    In 2002, for example, Ecolab launched a revolutionary foaming hand soap system for the janitorial and building service contractor markets. The EpiSoft foaming Lotion Soap System combines exceptional quality soap in a sleek dispenser.

    Cutting-edge technology is the key to EpiSoft's success. Its patented anti-drip dispenser prevents wasteful spills with an auto-retraction device that keeps unused soap inside the dispenser. The unique reservoir system holds up to seventy additional washes, which allows the soap container to drain completely before being replaced, lessening waste while ensuring a continuous supply of foaming soap.

"Ecolab's ongoing focus on research and development gives us a great competitive advantage," said Tim Mulhere, the company's vice president and general manager of the Professional Products Division. "EpiSoft combines superior foam and cleansing ingredients with innovative dispensing technology, which the janitorial segment hasn't been exposed to in the past."

The silky EpiSoft foam lathers faster and rinses more easily than conventional liquid soaps. Additionally, the superior quality and fresh scent of the foam encourages more frequent hand washing, which is the number one way to help reduce cross-infection and resulting illness and absenteeism.

Total assets: $3,716 million
Current ratio: 1.36
Common shares outstanding: 258 million
Return on 2004 shareholders' equity: 21.7%

|                      | 2004 | 2003 | 2002 | 2001 | 2000 | 1999 | 1998 | 1997 |
|----------------------|------|------|------|------|------|------|------|------|
| Revenues (millions)  | 4,185 | 3,762 | 3,404 | 2,321 | 2,264 | 2,080 | 1,888 | 1,640 |
| Net income (millions)| 310  | 277  | 210  | 188  | 209  | 176  | 155  | 134  |
| Earnings per share   | 1.19 | 1.06 | .80  | .73  | .79  | .66  | .58  | .50  |
| Dividends per share  | .33  | .29  | .27  | .26  | .24  | .21  | .19  | .16  |
| Price       high     | 35.6 | 27.9 | 25.2 | 22.1 | 22.8 | 22.2 | 19.0 | 14.0 |
|             low      | 26.1 | 23.1 | 18.3 | 14.3 | 14.0 | 15.8 | 13.1 | 9.1  |

Growth and Income

# Emerson Electric Company

8000 W. Florissant Avenue ❏ P. O. Box 4100 ❏ St. Louis, MO 63136–8506 ❏ (314) 553–2197 ❏ Dividend reinvestment plan available: (888) 213–0970 ❏ Web site: *www.gotoemerson.com* ❏ Listed: NYSE ❏ Ticker symbol: EMR ❏ Fiscal years end September 30 ❏ S&P rating: A ❏ Value Line financial strength rating: A++

"When David Farr became the Asia-Pacific president of Emerson Electric in 1992, the region was barely on the radar back at headquarters in St. Louis," said Russell Flannery, in an article in *Forbes* magazine on July 26, 2004. "Veteran chief executive Charles F. Knight saw potential, but told colleagues it was 'a young man's game.'

Farr was the young man. Asia was good for him, and good for Emerson, too. Twelve years later Farr, forty-nine, has succeeded Knight and is pushing the company ever more into emerging markets, especially China. The company's products, which keep industrial systems powered, flowing and cooled, are part of the backbone in manufacturing centers. First, Emerson created most new factory jobs overseas. Now, new white-collar hiring is shifting, too—jobs for engineers and product designers. There are two reasons for this. One is that overseas is where the business is coming from—manufacturing output, a proxy for demand for Emerson goods, is growing at 8 percent in emerging markets, compared with only 3 percent in the U.S. The other reason is that overseas is where the brainpower is. China hands out 220,000 basic engineering degrees a year. The U.S. hands out only 60,000—and at the graduate level half go to foreigners."

## Results in Fiscal 2004

In early fiscal 2005, CEO David N. Farr said, "In 2004, Emerson delivered strong financial and operational performance with record sales and operating cash flow, as well as a double-digit earnings-per-share increase. In addition, we continued to strengthen our global competitive position, advance technology leadership, and enhance our ability to deliver solutions to customers.

"Net sales were a record $15.6 billion, up 12 percent from $14 billion in fiscal 2003. Sales were driven by 20 percent gains in our major growth initiatives, including strong performance in the emerging markets of Asia-Pacific, Eastern Europe, Latin America, and the Middle East."

## Company Profile

Emerson is a leading manufacturer of a broad list of intermediate products such as electrical motors and drives, appliance components, and process-control devices. The company also produces hand and power tools, as well as accessories.

Founded 109 years ago, Emerson is not a typical high-tech capital goods producer. Rather, the company makes such prosaic things as refrigerator compressors, pressure gauges, and In-Sink Erator garbage disposals—basic products that are essential to industry.

Here are the company's five segments:

### Industrial Automation

This segment of the company provides integral horsepower motors, alternators, electronic and mechanical drives, industrial valves, electrical equipment, specialty heating, lighting, testing and ultrasonic welding, and cleaning products for industrial applications. Key growth drivers for the segment include the embedding of electronics into motors and other equipment to enable self-diagnosis and preventative maintenance functionality, as well as alternators for diesel and natural gas generator sets to create reliable distributed power solutions. The Industrial Automation segment had revenues of $2.9 billion in fiscal 2004, for a gain of 13 percent.

### Appliance and Tools

This operation includes the Emerson Storage Solutions, Emerson Tools, Emerson Appliance Solutions, and Emerson Motors brand platforms. Customer offerings feature an extensive range of consumer, commercial and industrial storage products; market-leading tools; electrical components and systems for appliances; and the world's largest offering of fractional horsepower motors. Key growth drivers include professional-grade tools serving the fast-growing home center market, as well as advanced electrical motors, which create entirely new market opportunities for Emerson. This part of the company had sales in 2004 of $3.7 billion, up 9 percent over the prior year.

### Climate Technologies

This segment is known for leading technologies and solutions for heating, air conditioning, and refrigeration applications that provide homeowners with a whole new level of comfort and efficiency, while lowering their energy bills. Climate Technologies's remote monitoring capabilities help assure food safety and quality for grocery stores. In 2004, this operation had revenues of $3 billion, up 14 percent over 2003.

### Process Management

Award-winning technologies help oil and gas, refining, power generation, chemical, pharmaceutical, and other process businesses increase plant uptime, improve productivity, and identify and eliminate problems before they occur. Emerson offers intelligent control systems and software, measurement instruments, valves, and expertise in engineering, project management, and consulting. In 2004, its sales were $3.7 billion, a gain of 9 percent.

## Network Power

Businesses depend on the company's Network Power for reliable power to run data centers, telecommunications networks, and other mission-critical applications. Emerson leads the industry in the design, manufacture, installation, and service of power solutions such as AC and DC backup systems and precision cooling equipment. Its revenues advanced 16 percent in 2004, to $2.7 billion.

## Shortcomings to Bear in Mind

- The trend of Earnings per share in recent years have been disappointing. The company earned $2.77 per share as far back as 1998. Although EPS climbed to $3 the following year and $3.30 in 2000, Emerson has failed to reach this level in the years since. On the other hand, 2004 was a solid step in the right direction.
- "HOLD-rated Emerson Electric Company's story has not changed much since our last note, a situation that has been mirrored by the static stock price over that time frame. While we applaud Emerson's dynamic merging markets strategy, which is targeting future sales from international markets at 60 percent of the total, up from 47 percent at present, we don't foresee any positive surprises in 2005 that would justify buying a stock that is priced very close to its fair value."

## Reasons to Buy

- "For the past few years, Emerson has been accelerating improvement in operating and capital efficiencies through extensive restructuring and a shift to global best-cost manufacturing," said CEO David M. Farr in early fiscal 2005. "Together with our lean manufacturing initiatives, these accomplishments have strengthened our global competitive position and helped us overcome the impact of increased material and pension costs during the period.

"This capital efficiency progress is reflected in our improved average trade working capital ratio, which declined to 19.6 percent of sales in 2004, from 21.2 percent last year, led by an 11 percent improvement in inventory turnover. The increase in the return on capital is a result of improvements in profitability, fixed asset utilization, and working capital efficiency and is an important measure of our success in effectively using shareholder resources."

- Mr. Farr also said, "We achieved that increase while investing during the fiscal year in strategic acquisitions that extend our global reach and capabilities. The acquisition of the outside plant and power systems business of Marconi Corporation PLC, renamed Emerson Network Power Energy Systems-North America, gave us a stronger position in the U.S. telecom power industry.

"We also added to our leading worldwide position in the process control business with the acquisition of Metran Industrial Group, one of the top suppliers of measurement instrumentation and services for the process industry in Russia and Eastern Europe."

- Technology is fundamental to Emerson's sales growth. As a consequence, the company has been increasing its investment in Engineering & Development, notably in such sectors as communications, software, and electronics. E&D investment, moreover, has risen every year since 1973.
- Emerson is now supplying the world's leading windmill manufacturer with more than 3,000 wind turbine generators, helping deliver electricity to the national grid for twenty-eight different countries.
- *Standard & Poor's Stock Reports* was upbeat about Emerson Electric on February 8, 2005, according analyst John F. Hingher, CFA. "We project an uptick in

some of the company's important end markets and believe that strong growth in emerging markets, particularly in Asia, Latin America, and Eastern Europe, will continue. We are optimistic regarding the short-term outlook and the company's solid cash flow generating ability."

- "A joint venture between BP, Sinopec, and Shanghai Petrochemical Corporation, SECCO will be the first of several new petrochemical facilities in China racing to meet the country's rapidly growing

need for plastics, including food packaging, computers, and automobile parts," said James G. Berges, president of Emerson Electric, in fiscal 2005. "The world's largest facility of its kind, SECCO chose Emerson's PlantWeb digital architecture to give it a complete solution, including measurement, valves, and services. This technology will help the facility maximize efficiency and speed to the market, enabling SECCO to seize opportunity ahead of the competition."

Total assets: $16,361 million
Current ratio: 1.48
Common shares outstanding: 420 million
Return on 2004 shareholders' equity: 18.4%

|  | | 2004 | 2003 | 2002 | 2001 | 2000 | 1999 | 1998 | 1997 |
|---|---|---|---|---|---|---|---|---|---|
| Revenues (millions) | | 15,615 | 13,958 | 13,748 | 15,480 | 15,545 | 14,270 | 13,447 | 12,299 |
| Net income (millions) | | 1,257 | 1,013 | 1,060 | 1,032 | 1,422 | 1,314 | 1,229 | 1,122 |
| Earnings per share | | 2.98 | 2.41 | 2.52 | 2.50 | 3.30 | 3.00 | 2.77 | 2.52 |
| Dividends per share | | 1.60 | 1.58 | 1.55 | 1.53 | 1.43 | 1.31 | 1.18 | 1.08 |
| Price | high | 70.9 | 65.0 | 66.1 | 79.6 | 79.8 | 71.4 | 67.4 | 60.4 |
|  | low | 56.2 | 43.8 | 41.7 | 44.0 | 40.5 | 51.4 | 54.5 | 45.0 |

---

Conservative Growth

# Energen Corporation

605 Richard Arrington Jr. Boulevard North ❑ Birmingham, AL 35203–2707 ❑ (205) 326–8421 ❑ Direct dividend reinvestment plan available: (800) 654–3206 ❑ Web site: *www.energen.com* ❑ Listed: NYSE ❑ Ticker symbol: EGN ❑ S&P rating: A ❑ Value Line financial strength rating: B++

"Energen has come a long way in just over eight years," said CEO Mike Warren in 2004. "We've invested a lot of capital in producing oil and gas properties. We've enhanced the profitability of those properties through development well drilling, recompletions, pay-adds and operational enhancements.

"We've maintained a disciplined approach to purchasing properties. We've worked hard to minimize the risks inherent in the oil and gas business; in particular, we have been aggressive hedgers as we have

sought to minimize the risk associated with volatile energy prices."

If some of those terms are a bit fuzzy, here are a few definitions from the company's annual report:

*Recompletion:* An operation within an existing wellbore whereby a completion in one zone is abandoned in order to attempt a completion in a different zone.

*Pay-add:* An operation within a currently producing wellbore that attempts to access and complete an addition pay zone(s) while maintaining production from the existing completed zone(s).

*Hedging:* The use of derivative commodity instruments such as futures, swaps, and collars to help reduce financial exposure to commodity price volatility.

*Development well:* A well drilled within the proved area of an oil or gas reservoir to the depth of a stratigraphic horizon known to be productive.

*Operational enhancement:* Any action undertaken to improve production efficiency of oil and gas wells and/or reduce well costs.

## Company Profile

Energen is a diversified holding company engaged primarily in the acquisition, development, exploration, and production of oil, natural gas, and natural gas liquids in the continental United States. It also has a stake in the purchase, distribution, and sale of natural gas, principally in central and north Alabama. Its two subsidiaries are Energen Resources Corporation and Alabama Gas Corporation (Alagasco).

Energen was incorporated in Alabama in 1978 in connection with the reorganization of its oldest subsidiary, Alagasco. Alagasco was formed in 1948 by the merger of Alabama Gas Company into Birmingham Gas Company, the predecessors of which had been in existence since the mid-1800s. Alagasco became a public company in 1953. Energen Resources was formed in 1971 as a subsidiary of Alagasco and became a subsidiary of Energen in the 1978 reorganization.

### Oil and Gas Operations

Energen's oil and gas operations focus on increasing production and adding proved reserves through the acquisition and development of oil and gas properties. To a lesser extent, Energen Resources explores for and develops new reservoirs, primarily in areas in which it has an operating presence. Sub-

stantially all gas, oil, and natural gas liquids production is sold to third parties. Energen Resources also provides operating services in the Black Warrior Basin in Alabama for its partners and third parties. These services include overall project management and day-to-day decision-making, relative to project operations.

At the end of the latest fiscal year, Energen Resources inventory of proved oil and gas reserves totaled 1,364.9 billion cubic feet equivalent (Bcfe). Substantially all of the company's 1.4 trillion cubic feet equivalent of reserves are situated in the San Juan Basin in New Mexico, the Permian Basin in west Texas, the Black Warrior Basin in Alabama, and the north Louisiana/east Texas region. About 81 percent of Energen Resources' year-end reserves are proved developed reserves. Energen Resources reserves are long-lived, with a year-end reserves-to-production ratio of sixteen. Natural gas represents about 65 percent of Energen Resources' proved reserves, with oil representing about 23 percent, and natural gas liquids making up the rest.

### Natural Gas Distribution

Alagasco is the largest natural gas distribution utility in the state of Alabama. Alagasco purchases natural gas through interstate and intrastate marketers and suppliers. It then distributes the purchased gas through its distribution facilities for sale to residential, commercial, and industrial customers and other end-users of natural gas. Alagasco also provides transportation services to industrial and commercial customers located on its distribution system. Those transportation customers, using Alagasco as their agent or acting on their own, purchase gas directly from producers, marketers, or suppliers and arrange for the delivery of the gas into the Alagasco distribution system. Alagasco charges a fee to transport such customer-owned gas through its distribution system to the customers' facilities.

Alagasco's service territory is situated in central and parts of north Alabama and includes some 185 cities and communities in twenty-eight counties. The aggregate population of the counties served by Alagasco is estimated to be 2.4 million. Among the cities served by Alagasco are Birmingham, the center of the largest metropolitan area in Alabama, and Montgomery, the state capital. During the most recent year, Alagasco served an average of 427,413 residential customers and 35,463 commercial, industrial, and transportation customers. The Alagasco distribution system includes about 9,810 miles of main and more than 11,494 miles of service lines, odorization and regulation facilities, and customer meters.

Alagasco's distribution system is connected to two major interstate natural gas pipeline systems: Southern Natural Gas Company (Southern) and Transcontinental Gas Pipe Line Company (Transco). It is also connected to several intrastate natural gas pipeline systems and to Alagasco's two liquefied natural gas (LNG) facilities.

## Shortcomings to Bear in Mind

- One Wall Street analyst said, "We think sustained strength in commodity prices could constrain Energen's ability to economically execute its plans for $800 million in acquisitions from 2005 through 2008."

## Reasons to Buy

- On December 15, 2004, Argus Research Company raised its appraisal of Energen to a BUY, with this comment by Gary F. Hovis, "We view this combination oil and gas E&P and local gas distribution company as having solid prospects for strong earnings growth over the next three years. Other factors in our investment conclusion are the company's strong balance sheet, an average risk profile, the potential for lower cash operating costs, a well-managed regulated utility operation,

and from the E&P division (Energen Resources), growing volumes of natural gas and crude oil production.

"Moreover, with Energen's top-line growth (revenue growth) in mind, we think natural gas prices at the wellhead will stay above $5 per thousand cubic feet through the remainder of 2004 and on into 2005, with the correlation that West Texas Intermediate crude oil is unlikely to fall below $36 per barrel in 2005."

- *Value Line Investment Survey* rated the stock an above-average 2 on December 17, 2004. Frederick L. Harris III said, "We are constructive about the company's 2007–2009 prospects, although our projections assume that energy prices are lower than current levels over that time frame. Energen Resources should be the major growth vehicle in the future, as management will likely continue to implement an aggressive expansion strategy. Alagasco should remain a steady earnings contributor, made possible partly by a Rate Stabilization and Equalization mechanism, which provides the utility the opportunity to earn a target return on equity of between 13.15 percent and 13.65 percent in a given year." What the analyst is referring to is a contract with the regulators that protects the company from extreme changes in temperature, such as a mild or warm winter. On the other hand, if the winter is really cold, the company is penalized to some degree.

- *Standard & Poor's Stock Reports* gave Energen a BUY rating on February 28, 2005. Its analyst, Yogeesh Wagle, said, "In our view, EGN continues to execute successfully on an acquisition-driven growth strategy backed by significantly hedged production and stable utility performance. The company, along with other gas utilities with significant E&P operations, should continue to benefit near term from high natural gas prices."

Energen Resources attempts to lower the risks associated with its oil and natural gas business. A key component of the company's efforts to manage risk is its acquisition versus exploration orientation and its preference for long-lived reserves. In pursuing an acquisition, Energen Resources primarily uses the then-current oil and gas futures prices in its evaluation models, the prevailing swap curve and, for the longer term, its own pricing assumptions.

After a purchase, Energen Resources may use futures, swaps and/or fixed-price contracts to hedge commodity prices on flowing production for up to thirty-six months to help protect targeted returns from price volatility. On an ongoing basis, the company may hedge up to 80 percent of its estimated annual production in any given year, depending on its pricing outlook.

Total assets: $33,790 million
Current ratio: 0.83
Common shares outstanding: 72 million
Return on 2004 shareholders' equity: 17.5%

|  | 2004 | 2003 | 2002 | 2001 | 2000 | 1999 | 1998 | 1997 |
|---|---|---|---|---|---|---|---|---|
| Revenues (millions) | 937 | 842 | 677 | 785 | 556 | 498 | 503 | 448 |
| Net income (millions) | 127 | 110 | 70.6 | 67.9 | 53.0 | 41.4 | 36.2 | 29.0 |
| Earnings per share | 1.75 | 1.55 | 1.05 | 1.09 | .88 | .69 | .62 | .58 |
| Dividends per share | .38 | .37 | .36 | .35 | .34 | .33 | .47 | .30 |
| Price    high | 30.1 | 21.0 | 15.0 | 20.1 | 16.8 | 10.6 | 11.3 | 10.3 |
|            low | 20.0 | 14.1 | 10.8 | 10.8 | 7.4 | 6.6 | 7.6 | 7.3 |

Conservative Growth

# The Estée Lauder Companies, Inc.

767 Fifth Avenue ❑ New York, NY 10153 ❑ (212) 572–4384 ❑ Direct dividend reinvestment plan is available: (888) 860–6295 ❑ Fiscal years end June 30 ❑ Listed: NYSE ❑ Web site: *www.elcompanies.com* ❑ Ticker symbol: EL ❑ S&P rating: A- ❑ Value Line financial strength rating: A

"In this exciting year, we announced the creation of a new division, BeautyBank, a think-tank for new brand concepts and global business opportunities." said Chairman Leonard A. Lauder in early fiscal 2005. "In October 2003, BeautyBank's first project was born. We entered into a strategic alliance with Kohl's department stores to build and manage new cosmetic departments for their stores. We are currently the sole provider of branded cosmetics and skin care for about 600 Kohl's stores.

"This fall, you will see three new brands developed by our BeautyBank entrepreneurs debuting at Kohl's:
• "American Beauty, a full collection of makeup skin care celebrating the beauty of American style.
• "Flirt!, a makeup line with more than 250 shades that encourages the consumer to flirt with the possibilities.
• "Good Skin, a skin care line that is easy to choose, easy to use and doctor-formulated to deliver targeted results.

"This year, we associated ourselves with some very exciting celebrities. Actress Ashley Judd is the ideal spokeswoman for our new American Beauty brand. We also signed a license agreement to create a line of fragrances and beauty products with Sean 'P. Diddy' Combs and his Sean John fashion label. Through his success in music and theater, and by most recently winning the Council of Fashion Designers in America Menswear Designer of the Year award, Mr. Combs is unquestionably a leading trendsetter of our times. Additionally, the Tommy Hilfiger Toiletries division created a new fragrance called True Star in cooperation with superstar Beyonce Knowles."

## Company Profile

One of the world's leading manufacturers and marketers of quality skin care, makeup, fragrance and hair care products, the company's products are sold in over 130 countries and territories.

### Brand names:

Estée Lauder, Aramis, Clinique, Prescriptives, Origins, MQAQC, La Mer, Bobbi Brown, Tommy Hilfiger, Donna Karan, Aveda, Stila, Jo Malone, Bumble and bumble, *kate spade beauty*, Darphin, Michael Kors, and Rodan and Fields.

### Products:

Skin care: moisturizers, creams, lotions, cleansers, sunscreens and self-tanning products.

Makeup: lipsticks, mascaras, foundations, blushes, eyeshadows, nail polishes, and powders. Also compacts, brushes, and other makeup tools.

Fragrance: eau de parfum sprays, colognes, perfumes, lotions, powders, creams, and soaps based on particular fragrances. This also includes bath and aromatherapy products.

Hair care: shampoos, conditioners, styling gels and cremes, hair coloring products, and hairsprays.

### Distribution:

The company sells its products principally through limited distribution channels to complement the images associated with its brands. They consist primarily of upscale department stores, specialty retailers, upscale perfumeries, and pharmacies and, to a lesser extent, freestanding company stores and spas, stores on cruise ships, and in-flight and duty free shops in airports and cities. With the acquisitions of Aveda, the company entered two new channels of distribution: self-select retail outlets and professional hair salons.

### Brand History:

The company was founded in 1946 by Mrs. Estée Lauder and her husband, Joseph Lauder. The flagship brand, Estée Lauder, was launched with four products: Super Rich All Purpose Creme, Creme Pack, Cleansing Oil, and Skin Lotion. Four additional brands were developed internally. Aramis, a line of prestige fragrance and grooming products for men, was launched in 1964. Clinique, the first dermatologist-guided, allergy-tested, fragrance-free cosmetics brand, followed in 1968. Prescriptives, a color authority with an advanced collection of highly individualized products, was founded in 1979. Origins Natural Resources, a line of skin care, makeup, bath/body, and Sensory Therapy products that use age-old remedies from nature that have been perfected by science for the modern world, was introduced in 1990.

In the 1990s the company acquired two important makeup artist brands: MQAQC and Bobbi Brown. The company acquired a majority equity interest in MQAQC in 1994, completing the acquisition in 1998. Bobbi Brown was acquired in 1995.

In 1997, the company acquired Sassaby, Inc., owner of the color cosmetics brand *jane,* and Aveda Corporation, a leader in the U.S. prestige hair care industry. In 1999, the company acquired Stila Cosmetics, Inc., a Los Angeles-based prestige cosmetics company, and Jo Malone, the London-based marketer of prestige skin care and fragrance products. In 2000, the company acquired a majority equity interest in New York-based Bumble and bumble LLC, a premier hair salon, and Bumble and bumble Products LLC, a developer, marketer and distributor of quality hair care products. In 2003 it acquired Darphin, a Paris-based prestige skin care company. The Estée Lauder Companies is also the global licensee for fragrances and cosmetics for the Tommy Hilfiger, Donna Karan New York (DKNY), and Kate Spade brands.

In November 1998, the company also began to sell certain of its products over the Internet. The Estée Lauder Companies created a new division, ELC Online, responsible for all online strategies and activities for all brands, in 1999. In 2000, the company acquired gloss.com. In 2000, Chanel and Clarins became partners with the company in gloss.com.

*Fiscal 2004 Highlights*
- William P. Lauder named CEO
- Announced strategic alliance with Kohl's department stores
- Acquired Rodan + Fields
- Signed Sean John license
- Announced a new Tommy Hilfiger fragrance, True Star, with Beyonce Knowles
- Sold *jane* brand
- 50 percent dividend increase
- Increased share-repurchase program by 10 million shares
- Raised full-year financial expectations twice
- Double-digit top- and bottom-line growth
- Outstanding gross and operating margin improvements
- $292 million preferred stock redeemed

**Shortcomings to Bear in Mind**
- On December 7, 2004, *Standard & Poor's Stock Reports* gave EL a HOLD rating. Its

analyst, Howard Choe, said "We expect strong growth in fiscal 2005, but see this skewed toward the second half, due to greater marketing spending in the first half on new product introductions and costs associated with the BeautyBank initiative at Kohl's stores. Fragrance sales have been soft for some time, and increased competition in the skin care category at department stores concern us. Coupled with what we view as difficult sales and earnings comparisons, we see lower visibility in the company's fiscal 2004 Earnings per share growth target of 18 percent. However, we think EL continues to control expenses well and believe the company has a solid track record of successfully introducing new products."

**Reasons to Buy**
- On November 3, 2004, Estée Lauder reported new sales for the first quarter of fiscal 2005 of $1.5 billion, a 12 percent increase over the same quarter of the prior year. The company reported net earnings from continuing operations of $95 million, up 22 percent over the 2004 quarter.

  William P. Lauder, the company's CEO, said "Our entrance into fiscal 2005 with strong double-digit top- and bottom-line growth sets the stage and gives us confidence that we are on our way to achieving our previously stated full-year financial objectives. Sales and earnings this quarter were led by a strong performance in our international business."
- "Lauder's prospects through the latter years of the decade remain rather attractive, due in part to its ongoing savings and sales-growth programs," said *Value Line* on December 31, 2004. Kenneth A. Nugent went on to say, "Through 2007–2009, management looks for a combination of sales growth initiatives,

operational efficiencies, and productivity gains to lift the top line (sales) at an average rate of 6 percent to 7 percent, with the bottom line (profits) improving by about 12 percent annually.

Investors with a long-term bias ought to consider this neutrally ranked equity. Indeed, at the current quotation (then $46.11) Estee Lauder stock's appreciation potential through the latter years of this decade is well above that of the *Value Line* median."

- "Over the years, we've insisted on being the best innovators and coming to the marketplace first with new ideas. Hundreds of scientists in our laboratories collaborate with researchers at universities and medical institutions around the world to find breakthroughs in dermatology, biophysics, molecular biology, immunology and chemistry," said Leonard A. Lauder.

He went on to say, "Our research insights led to this year's major launch of Clinique's revolutionary and patent-pending Repairwear, which optimizes the skin's natural repair processes while you sleep. We call the line's three products (Repairwear Intensive Night Cream, Repairwear Intensive Night Lotion and Repairwear Extra Help Serum) the 'Dream Team'—and they've been a dream come true for consumers and retailers alike.

"At Estée Lauder brand, our scientists triumphed by creating the brand's most technologically advanced volumizing mascara: MagnaScopic Maximum Volume Mascara. Its newly patented formula builds up the lashes, magnifying them up to four times their original thickness, without weight or clumping, through a unique lofting complex called Expandex and its dedicated Speed-Meter Brush. Color is intensified by 30 percent. Mascara has become enormously competitive this year with one major magazine referring to 'The Mascara Wars.' With our innovation, we are emerging as a leader in the mascara business."

Total assets: $3,708 million
Current ratio: 1.66
Common shares outstanding: 226 million
Return on 2004 shareholders' equity: 23.8%

|  | 2004 | 2003 | 2002 | 2001 | 2000 | 1999 | 1998 | 1997 |
|---|---|---|---|---|---|---|---|---|
| Revenues (millions) | 5,790 | 5,118 | 4,744 | 4,608 | 4,367 | 3,962 | 3,618 | 3,382 |
| Net income (millions) | 375 | 320 | 213 | 307 | 314 | 273 | 237 | 198 |
| Earnings per share | 1.48 | 1.26 | 0.78 | 1.17 | 1.20 | 1.03 | .89 | .73 |
| Dividends per share | .30 | .20 | .20 | .20 | .15 | .18 | .17 | .17 |
| Price    high | 49.3 | 40.2 | 38.8 | 44.3 | 55.9 | 56.5 | 43.3 | 28.2 |
| low | 37.6 | 25.7 | 25.2 | 29.3 | 33.8 | 37.3 | 23.3 | 19.5 |

Aggressive Growth

# Ethan Allen Interiors, Inc.

Ethan Allen Drive ❏ Danbury, CT 06811 ❏ (203) 743–8234 ❏ Web site: *www.ethanallen.com* ❏ Dividend reinvestment plan not available ❏ Fiscal years end June 30 ❏ Listed: NYSE ❏ Ticker symbol: ETH ❏ S&P rating: B+ ❏ Value Line financial strength rating: A

"Furniture sales typically pick up after a boom in home sales, once owners start buying new beds and draperies," said Dimitra DeFotis in a *Barron's* article dated October 4, 2004. "Although the economic recovery so far has been tepid, many consumers still have big empty houses to fill, and the latest data show that new-home sales remain strong. Plus, Ethan Allen is pushing new casual and contemporary styles—think leather and light, unadorned wood—and its planned increase in marketing should lure new shoppers.

"Meanwhile, by certain criteria, the stock is trading at a healthy discount to its peers. 'It is a good company, and it is cheap,' says Scott Goginsky, an analyst at Schwartz Investment Counsel, a money-management firm near Detroit. 'The single brand is a plus, and as a manufacturer, they are efficient.'

"A multiyear slowdown in the fragmented, roughly $70 billion U.S. retail-furniture industry, forced manufacturers to consolidate plants and seek cheaper labor overseas. Ethan Allen closed six small U.S. plants, kept twelve larger ones open and now has roughly 30 percent of its products manufactured abroad, especially in southeast Asia."

Dimitra DeFotis also said, "By controlling both the wholesale and retail sides of the business, Ethan Allen can track orders better than the typical wholesaler can. The result is operating margins near 15 percent, twice those of other residential furniture makers, says Joel Havard, an analyst at BB&T Capital Markets."

## Company Profile

Ethan Allen, one of the ten largest manufacturers of household furniture in the United States, sells a full range of furniture products and decorative accessories through a network of 311 retail stores in the United States and abroad, of which 127 are company-owned. The rest are owned and operated by independent dealers. However, all stores sell Ethan Allen products exclusively. Retail stores are located in the United States, Canada, and Mexico, with more than eighteen located overseas. The company has twelve manufacturing facilities, including two sawmills, located throughout the United States. In addition, Ethan Allen has six regional distribution centers situated throughout the U.S.

The company's stores (it prefers the term "galleries") are scattered across the country, with outlets in nearly every state. However, there are more than a dozen outlets in such states as California, Texas, and Florida. There is a also a concentrated cluster of Ethan Allen stores along the Eastern Seaboard in such states as New Jersey, Connecticut, and Massachusetts.

Within this fragmented industry, the company has the largest domestic furniture retail network utilizing the gallery concept. Comparable-store sales have benefited from a repositioning of the product mix to appeal to a broader consumer base, a program to renovate or relocate existing stores, coupled with more frequent advertising and promotional campaigns.

Ethan Allen is pursuing an aggressive growth strategy, including investments in technology, employee training and new stores. Margins have been enhanced by manufacturing efficiencies, lower interest expense and a strengthening of the upholstery and accessory lines.

With an efficient and flexible vertically integrated structure, a strong, dedicated retail network, an impressive 95 percent brand name recognition and a seventy-year reputation for exceptional quality and service, Ethan Allen is uniquely positioned as a dominant force in the home furnishings industry.

As Ethan Allen enters the new millennium, the company's philosophy of design remains the same as it was when it was founded more than seventy years ago. Styles may have changed from colonial to eclectic, but the company's commitment to exceptional quality, classical design elements, innovative style and functionality will continue to position Ethan Allen as a preferred brand for years to come.

In keeping with the way consumers live today, the company has organized its product programs into two broad style categories. "Classic" encompasses more historically inspired styles, from early European and French influences to designs from the eighteenth and nineteenth century masters. "Casual," on the other hand, captures a clean, contemporary line and an updated country aesthetic.

## Shortcomings to Bear in Mind

- On July 9, 2004, *Value Line Investment Survey* had an unfavorable Timeliness rating of 4 (below average) for Ethan Allen. Its analyst, Simon R. Shoucair, had this comment: "Pricing pressure from foreign competition could further undermine growth. The Department of Commerce recently issued a preliminary duty tax on wooden furniture from China in response to an anti-dumping petition. However, the tariff imposed was lower than the residential furniture industry expected. We believe the lower tariff will not derail the flow of imports, and cheaper Chinese goods are likely to continue to hurt pricing."

    On a more positive note, the analyst said, "We are cautiously optimistic about the long-term picture. At the current price ($35.91) the stock offers decent potential for capital gains out to 2007–2009."
- On January 7, 2005, the same analyst had these interesting words, "These shares are ranked to lag the broader market over the next six to twelve months. Sluggish growth throughout the home furnishings industry could continue to hamper

the company's near-term performance. However, a 13 percent increase in the stock price since our last review indicates that the market acknowledges these challenges as short-term concerns. Moreover, the stock's three- to five-year price appreciation potential is above average."

## Reasons to Buy

- The *Standard & Poor's* analyst, Amy Glynn, CFA, had this upbeat comment on February 22, 2005: "We think that ETH has a strong brand name, healthy balance sheet and a high quality of earnings. Over the next few years, we think that ETH will benefit from favorable demographic trends, recent housing market strength, and purchases by baby boomers in their peak spending years for household furnishings.
- The company employs a showcase gallery concept. Products are displayed in complete room ensembles, including furnishings, wall decor, window treatments, floor coverings, accents, and accessories. Ethan Allen believes the gallery concept leads to higher sales, as it encourages customers to buy a complete home collection, including case goods (furniture made of wood, rather than upholstered), upholstery, and accessories and offers designers an opportunity to offer additional services.
- Ethan Allen benefits from vertical integration. Because the company controls many aspects of its operations, it is self-sufficient, efficient, and cost-effective. Business decisions regarding everything from sales events to manufacturing locations are made by Ethan Allen management. That way, the company can position its strategies based on what works best. In other words, the company has eliminated the middle man and the waste, and it is able to avoid bottlenecks. This translates into productivity,

increased efficiency, satisfied customers, and steadily climbing profits.

- The company's new stores are situated in high-traffic shopping areas for customer convenience. Many existing stores have been relocated to better-traveled retail routes.

- Furniture is a fragile commodity. It's expensive to transport and can be damaged very easily. According to Mr. Kathwari, "About 12 years ago, we decided to take control of the logistics and deliver our products at one cost nationally. This was a major decision and a major risk, both in terms of servicing the consumer more effectively, while reducing our inventories on a national level. But we have been able to improve our profitability.

  "We have five national distribution warehouses, about 100 retail warehouses and a trucking fleet to service our business. Technology has helped us become more efficient. We have state-of-the-art computer systems, and warehousing systems that receive the product and prepare it for delivery to the customer."

- Operating a store in today's environment is a complicated business if management doesn't have the right structure in place. Ethan Allen is convinced that "You need to be able to keep the store beautiful and inspiring, help customers select the right products, train and motivate the sales staff, grow a complicated custom business, make accessory house calls and anticipate customer service requests—all at the same time."

To respond to these demands, Ethan Allen began testing new ways to staff its stores. For example, at its corporate headquarters in Danbury, Connecticut, management looked at its needs—especially on high-traffic weekends—and created an environment to better support the designers who were working on the front lines.

First, the company established the right sales management structure, so that designers were able to obtain the training and direction they needed to build their businesses. Then, Ethan Allen added specialists in the soft goods and accessories areas to help designers sell more of the complicated product programs. In addition, the company also added a merchandise manager to keep the store beautiful and a customer service specialist to address delivery and service issues.

Since this structure has been in place, traffic in the Danbury store increased about 19 percent. During that same period, the store's written business jumped up 35 percent.

Total assets: $654 million
Current ratio: 2.16
Common shares outstanding: 37 million
Return on 2004 shareholders' equity: 16.1%

| | 2004 | 2003 | 2002 | 2001 | 2000 | 1999 | 1998 | 1997 |
|---|---|---|---|---|---|---|---|---|
| Revenues (millions) | 955 | 907 | 892 | 904 | 856 | 762 | 693 | 572 |
| Net income (millions) | 80 | 75 | 82 | 80 | 91 | 81 | 72 | 49 |
| Earnings per share | 2.10 | 1.95 | 2.06 | 1.98 | 2.20 | 1.92 | 1.63 | 1.11 |
| Dividends per share | .60* | .25 | .16 | .16 | .16 | .12 | .09 | .06 |
| Price     high | 46.6 | 42.7 | 42.2 | 42.3 | 33.8 | 37.8 | 44.4 | 28.6 |
|            low | 33.4 | 27.1 | 27.2 | 26.5 | 20.5 | 24.7 | 15.7 | 12.3 |

* On May 10, 2004, the company paid a special, one-time dividend of $3 per share. The indicated dividend, however is $.60 per share.

# ExxonMobil Corporation

5959 Las Colinas Boulevard ❑ Irving, TX 75039–2298 ❑ (972) 444–1538 ❑ Direct dividend reinvestment plan is available: (800) 252–1800 ❑ Web site: *www.exxonmobil.com* ❑ Listed: NYSE ❑ Ticker symbol: XOM ❑ S&P rating: A- ❑ Value Line financial strength rating: A++

"What type of energy will be demanded in the future?" asked Exxon's CEO, Lee R. Raymond, when he addressed the Hong Kong General Chamber of Commerce on November 4, 2004. Mr. Raymond went on to say, "Without a doubt, for many decades most growth in energy will be for oil, natural gas, and coal. Put simply, these are abundant and affordable, and we have established technologies for finding and using them.

"We project that oil and gas demand will each grow by close to 40 million barrels a day oil equivalent by 2030 and coal by almost 30 million oil-equivalent barrels a day. The rest will come from other sources. These increases will come despite an improvement in global energy intensity, which is the amount of energy used per unit of economic output. That improvement we forecast to average about 1.1 percent per year, or about one-third faster than the pace since 1970.

## The Future of Alternative Energy Sources

"And the increase in petroleum and coal energy demanded will come about even as alternative energy sources grow even more rapidly. For example, we believe wind and solar energy may grow at about 10 percent per year, but because they are such small contributors today, they will remain less than 1 percent of total energy in 2030. These alternative energy sources are much discussed in the press, and they will become more important, but we cannot ignore the limitations that each have.

"For example, solar energy has very high costs. Wind and hydroelectric power have siting limitations. And there are constraints to significantly increasing biomass fuels due

to economics and competition with alternative needs for food crops and forests."

## How About Nuclear Power?

Mr. Raymond goes on to say, "Nuclear energy remains an important option, with rapid growth projected in China. However, nuclear power has generated considerable public opposition elsewhere, both to new plants and to waste disposal options. While we think nuclear will grow, with perhaps more upside in the longer term if its costs become more competitive, the factors I just mentioned will certainly constrain growth in many countries in the medium term.

"Another energy type—hydrogen—has been increasingly mentioned as a possible long-term option. However, it is important to remember that hydrogen is more a battery than a primary source of energy. Hydrogen has to be produced from other materials, either hydrocarbons or water, and this process uses lots of energy and is very expensive. In addition, broad consumer use of hydrogen poses important safety and infrastructure issues that will take decades to manage or resolve in the best of circumstances."

## The Obvious Conclusion

Finally, Mr. Raymond concluded with these words: "The limitations and dilemmas presented by these alternative energy sources are serious and can be overcome only with research, significant investments and time. Therefore, we are left with the reality that for many decades the vast majority of energy that we will use will be hydrocarbon energy. That is why we must face seriously the issues that arise when obtaining energy from hydrocarbons."

In essence, it seems obvious that companies such as Exxon—the largest in the world—will be around for a long time. Not to have one or two petroleum companies in your portfolio would be a serious omission.

## Company Profile

ExxonMobil is engaged in the exploration, production, manufacture, transportation, and sale of crude oil, natural gas, and petroleum products. It also has a stake in the manufacture of petrochemicals, packaging films, and specialty chemicals.

Divisions and affiliated companies of ExxonMobil operate or market products in the United States and some 200 other countries and territories. Their principal business is energy, involving exploration for, and production of crude oil and natural gas, manufacture of petroleum products and transportation and sale of crude oil, natural gas, and petroleum products.

The company is a major manufacturer and marketer of basic petrochemicals, including olefins, aromatics, polyethylene, and polypropylene plastics and a wide variety of specialty products. It also has interests in electric power generation facilities.

In a nutshell, here is ExxonMobil:

• The company conducts oil and gas exploration, development, and production in every major accessible producing region in the world.

• ExxonMobil has the largest energy resource base of any nongovernment company, and it is the world's largest nongovernment natural gas marketer and reserves holder.

• Consumers know the company best by its brand names: Exxon, Mobil and Esso.

• ExxonMobil is the world's largest fuels refiner and manufacture of lube base stocks used for making motor oils.

• The company has refining operations in twenty-six countries, 42,000 retail service stations in more than 100 countries, and lubricants marketing in almost 200 countries and territories.

• ExxonMobil markets petrochemical products in more than 150 countries. Ninety percent of the company's petrochemical assets are in businesses that are ranked number one or number two in market position.

## Shortcomings to Bear in Mind

▪ Although this is a growth and income stock, dividends have not advanced at a very impressive pace. In the 1994–2004 period, Dividends per share inched ahead from $0.73 to $1.06, a compound annual growth rate of only 3.8 percent. On the other hand, Earnings per share in that ten-year stretch climbed from $0.92 to $3.89, a compound annual growth rate of 15.5 percent.

▪ The analyst for the Argus Research Company had a lukewarm opinion of Exxon. On November 15, 2004, Jeb Armstrong said, "HOLD-rated ExxonMobil Corp. is the global leader of the energy industry. With a market capitalization of more than $300 billion, it is also one of the world's largest publicly traded companies. While its size limits its agility, it consistently ranks at or near the top among major integrated energy firms in important performance metrics. XOM's size gives its shares a greater level of stability relative to other energy companies, which has enhanced its attractiveness in the current market uncertainty. Burgeoning energy prices have also drawn in investors. As such, the shares have performed strongly while the market as a whole has moved sideways. We rate the share HOLD on valuation."

## Reasons to Buy

▪ On April 4, 2005, *BusinessWeek* had good things to say about Exxon: "Exxon-Mobil relishes its role as the 'boring' oil giant. That means producing consistent, industry-leading results, like last year's 24 percent return on capital employed. Sure, high oil and gas prices and strong refining and chemical margins lifted all boats in this industry. But the Irving (Tex.) company's worldwide scope, investing discipline, and leading technology keep it on top in oil booms and busts alike. It's spending heavily to find and produce oil and gas in places like Qatar and Russia. With more than $43 billion in cash from operations and asset sales last year, though, Exxon had plenty left over for shareholders."

- ExxonMobil's world-class, geographically diverse upstream portfolio consists of 72 billion oil-equivalent barrels of oil and gas resources and activities in nearly forty countries. Large, highly profitable oil and gas operations in established areas, including North America, Europe, Asia, and West Africa, are the foundations of this portfolio. These areas include long-life fields and have significant near-term potential as new opportunities are developed using existing infrastructure. ExxonMobil also holds a strong position in the Caspian, Eastern Canada, the Middle East, and Russia, as well as in the deep waters of West Africa and the Gulf of Mexico. According to a company official, "Our financial strength allows us to pursue all profitable opportunities. We continually invest in our existing assets to extend their economic life and have an industry-leading portfolio of more than 100 major new projects."

- "Amid increased investor concern about whether energy companies are finding enough new oil and natural gas, Exxon-Mobil Corp. became the latest energy giant to report that it ended 2004 with lower fossil-fuel reserves than it had at the start of the year," said Jeffrey Ball, writing for the *Wall Street Journal* on February 22, 2005.

   "But Exxon, the world's largest publicly traded oil company in terms of revenue and market value, dismissed the apparent hit as an accounting anomaly. By its own standards, the Irving, Texas, energy giant said it more than replaced the reserves of oil and gas it pumped out in 2004."

- ExxonMobil is the world's largest refiner, with an ownership interest in forty-six refineries in 26 countries and a total capacity of 6.3 million barrels per day. It has an extensive transportation network of oil tankers, pipelines and product terminals. Lube-refining capacity is 150 thousand barrels per day.

- Worldwide, ExxonMobil markets gasoline and other fuels at more than 40,000 service stations, serves more than 1 million industrial and wholesale customers, provides aviation services and products at more than 700 airports, and services ocean-going vessels in more than 300 ports.

- ExxonMobil is more than the world's leading energy company," said Andrew Bary, writing for *Barron's* on March 28, 2005. "It's the biggest company of any kind in market value . . . and arguably, the best run. Credit goes to the plain-speaking Raymond, sixty-six, a veteran oilman who was deemed so crucial to the company that he was asked to stay on past his scheduled retirement date in 2003.

   ". . . Exxon has the best returns among peers and the best balance sheet."

- *Standard & Poor's Stock Reports* gave the stock a BUY rating on December 3, 2004, with this comment by T. J. Vital, "XOM has benefited from high oil and natural gas prices through its exploration and production operations, but, in our view, is protected by its business diversification in the event of a downturn in oil prices. As the largest publicly traded oil company in the world, with leading market positions across all its business lines, we believe the company is well positioned to participate in 'big-pocket' growth opportunities in the deepwater, in liquefied natural gas (LNG), and in ventures with state-owned companies. We view its finding/development, proved acquisition and reserve replacement costs as in line with the peer average, and its reserve replacement as strong, with a three-year average organic rate of 108 percent."

Total assets: $195 billion
Current ratio: 1.40
Common shares outstanding: 6606 million
Return on 2004 shareholders' equity: 23.9%

|  | 2004 | 2003 | 2002 | 2001 | 2000 | 1999 | 1998 | 1997 |
|---|---|---|---|---|---|---|---|---|
| Revenues (millions) | 291,252 | 246,738 | 204,506 | 187,510 | 206,083 | 160,883 | 100,697 | 120,279 |
| Net income (millions) | 25,330 | 17,030 | 11,011 | 15,105 | 16,910 | 8,380 | 6,440 | 8,155 |
| Earnings per share | 3.89 | 2.56 | 1.69 | 2.18 | 2.41 | 1.19 | 1.31 | 1.64 |
| Dividends per share | 1.06 | .98 | .92 | .91 | .88 | .84 | .82 | .81 |
| Price      high | 52.0 | 41.1 | 44.6 | 45.8 | 47.7 | 43.6 | 38.7 | 33.6 |
|            low | 39.9 | 31.6 | 29.8 | 35.0 | 34.9 | 32.2 | 28.3 | 24.1 |

Aggressive Growth

# Family Dollar Stores, Inc.

10401 Old Monroe Road ❑ P. O. Box 1017 ❑ Charlotte, NC 28201–1017 ❑ (704) 847–6961 ❑ Dividend reinvestment program is not available ❑ Fiscal years end last Saturday in August ❑ Web site: *www.familydollar.com* ❑ Listed: NYSE ❑ Ticker symbol: FDO ❑ S&P rating: A+ ❑ Value Line financial strength rating: A

The typical Family Dollar customer is a female who shops for a family with a median annual income of less than 35,000, and in many instances, under $20,000. These families depend on Family Dollar to provide them with the good values they need to stretch their limited disposable income.

U.S. Census statistics and demographic trends support the fact that Family Dollar's targeted low-to-middle-income customer base is large and growing. More than 40 percent of households in the United States have incomes below $35,000. Hispanic shoppers, the nation's fastest-growing demographic segment, like the company's small store format. Retirees, another expanding sector of the population, view these smaller stores located in their neighborhoods as a convenient and more enjoyable alternative to the "big box" discounters. As more baby boomers approach retirement with the prospect of reduced and fixed incomes, they particularly appreciate Family Dollar's everyday low prices.

The company does not try to meet all merchandising needs of all people. However, most merchandise is priced under $10, and the assortment covers basic products, such as health and beauty aids, household chemicals, paper products, and food. Shoppers can also select from an assortment of giftware and seasonal items, apparel for the entire family, as well as domestic furnishings such as towels, sheets, and pillows.

In recent years, in response to customer feedback, the mix of merchandise has shifted to more hardline consumables, including nationally advertised brand names. To make room for the expanded assortment of consumables and other hardline categories, the company completed a major space reallocation program in its stores. Hanging apparel space was reduced, and aisles were widened to make shopping easier.

## Company Profile

Family Dollar Stores, Inc. is one of the fastest-growing discount store chains in the United States. During the last ten years, over 2,300 new stores have been added to the chain, of which more than 1,500 were added in the last five fiscal years. During the fiscal year ended August 30, 2004, the company opened 500 new stores and closed 61, bringing the number of stores in operation at the end of the year to 5,481.

The merchandising concept responsible for this growth provides customers with good values at low cost. The merchandise is sold at everyday low prices in a no-frills, low overhead, self-service environment. Most merchandise is priced under $10.

Stores are situated in a contiguous forty-four-state region, ranging northeast to Maine, southeast to Florida, as far northwest as North Dakota and southwest to Arizona. They generally range in size from 6,500 to 8,000 square feet, and most are operated under leases. The relatively small size permits the company to open new stores in rural areas and small towns, as well as in large urban centers. Within these markets, the stores are situated in shopping centers or as freestanding buildings convenient to the company's value-conscious customer base.

Since the opening of the first Family Dollar store in 1959, the store expansion program has been financed entirely with internally generated funds, and the company has no long-term debt.

Family Dollar's headquarters is based in Matthews, North Carolina, just outside Charlotte. The company operates automated, full-service distribution centers in Matthews; West Memphis, Arkansas; Front Royal, Virginia; Duncan, Oklahoma; and Morehead, Kentucky. A sixth distribution center was opened in 2003.

The company purchases its merchandise from about 1,800 suppliers. About 57 percent of merchandise is manufactured in the United States, with substantially all such goods obtained directly from the manufacturer, rather than through wholesalers. Imported products, however, are purchased directly from the manufacturer or from importers.

## Shortcomings to Bear in Mind

- Retail businesses rarely lack for competitors. New ideas in merchandising come along periodically and give fits to companies that are unable to adjust to a new environment. The "big boxes," for instance (such as Wal-Mart, Staples, Bed Bath & Beyond, Home Depot, and Lowe's) have punched holes in such companies as Montgomery Ward, Sears, J. C. Penney, and the thousands of mom-and-pop operations.

- *Standard & Poor's Stock Reports* had a mixed view of Family Dollar Stores in a report issued February 14, 2005. Its analyst, Jason N. Asaeda, had this comment: "Our recommendation is HOLD, based on our valuation. With its growing focus on consumables and name brands, we see an opportunity for FDO to improve its share of wallet with core customers. However, our outlook is tempered by challenges we see in opening and operating urban stores, which have historically had less predictable opening lead times and higher shrinkage (*loss by theft*) and turnover than rural stores. To resolve these issues, FDO has expanded its real estate team, made changes in training and hiring practices, and assigned priority to urban stores for systems upgrades. Given likely payoff of these initiatives and improving economic conditions for core customers, we look for a strengthening of sales and free cash flow over the longer term."

## Reasons to Buy

- Family Dollar Stores is the rare company with no long-term debt.

- In the 1994–2004 period, Earnings per share advanced from $.37 to $1.54, with no dips along the way. That amounts to a compound annual growth rate of 15.3 percent. During the same 10-year period, Dividends per share climbed from $.11 to $.33, a growth rate of 11.6 percent.

- The company is expanding at a fast clip. In fiscal 2001, for instance, it added 502 new outlets, including seventy-six in Texas, thirty-three in New York, twenty-seven in Michigan, twenty-three in Georgia, and twenty in both Florida and Louisiana. Similarly, in fiscal 2002, the company added 515 new stores, representing the largest number added in any given year. Nor did the pace slow in 2003, with another 475 added to the chain. What's more, another 500 new units were added in 2004.

- In commenting on fiscal 2004 and the company's plans for the year ahead, CEO Howard R. Levine said, "The 6.1 percent increase in net income in fiscal 2004 was achieved in a difficult economic environment for the company's low-to-middle-income customer base. While we did not achieve our targeted net income growth, we did continue to reinvest in the business. In fiscal 2004, 500 new stores were opened. Good progress was made in the implementation of the multiyear 'Store of the Future' project, including infrastructure investments so that our customers are able to use PIN-based debit cards in our stores.

  "We also completed the strategic assessment, concept testing and development of implementation plans for urban and cooler programs that will be key initiatives in fiscal 2005. The company maintains its strong financial position with no debt on the balance sheet. Cash dividends declared per share of common stock increased by 13.8 percent—the twenty-eighth consecutive year of cash dividend increases. We also repurchased about 5.6 million shares of common stock at a cost of about $176.7 million." (By purchasing its own shares, the company's profits per share tend to climb, even when profits in total do not. However, if total profits rise, per-share profits rise even more.)

- Mr. Levine listed these key initiatives for fiscal 2005:

  - "Urban Initiative—Investments being made in process changes, technology and people will improve the operating performance of more than 1,000 high-income stores in thirty large metropolitan markets. This initiative is being rolled out in waves, with about 250 stores to be impacted in the first quarter. It incorporates a number of 'Store of the Future' components, including an automated hiring process and organizational changes to support a more mobile and flexible workforce.

    "'Treasure Hunt' Merchandise—Family Dollar's basic assortment of merchandise is being supplemented by additional opportunistically purchased goods. These goods are designed to create more excitement in the stores throughout the year, with particular emphasis on the holiday season. An advertising circular will be distributed in early November 2004, to generate additional sales.

  - "Coolers—Beginning in January 2005, coolers for perishable food will be installed in selected stores. By the end of the fiscal year in August 2005, the current plan is to have coolers in about 500 stores. The company also plans to begin implementation by fiscal year-end of new point-of-sale software to facilitate the acceptance of food stamps in stores with coolers, simplify cashier training and speed up checkout processes."

Total assets: $2,167 million
Current ratio: 1.72
Common shares outstanding: 168 million
Return on 2004 shareholders' equity: 19.7%

| | 2004 | 2003 | 2002 | 2001 | 2000 | 1999 | 1998 | 1997 |
|---|---|---|---|---|---|---|---|---|
| Revenues (millions) | 5,282 | 4,750 | 4,163 | 3,665 | 3,133 | 2,751 | 2,362 | 1,995 |
| Net income (millions) | 263 | 247 | 217 | 190 | 172 | 140 | 103 | 75 |
| Earnings per share | 1.53 | 1.43 | 1.25 | 1.10 | 1.00 | .81 | .60 | .44 |
| Dividends per share | .33 | .28 | .26 | .24 | .22 | .20 | .18 | .16 |
| Price    high | 39.7 | 44.1 | 37.2 | 31.3 | 24.5 | 26.8 | 22.4 | 15.1 |
|        low | 25.1 | 25.5 | 23.8 | 18.4 | 14.3 | 14.0 | 11.5 | 6.3 |

Aggressive Growth

# FedEx Corporation

942 South Shady Grove Road ❑ Memphis, TN 38120 ❑ (901) 818–7200 ❑ Web site: *www.fedex.com* ❑ Direct dividend reinvestment plan is available: (800) 446–2617 ❑ Fiscal years end May 31 ❑ Listed: NYSE ❑ Ticker symbol: FDX ❑ Standard & Poor's rating: B+ ❑ Value Line financial strength rating: B++

FedEx has been a part of the China free-trade success story for twenty years, helping build the air transportation infrastructure needed to support China's growing economic demands. Over that time, FedEx Express has grown to become the largest international express carrier in the country, with service to more than 220 cities and plans to expand to 100 more during the next five years.

With eleven flights every week through three major gateways—Beijing, Shanghai, and Shenzhen—FedEx serves its customers with more flights into and out of China than any other U.S.-based cargo carrier. "FedEx is benefiting enormously from the surge in China trade," said Michael L. Ducker, executive vice president of FedEx Express. "But we're also helping drive it. For the economic revolution to continue, China will need greater access to the global marketplace. That's what FedEx provides."

## Company Profile

FedEx Corporation is the world's leading provider of guaranteed express delivery ser-

vices. Using a $4 million inheritance as seed money, Frederick W. Smith founded FedEx in 1971 when he was only twenty-seven.

The company offers a wide range of express delivery services for the time-definite transportation of documents, packages, and freight. Commercial and military charter services are also offered by FedEx. The company's operations are as follows:

FedEx Express is the world's largest express transportation company, providing fast, reliable delivery to 214 countries, including every address in the United States.

FedEx Ground is North America's second-largest ground carrier for small-package business shipments, including business-to-residential service through FedEx Home Delivery.

FedEx Freight is the largest U.S. regional less-than-truckload freight company, providing next-day and second-day delivery of heavyweight freight within the United States and from key international markets.

FedEx Custom Critical is the "24/7" option for urgent shipments, proving non-stop, door-to-door delivery in the contiguous United States, Canada, and Europe.

FedEx Trade Networks facilitates international trade as the largest-volume customs filer in the United States, and a one-stop source for freight forwarding, advisory services, and trade technology.

## Shortcomings to Bear in Mind

- Over the years, the relationship between FedEx managers and some of its 4,000 pilots has been strained, in part because of CEO Fred Smith's opposition to unions.

  "We had started with the dream that if the company rose to Fred's vision, we'd be at the top as well," said Don Wilson, a twenty-eight-year company veteran who helped organize the FedEx Pilots Union in 1992. "The company has exceeded beyond what anyone expected, but our pay and benefits have not," Mr. Wilson said.

  On the other hand, the company has had a reputation as a great place to work, with employees claiming they "bleed purple and orange"—the company's colors—and living by Smith's mantra: "people, service, profit." FedEx has repeatedly been on *Fortune* magazine's list of the "100 Best Companies to Work For" and its lists of best places for minorities and women to work.

## Reasons to Buy

- On a more positive note, Jim Corridore, an analyst with *Standard & Poor's Stock Reports,* rated FedEx as a STRONG BUY on December 17, 2004, and had this comment: "FDX has long UPS in a number of financial metrics, such as return on assets and return on invested capital, in our opinion. We see much of the company's future growth coming from less asset-intensive ground and freight operations, and from Kinko's

which has proved more accretive than we initially expected. We see the company closing the gap somewhat on these metrics. In our view, this argues for a valuation more closely rivaling that of UPS. We have a STRONG BUY recommendation on the shares."

- Still another analyst spoke favorably about FedEx on January 24, 2005. Suzanne Betts, with the Argus Research Company, said

  "BUY-rated FedEx Corp. continues to grow as it chips away at UPS's domestic market share and plans for increased international presence. FedEx appears to be unaffected by the competitive environment as cited by UPS in a recent earnings warning . . . While we expect the domestic market to remain highly competitive, economic expansion and international growth opportunities are likely to provide enough slices of pie for everyone.

  "FedEx plans to expand its presence in Europe with a goal of sales and volume growth in excess of 10 percent per annum. The company also plans to take the FedEx Kinko's segment beyond U.S. borders to tap the international market. In addition, FedEx will continue to ramp up service in China under the new air agreement and plans to add another 100 cities over the next several years. The company currently serves 220 cities in China."

- "As the digital revolution took hold in the late 1990s, FedEx didn't sit by and wait for its overnight delivery business to be eroded by e-mail and other new technologies," said the author of a *BusinessWeek* article on April 4, 2005. "It went on the offensive, snapping up major trucking outfits and extending its 'just in time' service into heavier freight and package delivery. Last year, FedEx acquired the Kinko's chain to position itself as the shipping and printing service of choice for home-based entrepreneurs. So even as its overnight document business has slipped, FedEx's diversification paid off in spades. Profits doubled in 2004."

- "How has FedEx stayed on top?" asks Matthew Boyle in a *Fortune* article entitled "Why FedEx is Flying High" on November 1, 2004. The answer to the question, says Mr. Boyle: "Through a combination of smart strategy, savvy acquisitions, and really good execution. The aggressive move into Asia is a prime example. FedEx has also enjoyed excellent results from its foray into less-than-truckload (LTL) freight forwarding—a little-known business in which it wasn't even involved six years ago. Founder and CEO Fred Smith, 60, built it by buying two regional freight haulers. Revenues for the LTL business, known as FedEx Freight, grew 27 percent in the past quarter, compared with the same period last year."

- "FedEx transportation services provide the single most important element that every shipper needs—certainty," said the company's CEO Frederick W. Smith, in 2003. "We deliver both shipments and the related information about them exactly as customers need, virtually anywhere in the world. We provide a broad portfolio of service options. And all of this is becoming crucial to businesses striving to transform complex supply chains into more efficient engines of growth and profitability."

- Increasingly, businesses are seeking strategic, cost-effective ways to manage their supply chains—the series of transportation and information exchanges required to convert parts and raw materials into finished, delivered products. According the management: "Experience tells us that customers prefer one supplier to meet all of their distribution and logistics needs. And FedEx has what

it takes: Our unique global network, operational expertise and air route authorities cannot be replicated by the competition. With FedEx, our customers have a strategic competitive weapon to squeeze time, mass and cost from the supply chain."

- In December of 2003, FedEx invested $2.4 billion to buy Kinko's, Inc., "a one-stop back office" for small and midsize businesses. By acquiring Kinko's, FedEx is adopting a strategy of UPS, which bought MailBoxes, Inc. in 2001 to reach more small businesses. Kinko's has 1,200 stores in ten countries. The acquisition is expected to lead to a major expansion of the Kinko's network. FedEx said there is room to "easily double" the number of Kinko's stores in the United States.

- FedEx has invested heavily in recent years to develop an international infrastructure. It presently can reach locations accounting for 90 percent of world GDP, with twenty-four- or forty-eight-hour service. International delivery services for documents and freight have been growing faster than domestic business in recent years.

- According to CEO Frederick W. Smith, "The new strategy we have put in place of the past several years has made us a full-service transportation company, offering the broadest array of services. With FedEx Express, FedEx Ground, FedEx Freight, FedEx Custom Critical and FedEx Trade Networks, we can offer our customers an unprecedented array of shipping and supply chain services quickly and conveniently across the globe."

- FedEx has a solid record of growth. In the last ten years (1994–2004), Earnings per share advanced from $.91 to $2.76, a compound annual growth rate of 11.7 percent. What's more, EPS declined only once in that span (from $2.32 to $2.26 in 2001).

Total assets: $19,134 million
Current ratio: 1.05
Common shares outstanding: 299 million
Return on 2004 shareholders' equity: 10.9%

|  | 2004 | 2003 | 2002 | 2001 | 2000 | 1999 | 1998 | 1997 |
|---|---|---|---|---|---|---|---|---|
| Revenues (millions) | 24,710 | 22,487 | 20,607 | 19,629 | 18,257 | 16,773 | 15,703 | 11,520 |
| Net income (millions) | 838 | 830 | 710 | 663 | 688 | 531 | 526 | 348 |
| Earnings per share | 2.76 | 2.74 | 2.39 | 2.26 | 2.32 | 2.10 | 1.75 | 1.51 |
| Dividends per share | .22 | .20 | Nil | — | — | — | — | — |
| Price high | 100.9 | 78.0 | 61.4 | 53.5 | 49.8 | 61.9 | 46.6 | 42.3 |
| low | 64.8 | 47.7 | 42.8 | 33.2 | 30.6 | 34.9 | 21.8 | 21.0 |

Growth and Income

# Fortune Brands, Inc.

300 Tower Parkway ❑ Lincolnshire, IL 60069–3640 ❑ (847) 484–4410 ❑ Dividend reinvestment plan available: (800) 225–2719 ❑ Web site: *www.fortunebrands.com* ❑ Listed: NYSE ❑ Ticker symbol: FO ❑ S&P rating: B ❑ Value Line financial strength rating: A

"We're driving sales growth and gaining share in a number of ways," said CEO Norm Wesley on October 22, 2004. "That includes successful investments to grow market-leading products such as the Titleist Pro V1 golf ball, new Moen faucets, and Jim Beam bourbon.

"As a partner of choice for major customers, we're benefiting from the rollout of successful kitchen and bath cabinet lines and entry doors at additional home-center stores, as well as expanded relationships with large builders, dealers, and wholesalers.

"Reflecting solid execution, we're successfully growing the high-return Therma-Tru doors brand that we acquired last November. And with a sharpened marketplace focus, our office products brands grew sales for the third quarter in a row. Beyond winning in the marketplace, we also added value for shareholders in the quarter with another double-digit dividend increase. We're pleased that we delivered such strong results in spite of challenging comparisons and higher commodities costs, which we were able to offset with higher volumes, supply chain efficiencies, and select price increases."

## Company Profile

Fortune Brands owns companies with leading consumer brands in home products, office products, golf equipment and spirits and wine. These brands include familiar names like Moen, Titleist, Jim Beam, Master Lock, Swingline, Day-Timer, FootJoy, Cobra, Kensington, ACCO, Wilson Jones, and Geyser Peak.

Named Fortune Brands only since 1997, the company was formerly known as American Brands and was incorporated in Delaware in 1985 as a holding company with subsidiaries in the above-mentioned businesses, as well as others in which it no longer has holdings.

Fortune Brands' roots were planted decades ago. In 1966, a former New Jersey-incorporated subsidiary changed its name to American Brands and began a diversification program with the acquisition of Sunshine Biscuits. The diversification extended to the distilled spirits business in 1967 with the acquisition of the company now known as Jim

Beam Brands Worldwide. The first home and office brands—including Swingline, Master Lock, and Wilson Jones—were acquired in 1970. The 1976 acquisition of Acushnet, with its premier Titleist brand, led the charge into the golf business. In the ensuing years, a wide range of businesses and brands were both acquired and divested to promote the goal of enhanced shareholder value.

In 1994, American Brands, by then a wide collection of businesses with annual net sales totaling more than $15 billion, began a fundamental transformation to focus solely on growing categories in which the company was a leader—home, office, golf, and distilled spirits. The company made significant divestitures in 1994, and in 1997, the company spun off its remaining noncore subsidiary. With its fundamental transformation complete, the company changed its name to Fortune Brands in June of 1997.

Today, fifteen brands have annual sales exceeding $100 million each. Moen, Titleist, and Jim Beam, the three largest brands, account for more than a quarter of sales. More than 80 percent of sales come from brands that are number one or number two in their markets, and more than 25 percent of sales come from new products. For two successive years, the company has been recognized by *Fortune* magazine's prestigious annual survey of executives, directors and securities analysts as the most admired company in the world in its category. The 1999 survey proclaimed Fortune Brands as one of the top five U.S. "National Champions" and as one of the top three companies in the world in innovativeness.

## Shortcomings to Bear in Mind

- *Value Line Investment Survey* had a guarded view of the company on January 28, 2005. Eric M. Gottlieb said, "Fortune Brands shares should outperform the market over the six-to-twelve-month period. But out to 2007–2009, the shares do not provide much capital gains

potential, since we expect the price/earnings ratio to fall, offsetting much of our projected earnings gains."

## Reasons to Buy

- On the other hand, Howard Choe, writing for *Standard & Poor's Stock Reports* on February 1, 2005, had a positive opinion. "Our STRONG BUY recommendation, based on total return (*capital gains plus dividends*), reflects our view of the high growth profile of the company, and attractive valuation. We believe consumers will continue to invest in new homes and remodel existing homes, aiding FO's home and hardware division, which markets the popular Moen faucet lines, and various kitchen cabinet lines. In addition, we believe the company's other operating segments of golf, wine and spirits and office products provide diversification benefits."

- The Therma-Tru doors business of consumer products will significantly increase its presence at North American home-improvement retailers and in attractive European markets due to two new growth initiatives, a company spokesman said in 2004.

  As a result of a newly expanded relationship with Lowe's, a new selection of fiberglass entry doors by Therma-Tru will be available for the first time on an in-stock basis at all 975 of the home-improvement retailer's North American stores over the next six to nine months. Separately, Fortune Brands also announced that Therma-Tru had acquired fast-growing Sentinel Doors Ltd., a leading brand of composite entry doors in the United Kingdom.

  "When we acquired Therma-Tru, we saw significant upside potential for the brand," said Mr. Wesley. "Expansion in the home center channel and development in international markets will help Therma-Tru accelerate its growth and diversify its growth profile. Replacing entry doors is one of the highest-return improvements homeowners can make, and the nationwide roll-out at Lowe's will help Therma-Tru gain share in the growing replace-and-remodel segment.

Therma-Tru is the leading brand of residential entry doors in the United States, and its market leadership is strongest in the industry's fastest-growing segment—high-performance fiberglass entry doors. Therma-Tru uses proprietary technology to create fiberglass entry doors that resemble wood but deliver superior thermal performance and durability.

- In 2003, the company introduced the new King Cobra SS-i iron line and the new King Cobra SS 380 model driver. These innovative new golf clubs build on strong momentum for the Cobra brand, which doubled its sales and market share in 2002 and became the fastest-growing club brand in the marketplace.

The new King Cobra SS-i irons deliver a variety of key enhancements to the original King Cobra SS design. The King Cobra SS-i iron line features an even larger "sweet spot," softer feel, and custom fitting options as the relevant points of difference, as compared with competitive products in the game-improvement strategy.

- In 2003, Fortune Brands announced that its kitchen and bath cabinets business had purchased Capital Cabinet Corporation, a supplier of cabinetry to homebuilders in the fast-growing Las Vegas and Southern California markets. With annual sales of about $30 million, Capital Cabinets became part of the company's Master-Brand Cabinets unit, the second-largest cabinet manufacturer in North America, with annual sales exceeding $1.2 billion.

"Through strong internal growth and successful high-return acquisitions, we're gaining significant share in kitchen and bath cabinetry," said CEO Norm Wesley. "In the second quarter (2003), our cabinets business continued to perform at the high end of our expectations. Capital Cabinets will help give us even better geographic and channel balance in a category with excellent long-term demographics."

- *Standard & Poor's Stock Reports* had good things to say about Fortune Brands on December 7, 2004, according to its analyst, Howard Choe: "Our strong BUY recommendation, based on total return, reflects our view of the high growth profile of the company, and attractive valuation. We believe consumers will continue to invest in new homes, and remodel existing homes, aiding FO's home and hardware division, which markets the popular Moen faucet lines and various kitchen cabinet lines. In addition, we believe the company's other operating segments of golf, wine and spirits, and office products provide diversification benefits. We believe management will continue to focus on bolstering the balance sheet as well as cash flows."

Total assets: $7,884 million
Current ratio: 1.30
Common shares outstanding: 144 million
Return on 2004 shareholders' equity: 26.4%

| | 2004 | 2003 | 2002 | 2001 | 2000 | 1999 | 1998 | 1997 |
|---|---|---|---|---|---|---|---|---|
| Revenues (millions) | 7,321 | 6,214 | 5,678 | 5,674 | 5,844 | 5,525 | 5,241 | 4,844 |
| Net income (millions) | 784 | 579 | 526 | 336 | 366 | 340 | 294 | 242 |
| Earnings per share | 5.23 | 3.86 | 3.41 | 2.49 | 2.29 | 1.99 | 1.67 | 1.41 |
| Dividends per share | 1.26 | 1.14 | 1.02 | .97 | .93 | .89 | .85 | .41 |
| Price      high | 80.5 | 71.8 | 57.9 | 40.5 | 33.3 | 45.9 | 42.3 | 38.0 |
| low | 66.1 | 40.6 | 36.8 | 28.4 | 19.2 | 29.4 | 25.3 | 30.4 |

Conservative Growth

# Gannett Company, Inc.

7950 Jones Branch Drive ❏ McLean, VA 22107 ❏ (703) 854–6917 ❏ Dividend reinvestment plan available: (800) 778–3299 ❏ Web site: *www.gannett.com* ❏ Listed: NYSE ❏ Ticker symbol: GCI ❏ S&P rating: A ❏ Value Line financial strength rating: A++

On November 19, 2004, Gannett acquired the assets of Home Town Communications Network, Inc., a community publishing company with newspapers, telephone directories, shoppers and niche publications in Michigan, Ohio and Kentucky.

The Home Town Communications Network features one daily and sixty-two weekly and twice-weekly community newspapers, with an aggregate, audited circulation greater than 740,000. The network also includes twenty-four community telephone directories with a total distribution of nearly 1,500,000; one shopping guide; and other specialty and niche publications. The company has a digital operation, with Web sites and Web-based services including design and production, as well as commercial typesetting and printing from four plants.

The newspaper group includes the recently launched *Daily Press & Argus* in fast-growing Livingston County, Michigan, and nondaily groups in the suburban areas near Detroit, Cincinnati/Northern Kentucky, and Lansing, Michigan.

"Home Town's publications are an excellent fit with Gannett's operations in these growth areas of Michigan, Ohio and Kentucky," said Gary Watson, president of Gannett's Newspaper Division. "We're very pleased that company founder Philip Power and his wife Kathleen looked to Gannett when they decided to retire. The Powers made very smart decisions in the nearly forty years they owned and operated Home Town and we plan to continue in that tradition."

"Gannett is one of the world's largest newspaper companies, with a demonstrated track record of capable professional management, great financial stability and high community involvement. I wanted the newspapers, telephone directories and other publications that I spent so much of my career building to wind up in good hands after I left. I believe Gannett's hands are the best available," said Philip Power, Home Town's chairman.

Home Town has about 780 employees and revenues in 2004 of about $85 million.

## Company Profile

Gannett Co., Inc. is a large diversified news and information company. Here is a brief rundown of its operations in the USA and abroad:

### Operations Worldwide

Gannett is an international company with headquarters in McLean, Virginia, and operations in forty-three states, the District of Columbia, Guam, the United Kingdom, Belgium, Germany, Italy, and Hong Kong.

### Newspapers

Gannett is the USA's largest newspaper group in terms of circulation. The company's 101 daily newspapers in the USA have a combined daily paid circulation of 7.6 million. They include *USA Today*, the nation's largest-selling daily newspaper, with a circulation of approximately 2.3 million. *USA Today* is available in sixty countries worldwide.

Gannett also owns a variety of nondaily publications and *USA Weekend*, a weekly newspaper magazine of 22.7 million circulation delivered in more than 600 Gannett and non-Gannett newspapers.

Newsquest plc, a wholly owned Gannett subsidiary acquired in mid-1999, is the second largest regional newspaper publisher in the United Kingdom with a portfolio of more than 300 titles. Its publications include seventeen daily newspapers with a combined circulation of approximately 725,000. Newsquest's nondaily publications include *Berrow's Worcester Journal,* the oldest continuously published newspaper in the world.

### Broadcasting
The company owns and operates twenty-one television stations covering 17.9 percent of the USA.

### On the Internet
Gannett has more than 130 Web sites in the United States including *www.usatoday. com,* one of the top newspaper sites on the Internet. Newsquest's award-winning Web network has more than eighty sites in the United Kingdom.

### Other Ventures
Other company operations include Gannett News Service; Clipper, a direct-mail advertising magazine company; Captivate, a network that delivers programming and advertising to television screens in elevators in premier office towers in North America; Gannett Retail Advertising Group; Gannett New Business and Product Development; Gannett Direct Marketing Services; Gannett Offset, a commercial printing operation; Gannett Media Technologies International; and Telematch, a database marketing company.

### History and Financial
Founded by Frank E. Gannett and associates in 1906, Gannett was incorporated in 1923, went public in 1967, and listed on the New York Stock Exchange in 1969. The company has about 53,000 employees. Its more than 272 million shares of common stock are held by some 12,800 shareholders of record in all fifty states and abroad.

### Shortcomings to Bear in Mind
- Some people consider newspapers a dying medium. In 1990, for instance, 113 million Americans read dailies; today, only 76.6 million do. Classifieds, which account for 27 percent of Gannett's annual revenues, seem destined to move to the Web.
- On January 7, 2005, Ford Equity Research awarded Gannett an uninspiring HOLD rating with this brief comment, "Over the past year, the stock has disappointed investors by producing weak relative performance."

### Reasons to Buy
- "Quality journalism also is a key to success, and our TV stations, newspapers and Internet sites consistently are award winners," said CEO Douglas H. McCorkindale in March of 2005. "Gannett properties in the United States and the United Kingdom won more than 1,230 local, state and national journalism awards in 2004. Among them: the coveted Pulitzer Prize for editorial cartooning for Matt Davies of the *Journal News* in Westchester County, N. Y.; the 2004 Scottish Newspaper of the Year for the *Sunday Herald* in Glasgow; two national Edward R. Murrow Awards for KARE-TV in Minneapolis-St. Paul, and one for KUSA-TV in Denver. Gannett's was the only local television group to win three national Murrows."
- On December 6, 2004, *Standard & Poor's Stock Reports* gave Gannett a BUY rating. William H. Donald had this comment: "We are cautious regarding the outlook for advertising in general, in light of uncertainty surrounding business and consumer spending amid uneven economic signals and oil price concerns. However, we see a 7.7 percent

rise in GCI's total revenues for 2005, to $7.94 billion, boosted in part by the addition of about $80 million from the planned acquisition of newspaper publisher Home Town Communication Network, subject to necessary approvals. Most of the growth that we expect in 2005 would come from newspaper publishing."

- "Our rating on Gannett Company is BUY," said John Eade, writing for the Argus Research Company on February 2, 2005. "Gannett is a very solid holding in the media sector due to its strong cash flow, solid balance sheet, and experienced management team. Its revenues are growing faster than most of its industry peers."

- "GCI's small and mid-sized markets are less reliant on volatile national advertising and help wanted advertising than its larger market-focused peers," said Steven Barlow, writing for Prudential Equity Group, LLC, on February 15, 2005. "At the same time, GCI's *USA Today* should provide investors with leverage to a national advertising upturn when it occurs. The company owns the number one and number two position in all of its local news markets. This is a great source of pride at GCI because more than 50 percent of the company's broadcast revenue comes from local news, and broadcast revenue is growing aggressively."

- Gannett Broadcasting's television stations are local market leaders. KARE-TV at Minneapolis-St. Paul, Minnesota; KSDK-TV at St. Louis, Missouri; and KUSA-TV at Denver, Colorado are the top three stations in the nation for late local news in the key selling demographic of adults twenty-five to fifty-four in recent ratings.

  KPNX-TV at Phoenix, Arizona joins them in the top ten in the country. WBIR-TV at Knoxville, Tennessee; WCSH-TV at Portland, Maine; and WMAZ-TV at Macon, Georgia are tops among the nation's medium-sized smaller markets.

  WGRZ-TV at Buffalo, New York; KTHV-TV at Little Rock, Arkansas; and WLTX-TV at Columbia, South Carolina, three stations purchased in the 1990s and all with a history of underperformance, made great strides since 2001. WGRZ went from third to first place in late news for the first time in the station's history. KTHV ranked number two in all news time periods with adults twenty-five to fifty-four.

- Most of the company's newspapers are the only daily publication in their respective cities. To be sure, that doesn't mean they have a monopoly on advertising, since there are other ways to advertise, such as TV, radio, and direct mail. Still, newspapers have always been an important advertising medium, and if you are the only game in town, it helps.

- As the Internet continues to be a growing part of people's lives, more Gannett newspapers are jumping into the World Wide Web. What's more, the online pioneers continue to enhance content and add new products, including those stemming from Gannett's participation in Classified Ventures and CareerPath.com.

  As leading information providers for their communities, the company's newspapers are aware that fresh information is essential to success online. *FLORIDA TODAY*'s Space Online (*www.flatoday. com*), for instance, covers space shuttle launches, literally as they blast off. Reporters with laptop computers file stories from the beach at Cape Canaveral, supplying live news online within moments of a launch.

Total assets: $15,121 million
Current ratio: 1.23
Common shares outstanding: 257 million
Return on 2004 shareholders' equity: 16%

| | 2004 | 2003 | 2002 | 2001 | 2000 | 1999 | 1998 | 1997 |
|---|---|---|---|---|---|---|---|---|
| Revenues (millions) | 7,381 | 6,711 | 6,422 | 6,300 | 6,222 | 5,260 | 5,121 | 4,730 |
| Net income (millions) | 1,317 | 1,211 | 1,160 | 831 | 972 | 919 | 816 | 713 |
| Earnings per share | 4.92 | 4.46 | 4.31 | 3.12 | 3.63 | 3.26 | 2.86 | 2.50 |
| Dividends per share | 1.04 | .98 | .94 | .89 | .86 | .82 | .78 | .74 |
| Price    high | 92.4 | 89.6 | 79.9 | 71.1 | 81.6 | 83.6 | 75.1 | 61.8 |
|          low | 78.8 | 66.7 | 62.8 | 53.0 | 48.4 | 60.6 | 47.6 | 35.7 |

Conservative Growth

# General Dynamics Corporation

2941 Fairview Park Drive, Suite 100 ❑ Falls Church, VA 22042–4513 ❑ (703) 876–3195 ❑ Dividend reinvestment plan not available ❑ Web site: *www.gendyn.com* ❑ Ticker symbol: GD ❑ S&P rating: B+ ❑ Value Line financial strength rating: A++

The U.S. Army Tank-Automotive and Armaments Command on December 2, 2004, awarded General Dynamics Land Systems three delivery orders valued at $206 million for 95 Stryker combat vehicles, including the first production of the Mobile Gun System and Nuclear, Biological, and Chemical Reconnaissance variants. The vehicles are part of a $4 billion order awarded in November 2000 to equip the Army's six new Stryker Brigade Combat Teams with 2,100 Stryker armored vehicles. General Dynamics Land Systems is a business unit of General Dynamics.

The Department of Defense approved the mobile gun variant and NBC reconnaissance vehicle for low rate initial production in October of 2004. Production of fourteen mobile guns, seventeen NBC vehicles, twenty-five infantry, and thirty-nine mortar carriers began in January 2005 at plants in Anniston, Alabama; Lima, Ohio; and London, Ontario. Production will be completed in February 2006. Subcomponents will be built at General Dynamics Land Systems

facilities in Eynon, Pennsylvania; Imperial Valley, California; Muskegon, Michigan; Tallahassee, Florida; and Westminster, Maryland.

The Army will have six Stryker Brigade Combat Teams by 2008. Stryker is the Army's highest-priority production combat vehicle program and the centerpiece of the ongoing Army Transformation. Significantly lighter and more transportable than existing tanks and armored vehicles, Stryker fulfills an immediate requirement to equip a strategically deployable (C-17/C-5) and operationally deployable (C-130) brigade capable of rapid movement anywhere on the globe in a combat-ready configuration.

Stryker is a family of eight-wheel drive combat vehicles that can travel at speeds up to 62 mph on highways, with a range of 312 miles. It operates with the latest C4ISR equipment as well as detectors for nuclear, biological, and chemical weapons. Stryker vehicle configurations include the nuclear, chemical, and biological reconnaissance vehicle; anti-tank guided missile and medical evacuation vehicles; and carriers for mortars, engineer squads, infantry squads, command groups, and fire support teams.

## Company Profile

General Dynamics was officially established February 21, 1952, although it has organizational roots dating back to the late 1800s. The company was formed after its predecessor and current operating division, Electric Boat, acquired the aircraft company Canadair Ltd. and began building the first nuclear-powered submarine, USS *Nautilus*.

Through the years, General Dynamics has applied the wisdom of its experience and insight to recognize and act on change to build its position in the defense and technology business sectors. Building upon its marine business, the company added its first Combat Systems business unit, Land Systems, in 1982; its first Information Systems and Technology business unit, Advanced Technology Systems, in 1997; and returned to the aerospace business with Gulfstream in 1999.

Today, General Dynamics has leading market positions in business aviation and aircraft services, land and amphibious combat systems, mission-critical information systems and technologies, and shipbuilding and marine systems. The company is a leading supplier of sophisticated defense systems to the United States and its allies, and sets the world standard in business jets.

General Dynamics has four main business segments. Aerospace designs, manufactures, and provides services for mid-size, large cabin, and ultralong range business aircraft. Combat Systems supplies land and amphibious combat machines and systems, including armored vehicles, power trains, turrets, munitions, and gun systems. Information Systems and Technology's expertise lies in specialized data acquisition and processing, in advanced electronics, and in battlespace information networks and management systems. Marine Systems

designs and builds submarines, surface combatants, auxiliary ships, and large commercial vessels.

### Information Systems and Technology

General Dynamics Information Systems and Technology is a leading integrator of transformational, network-centric command-and-control, communications, computing, intelligence, surveillance, and reconnaissance (C4ISR) systems using digital information-sharing technologies. These systems provide today's war-fighters with secure, on-demand access to more mission-critical information than ever before, enabling U.S. forces and allies to prevail on the battlefield.

### Combat Systems

General Dynamics Combat Systems is a market-leading provider of tracked and wheeled armored combat vehicles, armament systems, and munitions for customers in North America, Europe, the Middle East, and the South Pacific—and the only producer of America's main battle tanks.

### Marine Systems

General Dynamics Marine Systems designs, develops, manufactures, and integrates the complex naval platforms that are central to the U.S. Navy's transformation to a more lethal, flexible, network-centric sea force of the future. Its three advanced shipyards apply decades of development innovation, experience, and expertise to produce the world's most sophisticated maritime surface, sub-surface, and support systems.

### Aerospace

General Dynamics Aerospace is one of the world's leading designers and manufacturers of business-jet aircraft, and is a leading provider of services for private aircraft in select markets globally. Gulfstream business jets are among the most technologically advanced aircraft available, and the company provides a broad selection of planes to meet the demanding requirements of business and government customers alike.

## Shortcomings to Bear in Mind

- On January 4, 2005, the Argus Research Company had a HOLD rating on General Dynamics, according to Suzanne Betts, who said, "We are downgrading our rating on General Dynamics Corp. from BUY to HOLD, as the stock took a hit from proposed government budget cuts. While GD may not feel the brunt of the ultimate budget-cutting decision, the stock is likely to remain under pressure in the near term."

  She also said, "The recently unveiled proposals to slash defense spending over the next six years have sent the defense stocks into a tail spin. While the final verdict remains unclear, we do expect a portion of these proposals to take effect, thus impacting how these companies will perform in the long term."

- On January 27, 2005, Prudential Equity Group, LLC had a mixed view of the stock and gave it a NEUTRAL rating. Jared Muroff said, "We believe the company has some very attractive business lines. However, we believe its stock is appropriately valued at current levels ($102.30). Although we believe that the Land Combat Systems business is second-to-none globally, improvement at Gulfstream is likely, and that the company's information technology business performance should remain strong, we still have concerns surrounding the Marine Systems business, our expectation that earnings growth will be below the average we expect for our universe, and that at GD's current share price, the stock trades near the value we calculate on a discounted cash flow basis and above its historic multiples."

## Reasons to Buy

- "General Dynamics continues to benefit from its ground vehicle superiority," said Ian Gendler writing for *Value Line Survey* on March 25, 2005. "On February 17, 2005, the U.S. Army purchased 423 Strykers (wheeled combat vehicles) for a total of $582 million, to be delivered over the next two years. This segment should continue to perform well as the U.S. Army transforms itself into a more agile, faster-moving fighting force."

- The Information Systems and Technology Group secured several important contracts in 2003, including the Intelligence Information, Command and Control Equipment and Enhancements (ICE2) program, which provides IT support for U.S. defense and intelligence operations worldwide; the integration of the Army's Land Warrior system; and the Common Hardware/Software III program, which provides continuously updated computing technology to defense customers.

- Several activities of the Combat Systems Group in 2003 demonstrated the group's strength, including continued production of the Army's Stryker infantry carrier vehicles and specialized variants, and development of the U.S. Marine Corps's Expeditionary Fighting Vehicle (EFV). The group also was selected to develop manned ground vehicles and robotic technologies for the Army's Future Combat Systems program, and expanded its market in munitions, guided rockets, sensors, and composites.

- The Marine Systems group continuing partnership with the Navy was illustrated in 2003 by the Virginia-class submarine program and the T-AKE, the first new combat logistics ship design in almost twenty years. The group also is helping the Navy extend the utility of its Trident ballistic-missile submarines by converting four to tactical-strike SSGNs, and it was selected to develop preliminary designs for the fast, network-centric Littoral Combat Ship.

- The Aerospace group met several key milestones in 2003, including Federal Aviation Administration certification of the Collier Trophy-winning Gulfstream G550 aircraft, and introduction of the large-cabin, long-range G450 and G350.

The G450 also was designated as the platform of choice by a team competing for the U.S. military contract for an airborne intelligence, surveillance, and reconnaissance system.

**Total assets: $17,544 million**
**Current ratio: 1.36**
**Common shares outstanding: 200 million**
**Return on 2004 shareholders' equity: 18.4%**

|  |  | 2004 | 2003 | 2002 | 2001 | 2000 | 1999 | 1998 | 1997 |
|---|---|---|---|---|---|---|---|---|---|
| Revenues (millions) | | 19,178 | 16,617 | 13,829 | 12,163 | 10,356 | 8,959 | 4,970 | 4,062 |
| Net income (millions) | | 1,203 | 998 | 1,051 | 943 | 901 | 715 | 364 | 316 |
| Earnings per share | | 5.97 | 5.00 | 5.07 | 4.65 | 4.48 | 3.54 | 2.86 | 2.50 |
| Dividends per share | | 1.40 | 1.26 | 1.20 | 1.10 | 1.02 | .96 | .87 | .82 |
| Price | high | 110.0 | 90.8 | 111.2 | 96.0 | 79.0 | 75.4 | 62.0 | 45.8 |
| | low | 85.0 | 50.0 | 73.3 | 60.5 | 36.3 | 46.2 | 40.3 | 31.6 |

Growth and Income

# General Electric Company

3135 Easton Turnpike ❑ Fairfield, CT 06828 ❑ (203) 373–2468 ❑ Direct dividend reinvestment plan available: (800) 786–2543 ❑ Web site: *www.ge.com* ❑ Ticker symbol: GE ❑ S&P rating: A+ ❑ Value Line financial strength rating: A++

Some companies manufacture locomotives, and some engineer thermoplastics for a living.

Others design high-end cooktops; still others operate national TV networks.

Not many, though, offer a full range of economy-fueling financial services on a global scale.

Fewer still make jet engines.

Or sophisticated medical scanners.

Or multimegawatt gas-fired power turbines.

And only one company—just one— delivers on all these things.

Only GE.

## Company Profile

General Electric, a superbly managed company, provides a broad range of industrial products and services. Under the stewardship of CEO Jack Welch (now retired), GE transformed itself from operating as a maker of diverse industrial equipment, to being a provider of a broad range of commercial and consumer services.

In 1980, manufacturing operations generated about 85 percent of operating profits; currently, services operations generate 70 percent of total operating profits. GE Capital (the company's enormous financing arm, and the world's largest nonbank financial operation) alone generates nearly 30 percent of operating profits.

General Electric is one of the world's largest corporations. Although GE can trace its origins back to Thomas Edison, who invented the light bulb in 1879, the company was actually founded in 1892.

The company's broad diversification is clearly evident if you examine its components: Operations are divided into two groups: product, service, and media businesses and GE Capital Services (GECS).

Product, service and media includes 11 businesses: aircraft engines, appliances, lighting, medical systems, NBC, plastics, power systems, electrical distribution and control, information services, motors and industrial systems, and transportation systems.

In 2002, the company—often criticized for the complexity of its structure and the resulting opacity of its numbers—said it would break up GE Capital, by far its largest business, into four businesses. The new businesses are GE Commercial Finance, GE Insurance, GE Consumer Finance, and GE Equipment Management.

## Shortcomings to Bear in Mind

- "In a loss for General Electric Company, long-time GE customer All Nippon Airways selected Rolls-Royce PLC to supply engines for the 50 Boeing 7E7 jetliners that ANA plans to purchase," according to an article in the *Wall Street Journal* on October 14, 2004. Authors Daniel Michaels and Kathryn Kranhold went on to say, "Rolls-Royce, based in Britain, valued the deal at $1 billion. The 7E7 and the engines from GE of Fairfield, Conn., and Rolls-Royce are in development, with first deliveries planned for 2008. GE widely was expected to win the ANA engine competition with its GEnx model. It supplies eighty percent of ANA's engines and dominates the Japanese market."

- "General Electric has been paying lofty sums these days as it pushes to buy companies in high-growth businesses," said Kathryn Kranhold for the *Wall Street Journal* on December 2, 2004. Ms. Kranhold also said, "Just last week, GE Infrastructure, formed a year ago, agreed to pay $1.1 billion, plus the assumption of $200 million in debt, for water-treatment company

Ionics, Inc., a 48 percent premium based on its share price the day before the deal was announced."

- On October 13, 2004, a *Wall Street Journal* article had this negative article, written by Brooks Barnes: "The Peacock's feathers are fraying. After more than a decade as the dominant broadcast network, General Electric Company's NBC is having a rocky fall. So far this season, the network has endured double-digit ratings declines in both total viewers and viewers aged eighteen to forty-nine, the demographic that advertisers pay a premium to reach. Particularly troubling: For the first time since 1987, NBC is losing the ratings race on Thursdays, the night that by far draws the most advertising dollars and have been the bulwark of NBC's 'Must See TV' franchise."

## Reasons to Buy

- Nicholas Heymann, an analyst with Prudential Equity Group, had this comment on February 16, 2005, "As investors seek to prepare for slower economic growth ahead, as U.S. interest rates and global growth slow, we believe GE represents one of the best choices to outperform the overall averages with a likely series of positive catalysts which should begin to emerge later this spring and early winter. We strongly sense these are likely to further reinforce investor belief that the company's expected above-average growth will be achieved. Most importantly, since some 90 percent of GE's earnings come from long-cycle rather than flow businesses, we believe GE's return to double-digit earnings growth is likely to be sustainable for three to five years, and possibly the rest of the decade."

- Lehman Brothers, another leading brokerage firm, gave GE an OVERWEIGHT (*similar to BUY*) rating on March 3, 2005. The analyst said, "The company anticipates that 60 percent of its growth in the next decade will come from the developing world. But U.S. and Europe will contribute importantly as well. We continue to believe GE EPS (*Earnings per share*) growth in 2005–2007 could be 15 percent."

- "We expect cash flow from operating activities to grow annually at double-digit rates over the next several years," said Edward Plank, writing for *Value Line Investment Survey* on January 14, 2005. "GE plans to use its strong cash resources to fund growth at the financial services unit, as well as return value to shareholders. Indeed, the company recently raised its quarterly dividend 10 percent and authorized repurchase of up to $15 billion of its common stock over the next three years.

- *BusinessWeek* magazine had a favorable comment on October 11, 2004, written by Diane Brady: "While many companies boast a global workforce, few are as skilled at mobilizing experts from diverse disciplines and locales in pursuit of a common goal. The difference stems from culture more than from technology. At GE, executives are encouraged to think beyond the boundaries of their particular business.

  "They come together frequently for training or joint projects. Executives are apt to move among units several times in their careers, letting them build up a rich network of internal contacts. There's also a tradition of plucking people from their day jobs for other projects. At any given time, thousands of GE employees are on so-called bubble assignments—lending their skills to another function or business that pays their salaries for the duration of the project."

- On July 18, 2004, a *New York Times* article, written by Reed Abelson and Milt Freudenheim, had this comment: "With $14 billion in sales, GE's health care business is among the fastest-growing and most profitable units, and one that is central to the vision of its chief executive,

Jeffrey R. Immelt, who rose to the top job after running the company's medical systems unit. He is unapologetic about GE's growing role in providing management skills and financing, as well as hardware, to hospitals. GE is responsible for important advances in medical technology, he said, and can bring a businesslike efficiency to an industry that is badly in need of it."

In a later section, the *New York Times* writers said, "General Electric is famous for its sophisticated diagnostic imaging equipment. Using new CT scanners, doctors can take an image of the heart in five beats, to check for a narrowing of the arteries. Or they can perform a 'virtual colonoscopy' without the invasive procedure that patients find so unpleasant."

- The key to GE's business plan is the requirement that businesses be first or second in market share in their industries. Those that fail to achieve this status are divested.

- Jack Welch, the previous CEO, enhanced and augmented a defect-reduction program called Six Sigma. Six Sigma contributes mightily to GE's earning growth. Think of sigma as a mark on a bell curve that measures standard deviation. Most companies have between 35,000 and 50,000 defects per million operations, or about 3 sigma. For GE, a defect could be anything from the miss billing of an NBC advertiser to faulty wiring in locomotives. Four years ago, engineers determined that the company was averaging 35,000 defects per million operations—or about 3.5 sigma. (The higher the sigma, the fewer the errors.) That was a better-than-average showing, but not enough for Welch's restless mind. He's now maniacal about hitting his goal of reducing defects to the point where errors would be almost nonexistent; 3.4 defects per million, or 6 sigma.

- In an article written for the *Wall Street Journal* on October 4, 2004, Kathryn Kranhold said: "General Electric Company, the leader in manufacturing natural-gas-fired turbines for power plants, is negotiating with several electric companies to build new 'clean coal' power plants, as it moves to create a global market for the costly, environmentally friendly technology."

  The *Journal* writer went on to say, "GE has estimated the coal-generation market at about $25 billion a year as power companies start replacing aging plants. Smith Barney analyst Jeffrey Sprague stated in a recent report that the gasification technology 'has the potential of capturing a dominant share of the coal power generation capital expenditures' by the end of the decade. He notes it is in its 'embryonic stage.'"

- Since taking the reins in late 2001, CEO Jeffrey Immelt has overhauled the company's portfolio of businesses, investing more than $40 billion to expand into industries such as water services and security systems, as well as health care information technologies, and the film industry. What's more, Mr. Immelt has also scaled down the company's volatile—once giant—insurance business and focused on GE's consumer- and commercial-lending businesses.

Total assets: $750 billion
Current ratio: 2.09
Common shares outstanding: 10,572 million
Return on 2004 shareholders' equity: 17.4%

|  |  | 2004 | 2003 | 2002 | 2001 | 2000 | 1999 | 1998 | 1997 |
|---|---|---|---|---|---|---|---|---|---|
| Revenues (millions) |  | 151,299 | 134,187 | 131,698 | 125,913 | 129,853 | 111,630 | 100,469 | 54,515 |
| Net income (millions) |  | 16,593 | 15,589 | 14,118 | 13,684 | 12,735 | 10,717 | 9,296 | 8,203 |
| Earnings per share |  | 1.59 | 1.55 | 1.51 | 1.41 | 1.27 | 1.07 | .93 | .83 |
| Dividends per share |  | .82 | .77 | .73 | .64 | .57 | .48 | .42 | .36 |
| Price | high | 37.8 | 32.4 | 41.8 | 53.6 | 60.5 | 53.2 | 34.6 | 25.5 |
|  | low | 28.9 | 21.3 | 21.4 | 28.5 | 41.6 | 31.4 | 23.0 | 16.0 |

Growth and Income

# General Mills, Incorporated

P. O. Box 1113 ▢ Minneapolis, MN 55440–1113 ▢ (763) 764–7780 ▢ Dividend reinvestment plan available: (800) 670–4763 ▢ Web site: *www.generalmills.com* ▢ Listed: NYSE ▢ Fiscal years end last Sunday in May ▢ Ticker symbol: GIS ▢ S&P rating: A- ▢ Value Line financial strength rating: B++

"Sales for our consolidated international businesses grew 19 percent in fiscal 2004, to reach $1.55 billion," said a spokesman for General Mills in mid-2004. GIS is the nation's second-largest producer of ready-to-eat breakfast cereals and a leading producer of other well-known packaged consumer foods. "We continue to build the scale of our international operations and improve margins."

The GIS company official went on to say, "In Canada, unit volume increased 6 percent, with good growth from our cereal, vegetables, and frozen snacks. Retail sales for our ready-to-eat cereals were up 7 percent, led by a 23 percent sales increase of our Oatmeal Crisp cereal line. Pillsbury Pizza Pops frozen snacks continued to perform well, with unit volume up 8 percent.

"Outside of North America, we market three global brands. Haagen-Dazs holds the leading position in Europe's growing super-premium ice cream category. This spring (2004), we launched Haagen-Dazs Cream Crisp ice cream sandwiches in Europe, building on the success of our Haagen-Dazs Crispy Sandwich in Japan.

"In China, Wanchai Ferry dumplings posted a 36 percent volume increase, thanks to new pan-fried and steamed varieties. In Australia, we rolled out 18 new Betty Crocker dessert mixes for uniquely Australian treats such as Rock Cakes and Anzac Biscuits.

"In Latin America, volume of La Saltena fresh pasta in Argentina rose 10 percent. In addition, we've introduced a variety of Frescarini pasta shapes in Brazil. We expect our international businesses to generate excellent sales and margin growth in the years ahead."

## Company Profile

General Mills is the second-largest domestic producer of ready-to-eat breakfast cereals. It is also a leading producer of other well-known packaged consumer foods.

Major cereal brands, most of which bear the Big G label, include Cheerios, Wheaties, Lucky Charms, Total, and Chex cereals. Other consumer packaged food products include baking mixes (Betty Crocker and Bisquick); meals (Betty Crocker dry packaged dinner mixes), Progresso soups, Green Giant canned and frozen vegetables); snacks (Pop Secret microwave popcorn, Bugles snacks, grain and fruit snack products); Pillsbury refrigerated and frozen dough products, frozen breakfast products and frozen pizza and snack products; organic foods and other products, including Yoplait and Colombo

yogurt. Nor does this include many other brand names, such as Haagen-Dazs frozen ice cream and a host of joint ventures.

Net Sales Growth by Division (in millions):

|                | 2004    | 2003    | Growth |
|----------------|---------|---------|--------|
| Big G Cereals  | $2,071  | $1,998  | 5%     |
| Meals          | 1,749   | 1,702   | 3      |
| Pillsbury USA  | 1,518   | 1,438   | 6      |
| Yoplait/Other  | 1,011   | 932     | 8      |
| Snacks         | 828     | 788     | 5      |
| Baking Products| 586     | 549     | 7      |

The company's international businesses consist of operations and sales in Canada, Europe, Latin America, and the Asia/Pacific region. In those regions, General Foods sells numerous local brands, in addition to internationally recognized brands, such as Haagen-Dazs ice cream, Old El Paso Mexican foods and Green Giant vegetables. Those international businesses have sales and marketing organizations in thirty-three countries: Europe, 36 percent; Canada, 30 percent; Asia/Pacific, 21 percent; Latin America, 13 percent.

## Shortcomings to Bear in Mind

- The company's debt as a percentage of total capital is well above my guidelines, at 61 percent. However, management is endeavoring to improve its balance sheet in the years ahead. Here's what CEO Stephen W. Sanger had to say on the subject on July 29, 2004, "Strong cash flow enabled us to exceed our debt-reduction goal for 2004, pay out nearly 40 percent of earnings as dividends and make all of our planned capital investments to support future growth. General Mills' debt levels increased significantly in conjunction with our October 2001 acquisition of Pillsbury. We are committed to paying down $2 billion in net debt by the end of fiscal 2006 and targeted $450 million of that total in 2004. In fact, we reduced our debt balance by $572 million. This has improved our financial condition and puts us in good shape, relative to our three-year debt-reduction goal."

- For those investors looking for dividend growth, the record of recent years is not encouraging. The annual dividend was stuck at $1.10 for four years in a row. On a more positive note, the company took steps to enhance its payout with an increase to $1.24 in 2004, with the prospects of a further increase to $1.30 in 2005.

## Reasons to Buy

- According to Mr. Sanger, "The key driver of our results in 2005 will be the level of product innovation we bring to our brands and business categories. The number of new products will outpace the record level of 2004. And more importantly, our product innovation will bring meaningful, new health and convenience benefits to consumers.

  "We expect our product innovation, productivity initiatives and pricing actions to offset the hurdles we see in 2005 and enable us to meet or exceed our 2004 level of Earnings per share. And we expect another year of strong cash flows."

- Here is a comment by Ashley Smith, writing for Argus Research Company on December 23, 2004, "BUY-rated General Mills Inc. reported second-quarter sales and earnings and held a meeting with analysts on December 21, 2004. The company's second quarter earnings beat both our quarterly estimate of $0.89 and the Street's estimate of $0.87 per share. We continue to believe that General Mills' strong portfolio of products and focus on health-and-wellness-related products will drive growth over the next twelve months."

- General Mills has a solid market share in most of its product lines, generally number one or number two: ready-to-eat cereals (number two), refrigerated yogurt (one), frozen vegetables (one),

Mexican products (two), ready-to-serve soup (two), refrigerated dough (one), dessert mixes (one), frozen baked goods (one), microwave popcorn (two), frozen hot snacks (two), dry dinners (one), and fruit snacks (one).

- "Over the long haul, General Mills has delivered for consumers and investors, and there is little reason to believe that won't be the case in the future," said Andrew Bary, in a *Barron's* article dated March 1, 2004. "Since 1928, when the company began trading on the New York Stock Exchange at a split-adjusted price of 20 cents apiece, its stock has returned 7.6 percent annually, excluding dividends, beating the Dow Jones Industrial Average by three percentage points a year.

  "If General Mills can generate 5 percent annual sales growth and earnings gains of 8 percent to 9 percent, its stock should continue to rise by 7.6 percent a year or more in the next decade. Include dividends, and the total return could be closer to 10 percent, with limited downside risk. Think of it as the enduring power of Wheaties."

- Although some analysts are skeptical of the 2001 acquisition of Pillsbury, it now appears that the price paid was not excessive. According to the *Barron's* article, "In buying Pillsbury, its Minneapolis neighbor, General Mills doubled its annual sales. It picked up the leading maker of refrigerated dough; the Progresso, Old El Paso and Green Giant brands; a large domestic food-service business; international food operations; and one of the best-known corporate mascots, the Pillsbury Doughboy.

  "One unfortunate legacy, however, was the addition of debt, issued to fund the cash portion of the deal. In all, General Mills paid $6 billion in stock and $4 billion cash to Pillsbury's former owner, Diageo. The company's debt load is one of the food industry's highest."

In answer to the comments by *Barron's*, Mr. Sanger said, "We continue to believe that adding Pillsbury has made each of these growth strategies better. We think our mix of retail categories offer great opportunities for product and marketing innovation. We see exciting opportunities to expand distribution of our leading brands in fast-growing new retail channels, including natural and organic stores, and club stores. In addition, we've strengthened our opportunities to capture a growing share of away-from-home food sales.

"With the addition of the Pillsbury international business, we now generate more than $1 billion of our net reported sales in markets outside the United States. Through our wholly owned operations and our joint ventures, we expect to show continued strong growth in international sale and profits. And finally, we expect to drive margin expansion through a continuous focus on productivity savings. For our supply chain operations alone, productivity over the next three years is targeted at a cumulative $300 million pretax."

Total assets: $18,448 million
Current ratio: 1.17
Common shares outstanding: 378 million
Return on 2004 shareholders' equity: 22.4%

|  | 2004 | 2003 | 2002 | 2001 | 2000 | 1999 | 1998 | 1997 |
|---|---|---|---|---|---|---|---|---|
| Revenues (millions) | 11,070 | 10,506 | 7,949 | 7,078 | 6,700 | 6,246 | 6,033 | 5,609 |
| Net income (millions) | 1,055 | 917 | 581 | 643 | 614 | 567 | 522 | 475 |
| Earnings per share | 2.75 | 2.43 | 1.70 | 2.20 | 2.00 | 1.80 | 1.61 | 1.50 |
| Dividends per share | 1.10 | 1.10 | 1.10 | 1.10 | 1.10 | 1.08 | 1.06 | 1.02 |
| Price    high | 50.0 | 49.7 | 51.7 | 52.9 | 45.3 | 43.9 | 39.8 | 39.1 |
|          low | 43.0 | 41.4 | 37.4 | 37.3 | 29.4 | 32.5 | 29.6 | 28.9 |

Conservative Growth

# The Home Depot, Inc.

2455 Paces Ferry Road, N.W. ❏ Atlanta, GA 30339–4024 ❏ (770) 384–4388 ❏ Direct dividend reinvestment plan available: (877) 437–4273 ❏ Web site: *www.homedepot.com* ❏ Fiscal years end Friday closest to January 31 of following year ❏ Listed: NYSE ❏ Ticker symbol: HD ❏ S&P rating: A+ ❏ Value Line financial strength rating: A++

"When Bob Nardelli didn't win Jack Welch's vote of confidence to be CEO of General Electric in November 2000, he packed up and headed south to Atlanta to run the world's largest home-improvement retailer," said *Fortune* magazine's editor-at-large Patricia Sellers and writer Julie Schlosser on September 20, 2004. "The top spot at Home Depot, now the nation's thirteenth-largest company, was not only a respectable second prize but a chance to prove Welch wrong.

"It's been a tough slog. While the market rallied behind Nardelli in his first few months at the helm, Home Depot's stock price tumbled 47 percent by early 2003. Nardelli drew criticism for trying to impose GE's famously rigorous management techniques too quickly on the freewheeling Home Depot culture. But his recent performance has been a redemption of sorts. Despite pressure on multiple fronts—the challenging economic climate, rising lumber costs, fierce competition from Lowe's—Nardelli has increased revenues 42 percent, to $65 billion last year, and profits 67 percent, to $4.2 billion."

## Company Profile
Founded in 1978, Home Depot is the world's largest home-improvement retailer and the second-largest domestic retailer.

Home Depot operates more than 1,800 stores, including 1,602 Home Depot units in the United States, 110 Home Depot stores in Canada, and forty-two The Home Depot stores in Mexico. The company also operates fifty-four EXPO Design Centers, eleven The Home Depot Landscape Supply stores, five The Home Depot Supply stores, and two The Home Depot Floor stores.

The company's Home Depot stores are full-service warehouse-style outlets offering between 40,000 and 50,000 different kinds of building materials, home-improvement supplies, and lawn and garden products to do-it-yourselfers, home-improvement contractors, tradespeople, and building-maintenance professionals.

What's more, Home Depot operates EXPO Design Center stores, which offer products and services essentially related to design and renovation projects; Home Depot Landscape Supply stores, which service landscape professionals, and garden enthusiasts with lawn, landscape, and garden products; and Home Depot Supply stores, serving primarily professional customers. Finally, HD operates one Home Depot Floor Store, a test operation that offers only flooring products and installation services.

In addition, Home Depot has its fingers in a number of other pies. For instance, it offers its products through direct marketing channels. Its Maintenance Warehouse unit is a leading direct mail marketer of maintenance, repair, and operations products,

doing business with the multifamily housing and lodging facilities management market.

Nor has the company ignored the Internet. In fiscal 2001, HD began selling some 20,000 products online at its e-commerce site, *www.homedepot.com*. Finally, Home Depot also operates several subsidiaries. Atlanta-based Georgia Lighting offers an extensive collection of decorative lighting fixture, and accessories to commercial and retail customers. Apex Supply Company is a wholesale distributor of plumbing, HVAC, appliance and other related products. More recently, in the fall of 2002, Home Depot acquired three residential construction flooring businesses, making the company the largest supplier in a $12-billion market segment.

## Shortcomings to Bear in Mind
- Interest rates have been low, which has been a spur to home ownership and home-improvement projects, which helps Home Depot. If interest rates start to climb and mortgage rates follow suit, that ball game may come to an end.
- Lowe's push into major U.S. metro areas, where Home Depot has long dominated, could help Lowe's more than Home Depot. What's more, the smaller company's focus on enhancing customer experience through improved store layout, faster service and brand name appliances and fixtures could be a thorn in the side of Home Depot.

## Reasons to Buy
- "We are reiterating our BUY rating on Home Depot," said Christopher Graja, CFA, in a report issued by the Argus Research Company on February 23, 2005. "Our recommendation is based on the company's increasing return on capital, now over 20 percent, reasonable valuation, and financial strength. Our biggest concern with the recommendation is that we believe HD's earnings are vulnerable to

an unanticipated decline in the economy or the housing market. Nevertheless, we believe that the economy will continue to expand and that the company's strong financial position will support future opportunities for growth."

- On January 7, 2005, *Value Line Investment Survey* had an upbeat view of Home Deport, according to William W. Lee. At that time, *Value Line* rated the stock number one for Timeliness, its highest rating. "Home Depot is expanding beyond the typical 'big-box' structure and is seeking to capitalize on the emerging 'Do It for Me' market. The company acquired White Cap (a construction supply company) earlier this year, transforming it into a distribution business catering to large and mid-size professional contractor markets. Although this nonretail segment accounts for about 3 percent of total revenue, it is growing three times as fast as the company average."

- In January 2004, the company announced that it would spend $3.7 billion in 2004 to modernize its stores, upgrade technology, and open 175 new stores. Customer satisfaction at the stores is directly linked to technology improvements, such as self-checkout, cordless price scan guns, quick price lookup, as well as return policies that don't require receipts, said chief information officer, Bob DeRodes.

- "Our recommendation is BUY," said Michael Sauers, an analyst with *Standard & Poor's Stock Report*, on March 1, 2005. "We think recent and likely additional acquisitions in the fast-growing do-it-yourself segment should help maintain positive earnings momentum. We also see high consumer interest in home makeovers, healthy economic trends, and improved merchandise and consumer service as positive for the stock."

- "We believe HD can continue to improve its gross margin rate in the upcoming years with a more favorable merchandise mix, improved inventory shrinkage, and increase penetration of higher-margin imports and private brands," said Wayne Hood, writing for Prudential Equity Group, LLC, on February 23, 2005. "During 2004, HD invested close to $1 billion in modernizing new stores. This investment took the form of full remodels, relocations, minor touch ups, and extensive merchandise resets."

- In 2004, Home Depot announced the purchase of Creative Touch Interiors (CTI), a leading turnkey design center provider for major homebuilders in Southern California and Las Vegas. According to management, "CTI has become part of The Home Depot Supply's Builder Solutions Group, which offers turnkey solutions in flooring, countertops, window treatments and design services for the nation's largest homebuilders. The group targets the $25 billion in finished products and services consumed annually in new home construction. The acquisition of CTI extends the Builder Solutions Group's reach from coast to coast, by adding the Las Vegas and Southern California markets."

- "Nardelli, former head of General Electric's Power Systems unit, is remaking Home Depot, and doing it in classic GE style, according to an article in *BusinessWeek* on October 25, 2004, written by Brian Grow. "He's betting big on technology to boost productivity while plunging into services, this time to profit from those who want home improvements done for them. There is also a push to innovate, with spiffy new store designs, and a move into largely untapped foreign markets, such as China, where the company is scouting locations."

- *Barron's* financial weekly had some interesting comments on October 11, 2004. According to Christopher C. Williams, "The CEO has stated that he wants to build Home Depot into a $100-billion business and open upwards of 200 stores a year for 'the foreseeable future.' To do that, he must exploit new markets, and few are more appealing than Manhattan, where the company estimates home-improvement sales total $3 billion a year. 'We don't have too many $3 billion markets where we don't have stores,' says Tom Taylor, Home Depot's Eastern division president. 'There are more do-it-yourselfers in Manhattan than you might think.'"

■ In 2004, Mr. Nardelli had this to say about his plans for the future, "We are enhancing the core of our business through a more sophisticated focus on the market and on the customer. We are analyzing demographics, consumer trends, and

geographic locations to remain current or ahead of emerging customer trends. This includes a company-wide store modernization plan, the introduction of innovative, and distinctive merchandise and technological enhancements."

He also said, "Through our services business, we are positioned to capitalize on demographic shifts that are creating customers who want home improvement 'done for them.' Home Depot stores offer a variety of installation programs, ranging from counter-tops and kitchens to fencing and HVAC. We currently handle more than 10,000 projects each business day and expect this business to continue its double-digit growth rate."

Total assets: $38,907 million
Current ratio: 1.35
Common shares outstanding: 2,262 million
Return on 2004 shareholders' equity: 21.5%

| | 2004 | 2003 | 2002 | 2001 | 2000 | 1999 | 1998 | 1997 |
|---|---|---|---|---|---|---|---|---|
| Revenues (millions) | 73,094 | 64,316 | 58,247 | 53,553 | 45,738 | 38,434 | 30,219 | 24,156 |
| Net income (millions) | 5,001 | 4,304 | 3,664 | 3,044 | 2,581 | 2,320 | 1,614 | 1,160 |
| Earnings per share | 2.26 | 1.88 | 1.56 | 1.29 | 1.10 | 1.00 | .71 | .52 |
| Dividends per share | .34 | .28 | .21 | .17 | .16 | .11 | .08 | .06 |
| Price high | 44.3 | 37.9 | 52.6 | 53.7 | 70.0 | 69.8 | 41.3 | 20.2 |
| low | 32.3 | 20.1 | 23.0 | 30.3 | 34.7 | 34.6 | 18.4 | 10.6 |

Conservative Growth

# Hormel Foods Corporation

1 Hormel Place ❏ Austin, MN 55912–3680 ❏ (507) 437–5007 ❏ Dividend reinvestment plan available: (877) 536–3559 ❏ Fiscal years end on the last Saturday of October ❏ Listed: NYSE ❏ Web site: *www.hormel.com* ❏ Ticker symbol: HRL ❏ S&P rating: A ❏ Value Line financial strength rating: A

In 2001, 2002, 2003, and 2004, Hormel Foods was named one of "The Best Big Companies in America" by *Forbes* magazine. The company enjoys a strong reputation among consumers, retail grocers, foodservice, and industrial customers for products regarded for quality, taste, nutrition, convenience, and value.

These qualities were once again translated into sales and profits in 2004:

● Earnings per share advanced to $1.65, up from $1.33 in 2003.

● Dollar sales of $4.8 billion represented a gain of 14 percent over the prior year.

● Volume of goods sold climbed 6 percent over 2003.

• Jennie-O Turkey Store's operating profit surged 91 percent, even though sales rose a less-spectacular 14 percent.

• Refrigerated Foods' operating profit was up a handsome 37 percent, compared with a sales increase of 14 percent.

• A negative note: Grocery Products's operating profit dipped 16 percent in 2004 on a 4 percent decrease in volume and a dollar sales increase of a modest 1 percent.

• Finally, Specialty Foods' operating profit advanced 43 percent, and dollar sales did nearly as well, advancing 48 percent.

Commenting on the 2004 performance, CEO Joel W. Johnson had this comment on November 24, 2004: "Our strong fourth quarter was supported by a very good demand for our value-added pork and turkey products. As we noted in the November 11 earnings pre-announcement, our Jennie-O Turkey Store business delivered better-than-expected results, driven by outstanding demand for turkey products and excellent market conditions. We continue to see this strength into the first quarter of fiscal 2005, which gives us a great start to the new year."

Mr. Johnson also said, "Our International business reported strong growth, with volume up 25 percent. Business in China continues to be good, with double-digit growth in both retail and foodservice. We are excited about the opportunities in the Philippines, as well. To support this growth, we just opened our second plant in that country."

## Company Profile

Founded by George A. Hormel in 1891 in Austin, Minnesota, Hormel Corporation is a multinational manufacturer of consumer-branded meat and food products, many of which are among the best-known and trusted in the food industry. The company, according to management, "enjoys a strong reputation among consumers, retail grocers, and foodservice and industrial customer for products highly regarded for quality, taste, nutrition, convenience and value."

The company's larger subsidiaries include Jennie-O Turkey Store, the nation's largest turkey processor; Vista International Packaging, Inc., a manufacturer of casings; and Hormel Foods International Corporation, which markets Hormel products throughout the world.

The company's business is reported in five segments: Refrigerated Foods (accounting for 48.1 percent of total Hormel Foods sales in 2004 and 35.5 percent of operating profits), Grocery Products (15.9 percent and 32.4 percent), Jennie-O Turkey Store (22 percent and 19.8 percent), Specialty Foods, (9.8 percent and 6.5 percent), and All Other (4.2 percent and 5.8 percent).

The company's products include hams, bacon, sausages, franks, canned luncheon meats, stews, chilies, hash, meat spreads, shelf-stable microwaveable entrees, salsas, and frozen processed meats.

These selections are sold to retail, foodservice, and wholesale operations under many well-established trademarks that include: Black Label, by George, Cure 81, Always Tender, Curemaster, Di Lusso, Dinty Moore, Dubuque, Fast'n Easy, Homeland, Hormel, House of Tsang, Jennie-O-Kid's Kitchen, Layout Pack, Light & Lean 100, Little Sizzlers, May Kitchen, Old Smokehouse, Peloponnese, Range Brand, Rosa Grande, Sandwich Maker, Spam, and Wranglers.

These products are sold in all fifty states by a Hormel Foods sales force assigned to offices in major cities throughout the United States. Their efforts are supplemented by sales brokers and distributors.

The headquarters for Hormel Foods is in Austin, Minnesota, along with the Research and Development division and flagship plant. Company facilities that manufacture meat and food products are situated in such states as Iowa, Georgia, Illinois, Wisconsin, Nebraska, Oklahoma,

California, and Kansas. In addition, custom manufacturing of selected Hormel Foods products is performed by various companies that adhere to stringent corporate guidelines and quality standards.

Hormel Foods International Corporation (HFIC), a wholly owned subsidiary in Austin, has established a number of joint venture and licensing agreements in such countries as Australia, China, Colombia, Costa Rica, Denmark, England, Japan, Korea, Mexico, Panama, the Philippines, Poland, Spain, among others. HFIC exports products to more than forty countries.

## Shortcomings to Bear in Mind

- "We are maintaining our HOLD recommendation on the stock, as we believe the current valuation accurately reflects our expectations for an improving raw material environment, coupled with continued marketing investment in growing value-added product lines," said Joseph Agnese, an analyst with *Standard & Poor's Stock Reports,* on March 1, 2005. "However, we continue to believe the company is well-positioned for longer-term growth, with profitability expected to benefit as higher margin, value-added products become a larger part of the company's businesses."

## Reasons to Buy

- "In a fresh assault on bacterial contamination of food, some major meat processors have embraced a high-pressure processing technique that they say makes cold cuts, fruits, and other edibles safer without affecting taste," said Janet Adamy, writing for the *Wall Street Journal* on February 17, 2005. "Hormel Foods Corp., Perdue Farms Inc. and others are dunking pre-wrapped foods into tanks of pressurized water—a process that kills salmonella, e. coli and, listeria and allows food makers to add fewer preservatives. It also enables vendors to keep deli ham,

pre-cooked chicken strips and other meats in the food pipeline a lot longer. Hormel says its lunch meat now lasts for as long as 100 days—more than twice as long as before."

- Writing for the September 2004 issue of *Food & Drug Packaging,* Editor-in-Chief Lisa McTigue Pierce said, "Throughout the years, Hormel's leadership in culinary creativity and packaging prowess has been recognized by the food industry and the packaging community."

She also said, "Innovations extend across all divisions, but three recent ones from the company's Grocery Products group prove that Hormel earns its status as a packaging leader:

  • "The first U.S. application of a retortable carton for the Hormel and Stagg chili brands.

  • "A retort pouch for SPAM Single, a single-serve slice of SPAM luncheon meat.

  • "A package re-design and re-launch of Dinty Moore microwaveable meals.

"These exciting new packages have recharged Grocery Products sales, which in 2003 represented nearly 45 percent of the company's operating profits."

- On February 4, 2005, *Value Line Investment Survey* gave Hormel a 4 rating (*below average*) for Timeliness—short-term outlook. On the other hand, Justin Hellman had these positive thoughts: "The firm has completed a significant acquisition. In late December (2004), Hormel bought Clougherty Packing Company, a privately held pork processor based in southern California, for $186 million in cash. The deal will probably enhance the firm's profitability by increasing its value-added product mix. (Clougherty markets its goods under the popular Farmer John label.)" Mr. Hellman also said, "These shares have good total-return potential to 2007–2009. The issue is untimely for the year ahead, however."

- Value-added products are helping the Jennie-O Turkey Store. This segment now offers a broad selection of value-added branded products such as Thanksgiving Tonight oven-roasted turkey breast, which "delivers holiday flavor and everyday convenience."

  Demand for value-added turkey items, moreover, are growing faster than that for traditional products.
- Developing new products takes some effort. For Hormel, it means asking customers "about features that make their lives better." A case in point is the award-winning kid-friendly plastic packaging "of our popular Kid's Kitchen brand of microwave-ready foods."
- Under the leadership of CEO Joel Johnson (a former Kraft executive), Hormel has become a leader in the pork industry by focusing on offering more convenient, value-added products. The company has grown sales and earnings primarily by expanding into higher-margin, value-added meat products.
- The company's recent acquisition of Diamond Crystal Brands Nutritional Products and Cliffdale Farms further strengthened Hormel Foods' brand presence in the fast-growing managed healthcare foods business. Hormel Foods is among the top providers in this field, which has

strong growth prospects. The sixty-plus population worldwide is expected to double between 2000 and 2025.
- Thomas C. Morabito, an analyst with *Longbow Research,* had this comment on November 24, 2004: "We continue to believe that HRL is an attractive idea within the food space, given the company's excellent balance between the fast-growing protein business, and the relative safety and cash flow of its well-known packaged brands. In addition, today's results gives us further confidence that there remains additional upside to HRL's share price, despite the stock's 13 percent comeback over the past month. We are therefore maintaining our OUTPERFORM rating on the shares."
- Still another brokerage firm, Credit Suisse, had an upbeat view of the company on November 25, 2004: "We believe the greatest strength of HRL lies in upgrading and branding fresh pork and turkey and the strength in Refrigerated and Turkey divisions continues to support our thesis. We continue to believe that HRL is by far the best at adding value and marketing in the meat industry." The two analysts who cover this company for Credit Suisse are David C. Nelson and Robert Moskow.

Total assets: $2,534 million
Current ratio: 2.22
Common shares outstanding: 138 million
Return on 2004 shareholders' equity: 17.5%

| | 2004 | 2003 | 2002 | 2001 | 2000 | 1999 | 1998 | 1997 |
|---|---|---|---|---|---|---|---|---|
| Revenues (millions) | 4,780 | 4,200 | 3,910 | 4,124 | 3,675 | 3,358 | 3,261 | 3,257 |
| Net income (millions) | 232 | 186 | 189 | 182 | 170 | 160 | 122 | 106 |
| Earnings per share | 1.65 | 1.33 | 1.35 | 1.30 | 1.20 | 1.09 | .81 | .70 |
| Dividends per share | .45 | .42 | .39 | .37 | .35 | .33 | .32 | .31 |
| Price high | 32.1 | 27.5 | 28.2 | 27.3 | 21.0 | 23.1 | 19.7 | 16.5 |
| low | 24.9 | 19.9 | 20.0 | 17.0 | 13.6 | 15.5 | 12.8 | 11.8 |

# Illinois Tool Works, Inc.

3600 West Lake Ave. ❏ Glenview, IL 60025–5811 ❏ (847) 657–4104 ❏ Dividend reinvestment plan available: (888) 829–7424 ❏ Web site: *www.itw.com* ❏ Listed: NYSE ❏ Ticker symbol: ITW ❏ S&P rating: A+ ❏ Value Line financial strength rating: A

Illinois Tools' record of sustained quality earnings is the result of a very practical view of the world. The company relies on market penetration—rather than price increases—to fuel operating income growth. What's more, the company's conservative accounting practices serve as a reliable yardstick of financial performance. These results then generate the cash needed to fund ITW's growth—through both investing in core businesses and acquisitions.

Illinois Tool Works has an impressive record of growth. In the 1994–2004 period, Earnings per share climbed from $1.23 to $4.39, an annual compound growth rate of 13.6 percent. In the same 10-year stretch, dividends advanced from $0.28 to $1.00, for a growth rate of 13.6 percent.

## Company Profile

Illinois Tool Works is a multinational manufacturer of highly engineered fasteners, components, assemblies and systems. ITW's businesses are small and focused, so they can work more effectively in a decentralized structure to add value to customers' products.

The company has subsidiaries and affiliates in forty countries on six continents.

More than 600 ITW operating units are divided into several business segments:

### Premark International Inc.

In 1999, the company made its biggest purchase yet—Premark International Inc.—a $2.7-billion conglomerate making everything from industrial food equipment to gym equipment to residential flooring and appliances.

The Street did not take kindly to this huge acquisition. The day after the announcement, the stock dropped 8 percent, closing at

$73.69 on September 10, 1999. More than a year later, the stock was still under siege, as it sagged below $50. No one seemed to notice that 90 percent of Premark's revenue came from nonconsumer goods, making it, at least in management's view, a good fit for ITW.

### Engineered Products—North America

Businesses in this segment are located in North America and manufacture short-lead-time components and fasteners, and specialty products such as adhesives, re-sealable packaging, and electronic component packaging.

### Engineered Products—International

Businesses in this segment are located outside North America and manufacture short-lead-time components and fasteners and specialty products such as electronic component packaging and adhesives.

### Specialty Systems—North America

Businesses in this segment operate in North America and produce longer-lead-time machinery and related consumables, and specialty equipment for applications such as industrial spray coating, quality measurement, and static control.

### Specialty Systems—International

Operations in this segment do business outside North America. They have stakes in longer-lead-time machinery and related consumables, and specialty equipment for industrial spray coating and other applications.

### How Illinois Tool Works Got Started

Founded in 1912, Illinois Tool Works' earliest products included milling cutters and hobs used to cut gears. Today ITW is a multinational manufacturer of highly engineered components and systems.

In 1923, the company developed the Shakeproof fastener, a patented twisted tooth lock washer. This product's success enabled ITW to become the leader in a new industry segment—engineered metal fasteners.

Illinois Tool soon expanded the Shakeproof line to include thread-cutting screws, pre-assembled screws and other metal fasteners.

By the late 1940s, the line grew to include plastic and metal/plastic combination fasteners. Today, ITW units produce fasteners for appliance, automotive, construction, general industrial, and other applications.

After World War II, the company also expanded into electrical controls and instruments, culminating in the formation of the Licon division in the late 1950s. Today, ITW units provide a wide range of switch components and panel assemblies used in appliance, electronic, and industrial markets.

In the early 1960s, the newly formed Hi-Cone operating unit developed the plastic multipack carrier that revolutionized the packaging industry. Hi-Cone multipacks today are used to package beverage and food products as well as a variety of other products.

Also in the 1960s, the company formed Buildex to market existing Shakeproof fasteners as well as a line of masonry fasteners to the construction industry. Buildex today manufactures fasteners for drywall, general construction and roofing applications.

In the mid-1980s, ITW acquired Ramset, Phillips Drill (Red Head) and SPIT, manufacturers of concrete anchoring, epoxy anchoring and powder actuated systems; and Paslode, maker of pneumatic and cordless nailers, staplers, and systems for wood construction applications. Today, the construction industry is the largest market served by Illinois Tool Works.

In the 1970s, ITW purchased Devcon Corporation, a producer of adhesives, sealants and related specialty chemicals. Today the company's engineered polymers businesses offer a variety of products with home, construction and industrial applications.

In 1986, Illinois Tool acquired Signode Packaging Systems, a multinational manufacturer of metal and plastic strapping stretch film, industrial tape, application equipment, and related products. Today, ITW offers a wide range of industrial packaging systems, including Dynatec hot-melt adhesive application equipment.

In 1989, Illinois Tool Works acquired Ransburg Corporation, a leading producer of finishing equipment.

ITW expanded its capabilities in industrial finishing with the purchase of DeVilbiss Industrial/Commercial division in 1990. Today, DeVilbiss and Ransburg manufacture conventional and liquid electrostatic equipment, while Gema Volstatic (acquired with the Ransburg and DeVilbiss purchases) produces electrostatic powder coating systems.

The company acquired the Miller Group in 1993. Miller is a leading manufacturer of arc welding equipment and related systems. Miller's emphasis on new product development and innovative design fits well with ITW's engineering and manufacturing strategies.

## Shortcomings to Bear in Mind

- The stock has historically traded at a premium to the market, but based on its exceptional performance over the years, it would appear to be warranted. With some 600 businesses, Illinois Tool offers investors wide diversification by product line, geographic region and industry. This helps insulate the company from weakness in any one sector. Over the years, this has resulted in consistent performance despite the cyclicality of the automotive and construction sectors.

## Reasons to Buy

- There's no doubt that Illinois Tool Works is a superior company. I think CEO W. James Farrell explained why in 2004. "What drives these results? We believe it is our time-tested 80/20 business planning process. Simply put, our business units—big and small, new and old—focus their attention and resources on the 20 percent of customers and products that generate 80 percent of revenues."

  Mr. Farrell went on to say, "A prime example of the 80/20 process in action is ITW's 1999 merger with Premark International, our largest acquisition to date. As part of the five-year simplification process, we divested businesses that didn't fit strategically—most recently, the Florida Tile business in the fourth quarter of 2003. We increased operating margins from 9 percent in 1999 to 16 percent in 2003, despite the fact that growth in Premark's top product lines decreased nearly 10 percent for the past four years due to weak end markets. Now in the final year of our five-year profitability improvement plan, we are on track to double Premark's operating margin and reach our margin goal of 18 percent by the end of 2004. We expect that financial performance of the Premark businesses will continue to improve, driven by new product development and greater operating efficiencies."

- Acquisitions are likely to remain a key component of the company's growth strategy. ITW has grown steadily over the years by taking underperforming businesses and turning them into solid performers.

  In most years, the company completes a dozen or two "bottom-up" acquisitions—companies that are directly related to or integrated into an existing product line or market. These transactions, typically represent more than $1 billion in combined revenues, are normally initiated by operating management for both North American and international businesses. According to management, "Looking ahead, our pipeline of potential acquisitions remains full."

  A second type of acquisition, which the company undertakes far less frequently, is a major, or "top-down" proposition. These transactions are identified by senior management and represent entirely new businesses for ITW. Illinois Tool completed its largest transaction of this type by merging with Premark in 1999.

  This merger brought the company nearly eighty decentralized businesses with products marketed in more than 100 countries. Two principal lines of business—commercial food equipment and laminate product used in construction—represent about $2.5 billion in revenues. Their products have strong brand names such as Hobart, Wilsonart, Traulsen, Vulcan, and Wittco, established market positions, good distribution channels and benefit from value-added engineering—all the things ITW looks for in a successful acquisition.

Total assets: $11,352 million
Current ratio: 2.33
Common shares outstanding: 296 million
Return on 2004 shareholders' equity: 17.3%

| | 2004 | 2003 | 2002 | 2001 | 2000 | 1999 | 1998 | 1997 | 1996 |
|---|---|---|---|---|---|---|---|---|---|
| Revenues (millions) | 11,731 | 10,036 | 9,468 | 9,293 | 9,984 | 9,333 | 5,648 | 5,220 | 4,997 |
| Net income (millions) | 1,340 | 1,040 | 932 | 806 | 958 | 841 | 810 | 587 | 486 |
| Earnings per share | 4.39 | 3.37 | 3.02 | 2.63 | 3.15 | 2.99 | 2.67 | 2.33 | 1.97 |
| Dividends per share | 1.04 | .94 | .90 | .82 | .76 | .63 | .54 | .46 | .36 |
| Price high | 96.7 | 84.7 | 77.8 | 72.0 | 69.0 | 82.0 | 73.2 | 60.1 | 48.7 |
| low | 72.9 | 54.6 | 55.0 | 49.2 | 49.5 | 58.0 | 45.2 | 37.4 | 26.0 |

# Intel Corporation

2200 Mission College Boulevard ❏ Santa Clara, CA 95054–1549 ❏ (408) 765–1480 ❏ Dividend reinvestment plan available: (800) 298–0146 ❏ Web site: *www.intc.com* ❏ Listed: NASDAQ ❏ Ticker symbol: INTC ❏ S&P rating: A ❏ Value Line financial strength rating: A++

On November 11, 2004, Intel Corporation, the world's largest chip maker, selected Paul Otellini, age fifty-four, to succeed Craig R. Barrett, age sixty-five, as its new CEO. The promotion of Mr. Otellini was not a surprise, since he has been president and chief operating officer of the company since January 2002.

The new CEO, who studied economics at the University of San Francisco and received an MBA from the University of California, is the first Intel chief executive not formally trained as an engineer. However, he had plenty of on-the-job training, serving in a vast array of positions in marketing and management in his thirty years with the company. As a result of the move, Craig Barrett became chairman of the board, and Andrew S. Grove, age sixty-eight, stepped aside as chairman to assume the role of senior adviser to the board of directors and senior management.

Since joining Intel in 1974, Paul Otellini has held a number of positions, including general manager of the company's chipset business and later serving as an assistant to then-Intel president Andy Grove. In 1990, Mr. Otellini was named to oversee Intel's microprocessor business as general manager, leading the introduction of the Intel Pentium processor in 1993.

Mr. Otellini served from 1992 to 1998 as executive vice president of sales and marketing where he focused on extending Intel's global presence into emerging markets. In that role, he initiated Intel's leadership in the development and use of e-commerce for transacting business worldwide. From 1998 to 2002, the new chief executive served as executive vice president and general manager of the Intel Architecture Group, responsible for the company's microprocessor and chipset businesses and strategies. What's more, he took charge of Intel's business groups related to enterprise, mobile and desktop computing.

## Company Profile

It has been more than three decades since Intel introduced the world's first microprocessor, making technology history. The computer revolution that this technology spawned has changed the world. Today, Intel supplies the computing industry with the chips, boards, systems, and software that are the "ingredients" of computer architecture. These products are used by industry members to create advanced computing systems.

### Intel architecture platform products

Microprocessors, also called central processing units (CPUs) or chips, are frequently described as the "brains" of a computer, because they control the central processing of data in personal computers (PCs), servers, workstations, and other computers. Intel offers microprocessors optimized for each segment of the computing market. Chipsets perform essential logic functions surrounding the CPU in computers, and support and extend the graphics, video and other capabilities of many Intel processor-based systems. Motherboards combine Intel microprocessors and chipsets to form the basic subsystem of a PC or server.

## Wireless communications and computing products

These products are component-level hardware and software focusing on digital cellular communications and other applications needing both low-power processing and re-programmable, retained memory capability (flash memory). These products are used in mobile phones, hand-held devices, two-way pagers and many other products.

## Networking and communications products

System-level products consist of hardware, software and support services for e-Business data center and building blocks for communications access solutions. These products include e-Commerce infrastructure appliances; hubs, switches, and routers for Ethernet networks; and computer telephony components. Component-level products include communications silicon components and embedded control chips designed to perform specific functions in networking and communications applications, such as telecommunications, hubs, routers, and wide area networking. Embedded control chips are also used in laser printers, imaging, storage media, automotive systems, and other applications.

## Solutions and Services

These products and services include e-Commerce data center services as well as connected peripherals and security access software.

## Major Customers

- Original equipment manufacturers of computer systems and peripherals.
- PC users, who buy Intel's PC enhancements, business communications products and networking products through reseller, retail and OEM channels.

- Other manufacturers, including makers of a wide range of industrial and telecommunications equipment.

## Shortcomings to Bear in Mind

- According to Matthew Fordahl, writing for the *Associated Press* on November 12, 2004, "Intel has made big moves into server chips, including its Itanium processor, which has seen slow market acceptance after a decade of development. It's also expanded into providing processors for cell phone and handheld computers as well as flash memory.

  "At the same time, it's been trailing its much smaller competitor AMD, which beat Intel to market with next-generation PC and server processors that offered many of the advanced benefits of Itanium and more robust backward compatibility with existing software. After months of denying that the market was looking for such a chip, Intel changed course and announced a similar technology earlier this year."

- *Standard & Poor's Stock Reports* had a mixed view of the company on January 13, 2005, according to analyst Amrit Tewary, "We would HOLD the shares. We believe INTC's scale-based strengths in R&D, manufacturing and marketing should help it prosper in a semiconductor industry expansion that we expect to last through 2006."

## Reasons to Buy

- Nearly two-thirds of the world's fastest supercomputers now use Intel Itanium or Intel Xeon processors, according to the twenty-fourth edition of the "TOP500" list, illustrating the growing momentum toward the use of standard Intel components for the most demanding high-performance computing applications. The TOP500 project was started in 1993 to provide a reliable basis for tracking and detecting trends in high-performance computing. Twice a year, a list of the sites operating the 500 most powerful computer systems is assembled and released. Intel architecture-based platforms currently make up 64 percent of the top 500 systems, continuing the surge in the use of Intel processors that accounted for only nineteen systems in 2001—essentially a fifteen-fold increase in the past three years.

- "Intel Corp. on Wednesday introduced a new package of chips for wireless laptop computers, a move meant to increase the company's dominant position in notebook computers and expand its foothold in the consumer market," said Terril Yue Jones, writing for the *Los Angeles Times* on January 20, 2005. The article went on to say, "The chip package includes a faster laptop microprocessor and technology that allows more rapid communication with memory and peripherals. It also provides high-definition video and theater-like sound that have been available only in desktop computers."

- According to Don Clark, in an article in the *Wall Street Journal* on November 12, 2004, "During the past few years, Mr. Otellini has pushed for two major changes to move the company beyond gigahertz, a measure of 'clock speed' that increasingly is causing energy-consumption problems. He has advocated technology 'platforms'—composed of several chips rather than a microprocessor alone—for specific audiences such as mobile professionals and consumers seeking digital entertainment. Intel's Centrino technology for laptop computers is the first example.

"Mr. Otellini also has committed the company to shifting product development to putting the equivalent of multiple microprocessors in a single chip, starting with 'dual-core' chips expected next year. The move toward dual-core is really ushering in, in my mind, a new era in computing,' Mr. Otellini said. "And we intend to lead."

- On November 8, 2004, Intel said that the company had "enhanced its entire line of Intel Itanium 2 processors, delivering new versions of multi-, dual-, and low-voltage processors. The new processors are the next step toward the goal of using computing platforms based on industry standards to gain more market segment share from the $20-billion proprietary RISC market segment."

More than seventy OEMs (original manufacturers) are now shipping Itanium-based systems. The platform currently supports a choice of five leading operating systems and a "vast suite of software applications, increasing the choice and flexibility of Itanium-based solutions for IT managers worldwide."

Abhi Talwalkar, vice-president and general manager of the Enterprise Platforms Group at Intel, said, "The multi-billion-dollar RISC market segment is ripe for the Intel approach of delivering outstanding performance, choice of systems, and software at more affordable price points. Today's enhancements to the Itanium 2 processor lineup will further support customer migration away from costly, proprietary systems."

Already, the new Itanium 2 processors are being deployed for mission-critical applications, including powering one of the world's fastest supercomputers at NASA, a SGI Altix system, consisting of 10,240 Itanium 2 processors running the Linux operating system. Additionally, MGM MIRAGE, "a leading and respected hotel and gaming company, has deployed a Unisys system with sixteen Itanium 2 processors for a data-warehousing project based upon Microsoft Windows Server 2003 and Microsoft SQL Server 2000," according to the Intel report.

Total assets: $48,417 million
Current ratio: 3.0
Common shares outstanding: 6,665 million
Return on 2004 shareholders equity: 19.7%

|  | 2004 | 2003 | 2002 | 2001 | 2000 | 1999 | 1998 | 1997 |
|---|---|---|---|---|---|---|---|---|
| Revenues (millions) | 34,209 | 30,141 | 26,764 | 26,539 | 33,726 | 29,389 | 26,273 | 25,070 |
| Net income (millions) | 7,516 | 5,641 | 3,117 | 1,291 | 10,535 | 7,314 | 6,178 | 6,945 |
| Earnings per share | 1.16 | .85 | .46 | .19 | 1.51 | 1.17 | .89 | .97 |
| Dividends per share | .16 | .08 | .08 | .08 | .07 | .05 | .04 | .03 |
| Price    high | 34.6 | 34.5 | 36.8 | 38.6 | 75.8 | 44.8 | 31.6 | 15.5 |
|          low | 19.6 | 14.9 | 12.9 | 19.0 | 29.8 | 25.1 | 16.4 | 15.7 |

Aggressive Growth

# International Business Machines Corporation

New Orchard Road ❑ Armonk, NY 10504 ❑ (914) 499–7777 ❑ Direct dividend reinvestment plan available: (888) 426–6700 ❑ Web site: *www.ibm.com* ❑ Listed: NYSE ❑ Ticker symbol: IBM ❑ S&P rating: B+ ❑ Value Line financial strength rating: A++

"For the past couple of decades, if you were to look at IBM's performance in any given year or over several years, what would your see?" asked CEO Samuel J. Palmisano in 2004. "You'd see a very large global company in which some businesses are growing rapidly, some are flat, and some are declining. Add it up, and it would average out to some steady profitability—but perhaps uninspiring growth. For people with comparatively short memories, this might be the only IBM they'd ever known. And it would be legitimate to ask if the company is capable of more.

"The answer is: We certainly are. In fact, over most of our nearly 100-year history, IBM was consistently a company that outperformed others in our markets and generated superior returns. And that was because we were singularly focused on leading, and most often creating and defining, the high-value spaces in our industry.

"Of course, with a company of IBM's breadth and global presence, there are always ups and downs that result from economic cycles, product and technology transitions, and sometimes issues of execution. But it's also apparent that, somewhere along the line, we became more focused on defending our existing leadership position than on creating the next one. We weren't particularly bold or imaginative in getting into new markets or developing new businesses, products and services, even when our strategic analysis indicated that something new was coming. And, just as important, we hesitated to reinvent or get out of businesses that no longer represented high value for either clients or shareholders. In a word, we lost sight of IBM's mission, of what had always set us apart.

"Well, we've regained our focus now. IBM is an innovator—in every dimension of that word. We know that IBM and IBMers are at their best when they create value that our clients cannot get from anyone else. That means we will provide leading-edge technology, services, expertise and intellectual capital, and will integrate these capabilities for each client to provide them with competitive advantage."

Mr. Palmisano joined IBM in 1973 as a salesman in Baltimore. Later he became senior managing director of operations for IBM Japan; president of Integrated Systems Solutions Corporation, which is part of IBM's services division; and was senior vice president for the personal systems group, the enterprise systems group, the enterprise global services, and IBM global services. He became president and chief operating officer in 2000 and was elevated to CEO on March 1, 2002—assuming the executive mantle from the legendary Lou Gerstner; and was awarded the title of Chairman on January 1, 2003.

## Company Profile

Big Blue is the world's leading provider of computer hardware. IBM makes a broad range of computers, including notebooks, mainframes, and network servers. The company also develops software (it's number two, behind Microsoft) and peripherals. IBM derives about one-third of its revenues from an ever-expanding service arm that is the largest in the world. IBM owns Lotus Development, the software pioneer that makes the Lotus Notes messaging system.

The company's subsidiary, Tivoli Systems, develops tools that manage corporate computer networks. Finally, in an effort to keep up with the times, IBM has been making a concerted effort to obtain a slice of Internet business.

## Shortcomings to Bear in Mind

- On August 16, 2004, J. P. Morgan Chase & Company said it would bring back in-house a wide variety of core technology functions it had outsourced to IBM, ending a contract that had been expected to be worth about $5 billion. The deal, announced in late 2002, was among the largest outsourcing projects that IBM—or any other technology-services company—has taken on. It provided for some technology to be bought as services on demand, or as they are needed, a concept IBM had

heavily promoted as more efficient for companies than buying their own gear and running the operation themselves.

- "The jury is still out on whether IBM's $3.9 billion purchase of the Pricewaterhouse business in 2002 has been a success," said Charles Forelle, in an article in the *Wall Street Journal* dated January 20, 2005. "In the fourth quarter of last year (2004), revenue for IBM's Business Consulting Services unit, which includes the Pricewaterhouse assets, grew 12 percent from the year-earlier period, surpassing services growth as a whole—but in prior quarters it substantially lagged behind overall services growth."

## Reasons to Buy

- "After more than two years of playing second fiddle to Japan in supercomputers, the U.S. has clawed its way back to head of the pack," said an article written by Otis Port for *BusinessWeek* on January 17, 2005. "A machine from IBM called Blue Gene/L, now being installed at Lawrence Livermore National Laboratory, holds the world record for supercomputing speed, scoring 92 teraflops. That's a mind-blowing 92 trillion floating-point calculations every second."
- In 2004, Mr. Palmisano said, "Over the past several years, we've taken aggressive steps to re-mix our business so that we are positioned for long-term leadership and new opportunities in the high-value enterprise space, however that changes. We have, since 1997:
  - Exited or reduced our presence in such areas as application software, hard-disk drives, networking hardware, low-end printers and retail PCs—which we estimate have declined from 31 percent to 25 percent of IT industry revenue.
  - Entered or increased our presence in distributed middleware, nonhardware maintenance services, Intel-based servers, and mobile PCs—which have

grown from 40 percent of industry revenue to 46 percent and are expected to continue outperforming the overall IT market.

- Increased our revenue in business and technology consulting services, infrastructure services, and infrastructure software—which generate superior long-term revenue growth, profit, cash and return on invested capital—from 48 percent to 64 percent of our total, with expectations of increasing that going forward.

- Grown aggressively in emerging markets; in China, India, Russia, and Brazil we generated revenue of $3 billion last year and saw double-digit growth.

- Incubated successful new high-growth businesses such as life sciences, digital media, application management services, e-business hosting services, Linux and pervasive computing—each of which has already become a $1 billion-plus revenue stream. In the areas we're targeting within life sciences and digital media alone, third-party analysts see more than $60 billion of market opportunity in 2006."

- "We continue to have a STRONG BUY opinion on the shares," said M. Graham-Hackett, writing for *Standard & Poor's Stock Reports* on January 21, 2005. "We think IBM's consistent results in 2004 reflect the benefits of the company's broad solutions-focused product portfolio. We believe IBM has gained market share throughout the technology-spending downturn, and that these gains in services, software, and servers should strengthen results this year and next."

- When IBM announced in late 2004 that it was seeking a buyer for its personal computer business, Wall Street rewarded the company's shareholders with a solid boost in its stock price. At the time, IBM was asking between $1 and $2 billion for this unprofitable business, which ranked a distant third to Dell Computer and Hewlett-Packard, with only 5.2 percent of the market. On the plus side, IBM's sales are almost exclusively to corporate buyers, with most of those buyers being customers who also buy other equipment and services from Big Blue.

On December 7, 2004, it was learned that IBM and Lenovo Group Ltd. plan to create a new U.S.-based personal computer company that would own IBM's PC business. The new company would be majority owned by Lenovo, with IBM holding onto a minority stake small enough that its revenues and profit or loss would be excluded from operating results. Lenovo, based in China, is expected to earn up to $2 billion for the majority share in the IBM PC business. Lenovo paid IBM $1.25 billion in cash and stock for its share of the PC business.

- Although IBM is well-known as the titan of computer hardware, it is the Global Services division that is proving to be the company's star performer. While sales for the rest of Big Blue are barely inching ahead, the services division is averaging more than 10 percent sales growth a year. That has helped pull up overall growth at IBM to about 5 percent per year.

- Competing against everyone from Electronic Data Systems to Big Four accounting firms to boutique shops offering only Web services, IBM has emerged as the world's largest purveyor of technology services, according to *Business Week*. It counsels customers on technology strategy, helps them prepare for mishaps, runs all their computer operations, develops their applications, procures their supplies, trains their employees, and even gets them into the dot.com realm.

- IBM launched a security system that it expects will set the industry standard for protecting confidential documents such as those used in the growing sector of electronic commerce. Unlike previous security measures that rely on software "fireballs" that filter out unauthorized users of information, IBM has developed a security chip embedded within the computer hardware, which adds additional levels of security. "People from outside your organization can get at your software," said Anne Gardner, general manager of desktop systems for IBM. "People from the outside can't get to your hardware."

- On July 13, 2004, IBM introduced a new generation of servers that could vault the company ahead of such competitors as Sun Microsystems and Hewlett-Packard. It's a worldwide market valued at $21 billion. The P5 servers use IBM's new Power 5 chip and run on the Unix operating system and thus can be more competitive in a segment of the market long dominated by Sun and Hewlett-Packard. IBM says its new devices will offer faster performance and the ability to "micro-partition," or split up the functions of the Power 5 chip to mimic the function of up to ten separate servers.

Servers are high-capacity computers that form the backbone of corporate, government, and university networks. They operate e-mail systems, host Web sites, manage payroll, and run inventory programs, as well as other functions. People who do banking through personal computers or ATMs, who make airline and hotel reservations online or who shop at online stores probably are going through servers with Unix operating systems. In short, Unix servers are the workhorses of most computer data centers.

"I want to be first in Unix and first in overall servers," said Bill Zeitler, who heads IBM's server group. "We're very confident of our prospects." Mr. Zeitler said that he expects the P5 systems will help IBM extend its overall leadership in the market for larger computers, which was $46 billion in 2003. Over the next five years, he said, "we believe there will be another ten to fifteen points of market-share change, and IBM and Dell are the most likely to get it."

Total assets: $109,183 million
Current ratio: 1.18
Common shares outstanding: 1723 million
Return on 2004 shareholders' equity: 32.8%

| | 2004 | 2003 | 2002 | 2001 | 2000 | 1999 | 1998 | 1997 |
|---|---|---|---|---|---|---|---|---|
| Revenues (millions) | 96,503 | 89,131 | 81,186 | 83,067 | 88,396 | 87,548 | 81,667 | 78,508 |
| Net income (millions) | 8,448 | 7,583 | 3,579 | 7,495 | 8,093 | 7,712 | 6,328 | 6,093 |
| Earnings per share | 5.03 | 4.34 | 3.07 | 4.69 | 4.44 | 4.12 | 3.29 | 3.01 |
| Dividends per share | .70 | .66 | .60 | .55 | .51 | .47 | .44 | .39 |
| Price high | 100.4 | 94.5 | 124.0 | 124.7 | 134.9 | 139.2 | 95.0 | 56.8 |
| low | 81.9 | 73.2 | 54.0 | 83.8 | 80.1 | 80.9 | 47.8 | 31.8 |

Conservative Growth

# International Flavors & Fragrances, Inc.

Global Headquarters ❑ 521 West 57th Street ❑ New York, NY 10019 ❑ (212) 708–7146 ❑ Dividend reinvestment plan available: (800) 829–8432 ❑ Web site: *www.iff.com* ❑ Ticker symbol: IFF ❑ Listed: NYSE ❑ S&P rating: B ❑ Value Line financial strength rating: B++

International Flavors & Fragrances announced plans for the construction of a new specialty ingredients (aroma chemical) manufacturing plant in China in late 2004. A groundbreaking ceremony for the $29-million plant was held on November 9, 2004. The new facility will be situated on a 16.9-hectare site within the Hangzhou Economic and Technological Development Area (HEDA), a Chinese national-level development area. *A hectare is a metric unit equal to 2.471 acres.*

The plant will focus on the production of specialty ingredients and intermediates to satisfy global requirements and other products specifically for regional demand in Asia/Pacific. It is expected to open in late 2006 and reach fully optimized operation in 2008.

Of the new plant, IFF CEO Richard Goldstein said, "The ingredients business is a key part of IFF's ongoing strategy. We have made dramatic investments in this part of the business, and we are further affirming our commitment through the construction of this new facility in China."

## Company Profile

International Flavors & Fragrances is a leading creator and manufacturer of flavor and fragrance products used by other manufacturers to impart or improve flavor or fragrance in a wide variety of consumer products. Fragrance products are sold principally to manufacturers of perfumes, cosmetics, toiletries, hair care products, deodorants, soaps, detergents, and air care products. Flavor products are sold mainly to manufacturers of prepared foods, beverages, dairy foods, pharmaceuticals, and confectionary products.

International Flavors & Fragrances produces more than 35,000 unique compounds annually, of which 60 percent are flavors and 40 percent fragrances. In addition, the company continually creates new compounds to meet the many and varied characteristics and needs of its customers' end products.

No individual compound represents more than 1.5 percent of net sales.

The development of fragrances and flavors is a complex artistic and technical process calling upon the combined knowledge and talents of creative perfumers and flavorists and application research chemists. An important contribution to the creation of new fragrances and flavors is the development of new ingredients. IFF bears essentially all costs incurred in connection with the creation and development of new flavors and fragrances—and such formulae are protected under trade secrecy.

In 2000, the company acquired Bush Boake Allen, Inc., an international flavor, fragrance, and aroma chemical company with worldwide annual sales of $499 million. This acquisition enhanced the company's position as a global leader in flavor markets, strengthened the company's already leading global fragrance position, expanded the company's product line and customer base, particularly in certain emerging markets, and broadened and enhanced IFF's management pool.

International Flavors & Fragrances has thirty-four manufacturing facilities with the major manufacturing facilities situated in the United States, France, Great Britain, Ireland, The Netherlands, Spain, Switzerland, Argentina, Brazil, Mexico, India, Australia, China, Indonesia, Japan, and Singapore. The remaining manufacturing facilities are situated in nine other countries.

IFF maintains its own sales and distribution facilities in thirty-four countries and is represented by sales agents in other countries.

More than 5,000 different raw materials are purchased from many sources all over the world. The principal natural raw material purchases consist of essential oils, extracts, and concentrates derived from fruits, vegetables, flowers, woods, and other botanicals, animal products, and raw fruits. The principal synthetic raw material purchases consist of organic chemicals.

## Markets

Fragrance products are used by customers in the manufacture of consumer products such as soaps, detergents, cosmetic creams, lotions and powders, lipsticks, aftershave lotions, deodorants, hair preparations, candles, air fresheners, and all-purpose cleaners, as well as other consumer products designed solely to appeal to the sense of smell, such as perfumes and colognes.

The cosmetics industry, including perfume and toiletries manufacturers, is one of the company's two largest fragrance customer groups. Most of the major domestic companies in this industry are customers of the company, and five of the largest U.S. cosmetics companies are among the principal customers. The household products industry, including soaps and detergents, is the other important fragrance customer group. Four of the largest domestic household product manufacturers are major customers of International Flavors & Fragrances.

Flavor products are sold principally to the food and beverage industries for use in consumer products such as soft drinks, candies, baked goods, desserts, and alcoholic beverages. Two of the company's largest customers for flavor products are major producers of prepared foods, and beverages in the United States.

The company's principal fragrance and flavor products consist of compounds of large numbers of ingredients blended under proprietary formulas created by its perfumers and flavorists. Most of these compounds contribute the total fragrance or flavor to the company's products in which they are used. This fragrance or flavor characteristic is often a major factor in the public selection and acceptance of the consumer end product.

A smaller number of compounds are sold to manufacturers who further blend them to achieve the finished fragrance or flavor in their products. IFF produces thousands of compounds, and new compounds are constantly being created in order to meet the many and changing characteristics of its customers' end products. Most of the fragrance and flavor compounds are created and produced for the exclusive use of particular customers. The company's products are sold in solid and liquid form and in amounts ranging from a few pounds to many tons, depending on the nature of the product.

## Shortcomings to Bear in Mind

- *Value Line Investment Survey* was not exactly hopping up and down with joy over the prospects for IFF on March 18, 2005. Eric M. Gottlieb said, "Investors may want to look elsewhere for an investment with more potential. The average-ranked shares now trade within our Target Price Range for the 2008–2010 pull. The current price reflects successful 2004 results with high expectations for 2005. Although we believe the revamping will be accretive to earnings, we have some doubt as to the reliability of the company's continued success in increasing its market share."

- International Flavors & Fragrances has more than fifty competitors in the United States and world markets. While no single factor is responsible, the company's competitive position is based primarily on the creative skills of its perfumers and flavorists, the technological advances resulting from its research and development, the quality of its customer service, the support provided by its marketing and application groups, and its understanding of consumers. The company believes that it is one of the largest companies producing and marketing on an international basis a wide range of fragrance and flavor products.

## Reasons to Buy

- *Standard & Poor's* had good things to say about IFF on December 10, 2004, according to Richard O'Reilly, CFA, "We have a BUY recommendation on the shares on a total-return (*stock appreciation plus dividends*) basis. We see IFF renewing sales growth with an improved win rate of new business, especially in North American flavors and fine fragrances."

- J.P. Morgan had an upbeat appraisal of International Flavors on January 27, 2005. "IFF had an exceptionally good year in 2004, reflecting overall volume improvement in a market that typically grows at much slower rates. IFF gained share in every major region except for Europe, registering 9 percent local currency growth in North America, 7 percent in Latin America and 6 percent in Asia/Pacific. Fine fragrances were the highlight for the year, with 8 percent local currency growth overall (6 percent domestically and 5 percent in Europe) owing to new business wins."

- The demand for consumer products utilizing flavors and fragrances has been stimulated and broadened by changing social habits resulting from various factors such as increases in personal income, employment of women, teenage population, leisure time, health concerns, urbanization, and by the continued growth in world population.

  In the fragrance field, these developments have expanded the market for hair care, candles and air care products, and deodorant and personal wash products with finer fragrance quality, as well as the market for colognes, toilet waters, men's toiletries, and other products beyond traditional luxury items such as perfumes.

  In the flavor field, similar market characteristics have stimulated the demand for products such as convenience foods, soft drinks, and low-cholesterol and low-fat food products that must conform to expected tastes. New and improved methods of packaging, application, and dispensing have been developed for many consumer products that utilize some of the company's flavor or fragrance products.

- Scientists from various disciplines work in project teams with the perfumers and flavorists to develop flavor and fragrance products with consumer preferred performance characteristics. Scientific expertise includes: natural products research, plant science, organic chemistry, analytical chemistry, biochemistry, microbiology, process engineering, food science, material science, and sensory science.

Total assets: $2,362 million
Current ratio: 2.38
Common shares outstanding: 94 million
Return on 2004 shareholders' equity: 26.2%

| | 2004 | 2003 | 2002 | 2001 | 2000 | 1999 | 1998 | 1997 |
|---|---|---|---|---|---|---|---|---|
| Revenues (millions) | 2,034 | 1,901 | 1,809 | 1,844 | 1,463 | 1,439 | 1,407 | 1,427 |
| Net income (millions) | 216 | 200 | 184 | 135 | 150 | 189 | 204 | 218 |
| Earnings per share | 2.27 | 2.13 | 1.94 | 1.41 | 1.48 | 1.79 | 1.90 | 2.00 |
| Dividends per share | .67 | .62 | .60 | .60 | 1.29 | 1.52 | 1.49 | 1.45 |
| Price high | 43.2 | 36.6 | 37.4 | 31.7 | 37.8 | 48.5 | 51.9 | 53.4 |
| low | 32.8 | 29.2 | 26.0 | 19.8 | 14.7 | 33.6 | 32.1 | 39.9 |

# Johnson & Johnson

One Johnson & Johnson Plaza ❑ New Brunswick, N J 08933 ❑ (800) 950–5089 ❑ Dividend reinvestment plan available: (800) 328–9033 ❑ Web site: *www.jnj.com* ❑ Listed: NYSE ❑ Ticker symbol: JNJ ❑ S&P rating: A+ ❑ Value Line financial strength rating: A++

According to a report issued by Cordis Corporation (a Johnson & Johnson company) on September 23, 2004, women patients who received the Cypher Sirolimus-eluding Coronary Stent are five times more likely to avoid a repeat re-blockage in the treated arteries than patients treated with a bare metal stent. The Cordis report was based on an integrated analysis of data from multiple clinical trials.

What's more, benefits were also seen in women with increased risks of heart disease due to diabetes and/or smoking. While extensive clinical data prove that the Cypher Stent is helpful for a wide variety of patients with heart disease, this is the first data analysis to focus exclusively on the Cypher Stent's effectiveness in women.

"There has been no definitive analysis focused exclusively on the impact of drug-eluding stents on women," said Cindy L. Grines, M.D., Director of the Cardiac Catheterization Laboratories, William Beaumont Hospital, Royal Oak, Michigan. "This is significant because heart disease is the main killer of women in the United States, regardless of race, and most women don't even know it. The data may help us better treat our female patients with heart disease."

In April 2003, the Cordis Corporation received FDA approval to market its Cypher Sirolimus-eluding Coronary Stent, making it the first drug-eluting stent to be approved in the United States for the treatment of restenosis, also known as re-blockage, of arteries. The Cypher Stent is currently available in more than eighty countries and has been used by doctors to treat more than 900,000 patients worldwide.

Overall, more than 5 million Americans are treated each year for coronary disease— blockages in the vessels that supply oxygen and vital nutrients to the heart muscle. Some 1.1 million people undergo balloon angioplasty, with about 80 percent of those receiving a coronary stent. Among the patients who are treated with these and other therapies, 15 to 20 percent (150,000 to 200,000) develop restenosis, or re-blockage of the treated artery and have to undergo one or more repeat procedures to keep the artery open.

The Cypher Stent combines the action of a stent—which works like a scaffold to keep the artery propped open—with delivery of the drug Sirolimus into the vessel wall to prevent restenosis, or re-blockage, of the artery. Unlike open heart surgery or other more invasive medical procedures, with the Cypher Stent, a cardiologist inserts the stent using a guiding catheter through a small incision in the femoral artery (in the upper thigh), into the blocked artery where it is deployed.

## Company Profile

Johnson & Johnson is the largest and most comprehensive healthcare company in the world, with 2004 sales of more than $46 billion.

JNJ offers a broad line of consumer products, ethical and over-the-counter drugs, as well as various other medical devices and diagnostic equipment.

The company has a stake in a wide variety of endeavors: anti-infectives, biotechnology, cardiology and circulatory diseases, the central nervous system, diagnostics, gastrointestinals, minimally invasive therapies, nutraceuticals, orthopedics, pain management, skin care, vision care, women's health, and wound care.

Johnson & Johnson has more than 200 operating companies in fifty-four countries, selling some 50,000 products in more than 175 countries.

One of Johnson & Johnson's premier assets is its well-entrenched brand names, which are widely known in the United States as well as abroad. As a marketer, moreover, JNJ's reputation for quality has enabled it to build strong ties to healthcare providers.

Its international presence includes not only marketing, but also production and distribution capability in a vast array of regions outside the United States.

One advantage of JNJ's worldwide organization: Markets such as China, Latin America, and Africa offer growth potential for mature product lines.

The company's well-known trade names include Band-Aid adhesive bandages; Tylenol; Stayfree, Carefree and Sure & Natural feminine hygiene products; Mylanta; Pepcid AC, Neutrogena, Johnson's baby powder, shampoo and oil; and Reach toothbrushes.

The company's professional items include ligatures and sutures, mechanical wound closure products, diagnostic products, medical equipment and devices, surgical dressings, surgical apparel and accessories, and disposable contact lenses.

## Shortcomings to Bear in Mind

- John Watkins, an analyst with Argus Research Company had this somewhat negative comment on October 12, 2004: "We are maintaining our HOLD rating on Johnson & Johnson Inc. The shares are near our target at this time. We feel that, beginning in 2005, the company will struggle to grow the top line (revenues), as patent expirations loom and competition intensifies. The company's balance sheet is strong, and it has had a consistent record of delivering double-digit EPS (Earnings per

share) growth. That said, we think that over the next few years the company's growth will slow, as there appears to be a gap between upcoming patent expirations and new product approvals. The company does have a strong pipeline and should return to more rapid growth in a couple of years."

## Reasons to Buy

- "In a year when its drug company rivals were stumbling, Johnson & Johnson continued to prosper," said *BusinessWeek* in an article dated April 4, 2005. "Its broad portfolio of businesses offset weakness in one market with strength in other lines."

- In December 2004, JNJ made a bold move with the purchase of Guidant, one of the nation's largest makers of devices to treat heart and circulatory illnesses, plunking down a hefty $25.4 billion. The deal faces significant challenges and risks. It must pass muster with antitrust regulators, a process that lawyers say could push a closing to the fall of 2005—and may force Johnson & Johnson to sell off or license Guidant product lines. Rick Wise, an analyst with Bear Stearns & Company who covers both JNJ and Guidant, views these antitrust issues as tricky, but manageable.

  Guidant of Indianapolis will be merged with Cordis Corp., a JNJ unit, in a new franchise that will carry the Guidant name. Guidant is expected to generate about $4 billion in revenues in 2005. Michael Dormer, Johnson & Johnson's worldwide chairman for medical devices and diagnostics, said, "We believe that the combination will generate much better products and a much faster rate of product introduction."

- "Johnson & Johnson received FDA approval for the first spinal-disc implant to replace deteriorated natural shock absorbers between the bones of the lower back," said Scott Hensley, writing for the

*Wall Street Journal* on October 27, 2004. The article went on to say, "The disc from Johnson & Johnson, New Brunswick, N.J., consists of a plastic core that slides between two metal end plates. The product, called the Charite artificial disc, is expected to cost $11,500, not including the surgery. Other companies, including Medtronic Inc., are working on rival implants." One important benefit of the new disc is that it gives the patient greater flexibility, compared with the traditional surgery which fuses the bones around the degenerated disc.

- "I am pleased that Johnson & Johnson continues to achieve solid results in both sales and earnings," said CEO William C. Weldon in late 2004. "Our broadly based approach to health care continues to serve us well as competition intensifies across many of our businesses and products lines."

  Sales growth reflected the strong performances of Risperdal (an antipsychotic medication), Duragesic (a transdermal patch for chronic pain), Topamax (to treat epilepsy—and recently approved for use in the prevention of migraines), Remicade (a treatment for rheumatoid arthritis and Crohn's disease), Sporanox (an antifungal), Concerta (a treatment for attention deficit hyperactivity disorder), and Natrecor (a novel agent for the treatment of congestive heart failure).

- *Value Line Investment Survey* had some kind words to say about JNJ on March 4, 2005. Its analyst, George Rho, said "This timely issue represents a core long-term holding. J&J's robust presence in a host of healthcare sectors is certainly attractive. So, too, is its potent financial position, as this gives management ample flexibility. We think the stock will yield solid total returns to late decade."

- In 2003, Johnson & Johnson acquired Scios Inc. for $2.4 billion, bolstering its pharmaceutical pipeline and adding to its position in biotechnology. Scios' major product is Natrecor, a heart-failure drug. However, what attracted JNJ to Scios is an arthritis drug that is under investigation. Known as SCIO-469, it targets p38, an enzyme responsible for inflammation in rheumatoid arthritis and other afflictions. Now in its second round of tests, the drug could become a billion-dollar-a-year blockbuster, according to analysts.

  "Natrecor is a young product with room to grow, and the arthritis drug candidate is risky but potentially rewarding," said Scott Hensley and Robin Sidel, in a February 2003 article in the *Wall Street Journal.* "Those prospects could aid J&J as sales growth of some of its most important products begins to slow and before an increased investment in internal drug discovery pays off."

- Johnson & Johnson has thirty-four drugs with annual sales exceeding $50 million; twenty-four drugs with annual sales of more than $100 million; and more than 100 drugs that are sold in more than 200 countries.

- A revolutionary liquid bandage that is changing the way consumers treat minor cuts and scrapes was introduced by Johnson & Johnson Consumer Products Company. Band-Aid Brand Liquid Bandage provides superior protection and optimal healing and stays on hard-to-cover areas like fingers and knuckles.

  The bandage creates a clear seal that keeps out water and germs to help prevent infection and promote quick healing. It stays on until it naturally sloughs off as the wound heals. Band-Aid Brand Liquid Bandage contains 2-octyl cyanoacrylate, the same base material found in Dermabond Topical Skin Adhesive, a prescription device marketed by Ethicon Products. Both are manufactured by Closure Medical Corporation. Used by physicians to close wounds and incisions in place of stitches or staples, Dermabond adhesive acts as a barrier that seals out bacteria that can lead to infection.

Total assets: $53,317 million
Current ratio: 1.96
Common shares outstanding: 2,968 million
Return on 2004 shareholders' equity: 29%

|                       | 2004  | 2003  | 2002  | 2001  | 2000  | 1999  | 1998  | 1997  |
|-----------------------|-------|-------|-------|-------|-------|-------|-------|-------|
| Revenues (millions)   | 47,348| 41,862| 36,298| 32,317| 29,139| 27,471| 23,657| 22,629|
| Net income (millions) | 8,509 | 7,197 | 6,651 | 5,668 | 4,800 | 4,167 | 3,669 | 3,303 |
| Earnings per share    | 2.84  | 2.40  | 2.18  | 1.84  | 1.63  | 1.47  | 1.34  | 1.21  |
| Dividends per share   | 1.10  | .93   | .82   | .70   | .62   | .55   | .49   | .43   |
| Price      high       | 64.2  | 59.1  | 65.9  | 61.0  | 53.0  | 53.5  | 44.9  | 33.7  |
|            low        | 49.2  | 48.0  | 41.4  | 40.3  | 33.1  | 38.5  | 31.7  | 24.3  |

Conservative Growth

# Johnson Controls, Inc.

P. O. Box 591 ▫ Milwaukee, WI 53201–0591 ▫ (414) 524–2375 ▫ Direct dividend reinvestment plan available: (877) 602–7397 ▫ Fiscal years end September 30th ▫ Web site: *www.johnsoncontrols.com* ▫ Listed: NYSE ▫ Ticker symbol: JCI ▫ S&P rating: A+ ▫ Value Line financial strength rating: A

"As Wisconsin's largest public corporation, Johnson Controls is a rock of stability," said Thomas Content, a reporter for the *Milwaukee Journal Sentinel*.

"Its roots stretch to 1885, before other corporate mainstays such as Harley-Davidson and Briggs & Stratton were born.

"It still operates in the business of climate control for commercial buildings, a venture launched when Warren Johnson invented the electric room thermostat in 1883 while a professor at Whitewater State College.

"And Johnson Controls has consistently produced record earnings for more than a decade, and record sales for more than half a century—during times of recession or boom. This is a company that has embraced change, seizing on a dramatic shift in the auto industry to catapult itself into a dominant global player in the business of designing and building the interiors of cars and minivans."

## Company Profile

Johnson Controls, Inc. is a global market leader in automotive systems and facility management and control. In the automotive market, it is a major supplier of seating and interior systems, and batteries. For nonresidential facilities, Johnson Controls provides building control systems and services, energy management, and integrated facility management.

### Automotive Systems Group

• Global market leader in seating and interior systems for light vehicles, including passenger cars and light trucks.

• Systems supplied include seating, overhead, door, instrument panels, storage, electronics, and batteries.

• All systems are sold to the original equipment automotive market. However, the automotive replacement market is the major course of sales for batteries.

• Major customers include AutoZone, Costco, DaimlerChrysler, Fiat, Ford, General Motors, Honda, Interstate Battery Systems of America, John Deere, Mazda, Mitsubishi, Nissan, NUMMI, Peugeot, Renault, Sears, Toyota, Volkswagen, and Wal-Mart.

• 300 locations worldwide.

## Controls Group

• The Controls business is a leader in supplying systems to control heating, ventilating, air conditioning (HVAC), lighting, security, and fire management for buildings. Services include complete mechanical and electrical maintenance.

• World leader in integrated facility management, providing facility management and consulting services for many *Fortune* 500 companies. The company manages more than 1 billion square feet worldwide.

• Customers worldwide include education, healthcare, industrial, government, and office buildings.

• 300 locations worldwide.

## Shortcomings to Bear in Mind

■ "Just as the economy is supposed to be picking up steam, the auto sector is facing a new round of weak earnings and job cuts in part because of a new twist on an old demon: inflation," said Paul Glader and Neal E. Boudette, writing for the *Wall Street Journal* on October 19, 2004. The article quoted a comment by John Barth, CEO of Johnson Controls: 'You can't absorb all the raw-material costs and continue to provide the huge price reductions' required by the auto makers. Johnson Controls' automotive unit, which makes seats and interiors, is profitable and faring much better than many suppliers, but nevertheless announced last week that it was cutting 350 jobs at several Michigan locations to keep its costs down."

In a more optimistic report issued by the company on October 8, 2004,

Mr. Barth commented on prospects for 2005, "Automotive Group sales of seating, interiors, and batteries are projected to increase 8 to 10 percent, primarily due to the addition of $2.3 billion in new seating and interiors business and higher battery sales. This growth is expected to more than offset the assumption of a slight reduction in vehicle production in North America and Europe. Over the next three years, the company's incremental backlog of new interiors business totals $4.7 billion. Operating income as a percentage of automotive sales is expected to increase slightly due to the sales growth and increased efficiencies."

## Reasons to Buy

■ Johnson Controls had another good year in 2004. Sales increased to $26.6 billion, 17 percent higher than the prior year. The growth in revenues reflects a 20 percent increase in the Automotive Group sales of seating, interiors, and batteries, and a 9 percent increase in sales of the Controls Group. Net income for fiscal 2004 reached $818 million, up 20 percent, compared with 2003.

■ Over the past 10 years, 1994–2004, the company's Earnings per share increase without interruption, climbing from $0.90 to $4.24, an impressive annual compound growth rate of 16.8 percent. In the same ten-year span, dividends advanced from $.36 to $0.85, a solid growth rate of 9 percent.

■ Integration of electronics into vehicle interiors is one of the company's specialties, ranging from global positioning systems to digital compasses and Homelink. The company, moreover, is continuously developing new products and holds more patents than any other automotive interior supplier.

- The company's automotive business is expected to expand in the years ahead as automakers continue outsourcing seating and interior systems in North America and Europe, as well as in emerging global markets.

  What's more, the company's development of innovative features and application of new technologies for the automotive interior will strengthen the company's leadership position, as Johnson Controls makes its customers' vehicles more comfortable, convenient, and safe.

- Nearly every automotive system the company makes today includes electronics. New products such as the company's AutoVision, in-vehicle video system and PSI tire pressure-sensing system are electronics-based. What's more, electronics are a part of its seats and other interior systems as well. Innovative use of electronics creates new features and functions for car interiors, as well as new way for the company's automaker customers to differentiate their vehicles.

- Industry studies estimate that 75 percent of all tires are improperly inflated. The company's PSI system uses a radio-frequency transmitter in each tire, which sends air pressure information to an in-vehicle electronic display.

- The annual market for automotive electronics in North America reached a total of $28 billion in 2004. To help meet this demand, according to management, "We're expanding and accelerating our electronics capabilities and creating new partnering programs with leading electronics firms."

- According to a spokesman for the company, "With more than 110 years of experience in the controls industry, Johnson Controls understands buildings better than anyone else. That's why tens of thousands of commercial, institutional and government building owner and managers around the world turn to Johnson Controls to improve the quality of buildings' indoor environments by maximizing comfort, productivity, safety and energy efficiency."

- The company engineers, manufactures, and installs control systems that automate a building's heating, ventilating, and air conditioning, as well as its lighting and fire-safety equipment. Its Metasys Facility Management System automates a building's mechanical systems for optimal comfort levels while using the least amount of energy. In addition, it monitors fire sensors and building access, controls lights, tracks equipment maintenance, and helps building managers make better decisions.

- Building systems at some companies are critical to achieving their corporate missions. In the pharmaceutical industry, for example, the failure of a building's equipment or staff to maintain the proper laboratory conditions could mean the loss of years of new drug research and development. In a bank's data center, moreover, the failure of cooling equipment could shut down computer systems, delaying millions of dollars in transactions every minute.

- The company's Controls Group does business with more than 7,000 school districts, colleges, and universities as well as over 2,000 healthcare organizations. These customers benefit from performance contracting, a solution that lets them implement needed facility repairs and updates without up-front capital costs. Performance contracting uses a project's energy and operational cost savings to pay its costs over time. For instance, using a performance contract, Grady Health System in Atlanta was able to complete energy efficiency upgrades that will generate $20 million in savings over the next 10 years.

Total assets: $15,091 million
Current ratio: 0.97
Common shares outstanding: 190 million
Return on 2004 shareholders' equity: 17.3%

| | 2004 | 2003 | 2002 | 2001 | 2000 | 1999 | 1998 | 1997 |
|---|---|---|---|---|---|---|---|---|
| Revenues (millions) | 26,553 | 22,646 | 20,103 | 18,427 | 17,155 | 16,139 | 12,587 | 11,145 |
| Net income (millions) | 818 | 683 | 601 | 542 | 472 | 387 | 303 | 265 |
| Earnings per share | 4.24 | 3.60 | 3.18 | 2.56 | 2.55 | 2.07 | 1.63 | 1.43 |
| Dividends per share | .85 | .72 | .66 | .62 | .56 | .50 | .46 | .43 |
| Price      high | 63.2 | 58.1 | 46.6 | 41.4 | 32.6 | 38.4 | 31.0 | 25.5 |
|            low | 49.6 | 35.9 | 34.6 | 24.1 | 22.9 | 24.5 | 20.3 | 17.7 |

Conservative Growth

# Kellogg Company

One Kellogg Square ❏ P. O. Box 3599 ❏ Battle Creek, MI 49016–3599 ❏ (269) 961–6636 ❏ Dividend reinvestment plan available: (877) 910–5385 ❏ Web site: *www.kelloggcompany.com* ❏ Ticker symbol: K ❏ Listed: NYSE ❏ S&P rating: B+ ❏ Value Line financial strength rating: B++

"If there are limits to how hard a company can sell packaging over product, Kellogg is stretching them," said Robert Barker, writing for *BusinessWeek* on December 27, 2004. "Right now, it's pushing a 'Limited Edition' multigrain cereal called The Incredibles (10.5 ounces inside a $2.79 box), part of a joint promotion with Walt Disney and Pixar, makers of the hit movie of the same name.

"Such new frontiers in marketing—a key element in outgoing Chief Executive Carlos Gutierrez's strategy—have helped boost revenue this year (2004), not counting currency moves. Better yet, as cost cutting widens margins, full-year profits should be near $2.12 a share, up 10 percent or so from 2003. Since Gutierrez became chairman in April 2000, the stock has doubled.

"No wonder then, that the share price began wobbling after President George W. Bush named Gutierrez his next Commerce Secretary. Yet this may be an overreaction, because Kellogg has plenty of substance within, whoever's face is on the corporate package. New CEO James Jenness, who joined Kellogg's board in 2000, is making it plain he plans to stay on Gutierrez's course. More important, the company has the means to reward investors further. Kellogg has ample room to raise its dividend, and I'm betting it will before long."

## Company Profile
Dating back to 1906, Kellogg is the world's leading producer of cereal and a leading producer of convenience foods, including cookies, crackers, toaster pastries, cereal bars, frozen waffles, meat alternatives, pie crusts, and cones.

The company's brands include Kellogg's, Keebler, Pop-Tarts, Eggo, Cheez-It, Nutri-Grain, Rice Krispies, Special K, Murray, Austin, Morningstar Farms, Famous Amos, Carr's, Plantation, and Kashi.

Kellogg icons such as Tony the Tiger, Snap! Crackle! Pop!, and Ernie Keebler are among the most recognized characters in advertising. The company's products are manufactured in nineteen countries and marketed in more than 160 countries around the world.

## Shortcomings to Bear in Mind

- "A lot has happened to Kellogg Company since our November report," said *Value Line* analyst William G. Ferguson on February 4, 2005. "Of most importance was the resignation of Chairman and CEO Carlos Gutierrez, who was tapped by President Bush to be the nation's Secretary of Commerce. Mr. Gutierrez was the main cog behind the company's impressive turnaround. He was very instrumental in Kellogg's acquisition of Keebler, the cookie and cracker maker."

  On a more positive note, Mr. Ferguson also said, "It seems likely that Kellogg will strengthen its price/product mix this year. The company should also witness an increase in volume, since U.S. cereal consumption is expected to remain strong.

  The company's commitment to cost-cutting in recent years and the ongoing share-repurchase program should lend support to the bottom line, too."

- *Standard & Poor's Stock Reports* also had some reservations concerning the future of Kellogg on December 6, 2004, when Richard Joy said, "Our HOLD recommendation reflects our belief that improving trends for K's cereal and snack products and strong free cash flow growth will be balanced by rising costs and competitive pressures. Competition in the core ready-to-eat cereal business remains strong, but the company appears to be making solid dollar share gains, and the addition of Keebler has provided diversification and helped reduce dependence on cereal.

  "K appears to be focusing on improving profitability rather than on volume growth, and improvements in margins and cash flow trends are materializing. We view favorably the company's longer-term prospects and think the shares are a worthwhile holding, based on our projections of solid earnings growth, strong free cash flows, and improving returns."

## Reasons to Buy

- Departing CEO Carlos Gutierrez had this comment when James M. Jenness, age 58, was appointed to succeed him, "Jim is a strong leader with world-class marketing skills. During his thirty-year relationship with the company, he has been directly involved with building Kellogg brands around the world and most recently served as chairman of the Consumer Marketing Committee of the Kellogg Board of Directors. Jim has a unique relationship with the company. He has been instrumental in setting and implementing the company's current strategy; he knows our business, our culture, and our people well. His experience and knowledge of our company makes him an excellent choice for this role."

- In 2004, Mr. Gutierrez said, "We are a very focused company. Between cereal and wholesome snacks, the vast majority of our sales take place in a single aisle of most stores and channels. We believe it is a competitive advantage to concentrate our resources on categories in which we have scale, expertise, and leading brands, as opposed to participating in a large number of categories that can distract us from what we do best. Our strategy underscores our focus: Grow Cereal, Expand Snacks, Pursue Selective Growth Opportunities."

  He also said, "Ready-to-eat cereal accounts for more than half of our company's net sales. That's a good thing.

Cereal is a large and profitable category that reacts to brand building and innovation. It offers consumers convenience, fun, and great taste, and it contributes to a healthy, well-balanced diet. It's also what we do best. We have leading shares in this category across the globe, giving us the best opportunity to expand consumption. When managed well, we can generate strong, profitable growth in cereal."

- Commenting on the snack business, Mr. Gutierrez said, "Snacks, and particularly wholesome snacks, continue to grow faster than other food categories. We are well positioned to participate in this growth. We have strong, extendable brands and an expertise in grain- and fruit-based foods. In the U.S. and Mexico, we have direct store-door distribution, giving us an in-store advantage. And wholesome snacks are usually located right in the cereal aisle."

- Mr. Gutierrez went on to say, "Beyond cereal and snacks, we also participate in other nearby categories, using strong regional brands. For example, in the U.S., we have Pop-Tarts, number one in toaster pastries; Eggo, the leading frozen waffle brands; and Morningstar Farms, the largest frozen meat-alternatives brand. Brands like these offer good, profitable growth."

- Commenting on the company's recent stellar performance, Mr. Gutierrez said "In late 2000, we laid out our plan to return Kellogg to sustainable growth. We changed our strategy and our organizational structure. The year 2001 was to be a year of transition. We purchased Keebler Foods, the largest acquisition in our history. We essentially overhauled the entire company while still achieving our earnings goals. In 2002, we planned for a year of acceleration in sales and earnings, and we actually exceeded our targets that year. By 2003, our business was expected to exhibit momentum, and

it did. We surpassed our sales and earnings growth targets while reinvesting for the future."

- According to an article in the *Chicago Tribune* on April 7, 2003, "Pop-Tarts were an instant hit when they were test-marketed in Cleveland in 1963. Kellogg's sold out of all 45,000 cases of each of the four original, unfrosted flavors it had prepared for the test run.

  "The pioneering toaster pastry would go on to become the strongest brand for Kellogg's and a staple found in millions of American kitchens, office desk drawers, and college dorm rooms. Pop-Tarts also are sold in Canada and the United Kingdom.

  "Despite an expanding selection of convenience breakfast foods such as granola bars, fruit bars, and frozen sandwiches on the market, Pop-Tarts continue to grow in popularity, says Jeff Montie, president of Kellogg's morning foods division. The company now sells about 2 billion Pop-Tarts each year in the United States, which is double the sales of the early 1990s, he says. Today, Kellogg's offers twenty-eight varieties of Pop-Tarts. The most popular are frosted strawberry, frosted brown sugar cinnamon and S'Mores, the company says."

- In the words of a company official, "Latin America remains our fastest-growing region in the world. We have leading category shares, a long-standing presence, and a strong local management team that is adept at managing through the volatility inherent in that region. Per capita consumption of ready-to-eat cereal continues to grow, and yet remains well below levels of developed markets. This points to sustainable category growth. Furthermore, rising disposable income and increased snacking suggests very attractive potential for our small, but rapidly growing wholesome snacks business in key markets of Latin America."

Total assets: $10,790 million
Current ratio: 0.75
Common shares outstanding: 413 million
Return on 2004 shareholders' equity: 48.2%

|                      | 2004  | 2003  | 2002  | 2001  | 2000  | 1999  | 1998  | 1997  |
|----------------------|-------|-------|-------|-------|-------|-------|-------|-------|
| Revenues (millions)  | 9,614 | 8,812 | 8,304 | 8,853 | 6,955 | 6,984 | 6,762 | 6,830 |
| Net income (millions)| 890.6 | 787.1 | 710.7 | 532.8 | 651.9 | 606.2 | 548.9 | 704.5 |
| Earnings per share   | 2.14  | 1.92  | 1.73  | 1.31  | 1.61  | 1.50  | 1.35  | 1.70  |
| Dividends per share  | 1.01  | 1.01  | 1.01  | 1.01  | 1.00  | .96   | .92   | .87   |
| Price      high      | 45.3  | 38.6  | 37.0  | 34.0  | 32.0  | 42.3  | 50.2  | 50.5  |
|            low       | 37.0  | 27.8  | 29.0  | 24.3  | 20.8  | 30.0  | 28.5  | 32.0  |

Growth and Income

# Kimco Realty Corporation

3333 New Hyde Park Road ❑ Suite 100 ❑ New Hyde Park, NY 11042–0020 ❑ Listed: NYSE ❑ (516) 869–7288 ❑ Direct dividend reinvestment plan available: 1-(866) 557–8695 ❑ Web site: *www.kimcorealty.com* ❑ Ticker symbol: KIM ❑ S&P rating: A+ ❑ Value Line financial strength rating: B++

Kimco, the nation's largest publicly traded owner of neighborhood and community shopping centers, concentrates on increasing the cash flow and value of its properties through strategic re-tenanting, redevelopment, renovation, and expansion. It also makes selective acquisitions of neighborhood and community shopping centers that have below-market-rate leases or other cash flow growth potential. Kimco's current management has been developing neighborhood and community shopping centers for more than forty years.

Kimco has grown from 126 properties when it went public in 1991 to 720 today. Recent acquisitions include:

• Palm Aire Marketplace, a 140,000 square-foot property in Pompano, Florida, acquired through a partnership with DRA Advisors LLC, is 94 percent leased.

• The company acquired a portfolio of eleven properties in the New York Metropolitan area leased to national drug store chains and other local tenants with long-term below-market leases.

• Mission Bell, a 168,000 square-foot redevelopment project in Tampa, Florida, acquired from Kmart and anchored on a short-term lease.

• Kimco acquired a 50 percent partnership interest in a 170,000 square-foot shopping center in Valdosta, Georgia, anchored by a Lowe's Home Improvement store.

• RioNorte Shopping Center, a 237,000 square-foot shopping center in Laredo, Texas, was acquired as part of a joint venture with General Electric Company.

## Company Profile

Kimco Realty Corporation is the largest publicly traded real estate investment trust (REIT) that owns and operates a portfolio of neighborhood and community shopping centers (measured by gross leasable area). The company has specialized in the acquisition, development and management of well-located shopping centers with strong growth potential. Kimco has interests in 720 properties, comprised of 645 shopping centers, thirty-two retail store leases, and other projects totaling about 104 million square feet of leasable area in forty-two states, Canada, and Mexico.

Since incorporating in 1966, Kimco has specialized in the acquisition, development and management of well-located centers with strong growth potential. Self-administered and self-managed, the company's focus is to increase the cash flow and enhance the value of its shopping center properties.

A substantial portion of KIM's income consists of rent received under long-term leases, most of which provide for the payment of fixed-base rents and a pro rata share of various expenses. Many of the leases also provide for the payment of additional rent as a percentage of gross sales.

KIM's neighborhood and community shopping center properties are designed to attract local area customers and typically are anchored by a supermarket, discount department store or drugstore, offering day-to-day necessities rather than high-priced luxury items. Among the company's major tenants are Kmart, Wal-Mart, Kohl's, and TJX Companies.

Kimco's core strategy is to acquire older shopping centers carrying below-market rents. This space is then re-leased at much higher rates.

## Funds From Operations

REITs are not valued by Earnings per share (EPS), but rather by funds from operations (FFO) per share. FFO is calculated by adding net income and depreciation expense and then subtracting profits from the sale of assets. If a REIT pays out 90 percent or more of its taxable income in dividends, it is exempt from paying federal income taxes. FFO per share is in excess of net income because depreciation is added in. This means that a REIT such as Kimco pays out only about 66 percent of its FFO in dividends, with the balance of 34 percent available for acquisitions and improving existing properties.

## Shortcomings to Bear in Mind

- "Kimco Realty stock doesn't stand out," said John Marrin, writing for *Value Line Investment Survey* on January 21, 2005. "Our projections to the 2007–2009 horizon do not support a compelling case for a long-term investment. And with interest rates likely on the rise, income-oriented investors may soon begin to find alternatives that satisfy a lower risk/return profile."

- As most investors are aware, dividends under a new federal tax law, are now taxed at a maximum rate of 15 percent. Unfortunately, this does not apply to dividends paid out by REITS. That's because real estate investment trusts generally don't pay corporate income tax.

## Reasons to Buy

- *Standard & Poor's Stock Reports* gave Kimco a BUY rating on December 30, 2004, with this comment by R. McMillan, "Our twelve-month target price is $65, assuming Kim delivers FFO of $3.92 over the next four quarters, and that the shares trade at about 16.7 times our trailing twelve-month FFO projections.

  This is higher than the stock's historical price-to-FFO multiple of about 11.6 times, but in line with current levels, and we think it can be sustained by what we view as KIM's solid operating prospects, and investor enthusiasm for REITs and their relatively high dividends. In addition, we expect the dividend to continue to rise in tandem with future potential growth to meet the 90 percent REIT payout requirement."

- In the past ten years (1994–2004), the company's Earnings per share climbed from $0.78 to $2.38, a compound annual growth rate of 11.8 percent, a rather spectacular performance for an income stock. In the same span, Dividends per share advanced from $0.91 to $2.28, a growth rate of 9.6 percent, or far above the rate of inflation. What's more, the dividend was boosted every year during that ten-year period.

- Kimco's customers include some of the strongest and most rapidly growing chains in the United States, such as Costco, Home Depot, Circuit City, Best Buy, Wal-Mart, Value City, Target, and Kohl's.
- Nearly all of the company's revenue is contractual. This means that even when a retailer's sales slump, it does not change the rent they must pay to Kimco under the lease agreement or the value of the company's real estate.
- Knowledge of local markets and trends is crucial to success in the real estate sector. Kimco's decentralized asset management staff—situated in such cities as New York, Los Angeles, Chicago, Philadelphia, Dallas, Phoenix, Tampa, Charlotte, and Dayton, provides knowledge of real estate developments that are analyzed by professionals on the scene.
- Kimco's success comes not by accident but as the careful product of business principles that have remained firmly in place since the company was founded in the 1950s. The company invests in properties that are undervalued assets, where management knows it will be able to capitalize on the margin between the price at which it can buy the property and the price at which it can lease it. The average rent on properties in Kimco's portfolio remains below the market, providing the company with significant upside potential.
- To continue growing its portfolio and income, the company has established the following special-purpose ventures to acquire properties:
  - The Kimco Retail Opportunity Portfolio, a joint venture with GE Capital Real Estate.
  - Kimco formed a joint venture with RioCan real estate investment trust, Canada's largest REIT.

- In 1999, the company launched the Kimco Income REIT, which currently consists of more than $1.2 billion in assets.
- Anticipating new opportunities when the REIT Modernization Act became effective on January 1, 2001, Kimco formed Kimco Developers Inc. (KDI) which operates as a merchant developer. The new legislation allows KDI to immediately sell properties and capture the developer's profit for future reinvestment. KDI generated income of $8.1 million in its first full year of operations.
- "While you can't be sure whether REITs or rental properties will perform better, REITs do have one undeniable advantage: They are a lot less risky," said Jonathan Clements in a *Wall Street Journal* article dated September 10, 2003. Mr. Clements' columns appear nearly every Wednesday in the *Wall Street Journal*. I urge you to read them. His thinking and advice are nearly always exceptionally sound.

His piece on REITs went on to say, "If you invest in rental property, you are banking a ton of money on a single piece of real estate, rather than getting the diversification of REITs. Moreover, there is the problem of collecting those rent checks. 'If it takes you three months to evict a tenant, you're out a quarter of that year's return,' according to Chris Mayer, a finance professor at New York's Columbia Business School.

"The bottom line: Owning REITs is not only less risky, but it also involves far fewer hassles. 'It's easy to describe the difference,' between REITs and rental properties, says William Bernstein, an investment adviser in North Bend, Oregon. 'One is an investment and the other is a job. It also depends on your tolerance for broken toilet bowls and psychopathic tenants.'"

Total assets: $4,747 million
Current ratio: NA
Return on 2004 equity: 12.6%
Common shares outstanding: 111 million

| | 2004 | 2003 | 2002 | 2001 | 2000 | 1999 | 1998 | 1997 |
|---|---|---|---|---|---|---|---|---|
| Rental income (millions) | 517 | 480 | 433 | 450 | 459 | 434 | 339 | 199 |
| Net income (millions) | 517 | 480 | 451 | 469 | 459 | 434 | 339 | 199 |
| Earnings per share | 2.38 | 2.62 | 2.16 | 2.16 | 1.91 | 1.64 | 1.35 | 1.19 |
| Funds from operations | 3.55 | 3.23 | 2.93 | 2.99 | 2.69 | 2.41 | 2.02 | 1.75 |
| Dividends per share | 2.32 | 2.16 | 2.10 | 1.96 | 1.83 | 1.62 | 1.31 | 1.15 |
| Price    high | 59.3 | 45.9 | 33.9 | 34.1 | 29.8 | 27.2 | 27.8 | 24.1 |
|          low | 39.5 | 30.3 | 25.0 | 27.2 | 21.8 | 20.6 | 22.3 | 20.2 |

Growth and Income

# Kinder Morgan Energy Partners, L.P.

500 Dallas Street, Suite 1000 ❑ Houston, TX 77002 ❑ (713) 369–9490 ❑ Dividend reinvestment program not available ❑ Web site: *www.kindermorgan.com* ❑ Listed: NYSE ❑ Ticker symbol: KMP ❑ S&P rating: Not rated ❑ Value Line financial strength rating: B+

"For a company to be successful and deliver value to its unit holders (*similar to stockholders*), it has to have a solid strategy, and it must effectively executive that strategy," said Richard D. Kinder, CEO of Kinder Morgan Energy Partners. "At KMP, our game plan has remained simple and consistent. We own and operate quality midstream energy assets—primarily pipelines and terminals—that are core to the energy infrastructure of growing markets and which produce stable, fee-based cash flow and earnings.

"We run these assets in the most efficient, cost-effective way possible. We increase distributions due to internal volume growth, small rate increases, expansions, and extensions, and we maximize the tax efficiency of the master limited partnership (MLP) structure.

"In addition to a proven strategy, we have employed a philosophy that I believe helps us stand apart from many other companies. I receive $1 a year in salary—with no bonuses, no stock options, and no restricted stock.

"We limit base salaries for the rest of senior management to $200,000 a year, well below industry medians. To keep corporate costs low, we don't own corporate jets or fly first class. However, we don't cut corners in the field where maintenance and safety are key to our operations. We avoid businesses with direct commodity exposure as much as possible and hedge to minimize the risk when there is exposure. And, we have a very hands-on senior management team that pays great attention to detail."

## Company Profile

The Kinder Morgan family of companies includes three separate, publicly traded entities on the New York Stock Exchange: Kinder Morgan, Inc. (KMI), Kinder Morgan Energy Partners, L.P. (KMP), and Kinder Morgan Management, LLC (KMR).

Kinder Morgan, Inc. (KMI) is one of the largest energy transportation and storage companies in America, operating more than 35,000 miles of natural gas and products pipelines and approximately 135 terminals. Kinder Morgan, Inc. owns the general partner interest of Kinder Morgan Energy Partners, L.P., the largest publicly traded pipeline limited partnership in the U.S. in terms of market capitalization.

The general partner of KMP is owned by Kinder Morgan, Inc. (NYSE: KMI), one of the largest energy transportation and storage companies in America. Combined, the two companies have an enterprise value of approximately $26 billion.

Kinder Morgan Management, LLC (KMR) is a limited liability company, and its only significant assets are the partnership units it owns in KMP. KMR shareholders receive distributions in the form of additional shares equivalent in value to the cash distributions received by KMP common unit holders.

### Kinder Morgan Energy Partners, L. P.

Kinder Morgan Energy Partners, L.P. (KMP) is America's largest pipeline master limited partnership.

• KMP is the largest independent owner/operator of products pipelines in the country, transporting more than 2 million barrels a day of gasoline, jet fuel, diesel fuel, and natural gas liquids through more than 10,000 miles of pipelines. The Products Pipelines segment also includes associated storage terminals and transmix processing facilities.

• KMP's Natural Gas pipelines consist of approximately 15,000 miles of pipelines, with the capacity to transport 7.8 billion cubic feet per day (Bcf/d) and includes gathering, treating, processing, and storage facilities.

• KMP is the largest independent terminal operator in the U.S. The company's nearly 100 terminals handle over 60 million tons of coal and other dry-bulk materials annually and have a liquids storage capacity of approximately 60 million barrels for petroleum products and chemicals.

• KMP is the largest $CO_2$ marketer and transporter in the country. Kinder Morgan $CO_2$ Company, L.P. owns the most prolific source of carbon dioxide in the world and transports and markets more than 1 billion cubic feet per day of $CO_2$ through its network of more than 1,100 miles of pipelines. $CO_2$ is used for enhanced oil recovery projects.

• KMP's strategy is to focus on the development and acquisition of stable, fee-based midstream energy assets and to take advantage of the low-cost capital advantages of the master limited partnership structure. Since 1997, KMP's enterprise value (market equity plus debt) has grown from $325 million to about $13 billion.

## Shortcomings to Bear in Mind

■ Since Kinder Morgan is a limited partnership, which is not the same as a conventional stock, you will not receive your tax form in January. It will probably be sent at the end of February. I suggest you invest in Kinder Morgan in your IRA, not in your regular account.

■ Mr. Kinder pointed out some risks to owning Kinder Morgan Energy Partners. "Let me assure you that all companies have challenges, and KMP is not an exception. We operate more than 25,000 miles of pipelines and more than ninety terminals across America, which exposes us to both regulatory and operational risks. On the regulatory front, we face possible challenges to our rate structure, including the long-running case involving our Pacific system (part of our Products Pipelines businesses segment), along with increasingly stringent and expensive safety regulations. On the operational side, mishaps are possible regardless of how careful we are or how much money we spend to keep our pipelines and terminals operating safely."

## Reasons to Buy

- On January 21, 2005, *Standard & Poor's Stock Reports* rated this stock a BUY. Charles LaPorta, CFA, said "Management suggested a nearly 10 percent distribution growth rate in 2005, which was higher than our initial expectations. KMP continues to see enough growth opportunities on its terms, both organic and through acquisitions, to maintain its return on capital criteria. Given its long-term history of meeting or exceeding its prescribed targets, we are inclined to give management a lower threshold of skepticism."

- "Kinder Morgan Energy Partners is widely recognized for having one of the premier management teams in the energy industry. Consequently, its annual presentation is typically the most well-attended conference among MLPs by a wide margin."

  This comment was made on January 19, 2005, by analysts with the brokerage firm of Lehman Brothers who rated the stock OVERWEIGHT, which is their term for BUY.

- Argus Research Company also had an upbeat comment on February 16, 2005. Gary F. Hovis said, "We reiterate our BUY rating on Kinder Morgan Energy Partners, L.P. In this connection, we look for the partnership to earn a strong $2.35 per unit in 2005." He also said,

"We expect Kinder Morgan Energy Partners to post annual earnings growth of around 9 percent over the next four-to-five years. Our growth forecast is supported by the partnership's relatively high and expanding operating margin, a long-term debt load that remains in line with partnership capital, dominant and growing U.S. market share, successfully integrated and accretive acquisitions, and what we see as an impressive U.S. distribution system for both refined petroleum products and natural gas. Growth in both volume and earnings has been strong in recent years, reflecting a strong management team and operating assets that are strategically located near energy supply sources with direct connections to areas of growing demand. Overall, we think Kinder Morgan Energy Partners is well positioned to deliver solid long-term growth for KMP unit holders."

- The company is aggressive on the acquisition front. Here are its moves in 2004: Southeast Terminals (purchased for $129 million between February and November); Kaston Pipeline ($111 million in August); Global Materials (October for $80 million); TransColorado (November for 275 million); Cochin (November for $11.8 million); and Novolog ($15.8 million in December).

Total assets: $2,749 million
Current ratio: 0.69
Common shares outstanding: 203 million
Return on 2004 shareholders' equity: 25.2%

|  |  | 2004 | 2003 | 2002 | 2001 | 2000 | 1999 | 1998 | 1997 |
|---|---|---|---|---|---|---|---|---|---|
| Revenues (millions) |  | 7,933 | 6,624 | 4,237 | 2,947 | 816 | 429 | 323 | 74 |
| Net income (millions) |  | 832 | 694 | 608 | 442 | 278 | 175 | 117 | 18 |
| Earnings per share |  | 2.22 | 2.00 | 1.96 | 1.56 | 1.34 | 1.22 | 1.05 | .51 |
| Dividends per share |  | 2.81 | 2.58 | 2.36 | 2.08 | 1.60 | 1.39 | 1.19 | .81 |
| Price | high | 49.1 | 38.9 | 39.7 | 28.9 | 22.8 | 19.1 | 20.6 | 7.3 |
|  | low | 37.6 | 33.5 | 23.9 | 25.2 | 18.2 | 16.5 | 14.3 | 6.8 |

# Eli Lilly and Company

Lilly Corporate Center ❑ Indianapolis, IN 46285 ❑ (317) 277–1302 ❑ Direct dividend reinvestment plan available: (800) 833–8699 ❑ Web site: *www.lilly.com* ❑ Listed: NYSE ❑ Ticker symbol: LLY ❑ S&P rating: B+ ❑ Value Line financial strength rating: A++

The career of CEO Sidney Taurel was discussed in *Fortune* magazine on June 28, 2004 by John Simons. "Since arriving at Lilly straight from graduate school in 1971, Taurel had distinguished himself as a deft manager. Throughout the 1970s and early '80s, he was an ambassador of sorts, representing Lilly in marketing and managerial positions in Latin America, Eastern Europe and France. In 1986, Taurel left his position in London as vice president of European operations and moved to Lilly's Indianapolis headquarters to head up the company's international operations.

"Though Taurel had ascended to great heights at Lilly, he had earned a reputation as a micro-manager. 'There was a time when he would sit in a meeting and ask a question, the next question, and the next question. And then he'd want more information after the meeting,' said Randall Tobias (the previous CEO). Often micro-managers have trouble delegating. They hover around the details and can't see the bigger picture. That's the way people might have seen Sidney years ago.'

"By 1997, Taurel was focused on the big picture, ready to begin implementing Year X, (the year when the patent would run out on its biggest drug at that time, Prozac). The plan's centerpiece was an industry-leading increase in R&D spending, to 19 percent of revenues. (The industry average is roughly 15 percent.) The effort also called for reducing the number of experimental failures and shortening the time each drug spent in various testing stages. Within a year, Tobias felt Taurel had proved himself as CEO material. He had grown, says Tobias, but most important, he had shaken his micro-managing instincts."

## Company Profile

Eli Lilly is one of the world's foremost healthcare companies. With a solid dedication to R & D, Lilly is a leader in the development of ethical drugs—those available on prescription.

It is well-known for such drugs as Prozac (to treat depression); a number of antibiotics such as Ceclor, Vancocin, Keflex, and Lorabid; insulin and other diabetic care items. Some of its other important drugs include Gemzar (to treat cancer of the lung and pancreas); Evista (to treat and prevent osteoporosis); ReoPro (a drug used to prevent adverse side effects from angioplasty procedures); Zyprexa, its largest-selling drug (a breakthrough treatment for schizophrenia and bipolar disorder); Dobutrex (for congestive heart failure); Axid (a medication that reduces excess stomach acid); and Sarafem (for the treatment of premenstrual dysphoric disorder).

The company is a pioneer in the treatment of diabetes and sells several versions of insulin. Sales of insulin products are well over $2 billion a year.

Lilly also has a stake in animal health and agricultural products.

Like most drug companies, Lilly is active abroad and does business in 120 countries.

## Shortcomings to Bear in Mind

■ *Standard & Poor's Stock Reports* had some reservations about Lilly on February 9, 2005. H. B. Saftlas said, "We maintain our HOLD recommendation with anticipated benefits from what we consider to be one of the most promising new drug pipelines in the industry balanced against eroding sales of Zyprexa anti-psychotic agent, and uncertainty regarding ongoing Zyprexa patent litigation. Zyprexa, which accounts for 32 percent of LLY's profits in 2004, has come under considerable competitive pressure from new rivals such as Bristol-Myers Squibb's Abilify and AstraZeneca's Seroquel. Based on IMS data, Zyprexa's share of the new anti-psychotic Rx market shrank to 17 percent in December 2004, from 25 percent in November 2003.

"We also believe that slowing trends in the pharmaceutical industry, partly due to tougher pricing conditions in principal managed care markets and uncertainties with respect to the new Medicare drug benefit, have led to multiple compression in the sector."

## Reasons to Buy

- Lilly's CEO took issue with this negative view of its prospects, according to an article in the *Wall Street Journal* on December 10, 2004. The author, Leila Abboud, said, "Eli Lilly & Co. forecast higher profits for next year, saying sales of its newer drugs would offset a decline in its flagship drug Zyprexa.

"The Indianapolis drug maker said sales would grow 8 to 10 percent next year. Net income per share was forecast to be $2.80 to $2.90, compared with expected net this year of $2.13 to $2.20 a share.

The *Wall Street Journal* article went on to say, "Lilly is also waiting for a decision in a patent challenge to Zyprexa filed by generic-drug makers. A loss would allow a generic to market far earlier than Lilly expected.

"Lilly executives vowed to stem the erosion of Zyprexa with a retooled sales message emphasizing what they called the drug's superior effectiveness, especially in particularly sick patients."

Finally, Ms. Abboud said, "Lilly also touted growing international sales of Zyprexa: sales in Europe topped $1 billion this year. Charlie Golden, chief financial officer, said that a major part of the revenue growth would come from eight new drugs, for cancer, depression, and attention-deficit disorder among other diseases, which have been launched in the past two years."

- As the developer of the first insulin product and one of the world's major suppliers of insulin, Lilly has long been a global leader in the field. But diabetes, which affects more than 100 million people worldwide, continues to cause severe long-term complications, suffering, lost productivity, and death.

For many patients with this disease, diabetes is also inconvenient. Diabetics have to check their blood glucose several times a day. They may have to give themselves one or more shots of insulin or risk severe complications, such as blindness, poor circulation, amputations, and nerve damage.

Lilly believes that it has an answer that gives patients with diabetes a better quality of life—and a good deal more convenience. Humalog acts faster than traditional insulin to control blood-glucose levels. Patients take it right before a meal, compared with 30 to 45 minutes before with current products. Humalog provides them with more freedom, better health and fewer complications.

- The first new drug for ADHD in decades, Strattera is regarded as a potentially important drug because most of the existing treatments for the condition, such as Ritalin, generic methylphenidate, Adderall and Concerta, are stimulants and can interfere with sleep and appetite. What's more, they are controlled substances under federal law. This means that access to them is restricted, and that their sales are monitored by the federal Drug Enforcement Administration.

ADHD, which can be a subjective diagnosis, is believed to be widely over-diagnosed and yet quite prevalent. It is estimated that as many as 5 percent to 10 percent of school-age children have the affliction. ADHD involves compulsive behavior, great difficulty concentrating, and often a learning disability. Finally, the condition tends to be inherited and can continue into adulthood.

- On December 9, 2004, Eli Lilly and Company said at its annual meeting with the investment community that the company expects to add to its industry-leading new product flow in 2005 with three new product approvals in key markets—Cymbalta for depression in Europe followed by duloxetine for stress urinary incontinence and exenatide for type 2 diabetes in the United States. In addition, the company said it remains on track for a 2005 U.S. submission of ruboxistaurin for symptoms related to nerve damage caused by diabetes.

The company also detailed an additional nine compounds and ten new indications that are expected to be in mid-to-late stage development in 2005. These represent potential breakthrough treatments for cardiovascular disorders, diabetes, brain, and other cancers, fibromyalgia (pain disorder), urological disorders, osteoporosis, Alzheimer's disease, insomnia, and other central nervous system disorders. In addition, select molecules from the company's early-stage pipeline, including potential treatments for cancer and obesity, were reviewed.

"Our strategy of independence, innovation, partnering and productivity remain the best approach in the current business environment and positions Lilly well to deliver long-term value to patients and shareholders," said Sidney Taurel, Lilly's CEO.

"In the past three years, we have doubled our product line with the launch of eight innovative new medicines that address significant unmet medical needs. Also, within the past eighteen months, we've added seven new indications or formulations for our existing and new products. And our pipeline remains robust even after this recent surge of launches."

- "The stock of Eli Lilly & Co. has fallen from a high of $76 on May 6, 2004 to the mid-$50s," said John Watkins, writing for the Argus Research Company on February 9, 2005. "We feel that at current price levels the shares of Eli Lilly are an attractive investment. The company has a strong portfolio of new drugs and one of the best pipelines in the industry. Earnings growth is expected to accelerate as new drugs are released and begin to contribute to the top line (sales)." The stock was rated a BUY at that time.

**Total assets: $24,867 million**
**Current ratio: 1.69**
**Common shares outstanding: 1,132 million**
**Return on 2004 shareholders' equity: 17.5%**

|  | 2004 | 2003 | 2002 | 2001 | 2000 | 1999 | 1998 | 1997 |
|---|---|---|---|---|---|---|---|---|
| Revenues (millions) | 13,858 | 12,583 | 11,077 | 11,543 | 10,953 | 10,003 | 9,237 | 8,518 |
| Net income (millions) | 1,810 | 2,561 | 2,763 | 3,014 | 2,905 | 2,721 | 2,098 | 1,774 |
| Earnings per share | 1.66 | 2.37 | 2.55 | 2.76 | 2.65 | 2.28 | 1.94 | 1.57 |
| Dividends per share | 1.42 | 1.34 | 1.24 | 1.12 | 1.04 | .92 | .80 | .74 |
| Price     high | 76.9 | 73.9 | 81.1 | 95.0 | 109.0 | 97.8 | 91.3 | 70.4 |
|           low | 50.3 | 52.8 | 43.8 | 70.0 | 54.0 | 60.6 | 57.7 | 35.6 |

# Lowe's Companies, Inc.

1000 Lowe's Boulevard ❑ Mooresville, NC 28117 ❑ (704) 758–2033 ❑ Direct dividend reinvestment plan available: (877) 282–1174 ❑ Web site: *www.lowes.com* ❑ Fiscal years end Friday closest to January 31 of following year ❑ Listed: NYSE ❑ Ticker symbol: LOW ❑ S&P rating: A+ ❑ Value Line financial strength rating: A+

"Our strength and the strength of the home improvement industry is driven by several factors—demographic, social, and economic," said CEO Robert L. Tillman in fiscal 2005.

"First, evolving demographic trends have been, and will continue to be, a positive force for Lowe's and the home improvement industry. The large and influential baby boomer population is entering the peak second-home buying age and is driving a robust second-home market. Driven by this phenomenon, some estimates suggest that 150,000 second homes will be built each year for the rest of the decade. In addition, boomers are more time-strapped than ever and are looking for solutions that make their life easier. One-stop shopping convenience and an ever-expanding array of installation services makes Lowe's a destination to fulfill their needs.

"Generation Xers are in the family formation years and are looking for ways to improve their home's function, safety and appeal. This generation values information that allows it to initiate projects. Our informative signage and knowledgeable employees provide just the resources they're looking for at Lowe's.

"And finally, Echo boomers, also known as generation Y, are focused on customization, frequently changing everything from paint to flooring to faucets to fulfill their desire for distinctiveness. This generation is coming of age and is actively influencing many purchasing decisions today. With over 40,000 products in stock, and hundreds of thousands more available by special order, these customers can find the products they're looking for at Lowe's.

"The second force driving home improvement is diversity. Home ownership among minorities is growing rapidly in the U.S., driven by an immigrant population focused on the American dream of owning a home. Harvard's Joint Center for Housing Studies reports that in 2001, minorities accounted for 32 percent of first-time home buyers, and from 1995 to 2001, they represented 60 percent of the increase in households. Bilingual employees, targeted advertising and unique products to meet varying cultural styles are just a few of the things we're doing at Lowe's to meet the needs of our increasingly diverse customers.

"Third, Americans are more focused than ever on the comfort, security and warmth that home has to offer. As Americans deal with a tumultuous geopolitical environment and the stress of everyday life, keeping in touch with the people who matter remains a top priority, and they're doing it at home. Home ownership was a cornerstone of the American dream long before interest rates began their latest decline in 2001, and we believe a focus on the home and home improvement will remain part of the American dream even as interest rates rise.

"Finally, a growing trend in home improvement is a phenomenon known as 'serial remodeling.' Inspired by innovation and energy efficiency, home improvement is being driven less by need and more by a sense of style and a desire to trade up. Many customers are repainting their rooms with the most fashionable new color or replacing a working washer and dryer with new, more efficient appliances that clean better while using less water and energy. Innovation is the key, and we encourage vendors to ensure they are providing inspirational products for our customers."

## Company Profile

Lowe's Companies, Inc. is the second-largest domestic retailer of home-improvement products serving the do-it-yourself and commercial business customers. (Home Depot is number one.) Capitalizing on a growing number of U.S. households (about 100 million) the company has expanded from fifteen stores in 1962 and now operates 932 stores in forty-five states. Lowe's competes in the highly fragmented, $300-billion, home-improvement industry.

The company sells more than 40,000 home-improvement products, including plumbing and electrical products, tools, building materials, hardware, outdoor hard lines, appliances, lumber, nursery and gardening products, millwork, paint, sundries, cabinets and furniture. Lowe's has often been listed as one of the "100 Best Companies to Work for in America."

The company obtains its products from about 6,500 merchandise vendors from around the globe. In most instances, Lowe's deals directly with foreign manufacturers, rather than third-party importers.

In order to maintain appropriate inventory levels in stores and to enhance efficiency and distribution, Lowe's operates six highly automated, efficient, state-of-the-art regional distribution centers (RDCs). RDCs are strategically situated in North Carolina, Georgia, Ohio, Indiana, Pennsylvania, Washington, and Texas.

In 2000, the company broke ground in Findlay, Ohio on an $80-million regional distribution center. Completed in October of 2001, the 1.25-million-square-foot facility employs 500 people and supplies products to some 100 stores throughout the lower Great Lakes region.

Lowe's serves both retail and commercial business customers. Retail customers are primarily do-it-yourself homeowners and others buying for personal and family use. Commercial business customers include building contractors, repair and remodeling contractors, electricians, landscapers, painters, plumbers, and commercial building maintenance professionals.

During 1999, Lowe's acquired Eagle Hardware & Garden, a thirty-six-store chain of home-improvement and garden centers in the West. The acquisition accelerated Lowe's West Coast expansion and provided a stepping stone for the company into ten new states and a number of key metropolitan markets.

In recent years, the company has been transforming its store base from a chain of small stores into a chain of home-improvement warehouses. The current prototype store (the largest in the industry) has 150,000 square feet of sales floor and another 35,000 dedicated to lawn and garden products. The company is in the midst of its most aggressive expansion in company history. Lowe's is investing $2 billion a year and opening more than one store each week.

## Shortcomings to Bear in Mind

- Interest rates have been low, which has been a spur to home ownership and home improvement projects, which helps Lowe's. If interest rates start to climb and mortgage rates follow suit, that ball game may come to an end.
- By competing head-to-head with Home Depot in large metropolitan markets, Lowe's may find it has a formidable rival to deal with, compared to the small cities where it made its fast-growth reputation.

## Reasons to Buy

- *Standard & Poor's Stock Reports* likes Lowe's. Here's what Michael Sauers had to say on February 28, 2005, "We have a BUY recommendation on the shares. . . . We think continued strong GDP (*gross domestic product*) growth and a recovering job market will lead to strong consumer spending in 2005. We believe home improvement retailers, in particular, will see solid gains as consumers continue to view their homes as investments and should continue to allocate a good portion of their discretionary income on home improvement projects."

- William W. Lee, writing for *Value Line* on January 7, 2005, rated the stock 2 for Timeliness (*which is above average*) and had this comment, "Earnings will likely advance by about 25 percent in the coming year. Contributions from new stores and same-store sales should fuel a top-line (*sales*) gain of 15 percent to 18 percent. The company's current merchandise focus on installations, special orders, and commercial business customers should continue to aid sales momentum."

- The Argus Research Company also chimed in with some good words on February 24, 2005, according to Christopher Graja, CFA.

"We reiterate our BUY rating on Lowe's Companies Inc. Lowe's is continuing its aggressive store-building campaign with plans to add 150 stores, representing a 13 percent to 14 percent increase in square footage, in the current fiscal year. On a fundamental basis, the company's financial strength is solid, and stores are productive, with comparable sales increasing 6.6 percent in the just-completed fiscal year."

- To enhance its extensive line of national brands, such as DeWalt, Armstrong, American Standard, Olympic, Owens Corning, Sylvania, Harbor Breeze, and Delta, the company is teaming up with vendors to offer preferred brands exclusive to Lowe's. These include Laura Ashley, Sta-Green, Troy-Bilt, Alexander Julian, among others.

In categories where preferred brands are not available, Lowe's has created its own brands, including Kobalt tools, Reliabilt doors and windows, and Top Choice lumber.

Total assets: $21,209 million
Current ratio: 1.22
Common shares outstanding: 772 million
Return on 2004 shareholders' equity: 19.9%

|  |  | 2004 | 2003 | 2002 | 2001 | 2000 | 1999 | 1998 | 1997 |
|---|---|---|---|---|---|---|---|---|---|
| Revenues (millions) | | 36,464 | 30,838 | 26,491 | 22,111 | 18,779 | 15,905 | 12,245 | 10,137 |
| Net income (millions) | | 2,176 | 1,844 | 1,471 | 1,023 | 810 | 673 | 482 | 357 |
| Earnings per share | | 2.71 | 2.35 | 1.89 | 1.30 | 1.06 | .90 | .68 | .51 |
| Dividends per share | | .16 | .12 | .08 | .075 | .07 | .06 | .06 | .06 |
| Price | high | 60.5 | 60.4 | 50.0 | 48.9 | 33.6 | 33.2 | 26.1 | 12.3 |
| | low | 45.9 | 33.4 | 32.5 | 21.9 | 17.1 | 21.5 | 10.8 | 7.9 |

Conservative Growth

# McCormick & Company, Inc.

18 Loveton Circle ❑ P. O. Box 6000 ❑ Sparks, MD 21152–6000 ❑ (410) 771–7244 ❑ Web site: *www.mccormick.com* ❑ Direct dividend reinvestment plan available: (877) 778–6784 ❑ Fiscal years end November 30 ❑ Listed: NYSE ❑ Ticker symbol: MKC ❑ S&P rating: A ❑ Value Line financial strength rating: B++

McCormick completed the purchase of C. M. Van Sillevoldt B. V. on November 2, 2004. The company sells spices, herbs, and seasonings under the Silvo brand in The Netherlands and the India brand in Belgium. Silvo dates back to 1833. Today, the brand has a strong heritage and high recognition among consumers in The Netherlands. Net sales have increased at a 5 percent compound annual growth rate since 1999 and reached euro 38 million in 2003. The business is achieving growth through innovative products and packaging, with a focus on convenience, quality, and ethnic flavors. In 2003, Silvo transformed its direct-to-store distribution system that is leading to improvements in product merchandising, customer service, sales information, and distribution logistics.

Silvo is a market leader in the Dutch spices and herbs consumer market. Products are spice, herbs and seasonings (75 percent of sales) and specialty food items (25 percent). The company has a 63 percent share of spices and herbs in The Netherlands, with distribution in all major food retailers. Silvo also has a strong position in Belgium, with a 30 percent share, including brands and private label.

Robert J. Lawless, CEO of McCormick said, "A primary avenue of growth for McCormick is the acquisition of leading brands in key markets. Since the acquisition of Ducros in 2000, we have directed our efforts to expansion in Europe. The Silvo acquisition fits squarely within this strategy, extending our presence into The Netherlands, with a strong leading brand."

## Company Profile

McCormick, the world's foremost maker of spices and seasonings, is committed to the development of tasty, easy-to-use new products to satisfy consumer demand.

When investors hear the name McCormick, they think of the spices they use every day. Indeed, McCormick is the world's largest spice company. Yet, the company is also the leader in the manufacture, marketing and distribution of such products as seasonings and flavors to the entire food industry. These customers include foodservice and food-processing businesses, as well as retail outlets. This industrial segment was responsible for 49 percent of sales and 33 percent of operating profits. A majority of the top 100 food companies are MKC's customers.

Founded in 1889, McCormick distributes its products in about 100 countries.

McCormick's U.S. Consumer business (47 percent of sales and 67 percent of operating profits), its oldest and largest, is dedicated to the manufacture and sale of consumer spices, herbs, extracts, proprietary seasoning blends, sauces and marinades. They are sold under such brand names as McCormick, Schilling, Produce Partners, Golden Dipt, Old Bay, and Mojave.

Many of the spices and herbs purchased by the company are imported into the United States from the company of origin. However, significant quantities of some materials, such as paprika, dehydrated vegetables, onion and garlic, and food ingredients other than spices and herbs originate in the U.S.

McCormick is a direct importer of certain raw materials, mainly black pepper, vanilla beans, cinnamon, herbs, and seeds from the countries of origin.

The raw materials most important to the company are onion, garlic and capsicums (paprika and chili peppers), which are produced in the United States; black pepper, most of which originates in India, Indonesia, Malaysia, and Brazil; and vanilla beans, a large portion of which the company obtains from the Malagasy Republic and Indonesia.

### Highlights of 2004's Consumer Segment:

• In the Netherlands, acquired the Silvo business, gaining entry into the Dutch market with a 63 percent market share.

• Launched new products in the last three years that accounted for 6 percent of 2004 sales.

- In the United States, increased sales of the Zatarain's brand 20 percent with expanded product penetration and new items.
- In the United States, significantly increased the effectiveness of trade promotions. This was one of the key factors in a 17 percent sales increase in the Americas.
- In China, substantially improved the company's distributor network and streamlined its business to seventy-five well-qualified distributors. This was a reduction from 250 distributors in the network of 2003.
- Worldwide, sales of grinders expanded by 36 percent. This innovative package originated in France, under the Ducros label.
- Increased sales of the company's grilling products, including seasonings, marinade blends, and sauces, 8 percent worldwide.
- In the United States, strengthened a leading position with Hispanic consumers with new products and a focused expansion into the Texas and Chicago markets. In 2005, for the first time, McCormick began advertising on Hispanic networks.
- In the United Kingdom, the company converted more than 5,000 stores to new packaging and merchandising of the Schwartz brand spices and herbs in only two months. With this change, the company has significantly reduced the variety of packaging formats in Europe.

## Shortcomings to Bear in Mind

- The company purchases certain raw materials that are subject to price volatility caused by weather and other unpredictable factors. While future movements of raw material costs are uncertain, a variety of programs, including periodic raw material purchases and customer price adjustments, help McCormick address this risk. Generally, the company does not use derivatives to manage the volatility related to this risk.
- "After being ranked 3 (Average) for Timeliness since the late 1990s, McCormick's stock's rank has been lowered to 4 (Below Average)," said Dylan D. Cathers, writing for *Value Line Investment Survey* on February 4, 2005. "The spice company reported earnings of $0.62 a share to finish fiscal 2004 (year ended November 30, 2004). This was a bit below our estimate. It was apparently below Wall Street's view, as well, since the stock's price was hit after the announcement . . . Further, we don't think that there is much news to give the stock a jumpstart in the near term."

## Reasons to Buy

- On December 10, 2004, *Standard & Poor's Stock Reports* rated the stock a BUY, with the following comment by Richard Joy: "We see MKC's financial strength continuing to improve, and free cash flow generation is rising. Internal volume trends remain solid, in our opinion, with volume gains exceeding category growth for several core product lines. We think longer-term growth prospects are attractive, reflecting the company's dominant and expanding U.S. spice market share (more than 50 percent), as well as its leading share of the European consumer market (more than 20 percent)."
- On December 27, 2004, John W. Rogers Jr. had this comment on McCormick in his column in *Forbes* magazine: "You should take a look at another of my longtime Baltimore favorites: McCormick & Co. (37,MKC), the world's largest spice vendor and a 115-year-old business that continues to show new pizzazz. For a long time now, the company has scented each annual report with a different spice. That was not enough to whet Wall Street's appetite, and for years the shares languished. Since then, the intense focus on the core spice business and innovative new products have caught investors' attention. Zatarain's Ready-to-Serve rice and Grill Mates seasonings are very popular. Earnings are cooking."

- The market environment for McCormick's consumer products—such as spices, herbs, extracts, propriety seasoning blends, sauces, and marinades—varies worldwide. In the United States, for instance, usage is up, and consumers are seeking new and bolder tastes.

  Although many people use prepared foods and eat out, a *Parade Magazine* survey reports that 75 percent of families polled eat dinner together at least four nights a week. A study conducted by *National Panel Diary* indicates that 70 percent of all meals are prepared at home, and a Canned Food Association Survey reports that 51 percent of women eighteen to sixty-four actually "scratch-cook" meals six times a week.
- In the company's industrial business, said Mr. Lawless, "Our customers are constantly seeking new flavors for their products. In this environment, the ability to identify, develop and market winning flavors is essential. We flavor all kinds of products—spaghetti sauce, snack chips, frozen entrees, yogurt, a pack of chewing gum. In restaurants, we provide seasonings for a gourmet meal, salad dressings at a casual dining chain, and coating and sauce for a quick-service chicken sandwich.

  "To anticipate and respond to changing tastes in markets worldwide, we are investing in research and development staff, equipment, instrumentation, and facilities. These investments enable us not only to create innovative products but also to use sensory skills to make sure that the flavors we deliver are winners in the marketplace."
- McCormick has paid dividends every year since 1925 and has raised dividends in each of the past fifteen years. In the 1994–2004 period, dividends climbed from $.24 to $.58, a compound annual growth rate of 9.2 percent.
- Worldwide, the retail grocery industry continues to consolidate, creating larger customers. What's more, in many of McCormick's markets, the company has multiyear contracts with customers to secure the shelf space for its products. McCormick's capabilities in category management and electronic data interchange, along with its high-quality products and service, also forge a link to its increasingly larger customers.
- The company's past successes and future potential are rooted in the strength of the McCormick name. As a consequence, the company is now experiencing a 95 percent brand-awareness rating in the United States. This leadership role in the food industry ensures that consumers will enjoy a McCormick products at nearly every eating occasion. Grocery store aisles present more than 700 well-known products from major processors that rely on McCormick for seasoning or flavor.

Total assets: $2,370 million
Current ratio: 1.12
Common shares outstanding: 137 million
Return on 2004 shareholders' equity: 26.0%

|  | 2004 | 2003 | 2002 | 2001 | 2000 | 1999 | 1998 | 1997 |
|---|---|---|---|---|---|---|---|---|
| Revenues (millions) | 2,526 | 2,270 | 2,045 | 2,372 | 2,124 | 2,007 | 1,881 | 1,801 |
| Net income (millions) | 214 | 199 | 180 | 147 | 138 | 122 | 106 | 98 |
| Earnings per share | 1.52 | 1.40 | 1.29 | 1.05 | 1.00 | .85 | .72 | .65 |
| Dividends per share | .56 | .46 | .42 | .40 | .38 | .34 | .32 | .30 |
| Price    high | 38.9 | 30.2 | 27.3 | 23.3 | 18.9 | 17.3 | 18.2 | 14.2 |
| low | 28.6 | 21.7 | 20.7 | 17.0 | 11.9 | 13.3 | 13.6 | 11.3 |

# The McGraw-Hill Companies, Inc.

1221 Avenue of the Americas ❑ New York, NY 10020–1095 ❑ (212) 512–4321 ❑ Direct dividend reinvestment program available: (888) 201–5538 ❑ Web site: *www.mcgraw-hill.com* ❑ Listed: NYSE ❑ Ticker symbol: MHP ❑ S&P rating: not rated ❑ Value Line financial strength rating: A+

"When Harold (Terry) McGraw III took over the media giant that his great-grand-father co-founded 116 years ago, he could have easily left well enough alone," said Brett Pulley in an article in *Forbes* magazine in 2004. The writeup on McGraw-Hill came under the heading, *Best Managed Companies in America.*

"In 1990, the McGraw-Hill Cos., known for such magazines as *Business Week* and *Aviation Week,* received about half of its $1.9 billion in revenue from publications. But since becoming president in 1993 and chief executive five years later, McGraw, 55, has transformed the company into three separate units and made it far less vulnerable to the ups and downs of the advertising market.

"Today only 17 percent of the company's $4.8 billion in revenue comes from the ad-based information and media unit. Meanwhile, the company has bolstered its education and testing services, with that business quadrupling its revenue since 1990 and now accounting for 49 percent of the total. McGraw-Hill's *Standard & Poor's* operation, which does research on stocks (sold to investment managers) and on bonds (paid for mainly by the bond issuers), has tripled in size over the past decade, now representing 34 percent of sales."

## Company Profile

The McGraw-Hill Companies is a leading global information services provider aligned around three powerful and enduring forces essential to economic growth worldwide: the need for knowledge, the need for capital, and the need for transparency. MHP has

built strong businesses with leading market positions in financial services, education, and business information to meet those needs.

## McGraw-Hill Financial Services

• Standard & Poor's sets the standard for the global investment community by providing highly valued investment data, analysis, and opinions to financial decision-makers through its three businesses.

• Credit Market Services, which includes the world's largest network of credit ratings professionals, provides ratings for a wide array of credit obligations, as well as risk management and credit performance evaluation services.

• Investment Services provides institutional and retail investors with a wide range of investment information, analysis and opinions in equities, fixed-income, foreign exchange, and mutual fund markets. The S&P indexes are used more than any other index group around the world.

• Corporate Value Consulting is the U.S. market leader in providing valuation and value analysis for financial reporting, tax, business combinations, corporate restructuring, capital allocation, and capital structure purposes.

## McGraw-Hill Education

• McGraw-Hill Education is a global leader in education and professional information. With a broad range of products—from traditional textbooks to the latest in online and multimedia offerings—the company helps teachers teach and learners learn.

• The School Education Group is the domestic leader in the pre-K to twelve school market, providing educational, supplemental and testing materials across all subject areas.

• Through its Higher Education, Professional and International businesses, the company is a leader in the globally expanding market for college and post-college and post-graduate education, and the company's professional publishing businesses serve the rapidly expanding needs of the global scientific, healthcare, business, and computer technology fields.

## McGraw-Hill Information and Media Services

• Information and Media Services provides information, business intelligence and solutions that business executives, professionals and governments worldwide use to remain competitive in their fields and in the global economy.

• Well-known brands in this unit include *BusinessWeek*, the number one global business magazine. The franchise also includes *BusinessWeek* Online, conferences and events, and *BusinessWeek* TV.

• This business also includes Platts (the key provider of price assessments with the petroleum, petrochemical and power markets).

• *McGraw-Hill Construction* and *Aviation Week*, which serve the needs of construction, and aviation professionals worldwide, and ABC-affiliated television stations in Bakersfield, California; Denver, Colorado; Indianapolis, Indiana; and San Diego, California.

## Shortcomings to Bear in Mind

▪ One analyst pointed out that "risks include a sharp rise in interest rates, which could curtail growth in S&P's ratings division, or a prolonged economic slump that could negatively affect the publishing division."

## Reasons to Buy

▪ On October 21, 2004, CEO Harold McGraw III, said, "The success of our titles in Business and Economics was a key to capturing market share this year in the U.S. college and university market. The sixteenth edition of *McConnell's Economics,* the world's best-selling economics title, continues to win adherents. The other market standards, the seventh edition of Nickel's *Understanding Business,* an introductory text, and the seventeenth edition of the *Fundamentals of Accounting Principles* by Larson also contributed to our improved performance.

"We also benefited from increased sales of our lists for Science, Engineering and Math and the Humanities, Social Sciences, and Languages. Best-sellers include the eighth edition of Chang's *Chemistry,* the seventh edition of Raven's *Biology,* the seventh edition of Knorre's *Puntos de Partida* and the eighth edition of Lucas's *The Art of Public Speaking.*"

▪ S&P Indexes are the foundation for a growing array of investment funds and exchange-traded products that continue to generate new revenue. The company receives fees based on assets and trading activity. In addition, the recent volatility of the stock market has increased the revenue stream. Currently, more than $700 billion is invested in mutual funds tied to the S&P indexes.

▪ Europe contributes almost half of McGraw-Hill's international revenue, growing at a double-digit rate. With a push from the new Monetary Union, the European market will be a springboard for growth in many of the company's key businesses. Here are some expectations:

• European companies that once financed their growth mainly by borrowing from banks are shifting to the issuance of corporate bonds instead, while nontraditional financial instruments also boom. Those are both large opportunities for Standard & Poor's Rating Services, which has built the world's largest network of ratings professionals.

- Increases in investments by Europeans building retirement funds—the result of a transition to privately funded pension plans—will accelerate demand for global financial information. These are pluses for Standard & Poor's Financial Information Services.

- The continued growth of English in business communications and as a second language in everyday use widens. These will benefit the company's educational products and the European edition of *Business Week*.

- The promise of the global economy depends on educational training. This is a plus for McGraw-Hill's global publishing activities—most notably the company's business, finance, engineering, information technology and English instruction products.

■ In the construction industry, The McGraw-Hill Construction Information Group (MH-CIG) is the foremost source of information crucial to new construction projects and planning. MH-CIG has increasingly turned to the Internet and other electronic tools to gather and distribute information.

Dodge Plans is the latest of several MH-CIG electronic products stemming from print media. It provides access—online or by CD-ROM twice weekly—to the plans, specifications and bidding requirements for more than 60,000 new construction and renovation projects.

■ The McGraw-Hill Professional Book Group publishes nearly 800 titles per year in computing, business, science, technical, medical and reference markets. The group continues to expand by creating publishing alliances with partners such as Oracle and Global Knowledge, transforming key reference titles into Internet-based services. In addition, the Professional Book Group offers electronic products, ranging from Internet subscription services to CD-ROMs, and is building its capabilities in on-demand publishing.

■ "The education segment is expected to produce stronger growth in 2005," said Simon R. Shoucair, writing for *Value Line Investment Survey* on February 18, 2005. "Management indicates that it anticipates a sharp rebound in the kindergarten through the twelfth grade market this year. Some potential curriculum changes to specific subjects, including social studies, math, and science, have created growth opportunities."

The analyst also said, "The company's finances are in fine shape. McGraw-Hill has no debt, generates decent cash flow, and recently raised its dividend by 10 percent. Management also announced that is has expanded its share-repurchase program to between 3 million and 5 million shares."

■ The Argus Research Company had good things to say about McGraw-Hill on March 11, 2005. John Eade said, "Our investment rating on Focus List selection McGraw-Hill Companies, Inc. is BUY. Once again, management underpromised Wall Street and overdelivered corporate results.

"McGraw-Hill has recently announced several acquisitions. The company purchased JD Power Associates, the consumer rating organization, which it will operate in its Information and Media Services Group. McGraw-Hill has also purchased Vista Research, a primary investment research company, which it will fold into its Financial Services division. In addition, the company purchased an Australian financial data company."

Total assets: $5,394 million
Current ratio: 1.17
Common shares outstanding: 380 million
Return on 2004 shareholders' equity: 27%

| | 2004 | 2003 | 2002 | 2001 | 2000 | 1999 | 1998 | 1997 |
|---|---|---|---|---|---|---|---|---|
| Revenues (millions) | 5,250 | 4,828 | 4,640 | 4,646 | 4,308 | 3,992 | 3,729 | 3,534 |
| Net income (millions) | 736 | 629 | 572 | 380 | 481 | 402 | 342 | 291 |
| Earnings per share | 1.91 | 1.64 | 1.48 | 1.23 | 1.21 | 1.01 | .86 | .73 |
| Dividends per share | .60 | .54 | .51 | .49 | .47 | .43 | .39 | .36 |
| Price     high | 45.8 | 35.0 | 34.9 | 35.5 | 33.9 | 31.6 | 25.9 | 18.9 |
|           low | 34.3 | 25.9 | 25.4 | 24.4 | 21.0 | 23.6 | 17.2 | 11.2 |

Growth and Income

# MDU Resources Group, Inc.

Schuchart Building ❑ P. O. Box 5650 ❑ Bismarck, ND 58506–5650 ❑ (800) 437–8000 Ext. 7621 ❑ Direct dividend reinvestment plan available: (877) 536–3553 ❑ Web site: *www.mdu.com* ❑ Listed: NYSE ❑ Ticker symbol: MDU ❑ S&P rating: A ❑ Value Line financial strength rating: A+

MDU Resources Group, with operations in seven businesses—mostly connected with energy and public utilities—has an impressive record, as summarized below:

• Paid quarterly common stock dividends continuously since 1937.

• Increased the quarterly common stock dividend each of the last thirteen years.

• Has a strong balance sheet.

• *Forbes* magazine named MDU Resources the Best Managed Company in the utilities industry from its Platinum 400 list of America's best big companies.

• Named to *Fortune's* list of 100 Fastest growing companies.

• Member of the S&P Midcap 400 Index.

• According to the list published in the April 5, 2004 issue of *Fortune* magazine, MDU Resources ranked as number one in the energy industry in profits as a percentage of revenues, and number two in total return to investors and in annual growth

rate of Earnings per share for the years 1993–2003.

• CEO Martin White received an American Business Award for Best Executive in 2004.

## Company Profile

MDU Resources Group, Inc. is a natural resource company. The company's diversified operations, such as oil and gas and construction materials should help MDU Resources grow at a better rate than electric utilities that depend entirely on their electric business.

MDU Resources Group has a number of operations:

### Electric Distribution

Montana-Dakota Utilities Company generates, transmits, and distributes electricity, and provided related value-added products and services in the Northern Great Plains. Electric business earnings for 2004 totaled $12.8 million, compared with $16.9 million the prior year.

THE 100 BEST STOCKS YOU CAN BUY 2006

## Natural Gas Distribution

Montana-Dakota Utilities Company and Great Plains Natural Gas Company distribute natural gas and provide related value-added products and services in the Northern Great Plains. This segment reported 2004 earnings of $2.2 million, down from $3.9 million in the 2003 period.

## Utility Services

Operating throughout most of the United States, Utility Services, Inc. is a diversified infrastructure construction company specializing in electric, natural gas, and telecommunication utility construction, as well as interior industrial electrical, exterior lighting and traffic stabilization.

Earnings from this business were a loss of $5.6 million for 2004, down substantially from a profit of $6.2 million in 2003.

## Independent Power Production

Centennial Energy Resources owns electric generating facilities in the United States and Brazil. Electric capacity and energy produced at these facilities is sold under long-term contracts to nonaffiliated entities.

Earnings were $26.3 million in 2004, compared with $11.4 million in 2003.

## Pipeline and Energy Services

WBI Holdings, Inc. provides natural gas transportation, underground storage, and gathering services through regulated and nonregulated pipeline systems and provides energy marketing and management throughout the United States. Operations are situated primarily in the Rocky Mountain, Midwest, Southern, and Central regions of the United States.

Pipeline and energy services segment earnings for 2004 totaled $8.9 million, down from $18.2 million the year before.

## Natural Gas and Production

Fidelity Exploration & Production Company is engaged in oil and natural gas acquisition, exploration and production throughout the United States and in the Gulf of Mexico. Earnings at this segment were $110.8 million in 2004, or well above the $63.0 million of the prior year.

## Construction Materials and Mining

Knife River Corporation mines and markets aggregates and related value-added construction materials products and services in the western United States, including Alaska and Hawaii. It also operates lignite and coal mines in Montana and North Dakota.

Earnings for 2004 for this business segment totaled $50.7 million, compared with $54.4 million in 2003.

## Highlights for 2004

• Earnings per common share increased 14 percent to $1.76.

• Record consolidated earnings of $206.4 million, up from $174.6 million.

• Reaffirms 2005 Earnings per share guidance in range of $1.70 to $1.90. Earnings for 2003 included a $7.6 million after-tax noncash transition charge, reflecting the cumulative effect of a change in accounting for asset retirement obligations as required by the adoption of Statement of Financial Accounting Standards No. 143.

"Our diversification strategy continues to show excellent results, with another record year of earnings," said CEO Martin A. White. "Our natural gas and oil production segment had an outstanding year. In addition to benefiting from the strong pricing environment, we increased natural gas production and added to our reserve base. Our independent power production business also saw significant growth in 2004, with new operations both domestically and internationally.

"We are excited about the future and our opportunities to provide the products and services that are essential to our country's infrastructure. We look forward to continuing to help build a strong America."

## Shortcomings to Bear in Mind

- *Value Line Investment Survey* had a lukewarm opinion of MDU Resources on February 11, 2005, according to Paul E. Debbas, CFA, "Finances are strong. The fixed-charge coverage and common-equity ratio are high. Accordingly, MDU merits a Financial Strength rating of A+, and its stock carries a top-notch Safety rank.

  "This stock's yield is comparable to that of a highly diversified utility. Its Timeliness rank is 3 (Average). MDU has a long record of annual dividend increases, and we expect this to continue to 2007–2009. Total return potential over that time is very modest, however."

- *Standard & Poor's Stock Reports* also had some reservations. On February 9, 2005, Yogeesh Wagle said, "With natural gas and oil price hedges (30 percent to 35 percent for 2005) well below most peers, we see returns from MDU's exploration and production operations as more volatile. Despite what we view as the difficulty of boosting earnings from levels spurred by unusually high natural gas prices, we see MDU's diversified businesses generating long-term EPS (*Earnings per share*) in line with more regulated utility peers."

- Public utilities are often hurt by rising interest rates, since they have to borrow money to build new facilities. As the economy strengthens, it seems logical to assume that interest rates will climb from the depressed levels of recent years.

## Reasons to Buy

- MDU Resources Group, Inc. announced financial results for 2004, showing consolidated earnings of $206.4 million, compared to $174.6 million for 2003. Earnings per common share, diluted, totaled $1.76, compared to $1.55 for 2003.

- In its January 10, 2005 issue, *Forbes* magazine named MDU Resources to its Platinum 400 list of the best big companies in America. The magazine's criteria for the list include such things as corporate governance and accounting practices, as well as long- and short-term sales and earnings growth and stock market performance. This is the fifth consecutive year that MDU Resources has been on the list.

- Over the past ten years (1994–2004), Earnings per share advanced from $0.61 to $1.76, a compound annual growth rate of 11.2 percent, an enviable record for a public utility. To be sure, MDU Resources is not a typical utility, since it has many diverse businesses.

- The Argus Research Company had some favorable comments on January 14, 2005, according to Gary F. Hovis, "We reiterate our BUY rating on MDU Resources Group." He went on to say, "As for valuation metrics, the MDU shares are now trading at a forward multiple of some thirteen times, a discount to the rest of the diversified electric and gas utility group. Looking ahead, we think the MDU equity is deserving of a premium multiple, given the improving balance sheet and the future growth aspects pertaining to the company's nonregulated oil and gas and construction materials businesses. In short, we believe that MDU management will continue to leverage the company's diverse operations to deliver earnings growth and enhanced shareholder value."

- MDU Resources has an established position in the coal bed natural gas fields in the Powder River Basin of Wyoming and Montana. This provides the company's natural gas and oil production segment with additional reserve potential of low-cost coal bed natural gas.

  In addition, MDU continues enhancing production from its existing gas fields in Colorado and Montana. The company's strong reserve position, both onshore and offshore in the Gulf of Mexico, provides this group a large geographic base upon which to expand.

- Over the past five years (ended December 31, 2004), MDU's total annual return was 19 percent, compared with its peer group average return of 16 percent. Even more striking, this enviable record contrasted with the Standard & Poor's 500 Index, with its average annual return in that five-year span of a minus 2 percent.

**Gross Property: $3,733 million**
**Operating Ratio: 91.4%**
**Common shares outstanding: 118 million**
**Return on 2004 shareholders' equity: 13.2%**

|  |  | 2004 | 2003 | 2002 | 2001 | 2000 | 1999 | 1998 | 1997 |
|---|---|---|---|---|---|---|---|---|---|
| Revenues (millions) |  | 2,719 | 2,352 | 2,032 | 2,224 | 1,874 | 1,280 | 897 | 608 |
| Net income (millions) |  | 206 | 175 | 148 | 156 | 110 | 83 | 74 | 55 |
| Earnings per share |  | 1.76 | 1.55 | 1.38 | 1.53 | 1.20 | 1.01 | .44 | .83 |
| Dividends per share |  | .70 | .66 | .63 | .60 | .57 | .54 | .52 | .50 |
| Price | high | 27.7 | 24.4 | 22.3 | 26.9 | 22.0 | 18.1 | 19.2 | 14.9 |
|  | low | 21.8 | 16.4 | 12.0 | 14.9 | 11.8 | 12.5 | 12.6 | 9.3 |

Aggressive Growth

# Medtronic, Inc

710 Medtronic Parkway N. E. ❑ Minneapolis, MN 55432–5604 ❑ Listed: NYSE ❑ 1-(763) 505–2692 ❑ Dividend reinvestment plan available: (888) 648–8154 ❑ Web site: *www.medtronic.com* ❑ Ticker symbol: MDT ❑ Fiscal years end April 30 ❑ S&P rating: A- ❑ Value Line financial strength rating: A+

"Medtronic's mission of applying biomedical engineering to 'alleviate pain, restore and extend life' has guided our company since founder Earl Bakken wrote it in 1960," said CEO Arthur D. Collins, Jr. in fiscal 2005. "Strong commitment to the mission in 2004 allowed Medtronic to reach more patients and again deliver record financial results. New product introductions and market-share gains helped drive a 19 percent increase in revenues, to $9.087 billion, or $1.60 per share, up 23 percent from the previous year."

Mr. Collins went on to say, "While delivering these record financial results, we also made substantial investments to help ensure strong, long-term growth. Research and development (R&D) spending increased by 14 percent, to $852 million. R&D expenditures continued to fuel a number of new product introductions, which contributed significantly to our record financial performance. Approximately two-thirds of current revenues were from products introduced within the past two years.

"Investments we made in expanding clinical trials also paid dividends last year. The NIH-sponsored Sudden Death Cardiac Death in Heart Failure Trial (SCD-HeFT)—the largest ICD trial ever conducted and one of the most important trials ever backed by Medtronic—showed that ICD (implantable cardioverter defibrillator) therapy reduced death by 23 percent in patients with moderate heart failure. As a result, the SCD-HeFT trial may expand the number of patients indicated for ICD therapy."

Mr. Collins also said, "By design, Medtronic is well-positioned in a number of very large and underserved global markets—for chronic conditions such as sudden cardiac arrest, diabetes, and movement disorder—which are only 10-to-20 percent penetrated. In fact, in most of the markets we serve, only a small percentage of patients with clear indications for Medtronic products actually receive them.

"Currently, we do business in more than 120 countries, providing products that support a wide range of therapies to treat major medical problems—including congestive heart failure, cardiovascular disease, numerous spinal and neurological disorders, and a range of urological and gastrointestinal problems. Expanding access in these markets not only benefits patients, it also provides significant growth potential for Medtronic."

## Company Profile

Medtronic is the world's leading medical technology company, providing lifelong solutions for people with chronic disease. Here are its key businesses:

Medtronic Cardiac Rhythm Management develops products that restore and regulate a patient's hearth rhythm, as well as improve the heart's pumping function. The business markets implantable pacemakers, defibrillators, cardiac ablation catheters, monitoring and diagnostic devices, and cardiac re-synchronization devices, including the first implantable device for the treatment of heart failure.

Medtronic Cardiac Surgery develops products that are used in both arrested and beating heart bypass surgery. The business also markets the industry's broadest line of heart valve products for both replacement and repair, plus autotransfusion equipment and disposable devices for handling and monitoring blood during major surgery, as well as cardiac ablation devices to treat a variety of heart conditions.

Medtronic Vascular develops products and therapies that treat a wide range of vascular diseases and conditions. These products include coronary, peripheral and neuro-vascular stents, stent graph systems for diseases and conditions throughout the aorta, and distal protection systems.

Medtronic Neurological and Diabetes offers therapies for movement disorders, chronic pain, and diabetes. It also offers diagnostics and therapeutics for urological and gastrointestinal conditions, including incontinence, benign prostatic hyperplasia (BPH), enlarged prostate, and gastroesophageal reflux disease (GERD).

Medtronic Spinal, ENT, and SNT develops and manufactures products that treat a variety of disorders of the cranium and spine, including traumatically induced conditions, deformities, and tumors.

## Shortcomings to Bear in Mind

- "Medtronic and other ICD makers expect more people to get the devices thanks to a recent Medicare decision to expand coverage," said Daniel Rosenberg, writing for the *Wall Street Journal* on February 23, 2005. "But Jay Warren, president of closely held Cameron Health, Inc., thinks what is needed is a new, easier-to-use product. 'Today's devices require invading the chest and literally touching the heart,' Mr. Warren said in a telephone interview. 'To get a device in today . . . we have to thread a wire through the vein to the heart, and that's a real problem.'

  "ICDs consist of a generator implanted in the chest connected to the heart by wires called leads. Because feeding those wires to the heart is complex, Mr. Warren said, many doctors don't have the technical capability to put in an ICD. Specialty physicians, called electro-physiologists, implant the devices. To get ICDs to more patients, a device must be built that more doctors can insert."

## Reasons to Buy

- On December 7, 2004, the Argus Research Company had a BUY rating on Medtronic. David H. Toung gave three reasons:

- "News reports of Johnson & Johnson's bid for Guidant shows the attractiveness of the businesses and the strong position in cardiac rhythm management held by Medtronic Inc.
- "We reaffirm our BUY-rating on the MDT shares with a $58 target price.
- "Expanded Medicare reimbursement of ICD devices and wider availability of new implantable defibrillator products should drive sales in the second half of fiscal 2005."

■ Medtronic has an impressive record of growth. In the 1994–2004 period, Earnings per share climbed from $.32 to $1.60, a compound annual growth rate of 17.5 percent. In the same 10-year span, Dividends per share advanced from $.05 to $.28, a growth rate of 18.8 percent.

■ Medtronic is a pioneer in the emerging field of medicine that promises to restore normal brain function and chemistry to millions of patients with central nervous system disorders. The company's implantable neuro-stimulation and infusion systems treat disorders by modulating the nervous system with electrical stimulation, chemicals, and biological agents delivered in precise amounts to specific sites in the brain and spinal cord.

■ Since its origin, Medtronic has held a clear market leadership in cardiac pacing, chiefly with pacemakers designed to treat bradycardia (hearts that beat irregularly or too slow) and more recently, tachyarrhythmia (hearts that beat too fast or quiver uncontrollably, called tachycardia and fibrillation). Today, more than half the cardiac rhythm devices and leads implanted throughout the world come from Medtronic.

■ The worldwide coronary vascular market is estimated at $4 billion and is expected to grow because it serves significant, unmet medical needs. Medtronic's coronary vascular products include several types of catheters used to unblock coronary arteries, stents that support the walls of an artery and prevent more blockage, and products used in minimally invasive vascular procedures for coronary heart disease, the chief cause of heart attack and angina.

■ Medtronic's cardiac surgery group offers superior products to support cardiac surgeons, including tissue heart valves that are best represented by the Freestyle stentless valve, the Mosaic stented tissue valve, and the Hall mechanical valve. In addition, the company is expanding its leadership in cardiac cannulae used to connect a patient's circulatory system to external perfusion systems used in conventional and minimally invasive surgeries.

■ Medtronic has a pipeline filled with treatments for a number of profitable (but uncrowded) markets. Its Activa, for example, which uses electronic stimulation to alleviate many of the symptoms associated with Parkinson's Disease, received approval in 2002 from the U.S. Food & Drug Administration (USFDA).

Parkinson's Disease impacts the lives of an estimated 1 million people in the U.S. and 2 million worldwide. Activa, according to the company "utilizing our brain pacemaker, can significantly reduce shaking, slowness, and stiffness for patients who live with this debilitating disease. The dramatic benefits of this therapy were vividly demonstrated during an extensive media campaign that followed USFDA approval, including a report that aired on CBS Television's '60 Minutes' in February 2002."

In another realm, Medtronic's InSync ICD system is one of the only treatments for heart failure that does not rely on the use of drugs. Heart failure, the progressive deterioration of the heart's pumping capability, afflicts more than 22 million people worldwide and more than 5 million in the United States.

According to management, the company's InSync and InSync ICD cardiac devices address "one of the largest and fastest-growing new market opportunities. As reported in the *New England Journal of Medicine*, it is estimated that more than 3 million heart failure patients around the world can experience improved quality of life from this new bi-ventricular pacing therapy.

"Sudden Cardiac Arrest strikes one American every two minutes and is the leading cause of death in the U.S. Research data reported in the *New England Journal of Medicine* shows dramatically reduced mortality from sudden cardiac arrest in the heart attack survivors who receive implantable cardioverter defibrillators

(ICDs). This expanded indication for ICDs approximately doubles the market potential to more than 600,000 patients a year in the U.S. alone."

- Diabetes afflicts more than 170 million people worldwide and about 20 million in the United States. It's the most costly chronic condition, with annual expenditures exceeding $130 billion in the U.S. alone. People with diabetes are also much more likely to suffer from numerous other medical complications, including cardiovascular disease, kidney disease, blindness and amputation. As the world leader in external insulin pumps, Medtronic is expanding its product offering to help insulin-dependent diabetes patients better manage their glucose levels and their disease.

Total assets: $14,111 million
Current ratio: 1.25
Common shares outstanding: 1,212 million
Return on 2004 shareholders' equity: 23.1%

|  |  | 2004 | 2003 | 2002 | 2001 | 2000 | 1999 | 1998 | 1997 |
|---|---|---|---|---|---|---|---|---|---|
| Revenues (millions) | | 9,087 | 7,665 | 6,411 | 5,552 | 5,015 | 4,134 | 2,605 | 2,438 |
| Net income (millions) | | 1,959 | 1,600 | 984 | 1,282 | 1,111 | 905 | 595 | 530 |
| Earnings per share | | 1.60 | 1.30 | .80 | .85 | .90 | .40 | .48 | .56 |
| Dividends per share | | .28 | .25 | .20 | .12 | .15 | .12 | .10 | .08 |
| Price | high | 53.7 | 52.9 | 49.7 | 62.0 | 62.0 | 44.6 | 38.4 | 26.4 |
| | low | 45.5 | 42.2 | 32.5 | 36.6 | 32.8 | 29.9 | 22.7 | 14.4 |

Conservative Growth

# Meredith Corporation

1716 Locust Street ❑ Des Moines, IA 50309–3023 ❑ (515) 284–2633 ❑ Dividend reinvestment plan not available ❑ Fiscal years end June 30 ❑ Listed: NYSE ❑ Web site: *www.meredith.com* ❑ Ticker symbol: MDP ❑ S&P rating: A- ❑ Value Line financial strength rating: B+

Meredith Corporation, one of the nation's leading magazine publishers, once again distinguished itself in the fifteenth annual edition of *Advertising Age's* "Magazine 300" Special Report, released in September 2004.

Three magazines, *More, Midwest Living,* and *Ladies' Home Journal,* ranked among the Top 25 publications for advertising page growth. What's more, *Country Home, More,* and *Traditional Home* were listed among the Top 25 magazines for paid circulation growth. *Better Homes and Gardens* was named as the top home service/home consumer magazine, while maintaining its fifth-place spot in the Top 300 rankings. Several Meredith magazines included in the Top 300 improved their rankings over the prior year's report:

• *Ladies' Home Journal* moved up four spots, to seventeen.

• *Country Home* moved up seven spots, to fifty-two.

• *Traditional Home* moved up twelve spots, to eighty-three.

• *Midwest Living* moved up eighteen spots, to 113.

• *More* moved up twenty-seven spots, to 122.

• *WOOD* moved up twenty-two spots, to 193.

*American Baby* (acquired in late 2002) and *Successful Farming* were also included in the top 300. The rankings are based on total advertising and circulation gross revenue in 2003, as compiled by *Advertising Age.*

"These rankings confirm that Meredith magazines are uniquely positioned to serve the Baby Boomer market," said Meredith Publishing Group President, Jack Griffith. "Readers crave our content, and advertisers know that no one can deliver these consumers better than Meredith."

## Company Profile

Meredith Corporation is one of America's leading media and marketing companies. Its business centers on magazine and book publishing, television broadcasting, interactive media and integrated marketing. The company's roots go back to 1902, when it was an agricultural publisher.

The Meredith Publishing Group is the country's foremost home and family publisher. The group creates and markets magazines, including *Better Homes and Gardens, Ladies' Home Journal, Country Home, Creative Home, Midwest Living, Traditional Home, WOOD, Hometown Cooking, Successful*

*Farming, More, Renovation Style, Country Gardens, American Patchwork & Quilting, Garden Shed, Do It Yourself, Garden, Deck and Landscape, Decorating,* and about 150 special-interest publications.

In late 2002, the company acquired American Baby Group, a publisher with titles geared toward mothers-to-be and young mothers. American Baby's magazines include: *American Baby, First Year of Life, Childbirth, Healthy Kids en Espanol, Pimeros 12 Meses,* and *Espera.* American Baby produces television shows; owns six consumer sampling programs; provides custom publishing; and owns the American Baby Family Research Center and two Web sites. The company expected the acquisition to attract younger readers and to tap the fast growing domestic Hispanic market.

The Publishing Group also creates custom marketing programs through Meredith Integrated Marketing, licenses the *Better Homes and Gardens* brand and publishes books created and sold under Meredith and Ortho trademarks. Meredith has nearly 300 books in print and has established marketing relationships with some of America's leading companies, including Home Depot, Daimler-Chrysler, and Carnival Cruise Lines. Meredith's most popular book is the red-plaid *Better Homes and Gardens New Cook Book.*

The Meredith Broadcasting Group includes 13 television stations in locations across the continental United States, in such cities as Atlanta; Phoenix; Portland, Oregon; Hartford-New Haven, Connecticut; Kansas City, Missouri; Nashville; Greenville-Spartanburg-Anderson, South Carolina; Asheville, North Carolina; Las Vegas; Flint-Saginaw, Michigan; and Bend, Oregon. The network affiliations include CBS (five affiliates), NBC (one), UPN (one), and FOX (4).

Meredith's consumer database contains more than 75 million names, making it one of the largest domestic databases among media companies. These databases enable magazine and TV advertisers to precisely target marketing campaigns. In addition, the company has an extensive Internet presence, including branded anchor tenant positions on America Online.

## Shortcomings to Bear in Mind

- The company's profits depend heavily on advertising revenues. The recession in the early part of the decade was particularly hard on advertising, which can be a volatile factor. When a company's profits are hurting, they often lay off employees and pare back advertising.
- Stuart Plesser, an analyst with *Value Line Investment Survey,* had this comment on February 18, 2005: "Meredith's Publishing business is experiencing an advertising slump. Ad revenues declined 5 percent in the second quarter of fiscal 2005 (year ends June 30). And, we expect this trend to continue into the third quarter, with ad revenues declining in the low single digits. Part of the problem, we believe, is difficult year-over-year comparisons. Also, advertisers appear to be uncertain as to the direction of the economy and, as a result, may be holding back spending."

## Reasons to Buy

- In the 1994–2004 period, Earnings per share advanced from $.41 to $2.14, a compound annual growth rate of 18 percent. In the same ten-year span, however, Dividends per share expanded less impressively, from $.17 to $.43, a growth rate of 9.7 percent.
- "Americans are coming home," said a company spokesman. "Research shows they are devoting more time to their homes and their families, and the Meredith Publishing Group is ideally positioned to serve them. Through our century-long commitment to quality service journalism, we have built a reputation as a trusted source of information. Our subscription magazines, special interest publications, book, Web sites and other materials are respected resources for Americans seeking to enrich their homes through remodeling, decorating, gardening and cooking."
- Meredith serves more than 80 million American consumers each month through its magazines, books, custom publications, Internet presence, and television stations. What's more, the company's database contains 75 million names, with 300 data points on seven of the ten domestic home-owning households.
- The company's products dominate the industry sweet spot of Americans in the thirty-five to fifty-four age group, the nation's largest purchasers. This age group does a disproportionate amount spending in Meredith specialties—remodeling, decorating, cooking, and gardening.
- The national recognition of titles such as *Better Homes and Gardens, Ladies' Home Journal, American Baby,* and *Country Home,* combined with the strong local reputation of many of its TV stations, provide a solid foundation for continued growth.
- William H. Donald, an analyst with the *Standard and Poor's Company Reports,* had this favorable view of MDP on January 28, 2005: "The stock has historically traded at what we view as high P/E multiples, and toward the high end of its peer group range. Based on cash flow and earnings growth comparisons with peers, we think a premium valuation is warranted. We expect the company to continue to expand in growing markets. We see favorable demographic trends and think MDP should continue to benefit, in terms of business growth and asset values, from its position as the largest publisher of shelter magazines and as a major group broadcaster. The company continues to outperform the magazine industry in circulation and advertising gains. We expect EPS *(Earnings per share)* growth to average in the mid- to high teens over the next five years."

Total assets: $1,466 million
Current ratio: 0.85
Common shares outstanding: 50 million
Return on 2004 shareholders' equity: 20.4%

| | 2004 | 2003 | 2002 | 2001 | 2000 | 1999 | 1998 | 1997 |
|---|---|---|---|---|---|---|---|---|
| Revenues (millions) | 1,162 | 1,080 | 988 | 1,053 | 1,097 | 1,036 | 1,010 | 855 |
| Net income (millions) | 110.7 | 91.1 | 70.1 | 71.3 | 71.0 | 89.7 | 79.9 | 67.6 |
| Earnings per share | 2.14 | 1.80 | 1.38 | 1.55 | 1.71 | 1.64 | 1.46 | 1.22 |
| Dividends per share | .43 | .37 | .35 | .33 | .31 | .29 | .27 | .24 |
| Price　　high | 55.9 | 50.3 | 47.8 | 39.0 | 41.0 | 42.0 | 48.5 | 36.9 |
| 　　　　low | 48.2 | 36.9 | 33.4 | 26.5 | 22.4 | 30.6 | 26.7 | 22.1 |

Conservative Growth

# Microsoft Corporation

One Microsoft Way ❑ Redmond, WA 98052–6399 ❑ (425) 706–3703 ❑ Direct dividend reinvestment plan available: (800) 285–7772 ❑ Web site: *www.microsoft.com* ❑ Listed: NASDAQ ❑ Fiscal year ends June 30 ❑ Ticker symbol: MSFT ❑ S&P rating: B+ ❑ Value Line financial strength rating: A++

According to Jay Greene, writing for *BusinessWeek* on August 2, 2004, "Most stock analysts expect the $36 billion company to grow in the single digits for the next few years. But if the stars align, it could produce a surge toward the end of the decade. Here's how the scenario would work: The company is betting big on the next major update of Windows, called Longhorn, which is expected out in 2006. Since there hasn't been a major upgrade since 2001, you can expect to see pent-up demand from both corporations and consumers.

"Right after that, Microsoft plans a second wave of product upgrades, including new versions of its Office productivity suite and its applications for small and medium-size businesses. If things work right, it could also be reaping rewards from investments in the Xbox video game console and MSN Web site at the same time. Analyst Rick Sherlund of Goldman, Sachs & Company says growth could reach as high as 15 percent in fiscal 2007 or 2008."

## Company Profile

Microsoft is the dominant player in the PC software market. It climbed to prominence on the popularity of its operating systems software and now rules the business-applications software market. Microsoft, moreover, has set its sights on becoming the leading provider of software services for the Internet.

By virtue of it size, market positioning and financial strength, Microsoft is a formidable competitor in any market it seeks to enter. Earnings have shown explosive growth in recent years, enhanced by a strong PC market in general, along with new product introductions and market-share gains. Of course, the last couple years have seen the PC market sag, along with most everything else. But better times should return.

Microsoft is best known for its operating-systems software programs, which run on close to 90 percent of the PCs currently in use. Its original DOS operating system, of course, gave way to Windows, a graphical user interface program run in conjunction with DOS, which made using a PC easier.

The company entered the business-applications market in the early 1990s via a line-up of strong offerings, combined with aggressive and innovative marketing and sales strategies. The company's Office 97 suite, which includes the popular Word (word processing), Excel (spreadsheet) and PowerPoint (graphics) software programs, is now by far the best-selling applications software package.

## Shortcomings to Bear in Mind

- Here's an interesting quote from an article in *BusinessWeek* on January 24, 2005, written by Steve Hamm: "How's this for a mismatch? On one side, you have Microsoft Corp., the largest software company in the world, with $37 billion in revenues and 57,000 employees. On the other side, there's the Mozilla Foundation, a not-for-profit organization with a $2 million budget and just sixteen employees wedged into a single room in an office park in Mountain View, Calif. It's Godzilla vs. Mozilla, and Mozilla is a midget.

  "Yet Mozilla foundation is pulling off a feat that would have seemed preposterous a year ago: It's taking share from Microsoft in the market for Internet browsing. According to a survey released on January 12, by WEB site analytics firm WebSideStory Inc., Mozilla's free Firefox browser has grabbed 4.6 percent share over the past six months and seems well on the way to its stated goal of 10 percent. Meanwhile, Microsoft's Internet Explorer has slipped 4.9 percentage points, to 90.6 percent, the lowest in three years."

- "What could go wrong?" asks Jay Greene of *BusinessWeek*. "Microsoft is facing the most serious threat to its operating system monopoly that it has seen in years. Its chief adversary is not another software company but Linux, the open-source operating system. Governments around the world, leery of becoming too dependent on Microsoft, are encouraging their agencies and local companies to favor Linux over Windows. That's causing Microsoft trouble in one of the industry's biggest growth areas—emerging markets such as China, India, and Russia."

## Reasons to Buy

- George A. Niemond, an analyst with *Value Line Investment Survey*, had this comment on February 25, 2005, "Microsoft is rolling out new products, such as upgraded versions of the Visual Studio applications development tool, the SQL database, and a version of Office aimed at small business management. Then, too, we expect to see an upgraded Xbox in time for the 2005 holiday season."

- Writing for the *Standard & Poor's Stock Reports* on February 4, 2005, Jonathan Rudy, CFA, had this favorable observation: "We have a STRONG BUY recommendation on MSFT, primarily due to its strong balance sheet, market leadership, and discount to our estimated intrinsic value, based on discounted cash-flow analysis." Mr. Rudy also said, "Microsoft has continued to diversify its revenue stream into new areas, resulting in solid growth and profitability, while many competitors were severely affected by the technology downturn. The company's notable cash and short-term investment balance of over $34.5 billion, with no debt, provided the flexibility for the significant announcement of the planned stock buyback, special dividend, and the doubling of its regular dividend."

- On January 28, 2005, Lehman Brothers had an OVERWEIGHT (*buy*) rating on Microsoft. "We believe that the pipeline is healthy and that bookings remain strong. While deferred revenue was up nicely in the second quarter, accounts receivable also jumped. We believe the outlook for MSFT remains extremely strong and expect the server business to be a key economic driver in the coming quarters."

- With more than 250 million unique users worldwide each month, MSN is now one of the most popular destinations on the Internet. And with the launch of the newest version of MSN in 2002, the momentum continues. This latest offering includes a new home page design, improved performance, and several updates to help users better communicate and enjoy digital media. It also provides fast and reliable Internet access in the United States with the new MSN Broadband service.

- Xbox is Microsoft's future-generation video game system that gives the game players experiences they have yet to imagine. With a built-in hard disk drive, Xbox delivers much richer game worlds. And with Dolby Digital 5.1 sound, gamers will actually feel what's happening. Xbox is the only system designed to enable players to compete or collaborate with other players around the world through broadband online gaming.

- In the words of Eric J. Savitz, writing for *Barron's*—the nation's most prestigious weekly investment publication—on July 26, 2004, "Investors are interpreting the software giant's new plan to pay out a mountain of cash to shareholders as a signal that its days as a growth stock are over. But the opposite is true: Microsoft is gearing up for further revenue gains and accelerating profits. The company has never been better positioned, and the stock has rarely been more attractive.

  In part, this is a reflection of the fact that for the last two years, as the stock market rediscovered technology stocks, Microsoft shares have been weighed down by a lengthy list of woes, real and imagined. Investors have worried about litigation risk over antitrust issues. They have wrung their hands over the competitive threat posed by Linux, the freely distributed operating system. They have fretted over the revenue impact of a push

by Microsoft to get corporate customers to sign long-term licensing deals."

Mr. Savitz also said, "And perhaps most significantly, they have wondered if the company's days as a growth company are over.

Freighted with all of that, it's no wonder that the stock has been dead in the water. But the company has been attacking those issues, one by one. And the result is, Microsoft is reemerging as a stock that growth investors are interested in again."

- Nor is *Barron's* the only major publication recommending Microsoft. On August 9, 2004, *Fortune* magazine writer Adam Lashinsky said, "Microsoft has a spate of new products on the way, notably next year's Yukon server software, followed in 2006 or 2007 by Longhorn, the long-awaited overhaul of Windows. Longhorn in particular represents the company's next big opportunity because Microsoft could use it to increase its revenues from customers who take out continuing subscriptions for software and services. 'It could be a huge home run,' says Rob Gensler, who owns Microsoft in his T. Rowe Price Global Technology fund.

  "The ultimate reason for confidence in Microsoft is that unlike many other companies—especially in the tech sector—it isn't likely to come unhinged anytime soon, especially with so much of its bad news behind it."

  Mr. Lashinsky went on to say, "Is Microsoft a sure thing? Of course not. Otherwise it would have shot up on the dividend news. Instead, it rose briefly, then fell back after a mildly disappointing earnings report—further proof that plenty of Microsoft skeptics remain. 'You always want to buy stocks during periods of transition and uncertainly,' says T. Rowe Price's Gensler. 'If you believe they can pull it off, this will be a great long-term stock.'"

Total assets: $92,389 million
Current ratio: 4.71
Common shares outstanding: 10,862 million
Return on 2004 shareholders' equity: 11.7%

| | 2004 | 2003 | 2002 | 2001 | 2000 | 1999 | 1998 | 1997 |
|---|---|---|---|---|---|---|---|---|
| Revenues (millions) | 36,835 | 32,187 | 28,365 | 25,296 | 22,956 | 19,747 | 14,484 | 11,358 |
| Net income (millions) | 8,168 | 9,993 | 7,829 | 7,785 | 9,421 | 7,625 | 4,786 | 3,454 |
| Earnings per share | .75 | .92 | .70 | .69 | .85 | .70 | .45 | .36 |
| Dividends per share | .16 | .08 | Nil | — | — | — | — | — |
| Price      high | 27.5 | 30.0 | 35.3 | 38.1 | 58.6 | 60.0 | 36.0 | 18.9 |
|            low | 21.6 | 22.6 | 20.7 | 21.3 | 20.2 | 34.0 | 15.6 | 10.1 |

Aggressive Growth

# Oshkosh Truck Corporation

2307 Oregon Street ❑ P. O. Box 2566 ❑ Oshkosh, WI 54903–2566 ❑ (920) 233–9332 ❑ Web site: *www. oshkoshtruckcorporation.com* ❑ Dividend reinvestment plan not available ❑ Fiscal years end September 30 ❑ Listed: NYSE ❑ Ticker symbol: OSK ❑ S&P rating: A- ❑ Value Line financial strength rating: not covered

In recent years, Oshkosh Truck has impressed a host of writers and publications. Here is a sample of their comments:

• "Saddam may have been pried from his hole, but the ongoing military operations in Iraq and Afghanistan continue to deliver a big payload of $1.9 billion (sales) Oshkosh Truck. The U.S. military's need for heavy transport equipment and spare parts in both nations pushed the Oshkosh, Wisconsin-based truckmaker's defense sales to $199 million in 2003's fourth quarter, 18 percent ahead of the year-ago period. Total net income for the full year rose 27 percent, to $76 million, from $60 million," said *Forbes* magazine, January 12, 2004.

• "In the past decade at the helm of the top-performing fund at T. Rowe Price, Brian Berghuis has averaged a return of nearly 14 percent annually. He likes to focus on companies flying below the radar because he finds he gets easier access to management. That, in turn, allows him to gain a better understanding of the catalysts that drive the company. Right now, Berghuis is excited about Oshkosh Truck. The Wisconsin company makes specialty trucks used by the military, garbage haulers, and cement layers. It also has a 29 percent share of the U.S. fire truck market. And sales are sizzling. Profits have grown 30 percent annually over the past five years," said *Fortune* magazine, December 22, 2003.

• "Five years ago, Oshkosh Truck was losing money, and its stock was stuck in single digits. Then came a revival. Oshkosh, based in Oshkosh, Wisconsin, borrowed to acquire some specialized businesses with the intention of becoming a rapidly growing manufacturer. Manufacturing isn't usually considered sexy, but consider this: Since October 1997, when Robert Bohn was elevated to CEO, the shares are up by five times, and profits have soared," said *Kiplinger's Personal Finance,* April 2002.

• "Since 1997, Oshkosh's earnings have risen from $10 million to about $51 million. Sales have grown to $1.4 billion, from $683 million. And now, the company's growth is about to get a shot in the arm. Given that, the stock appears reasonably valued at 19 times the past four quarter's earnings, 2.6 times book value, and 0.6 times revenue. Though with a market cap of $895 million, the firm is small by my standards, *Forbes* magazine recently named Oshkosh to the number eleven position on its list of best big companies." *Bloomberg Personal Finance* magazine, April 2002.

## Company Profile

Oshkosh Truck is a manufacturer of a broad range of specialty commercial, fire and emergency and military trucks and truck bodies. It sells mostly to customers in domestic and European markets. The company sells trucks under the Oshkosh and Pierce trademarks; truck bodies under the McNeilus, MTM, Medtec, Geesink, and Norba trademarks; and mobile and stationary compactors under the Geesink Kiggen trademark.

Oshkosh began business in 1917 and was among the early pioneers of four-wheel drive technology.

The company's commercial truck lines include refuse truck bodies, rear and front-discharge concrete mixers and all-wheel drive truck chassis. Its custom and commercial fire apparatus and emergency vehicles include pumpers; aerial and ladder trucks; tankers; light-, medium- and heavy-duty rescue vehicles; wildland and rough-terrain response vehicles; and aircraft rescue and firefighting vehicles and ambulances, and snow-removal vehicles.

As a manufacturer of severe-duty, heavy-tactical trucks for the United States Department of Defense, Oshkosh Truck manufactures vehicles that perform a variety of demanding tasks, such as hauling tanks, missile systems, ammunition, fuel, and cargo for combat units.

More than 6,500 Oshkosh trucks have been in service in Iraq.

## Shortcomings to Bear in Mind

- *Standard & Poor's Stock Reports* had the following opinion of Oshkosh Truck on

February 1, 2005. Anthony M. Fiore, CFA, said, "We believe near-term growth prospects are strong for this company, and we have confidence in management's ability to execute its strategic initiatives over the long term. However, we are maintaining our HOLD opinion on OSK shares, based on valuation considerations."

- On November 22, 2004, Mr. Bohn discussed some negative factors to bear in mind: "Even a year of significant achievement is not without its disappointments. In October 2004, we learned that Oshkosh had not been selected to supply the United Kingdom Ministry of Defense with the next generation of Support Vehicles. If passion and dedication had determined the winner, this team would have brought the contract home. I'm proud of our efforts to win the program. Now we've moved on and are actively pursuing other international defense opportunities to supplement our strong U.S. Sales.

  "Finally, no discussion of fiscal 2004 would be complete without commenting on the sharp rise of steel costs. It was an influential factor on our performance this year. Despite several price increases that we levied in our commercial and fire and emergency segments, we still took a bit of a hit of $0.17 per share this year."

## Reasons to Buy

- In reviewing the accomplishments of fiscal 2004, CEO Robert J. Bohn said, "Fiscal 2004 has been an outstanding year for Oshkosh Truck Corporation. For the first time in company history, sales topped the $2 billion mark, at $2.3 billion, up 17.5 percent from fiscal 2003. We generated $112.8 million in net income, up 49.2 percent year-over-year, and our return on invested capital reached 18.3 percent, up from 14.4 percent in fiscal 2003.

  "We generated real growth this year. Most notable was the performance of our defense segment, which was the primary driver behind the 44.9 percent growth in EPS (Earnings per share), from $2.16 to $3.13 per share. Defense operating results served to balance weak profit performance in our commercial business segment, once again demonstrating the strength of our diversified business model.

"Several significant events have shaped company performance in fiscal 2004 and provide fuel to move full throttle into 2005. To begin, defense sales and operating income reached record levels. Although there are a number of drivers for these results, three stand out. First, our ability to fulfill parts and service requirements—made possible by our in-theater support and fast response. Second, the need to recapitalize, or reset, trucks returning from Iraq to like-new condition. And, finally, a renewed emphasis on armoring logistics fleets.

"McNeilus Companies inked a five-year contract to be a key supplier for Waste Management, Inc. This deal has a potential value of $250 million over the life of the contract, providing a solid base for McNeilus's refuse business."

■ In fiscal 2004, the company announced that its subsidiary, Geesink Norba Group, Europe's leading manufacturer of refuse collection bodies, had unveiled a new line of rear loader. Called GPM III, this is the third generation of Geesink's best-selling product line and the first to feature a smooth-sided body for greater packing capability. The curved body design provides added strength and durability to help reduce maintenance costs and is equipped with a host of high-tech features to increase productivity for refuse haulers on a variety of routes.

■ The development of the ProPulse hybrid electric drive systems exemplifies Oshkosh Truck's ability to deliver new technologies to meet the changing demands of all Oshkosh business segments. ProPulse alternative drive technology increases fuel economy up to 40 percent and generates 400 kilowatts of electricity on-board, enough to power an airport, hospital, command center or an entire city block.

According to a company executive, "Oshkosh was the first company to apply hybrid technology to severe-duty vehicles. With some of the most experienced engineers in the industry working on the project, the Oshkosh team developed many breakthrough technologies for the ProPulse project. Oshkosh has patents pending for many of the technologies incorporated into the ProPulse system.

"The ProPulse technology has applications well beyond the military use, including refuse trucks, fire apparatus, snow removal and other commercial vehicles. In fact, Oshkosh is already adapting the ProPulse technology to a refuse-hauling vehicle."

■ Perhaps the most cutting-edge initiative of fiscal 2004 was Oshkosh Truck's work in developing an autonomous defense vehicle—the TerraMax makes its own decisions on route planning, obstacle avoidance, and speed, without any human interaction.

"Fiscal 2004 was another strong year for Pierce Manufacturing with multiple new product introductions," said John W. Randjelovic, executive vice president and president of Pierce Manufacturing, Inc. "Pierce filled the last major gap in its aerial product line with the debut of a 75-foot aluminum aerial. This product addresses a niche market in the fire service and targets incremental sales.

"A new version of Pierce's flagship chassis, the Quantum, was also introduced. It features a distinctive new design and incorporates best-in-class safety features, such as TAK-4 independent front suspension, side-roll protection, and Command Zone advanced electronics."

Total assets: $1,452 million
Current ratio: 1.05
Common shares outstanding: 36 million
Return on 2004 shareholders' equity: 19.5%

|  | 2004 | 2003 | 2002 | 2001 | 2000 | 1999 | 1998 | 1997 |
|---|---|---|---|---|---|---|---|---|
| Revenues (millions) | 2,262 | 1,926 | 1,744 | 1,445 | 1,324 | 1,165 | 903 | 683 |
| Net income (millions) | 113 | 75.6 | 59.6 | 50.9 | 48.5 | 31.2 | 16.3 | 10.0 |
| Earnings per share | 3.13 | 2.16 | 1.72 | 1.49 | 1.48 | 1.20 | .64 | .39 |
| Dividends per share | .26 | .15 | .17 | .18 | .17 | .17 | .17 | .17 |
| Price      high | 69.0 | 52.7 | 32.7 | 22.9 | 22.0 | 19.2 | 11.7 | 7.1 |
|            low | 62.3 | 26.1 | 23.1 | 15.9 | 10.8 | 9.7 | 5.8 | 3.4 |

Aggressive Growth

# Patterson Companies, Inc.

(formerly Patterson Dental Company) ❏ 1031 Mendota Heights Road ❏ St. Paul, MN 55120–1419 ❏ (651) 686–1600
❏ Web site: *www.pattersondental.com* ❏ Dividend reinvestment not plan available ❏ Fiscal years end last Saturday in April ❏ Listed: Nasdaq ❏ Ticker symbol: PDCO ❏ Standard & Poor's rating: B+ ❏ Value Line financial strength rating: A

Patterson Companies (formerly Patterson Dental Company) entered the estimated $5-billion worldwide rehabilitation-supply market in fiscal 2004 by acquiring AbilityOne Products Corp., the world's leading distributor of rehabilitation supplies, equipment, and nonwheelchair assistive living products. As the only one-stop shop in the rehabilitation marketplace, AbilityOne provides its customers with the convenience of a single source of supply for all of their product needs.

AbilityOne owns many of the leading brands on the global rehabilitation market, including Sammons, Preston, and Rolyan in the United States and Homecraft in Europe. As a result, no competitor comes close to matching the breadth, and leadership positions of AbilityOne's offerings, which include:

• Braces, splints, and continuous passive motion machines for the orthopedic market.

• Dressings, dining, and bathing devices for the assistive living segment.

• A full range of rehabilitation equipment, including treatment tables, mat platforms, and stationary bicycles.

• Clinical products, such as exercise bands, weights, balls, and mats.

• Walkers, canes, and wheelchair accessories in the mobility category.

## Company Profile

Patterson Companies, Inc. is a value-added distributor serving the dental, companion-pet veterinarian and rehabilitation supply markets. The company recently changed its name from Patterson Dental Company to reflect its expanding base of business, which now encompasses the veterinary and rehabilitation supply markets, as well as its traditional base of operations in the dental supply market.

## Dental Market

As Patterson's largest business, Patterson Dental Supply provides a virtually complete range of consumable dental products, equipment, and software, turnkey digital solutions and value-added services to dentists and dental laboratories throughout North America.

## Veterinary Market

Webster Veterinary Supply is the nation's second-largest distributor of consumable veterinary supplies, equipment, diagnostic products, vaccines and pharmaceuticals to companion-pet veterinary clinics.

## Rehabilitation Market

AbilityOne Products Corp. is the world's leading distributor of rehabilitation supplies and nonwheelchair assistive patient products to the physical and occupational therapy markets. The unit's global customer base includes hospitals, long-term-care facilities, clinics, and dealers.

## Recent Business Developments

During fiscal 2004, Patterson made four strategic acquisitions that have added a large new market to the company's mix of businesses and strengthened its competitive position in its two pre-existing markets.

- As noted above, Patterson entered the worldwide rehabilitation supply and equipment market by acquiring AbilityOne Products Corp.

- In April 2004, Patterson acquired ProVet, a value-added distributor of companion-pet veterinary supplies in the Midwest and Northwest, to strengthen the national market position of the company's Webster unit.

- As part of the company's strategy for consolidating the fragmented rehabilitation market, Patterson acquired Medco Supply Company, Inc. in May 2004. Medco is a leading national distributor of sports medicine, first aid, and medical supplies.

- To equip Patterson's Dental Supply's sales force with an important value-added service, the company acquired CAESY Education Systems, Inc. in May 2004. CAESY is the leading provider of patient education services to North American dental practices.

## Shortcomings to Bear in Mind

- As noted below, Patterson Dental has a most impressive record of consistent growth. It is not surprising that the stock normally sells at a lofty P/E ratio.

- Massimo Santicchia, an analyst with *Standard & Poor's Stock Reports,* had this comment on February 10, 2005: "We recently downgraded our recommendation to HOLD, from BUY, after the stock reached our twelve-month target price. The shares traded recently at a significant premium to the S&P 500, at 30 times our fiscal 2005 EPS *(Earnings per share)* estimate of $1.62. Despite the company's strong track record of consistent earnings and cash flow growth, and return on equity above 20 percent, we would take a more cautious stance at current valuation levels."

## Reasons to Buy

- On the other hand, the analyst with *Value Line Investment Survey* had a more positive observation on March 4, 2005. Erik Antonson said, "Patterson Companies is on track to post 20 percent to 25 percent bottom-line *(profits)* gains for fiscal 2004 and 2005. The results are being driven by strong internal revenue growth across all three of the company's units. Indeed, Patterson's sales force has been growing steadily at a rate of 8 percent to 10 percent a year. Furthermore, recent acquisitions of ProVet, Medco, CAESY, and Milburn will likely help drive positive results going forward."

- According to CEO Peter L. Frechette, "Sales of Patterson Dental Supply, our largest business, rose 10 percent, to $1.6 billion in fiscal 2004, paced by the continuation of strong demand for dental equipment. Sales of new-generation equipment, including the CEREC 3D dental restorative system, digital radiography, and office networking gear, were strong throughout the year. In addition, demand was robust for such core equipment as chairs, lights, and units. It is clear that dental practices are continuing to invest heavily in a wide range of equipment designed to increase productivity, improve clinical outcomes, and generate new revenue opportunities.

"It is also important to realize that we are still in the early stages of penetrating the North American market with new-generation dental equipment, a factor that should continue driving growth of our dental business for some time."

Mr. Frechette went on to say, "Sales of the Webster Veterinary Supply unit increased 13 percent in fiscal 2004, paced by growth in existing markets, internal expansion into several new markets, and the April 16, 2004 acquisition of ProVet, a distributor of companion-pet supplies.

- In the 1994–2004 period, Earnings per share climbed—without interruption—from $0.15 to $1.09, a compound annual growth rate of 22.3 percent, which makes this an aggressive growth stock.

- The CEREC 3 dental restorative system is a clear example of new-generation equipment that benefit both the patient and the dentist. In addition to providing certain clinical advantages in comparison to traditional restoration techniques, the CEREC 3D increases office productivity by eliminating the need for a second office visit to complete a tooth restoration. As a result, CEREC 3D enables a dentist to treat additional patients, thus creating a revenue-generating opportunity.

- Webster Veterinary Supply serves the $2.2 billion domestic companion-pet veterinary supply market, which the company believes to be growing at a 6 percent to 7 percent rate. Small-animal or companion-pet veterinarians are the largest and fastest-growing segment of the overall veterinary market.

A variety of factors are driving the growth of this segment, including rising pet ownership. It is currently estimated that about 31 million U.S. households own dogs, while 27 million own cats. Consistent with the growth of pet ownership, annual consumer spending on veterinary care is far higher today than it was a decade ago. The willingness of owners to spend more on their pets is related in part to the advent of new procedures and drugs that significantly improve clinical outcomes.

Total assets: $1,589 million
Current ratio: 2.95
Common shares outstanding: 136 million
Return on 2004 shareholders' equity: 20.8%

|                      | 2004 | 2003 | 2002 | 2001 | 2000 | 1999 | 1998 | 1997 |
|----------------------|------|------|------|------|------|------|------|------|
| Revenues (millions)  | 1,969 | 1,657 | 1,416 | 1,156 | 1,040 | 879 | 778 | 662 |
| Net income (millions) | 150 | 116 | 95.3 | 76.5 | 64.5 | 49.9 | 40.8 | 32.4 |
| Earnings per share   | 1.09 | .85 | .70 | .57 | .48 | .37 | .31 | .25 |
| Dividends per share  | Nil | — | — | — | — | — | — | — |
| Price        high    | 43.7 | 35.8 | 27.6 | 21.1 | 17.3 | 12.6 | 11.6 | 7.7 |
|              low     | 29.7 | 17.7 | 19.1 | 13.8 | 8.2 | 8.3 | 7.1 | 4.5 |

# PepsiCo, Inc.

700 Anderson Hill Road ❑ Purchase, NY 10577–1444 ❑ (914) 253–3691 ❑ Dividend reinvestment plan available: (800) 226–0083 ❑ Web site: *www.pepsico.com* ❑ Listed: NYSE ❑ Ticker symbol: PEP ❑ S&P rating: A+ ❑ Value Line financial strength rating: A++

"Few companies seems as pained by the thought of missing a customer as PepsiCo Company," said Diane Brady, writing for *Business Week* on June 14, 2004. "Every year, the food and beverage giant adds more than 200 product variations to its vast global portfolio—which ranges from Quaker Soy Crisps to Gatorade Xtremo Thirst Quencher. Steven S. Reinemund, chairman and chief executive officer, believes that constant quest for change, more than even quality and value, is what has driven the Purchase (N.Y.) company to consistent double-digit earnings growth."

Ms. Brady went on to point out that Mr. Reinemund seems "far more obsessed with understanding and catering to changing tastes than in trying to shape them. To capitalize on the growing market for New Age herbally enhanced beverages, for example, the company acquired SoBe Beverages for $370 million in 2001. Since then, the company has extended the brand with such offerings as the energy drink SoBe No Fear, SoBe Synergy targeted at the school-aged market with 50 percent juice, and SoBe Fuerte, aimed at the Hispanic market.

"PepsiCo's huge Frito-Lay division, which dominates 60 percent of the U.S. chip market and had $9.1 billion in revenues last year, has been equally adept at coming up with products to reflect changing tastes and demographics. Even amid the low-carb craze, it racked up 4 percent volume growth last year, thanks to new flavors and healthier ingredients."

## Company Profile

The company consists of the snack businesses of Frito-Lay North America and Frito-Lay International; the beverage businesses of Pepsi-Cola North America, Gatorade/Tropicana North America and PepsiCo Beverages International; and Quaker Foods North America, manufacturer and marketer of ready-to-eat cereals and other food products. PepsiCo brands are available in nearly 200 countries and territories.

Many of PepsiCo's brand names are more than 100 years old, but the corporation is relatively young. PepsiCo was founded in 1965 through the merger of Pepsi-Cola and Frito-Lay. Tropicana was acquired in 1998 and PepsiCo merged with The Quaker Oats Company, including Gatorade, in 2001.

### Frito-Lay North America and Frito-Lay International

PepsiCo's snack food operations had their start in 1932 when two separate events took place. In San Antonio, Texas, Elmer Doolin bought the recipe for an unknown food product—a corn chip—and started an entirely new industry. The product was Fritos brand corn chips, and his firm became the Frito Company.

That same year in Nashville, Tennessee, Herman W. Lay started his own business distributing potato chips. Mr. Lay later bought the company that supplied him with product and changed its name to H.W. Lay Company. The Frito Company and H.W. Lay Company merged in 1961 to become Frito-Lay, Inc.

Today, Frito-Lay brands account for more than half of the U.S. snack chip industry.

PepsiCo began its international snack food operations in 1966. Today, with operations in more than 40 countries, it is the leading multinational snack chip company, accounting for more than one quarter of international retail snack chip sales. Products are available in some 120 countries. Frito-Lay North America includes Canada and the United States. Major Frito-Lay International markets include Australia, Brazil, Mexico, the Netherlands, South Africa, the United Kingdom, and Spain.

Often Frito-Lay products are known by local names. These names include Matutano in Spain, Sabritas and Gamesa in Mexico, Elma Chips in Brazil, Walkers in the United Kingdom, and others. The company markets Frito-Lay brands on a global level, and introduces unique products for local tastes.

Major Frito-Lay products include Ruffles, Lay's and Doritos brands snack chips. Other major brands include Cheetos cheese-flavored snacks, Tostitos tortilla chips, Santitas tortilla chips, Rold Gold pretzels, and SunChips multigrain snacks. Frito-Lay also sells a variety of snack dips and cookies, nuts, and crackers.

### Pepsi-Cola North America and PepsiCo Beverages International

PepsiCo's beverage business was founded at the turn of the century by Caleb Bradham, a New Bern, North Carolina, druggist, who first formulated Pepsi-Cola. Today consumers spend about $33 billion on Pepsi-Cola beverages. Brand Pepsi and other Pepsi-Cola products—including Diet Pepsi, Pepsi-One, Mountain Dew, Slice, Sierra Mist, and Mug brands—account for nearly one-third of total soft drink sales in the United States, a consumer market totaling about $60 billion.

Pepsi-Cola also offers a variety of non-carbonated beverages, including Aquafina bottled water, Fruitworks, and All Sport.

In 1992 Pepsi-Cola formed a partnership with Thomas J. Lipton Co. Today Lipton is the biggest selling ready-to-drink tea brand in the United States. Pepsi-Cola also markets Frappuccino ready-to-drink coffee through a partnership with Starbucks.

In 2001 SoBe became a part of Pepsi-Cola. SoBe manufactures and markets an innovative line of beverages including fruit blends, energy drinks, dairy-based drinks, exotic teas, and other beverages with herbal ingredients.

Outside the United States, Pepsi-Cola soft drink operations include the business of Seven-Up International. Pepsi-Cola beverages are available in about 160 countries and territories.

### Gatorade/Tropicana North America

Tropicana was founded in 1947 by Anthony Rossi as a Florida fruit packaging business. The company entered the concentrate orange juice business in 1949, registering Tropicana as a trademark.

In 1954 Rossi pioneered a pasteurization process for orange juice. For the first time, consumers could enjoy the fresh taste of pure not-from-concentrate 100 percent Florida orange juice in a ready-to-serve package. The juice, Tropicana Pure Premium, became the company's flagship product.

In 1957 the name of the company was changed to Tropicana Products, headquartered in Bradenton, Florida. The company went public in 1957, was purchased by Beatrice Foods Co. in 1978, acquired by Kohlberg Kravis & Roberts in 1986 and sold to The Seagram Company Ltd. in 1988. Seagram purchased the Dole global juice business in 1995. PepsiCo acquired Tropicana, including the Dole juice business, in August 1998.

Today the Tropicana brand is available in sixty-three countries. Principal brands in North America are Tropicana Pure Premium, Tropicana Season's Best, Dole Juices, and Tropicana Twister. Internationally, principal brands include Tropicana Pure Premium and Dole juices along with Frui'Vita, Loóza, and Copella. Tropicana Pure Premium is the third largest brand of all food products sold in grocery stores in the United States.

Gatorade sports drinks was acquired by the Quaker Oats Company in 1983 and became a part of PepsiCo with the merger in 2001. Gatorade is the first isotonic sports drink. Created in 1965 by researchers at the University of Florida for the school's football team, "The Gators," Gatorade is now the world's leading sport's drink.

### Quaker Foods North America

The Quaker Oats Company was formed in 1901 when several American pioneers in oat milling came together to incorporate. In Ravenna, Ohio, Henry D. Seymour and William Heston had established the Quaker Mill Company and registered the now famous trademark.

The first major acquisition of the company was Aunt Jemina Mills Company in 1926, which is today the leading manufacturer of pancake mixes and syrup.

In 1986, The Quaker Oats Company acquired the Golden Grain Company, producers of Rice-A-Roni.

PepsiCo merged with The Quaker Oats Company in 2001. Its products still have the eminence of wholesome, good-for-you food, as envisioned by the company over a century ago.

### Shortcomings to Bear in Mind

- According to one analyst, there is some risk from unfavorable weather conditions in the company's markets, inability to meet volume and revenue growth targets, increased popularity of low-carbohydrate diets, and consumer acceptance of new product introductions.

### Reasons to Buy

- *Standard & Poor's* analyst, Richard Joy, had an upbeat comment on February 15, 2005: "We have a STRONG BUY on the shares, based on our view of strong profit and free cash flow growth and what we view as solid EPS (Earnings per share) visibility and consistency. Based on the company's leading positions in several fast-growing food and beverage categories, we believe PEP is poised to deliver 11 percent to 12 percent annual EPS growth for the longer term."

- Similarly, Stephen Sanborn, CFA, an analyst with *Value Line Investment Survey*, had this encouraging assessment on February 4, 2005: "PepsiCo is well-positioned to grow in the years out to 2007–2009. The Frito-Lay, Pepsi-Cola, Quaker Oats, Gatorade, and Tropicana brands all have strong market positions in North America, and there is good reason to think they will continue to expand. International opportunities look even brighter, and sales abroad are likely to provide much of the company's growth in coming years. New products will always be of key importance in supporting growth, and Pepsi's management has an outstanding record for developing new products and expanding existing ones."

- "The Pepsi Generation has never looked stronger," said Andrew Bary, writing for *Barron's* on March 28, 2005. "PepsiCo is trouncing Coca-Cola in both the supermarket and the stock market.

  With Coke struggling for a growth strategy, Pepsi has pushed hard into non-carbonated drinks, offering the leading brands in water, tea, juice, and sports drinks. That's important because the soda business has gone flat. Pepsi's powerhouse Frito-Lay division, meanwhile, dominates the U.S. snack-food market and is the biggest contributor to the company's profits."

Total assets: $27,987 million
Current ratio: 1.28
Common shares outstanding: 1,678 million
Return on 2004 shareholders' equity: 22.3%

|                     | 2004   | 2003   | 2002   | 2001   | 2000   | 1999   | 1998   | 1997   |
|---------------------|--------|--------|--------|--------|--------|--------|--------|--------|
| Revenues (millions) | 29,261 | 26,971 | 25,112 | 23,512 | 25,480 | 20,367 | 2 2,348 | 20,917 |
| Net income (millions) | 4,174 | 3,494 | 3,313 | 2,660 | 2,540 | 1,845 | 1,760 | 1,730 |
| Earnings per share  | 2.44   | 2.01   | 1.85   | 1.47   | 1.42   | 1.23   | 1.16   | 1.10   |
| Dividends per share | .85    | .63    | .60    | .58    | .56    | .54    | .52    | .49    |
| Price    high       | 55.7   | 48.9   | 53.5   | 50.5   | 49.9   | 42.6   | 44.8   | 41.3   |
|          low         | 45.3   | 36.2   | 34.0   | 40.3   | 29.7   | 30.1   | 27.6   | 28.3   |

Aggressive Growth

# Pfizer Inc.

235 East 42nd Street ❑ New York, NY 10017–5755 ❑ (212) 573–2323 ❑ Direct dividend reinvestment plan available: (800) 733–9393 ❑ Web site: *www.pfizer.com* ❑ Listed: NYSE ❑ Ticker symbol: PFE ❑ S&P rating: A ❑ Value Line financial strength rating: A++

"Pfizer's pharmaceutical business has again shown its industry-leading ability to perform in a challenging global environment," said Karen Katen, executive vice president of the company and president of Pfizer Global Pharmaceuticals, on October 20, 2004. "Our portfolio is strong. While our environment is tough, we're tougher. And we're attending to both the top line *(sales)* and bottom line *(profits)* with disciplined strategies to sustain future business performance."

Ms. Katen went on to say, "Human pharmaceutical year-to-date revenue growth has been driven largely by the strong global growth of Lipitor (up 15 percent), Neurontin (up 17 percent), Zoloft (up 8 percent), Norvasc (up 4 percent), Geodon (up 31 percent), Vfend (up 47 percent), Relpax (up 102 percent), and several key products added in the Pharmacia acquisition—Celebrex, Bextra, Xalatan, Detrol, and Zyvox."

Ms. Katen also said, "Thirteen Pfizer medicines lead their respective therapeutic categories, and six of the world's twenty-five top-selling medicines are marketed by Pfizer.

The company's top five medicines—Lipitor, Norvasc, Zoloft, Celebrex, and Neurontin—together account for slightly more than half of human pharmaceutical revenues year-to-date. Each has delivered at least $2 billion in sales already this year, while Viagra, and Zithromax have each surpassed $1 billion."

## Company Profile

Pfizer traces its history back to 1849 when it was founded by Charles Pfizer and Charles Erhart. In those early days, Pfizer was a chemical firm. Today, it is a leading global pharmaceutical manufacturer, creating and marketing a wide range of prescription drugs.

In the prescription drug realm, Pfizer has some of the world's best-selling drugs. Principal cardiovascular drugs include Lipitor, the world's largest-selling cholesterol-lowering agent, and antihypertensives such as Norvasc, Cardura, and Accupril. Infectious disease drugs consist of Zithromax broad-spectrum macrolide antibiotic; key central nervous system medicines are Zoloft antidepressant and Neurontin anti-convulsant.

Nor is that all. Pfizer's prescription drugs also include Viagra for male erectile dysfunction, Zyrtec, an antihistamine and Glucotrol XL for type 2 diabetes.

In the over-the-counter sector, the company's consumer products include such well-known brands as Ben-Gay, Desitin, Sudafed, Benadryl, Listerine, Trident, Dentyne, Certs, Halls cough drops, and Schick shaving products. In 2003, Schick was sold to Energizer for $930 million.

PFE also has an important stake in hospital products, and animal health products.

Pfizer's growth over the past half century was paced by strategic acquisitions, new drug discoveries and vigorous foreign expansion. Its most recent move involved the giant acquisition of Warner-Lambert in 2000, making the new firm the largest pharmaceutical company in the world—and even larger when it acquired Pharmacia Corporation in December of 2002.

## Shortcomings to Bear in Mind

- "Two months ago, Pfizer was talking about financing research to show that Celebrex, the world's most-prescribed painkiller, might help prevent heart attacks," said Barnaby J. Feder in a December 18, 2004, article for the *New York Times.* "Now, it may face a flood of lawsuits charging that Celebrex is more likely to cause them. Pfizer's announcement yesterday that patients in a cancer study who used Celebrex had a heightened incidence of heart attacks left lawyers wondering whether the legal troubles will grow to match those of Merck, which withdrew its own painkiller, Vioxx, from the market on Sept. 30, 2004."

  Mr. Feder went on to say, "But many lawyers, even those who have sued Merck on behalf of patients who took Vioxx, said yesterday that there are clear-cut differences. The case against Pfizer does not appear as strong at this point, they said, because major clinical studies suggest

that Celebrex does not pose as great a risk as Vioxx. Nor have any documents yet emerged, as they did for Merck, suggesting that Pfizer had doubts about its drug."

## Reasons to Buy

- "Pfizer Inc., facing a string of patent expirations on blockbuster drugs, plans to cut about $2 billion from its costs and to overhaul the way it markets drugs to doctors," said Scott Hensley, writing for the *Wall Street Journal* on February 11, 2005. "The planned reorganization at the world's biggest drug maker also is expected to include a redeployment of about $2 billion of Pfizer's resources into more productive areas. The proposed cost cuts and redirected spending would take a bite out of the company's overall spending. Last year (*2004*), Pfizer, of New York, had selling, general and administrative expenses of $16.9 billion, and research-and-development expenses of $7.68 billion."

- On December 31, 2004, the U.S. Food and Drug Administration approved Lyrica for the treatment of pain caused by nerve damage from diabetes or shingles. This pain is often described as burning, tingling, sharp, stabbing, or pins and needles in the feet, legs, hands, or arms. "Lyrica is an important new therapy for millions of people suffering from the two most common neuropathic pain conditions, as it provides rapid and sustained pain relief," said Dr. Joseph Feczko, president of Worldwide Development at Pfizer. The company estimates that about 3 million diabetes patients in the United States who will develop this affliction sometime during their diabetic life. Another 150,000 develop nerve damage from shingles each year.

- "Many patients who are taking Merck & Company's Vioxx, a pain drug most often used to treat arthritis, are switching to other prescription drugs, particularly two Vioxx competitors sold by Pfizer," said Scott Hensley, writing for the *Wall Street Journal* on October 6, 2004. "Some 2.4 percent of current Vioxx users in the U.S. got prescriptions for new medicines within twenty-four hours of Merck's announcement on Thursday that it was withdrawing the drug from the market." Studies had shown that patients using Vioxx—the Merck's largest-selling product—had double the risk of having a heart attack or stroke.

- On March 14, 2004, columnist Kenneth N. Gilpin interviewed Barbara A. Ryan for the *New York Times*. Ms. Ryan is a managing director and pharmaceutical analyst at Deutsche Bank. Here is what she said about Pfizer: "Pravachol and Zocor will go off patent in June 2006. Lipitor's patent will come off in 2010 and 2011. And Crestor will go out much further, probably in 2015.

"By the time Lipitor goes off patent, the market will be on to something else. Right now Pfizer is working on C.E.T.P. (cholesteryl ester transfer protein) inhibitor, which could be combined with Lipitor to raise H.D.L., good cholesterol, by 50 percent."

She also said, "We have had a top rating on Pfizer for some time. The industry is going through a lot of challenges, and the one company that has changed its model to respond to those challenges is Pfizer. It doesn't get any credit for having a lower risk profile than most of the other big drug companies."

- Each day, 20,000 people around the world go to work promoting Pfizer products to the medical profession. They fill their "detail" bags with free samples of popular drugs such as Viagra and Zithromax, and they quote favorable conclusions from scientific studies (often company-sponsored) that show how Lipitor is the most potent way to control cholesterol and should be used instead

of Merck's Zocor. By nearly all counts, Pfizer is the industry's largest, and most effective, sales force.

According to Henry A. McKinnell, Ph.D., who became the company's CEO in 2001, "Pfizer has never been stronger and today possesses strengths and capabilities unequaled in the pharmaceutical industry. Our U.S. sales force, for example, was recently ranked as best in class in a survey of physicians, the sixth year in a row for this honor."

- Pfizer's Animal Health Group (AHG) in not only one of the largest in the world, but is also noteworthy for the breadth of its product lines and its geographic coverage. Innovative marketing has become an AHG hallmark in its efforts to succeed in a highly competitive market. An independent survey of U.S. veterinarians, for example, named the Pfizer sales force the best in the industry.

- Pfizer regularly makes use of partnerships and licensing agreements to extend its reach. Although the company must share the profits from any products developed with a partner, the deals take some pressure off Pfizer's research arm. Given its marketing expertise and reputation for successful collaborations, many smaller drug companies are reported to view Pfizer as their first choice as a partner. A recent example is Aricept, a drug developed by Eisai Company of Japan. It was co-promoted by Pfizer and quickly became the leading treatment for Alzheimer's disease in the United States.

- On February 22, 2005, the Argus Research Company rated Pfizer as a BUY. John Watkins said, "The advisory committee had several options. It could recommend the whole class be withdrawn from the market, that some Cox-II's be withdrawn from the market, or that 'black box' warning labels be put on the drugs.

"Two of the prominent Cox-II inhibitors (Celebrex and Bextra) are marketed by Pfizer. The committee looked at the data behind each drug separately. On Celebrex, a first voting was that the committee felt Celebrex carried cardiovascular risk. A second vote overwhelmingly (32 for and one against) recommended that Celebrex stay on the market.

"The committee then evaluated Bextra. Again, the committee voted that Bextra carries cardiovascular risk—and again voted (17 for and three against) to recommend that Bextra stay on the market.

"This is clearly good news for Pfizer, as the company will be facing a number of patent expirations over the next several years."

Total assets: $120,058 million
Current ratio: 1.46
Common shares outstanding: 7,551 million
Return on 2004 shareholders' equity: 22.5%

|  | 2004 | 2003 | 2002 | 2001 | 2000 | 1999 | 1998 | 1997 |
|---|---|---|---|---|---|---|---|---|
| Revenues (millions) | 52,516 | 45,188 | 32,373 | 32,259 | 29,574 | 16,204 | 13,544 | 12,504 |
| Net income (millions) | 11,361 | 3,910 | 9,126 | 7,788 | 6,495 | 3,360 | 2,627 | 2,213 |
| Earnings per share | 1.49 | .54 | 1.53 | 1.31 | 1.02 | .87 | .67 | .57 |
| Dividends per share | .68 | .60 | .52 | .44 | .36 | .31 | .25 | .23 |
| Price       high | 38.9 | 36.9 | 42.5 | 46.8 | 49.3 | 50.0 | 43.0 | 26.7 |
|             low | 23.5 | 27.0 | 25.1 | 34.0 | 30.0 | 31.5 | 23.7 | 13.4 |

Income

---

# Piedmont Natural Gas Company, Inc.

P. O. Box 33068 ▫ Charlotte, NC 28233 ▫ (704) 731–4438 ▫ Dividend reinvestment program is available: (800) 937–5449 ▫ Fiscal years end October 31 ▫ Listed: NYSE ▫ Web site: *www.piedmontng.com* ▫ Ticker symbol: PNY ▫ S&P rating: A- ▫ Value Line financial strength rating: B++

"The company is an industry leader, located in a geographic area of above-average customer growth and is favorably impacted by fair and balanced regulatory environment," said David M. Schanzer, first vice president of the brokerage firm, Janney Montgomery Scott LLC, on October 6, 2004.

The analyst went on to say, "Led by a capable, deep management team, the company has been able to execute on its transparent utility-based strategy. Management has shown a narrowing of focus and a renewed commitment to the company's basic business, having exited two businesses that no longer fit the mold. The company's recent expansion to service a larger area of North Carolina will allow the company to attain above-average growth in the coming years."

CEO Thomas E. Skains would certainly agree with this assessment of Piedmont Natural Gas. Here is what he said on January 10, 2005. "Fiscal year 2004 was truly an exciting and rewarding year for the company. Consider the following accomplishments:

• "Record net income and Earnings per share.

• "Total shareholder return at the top of our industry peer group.

• "Exceptional performance from nonutility joint ventures.

- "Completion of permanent financing of the North Carolina Natural Gas (NCNG) acquisition.
- "Successful integration of NCNG operations.
- "Customer growth at a rate in excess of 3 percent.
- "A new continuous business process improvement (CBPI) program.
- "Establishment of the Piedmont Natural Gas Foundation."

## Company Profile

Incorporated in 1950, Piedmont Natural Gas is an energy services company, primarily engaged in the transportation, distribution and sale of natural gas and propane to residential, commercial and industrial customers in North Carolina, South Carolina, and Tennessee.

The company is the second-largest natural gas utility in the Southeast, serving 960,000 natural gas customers. Piedmont Natural Gas and its nonutility subsidiaries and divisions are also engaged in acquiring, marketing, transporting, and storing natural gas for large-volume customers, in retailing residential and commercial gas appliances.

Other business interests in which the company is engaged that are not subject to state utility regulation include the sale of propane and investments in a natural gas pipeline and an interstate LNG (liquefied natural gas) storage facility and marketing natural gas and other energy products and services to deregulated markets.

PNY's Joint Ventures:
- SouthStar Energy Services LLC—an equity participant (or part owner) in Georgia's largest retail natural gas marketer.
- Pine Needle LNG Company, LLC—an equity participant in a liquefied natural gas facility that's among the nation's largest.
- Cardinal Pipeline Company, LLC—an equity participant in a 102-mile

intrastate pipeline serving portions of North Carolina.
- EasternNC Natural Gas—an equity participant in a venture that is expanding natural gas distribution into fourteen counties in eastern North Carolina.

## Shortcomings to Bear in Mind

- The company has benefited from extraordinary growth in its service territory. However, customer growth can be a double-edged sword, as it is expensive to continuously expand an underground pipe system to keep up with new construction. On the other hand, Piedmont has effectively lowered its cost to connect a customer to about $1,800, a significant decline over prior years. Analysts, moreover, expect this cost to continue to decline, which would contribute to future earnings growth.
- Piedmont Natural gas has increased its dividend for 26 consecutive years. In the 1994–2004 period, dividends expanded from $0.51 per share to $0.86, a compound annual growth rate of 5.4 percent, or well ahead of the pace of inflation—but not exactly spectacular. If you are looking for growth, this may not be a good choice. That's why I have categorized this stock for "income."

## Reasons to Buy

- "Record earnings were achieved in 2004 due to solid results in our core utility operations and a strategic restructuring of and strong operating performance from our nonutility joint ventures, including certain one-time items," said CEO Skains on January 10, 2005. "Net income for 2004 was $95.2 million, or $1.27 per diluted share (*this assumes that convertible securities are converted into common stock. Actually, in this instance, the difference is minuscule, since Earnings per share without dilution were $1.28, but* *in some companies the difference is much greater).* This compares with net income of $74.4 million, or $1.11 per diluted share in 2003. Weather in our gas utility market area in 2004 was 9 percent warmer than 2003 and 5 percent warmer than normal."

Mr. Skains also said, "Our nonutility joint ventures contributed $20 million to net income in 2004, including $4.6 million in one-time gains. Of the total amount, SouthStar Energy Services provided $11.8 million (including a one-time gain of $1.5 million due to the resolution of certain disproportionate sharing issues), Pine Needle LNG $2.4 million and Cardinal Pipeline $1.1 million. Heritage Propane contributed $4.7 million (including a one-time gain of $3.1 million from the sale of our interest). This compares with a total contribution of $10.7 million to net income in 2003 from our nonutility joint ventures.

"We are pleased with the performance of these joint ventures and remain committed to our strategic process of seeking and investing in complementary wholesale and retail energy assets. Consistent with that strategy, we recently announced our 50 percent equity participation in the proposed Hardy Storage Project with Columbia Gas Transmission, a subsidiary of NiSource. This $100 million, 12.4 Bcf (*billion cubic feet*) interstate storage project is both an attractive nonutility investment opportunity and a strategic cost-effective supply source to meet our growing demand for seasonal gas service."

- Piedmont Natural Gas has an impressive record of acquisitions:
  - Effective January 1, 2001, the company purchased for cash the natural gas distribution assets of Atmos Energy Corporation, situated in the city of Gaffney and portions of Cherokee Country, South Carolina. It added 5,400 customers to PNY's operations.
  - Effective September 30, 2002, the company purchased for $26 million in cash substantially all of the natural gas distribution assets of North Carolina Gas Service, a division of NUI Utilities, Inc. This added 14,000 customers to PNY's distribution system in the counties of Rockingham and Stokes, North Carolina.
  - Effective September 30, 2003, the company purchased for $417.5 million in cash 100 percent of the common stock of NCNG from Progress Energy, Inc., a natural gas distributor serving some 176,000 customers in eastern North Carolina.
  - In the first quarter of 2004, the company completed the permanent debt and equity financing of its acquisition of NCNG. Mr. Skains said, "We established our historically strong capital structure with an equity capitalization of 56 percent, as of October 31, 2004. In April, the rating agencies recognized these accomplishments by raising their outlook for Piedmont to 'stable' along with credit ratings of 'A' and 'A3.' Your company is financially strong and well-positioned to take advantage of future strategic opportunities in a disciplined fashion."

According to another officer of the company, "The primary reasons for these acquisitions are consistent with our strategy of pursuing profitable growth in our core natural gas distribution business in the Southeast. The reasons for the acquisitions and the factors that contributed to the goodwill include:
  - "A reasonable purchase price, slightly above book value.

- "The prospect of entering a market contiguous to our existing North Carolina service areas where, as a combined company, we could realize ongoing system benefits.
- "The prospect of acquiring an operation that could be integrated into our existing business systems and processes.
- "The opportunity to grow within a regulatory environment with which we are familiar."

■ Piedmont Natural Gas enjoys an economically robust and diverse service area that is among the fastest growing in the nation. The company's three-state service area consists of the Piedmont region of the Carolinas—Charlotte, Salisbury, Greensboro, Winston-Salem, High Point, Burlington, and Hickory in North Carolina and Anderson, Greenville and Spartanburg in South Carolina—and the metropolitan area of Nashville, Tennessee. Both *Plant Sites and Parks* and *Site Selection* magazines continue to rank the Carolinas and Tennessee among the best in the nation for business relocation and expansion and business climate.

The center of the Piedmont Carolinas area is the Greater Charlotte urban region—sixth largest in the nation—with more than 6 million people within a 100-mile radius. Charlotte is the nation's second-largest financial center. It is headquarters city for Bank of America, the nation's second-largest bank, and for First Union National bank, the sixth largest. Wachovia Corporation, the nation's fifth-largest bank, is headquartered in Winston-Salem.

Charlotte/Douglas International Airport, with over 500 flights per day and 23 million passengers annually, is US Airways' largest hub and the twentieth busiest airport in the world.

The Nashville region is a diverse center of a retail trading area of more than 2 million people, where health care is the largest industry. It is also home to major transportation, publishing, printing, financial, insurance, and communications companies as well as twenty colleges and universities.

■ An important factor in analyzing any public utility is the region's regulatory environment. In Piedmont's states, regulators have generally been supportive of the company's regulatory needs over the past few years. In the opinion of Daniel M. Fidell and Tracey W. McMillin, analysts with A. G. Edwards, "Our conclusion is based on several factors, such as purchased gas and weather normalization mechanisms in rates that serve to smooth the impact of changes in gas prices and abnormal weather conditions. In addition, PNY has benefited from fair and timely rate relief in the past to recover costs associated with extensive system growth."

Total assets: $2,336 million
Current ratio: 1.09
Common shares outstanding: 77 million
Return on 2004 shareholders' equity: 12.8%

|                      |        | 2004  | 2003  | 2002  | 2001  | 2000 | 1999 | 1998 | 1997 |
|----------------------|--------|-------|-------|-------|-------|------|------|------|------|
| Revenues (millions)  |        | 1,530 | 1,221 | 832   | 1,108 | 830  | 686  | 765  | 776  |
| Net income (millions)|        | 95    | 74    | 62    | 65    | 64   | 58   | 60   | 55   |
| Earnings per share   |        | 1.27  | 1.11  | 1.04  | 1.01  | 1.00 | .93  | .98  | .90  |
| Dividends per share  |        | .86   | .82   | .79   | .76   | .72  | .68  | .64  | .60  |
| Price                | high   | 24.4  | 22.0  | 19.0  | 19.0  | 19.7 | 18.3 | 18.1 | 18.2 |
|                      | low    | 19.2  | 16.6  | 13.7  | 14.6  | 14.3 | 13.9 | 11.0 | 10.2 |

# Pitney Bowes, Inc.

World Headquarters ❑ 1 Elmcroft Road ❑ Stamford, CT 06926–0700 ❑ (203) 351–6349 ❑ Dividend reinvestment plan available: (800) 648–8170 ❑ Web site: *www.pitneybowes.com* ❑ Ticker symbol: PBI ❑ Listed: NYSE ❑ S&P rating: A- ❑ Value Line financial strength rating: A

In 2004, Pitney Bowes said that eBay, The World's Online Marketplace, selected PBI as the technology provider for a completely browser-based online postage solution that gives both eBay.com and PayPal customers quick and easy access to shipping services. The new online postage solution simplifies the process of calculating and paying for postage and accessing shipping services offered by the U.S. Postal Service.

"We are very pleased to team up with eBay to deliver the world's first completely browser-based Internet postage application," said Neil Metviner, president, Pitney Bowes Direct, which serves the small business marketplace. "Our application represents the next generation of Internet postage technology. It is designed to deliver maximum customer convenience and postal revenue security. This solution is another step in our strategy to deliver innovative mailing solutions to an expanded customer set, including consumers and small businesses."

The new solution, which is based on Pitney Bowes Internet postage technology, enables customers to select a shipping option, print the shipping label, and pay for the postage via their PayPal account. This new streamlined process eliminates the need to download software, provide unique registration, and pre-fund a postage account. Once the label is purchased, both the buyer and seller are now able to track the delivery status of the package online.

"Now, without leaving the eBay or PayPal sites, our customers can simply purchase postage online and print shipping labels from their computer," said Gary Dillabough, vice president of eBay Strategic Partnerships.

"This technology provided by Pitney Bowes is an integral part of eBay's Online Postage solution, allowing us to make shipping more integrated, fast, and reliable for eBay buyers and sellers."

## Company Profile

Pitney Bowes is the world's leading provider of integrated mail and document management systems, services, and solutions. The $5-billion company helps organizations—both large and small—to efficiently and effectively manage their mission-critical mail and document flow in physical, digital, and hybrid formats.

Its solutions range from addressing software and metering systems to print stream management, electronic bill presentment, and pre-sort mail services. The company's eighty-plus years of technological leadership has produced many major innovations in the mailing industry and more than 3,500 active patents with applications in a variety of markets, including printing, shipping, encryption, and financial services. With about 33,000 employees worldwide, PBI serves more than 2 million businesses through direct and dealer operations.

Pitney Bowes operates in three business segments, as follows:

• Global Mailstream Solutions, Global Enterprise Solutions, and Capital Services. The Global Mailstream Solutions segment includes worldwide revenue and related expenses from the rental of postage meters and the sale, rental, and financing of mailing equipment, including mail finishing and software-based mail creation equipment.

In 2004, this segment's revenue increased 12 percent, and earnings before interest and taxes (EBIT) increased 8 percent, when compared with the prior year. Outside the U.S., revenue grew organically (*not counting acquisitions*) at a double-digit pace, due primarily to strong growth in Europe, led by excellent results in the United Kingdom.

- The Global Enterprise Solutions segment includes Pitney Bowes Management Services and Document Messaging Technologies.

In 2004, this segment had a revenue increase of 15 percent, while EBIT increased 36 percent, compared with 2003.

- The Capital Services segment consists of financing for non-Pitney Bowes equipment. In the fourth quarter of 2004, this operation's revenue declined 8 percent, and EBIT declined 29 percent due to a smaller asset base. During the latter part of the year, Pitney Bowes management indicated that it would spin off its external financing business.

The company maintains field service organizations in the United States and some other countries to provide support services to customers who have rented, leased, or purchased equipment.

## Shortcomings to Bear in Mind

- "Pitney Bowes remains the number one maker of postal meters in the world," said Matthew Lubanko, writing for the *Hartford Courant* on June 6, 2004. "And with a 62 percent share of the global market for postal meters, the company has a nearly three-to-one lead over its nearest rival: Neopost SA of Bagneux, France."

The article went on to say, "But a kingdom in the mailroom is not the secure throne that it once was. In just three years, annual volume of first-class letters has slipped 4.3 percent, from 103.5 billion in 2000 to 99 billion in 2003, according to the U.S. Postal Service, also a chief customer of Pitney Bowes.

"Many blame e-mail, and other electronic messaging systems, for reducing the flow of traditional mail. The mail decline has impelled Pitney Bowes to fight harder to retain old customers and attract new ones. Intensified competition has clipped profit margins—the pennies earned from each dollar in sales—by 32 percent over the last three years."

## Reasons to Buy

- "The company is in the forefront of a shift toward digital mailing systems," according to David R. Cohen, an analyst with *Value Line Investment Survey.* On January 14, 2005, he went on to say, "A migration from mechanical to electronic meters mandated by U.S. Postal Service regulations helped boost earnings considerably in the late Nineties. A similar move to digital meters has been under way since early 2002, and the switch ought to be mostly completed by the close of 2006."
- *Standard & Poor's Stock Reports* rated the stock a BUY on February 10, 2005. Megan Graham Hackett said, "We find the shares attractive based on our view of PBI's large recurring revenue stream, a leadership position within its market, and a better-than-average dividend yield of nearly 3 percent. In addition, we see a strengthening economy, synergies from recent acquisitions, and new product introductions focusing on digital technology leading to steady revenue growth and widening margins in coming periods."
- In late 2004, Pitney Bowes signed a definitive agreement to acquire a substantial portion of the assets of Ancora Capital & Management Group LLC, for about $35 million net of cash and assumed liabilities. Ancora is a provider of first class, standard letter, and international mail processing and pre-sort services with five operations in Southern California, Pennsylvania, and Maryland.

"This acquisition is another step in our evolution to deliver enhanced customer and shareholder value," said CEO Michael J. Critelli. "Pre-sort operations help customers prepare, sort and aggregate mail to earn postal discounts and expedite delivery. Our growing national pre-sort network helps customers be more successful by enhancing their ability to communicate more efficiently. This acquisition helps us to continue to increase the volume of mail we touch, grow the value we add to each mailpiece, provide more mail services and expand our presence in the mailstream."

Pitney Bowes initiated its strategic entry into the multibillion-dollar pre-sort industry in 2002. Ancora employs about 900 people and is headquartered in San Fernando, California.

- On July 20, 2004, Pitney Bowes announced the acquisition of Group 1 Software, Inc., at a net cost of $321 million. Group 1 is an industry leader in software that enhances mailing efficiency, data quality, and customer communications.

"We are pleased to complete the acquisition of Group 1," said Mr. Critelli. "Their industry-leading infrastructure, expertise and solutions will help us better serve our customers, while expanding our global reach, growing our mailstream participation and laying the foundation for profitable expansion in the customer communication management market."

Group 1, based in Lanham, Maryland, employs some 600 people worldwide, with sales offices in the United States, the United Kingdom and Europe, Japan, South Korea, Singapore, Malaysia, and China. It also has development centers in Lanham, Maryland; Austin, Texas; Minneapolis, Minnesota; Boulder, Colorado, Mountain View, California; Toronto, Canada; and London, England.

- On December 16, 2004, Pitney Bowes acquired Groupe MAG, a distributor of finishing equipment used by commercial printers, and production mail equipment, software, and service in France, Belgium, and Luxembourg. This business will be managed as a separate unit with the company's International operation.

"Today's transaction is another step in our strategy to enhance customer value and grow our business," said Mr. Critelli. "With this acquisition, we continue to extend our distribution capabilities and reconfirm our commitment to Document Messaging Technologies in our International markets."

For the fiscal year ended March 31, 2004, Groupe MAG generated revenue of Euros 43 million. In accordance with French labor law, the transaction received a positive opinion from Groupe MAG's employee representatives. The company has some 225 employees in six offices in France and one in Belgium.

Total assets: $9,821 million
Current ratio: 0.82
Common shares outstanding: 231 million
Return on 2004 shareholders' equity: 40.5%

| | 2004 | 2003 | 2002 | 2001 | 2000 | 1999 | 1998 | 1997 |
|---|---|---|---|---|---|---|---|---|
| Revenues (millions) | 4,957 | 4,577 | 4,410 | 4,122 | 3,881 | 4,433 | 4,220 | 4,100 |
| Net income (millions) | 594 | 569 | 572 | 556 | 626 | 630 | 568 | 526 |
| Earnings per share | 2.54 | 2.41 | 2.37 | 2.25 | 2.44 | 2.31 | 2.03 | 1.82 |
| Dividends per share | 1.22 | 1.20 | 1.18 | 1.16 | 1.14 | 1.02 | .90 | .80 |
| Price high | 47.0 | 42.8 | 44.4 | 44.7 | 54.1 | 73.3 | 66.4 | 45.8 |
| low | 38.9 | 29.5 | 28.5 | 32.0 | 24.0 | 40.9 | 42.2 | 26.8 |

# Praxair, Inc.

39 Old Ridgebury Road ❑ Danbury, CT 06810–5113 ❑ (203) 837–2354 ❑ Dividend reinvestment plan available: (800) 368–5948 ❑ Web site: *www.praxair.com* ❑ Listed: NYSE ❑ Ticker symbol: PX ❑ S&P rating: A ❑ Value Line financial strength rating: B++

In recent years, Praxair, the largest supplier of industrial gases in North and South America, has been the recipient of a host of honors:

• "The Best CEOs in America" from *Institutional Investor* magazine—Praxair's CEO Dennis Reilley tops the basic materials category, January 2004.

• "The Best CFOs in America," *Institutional Investor* magazine—Praxair's CFO, James Sawyer is among the top ten, February 2004

• "Best Managed Companies in America," *Forbes* magazine—Praxair headlines the chemical company section, January 2004.

• "Leader for the 21st Century," *Treasury and Risk Management* magazine— Praxair's CFO, James Sawyer, is one of the three selected, January 2004.

• "Top Governance Practices Rating," *Governancemetrics International,* July 2003 and February 2004.

• "Senior Financial Officer of the Year," *Chemical Week* magazine—Praxair's CFO, James Sawyer, April 2003

• "Most Admired Companies," *Fortune* magazine—Praxair ranked third among chemical companies, March 2003 and March 2004.

## Company Profile

Praxair, Inc. is a global, *Fortune* 500 company that supplies atmospheric, process and specialty gases, high-performance coatings, and related services and technologies.

Spun off to Union Carbide shareholders in June 1992, it is the largest producer of industrial gases in North and South America; it is the third-largest company of its kind in the world.

Praxair's primary products are: atmospheric gases—oxygen, nitrogen, argon, and rare gases (produced when air is purified, compressed, cooled, distilled and condensed), and process and specialty gases—carbon dioxide, helium, hydrogen, semiconductor process gases, and acetylene (produced as by-products of chemical production or recovered from natural gas).

The company also designs, engineers, and constructs cryogenic and noncryogenic supply systems. Praxair Surface Technologies is a subsidiary that applies metallic and ceramic coatings and powders to metal surfaces in order to resist wear, high temperatures and corrosion. Aircraft engines are its primary market, but it serves others, including the printing, textile, chemical, and primary metals markets, and provides aircraft engine and airframe component overhaul services. Praxair adopted its name in 1992, from the Greek word "praxis," or practical application, and "air," the company's primary raw material. PX was originally founded in 1907 when it was the first company to commercialize cryogenically separated oxygen. Over the near century of its existence, Praxair has remained a leader in the development of processes and technologies that have revolutionized the industrial gases industry. The company introduced the first distribution system for liquid gas in 1917, and developed on-site gas supply by the end of World War II. In the 1960s, Praxair introduced noncryogenic means of air separation, and since then has continued to introduce innovative applications technologies for various industries. PX holds almost 3,000 patents. Praxair serves a wide range of industries: food and beverages, healthcare, semiconductors, chemicals, refining, primary metals, and metal fabrication, as well as other areas of general industry.

## Shortcomings to Bear in Mind

- "We have a HOLD opinion on the shares," said *Standard & Poor's* analyst Richard O'Reilly, CFA, on February 4, 2005. "The stock's P/E multiple, based on our 2005 EPS (*Earnings per share*) estimate, is at what we view as an appropriate premium to that of the S&P 500, versus a discount prior to 2004. The company is concentrating on several less-capital-intensive, faster-growing global markets. We believe that a continuing pickup in the U.S. industrial economy will translate into strong U.S. volume growth."

## Reasons to Buy

- In June 2004, the company acquired Home Care Supply, Inc., the largest private domestic home respiratory and medical equipment provider, for $245 million. With annual sales of $170 million, the acquisition doubled Praxair's U.S. homecare business.
- On January 27, 2005, a major brokerage firm, Lehman Brothers, had this favorable assessment of Praxair:

  Summary

  1. Sales grew at a rate of 22 percent, year-over-year, driven mainly by strong volume growth in North America, South America, and especially Asia.
  2. The company's hydrogen business continues to be the leading growth platform. On-site hydrogen volumes were up 11 percent, year-over-year, as the two new plants began contributing to profits in mid-2004. The outlook for hydrogen growth remains strong beyond 2005–2006 as well.

  3. The PX outlook for 2005 remains strong, with the strongest growth expected in North American hydrogen and homecare, improvements in the South American industrial and export markets and electronics in Asia."

- In 2004, Praxair and CSPC, a joint venture between China National Offshore Oil Corporation (CNOOC) and Shell Petrochemicals Company Ltd., announced an agreement for Praxair to supply CSPC with its oxygen and nitrogen requirements for its new $4.3 billion integrated petrochemical complex in Daya Bay, Huizhou, in Guangdong Province, China.

  The heart of the complex is a world-scale condensate or naphtha cracker producing 800,000 tons per year of ethylene and 430,000 tons per year of propylene, integrated with downstream products. It will be the largest capital investment for a Sino-foreign joint venture project in China.

  Under the agreement, Praxair will supply high-purity oxygen and nitrogen from new air separation units that will be built adjacent to the CSPC site in the center of the new chemical enclave in Daya Bay Economic and Technical Development Zone. The supply of these products is scheduled to begin in May 2005. Praxair will also produce liquid oxygen, nitrogen and argon and distribute these products to customers in the rapidly growing Guangdong region.

- Hydrogen is part of a comprehensive portfolio of bulk and specialty gases, technologies and services Praxair provides refining and chemical customers worldwide. For example, Praxair supplies more than fifty refineries and petrochemical plants from its 280 miles of pipeline along the Texas and Louisiana Gulf Coast. Other Praxair pipeline enclaves serving these industries are situated in Ecorse, Michigan; Edmonton, Alberta,

Canada; Salvador, Brazil; Antwerp, Belgium; and Beijing, China.

- Beyond its longstanding supply of pure oxygen and bulk storage equipment to hospitals and other medical facilities worldwide, Praxair delivers respiratory therapy gases and equipment, and a host of on-site gas-management services, including asset, inventory, transaction and distribution management. Praxair's home oxygen services, moreover, provide respiratory patients with life support, as well as therapies to help with sleep disorders or other illnesses in the home environment.

- The company sees opportunities to differentiate its offering in the food and beverage segment, based on the need for higher standards of food safety. Praxair is bringing the potential to save more than 15 billion gallons of water and $70 million each year to the U.S. poultry processing industry through a water recycling system that helps increase production and reduce water consumption without compromising food safety.

- The sparkle in soft drinks, the freshness of pastries, the crunch in an apple—chances are, Praxair carbon dioxide or nitrogen had something to do with it. At Praxair's Food Technology Laboratory—the only one of its kind in the industry—technologies and equipment are developed and tested to assist bakers, meat processors, and specialty foods producers deliver products that retain their taste and freshness.

- In 2004, Praxair announced that it had installed and completed startup operations of its new ultra performance cryogenic spiral freezer at DESCO Inc. in Boisbriand, Quebec, Canada. The patented freezer technology benefits customers by extracting more cooling power from the cryogen by capturing more of the refrigeration potential available in the cryogenic vapor. At DESCO, the results have shown up to 30 percent more production in the same equipment footprint when compared with existing cryogenic spiral systems.

"We recognize the opportunity to increase productivity, reduce product yield loss and lower overall labor costs with the new Praxair freezing technology," said Guy Chevalier, DESCO president.

"We were excited to be able to present the ColdFront ultra performance concept to DESCO," said Praxair's Talaat Girgis, national food technology and marketing manager. "DESCO produces high quality deli products and further processed poultry products and, like many of our customers, understands the value of rapid cryogenic freezing to preserve product quality."

- "Praxair is making headway in several end markets, such as refinery hydrogen, healthcare, and electronics," said Edward Plank, writing for *Value Line Investment Survey* on March 18, 2005. "We look for growth in these areas to contribute to earnings going forward. Although the company's Surface Technologies division has held its head above water, it remains burdened by a lackluster aircraft industry, which has crimped demand for aviation repair. Once the aerospace industry recovers, the division should be in a position to reap good gains."

- On January 12, 2005, Argus Research Company had this favorable comment, according to Bill Selesky, "We continue to rate the shares of Praxair, Inc. as BUY. In addition to having an attractive valuation, the PX stock has the potential to post above-average earnings and margin growth over the short and long term."

Total assets: $9,878 million
Current ratio: 0.93
Common shares outstanding: 325 million
Return on 2004 shareholders' equity: 20.8%

| | 2004 | 2003 | 2002 | 2001 | 2000 | 1999 | 1998 | 1997 |
|---|---|---|---|---|---|---|---|---|
| Revenues (millions) | 6,594 | 5,613 | 5,128 | 5,158 | 5,043 | 4,639 | 4,833 | 4,735 |
| Net income (millions) | 697 | 585 | 548 | 432 | 432 | 441 | 425 | 416 |
| Earnings per share | 2.10 | 1.77 | 1.66 | 1.50 | 1.49 | 1.36 | 1.30 | 1.27 |
| Dividends per share | .60 | .46 | .38 | .34 | .31 | .28 | .25 | .22 |
| Price      high | 46.2 | 38.3 | 30.6 | 28.0 | 27.5 | 29.1 | 26.9 | 29.0 |
|            low | 34.5 | 25.0 | 22.4 | 18.3 | 15.2 | 16.0 | 15.3 | 19.6 |

Conservative Growth

# The Procter & Gamble Company

P. O. Box 599 ❑ Cincinnati, OH 45201–0599 ❑ (513) 983–2414 ❑ Direct dividend reinvestment plan available: (800) 764–7483 ❑ Web site: *www.pg.com* ❑ Listed: NYSE ❑ Fiscal years end June 30 ❑ Ticker symbol: PG ❑ S&P rating: A ❑ Value Line financial strength rating: A++

On January 28, 2005, Procter & Gamble announced that it would acquire Gillette Company for about $57 billion. "This merger is going to create the greatest consumer products company in the world," said Warren E. Buffett, CEO of Berkshire Hathaway, Inc., Gillette's largest shareholder. "It's a dream deal."

Here is what Gillette looks like:

Founded in 1901, The Gillette Company is the world leader in male grooming, a category that includes blades, razors and shaving preparations. Gillette also holds the number one position worldwide in selected female grooming products, such as wet shaving products and hair epilation devices.

The company holds the number one position worldwide in manual and power toothbrushes and is the world leader in alkaline batteries.

According to the company, "Our focus is on placing resources behind Gillette's three core businesses: grooming, batteries and oral care. Our core businesses account for nearly 80 percent of our sales and 90 percent of our profits. We are—in all three—the undisputed global leader.

"Some of our core brands include:

- Gillette Mach3
- Gillette for Women Venus
- Gillette Series
- Right Guard
- Duracell Copper Top
- Oral-B
- Braun Oral-B
- Braun"

Gillette manufacturing operations are conducted at thirty-four facilities in fifteen countries. Products are distributed through wholesalers, retailers, and agents in more than 200 countries and territories.

## Company Profile

Procter & Gamble dates back to 1837, when William Procter and James Gamble began making soap and candles in Cincinnati. The company's first major product introduction took place in 1879, when it launched Ivory soap. Since then, P&G has traditionally created a host of block-buster products that have made the company a cash-generating machine.

Procter & Gamble is a uniquely diversified consumer-products company with a strong global presence. P&G today markets its broad line of products to nearly 5 billion consumers in more than 160 countries.

Procter & Gamble is a recognized leader in the development, manufacturing and marketing of superior quality laundry, cleaning, paper, personal care, food, beverage, and healthcare products, including prescription pharmaceuticals.

Among the company's nearly 300 brands are Tide, Always, Whisper, Didronel, Pro-V, Oil of Olay, Pringles, Ariel, Crest, Pampers, Pantene, Vicks, Bold, Dawn, Head & Shoulders, Cascade, Iams, Zest, Bounty, Comet, Scope, Old Spice, Folgers, Charmin, Tampax, Downy, Cheer, and Prell.

Procter & Gamble is a huge company, with 2004 sales of more than $51 billion. In the same fiscal year (which ended June 30, 2004), Earnings per share advanced from $1.85 to $2.32. Dividends also climbed—as they have for many years—from $0.82 to $0.93. The company has nearly 110,000 employees working in more than eighty countries.

## Shortcomings to Bear in Mind

- "Just consider this fact: In seven of the nine largest mergers in history that were completed, the acquirer's share price is down more than 46 percent from right before the merger was announced, according to research company FactSet Mergerstat," said Rachel Beck, writing for *The Associated Press* on February 5, 2005. That certainly doesn't sound too rewarding for anyone waiting for all those promising synergies to kick in."

  She went on to say, "Still, P&G and Gillette executives made lots of lofty promises when announcing their deal last week. They said the combined company will develop new products, boost

its international presence and use its increased clout to work on advertising and product deals with retailers."

- "Retailers are sometimes competitors as well as partners," said Mr. Lafley. "Their own brands are growing as the retailers, themselves, grow. Private labels, or store brands, strive to match innovation quickly and try to present a compelling value alternative in many categories. This is healthy, in my opinion. It requires that we continue to lead innovation and price P&G products competitively. Further, the growing strength of store brands underscores the importance of always being the number one or number two brand in any category. Brands that can't maintain this leadership stature will find it difficult to compete effectively with the best store brands. Based on our internal global share measures, we have the number one or number two brand in seventeen of our nineteen key global categories—categories that account for about 70 percent of sales and earnings. P&G is in a strong position, and ready to become an even better retail partner."

## Reasons to Buy

Procter & Gamble exceeded all its financial goals in fiscal 2004:

- Volume of goods sold was up 17 percent.
- Sales reached $51.4 billion, up 19 percent.
- Earnings climbed to $6.5 billion, a gain of 25 percent.
- Earnings per share advanced to $2.32, up 25 percent.
- Free cash flow climbed to $7.3 billion, or 113 percent of earnings.
- Annualized dividends advanced by 13 percent.
- Growth was broad-based. All five global business units delivered at or above the sales goal; four of five were at or above the earnings goal.

  What's more, cumulative results over the past three years were equally impressive:

- P&G's 2004's cumulative sales in that period grew by 30 percent. Fiscal 2004 marked the first time in company history that annual revenues exceeded $50 billion.
- Earnings per share expanded by 40 percent, cumulatively, compared with three years earlier.
- P&G businesses generated more than $20 billion in cumulative free cash flow.
- Most important, Procter & Gamble has delivered cumulative shareholder return of 81 percent over that three-year span, and the price of P&G's stock has increased more than 70 percent. In fact, over the past four years, cumulative shareholder return is more than 100 percent.
- P&G is the only company to appear on all seven *Fortune* magazine company lists in 2003, including:
  - Best Companies to Work For
  - Most Admired
  - Best Companies for Minorities
  - MBA's Top Employers
- In a recent U.S. survey by Cannondale Associates, retailers were asked to rank manufacturers on a number of competencies. P&G was ranked number one in virtually every category:
  - Clearest company strategy
  - Brands most important to retailers
  - Best brand marketers overall
  - Most innovative marketing programs
- In its April 5, 2004 edition, *Business Week* ranked Procter & Gamble No. 26 on its annual list of *The Business Week Fifty.*
- P&G made the biggest deal in its history in March 2003 with the purchase of a controlling interest in the German hair care company, Wella AG, strengthening its position in the fast-growing global hair care business. The deal exceeds the 2001 purchase of Clairol for $4.95 billion. In this transaction, Procter & Gamble paid $5.75 billion for a 77.6 percent interest in Wella. Professional salon hair care sales are $10 billion a year worldwide. Wella estimates that it has a 22 percent global share—number two behind L'Oreal (a French company regarded as a model of best practices in the sector), which is P&G's biggest competitor. Overall retail hair care is a $34 billion industry worldwide.

  Mr. Lafley says that Procter won't disturb Wella's salon business, the company's crown jewel. Unlike the purchase of Clairol, this transaction puts Procter & Gamble in the business of serving a new type of customer: professional hair dressers. Wella generated half of its $3.6 billion sales in 2002 selling its products in salons. Meanwhile, P&G will do what it knows best—plow Wella's shampoo, conditioner, and styling brands through mass-market retailers such as Wal-Mart.

  Finally, Mr. Lafley intends to incorporate Wella's fragrance brands, which include Gucci, Rochas, and Escada, into its own fragrance business, where it licenses brands like Hugo Boss and Lacoste. This strategy will enhance the geographic reach of Wella's brands.
- Procter & Gamble is known for product innovation. More than 8,000 scientists and researchers are accelerating the pace of new products. The company has a global network of eighteen technical centers in nine countries on four continents. What's more, P&G holds more than 27,000 patents and applies for 3,000 more each year. Not surprisingly, the company is among the ten patent-producing companies in the world—well ahead of any other consumer-products manufacturer.
- Procter & Gamble believes in product quality. One of the reasons given for the company's problems in 2000 was its refusal to get into the lower-quality, lower-cost private-label business. That just goes against the grain.

P&G believes that the consumer will reward even minor product advantages, and it will not launch a brand if it does not have a competitive advantage. Then, it will continually improve its products and make every effort to maintain that advantage. Tide, for example, has been improved more than seventy times over the years.

- While most stocks have been a huge disappointment since the market hit a peak on March 24, 2000, Procter & Gamble has made an impressive comeback. Much of its recent success can be attributed to its CEO, Alan G. Lafley who took the reins of the company in June of 2000, when it was "the sort of ink-stained mess you'd find in a Tide commercial," according to Katrina Brooker, writing for *Fortune* magazine in the fall of 2002.

In the words of Ms. Brooker, "Since he's been P&G's chief, Lafley has managed to pull off what neither of his two predecessors

could—turn around the global behemoth. And he did it in the midst of a world economic slowdown to boot."

Ms. Brooker also points out that Mr. Lafley "is a listener, not a storyteller. He's likable but not awe-inspiring. He's the type of guy who gets excited in the mop isle of a grocery store. His plan to fix P&G isn't anything ground-breaking, but rather a straightforward, back-to-the-basics tack. And so far it's worked. He has rallied his troops not with big speeches and dazzling promises, but by hearing them out (practically) one at a time. It's a little dull, perhaps. Workaday dull."

In another part of the *Fortune* article, Katrina Brooker said, "Lafley, who got his start at P&G a quarter century ago as a brand assistant for Joy dishwashing liquid, wouldn't be all that interesting to watch—were it not for the fact that he's so darn good at his job."

Total assets: $57,048 million
Current ratio: 0.77
Common shares outstanding: 5,188 million
Return on 2004 shareholders' equity: 38.7%

|  | 2004 | 2003 | 2002 | 2001 | 2000 | 1999 | 1998 | 1997 |
|---|---|---|---|---|---|---|---|---|
| Revenues (millions) | 51,407 | 43,377 | 40,238 | 39,244 | 39,951 | 38,125 | 37,154 | 35,764 |
| Net income (millions) | 6,481 | 5,186 | 4,352 | 2,922 | 4,230 | 4,148 | 3,780 | 3,415 |
| Earnings per share | 2.32 | 1.85 | 1.54 | 1.04 | 1.24 | 1.30 | 1.28 | 1.22 |
| Dividends per share | .93 | .82 | .76 | .70 | .64 | .57 | .51 | .45 |
| Price      high | 57.4 | 50.0 | 47.4 | 40.9 | 59.2 | 57.8 | 47.4 | 41.7 |
|             low | 48.9 | 39.8 | 37.1 | 28.0 | 26.4 | 41.0 | 32.6 | 25.9 |

Aggressive Growth

# Progressive Corporation

6300 Wilson Mills Road ❑ Mayfield Village, OH 44143 ❑ (440) 446–2851 ❑ Dividend reinvestment plan not available ❑ Web site: *www.progressive.com* ❑ Listed: NYSE ❑ Ticker symbol: PGR ❑ S&P rating: B+ ❑ Value Line financial strength rating: A

"The Progressive story isn't familiar because car insurance is hardly a scintillating topic, and the company doesn't talk much to Wall Street or the media," said Andrew Bary, in an article in *Barron's* on November 1, 2004. "But Progressive's record speaks for itself.

Since the sixty-seven-year-old company went public in 1971, its shares have risen more than 1,000-fold, matching the extraordinary record of Warren Buffett's Berkshire Hathaway. An initial purchase of 100 shares at $18 would now be worth over $2 million, excluding dividends. Progressive shares fetch a record $92, eight times their price a decade ago, giving the insurer a market value of $18 billion."

Mr. Bary goes on to say, "Progressive is a rarity; an innovative high-growth financial company that has avoided major trouble. The third-largest U.S. auto-policy issuer, it consistently has the industry's highest profit margins, while offering low rates to motorists. It has defied convention, profitably serving even bad drivers and deftly handling the conflict of offering insurance both through agents and directly, via telephone and the Internet."

## Company Profile

Progressive Corporation is an insurance holding company with sixty-eight subsidiaries, one mutual insurance company affiliate, and one reciprocal insurance company affiliate. The company's insurance subsidiaries and affiliates provide personal automobile insurance and other specialty property-casualty insurance and related services throughout the United States.

Progressive is the third-largest writer of personal auto insurance in the United States, with about 7 percent of the market.

The company has a conservative balance sheet and pays a minimal dividend. Management owns about 10 percent of the outstanding shares. This is far more than most large companies and gives company executives a solid reason to do a good job for shareholders.

Its property-casualty insurance products protect its customers against collision and physical damage to their motor vehicles and liability to others for personal injury or property damage arising out of the use of those vehicles.

The company's noninsurance subsidiaries generally support the company's insurance and investment operations. Progressive offers a number of personal and commercial property-casualty insurance products primarily related to motor vehicles.

Historically, the bulk of the company's core business consisted of nonstandard insurance programs, which provide coverage for accounts rejected or canceled by other companies. However, for the past fifteen years, as part of a strategy to expand its share of the personal automobile insurance market, PGR has been underwriting standard and preferred-risk automobile insurance coverage.

## Shortcomings to Bear in Mind

- On February 9, 2005, *Standard & Poor's Stock Reports* gave Progressive an unenthusiastic HOLD rating. Catherine A. Seifert said, "While we acknowledge PGR's above-average rate of premium growth and its historically superior (to peers) underwriting results, we remain concerned about the sustainability of both of these trends. At current levels, the shares trade at a premium to peers, both on a forward price/earnings and a price/book basis. Consequently, we would not add to holdings."
- On February 11, 2005, the Argus Research Company said to SELL Progressive. David Anthony explained, "On February 10, the property casualty insurance industry, along with companies in other industries achieved a victory when the Senate approved a measure restricting class-action lawsuits. These lawsuits have covered a multitude of disciplines and industries. Within the property casualty insurance industry, the suits have typically focused on medical malpractice, directors' and officers' liability, and product liability. Because of these lawsuits, legal costs for many companies have soared."
- In a recent nine-month period, insiders (such as officers and board members) were net sellers of their own shares. In that

span, there were twenty-two sales—and no purchases.

## Reasons to Buy

- "Glenn Renwick (CEO of Progressive) is proof that nothing succeeds like a successor," said Andrew Bary, writing for *Barron's* on March 28, 2005. "Since 2001 he has ably taken the place of Peter Lewis, the force behind Progressive's rise over three decades from a tiny Cleveland outfit to the country's third-largest insurer. When Renwick, 49, took over, Progressive was going through a rough patch because it had underpriced policies. Renwick, a statistics whiz from New Zealand, addressed the problems, and profits surged to $7.40 a share last year, from $0.25 in 2000."

- "Auto insurers had a smooth ride last year, thanks in part to rising rates and fewer accident claims," said *BusinessWeek* in an article dated April 4, 2005. "But with its low-cost advantage and high-touch service, Progressive zoomed ahead—fattening underwriting margins from 12.7 percent to 14.9 percent and boosting net income by 31 percent. Revenue growth . . . is likely to slow this year as cash-flush competitors chase new business and drive down prices. But with innovations such as Progressive's 'concierge' service, which handles nearly every aspect of a customer's car repairs, the potholes should be minor."

- "On a March 3 conference call, Progressive provided a more optimistic outlook for growth than it had previously, noting that early indications from its new advertising campaign were good and that it may see double-digit growth in its direct campaign in 2005," said an analyst with Lehman Brothers (a major brokerage firm) on March 4, 2005. "We are reiterating our OVERWEIGHT recommendation." That translates into BUY.

- "Investment income should gradually rise over the next few years," said Randy Shrikishun, writing for *Value Line* on December 24, 2004. "The rising interest-rate environment along with the continuous increase of invested assets will probably aid in lifting investment income by roughly 10 percent annually in 2005 and 2006. We think that higher interest rates will lead management to shift some assets to higher-yielding investments and to diversify the portfolio further to limit the greater risks."

- "Progressive is perhaps best known for selling insurance over the phone and Internet—mostly because its marketing campaigns typically focus on those channels—but the Mayfield Village, Ohio company sells about two-thirds of its policies through independent agents," said Christopher Oster, writing for the *Wall Street Journal* on November 4, 2004. "Progressive's ad campaign will stress what it sees as the positive aspects of working through an independent agent—the most obvious advantage being that an independent agent can offer policies from multiple insurers. State Farm and Allstate sell the policies through captive agents who peddle only their policies. Consumers buy about 80 percent of their auto insurance through agents, and about two-thirds of that is sold through captive agents.

  "'Ultimately that's where the business is—within the captive distribution channel,' said Bob Williams, head of Progressive's agency business. 'We've surmised there are a lot of potential customers out there we're not getting a shot at, and we're going to go after them.'"

- Progressive has been first in the industry to offer such innovations as:
  - Drive in claims. (1937)
  - Immediate Response claims service, becoming the only auto insurance company to serve customers where and when they need it most—at the accident scene. (1990)
  - Free rate comparison services, making it the only company to offer "apples to

apples" comparison rates from Progressive and up to three other companies. (1994)

- A fleet of 2,600 Immediate Response vehicles fitted with laptop computers, intelligent software, and wireless access to the Internet and the company's claims department. (1994)
- The first insurance company to go online with a Web site—w*ww. progressive.com*. (1995)
- The first to sell insurance online at Progressive.com, allowing customers to purchase auto policies in real-time over the Internet. (1997)
- The first to introduce interactive customer service on the Web with personal.Progressive.com. (1998)
- A patented insurance product that determines rates based primarily on how much, when, and where you drive. (1998)
- The first insurance company to sell online boat and motorcycle coverage. (2000)
- The first insurance company to offer instant online quotes for RV insurance. (2000)
- Wireless access to Progressive.com via mobile phones and personal digital assistants—allowing customers to make payments, check claims history, and contact customer service. (2000)
- The first publicly held company to report underwriting results monthly. (2001)

- The first insurance company to offer insurance for the Segway Human Transporter. (2003)
- First insurance company to open "Claims Service Centers" which combine retail-like front office space with body shop-line space where claims representatives inspect vehicles and prepare estimates. Progressive is the first to handle the entire claims/repair process, providing one-stop convenience and peace of mind to consumers in select markets around the country. (2003)
- Consumers can purchase Progressive auto insurance through more than 30,000 independent agencies around the country, making the company the largest writer of auto insurance through independent agencies.
- In 2002, the Web Marketing Association named Progressive.com "Best Insurance Web Site" of more than 1,300 sites judged.
- Progressive was named to the annual list of "Fast 50 Champions of Innovation" in the March 2003 issue of *Fast Company*.
- Progressive is willing to abandon big markets if condition aren't right. It left New Jersey and Massachusetts, two states that make it tough for insurers to earn reasonable returns. And it withdrew from California in 1988, after voters approved a proposition that rolled back insurance rates. The company went back into the Golden State in 1993, but its share there is only 3 percent, less than half of its national rate.

Total assets: $17,184 million
Property and casualty combined ratio: 84.6%
Common shares outstanding: 200 million
Return on 2004 shareholders' equity: 32.4%

| | 2004 | 2003 | 2002 | 2001 | 2000 | 1999 | 1998 | 1997 |
|---|---|---|---|---|---|---|---|---|
| Assets (millions) | 17,184 | 16,282 | 13,564 | 11,122 | 10,052 | 9,705 | 8,463 | 7,560 |
| Net income (millions) | 1,649 | 1,245 | 718 | 411 | 66 | 297 | 457 | 400 |
| Earnings per share | 7.63 | 5.65 | 3.22 | 1.83 | .30 | 1.33 | 2.04 | 1.77 |
| Dividends per share | .11 | .10 | .10 | .09 | .09 | .09 | .08 | .08 |
| Price high | 97.3 | 84.7 | 60.5 | 50.6 | 37.0 | 58.1 | 57.3 | 40.3 |
| low | 73.1 | 46.3 | 44.8 | 27.4 | 15.0 | 22.8 | 31.3 | 20.5 |

# RPM International, Inc.

P. O. Box 777 ❑ 2628 Pearl Road ❑ Medina, OH 44258 ❑ (330) 273–8820 ❑ Direct dividend reinvestment plan available: (800) 988–5238 ❑ Web site: *www.rpminc.com* ❑ Listed: NYSE ❑ Fiscal years end May 30 ❑ Ticker symbol: RPM ❑ S&P rating: A- ❑ Value Line financial strength rating: B

An old fable tells of a traveler who was strolling down a road when he came upon a man carrying a basket full of rocks. "What are you doing?" the traveler asked. "I have no idea," the worker replied. "They told me to start hauling, so I did—some life I have!"

The traveler walked a few more yards and came upon another man carrying a basket of rocks. "What are you doing?" he asked again. "I'm getting paid to drag these rocks up the mountain," the laborer said.

Further on, a third man toting a basket of rocks came into view. "What are you doing?" the traveler asked yet again. The response: "My fellow workers and I are building a cathedral and, when we are finished, it will be the most spectacular cathedral in the world."

"RPM is not a monolith, but a mosaic of superior products, services, technologies, companies, and, of course, people," said CEO Frank C. Sullivan in early fiscal 2005. "Just as a cathedral is erected stone by stone, so these individual elements have combined over the decades to produce year upon year of record growth.

"Our cathedral began with the roof coating Alumanation, the first product of the company my grandfather founded in 1947. In the years since, the RPM portfolio of products has grown larger and stronger as we have expanded our businesses and market share through strategic acquisitions and continued product innovation.

Mr. Sullivan also said, "We marked another year of strong financial performance and notable operational accomplishments in fiscal 2004, our fifty-seventh consecutive record year of growth.

"We achieved revenue growth of 12 percent, to a record $2.3 billion. Roughly 7 percent of this growth was internal, exceeding our 5 percent target. Acquisitions contributed another 3 percent, and favorable foreign exchange rates accounted for the remainder."

Mr. Sullivan went on to say, "We set out to increase our operating margins in fiscal 2004, and we succeeded despite rising raw material costs, largely because we drove productivity improvements in our manufacturing plants and leveraged our purchasing power in the marketplace.

"In a now-familiar sign of our strong cash generation, we raised our dividend for the thirtieth consecutive year. Raising our dividend annually is a long-term commitment, and companies like RPM are now more respected than ever by investors who value the dependability and compounding return that a consistently growing dividend payment represents."

## Company Profile

RPM International, Inc., a holding company, owns subsidiaries that are world leaders in specialty coatings serving both industrial and consumer markets. RPM has 87,000 shareholders, 7,900 employees, and hundreds of independent sales and technical representatives.

The company's products are sold in more than 130 countries and are manufactured at sixty-eight plant locations in seventeen countries.

### RPM's Industrial Maintenance Products

RPM's industrial customers are served by: waterproofing products, including Tremco roofing systems, Alumanation roofing coatings, Paraseal membranes and Vulkem, Dymeric and Monile sealants; corrosion protection coatings sold under the brand names of Carboline, Plasite, Mathys, Westfield, and TCI; Dryvit exterior insulation finishing systems (EIFS); Stonhard and Duracon industrial and commercial floor coatings; and specialized industrial products, including Day-Glo fluorescent colorants and pigments; Wolman industrial lumber treatments; Fibergrate and Chemgrate fiberglass reinforced plastic grating; and Euco concrete admixtures sold by Euclid Chemical Company.

## RPM's Consumer Products

Consumers, primarily in North America, are served by the company's do-it-yourself home improvement coatings and related products, including: Rust-Oleum and Stops-Rust rust-preventative coatings and decorative coatings marketed under the brands of Painter's Touch, American Accents, and others; the Zinsser family of primer-sealers, including B-I-N, Bulls Eye 1-2-3, Perma-White Mildew Proof Paint, and Cover-Stain; Zinsser's wall covering preparation and removal products, including DIF, Shieldz, and PaperTiger; Bondex and Plastic Wood patch and repair products; Wolman desk coatings, sealants, and brighteners; Thibaut wall coverings; Bondo and Masson auto repair compounds and Mar-Hyde auto body paints and specialty products for the automotive aftermarket; Varathane, Watco, Mohawk, Guardian, and Chemical Coatings woodworking and wood finishing products; the Testors and Floquil brands of model kits, coating, and accessories for the hobbyist market; Pettit, Woolsey, and Z-Spar marine coatings; and DAP caulks and sealants.

## Shortcomings to Bear in Mind

- "After the current litigation fund is exhausted, probably in 2007, it is likely that the creation of an additional fund will be necessary," said Edward C. Muztafago, writing for *Value Line Investment Survey* on March 18, 2005. "Asbestos claims are apt to continue through the current decade. The size of the allotment is, however, unquantifiable. With the successful passing of legislation to constrain many class-action suits to the federal court system, the prospects for the proposed law limiting payouts on asbestos claims is somewhat brighter. The success or failure of this proposed law would have a major effect upon future profitability."

## Reasons to Buy

- John F. Hingher, CFA, an analyst with *Standard & Poor's Stock Reports,* had a more positive outlook on RPM, despite the asbestos problem. On January 10, 2005, he said: "RPM has historically been able to deliver consistent earnings growth regardless of economic conditions due to its diverse product portfolio serving both the industrial and consumer end markets.

  "Our BUY recommendation is based, in part, on our view of improving end markets, powerful cash flow, and improving visibility regarding potential asbestos-related expenses, as well as RPM's current yield of 3.2 percent and its record of increasing dividends for thirty consecutive years."

- RPM has a solid record of growth. In the 1994–2004 period, Earnings per share advanced from $0.57 to $1.22, a compound annual growth rate of 7.9 percent. In the same 10-year span, Dividends per share expanded from $0.33 to $0.55, a growth rate of 5.2 percent. Even though this is not a spectacular pace, the stock should be considered a good choice for a combination of growth and income, since the dividend yield is well above average.

- At the heart of RPM's growth strategy is its acquisition program, which has accounted for roughly half of the company's historic growth. Having completed more than 100 acquisitions in the last forty years, RPM is recognized as an industry consolidator.

Within the past two years, RPM's acquisition strategy has driven the completion of twelve such acquisitions, enabling the company to enter new markets, integrate new product lines, and augment its European base.

RPM has become the leading manufacturer of water-proofing products for new residential construction in North America, thanks to the addition of what is now known as Tremco Barrier Solutions.

This growing $38-million business offers proprietary, spray-applied membranes and systems under such well-known brand names as Tuff-N-Dri and Watchdog Waterproofing.

Fulfilling a goal to expand its European presence, RPM Europe S.A. made two modest, but important, acquisitions in fiscal 2004: Ecoloc N.V./Lock-Tile Belgium N.V., a commercial and industrial tile flooring manufacturer, and Compakta/Pactan, a German-based producer of specialty silicone-based adhesives, joint fillers, and sealers.

Total assets: $2,353 million
Current ratio: 2.08
Common shares outstanding: 116 million
Return on 2004 shareholders' equity: 15.3%

|  | 2004 | 2003 | 2002 | 2001 | 2000 | 1999 | 1998 | 1997 |
|---|---|---|---|---|---|---|---|---|
| Revenues (millions) | 2,342 | 2,083 | 1,986 | 2,008 | 1,954 | 1,712 | 1,615 | 1,351 |
| Net income (millions) | 142 | 123 | 102 | 63 | 79 | 95 | 88 | 78 |
| Earnings per share | 1.22 | 1.06 | .97 | .62 | .73 | .86 | .84 | .76 |
| Dividends per share | .55 | .52 | .50 | .50 | .49 | .46 | .44 | .41 |
| Price       high | 19.9 | 16.5 | 17.9 | 15.0 | 11.3 | 16.5 | 18.0 | 16.8 |
|              low | 13.3 | 9.1 | 11.6 | 7.9 | 7.8 | 9.9 | 12.8 | 12.5 |

Conservative Growth

# Ruby Tuesday, Inc.

150 West Church Avenue ❑ Maryville, TN 37801 ❑ (865) 379–5700 ❑ Web site: *www.ruby-tuesday.com* ❑ Dividend reinvestment plan not available ❑ Fiscal years end first Tuesday after May 30 ❑ Listed: NYSE ❑ Ticker symbol: RI ❑ Standard & Poor's rating: B+ ❑ Value Line financial strength rating: B++

Since its inception in 1972, Ruby Tuesday, a key component of the casual dining segment, has consistently expanded its chain of restaurants, as it did once again in fiscal 2004. Some of the highlights of that year follow:

• Diluted Earnings per share increased 20.6 percent, to $1.64, up from $1.36.

• Net income increased 24.3 percent, to $110,009,000, from $88,484,000.

• Sales at franchise (including franchise partnership and traditional franchise) Ruby Tuesday restaurants totaled $453,983,000 and $387,592,000 for fiscal year 2004 and fiscal year 2003, respectively. These sales are the basis for determining royalty fees included in franchise income on the company's income statement.

• Same-store sales increased 2.3 percent at company-owned Ruby Tuesday restaurants and 4 percent at its domestic franchised units.

• Return on equity was 23.4 percent, once again among the highest in the industry, and especially significant because Ruby Tuesday has about twice as many company-owned restaurants as it does franchised outlets. *(Return on equity is a key measure of management's ability. Anything over 15 percent is considered good.)*

• Pre-tax margins, again among the highest in the industry, increased to 16.4 percent, from 14.9 percent in 2003—and up from 5.9 percent seven years ago.

• Fifty company-owned Ruby Tuesday restaurants were opened, and six were closed.

• Forty franchise restaurants were opened, and five were closed.

• The company exercised its right to acquire an additional 49 percent interest in four of the franchise partnerships during the year. As of June 1, 2004, the company held a 50 percent interest in thirteen franchise partnerships collectively, operating 137 Ruby Tuesday restaurants.

• The company repurchased 1.2 million shares of its common stock. *(Whenever a company repurchases its own stock, the Earnings per share automatically increase— although total earnings are not affected.)*

## Company Profile

Ruby Tuesday, Inc. owns and operates Ruby Tuesday casual dining restaurants. The company also franchises the Ruby Tuesday concept in selected domestic and international markets. As of July 14, 2004, the company owned and operated 484 restaurants, while U.S. franchisees and international franchisees operated 216 and 36 restaurants, respectively. The Ruby Tuesday chain includes restaurants in 41 states, Washington, D.C., Puerto Rico, and twelve foreign countries.

The first Ruby Tuesday restaurant was opened in 1972 in Knoxville, Tennessee. The Ruby Tuesday concept, which consisted of sixteen units, was acquired by Morrison Restaurants Inc. in 1982.

During the following years, Morrison added other casual dining concepts, including the internally developed American Café. In 1995, Morrison completed the acquisition of Tias Inc., a chain of Tex-Mex restaurants. In a spin-off transaction that took place in March 1996, shareholders of Morrison approved the distribution of two separate businesses of Morrison to its shareholders. In conjunction with the spin-off, Morrison was reincorporated in the state of Georgia and changed its name to Ruby Tuesday, Inc.

Ruby Tuesday restaurants are casual, full-service restaurants with warm woods, whimsical artifacts and classic Tiffany-style lamps which create a comfortable, nostalgic look and feel. The menu is based on variety, with something for just about everyone. Some of Ruby Tuesday's most popular entree items, which are prepared fresh daily are: fajitas, ribs, chicken, steak, seafood, pasta, burgers, soups, sandwiches, the company's signature salad bar, and signature Tallcake desserts in strawberry and chocolate varieties. Entrees range in price from $6.49 to $16.99.

## Shortcomings to Bear in Mind

▪ According to some analysts, there is some risk here, which include rising food and labor costs that could cause margins to narrow. Then, too, the company might suffer from the aggressive expansion by its competitors, which could hurt operating earnings in the bar and grill segment of the entire casual dining segment.

## Reasons to Buy

▪ Growth in the casual-dining category of food service, in which Ruby Tuesday is a major national player, has outpaced the entire restaurant industry and is projected to continue to do so. The bar-and-grill segment, where Ruby Tuesday is one of the four leading brands, represents about half of all casual dining sales.

According to CEO Sandy Beall, "This segment is projected to continue to grow an annual compound rate of 9 percent, compared to a projected rate of 6 percent for the overall casual-dining category, with the majority of new units coming from large national chains–like ours. And while the total number of casual-dining units has remained basically flat in recent years, unit growth by major chains has continued growing, and the number of independents and small chains has declined.

"Casual-dining chains currently have a 30 percent market share, and we believe their share in the coming years will mirror that of the fast-food category, where chains now represent 66 percent of total outlets.

"With continued opportunity for significant growth, our developing strategy includes a focus on opening low-risk, high-return company-owned restaurants in markets in the eastern United States where we have current units that are proven successes."

Mr. Beall went on to say, "Every potential new site is visited and approved or rejected by the CEO, and each new restaurant is led by a managing partner who invests in the potential and the performance of his or her unit."

- Earnings per share have advanced at a good clip since 1996, climbing from $0.28 to $1.64, a compound annual growth rate of 24.7 percent.

- Dennis Milton, an analyst with *Standard & Poor's Company Reports,* had this favorable comment on January 10, 2005: "Our recommendation is BUY. We view RI as well-positioned, based on its expansion plan, to capitalize on favorable demographic fundamentals that should drive strong sales growth in the casual dining sector for several years."

- "The recent launch of a television advertising campaign should increase brand awareness," said Warren Thorpe, writing for *Value Line Investment Survey* on December 10, 2004. "Management commissioned a study that found that 68 percent of consumers in the markets Ruby serves are unaware of the brand name. Given that, we think TV advertising has a lot of potential to bring traffic through the door.

"Ruby Tuesday stock has long-term appeal. By our estimation, share profits are likely to advance on average by about 16 to 17 percent annually over the next three to five years."

- "Americans are dining out again, putting an end to the worst downturn in the restaurant business in a decade," said Katy McLaughlin, in the *Wall Street Journal* on March 30, 2004. "After a sharp downturn in sales growth that lasted three years, customers are returning to the table as a result of a healthier economy and an uptick in consumer confidence. The largest chains are reporting 5 percent to 6 percent sales growth in January and February compared with the year-earlier period, says market research firm NPD Group." She went on to say, "Fast-food establishments and major chains like Olive Garden, a unit of Darden Restaurants, are rebounding the fastest."

- According to Mr. Beall, "Our menu will continually improve through evolution, not revolution. Twice a year, we enhance existing products, add new choices, and simplify preparation to assure consistency and improve speed of service. This year we added more choices for health-conscious guests with Ruby Tuesday Smart Eating that includes more than thirty low-carb items and more than twenty lower-fat, lower-calories dishes. We also provide nutrition information and a guide to a healthier lifestyle on the tables in every one of our restaurants. We have quickly become the leader in healthy eating choices in the casual dining segment, and we intend to keep it that way."

- Mr. Beall commented on the care and training of employees. "Because approximately 80 percent of our managers come from within the ranks of hourly team members, we have to be good at training and development. We are 100 percent committed to take care of the people who take care of our guests. We do that by offering healthcare benefits from the first day an employee joins our team, with performance-based compensation and stock options and a career pathway that certifies competency and enables outstanding performers to become future leaders of the company.

"All of our general managers, district sales and standard partners, regional directors and vice presidents, and the 'A' players in our performance management system spend time throughout the year at Wow University (WOW-U), our training facility in Maryville, Tennessee. They are hands-on participants in skill-development classes and workplace simulations. They are assessed for readiness and tested for certification before they are promoted to new levels of responsibility and ownership. WOW-U is also where new initiatives and processes are presented before being rolled out to our restaurants."

Total assets: $919 million
Current ratio: 0.65
Common shares outstanding: 67 million
Return on 2004 shareholders' equity: 23.4%

|  | | 2004 | 2003 | 2002 | 2001 | 2000 | 1999 | 1998 | 1997 |
|---|---|---|---|---|---|---|---|---|---|
| Revenues (millions) | | 1,041 | 914 | 833 | 790 | 798 | 722 | 711 | 655 |
| Net income (millions) | | 110 | 88.5 | 58.3 | 59.2 | 36.5 | 36.5 | 29.1 | 25 |
| Earnings per share | | 1.64 | 1.36 | 1.15 | .91 | .72 | .54 | .42 | .35 |
| Dividends per share | | .05 | .05 | .05 | .05 | .05 | .05 | .02 | Nil |
| Price | high | 33.0 | 30.0 | 27.2 | 21.7 | 16.6 | 11.0 | 10.6 | 7.2 |
|  | low | 22.6 | 15.9 | 14.2 | 13.3 | 7.8 | 8.2 | 6.0 | 4.2 |

- The company was part of Morrison Restaurants prior to early 1996.

---

Aggressive Growth

# St. Jude Medical, Inc.

One Lillehei Plaza ❑ St. Paul, MN 55117 ❑ (651) 766–3029 ❑ Dividend reinvestment program is not available ❑ Web site: *www.sjm.com* ❑ Listed: NYSE ❑ Ticker symbol: STJ ❑ S&P rating: B ❑ Value Line financial strength rating: B++

On February 15, 2005, St. Jude Medical announced today it has signed a definitive agreement to acquire the business of Velocimed, LLC ("Velocimed"), a privately owned company located in Maple Grove, Minnesota. Velocimed develops and manufactures specialty interventional cardiology devices. Under the terms of the agreement, St. Jude will acquire Velocimed's business for a cash purchase price of $82.5 million, less an estimated $8.5 million of cash to Velocimed upon closing, plus additional contingent payments tied to revenues in excess of minimum future targets.

Velocimed was founded in 2001 to develop, manufacture, and market specialty interventional cardiology devices. Velocimed has developed three product platforms: the

Premere patent foramen ovale (PFO) closure system; the Proxis proximal embolic protection device; and the Venture guidewire control catheter for accessing difficult anatomy and crossing chronic total occlusions in interventional catheterization procedures.

Commenting on the agreement to acquire Velocimed, St. Jude's CEO Daniel J. Starks said, "The acquisition of Velocimed supports our objective of building on the market leadership of our Angio-Seal vascular closure product line through selective investments in emerging therapies that represent significant new growth opportunities for interventional catheterization procedures. We look forward to completing this transaction and welcoming the employees of Velocimed to St. Jude Medical."

Paul R. Buckman, president of the company's Cardiology Division, said, "In July 2004, St. Jude Medical announced the formation of the Cardiology Division. With this transaction, St. Jude Medical gains immediate access to three product platforms that serve growing segments of the interventional cardiology market and that we are particularly interested in bringing to our customers."

About Velocimed's Products: A patent foramen ovale (PFO) is a structural defect of the heart where a small hole at birth between the right and left atria (upper chambers of the heart) fails to close in infancy. An estimated 25 percent of the adult population has a PFO. Though usually considered benign, this condition has been associated with an elevated risk of a stroke. More than 200,000 patients worldwide who survive a stroke each year have a PFO and are potential candidates for PFO therapy. The Premere PFO closure system already is approved in Europe. Efforts to initiate a U.S. clinical study of the Premere system under an investigational device exemption (IDE) are underway.

Embolic protection devices are used to help minimize the risk of heart attack or stroke if plaque or other debris are dislodged into the blood stream during interventional cardiology procedures. Interest in the embolic protection market has increased based on recent studies involving saphenous vein grafts (SVG) where a reduction of major adverse coronary events (MACE) occurred when other embolic protection devices were deployed. The Proxis device has CE Mark approval for SVG use in Europe and is currently being evaluated in the United States in a clinical study under an approved IDE granted by the FDA.

## Company Profile

St. Jude Medical, Inc. is dedicated to the design, manufacture, and distribution of cardiovascular medical devices of the highest quality, offering physicians and patients unmatched clinical performance and demonstrated economic value. The company's product portfolio includes pacemakers, implantable cardioverter defibrillators (ICDs), vascular closure devices, catheters, and heart valves.

In the Cardiac Rhythm Management therapy area, St. Jude Medical has assembled a broad array of products for treating heart rhythm disorders—including atrial fibrillation—as well as heart failure. Its innovative product lines include sophisticated ICDs, state-of-the-art pacemaker systems, and a variety of diagnostic and therapeutic electrophysiology catheters.

*Atrial fibrillation, a quivering chaotic rhythm in the upper chamber of the heart (atria) is the world's most common cardiac arrhythmia, affecting more than 5 million people worldwide. It reduces the normal output of the heart, is a known risk factor for stroke, is often associated with heart failure, and can greatly impair a person's quality of life. AF is encountered by all of the company's physician customers—and today it remains one of the most difficult conditions for the medical profession to treat.*

In addition to its electrophysiology catheters, the company develops catheter technologies for the Cardiology/Vascular Access therapy area. Those products include industry-leading hemostasis introducers, catheters, and the market's leading vascular closure device. From access to closure, those products represent a complete set of tools for vascular access site management.

In the Cardiac Surgery therapy area, the company has been the undisputed global leader in mechanical heart valve technology for more than twenty-five years. St. Jude Medical also develops a line of tissue valves and valve-repair products. In 2003, the company expanded its presence in cardiac surgery with a minority investment in Epicor Medical, Inc., which is developing a unique surgical approach for atrial fibrillation.

St. Jude Medical products are sold in more than 120 countries. The company has twenty principal operations and manufacturing facilities around the world.

## Shortcomings to Bear in Mind

- To be sure, St. Jude is an exceptional company with an impressive record. However, the market knows this and gives it a lofty P/E ratio, typically above thirty times earnings.
- *Value Line Investment Survey* tended to agree with me on March 4, 2005, when its analyst, Lucien Virgile, had this guarded comment: "We're lowering our enthusiasm beyond 2005. Limited funds may not permit growth rates to be as strong as before. And, especially so, as inflation fears, push up interest rates."

## Reasons to Buy

- On January 31, 2005, Bill Alpert, writing for *Barron's* financial weekly, had this to say, "Medicare extended coverage for implantable cardioverter defibrillators Thursday to hundreds of thousands of patients, ensuring a growth spurt for Medtronic, Guidant, and St. Jude Medical. The government funding seems as if it's coming just in the nick of time for

the companies. Both Guidant and St. Jude showed ICD sales growth that was slightly less than expected when they reported their December-quarter results last week."

- The Argus Research Company rated the stock a BUY on December 1, 2004. David H. Toung said, "We believe the company's new cardiac resynchronization therapy devices (CRT-Ds) will drive sales and profitability growth in 2005. In the few months since the Epic HF and Atlas HF family of CRT-Ds were introduced, they have already helped St. Jude expand market share in the implantable cardioverter defibrillator (ICD) market. ICDs are devices that regulate a dangerously fast heartbeat. The worldwide ICD market grew 25 percent in the first nine months of 2004. We expect the strong growth to continue in 2005, as additional countries approve ICDs for reimbursement.

  "The Epic and Atlas products are expanding share because they have important advantages over competitors. Atlas has a very high electrical output and charge time of eight seconds, which is twice as fast as its competitors. This means that the capacitor can more quickly build up the charge needed to send the electrical shock to the heart. The Epic and Atlas products give the company a full product suite that will enable it to pursue larger hospital contracts."
- *Standard & Poor's Stock Reports* also had favorable thoughts on the stock on February 2, 2005, according to Robert M. Gold: "Our recommendation is STRONG BUY. We believe St. Jude is well-positioned to capitalize on a rising level of ICD sales in the United States, aided by expanding Medicare and private pay reimbursements and favorable clinical trial data that is fueling a rising number of physician referrals."
- In 2004, the company's sales and profits continued to surge. Net sales reached

$2,294 million, an increase of 19 percent. Net earnings climbed to $410 million, or $1.10 per diluted share. That was an increase of 21 percent. According to CEO Daniel J. Stark, "The most significant event for the company in 2004 was the launch of our high-voltage cardiac resynchronization products to treat heart failure in the United States. We now have two full quarters experience in the U. S. CRT-D market. We are encouraged by our gain of market share and are optimistic we are well-positioned for continued success in the CRT market, one of the most attractive and fastest-growing medical technology markets. We view the publication last week in the *New England Journal of Medicine* of the results of the SCD-HeFT clinical trial as a catalyst to help drive penetration into a large pool of low ejection fraction patients who, until now, have not been candidates for ICDs."

- St. Jude Medical has been active on the acquisition front over the years. In 2003, for instance, the company completed the acquisition of Getz Japan, a distributor of medical technology products in Japan and the company's largest volume distributor in that Asian country. St. Jude paid 26.9 billion Japanese yen in cash to acquire 100 percent of the outstanding stock of Getz Japan. Net consideration paid was $219.2 million.

Although St. Jude markets its products in more than 120 countries, its largest geographic markets are the United States, Europe, and Japan.

Total assets: $3,231 million
Current ratio: 3.03
Common shares outstanding: 358 million
Return on 2004 shareholders' equity: 20.8%

| | 2004 | 2003 | 2002 | 2001 | 2000 | 1999 | 1998 | 1997 |
|---|---|---|---|---|---|---|---|---|
| Revenues (millions) | 2,294 | 1,932 | 1,590 | 1,347 | 1,179 | 1,114 | 994 | 809 |
| Net income (millions) | 410 | 339 | 276 | 203 | 156 | 144 | 129 | 97 |
| Earnings per share | 1.10 | .92 | .76 | .57 | .46 | .43 | .38 | .27 |
| Dividends per share | Nil | — | — | — | — | — | — | — |
| Price    high | 42.9 | 32.0 | 21.6 | 19.5 | 15.6 | 10.2 | 9.9 | 10.7 |
|       low | 29.9 | 19.4 | 15.3 | 11.1 | 5.9 | 5.7 | 4.8 | 6.8 |

Conservative Growth

# Sherwin-Williams Company

101 Prospect Avenue, N.W. ❑ Cleveland, OH 44115–1075 ❑ (216) 566–2102 ❑ Dividend reinvestment program is available: (866) 537–8703 ❑ Web site: *www.sherwin-williams.com* ❑ Listed: NYSE ❑ Ticker symbol: SHW ❑ S&P rating: A ❑ Value Line financial strength rating: A

On August 10, 2004, Sherwin-Williams Company announced that it has entered into a definitive agreement for the purchase of 100 percent of the stock of privately held Paint Sundry Brands Corporation. Paint Sundry Brands is a leading marketer and manufacturer of high-quality paint brushes and rollers for professional contractors and do-it-yourself users. The transaction for the equity and other consideration, including the assumption of certain financial obligations at closing, is valued at about $295 million. Additional financial details for Paint Sundry Brands were not disclosed.

Christopher M. Connor, CEO of Sherwin-Williams Company, said, "We are pleased to have reached an agreement to bring the Paint Sundry Brands organization, which we have long respected, into The Sherwin-Williams family. The well-known quality associated with the Purdy and Bestt Liebco brands will give us a strong branded presence in the important coatings applicator category.

"The acquisition strengthens the continued implementation of our coatings growth strategy, which is to provide high quality products and services to professional paint contractors and do-it-yourself users in various channels of distribution. Paint Sundry Brands will also enhance our coatings applicator manufacturing and distribution infrastructure, which will enable us to better serve the applicator needs of all current and potential customers."

## Company Profile

Sherwin-Williams has been in business since 1866. The company's core business is the manufacture, distribution, and sale of coatings and related products. The company sells Sherwin-Williams labeled architectural coatings, industrial finishes, and associated supplies through company-operated paint and wall covering stores in fifty states, Canada, and some countries of Latin America. SHW also manufactures and sells coatings such as Dutch Boy, Pratt & Lambert, Martin-Senour, Dupli-Color, Krylon, Thompson's, and Minwax plus private label brands to independent dealers, mass merchandisers and home improvement centers. Sherwin-Williams produces coatings for original equipment manufacturers in a number of industries and special purpose coatings for the automotive aftermarket, industrial maintenance, and traffic paint markets. Sherwin-Williams has annually increased dividends since 1979.

## Operating Segments

### Paint Stores:

*Products sold:* Paints, stains, caulks, applicators, wall coverings, floor coverings, spray equipment, and related products.

*Markets Served:* Do-It-Yourselfers, professional painting contractors, home builders, property managers, architects, interior designers, industrial, marine, aviation, flooring, and original equipment manufacturer (OEM) product finishes.

*Major Brands Sold:* Sherwin-Williams, ProMar, SuperPaint, A-100, PrepRite, Classic 99, Duration, Master Hide, Sher-Wood, and Powdura.

*Outlets:* 2,688 Sherwin-Williams stores in the United States, Canada, Mexico, Puerto Rico, and the Virgin Islands.

### Consumer:

*Products Sold:* Branded, private label, and licensed brand paints, stains, varnishes, industrial products, wood finishing products, applicators, corrosion inhibitors, aerosols, and related products.

*Markets Served:* Do-It-Yourselfers, professional painting contractors, and industrial maintenance.

*Major Brands:* Dutch Boy, Krylon, Minwax, Cuprinol, Thompson's WaterSeal, Formby's, Red Devil, Pratt & Lambert, Martin Senour, H&C, White Lightning, Dupli-Color, and Rubberset.

*Outlets:* Leading mass-merchandisers, home centers, independent paint dealers, hardware stores, automotive retailers and industrial distributors in the United States, Canada, and Mexico.

### Automotive Finishes:

*Products Sold:* High-performance interior and exterior coatings for the automotive, fleet, and heavy truck markets, as well as associated products.

*Markets Served:* Automotive jobbers, wholesale distributors, collision repair facilities, dealerships, fleet owners, and refinishers, production shops, body builders, and OEM product finishers.

*Major Brands:* Sherwin-Williams, Martin Senour, Western, Lazzuril, Excelo, Baco, and ScottWarren.

*Outlets:* 194 company-operated branches, in the United States, Canada, Jamaica, Chile, and Peru, and other operations throughout North and South America, the Caribbean Islands, and Europe.

### International Coatings

*Products Sold:* Architectural paints, stains, varnishes, industrial maintenance products, aerosols, product finishes, wood finishing products, and related products.

*Markets Served:* Do-It-Yourselfers, professional painting contractors, independent dealers, industrial maintenance, and OEM product finishes.

*Major Brands Sold:* Sherwin-Williams, Dutch Boy, Krylon, Kem-Tone, Martin Senour, Pratt & Lambert, Minwax, Sumare, Ronseal, Globo, Pulverlack, Colorgin, Andina, TriFlow, Thompson's WaterSeal, and Marson.

*Outlets:* Distribution in twenty-two countries through wholly owned subsidiaries, joint ventures, and licensees of technology, trademarks, and trade names, including sixty-one company-operated architectural and industrial stores in Chile, Brazil, Uruguay, and Argentina.

### Shortcomings to Bear in Mind

- Sherwin-Williams is not without competitors, according to an official of the company, "We experience competition from many local, regional, national, and international competitors of various sizes in the manufacture, distribution and sale of our paints, coatings and related products. We are a leading manufacturer and retailer of paints, coatings and related products to professional, industrial, commercial, and retail customers; however, our competitive position varies for our different products and markets.

"In the Paint Stores Segment, competitors include other paint and wallpaper stores, mass merchandisers, home centers, independent hardware stores, hardware chains, and manufacturer-operated direct outlets.

"In the Consumer and International Coatings Segments, domestic and foreign competitors include manufacturers and distributors of branded and private labeled paints and coatings products."

### Reasons to Buy

- The company had impressive results in 2004. In the fourth quarter, sales shot up 16.7 percent and increased 13.1 percent for the full year. Similarly, diluted net income was up a solid 16.5 percent in the final quarter of 2004 and a hefty 18.4 percent for the full year.

- On September 1, 2004, Sherwin-Williams completed its previously announced acquisitions of 100 percent of the stock of Duron, Inc. and Paint Sundry Brands Corporation. The aggregate consideration for these acquisitions, including the assumption of certain financial obligations, is about $625 million. Sherwin-Williams will finance the acquisitions through the use of cash, liquidated short-term investments, and $350 million in proceeds from the sale of commercial paper under its existing commercial paper program.

  Duron, Inc. is a leading coatings company in the eastern portion of the United States servicing the professional painting contractor, builder, and do-it-yourself markets through 230 company-owned stores. Duron customers will continue to be supported by Duron employees through existing Duron stores and manufacturing facilities.

- "Sherwin-Williams's results are getting a boost from acquisitions," said Adam Rosner, writing for *Value Line Investment Survey* on March 18, 2005. "The paint

store segment, which accounts for about 64 percent of total sales, is benefiting from the recent purchase of Duron, Inc. and Paint Sundry Brands. These purchases contributed about 240 stores in 2004, helping the company add a total of 300 stores during the year. We expect Sherwin-Williams to open about 80–90 new locations in 2005 and to continue renovating many of its older retail centers. In addition, demand for architectural paints should remain strong, due to increased home renovation and a strong housing market."

- *Standard & Poor's Stock Reports* also had some positive comments on February 10, 2005. Here's what Michael Sauers had to say, "We have a BUY recommendation on the shares. In our opinion, favorable economic indicators such as continued strength in building materials retail sales and existing home sales, although likely at a slower pace compared to 2004, should continue to support DIY (*do it yourself*) activity in 2005. Furthermore, we antici-

pate that improved business spending will boost growth in industrial maintenance and product finish applications."

- Rarely does a single product introduction create enough momentum to energize an entire paint category, but that's just what occurred with the launch of Krylon Fusion for Plastic, the first aerosol paint that bonds to plastic. This long-sought-after technology has generated high interest among consumers as well as earnings industry praise. Krylon Fusion for Plastic earned both an Innovation Award from *Handy* magazine, and an Editor's Choice Award from *Popular Mechanics*.

What's more, the recent introduction of SHW's new Dupli-Color Scratch Fix 2-in-1 has enabled the company to gain broader distribution with the nation's leading automotive after-market retailers. As the market leader in aerosol paints, Sherwin-Williams continues to benefit from its private-label manufacturing relationships with several mass merchants and distributors.

Total assets: $4,274 million
Current ratio: 1.17
Common shares outstanding: 141 million
Return on 2004 shareholders' equity: 27%

|  | 2004 | 2003 | 2002 | 2001 | 2000 | 1999 | 1998 | 1997 |
|---|---|---|---|---|---|---|---|---|
| Revenues (millions) | 6,114 | 5,408 | 5,185 | 5,066 | 5,212 | 5,004 | 4,934 | 4,881 |
| Net income (millions) | 393 | 332 | 311 | 263 | 310 | 304 | 273 | 261 |
| Earnings per share | 2.72 | 2.26 | 2.04 | 1.68 | 1.90 | 1.80 | 1.57 | 1.50 |
| Dividends per share | .68 | .62 | .60 | .58 | .54 | .48 | .45 | .40 |
| Price    high | 45.6 | 34.8 | 33.2 | 28.2 | 27.6 | 32.9 | 37.9 | 33.4 |
| low | 33.0 | 24.4 | 21.8 | 19.7 | 17.1 | 18.8 | 19.4 | 24.1 |

Growth and Income

# J.M. Smucker Company

One Strawberry Lane ❑ Orrville, OH 44667–0280 ❑ (330) 684–3838 ❑ Dividend reinvestment plan available: (800) 456–1169 ❑ Web site: *www.smuckers.com* ❑ Listed: NYSE ❑ Fiscal years end April 30 ❑ Ticker symbol: SJM ❑ S&P rating: A- ❑ Value Line financial strength rating: B++

In mid-2004, The J.M. Smucker Company acquired International Multifoods in a transaction valued at about $840 million, which includes the assumption of $340 million in debt. The acquisition added an attractive array of North American icon brands. In addition to its Smucker's, Jif, and Crisco brands, Smucker's expanded portfolio now includes icon brands that hold leadership positions in virtually all of their categories or markets.

Multifoods's primary domestic brands include: Pillsbury baking mixes and ready-to-spread frostings; Hungry Jack pancake mixes, syrup, and potato side dishes; Martha White baking mixes, and ingredients; and Pet evaporated milk, and dry creamer. In Canada, Smucker significantly increased its existing presence with the addition of such number one brands as Robin Hood flour and baking mixes, and Bick's pickles and condiments, and also participates in a growing ethnic food category with Golden Temple flour and rice.

## Company Profile

The J.M. Smucker Company was founded in 1897 when the company's namesake and founder sold his first product—apple butter—from the back of a horse-drawn wagon. Today, more than a century later, the company is the market leader in fruit spreads, peanut butter, shortening and oils, ice cream toppings, and health and natural foods beverages in North America under such icon brands as Smucker's, Jif, and Crisco.

In June 2004, the company expanded its family of products to include such brands as Pillsbury baking mixes and ready-to-spread frostings; Hungry Jack pancake mixes, syrups, and potato side dishes, and Martha White baking mixes and ingredients in the United States, along with Robin Hood flour and baking mixes, and Bick's pickles and condiments in Canada.

Major trademarks, apart from the Jif and Crisco brands acquired in June 2002,

include Smucker's, The R.W. Knudsen Family, After The Fall, Simply Nutritious, Mary Ellen, Dickinson's Lost Acres, Adams, Laura Scudder's, Simply Fruit, Good Morning, Double Fruit, Goober, Magic Shell, Sundae Syrup, Recharge, Santa Cruz Organic, Spritzer, Smucker's Snackers, Uncrustables, and IXL.

For more than 107 years, The J.M. Smucker Company has been headquartered in Orrville, Ohio, and has been family-run for four generations. The J.M. Smucker Company was recognized as the top company in *Fortune* magazine's 2003 annual survey of The 100 Best Companies to Work For and has ranked consistently in the top twenty-five companies each year since *Fortune* began the list in 1998. The J.M. Smucker Company has more than 4,500 employees worldwide and distributes products in more than forty-five countries.

## Shortcomings to Bear in Mind

- *Value Line Investment Survey* was not too keen on Smucker's acquisition of International Multifoods in 2004. William G. Ferguson, the *Value Line* analyst, had this comment on August 6, 2004: "Smucker may have overpaid for the business. International Multifoods's primary business is coming off two consecutive very difficult baking seasons. The baking products unit also faces stiff competition from Pinnacle's Duncan Hines and General Mills' Betty Crocker brands."

  On February 4, 2005, the same analyst was still singing a negative tune. He said, "These good-quality shares offer above-average three- to five-year appreciation potential. For the time being, however, elevated ingredient and energy costs and higher-than-anticipated startup expenses may lead to some near-term earnings volatility."

- *Standard & Poor's Stock Reports* did not speak highly of Smucker on February 22, 2005. Richard Joy said, "Our HOLD opinion on the stock reflects our view that its current valuation reasonably reflects expected near-term growth prospects, as we think that the oils and baking mix business will face a more competitive operating environment over the next few quarters."

## Reasons to Buy

- "Timothy P. and Richard K. Smucker, the brothers who serve as co-chief executives of J.M. Smucker Co., are unabashedly old-fashioned," said Joseph Weber in a *BusinessWeek* article on October 4, 2004. "The deeply religious pair refuses to advertise their jams, jellies, peanut butter, and cooking oil on some of television's biggest hits because they deem the content offensive.

     "Even as they build their once-sleepy foodmaker into a global powerhouse, they keep it based in tiny Orrville, Ohio, a town where tractors may only slightly outnumber churches. And as consolidation sweeps the food industry, the brothers are determined to keep their 107-year-old company independent—a stance backed by five younger Smuckers in management and other family shareholders."

     Mr. Weber also said, "Family has always been at the heart of the brothers' approach. Richard and Tim, who have been close ever since they were boys growing up in Orrville, began working at the company as teens. After both graduated from the University of Pennsylvania's Wharton School of Business, they started working closely with their father, Paul, who had been Smucker's longtime CEO. Paul died in 1998, and the brothers formally assumed the CEO title in 2001.

     "The outgoing Richard, age 56, also serves as chief financial officer and handles much of the communication with Wall Street. The more reserved Tim, 60, who is chairman, tends to handle tasks such as human resources and information technology. The two rarely squabble.

'If there is any friction, I've never seen it,' says Elizabeth Valk Long, a former *Time* magazine president and a Smucker's director since 1997."

- In addition to acquiring North American icon brands, the acquisition of Multifoods provided Smucker with several key strategic benefits, including:

  - A stronger platform for growth. The combined company now has greater scale and marketing representation and is able to take advantage of increased cross-branding/cross-promotion opportunities in the center of the store. Smucker says that it expects to increase overall marketing support for those brands to help drive increased sales.

  - Significant cost savings. The transaction is expected to generate synergies that will result in significant cost savings, ranging from $40 million to $60 million by the end of the third year after the closing. Synergies will come from the efficiencies of combining two companies, supplying-chain enhancements, and leveraging the current selling, marketing, and distribution networks.

  - Enhanced financial strength. The transaction should improve earnings and cash flow, which provides a solid foundation to accelerate growth and enhance shareholder value. For fiscal 2005, Smucker expects the acquisition to be modestly accretive, excluding merger and integration costs, as the additional marketing investment will offset a significant portion of the expected savings for the year. Management said it expected to incur merger and integration costs of about $20 million over the period of twelve to eighteen months following the takeover of International Multifoods.

- Commenting on the company's performance in fiscal 2004, Tim Smucker said, "We achieved record results in fiscal

2004, creating a strong base for future growth. Sales were $1.4 billion, up 8 percent. Earnings were $111 million, up 16 percent. Our earnings number is significant, as it is more than three times greater than it was just two years ago. Earnings per share were $2.21, up 9 percent and reflect increased shares outstanding as a result of the Jif and Crisco merger."

Mr. Smucker also said, "Our company's strong performance was broad-based, with all of our primary brands—Smucker's, Jif, Crisco, and R. W. Knudsen Family—achieving record sales and earnings levels."

Mr. Smucker went on to say, "U.S. Retail, our largest segment, had another

outstanding year, with total sales up 13 percent. This segment includes sales of Smucker's, Jif, and Crisco products to grocery, drug, mass retail, and warehouse club channels. Important, too, is the wide array of choices we offer in terms of varieties, flavors, sizes, packaging, and ingredients. We continue to respond to consumers who seek products to satisfy individual dietary needs. Most recent examples include our Sugar Free and Low Sugar fruit spreads and Simply Jif peanut butter, which appeal to consumers who are watching their carbohydrate intake, as well as our recently introduced zero grams trans fat per serving Crisco shortening."

Total assets: $1,684 million
Current ratio: 2.43
Common shares outstanding: 58 million
Return on 2004 shareholders' equity: 9.5%

|  |  | 2004 | 2003 | 2002 | 2001 | 2000 | 1999 | 1998 | 1997 |
|---|---|------|------|------|------|------|------|------|------|
| Revenues (millions) |  | 1,417 | 1,312 | 687 | 651 | 632 | 602 | 565 | 543 |
| Net income (millions) |  | 111 | 96 | 31 | 32 | 26 | 38 | 36 | 31 |
| Earnings per share |  | 2.21 | 2.02 | 1.24 | 1.23 | .92 | 1.29 | 1.24 | 1.06 |
| Dividends per share |  | .76 | .76 | .64 | .60 | .59 | .55 | .52 | .52 |
| Price | high | 53.5 | 46.8 | 40.4 | 37.7 | 29.0 | 25.8 | 28.2 | 30.0 |
|  | low | 40.8 | 33.0 | 28.7 | 22.6 | 15.0 | 18.4 | 20.6 | 16.0 |

---

Aggressive Growth

# Staples, Inc.

500 Staples Drive □ Framingham, MA 01702 □ (508) 253–4080 □ Web site: *www.staples.com* □ Direct dividend reinvestment plan is available: (888) 875–9002 □ Fiscal years end Saturday closest to January 31 □ Listed: NASDAQ □ Ticker symbol: SPLS □ S&P rating: B+ □ Value Line financial strength rating: A

"First come the people, then the pens, paper and Post-Its. Now that offices across the country are once again staffing up, they're busily restocking their supply cabinets," said Robin Goldwyn Blumenthal, writing for *Barron's* on November 15, 2004. *Barron's* has a long history of covering the investment scene with its insightful and

sophisticated weekly magazine that is part of the same parent firm—Dow Jones & Company—that also publishes the *Wall Street Journal*.

Ms. Blumenthal went on to say, "And that is bringing new life to the rivalry between the nation's two biggest superstores for office supplies, Office Depot and Staples.

Each is posting double-digit sales gains and, to keep up the momentum, each is mounting a big expansion into the other's turf.

"Staples, the bigger of the two, with about fourteen hundred North American stores and annual sales of more than $13 billion, looks to have a clear performance edge. It has been reaping the benefits of a plan put in place four years ago to remodel its stores and improve operating efficiency; the company's operating margins, at 6 percent, smartly outpace Office Depot's 3.8 percent."

## Company Profile

Staples, Inc. launched the office supplies superstore industry with the opening of its first store in Brighton (near Boston) Massachusetts in May 1986. Its goal was to provide small business owners the same low prices on office supplies previously enjoyed only by large corporations. Staples is now a $13 billion retailer of office supplies, business services, furniture and technology to consumers and businesses from home-based businesses to *Fortune* 500 companies in the United States, Canada, the United Kingdom, France, Italy, Spain, Belgium, Germany, the Netherlands, and Portugal. Customers can shop with Staples in any way they choose, by either walking in, calling in, or logging on.

Staples is the largest operator of office superstores in the world, serving customers in 1,600 office superstores, mail order catalogs, e-commerce, and a contract business.

The company operates three business segments: North American Retail, North American Delivery, and European operations.

The company's North American Retail segment consists of the company's U.S. and Canadian business units that sell office products, supplies, and services.

Staples North American Delivery segment consists of the company's U.S. and Canadian contract, catalog, and Internet business units that sell and deliver office

products, supplies, and services directly to customers.

Staples European Operations segment consists of the company's business units which operate 201 retail stores in the United Kingdom (93), Germany (53), the Netherlands (40), Portugal (14), and Belgium (1). The company also sells and delivers office products and supplies directly to businesses throughout the United Kingdom and Germany. The company's delivery operations comprise the catalog business (Staples Direct and Quill Corporation), the contract stationer business (Staples National Advantage and Staples Business Advantage), and the Internet e-commerce business (Staples.com). Quill, acquired in 1998, is a direct mail catalog business, serving more than 1 million medium-sized businesses in the United States.

In 2002, SPLS acquired, for $383 million, Medical Arts Press, a leading provider of specialized printed products and supplies for medical offices. In 2002, the company acquired Guilbert's European mail order business for about $788 million.

At the retail level, stores operate under the names Staples-The Office Superstore and Staples Express. The prototype store had, up until recently, about 24,000 square feet of sales space, which the company reduced to 20,000 in fiscal 2003. Stores carry about 8,500 stock items.

Express stores are much smaller, with between 6,000 square feet and 10,000 square feet of sales space. They also handle fewer items, generally about 6,000, and are situated in downtown business sectors. By contrast, the larger units tend to be situated in the suburbs.

Sales by product are: North American Retail, 59 percent; North American Delivery, 28 percent; and Europe, 13 percent. Sales by product line are: office supplies and services, 42 percent; business machines and telecommunications services, 30 percent; computers and related products, 21 percent; and office furniture, 7 percent.

## Shortcomings to Bear in Mind

- If you are looking for a conservative stock, you had better avoid Staples. It has a beta coefficient of 1.35, which means it is very volatile. In other words, if the stock market rises or falls a certain percentage, SPLS will rise or fall 35 percent more.
- Goldman Sachs, a large and prestigious brokerage firm, had this comment on November 17, 2004: "SPLS continues to drive the highest-quality results in the office products group, achieving consistently strong same-store sales growth, expanding profit margins, and working capital management." However, the Goldman Sachs analyst also said, "We are lowering our rating on Staples to In-Line from Outperform. Our coverage view is Neutral. We are maintaining our earnings estimates, and see no near-term earnings risk for SPLS. Our downgrade reflects apparent peaking in industrial production trends, a helpful macro indicator for SPLS's same-store trend; potentially aggressive revenue growth guidance; relatively full valuation; and the risk of 'noise' in the sector as competitors struggle and contemplate more aggressive moves to capture share."

## Reasons to Buy

- *Value Line Investment Survey* gave Staples a two rating (its second best) on January 14, 2005. David R. Cohen said, "Earnings, on average, during the 2007–2009 period, ought to be almost twice fiscal 2004's estimated level." He also said, "This timely stock offers good appreciation potential to 2007–2009. Moreover, cash assets, currently at $1.6 billion, and free cash flow (estimated at $650 million next year) appear ample to fund potential acquisitions, as well as sustain a recently authorized share-repurchase program."
- *Standard & Poor's Stock Reports* had an upbeat tone, as well, according to the analyst, Michael Sauers. On March 2, 2005, he said, "We have a BUY recommendation on the shares. We believe greater business spending, particularly by small to medium-size businesses, and an improving job market bode well for SPLS. We think Europe will continue to offer growth opportunities in retail and in the delivery business, and a new joint venture in China should provide ample opportunity for future growth in China's $25 billion office products market."
- Argus Research Company had a favorable comment on December 10, 2004, according to its analyst, Christopher Graja: "BUY-rated Focus List Selection, Staples is the leader in office supply retail. We like Staples' prospects because it is trying to boost growth on several fronts, by adding stores, increasing margins, expanding internationally, and taking share in a market that we believe is still quite fragmented."
- Prudential Equity Group, LLC gave the stock an OVERWEIGHT rating, which is similar to a BUY. Mark Rowen said "Why we rate SPLS an OVERWEIGHT:
  - With a rate of growth that continues to outpace the competition in just about every segment of the business, in our opinion, SPLS is the best operator in the office superstore sector and it should benefit from improving in business spending.
  - The small business customer, as opposed to the consumer, is the target audience of Staples stores, and in addition, a significant portion of the company's revenue comes from delivery operations, which are primarily geared toward business customers.
  - North American Retail is the largest business segment at Staples, accounting for almost 60 percent of company-wide revenues. While this segment faces limited future growth opportunities due to the relative maturity of the concept, comparable-store sales

growth has accelerated recently, which we believe reflects an improving economic environment, as well as market share gains from the competition."

■ "As Ronald Sargent was about to assume the chief executive post at Staples Inc. about five years ago, he called a staff meeting to discuss a radical idea: eliminating more than 800 items from the chain's shelves," said Joseph Pereira, in an article that appeared in the *Wall Street Journal March* 5, 2003.

"The nixed items were aimed at casual shoppers, and included cheap printers, cartoon-themed notepads, and novelty pens adorned with feathers or edible candies.

"Mr. Sargent argued that the company needed to shift focus, de-emphasizing occasional shoppers, looking for discounts in favor of bigger-spending small businesses and 'power users.' Although a group of Staples sales and merchandising executives balked, arguing that the company couldn't afford to alienate any potential customers in the midst of the post-Sept.11 downturn, Mr. Sargent prevailed."

■ Mr. Sargent, now in this sixth year in the corner office, has no plans to let up. He tells *Barron's* there's room for 25 percent growth in the industry-wide count of 3,200-plus office superstores in North America. And Staples plans to grow its own base 5 percent for the next few years, as well as opening smaller stores in downtown markets. In total, Sargent figures Staples can add about one hundred stores a year for the next few years.

■ Staples has a solid balance sheet, with 87 percent of its capitalization in shareholders' equity. Total interest coverage, moreover, is impressive, at twenty-eight times.

Total assets: $7,071 million
Current ratio: 1.72
Common shares outstanding: 747 million
Return on 2004 shareholders' equity: 18.2%

|  |  | 2004 | 2003 | 2002 | 2001 | 2000 | 1999 | 1998 | 1997 |
|---|---|---|---|---|---|---|---|---|---|
| Revenues (millions) |  | 14,448 | 13,181 | 11,596 | 10,744 | 10,674 | 8,937 | 7,132 | 5,181 |
| Net income (millions) |  | 708 | 552 | 417 | 307 | 264 | 315 | 238 | 149 |
| Earnings per share |  | .93 | .75 | .63 | .44 | .39 | .45 | .35 | .26 |
| Dividends per share |  | Nil | — | — | — | — | — | — | — |
| Price | high | 22.5 | 18.6 | 15.0 | 13.0 | 19.2 | 23.9 | 20.5 | 8.9 |
|  | low | 15.8 | 10.5 | 7.8 | 7.3 | 6.9 | 10.9 | 7.1 | 5.1 |

Aggressive Growth

# Stryker Corporation

P. O. Box 4085 ❑ Kalamazoo, MI 49003–4085 ❑ (616) 385–2600 ❑ Web site: *www.strykercorp.com* ❑ Listed: NYSE ❑ Dividend reinvestment plan not available ❑ Ticker symbol: SYK ❑ S&P rating: B+ ❑ Value Line financial strength rating: A

"When John Brown, seventy, retires as CEO of Stryker Corporation on January 1, 2005, he will leave behind a powerhouse company built on weak knees," according to an article in *Business Week,* dated December 6, 2004. The authors, Kathleen Kerwin and Michael Arndt, went on to say, "Over twenty-seven years, Brown racked up average annual earnings growth of 22 percent. He transformed a $17-million hospital-bed company into a $4-billion provider of artificial joints, implants, and surgical instruments."

The *Business Week* article went on to say, "The job of filling Brown's shoes—and calming those nervous investors—falls to Stephen P. MacMillan. A former pharmaceuticals executive, MacMillan, forty-one, is betting he can create a new growth engine through biotechnology. He has high hopes for OP-1, a compound for promoting bone growth that Stryker has been developing for two decades. He also plans to continue Brown's strategy of adding products through judicious acquisitions.

"MacMillan arrived in June 2003, from Pharmacia Corporation, where he turned around a $2-billion unit that included such underperforming operations as consumer health care and diagnostics. Previously, MacMillan spent most of his career at Johnson & Johnson, where he marketed Tylenol and later ran European marketing. That background should come in handy as Stryker appeals more directly to consumers via newspaper and TV ads."

## Company Profile

Stryker Corporation was founded in 1941 by Dr. Homer H. Stryker, a leading orthopedic surgeon and the inventor of several orthopedic products. The company now ranks as a dominant player in a $12-billion global orthopedics industry. SYK has a significant market share in such sectors as artificial hips, prosthetic knees and trauma products.

Stryker develops, manufactures and markets specialty surgical and medical products worldwide. These products include orthopedic implants, trauma systems, powered surgical instruments, endoscopic systems and patient care and handling equipment.

Through a network of 374 centers in twenty-six states, Stryker's Physiotherapy Associates division provides physical, occupational, and speech therapy to orthopedic and neurology patients. The physical therapy business represents a solid complementary business for Stryker, in view of the high number of its surgeon customers who prescribe physical therapy following orthopedic surgery.

A major component of Stryker's success is the optimal use of resources in manufacturing and distribution. Taking advantage of both information technology and leading-edge workflow management practices, the company monitors quality and service levels at its 16 plants throughout North America and Europe for continuous improvement. This attention to operations has resulted in the inclusion of Stryker facilities in the elite *Industry Week* Best Plants list twice in the last three years. The Stryker Instruments plant in Kalamazoo, Michigan, was named one of the Best Plants in 2000, and the Howmedica Osteonics facility in Allendale, New Jersey, was honored in 1998.

## Shortcomings to Bear in Mind

- In the past 10 years (1994–2004), Stryker's Earnings per share advanced without a dip, from $0.19 to $1.43, a compound annual growth rate of 22.4 percent. It's hard to find a company growing at this pace that you can buy for a reasonable PE ratio. Nor can you invest in Stryker at a bargain-basement share price. It is nearly always selling at a premium to the market. Let's hope it continues to be worth it.

## Reasons to Buy

- *Value Line Investment Survey* had some positive comments on March 4, 2005, according to analyst George Rho, "We like these good-quality shares for the long haul. Given prevailing demographic and socioeconomic trends, both here and abroad, industry fundamentals are likely to stay sound for years to come.

  This should allow Stryker to maintain its market-leading performance for the foreseeable future."

- Argus Research Company rated Stryker a BUY on January 21, 2005. Analyst David H. Toung said, "When BUY-rated Stryker announced its fourth-quarter and 2004 results on January 26, it marks the first earnings call provided over by new CEO Stephen MacMillan, who takes over after twenty-seven years of leadership by John Brown. While the company has strong franchises in replacement hips and knees, reconstructive implants for trauma cases, and powered surgical instruments, it also faces increased competition for its leading products, such as its ceramic-on-ceramic replacement hip joint and Triathlon knee replacement. . . . We are predicating our 20 percent growth estimate on continued strong sales of reconstructive and surgical products as well as the completion of a major reorganization of the sales force. . . . One of the company's most promising products, OP-1 is a proprietary recombinant version of the bone growth factor osteogenic protein 1. Preclinical studies showed that OP-1 induced the formation of new bone when implanted into bony defect sites. OP-1 has been approved for use in Europe, Australia, and Canada. In the U.S., commercialization of OP-1 has proceeded more slowly."

- "Minimally invasive techniques for reconstructive joint replacement are of great interest to surgeons and their patients, and Stryker is making substantial progress in supporting this surgical preference with responsible science," said then-CEO John W. Brown in 2004. "Following a multicenter clinical study, in 2003 we introduced the Scorpio Total Knee Minimally Invasive Instrumentation, a new line of instruments to complement the minimally invasive knee replacement technique developed by Peter Bonutti, M.D., using our Scorpio knee implant.

  "We have also invested significant resources to create best-in-class instruments for minimally invasive total hip replacement. We continue to make advances in image-guided joint replacement surgery, another less-invasive approach. We have launched the second generation of our knee navigation software and are developing our initial hip navigation platform."

- Peter M. Bonutti, M.D., F.A.C.S., has been developing approaches to minimally invasive total knee arthroplasty for over a decade, and he has collaborated with Stryker throughout the development process to create smaller instruments that spare soft tissue. This instrument line was introduced commercially by Stryker in late 2003.

  "My long-term goal is not simply to reduce postoperative pain and hasten rehabilitation, but to enable patients to resume all activities of daily living," says Dr. Bonutti. "Stryker has helped us develop instrumentation that reduces soft tissue disruption in knee replacement. Working together, we are continuing to evolve this technology for even greater long-term patient benefits." Dr. Bonutti directs the Bonutti Clinic in Effingham, Illinois, and is Associate Clinical Professor at the University of Arkansas in Little Rock.

- Analysts believe that industry trends are setting the stage for continued growth for Stryker in the years ahead. Virtually all market dynamics point in that direction. These are the key factors:

  - The population as a whole is aging. In fact, the target population for orthopedic implants for knees and hips is expected to increase 68 percent in the next nine years, according to a report issued by Gerard Klauer Mattison & Company, Inc., a brokerage firm headquartered in New York City.

  - Mild inflation in average selling prices for orthopedic implants in the United States compares favorably to the declining price environment of the past decade.

- Consolidation among orthopedic implant and device manufacturers over the past few years has greatly decreased the number of competitors in sectors such as orthopedic implants, spinal devices, arthroscopy products and other orthopedic products. This serves to consolidate market share and mitigates price competition.
- Advances in orthopedic technology— much of which has taken place in the past decade—have markedly decreased operating and recovery times. These advances have decreased the amount of time a surgeon must spend with each patient, thus giving the surgeon more time to perform more operations

in a period. Consequently, according to the Gerard Klauer Mattison report, "we believe that procedural volume will increase."

For its part, Stryker has set itself up to benefit from these microeconomic dynamics, according the report issued by this same brokerage house. "For example, Stryker has strategically used acquisitions over the past few years to broaden and deepen its product portfolio. Furthermore, innovation in orthopedic implants and instrumentation has provided the company with certain competitive advantages that should be important ingredients for gaining market share in the coming years."

Total assets: $4,084 million
Current ratio: 1.92
Common shares outstanding: 402 million
Return on 2004 shareholder's equity: 19%

|  |  | 2004 | 2003 | 2002 | 2001 | 2000 | 1999 | 1998 | 1997 |
|---|---|---|---|---|---|---|---|---|---|
| Revenues (millions) |  | 4,262 | 3,625 | 3,012 | 2,602 | 2,289 | 2,104 | 1,103 | 980 |
| Net income (millions) |  | 586 | 454 | 346 | 272 | 221 | 161 | 150 | 125 |
| Earnings per share |  | 1.43 | 1.12 | .88 | .67 | .55 | .41 | .39 | .32 |
| Dividends per share |  | .09 | .07 | .05 | .04 | .035 | .035 | .03 | .03 |
| Price | high | 57.7 | 42.7 | 33.8 | 31.3 | 28.9 | 18.3 | 14.0 | 11.4 |
|  | low | 40.3 | 29.9 | 21.9 | 21.7 | 12.2 | 11.1 | 7.8 | 6.1 |

Aggressive Growth

# Sysco Corporation

1390 Enclave Parkway ❑ Houston, TX 77077–2099 ❑ (281) 584–1458 ❑ Web site: *www.sysco.com* ❑ Dividend reinvestment plan available: (800) 730–4001 ❑ Fiscal years end the Saturday closest to June 30 ❑ Listed: NYSE ❑ Ticker symbol: SYY ❑ Standard & Poor's rating: A+ ❑ Value Line financial strength rating: A++

With the advent of two household incomes, with both husband and wife working outside the home, it is not surprising that no one wants to come home after eight hours at the office and still have to face cooking supper. Not to mention cleaning up after the repast.

Today, about half of Americans' food dollars are spent on meals prepared away from home. That figure far surpasses the 37 percent that was spent on away-from-home meals in 1972. It reveals how heavily our society now depends on foodservice operations to satisfy consumers' nutritional needs by providing a variety of quality meals at affordable prices.

According to Gail E. Allen, president and CEO of Sysco Food Services of Albany, "Sysco's $29.3 billion in sales translates into an approximate 14 percent share of a growing market. We are in a wonderful industry with great upside potential. Two-income families have more disposable income to spend. As the population ages, the fifty- and sixty-five-year-olds also have more time and money to eat meals cooked in someone else's kitchen.

"In addition, retirees are healthier and living longer, and many are in retirement communities that serve meals on site. Of course, the twenty-to-forty-year-old segment, has grown up with parents who worked outside the home, so eating out comes naturally to them, and many just don't have the time, skills or desire to cook."

## Company Profile

As they go about their lives, many people encounter the familiar Sysco trucks, bearing giant blue lettering, delivering products to customers. Few are aware, however, of Sysco's far-reaching influence on meals served daily throughout North America. As the continent's largest marketer and distributor of foodservice products, Sysco operates 150 distribution facilities across the United States and Canada (including 84 broadline facilities, seventeen hotel supply locations, sixteen specialty produce facilities, fifteen SYGMA distribution centers, twelve custom-cutting meat locations, and two distributors specializing in the niche Asian foodservice market). These distribution facilities serve about 415,000 restaurants, hotels, schools, hospitals, retirement homes, and other locations where food is prepared to be eaten on the premises or taken away and enjoyed in the comfort of the diner's chosen environment.

Sysco is by far the largest company in the foodservice distribution industry. In sales,

Sysco dwarfs its two chief competitors, US Foodservice and Performance Food Group.

In 2004, the company's revenue breakdown was as follows: restaurants (64 percent sales), hospitals and nursing homes (10 percent), schools and colleges (5 percent), hotels and motels (6 percent), other (15 percent).

With annual sales in 2004 of $29.3 billion, Sysco distributes a wide variety of fresh and frozen meats, seafood, poultry, fruits and vegetables, plus bakery products, canned and dry foods, paper and disposables, sanitation items, dairy foods, beverages, kitchen and tabletop equipment, as well as medical and surgical supplies.

Sysco's innovations in food technology, packaging, and transportation provide customers with quality products, delivered on time, in excellent condition, and at reasonable prices.

## Shortcomings to Bear in Mind

- Insiders, such as executives and board members, have been selling their Sysco shares in recent months. In one nine-month period, there were twenty-two sales—and not a single purchase.

- CEO Richard J. Schnieders pointed out on September 27, 2004, two factors that had a negative impact on fiscal 2004. "Our performance was particularly noteworthy in a year marked by considerable uncertainty in the foodservice industry. Sysco's product cost inflation, normally ranging from 1 percent to 3 percent, jumped to 5 percent at the beginning of the year and remained above that all year, resulting in 6.3 percent inflation for the year. This has proved difficult for our customers, who have been faced with choosing between raising menu prices, taking lower profits, lowering quality standards, or substituting products. Our marketing associates' ability to guide them through these difficult choices has been admirable, but we remain vigilant about the effects of prolonged product inflation.

"Similarly, sustained higher fuel costs, while a small part of our expense structure, presented another challenge. Our operating companies met this obstacle by more efficient routing, fuller trucks, and attention to minute detail, helping us continue to drive down expense ratios.

"Finally, the restaurant consumer exhibited signs of uncertainty during the year, which leads us to the conclusion that the foodservice industry did not grow as strongly this year as in the past. Thus, our emphasis on growing our profitable customers' businesses served us well, since firmly established restaurants are best positioned to react quickly to market changes."

## Reasons to Buy

- According to industry sources, there are nearly 900 thousand foodservice locations in the United States—such as restaurants, hospitals, nursing homes, cruise ships, summer camps, sports stadiums, theme parks, schools, colleges, hotels, motels, corporate dining rooms and cafeterias, and retirement homes—and more than sixty-three thousand in Canada. Sales of foodservice products in 2005 at the consumer level are projected to reach more than $440 billion in the United States and more than $45 billion in Canada.

- Whether dining in an upscale restaurant or picking up pasta as the entree for a meal at home, people spend less time on food preparation than ever before. They want variety and flavor in the foods they choose to eat, yet their time to prepare meals is constantly in competition with work and leisure activities. More than ever, people are turning to meals prepared away from home for greater convenience, quality and, most of all, choice.

It is a trend that started in World War II, as women began to work outside the home. Business cafeterias, coffee shops, school lunchrooms, and restaurants broadened the range of dining choices for people who were used to much simpler fare. Twenty-five years ago, not many consumers could identify kiwi fruit. During the past three decades, foodservice offerings have moved from fruit cocktail with a cherry on top to kiwi and other exotic fare; from steak and potatoes to fajitas with all the trimmings.

- As the largest distributor of foodservice products in North America, Sysco assists customers in creating a vast array of dining choices. Menus have greatly improved since a French chef named Boulanger offered a choice of soups, or "restorative" to patrons who paused at his inn to refresh themselves as they traveled during the 1700s. The sign in French read "restaurant," and his establishment may have been the first to offer a menu.

Today's diverse menu choices could not have been imagined then—raspberries from Australia served fresh in Wisconsin in January; gourmet pesto sauce rich with garlic, fresh basil and pine nuts delivered to a Vancouver chef's doorstep; or artfully prepared hearts of lettuce served in an Arizona college cafeterias each day. Providing choices from soup to nuts, and everything in between, Sysco leads the way in helping chefs in restaurants, schools, business cafeterias, healthcare locations, lodging, and other facilities increase the variety and quality of food choices in North America.

- Unlike some of its competitors, who order all their products from headquarters, Mr. Cotros encourages his seventy-eight branches to reach their own decisions about which products to carry and how to price them. Sysco's 13,500 sales representatives carry laptop computers that can instantly place orders and confirm inventory. By contrast, smaller distributors still take orders with pads and pencils and are often unsure which items are on the warehouse shelf.

- Sysco keeps margins high by selling products under its own label, a strategy it began a year after its founding. It saves on national advertising and passes some of the savings along to its customers. Its private-label business carries an estimated 24 percent gross margin, or 10 percent more than it earns on national brands.
- Sysco has an exceptional record of growth. In the past ten years (1994–2004), Earnings per share advanced from $0.30 to $1.37 (with no dips along the way), a compound annual growth rate of 16.4 percent. In the same decade, Dividends per share climbed from $0.08 to $0.48, a growth rate of 19.6 percent. Sysco has increased its quarterly cash dividend thirty-four times in its thirty-three years as a public company.
- Many of Sysco's operations have been the result of acquisitions. For instance, the 2002 acquisition of SERCA Foodservice, Inc., a division of Sobeys, Inc., significantly expanded the company's presence coast to coast in the $9-billion Canadian foodservice distribution market, completing Sys-

co's strategy of broadening its geographic reach. Foodservices, Inc. now operates from seventeen locations in eight provinces of Canada, providing products and services to 65,000 customers.

In 2004, "Sysco's strong capabilities in fresh produce were enhanced by the acquisition of FreshPoint, particularly in the upscale menu arena," said Verne Lusby, president, FreshPoint of Southern California. "Together, Sysco and Fresh-Point are the largest foodservice purchasers of produce in North America.

"At FreshPoint, we work extensively with the growers to develop the best in a particular type of crop and continually amaze our customers with one-of-a-kind items that make a menu extraordinary. We can offer highly specialized produce like exotic fruits and vegetables, rare and unusual herbs, heirloom tomatoes, unique varieties and micro-greens that chefs increasingly demand. Since we operate smaller vehicles and make more frequent deliveries, we are a great fit for customers who require multiple deliveries per week."

Total assets: $7,848 million
Current ratio: 1.23
Common shares outstanding: 639 million
Return on 2004 shareholders' equity: 38.7%

|  | 2004 | 2003 | 2002 | 2001 | 2000 | 1999 | 1998 | 1997 |
|---|---|---|---|---|---|---|---|---|
| Revenues (millions) | 29,335 | 26,140 | 23,351 | 21,784 | 19,303 | 17,423 | 15,328 | 14,455 |
| Net income (millions) | 907 | 778 | 680 | 597 | 454 | 362 | 325 | 302 |
| Earnings per share | 1.37 | 1.18 | 1.01 | .88 | .68 | .54 | .48 | .43 |
| Dividends per share | .48 | .40 | .36 | .28 | .22 | .19 | .16 | .15 |
| Price high | 41.3 | 37.6 | 32.6 | 30.1 | 30.4 | 20.6 | 14.4 | 11.8 |
| low | 29.5 | 22.9 | 21.2 | 21.8 | 13.1 | 12.5 | 10.0 | 7.3 |

Conservative Growth

# T. Rowe Price Group, Inc.

100 East Pratt Street ❑ Baltimore, MD 21202 ❑ (410) 345–2124 ❑ Dividend reinvestment plan not available ❑ Web site: *www.troweprice.com* ❑ Ticker symbol: TROW ❑ Listed: NASDAQ ❑ S&P rating: A ❑ Value Line financial strength rating: A+

"While no one was looking, T. Rowe Price has become the country's third-largest direct marketer of funds," said Ira Carnahan, writing for *Forbes* magazine on January 31, 2005. "Its secrets of success have powered it through the dark days of the bear market, scoring good returns that nicely exceed the market. Like the USS *Constellation*, an elegant 19th century wood-hulled warship moored in the nearby harbor, the old investment firm was once written off as a relic. Hardly.

"With $212 billion under management, the venerable company, founded in 1937, has become a force in funds, retirement plans, and institutional investing by playing it safe and offering customers a good deal. Its strong suits are low risk, and low expenses. Such attributes made it stodgy-looking in the Internet mania of the late 1990s but enabled it to breeze by go-go shop Janus when the bubble burst.

"Over the past five years, 83 percent of T. Rowe Price's mutual funds have beaten the average return for their category. The shares of T. Rowe's funds rated by Morningstar that earn four or five stars stand at 64 percent—more than double the average for funds as a whole."

## Company Profile

T. Rowe Price is an investment management firm offering individuals and institutions around the world investment management guidance and expertise.

The company's investment approach strives to achieve superior performance but "is always mindful of the risks incurred relative to the potential rewards. Our consistent investment philosophy helps mitigate unfavorable changes and takes advantage of favorable ones. We provide our clients with world-class investment guidance as well as attentive service."

Founded in 1937 by Thomas Rowe Price, Jr., the company offers separately managed investment portfolios for institutions and a broad range of mutual funds for individual investors and corporate retirement accounts. Mutual funds are pooled investments representing the savings of many thousands of individuals that are invested in stocks, bonds, and other assets managed by a portfolio manager or managers in the hope of either outperforming a market average—such as the S&P 500 of the Dow Jones Industrial Average—or meeting a similar goal. No-load funds are sold without a sales commission. However, this does not infer there is no cost. All mutual funds have expenses, such as salaries, office rent, advertising, travel, and the like. This averages about 1.6 percent per year, but does not include the cost of buying and selling stocks. T. Rowe Price is a low-cost manager.

In founding his firm, Mr. Price followed a very simple principle: What is good for the client is also good for the firm. Rather than charge a commission, as was then the practice in the securities business, Mr. Price charged a fee based on the assets under management. If the client prospered, so did T. Rowe Price.

Mr. Price is best known for developing the growth stock style of investing. Although he was trained as a chemist, he had a passion for investing. Mr. Price believed that investors could earn superior returns by investing in well-managed companies in fertile fields whose earnings and dividends could be expected to grow faster than inflation and the overall economy. The core of Mr. Price's approach, proprietary research to guide investment selection and diversification reduce risk, has remained part of the firm's bedrock principles.

Today, growth stock investing is one of the many investment styles the firm currently follows. T. Rowe Price also employs value-oriented, sector-focused, tax-efficient, and quantitative index-oriented approaches in managing mutual funds and institutional portfolios.

## Shortcomings to Bear in Mind

- Stephen Sanborn, CFA, writing for *Value Line Investment Survey* on February 25, 2005, was lukewarm about T. Rowe Price. He said, "Price could be a beneficiary of any move to privatize Social Security. In fact, that is the reason the stock rose after the reelection of George Bush. However, privatization remains very controversial and would by most accounts be extremely costly. Any major changes to Social Security are likely to be made gradually over many years, and any benefits to Price or others in the mutual fund industry are likely to be slow in coming."

- Similarly, Argus Research Company was less than enthusiastic about the company on December 21, 2004. David Anthony said, "We are maintaining our HOLD rating on T. Rowe Price Group. The stock is up 30 percent this year after appreciating 74 percent in 2003. With a P/E of 21.4 on our 2005 projected earnings, the stock now carries what we believe is a more than generous 27 percent premium to the general market multiple."

## Reasons to Buy

- By contrast, Robert Hansen, CFA, an analyst with *Standard & Poor's Stock Reports,* had this to say on December 10, 2004: "We believe the shares should trade at a significant premium to peers, based on our view of the company's impressive EPS (Earnings per share) growth, consistent net inflows, and high proportion of client assets in equity funds. We think a premium valuation is also justified, given the company's low debt balances, and diversified client base. We believe T. Rowe Price's broad line of no-load mutual funds makes its easy for investors to reallocate assets among funds—which is not the case at some smaller fund companies—contributing to increased client retention, in our opinion."

- Lehman Brothers, a leading brokerage house, had this positive statement on January 11, 2005: "We are raising our estimates for TROW, to reflect the appreciation of managed assets, since our last formal revisions in October. With stock option expensing apparently pending for the second half of 2005, we have also increased our subjective assumptions for related expense accruals, as management appears to be inclined to continue to issue options."

- On December 30, 2004, Prudential Equity Group had this to say, "We are increasing our 2004 fourth quarter EPS estimate to $0.67 and our 2005 estimate to $2.95. We are introducing our 2006 earnings estimate of $3.40 per share. Using our proprietary model, we are forecasting that TROW's year end AUMs (assets under management) exceed $230 billion. Investment performance has remained robust, and we expect the company to attract fund flows totaling $5 billion to $6 billion in the fourth quarter." The report also said, "T. Rowe Price's strong investment performance points to continued above-peer net flows into 2005, in our opinion."

- According to the January 2005 issue of *Better Investing* (which I subscribe to), "It's a rarity in the world of active management: a fund with strong performance, low expenses, and a manager with a long-term buy-and-hold investing philosophy. Brian Rogers, manager of T. Rowe Price Equity Income Fund, seeks companies selling at reasonable valuations with strong dividends. His strategy has paid off in the nearly twenty years he's been at its helm."

- In December of 2004, the company boosted its dividend by 21 percent. It was the 18th consecutive year of dividend increases.

- On February 6, 2004, CEO George A. Roche said, "This positive economic and market backdrop was tarnished by some shocking news concerning trading abuses by several firms in the investment management industry, including allegations that executives at certain fund companies permitted excessive trading or illegal after-hours trading. In addition, certain intermediaries that process fund transactions allegedly assisted some investors in executing improper mutual fund trades. The investigations have led to charges of improper mutual fund trading by some fund company executives and portfolio managers.

"I want T. Rowe Price stockholders to know that we emphatically condemn the abuses that have been revealed or alleged against other firms in the industry. We unequivocally oppose inappropriate trading. We have conducted a thorough review of our policies, procedures, and practices with respect to late trading and market timing, and we found that they are sound. T. Rowe Price has not entered into any agreements that authorize market timing by any party."

- In 2004, a company official said, "While financial markets are distinguished by change, T. Rowe Price is distinguished by discipline. Too often, short-term trends and emotions are allowed to dictate investment decisions, but our philosophy embraces the notion that consistent long-term results require discipline—in approach, process, and goals.

"T. Rowe Price investment professionals practice 'bottom-up' investing, exploiting fundamental research to uncover promising opportunities. (*Bottom-up investing means concentrating on picking well-managed companies, regardless of their industry or economic condition. By contrast, top-down investing may begin with economic trends and industries—and then picking appropriate stocks.*) This approach also leverages sophisticated risk management techniques to avoid wide fluctuations in returns for investors. Extreme volatility can tempt investors—including professionals—to make short-term decisions that may be counter to long-term goals.

"More than eighty-five stock and bond analysts cast a wide net around the globe to gather first-hand information in developing out independent research. Meeting with corporate managers is a key part of the research process, along with analyzing financial data and assessing information from myriad sources.

"Our analysts conduct more than 2,000 company visits per year. They discuss companies with their suppliers and clients and even observe the company grounds to glean useful insights. This information, distilled by our analysts and fused with rigorous valuation analysis, ultimately determines whether an investment is purchased at a reasonable price or sold at an advantageous price. Hands-on research and valuation disciplines, combined with prudent diversification define our approach to risk management."

### Total assets: $1,929 million
### Current ratio: 3.50
### Common shares outstanding: 130 million
### Return on 2004 shareholders' equity: 19.9%

|  |  | 2004 | 2003 | 2002 | 2001 | 2000 | 1999 | 1998 | 1997 |
|---|---|---|---|---|---|---|---|---|---|
| Revenues (millions) |  | 1,280 | 996 | 924 | 1,028 | 1,212 | 1,036 | 886 | 755 |
| Net income (millions) |  | 337 | 227 | 194 | 195 | 269 | 239 | 174 | 144 |
| Earnings per share |  | 2.51 | 1.77 | 1.52 | 1.52 | 2.08 | 1.85 | 1.34 | 1.13 |
| Dividends per share |  | .80 | .70 | .65 | .61 | .54 | .43 | .36 | .28 |
| Price | high | 63.4 | 47.6 | 42.7 | 43.9 | 49.9 | 43.3 | 42.9 | 36.9 |
|  | low | 43.8 | 23.7 | 21.3 | 23.4 | 30.1 | 25.9 | 20.9 | 18.3 |

# Teva Pharmaceutical Industries, Ltd.

5 Basel Street ❑ P.O. Box 3190 ❑ Petach Tikva, Israel 49131 ❑ ++972–3-926–7554 ❑ (215) 591–8912 ❑ Dividend reinvestment not plan available ❑ Web site: *www.tevapharm.com* ❑ Listed: NASDAQ ❑ Ticker symbol: TEVA ❑ S&P rating: not rated ❑ Value Line Financial Rating: A

"Teva Pharmaceutical Industries is the world's largest maker of generic drugs," said Michael Sivy, writing for the February 2004 issue of *Money* magazine. "Generics already represent more than half of all prescriptions dispensed, up from a third 10 years ago. And the new Medicare drug benefit is expected to boost demand further.

"Generics producers spend relatively little on research and development—mostly, they wait until hot products become available for generic use. And now, analysts say, the pipeline of drugs soon to come off patent is actually more attractive than the pipeline of newly developed drugs awaiting approval.

"Teva markets around 140 products in more than 400 versions (different dosages, for example) in the United States and an even larger variety in Europe. And though it's based in Israel, which is a possible risk factor, Teva has been in business for nearly 60 years and has most of its production facilities in the United States and Europe. Earnings are projected to grow at an impressive 24 percent rate over the next five years."

## What Are Generic Drugs?

"All drugs—whether prescription or over the counter—have a nonproprietary name (also called a generic name, it's the name of a drug that's not subject to being trademarked), but only some are sold as generic drugs," said Robert S. Dinsmoor, a Contributing Editor of *Diabetes Self-Management*. The article appeared in the January/February 2004 issue of this leading publication devoted to the treatment of diabetes. "If and when a drug can be sold as a generic depends on when the patent (or

patents) held by the developer of the drug expire. A patent gives the drug developer the exclusive right to market the drug under its brand name for a certain amount of time."

Mr. Dinsmoor went on to explain, "Generic drugs usually sell for a fraction of the cost of the brand-name drugs. Generic metformin, for example, costs about two-thirds as much as the brand-name product. The price drop that occurs when generics enter the market is attributable to several factors, including competition and the lower overhead of generic-drug manufacturers. When companies compete with each other to sell the same product, market theory argues that prices will tend to go down. Manufacturers of generics are also able to offer lower price because, unlike the developer of the original brand-name drug, they do not have to recoup large investments in research and development or engage in expensive marketing and advertising campaigns."

## Company Profile

Teva was founded in Jerusalem in 1901 as a small wholesale drug business that distributed imported medicines loaded onto the backs of camels and donkeys to customers throughout the land. The company was called Salomon, Levin and Elstein, Ltd., after its founders.

Teva Pharmaceutical Industries Ltd. is a global pharmaceutical company specializing in generic drugs. The company has major manufacturing and marketing facilities in Israel, North America, and Europe.

Teva's scope of activity extends to many facets of the industry, with primary focus on the manufacturing and marketing of products in the following categories:

• Human pharmaceuticals. Teva produces generic drugs in all major therapeutic realms in a variety of dosage forms, from tablets and capsules to ointments, creams, and liquids. Teva manufactures innovative drugs in niche markets where it has a relative advantage in research and development.

• Active Pharmaceutical Ingredients (API). Teva competitively distributes its API to manufacturers worldwide as well as supports its own pharmaceutical production.

These activities, which comprise the core businesses of the company, account for 90 percent of Teva's total sales.

## Shortcomings to Bear in Mind

■ According to an article by Leila Abboud in the *Wall Street Journal* on October 28, 2004, "Teva now faces challenges in keeping up its rapid growth because its top market, the U.S., is turning tougher for generic drug makers. In the U.S., the first generic company to win approval for copying a branded drug gets six months of marketing exclusivity—an advantage that traditionally accounts for much of generic companies' profits. Now branded companies are fighting back by licensing their drugs to 'authorized' generic makers or selling their own generics through subsidiaries. These tactics cut into the profits the first generic reaps in the first six months."

## Reasons to Buy

■ On a more positive note, Ms. Abboud said, "U.S. generic makers tend to be scrappy upstarts with short histories and sometimes-rapid turnover. At Teva, many employees have been around for decades. The company has a paternalistic streak that would be more familiar at a long-established European company. It pays the tab for employees' vacations and subsidizes their children's educations."

Ms. Abboud also said, "Being global allows Teva to start manufacturing generic copies of drugs even before they lose patent protection in the U.S. For example, the Kfar Saba factory is already making generic versions of Merck & Company's big-selling anti-cholesterol drug Zocor, even though Zocor's U.S. patents don't expire until 2006. Teva sells the pills in parts of Europe where Zocor patents have expired. When the U.S. market opens, it'll be ready to pounce."

■ "We believe the generic industry remains highly attractive with growing demand and consolidating supply," said Lehman Brothers on February 18. 2005. "Teva's global leadership will play an important role in this marketplace." The stock was rated OVERWEIGHT *(similar to BUY)*.

■ In 2004, Teva Pharmaceutical Industries completed the acquisition of Sicor Inc. Sicor Inc. is a vertically integrated, multinational pharmaceutical company that focuses on generic finished dosage injectable pharmaceuticals, active pharmaceutical ingredients, and generic bio-pharmaceuticals. Using internal research and development capabilities, together with operational flexibility and manufacturing and regulatory expertise, Sicor is able to take a wide variety of products from the laboratory to the worldwide marketplace.

Leveraging these capabilities, Sicor concentrates on products and technologies that present significant barriers to entry and offer first-to-market opportunities. Sicor operates several manufacturing facilities in the U.S., Western and Eastern Europe, and Mexico. It is headquartered in Irvine, California.

Israel Makov, Teva's CEO, said "This acquisition brings together two premier generic pharmaceutical companies and further enhances Teva's position of leadership within the industry. Our expanded customer base will enjoy the benefits of having access to a truly global supplier, possessing an unmatched product portfolio and the deepest pipeline of new products."

■ On December 10, 2003, Teva Pharmaceutical Industries and Andrx Corporation jointly announced that they had entered into a strategic collaboration to develop and market generic oral contraceptive pharmaceutical products. Under the terms of the agreement, Teva received exclusive marketing rights in the United States and Canada to Andrx's line of generic oral contraceptive products currently pending regulatory approval. For its part, Andrx will be responsible for all formulations, U.S. regulatory submissions, and manufacturing of products covered under the pact.

Larry Rosenthal, the president of Andrx, said, "Andrx is very pleased to be working with Teva, one of the premier generic companies, in this unique marketplace, and believes that this collaboration will enhance the marketability of our oral contraceptive product line, thereby increasing Andrx's overall profitability."

Mr. Makov, Teva's CEO, said, "We are pleased to be partnering with Andrx, which has made a significant commitment to the development of oral contraceptive products, including the construction of a specialized manufacturing area. This agreement is a natural extension of our strategy of market leadership, with enables us to offer our customers the most extensive portfolio of affordable, generic pharmaceuticals."

■ In addition to the production and sale of finished pharmaceutical products, Teva is a large manufacturer and provider of Active Pharmaceutical Ingredients, the vital raw materials of the drug manufacturing industry. In addition to supplying a major share of Teva's own needs, the API division is an active competitor in world markets, investing both in development of new products and manufacturing processes and in the upgrading of production facilities, it also provides an essential link in Teva's strategic marketing chain. The division also spearheads the company's entry into new drug markets, providing a cost-effective source of materials with which to commence local manufacturing and establishing viable distribution channels.

■ "A federal appeals court dealt a new blow to Merck & Co. by invalidating a patent that protects the company's second-biggest drug, the osteoporosis pill Fosamax," said Leila Abboud, writing for the *Wall Street Journal* on January 31, 2005. Merck's stock plunged 10 percent after generic drug maker Teva Pharmaceutical Industries Ltd., based in Israel, won the right to market a version of Fosamax in February 2008, a decade earlier than Merck expected.

"Fosamax comes in both daily and weekly formulations; the surprise legal setback concerns the patent protecting the popular weekly medication. The weekly pill accounts for about 90 percent of Fosamax's worldwide sales of $3.2 billion."

Total assets: $9,632 million
Current ratio: 1.91
Common shares outstanding: 555 million
Return on 2004 equity: 22.2%

| | 2004 | 2003 | 2002 | 2001 | 2000 | 1999 | 1998 | 1997 |
|---|---|---|---|---|---|---|---|---|
| Revenues (millions) | 4,799 | 3,276 | 2,519 | 2,077 | 1,750 | 1,282 | 1,116 | 1,117 |
| Net income (millions) | 965 | 691 | 410 | 278 | 148 | 118 | 69 | 101 |
| Earnings per share | 1.42 | 1.04 | .76 | .53 | .29 | .24 | .15 | .21 |
| Dividends per share | .16 | .14 | .09 | .06 | .07 | .03 | .03 | .04 |
| Price      high | 34.7 | 31.2 | 20.1 | 18.6 | 19.7 | 9.1 | 6.4 | 8.6 |
|            low | 22.8 | 17.3 | 12.9 | 12.1 | 8.0 | 4.9 | 4.0 | 5.3 |

# Textron, Inc.

40 Westminster Street □ Providence, RI 02903 □ (401) 457–2288 □ Dividend reinvestment program is available: (800) 829–8432 □ Listed: NYSE □ Web site: *www.textron.com* □ Ticker symbol: TXT □ S&P rating: B+ □ Value Line financial strength rating: A

"As a multi-industry company, our ability to maintain the right mix of businesses is critical to success," said CEO Lewis B. Campbell in 2004. "Whether it's acquisitions or divestitures, portfolio management is an essential component of multi-industry leadership, and we intend to become the very best at it.

"Over time, we will enhance and reshape our portfolio by divesting noncore assets and reinvesting in branded businesses in attractive industries with substantial long-term growth potential. By the end of the decade, Textron will have a streamlined portfolio of leading global brands, each generating $1 billion or more in annual revenue with returns of at least 400 basis points above our cost of capital. *There are 100 basis points in one percentage point.*

"We are developing rigorous processes to support our portfolio management capability. We have also established a comprehensive set of acquisition evaluation criteria, and in 2003 applied them to our existing portfolio and developed a strategic investment plan for each business.

"In 2003, we divested our OmniQuip business, noncore portfolios from Textron Financial, our interest in an Italian automotive joint venture, and a unit of Textron Fastening Systems. Over the past three years, we have divested some $2.3 billion of revenue in noncore businesses, allowing us to allocate capital to our stronger, faster-growing businesses."

## Company Profile

Textron Inc. is one of the world's largest and most successful multi-industry companies. Founded in 1923, the company has grown into a network of businesses with total revenues of $10 billion, and more than 44,000 employees in nearly forty countries, serving a diverse and global customer base. Textron is ranked 194th on the *Fortune* 500 list of largest U.S. companies. Organizationally, Textron consists of numerous subsidiaries and operating divisions, which are responsible for the day-to-day operation of their businesses.

### Bell

Bell is a leader in vertical takeoff and landing aircraft for commercial and military applications and the pioneer of the revolutionary tiltrotor aircraft. This segment also includes Textron Systems, a provider of advanced technology solutions for the aerospace and defense industries, and Lycoming aircraft engines. Bell's revenues are comprised of Bell Helicopter (75 percent of division revenues) and Textron Systems (25 percent). Overall, the Bell segment represents 24 percent of Textron, Inc.

Textron Systems provides innovative, advanced technology solutions to meet the needs of the global aerospace and defense industries. The Textron brand is well-known within these industries for its precision strike weapons, mobility, surveillance systems, specialty marine craft, and Cadillac Gage armored vehicles.

Lycoming is the world leader in the design and manufacture of reciprocating piston aircraft engines for the global general aviation industry. In addition to new engines, Lycoming provides after-market parts and service for its installed base of engines.

### Cessna Aircraft

The world's largest manufacturer of light and mid-size business jets, utility turboprops, single-engine business jets, utility turbo-props, and single-engine piston aircraft. The segment also includes a joint venture in CitationShares fractional jet ownership business. Cessna's annual revenues make up 23 percent of Textron, Inc.

## Fastening Systems

Textron Fastening Systems is the premier full-service provider of value-based fastening solutions, making up 18 percent of Textron, Inc. Its products and services are as follows:

### Threaded Fasteners (TFS)

TFS offers the most comprehensive threaded fasteners product line available in the industry. The TFS line of threaded fasteners is globally recognized in a broad range of markets and includes the Torx Plus Drive System, Taptite, Plastite, PT, and Mag-Form thread-forming fasteners and Drillite self-drilling fasteners, as well as nuts and washers.

TFS has more than forty manufacturing facilities in seventeen countries and serves customers in more than 100 countries.

## Engineered Products

To lower assembly costs, manufacturers utilize TFS-engineered products and assemblies, as well as TFS's extensive capabilities in cold forming, metal stamping, plastic molding, die-casting, and modular assemblies. Each TFS-engineered assembly is designed to meet the specific form, fit, and function requirements of the application.

## Blind Fasteners

The globally recognized Avdel and Cherry brands offer a broad range of installation tools and blind fasteners, including threaded inserts and structural, breakstem, and speed fasteners.

## Automated Systems

For full fastener assembly automation, TFS offers a vast array of solutions. TFS automation systems enable customers to automate their fastener installation processes to lower costs and greatly improve productivity.

## Industrial

The Industrial segment is comprised of five businesses that manufacture and market branded industrial products worldwide. This part the company is responsible for 29 percent of Textron's revenues. It consists of five groups:

### E-Z-GO (11 percent of the segment)

E-Z-GO offers the world's most comprehensive line of vehicles for golf courses, resort communities, and municipalities, as well as commercial and industrial users, such as airports and factories. Products include electric-powered and internal-combustion-powered golf cars and multipurpose utility vehicles.

### Jacobsen (12 percent)

Jacobsen offers the world's most comprehensive line of turf-care products for golf courses, resort communities, and municipalities, as well as commercial and industrial users and professional lawn-care services.

### Greenlee (12 percent)

Greenlee, a leader in wire and cable installation systems, is the premier source for professional grade tools and test instruments to the electrical contractor and voice/data/video contractor markets, as well as the telecommunications and CATV markets.

### Kautex (50 percent)

Kautex is a leading global supplier of plastic fuel systems, including plastic and metal fuel filler assemblies. Kautex also supplies automotive clear vision systems (windshield and headlamp cleaning), blow-molded ducting and fluid reservoirs, and other components, such as cooling pipes and acoustic components.

### Textron Fluid & Power (15 percent)

Textron Fluid & Power manufactures industrial pumps, gears, and gearboxes for hydrocarbon processing, polymer process-ing, industrial mining, mobile equipment, and defense applications.

### Finance

Textron Finance is a diversified commercial finance company with core operations in distribution finance, aircraft finance, golf finance, resort finance, structured capital, and asset-based lending. Textron Finance also pro-vides financing programs for products manu-factured and services by Textron, Inc. It makes up 8 percent of the company's revenues.

## Shortcomings to Bear in Mind

- On February 22, 2005, *Standard & Poor's Stock Reports* rated Textron as a HOLD. Robert E. Friedman, CPA, had this to say, "Looking at TXT's long-term finan-cial prospects, we believe the mature and highly cyclical aircraft and automotive markets may prevent the company from generating outsized sustainable earnings growth and profitability returns. How-ever, we believe free cash earnings could still expand at a 7 percent compound annual growth rate, with return on equity averaging about 15 percent at best."
- The Argus Research Company had this lukewarm appraisal of Textron on January 19, 2005. Suzanne Betts said, "Despite concerns over how future defense dollars will be spent, or not spent, we are main-taining our HOLD rating on Textron at this time. The biggest exposure for Tex-tron is the V-22 program, which could see $1 billion in funding cut under the most recent proposal. However, it remains to be seen how funding will be allocated in the final budget. The company's diversi-fication outside the defense industry will be unaffected by any proposed cuts in defense spending."

## Reasons to Buy

- "The company continues to benefit from strong demand for business jets," said Perry

H. Roth, writing for *Value Line Investment Survey* on January 28, 2005. "TXT's air-craft subsidiary, Cessna, introduced three new Citation jet models last year *(2004)*. The latest model, the Citation CJ3, was rolled out last December. The Citation CJ3 features the most comfortable cabin in its class and an advanced avionics sys-tem. Cessna has received more than 130 orders for the CJ3, valued at more than $800 million. In 2005, the company expects to receive FAA certification for Citation CJ2+. The CJ2+ is an enhanced version of the CJ2, currently the bestsell-ing light business jet in the market."

- Cessna Citations are operated in more than seventy-five countries, representing the largest fleet of business jets in the world. In its seventy-five-year history, Cessna has delivered more than 185,000 aircraft, including more than 150,000 single-engine airplanes, more than 1,400 Caravans; more than 2,000 military jets, and more than 4,000 Citation business jets. Cessna has delivered 34 percent more business jets than its closest competitor.
- "Our powerful brands, such as Bell, Cessna, E-Z-GO, Jacobsen, Kautex, Greenlee, and others, continue to lead their industries with technological inno-vation, generating new products that promise impressive revenue and earn-ings through the end of the decade and beyond," said CEO Campbell in 2004. "In 2003 alone, we brought more than 120 new and upgraded products and services to market, creating opportuni-ties for our customers to realize benefits unavailable elsewhere in our industries."
- At the end of 2004, Bell's backlog of $2.8 billion was up from $1.4 billion compared with year-end 2003. At Cessna, backlog from unaffiliated customers of $5.4 bil-lion was up from $3.9 billion, compared with a year earlier. In addition, Cessna also had orders from its CitationShares joint venture totaling $497 million.

Total assets: $15,875 million
Current ratio: 1.59
Common shares outstanding: 137 million
Return on 2004 shareholders' equity: 12.8%

|  | 2004 | 2003 | 2002 | 2001 | 2000 | 1999 | 1998 | 1997 |
|---|---|---|---|---|---|---|---|---|
| Revenues (millions) | 9,792 | 9,287 | 10,028 | 11,612 | 12,399 | 11,116 | 9,316 | 8,333 |
| Net income (millions) | 471 | 281 | 364 | 166 | 277 | 623 | 443 | 558 |
| Earnings per share | 3.36 | 2.05 | 2.60 | 1.16 | 1.90 | 4.05 | 2.68 | 3.29 |
| Dividends per share | 1.30 | 1.30 | 1.30 | 1.30 | 1.30 | 1.30 | 1.14 | 1.00 |
| Price        high | 74.9 | 58.0 | 53.6 | 60.5 | 76.3 | 98.0 | 80.9 | 70.8 |
|              low | 50.6 | 26.0 | 32.2 | 31.3 | 40.7 | 65.9 | 52.1 | 45.0 |

Conservative Growth

# 3M Company

3M Center, Building 225–01-S-15 ❑ St. Paul, MN 55144–1000 ❑ (651) 733–8206 ❑ Web site: *www.3M.com* ❑ Listed: NYSE ❑ Dividend reinvestment plan available: (800) 401–1952 ❑ Ticker symbol: MMM ❑ S&P rating: A- ❑ Value Line financial strength rating: A++

New products are the engine of 3M's growth, as the company continues to develop innovative products that make life better for people around the world. One of 3M's largest and fastest-growing product lines—Vikuiti Display Enhancement Films—make electronic displays brighter, more colorful and easier to read, while also extending battery life. Vikuiti films are extensively used in notebook computers, color cellular phones, personal digital assistants, and other portable electronic products, as well as in LCD desktop computer monitors. And now they're being used in LCD televisions, too.

Another 3M product platform showing rapid growth is immune response modifiers (IRMs). This unique class of drugs stimulates the body's immune system to fight virus-infected cells and tumor cells. The company's first-approved IRM—Aldara (imiquimod) Cream, 5 percent—is a patient-friendly prescription drug that attacks the virus that causes genital warts, a common sexually transmitted disease. In March 2004, the U.S. Food and Drug Administration granted 3M marketing approval for Aldara cream for the treatment of actinic keratosis, a precancerous skin condition affecting about 10 million Americans.

3M ingenuity is transforming a broad range of industries. For example, a new-generation 3M security laminate—combining advanced film, retro-reflective, and imaging technologies—makes it virtually impossible to counterfeit or alter passports, driver's licenses, and other security documents. What's more, 3M Composite Conductors, for use in overhead power transmission, represent one of the most important industry advances in nearly a century and were named by *R&D Magazine* as one of the 100 most technologically advanced products introduced in 2003.

## Company Profile

Minnesota Mining and Manufacturing—now known as 3M Company—is a $20-billion diversified technology company with leading positions in industrial, consumer and office, health care, safety, electronics, telecommunications, and other markets. The company has operations in more than 60 countries and serves customers in nearly 200 countries.

3M has a vast array of products (more than 50,000), including such items as tapes, adhesives, electronic components, sealants, coatings, fasteners, floor coverings, cleaning agents, roofing granules, fire-fighting agents, graphic arts, dental products, medical products, specialty chemicals, and reflective sheeting.

The company's Industrial and Consumer Sector is the world's largest supplier of tapes, producing more than 900 varieties. It is also a leader in coated abrasives, specialty chemicals, repositionable notes, home cleaning sponges and pads, electronic circuits, and other important products.

The Life Sciences Sector is a global leader in reflective materials for transportation safety, respirators for worker safety, closures for disposable diapers, and high-quality graphics used indoors and out. This sector also holds leading positions in medical and surgical supplies, drug-delivery systems, and dental products.

3M has a decentralized organization with a large number of relatively small profit centers, aimed at creating an entrepreneurial atmosphere.

## Shortcomings to Bear in Mind

- When MMM announced its results for 2004, one analyst had a rather guarded comment, according to an article in the *Wall Street Journal* by Erik Ahlberg on January 19, 2005. "Analyst Dmitry Silversteyn of Longbow Research said company executives sounded 'a little cautious' about the direction of the economy and 3M's prospects for this year, though the company often takes such a conservative stance regarding its earnings outlook." On the other hand, the company's sales and earnings both advanced in 2004, compared with the prior year.

## Reasons to Buy

- "Three M's results are heavily dependent upon the health of the domestic industrial economy," said Jeremy J. Butler, an analyst with *Value Line Investment Survey*, on February 18, 2005. He goes on to say, "And given the fact that most economists believe GDP (*Gross Domestic Product*) will grow about 3.5 percent this year, 3M should benefit accordingly. The company is also well diversified geographically, as well as by business line. It has a huge cash hoard, which it will probably use to acquire companies to supplement its fast-growing Healthcare and D&G businesses, buy back shares on temporary weakness, and increase the dividend payout."

- MMM has many strengths:
  - Leading market positions. Minnesota Mining is a leader in most of its businesses, often number one or number two in market share. In fact, 3M has created many markets, frequently by developing products that people didn't even realize they needed.
  - Strong technology base. The company draws on more than 30 core technologies—from adhesives and nonwovens to specialty chemicals and microreplication.
  - Healthy mix of businesses. 3M serves an extremely broad array of markets—from automotive and health care to office supply and telecommunications. This diversity gives the company many avenues for growth, while also cushioning the company from disruption in any single market.
  - Flexible, self-reliant business units. 3M's success in developing a steady stream of new products and entering new markets stems from its deep-rooted corporate structure. It's an environment in which 3M people listen to customers, act on their own initiative, and share technologies and other expertise widely and freely.

- Worldwide presence. Minnesota Mining has companies in more than 60 countries around the world. It sells its products in some 200 countries.
- Efficient manufacturing and distribution. 3M is a low-cost supplier in many of its product lines. This is increasingly important in today's value-conscious and competitive world.
- Strong financial position. 3M is one of a small number of domestic companies whose debt carries the highest rating for credit quality.

- To sustain a strong flow of new product, 3M continues to make substantial investments—about $1 billion a year—in research and development.
- 3M Company is a global leader in industrial, consumer, office, health care, safety, and other markets. The company draws on many strengths, including a rich pool of technology, innovative products, strong customer service and efficient manufacturing.
- The unrelenting drive toward smaller, lighter, more powerful, and more economical electronic products creates strong demand for leading-edge 3M Microflex Circuits. 3M is the world's No. 1 supplier of adhesive-less flexible circuitry. 3M microflex circuits connect components in many of the world's ink-jet printers. They also link integrated circuits to printed circuit boards efficiently and reliably, making it possible to develop even smaller cellular phones, portable computers, pagers, and other electronic devices.
- 3M supplies a wide variety of products to the automotive market, including high-performance tape attachment systems; structural adhesives; catalytic converter mounts; decorative, functional and protective films; and trim and identification products.
- The Life Sciences Sector produces innovative products that improve health and safety for people around the world. In consumer and professional healthcare,

3M has captured a significant share of the first-aid market with a superior line of bandages. 3M Active Strips Flexible Foam Bandages adhere better to skin—even when wet—and 3M Comfort Strips Ultra Comfortable Bandages set new standards for wearing comfort. Under development are tapes, specialty dressings, and skin treatments that will reinforce and broaden the company's leading market positions and accelerate sales growth.

- In pharmaceuticals, 3M is a global leader in technologies for delivering medications that are inhaled or absorbed through the skin, and the company is expanding its horizons in new molecule discovery.
- Hostile conditions lie under any vehicle's hood, but 3M's Dyneon Fluoropolymers withstand the heat. Found in seals, gaskets, O-rings, and hoses in automotive and airplane engines, the company's fluoropolymers outperform the competition when high temperatures and chemicals cross paths. And 3M technology isn't merely under the hood. Minnesota Mining also makes products for the vehicle's body and cabin that identify, insulate, protect and bond—such as dimensional graphics, Thinsulate Acoustic Insulation, cabin filters, and super-strong adhesives and tapes that replace screws and rivets. The company is also developing window films that help keep the cabin cool by absorbing ultraviolet light and reflecting infrared light.
- Post-it Notes were named one of the twentieth century's best products by *Fortune* magazine, and Scotch Tape was listed among the century's 100 best innovations by *BusinessWeek* magazine. Also, 3M ranked as the world's most respected consumer-goods company and 15th overall in a survey published by the *Financial Times of London*. Finally, 3M has received Achieved Vendor of the Year status from four leaders in the office-supply industry.

- In 2003, the company announced the creation of a Corporate Research Laboratory to energize its "cutting-edge" science and technology development, while also aligning a portion of its existing technology center resources to drive accelerated growth in the seven market-focuses businesses. 3M has 6,500 technical employees.

"Developing innovative technologies and matching them to customer needs is what 3M has always done best, and it remains our primary growth engine," said W. James McNerney, Jr., chairman and CEO. "By bringing more of our technology people into 3M businesses, we are strengthening our ability to commercialize new products, now and well into the future."

Mr. McNerney called the shift a "natural and essential step" in bringing 3M technology into alignment with customer needs. "By shifting more of 3M's R&D resources to the front lines, we enhance the ability of our R&D employees to make an even greater difference, to create more winning products that will make an even bigger impact in the marketplace."

Total assets: $20,708 million
Current ratio: 1.44
Common shares outstanding: 774 million
Return on 2004 shareholder's equity: 32.7%

| | 2004 | 2003 | 2002 | 2001 | 2000 | 1999 | 1998 | 1997 |
|---|---|---|---|---|---|---|---|---|
| Revenues (millions) | 20,011 | 18,232 | 16,332 | 16,079 | 16,724 | 15,659 | 15,021 | 15,070 |
| Net income (millions) | 2,990 | 2,403 | 1,974 | 1,430 | 1,782 | 1,711 | 1,526 | 1,626 |
| Earnings per share | 3.75 | 3.09 | 2.50 | 1.79 | 2.32 | 2.11 | 1.87 | 1.94 |
| Dividends per share | 1.44 | 1.32 | 1.24 | 1.20 | 1.16 | 1.12 | 1.10 | 1.06 |
| Price high | 90.3 | 85.4 | 65.8 | 63.5 | 61.5 | 51.7 | 48.9 | 52.8 |
| low | 73.3 | 59.7 | 50.0 | 42.9 | 39.1 | 34.7 | 32.8 | 40.0 |

Conservative Growth

# UnitedHealth Group Inc.

9900 Bren Road East ❑ Minneapolis, MN 55343 ❑ Listed: NYSE ❑ (952) 936–7265 ❑ Dividend reinvestment plan is not available ❑ Web site: *www.unitedhealthgroup.com* ❑ Ticker symbol: UNH ❑ S&P rating: A ❑ Value Line financial strength rating: A+

"UnitedHealth Group, Inc. said it will acquire Definity Health Corp., a specialist in 'consumer-driven' health benefits, for $300 million,' said Vanessa Fuhrmans, writing for the *Wall Street Journal* on November 30, 2004.

"The deal by UnitedHealth, the country's largest managed-care company in terms of members, is a bid to expand in the fast-growing area of high-deductible health plans coupled with medical spending accounts."

The *Wall Street Journal* article also said, "With the advent of Health Savings Accounts, a portable tax-saving account legislated into the Medicare drug bill passed last year (2003) high-deductible plans are expected to become even more widespread. A survey released by Mercer Human Resource Consulting last week said 1 percent of all companies offered consumer-driven plans this year. But 26 percent of large employers are likely to add one by 2006."

## Corporate Profile

UnitedHealth Group is a U.S. leader in health-care management, providing a broad range of health-care products and services, including health maintenance organizations (HMOs), point of service (POS) plans, preferred provider organizations (PPOs) and managed fee for service programs. It also offers managed behavioral health services, utilization management, workers' compensation, and disability management services, specialized provider networks, and third-party administration services. Here are its four segments.

UnitedHealthcare coordinates network-based health and well-being services on behalf of local employers and consumers in six broad regional markets, including commercial, Medicare, and Medicaid products and services.

Ovations offers health and well-being services for Americans age fifty and older and their families, including Medicare supplement insurance, hospital indemnity coverage, and pharmacy services for members of the health insurance program of AARP. Ovations also provides health and well-being services for elderly, vulnerable, and chronically ill populations through Evercare.

Uniprise provides network-based health and well-being services, business-to-business infrastructure services, consumer connectivity and service, and technology support services for large employers and health plans.

Specialized Care Services offers a comprehensive array of specialized benefits, networks, services, and resources to help consumers improve their health and well-being, including employee assistance/counseling programs, mental health/substance abuse services, solid organ transplant programs and related services, twenty-four-hour health and well-being information services and publications, dental benefits, vision care benefits, life, accident and critical illness benefits, and chiropractic, physical therapy, and complementary medicine benefits.

Ingenix serves providers, payers, employers, governments, pharmaceutical companies, and medical device manufacturers and academic and other research institutions through two divisions. Ingenix Health Intelligence offers business-to-business publications, and data and software analytic products. Ingenix Pharmaceutical Services is a global drug development and marketing services organization offering clinical trial management services, consulting services, medical education, and epidemiological and economic research.

## Shortcomings to Bear in Mind

- Phillip M. Seligman, an analyst with *Standard & Poor's Stock Reports* had this lukewarm comment on October 20, 2004, "We believe that UNH has shown strong, consistent performance and continues to have a robust operating outlook. Nevertheless, we do not anticipate much price appreciation for the shares for the foreseeable future."

  On January 25, 2005, Mr. Seligman had changed his rating to BUY, with this comment: "We believe that UNH has shown strong, consistent performance and continues to have a robust operating outlook. We are encouraged by the company's acquisitions."
- Argus Research Company was not enthusiastic on January 11, 2005. David H. Toung said, "We are maintaining our HOLD rating on the UNH shares because we believe that the stock's valuation (trading at 18.5 times our 2005 estimate) fairly reflects the company's strong growth prospects."

## Reasons to Buy

- On April 4, 2005, *BusinessWeek* had this comment: "Through employers, associations such as AARP, and state governments, UnitedHealth now counts a staggering 55 million Americans among its customers. A serial acquirer in a fast-consolidating industry, the diversified healthcare management firm added the Oxford Health Plans in the New York area in 2004. Such deals help drive rich gains, such as 2004's 42 percent rise in net earnings. To keep the gains coming, the Minnetonka (Minn.) outfit is moving into serving state Medicaid programs and health-related transaction processing."

■ On March 26, 2005, *Value Line Investment Survey* gave this stock its best Timeliness rating of 1. Mario Ferro said, "Demographic trends are playing into UnitedHealth's favor. Healthcare demand has continued to expand and is now the fastest-growing sector of the U.S. economy. And with the large number of baby boomers heading into their senior years, the company is positioned to benefit from increased demand for its products and services in the years ahead."

■ I'm not the only person who likes United-Health Group. Here are some recent awards:

• *Fortune* magazine (April 16, 2001) ranked UnitedHealth Group Number 91 in the 2001 rankings of the 500 largest U.S. corporations, based on 2000 revenues. *Fortune* also ranked UnitedHealth Group number two in the healthcare industry (based on 2000 revenues).

• UnitedHealth Group Chairman and CEO Bill McGuire was ranked number 26 on *Worth* magazine's Top 50 CEO list (May 2001). The magazine selected business leaders based on their foresight, judgment, and competitive edge.

• The company was ranked number 12 on *Barron's* 500 (April 23, 2001), a report card that grades companies' overall performance for investors.

• *Fortune* magazine has ranked UnitedHealth Group the first or second most admired healthcare company in America every year since 1995.

• For the second consecutive year, CareData, the health-care division of J.D. Power and Associates (September 19, 2000), ranked UnitedHealthcare the number one managed healthcare organization in a member satisfaction survey of leading national health plans.

• *Computerworld* magazine (June 4, 2001) listed UnitedHealth Group in its annual list of the 100 Best Places to Work in IT for the eight consecutive year.

■ In the past 10 years (1994–2004) Earnings per share advanced sharply, from $0.44 to $3.94, a compound annual growth rate of 24.5 percent. The only exception was 1996, when earning fell from $0.53 to $0.44.

■ Since its inception, UnitedHealth Group and its affiliated companies have led the marketplace by introducing key innovations that make healthcare services more accessible and affordable for customers, improving the quality and coordination of healthcare services, and help individuals and their physicians make more informed healthcare decisions.

## Time Line of Selected Highlights and Innovations

1974. Charter Med incorporated is founded by a group of physicians and other healthcare professionals.

1977. UnitedHealthcare Corporation is created and acquires Charter Med Incorporated.

1979. UnitedHealthcare Corporation introduces the first network-based health plan for seniors and participates in the earliest experiments with offering a private-market alternatives for Medicare.

1984. UnitedHealthcare Corporation becomes a publicly traded company.

1989. William W. McGuire, M.D. assumes leadership of the company. Annual revenues are just over $400 million. Today they are over $26 billion.

1995. The company acquires The MetraHealth Companies Inc. for $1.65 billion. MetraHealth is a privately held company that was formed by combining the group health-care operations of The Travelers Insurance Company and Metropolitan Life Insurance Company.

1996. The company patented artificial intelligence system AdjudiPro, which is entered into the permanent research collection of the Smithsonian Institution, and is awarded the CIO Enterprise Value Award.

1998. UnitedHealthcare Corporation becomes known as UnitedHealth Group and launches a strategic realignment into independent but strategically linked business segments—UnitedHealthcare, Ovations, Uniprise, Specialized Care Services, and Ingenix.

1998. The first release of Clinical Profiles takes place. Clinical Profiles, produced by Ingenix, provides network physicians with data comparing their clinical practices to nationally accepted benchmarks for care.

2001. UnitedHealthcare uses Web-enabled technology to simplify and improve service for physicians, enabling them to check benefit eligibility for patients and submit and review claims. The company also launches a Web-based distribution portal to serve small business brokers.

2002. Ingenix continues to introduce new knowledge and information products—including Parallax i iCES and Galaxy clinical and financial insights and improve the quality of health-care delivery and administration. (Parallax i iCES aggregates health data from multiple systems, enabling users to identify and analyze multifaceted benefit issues.)

Total assets: $27,879 million
Current ratio: 0.73
Common shares outstanding: 1.308 million
Return on 2004 shareholders' equity: 32.7%

| | 2004 | 2003 | 2002 | 2001 | 2000 | 1999 | 1998 | 1997 |
|---|---|---|---|---|---|---|---|---|
| Revenues (millions) | 37,218 | 28,823 | 25,020 | 23,454 | 21,122 | 19,562 | 17,355 | 11,794 |
| Net income (millions) | 2,587 | 1,825 | 1,352 | 913 | 705 | 563 | 509 | 460 |
| Earnings per share | 1.97 | 1.48 | 1.07 | .70 | .53 | .40 | .33 | .22 |
| Dividends per share | .015 | .01 | .01 | .01 | .005 | .005 | .005 | .005 |
| Price  high | 43.8 | 29.4 | 25.3 | 18.2 | 15.9 | 8.8 | 9.3 | 7.5 |
|      low | 27.7 | 19.6 | 17.0 | 12.7 | 5.8 | 4.9 | 3.7 | 5.3 |

Aggressive Growth

# United Parcel Service, Inc.

55 Glenlake Parkway N.E. ❑ Atlanta, GA 30328 ❑ (404) 828–6977 ❑ Dividend reinvestment plan is available: (800) 758–4674 ❑ Web site: *www.ups.com* ❑ Listed: NYSE ❑ Ticker symbol: UPS ❑ S&P rating: Not rated ❑ Value Line financial strength rating: A+

"UPS this week began the first of twelve new flights to China with MD-11 service to Shanghai," said a company official on November 4, 2004. "The new flights will triple the current service from six to eighteen flights a week and comes on the heels of UPS's impressive 129 percent growth in China export volume in the third quarter."

"Thanks to these flights, we are moving ahead of customer demand with even greater access to the world's fastest-growing economy," said David Abney, president, UPS International. "China is probably the most exciting business opportunity in a generation, and our growth numbers from the country show that customers are turning to UPS for the efficiency and reliability of its worldwide network."

According to economic and industrial experts, China will become the world's second-largest economy within eleven years, and the largest by 2039.

UPS has been serving China since 1988 and is the only U.S. cargo carrier providing daily, nonstop service to and from the United States and China, which started when the company was first granted China aviation rights in 2001. "These most recent grants of access will increase UPS's Shanghai service to twelve flights per week. Then, next year, UPS will inaugurate the remaining six flights to provide the first-ever nonstop service between the U.S. and Guangzhou in the fast-growing Pearl River Delta."

## Company Profile

United Parcel—also known as Big Brown— is one of the largest employee-owned companies in the nation. With a fleet of 88,000 vehicles and 600 aircraft, UPS delivers 13.5 million packages and documents each day, or well over 3 billion a year.

The company's primary business is the delivery of packages and documents throughout the United States and in more than 200 other countries and territories. In addition, UPS provides logistic services, including comprehensive management of supply chains, for major companies worldwide.

United Parcel has built a strong brand equity by being a leader in quality service and product innovation in its industry. UPS has been rated the second-strongest business-to-business brand in the United States in a recent Image Power survey and has been *Fortune*

magazine's Most Admired Transportation Company in the mail, package, and freight category for sixteen consecutive years.

UPS entered the international arena in 1975. It now handles more than 1.2 million international shipments each day. What's more, its international package-delivery service (17 percent of revenues) is growing faster than its domestic business, and this trend is likely to continue. The company is also moving to expand its presence in Asia. In 2001, the Department of Transportation awarded UPS the right to fly directly from the U.S. to China.

Nonpackage businesses, although only 8 percent of revenues, comprise the company's fastest-growing segment. These operations include UPS Logistics Group and UPS Capital Corporation. A truck leasing business was sold in 2000. The logistics business provides global supply chain management, service parts logistics, and transportation and technology services. UPS Capital, launched in 1998, provides services to expedite the flow of funds through the supply chain.

The UPS shares sold in late 1999 represent about 10 percent of the company's total ownership. The rest is still owned by about 125,000 of its managers, supervisors, hourly workers, retires, foundations and descendants of the company's early leaders. The company sold only Class B shares to the public. Each share has one vote, compared with the Class A stock, which has ten votes per share.

## Shortcomings to Bear in Mind

- Good companies often have a high price tag. UPS falls into that category. You may find that its P/E ratio is more than thirty. If so, it might pay to delay your purchase until its multiple sags down to twenty-five or so.
- On January 28, 2005, Rick Brooks, writing for the *Wall Street Journal*, said, "United Parcel Services, Inc. reported a lackluster 1.2 percent rise in fourth-

quarter earnings." He went on to say, "The single biggest factor in the fourth quarter's results was the slowdown in U.S. package volume, which generated 90 percent of the company's average daily load of 15.5 million shipments but rose 1.6 percent—its slowest pace since mid-2003."

## Reasons to Buy

- United Parcel Service—popularly known as UPS—introduced UPS World Ease in 2003. UPS World Ease combines the speed and tracking of express delivery with the efficiency and cost savings of consolidated customs clearance, a service that allows customers to ship multiple packages to many destinations in the same country as one consolidated shipment. This allows goods to move directly through customs as a single unit, reducing the need for warehousing, inventory and shipping.

  "This means that UPS's transportation network becomes a sort of 'in-transit warehouse' for us, eliminating our added expense of warehouse inventory," said Anil Agrawal, chief operating officer of EcoQuest International. Tennessee-based EcoQuest, a UPS customer that manufactures and markets air and water purification systems, already projects a world of difference using World Ease. "Because our shipments clear customs all at once, we can get our systems to international customers within days, instead of weeks. Adding World Ease will save at least $1 million in supply chain costs over the next five years."

  UPS World Ease is a contract service that works through the UPS small package network. Once the shipment clears customs, it is separated back into smaller shipments for final destination delivery throughout a country by UPS. UPS World Ease is available in sixty-one countries, in combination with delivery services UPS Worldwide Express, UPS Worldwide Expedited and UPS Standard services.

- UPS obtains the vast majority of its revenue from small-package deliveries here at home. On the other hand, overseas shipments, finance, and supply-chain management are growing at a fast clip—and that's where the company believes its future is headed.

- UPS stands out from the crowd in scores of ways:
  - The company's mobile radio network transmits more than 3 million packets of tracking data each day.
  - The company's maintenance capacity allows the transmission of more than 22 million instructions per second.
  - UPS shipping tools are embedded in more than 65,000 customer Web sites.
  - Using Global Positioning Satellite technology, has the capacity to pinpoint a package within thirty feet of its location.
  - UPS Supply Chain Solutions has operations in more than 120 countries. The Supply Chain Solutions Group provides logistics and distribution services, international trade management, and transportation and freight using multimodal transportation.
  - UPS Supply Chain Solutions files more than 4 million customer entries in the United States, making it the nation's largest broker.
  - UPS Supply Chain Solutions has hundreds of engineers to help remap supply chains for greater efficiency and market responsiveness.
  - UPS Supply Chain Solutions was rated as the number one logistics provider in *Inbound Logistics* annual "Top 10 3PL Excellence Award" survey.
  - UPS is ranked as the largest third-party logistics provider in North America by *Traffic World* magazine.
  - UPS has 4,500 retail locations worldwide—more than all other franchised shipping chains put together.

- In the United States and Canada, UPS has more than 41,000 drop boxes.
- There are 7,500 third-party retail pack-and-ship locations.
- The company operates 1,400 customer centers with its operating facilities worldwide.
- UPS has more than 12,900 in-store shipping locations and commercial counters.
- The company serves more than 850 airports around the world, flying more than 1,800 flight segments each day.
- UPS operates the eleventh-largest airline in the world.
- Local country management people average fourteen years of UPS experience.
- With expanded air rights to Hong Kong, UPS now offers direct service to its two largest hubs in Europe and Asia and enhanced service to China's fastest-growing express and cargo region.
- The company has under construction a $135-million, 30,000-square-meter facility at Cologne/Bonn Airport in Germany. It will be the largest UPS facility outside the United States.
- UPS has a ninety-seven-year history of revenue growth.
- UPS is one of seven companies in the United States that has a triple-A credit rating from both Standard & Poor's and Moody's.
- Active and former employees and their families own more than 50 percent of UPS stock. That may be why you rarely see a UPS driver walking—they insist on running at top speed.

■ Argus Research Company had some kind of words to say about UPS—rated a BUY—on January 21, 2005. Suzanne Betts said, "We remain optimistic about the company's growth outlook for 2005. Domestic competition from the US Postal Service and FedEx, and to a smaller degree from DHL, is likely to continue. However, UPS has significant growth opportunities in its international markets as it expands its presence in Asia over the coming year."

Total assets: $33,026 million
Current ratio: 1.94
Common shares outstanding: 1124 million
Return on 2004 shareholders' equity: 21.3%

|  |  | 2004 | 2003 | 2002 | 2001 | 2000 | 1999 | 1998 | 1997 |
|---|---|---|---|---|---|---|---|---|---|
| Revenues (millions) |  | 36,582 | 33,485 | 31,272 | 30,321 | 29,771 | 27,052 | 24,788 | 22,458 |
| Net income (millions) |  | 3,333 | 2,898 | 3,182 | 2,425 | 2,795 | 2,325 | 1,741 | 909 |
| Earnings per share |  | 2.90 | 2.55 | 2.84 | 2.10 | 2.38 | 2.04 | 1.57 | * |
| Dividends per share |  | 1.12 | .92 | .76 | .76 | .68 | .58 | .43 | * |
| Price | high | 89.1 | 74.9 | 67.1 | 62.5 | 69.8 | 76.9 | * | * |
|  | low | 67.2 | 53.0 | 54.3 | 46.2 | 49.5 | 61.0 | * | * |

* United Parcel was a private company prior to 1999, and thus no additional statistics are available.

Conservative Growth

# United Technologies Corporation

One Financial Plaza ❑ Hartford, CT 06103 ❑ (860) 728–7912 ❑ Listed: NYSE ❑ Dividend reinvestment plan available: (800) 519–3111 ❑ Web site: www.utc.com ❑ Listed: NYSE ❑ Ticker symbol: UTX ❑ S&P rating: A+ ❑ Value Line Financial Strength A++

"Getting a handle on George David (CEO of United Technologies) isn't easy," said Diane Brady in a *BusinessWeek* article dated October 25, 2004. "An ardent student of both history and management, he has the air of an academic and talks like some modern-day Plato in a production plant.

"But David, sixty-two, is more than just a head-in-the-clouds theorist. He has transformed this old-line industrial conglomerate into a \$31-billion powerhouse of productivity with relentless attention to detail. He has taken what are essentially commodity products such as elevators and air conditioners and, thanks to constant innovation and superior technology, turned them into high-margin businesses that dominate from Boston to Beijing.

"He pontificates on abstruse historical and macro-economic issues one minute and obsesses over a tiny improvement in the farthest corner of the UTC empire the next. And while he can terminate thousands of workers at a stroke in the name of efficiency, he also has crafted one of the most progressive employee education programs in the world—even extending benefits to laid-off workers.

"Together, these disparate impulses have yielded big results. In David's decade at the helm, in fact, this philosopher king of manufacturing has more than quadrupled Earnings per share and outperformed even the mythic General Electric Company in returns to investors. UTC's total returns have risen about 600 percent in the past ten years, vs. roughly 400 percent for GE."

## Company Profile

United Technologies provides high-technology products to the aerospace and building systems industries throughout the world. Its companies are industry leaders and include Pratt & Whitney, Carrier, Otis, Sikorsky, International Fuel Cells, and Hamilton Sundstrand. Sikorsky and Hamilton Sundstrand make up the Flight Systems segment.

## Pratt & Whitney

### Products and Services

Large and small commercial and military jet engines, spare parts and product support, specialized engine maintenance and overhaul and repair services for airlines, air forces and corporate fleets; rocket engines and space propulsion systems; industrial gas turbines.

### Primary Customers

Commercial airlines and aircraft-leasing companies; commercial and corporate aircraft manufacturers; the U.S. government, including NASA and the military services; regional and commuter airlines.

## Carrier

### Products and Services

Heating, ventilating, and air conditioning (HVAC) equipment for commercial, industrial, and residential buildings; HVAC replacement parts and services; building controls; commercial, industrial, and transport refrigeration equipment.

Carrier emphasizes energy-efficiency, quiet operation, and environmental stewardship in its new residential and commercial products. The new WeatherMaker residential air conditioner using Puron, a nonozone-depleting refrigerant, provides the domestic market with low operating costs and sound levels—about the same as a refrigerator's. The Puron unit gives Carrier a healthy lead over competitors, as chlorine-free refrigerants become the standard.

### Primary Customers

Mechanical and building contractors; homeowners, building owners, developers, and retailers; architects and building consultants; transportation and refrigeration companies; shipping operations.

## Otis

### Products and Services

Elevators, escalators, moving walks, shuttle systems, and related installation, maintenance, and repair services; modernization products and service for elevators and escalators.

### Primary Customers
Mechanical and building contractors; building owners and developers; homeowners; architects and building consultants.

## Flight Systems
### Products and Services
Aircraft electrical and power distribution systems; engine and flight controls; propulsion systems; environmental controls for aircraft, spacecraft, and submarines; auxiliary power units; space life support systems; industrial products including mechanical power transmissions, compressors, metering devices, and fluid handling equipment; military and commercial helicopters; spare parts; civil helicopter operations; and maintenance services for helicopters and fixed-wing aircraft.

### Primary Customers
The U.S. government, including NASA, FAA and the military services; non-U.S. governments; aerospace and defense prime contractors; commercial airlines; aircraft and jet engine manufacturers; oil and gas exploration companies; mining and water companies; construction companies; hospitals and charters.

## Shortcomings to Bear in Mind
- "Last March, United Technologies Corp. CEO David made it clear how important it was for his company's Sikorsky helicopter unit to land the contract for the U.S. president's next helicopter," said J. Lynn Lunsford, writing for the *Wall Street Journal* on January 31, 2005. 'We'll win it or drop dead,' he said. Now, how many people in the industry will be watching to see exactly what Mr. David meant by 'drop dead.'

   "On Friday, the U.S. Navy put an end to the bitter competition by announcing that Lockheed Martin Corp. had won the coveted Marine One contract—one that Sikorsky had controlled since Dwight Eisenhower was president."

## Reasons to Buy
- *Value Line Investment Survey's* analyst, Erik M. Manning, had some good words to say about United Technologies on January 28, 2005: "United Technologies's share net rose by 16 percent in 2004. The best-performing divisions during the twelve-month period were Pratt & Whitney (engines) and Otis (elevators). Additionally, the company met both goals that it set early in the campaign by using more than $800 million of cash flow from operations to pay down its pension plan deficit, and by buying back more than $900 million of its shares. And restructurings to lower UTX's cost structure that took place during the year should lead to an improved bottom line (*profits*) and operating margin expansion in 2005"
- Dana Richardson, writing for the Argus Research Company on January 24, 2005, had this favorable view: "UTX is widely considered one of the world's best-managed companies. Its smooth earnings growth, attested to by nine up years out of the last ten, and 17 percent annualized EPS growth over that period, is highly unusual for a large industrial company. It has achieved this record by means of a consistent strategy of free cash flow-funded acquisitions and their integration. In concert with the acquisition strategy, segment operating margin expansion from 5 percent 14 percent over the last ten years has been instrumental in its success."
- In December 2004, United Technologies bought Kidde, a British fire-safety company, for $2.8 billion. Kidde, based in Slough, England, supplies fire extinguishers and alarms to homes, commercial

buildings and industries, such as airlines and oil platforms. The company has 7,750 employees in twenty-nine countries and had $1.53 billion in revenues in 2003. Kidde was particularly attractive because in addition to its commercial and residential fire and safety products, it is an important player in similar products used widely on commercial airlines. Earlier in 2004, Kidde won a contract to provide the fire-protection system for Boeing's new 7E7 Dreamliner aircraft.

- Through internal growth and acquisition, Carrier's commercial refrigeration business has become a leader in the highly fragmented $17-billion global industry. Carrier's acquisition of Electrolux Commercial Refrigeration will broaden its offerings to supermarkets, convenience stores, and food and beverage markets, particularly in Europe. A new transport refrigeration unit, the Vector, can cool a trailer from 30 degrees C to minus 20 degrees C twice as fast as a conventional unit can.

- Pratt & Whitney scored a major coup by being chosen by the Pentagon as the lead engine supplier on both versions of the Joint Strike Fighter, as well as the F-22 fighter, two of the military's highest-profile new programs. Pratt is also tapping into markets it once chose to leave to others, aggressively seeking commercial-engine overhaul and maintenance business that could be valued at more than $1 billion a year. What's more, the company also has seized on an opportunity provided by the nation's power woes: It expects to sell fifty-four modified JT8D engines for industrial electric generation for major power companies in need of cheap and quickly obtainable electric power.

- Otis Elevator Company won the contract to supply elevators and escalators for Beijing's biggest public transit project, a new facility under construction in preparation for the Olympic Summer Games in Beijing in 2008. Otis will supply and install eleven elevators and thirty-eight escalators for the Transit Center.

- The Comanche is a new helicopter under development for the U.S. Army by the Boeing-Sikorsky team. This sophisticated piece of hardware will more accurately and effectively relay critical information from the battlefield to the command center than any other system in place today. Sikorsky is part of United Technologies' Flight Systems, one of the company's four segments.

While it has the ability to carry out light attack missions, the Comanche will mainly serve as a reconnaissance aircraft that will coordinate the many aircraft and ground forces involved in a combat mission. For this reason the U.S. Army has called the Comanche critical to the twenty-first century Objective Force.

The Comanche is designed, manufactured, and tested by the Boeing-Sikorsky team, with help from more than fifteen leading aerospace manufacturers. In addition to Sikorsky, another one of UTX's subsidiaries, Hamilton Sundstrand, will provide the electrical power generating system and the environmental control system for the Comanche.

The battlefield of the twenty-first century will be almost entirely digitalized. As such, the Comanche, which carries highly advanced electronic equipment, will be essential for receiving and processing intelligence and sending it on to other assets. This aircraft can visually detect and classify targets seven times quicker than any other U.S. Army surveillance device today, and it can hand off precise coordinates to shooters within seconds. What's more, it can operate any time of the day and in all weather conditions. The Comanche has been undergoing rigorous testing for almost ten years. Initial deployment is scheduled for the end of the decade.

Total assets: $40 billion
Current ratio: 1.20
Return on 2004 equity: 21.7%
Common shares outstanding: 1,024 million

|  | 2004 | 2003 | 2002 | 2001 | 2000 | 1999 | 1998 | 1997 |
|---|---|---|---|---|---|---|---|---|
| Revenues (millions) | 37,445 | 31,034 | 28,212 | 27,897 | 26,583 | 24,127 | 25,715 | 24,713 |
| Net income (millions) | 2,788 | 2,361 | 2,236 | 1,938 | 1,808 | 841 | 1,255 | 1,072 |
| Earnings per share | 2.76 | 2.35 | 2.21 | 1.92 | 1.78 | .83 | 1.27 | 1.06 |
| Dividends per share | .70 | .57 | .49 | .45 | .42 | .38 | .35 | .31 |
| Price    high | 53.0 | 48.4 | 38.9 | 43.8 | 39.9 | 39.0 | 28.1 | 22.3 |
|       low | 40.4 | 26.8 | 24.4 | 20.1 | 23.3 | 25.8 | 16.8 | 16.3 |

Conservative Growth

# Valspar Corporation

1101 Third Street South ▢ Minneapolis, MN 55415–1259 ▢ (612) 375–7702 ▢ Web site: *www.valspar.com*
▢ Direct dividend reinvestment plan is available: (800) 842–7629 ▢ Fiscal years end Friday before October 31
▢ Listed: NYSE ▢ Ticker symbol: VAL ▢ Standard & Poor's rating: A- ▢ Value Line financial strength rating: B+

In 2004, Valspar continued its long record of building the company through acquisition and strategic alliances. This time, it is teaming up with Quikrete, the number one name in concrete. Founded in 1940, Atlanta-based Quikrete Companies manufactures an extensive line of cement and concrete-related products for the do-it-yourself and commercial markets. The company has seventy-five manufacturing facilities in the United States, Canada, Puerto Rico, and South America, producing more than 200 products. It is unsurpassed in product depth and distribution.

In the fall of 2004, the two companies announced that they would combine their talents with the manufacture of the market's first complete line of premium concrete coatings. Going on sale in early 2005, the new line is being made and sold jointly by Valspar and Quikrete under the brand name, "Quikrete Professional Concrete Coatings." The line features fourteen technologically advanced products, from sealers to floor coatings to water-proofers. The flagship product of the new line is the Quikrete Epoxy Garage Floor Coating Kit, an all-in-one, easy-to-use kit that features Bond-Lok technology to deliver a coating that is actually twice as strong as concrete itself.

The new product was born out of a mutual desire to leverage a respected brand name to address an underserved sector of the coatings marketplace. "Concrete coatings is currently a fragmented category that is confusing for customers," said Bill Mansfield, Valspar's executive vice president and chief operating officer. "There is definitely a need in the marketplace for a comprehensive program. With the home-improvement industry booming, and Americans investing more in their homes than ever before, the time is ripe for this category to reach into the twenty-first century. With Quikrete, this strategic alliance will create a synergistic force in the concrete coatings category and maximize growth in the retail environment."

For its part, Quikrete's executive vice president, Dennis Winchester, said, "Quikrete and Valspar each bring something unique to this relationship. We bring unparalleled concrete knowledge, and Valspar brings coatings expertise. Utilizing these joint technologies allows us to horizontally diversify our business, and has all the signs of a profitable end result for the companies involved and the retailers we serve."

## Company Profile

Founded in 1806, The Valspar Corporation is the manufacturer of the nation's first varnish. VAL represents the combination of many pioneer coatings firms. Now one of the five largest North American manufacturers of paint and coatings, the company has expanded in recent years, largely through a host of acquisitions. More recently, it has moved aggressivly abroad, with close to a third of its revenues from that sector. Its largest customer is Lowe's Companies, which accounts for about 10 percent of the company's revenues.

The Valspar Corporation provides coatings and coating intermediates to a wide variety of customers. The company's products include:

• Industrial coatings for wood, metal, and plastic for original equipment manufacturers.

• Coatings and inks for rigid packaging, principally food and beverage cans, for global customers.

• Paints, varnishes, and stains, primarily for the do-it-yourself market.

• Coatings for refinishing vehicles.

• High-performance floor coatings.

• Resins and colorants for internal use and for other paint and coatings manufacturers.

Valspar's long-term objective is 15 percent growth in both sales and earnings through a combination of internal growth and acquisitions to enhance and complement its existing businesses. Management's goal is to be the lowest-cost supplier with the leading customized technology.

## Shortcomings to Bear in Mind

■ According to one analyst, "there is the risk of dilutive acquisitions, climbing raw-material costs, deterioration of relationships with large retailers and potential negative rulings in lead paint lawsuits."

■ "We are optimistic about an earnings rebound in fiscal 2006," said Jeremy J. Butler, writing for *Value Line Investment Survey* on March 18, 2005. "It must be noted, however, that our estimates are predicated on a reduction in oil prices. Given that scenario, we think growing demand from abroad, specifically China, a cyclical recovery in the domestic paint and coatings market, and the selling price hikes already in place should result in a widening of the operating margin."

That's the good news. Mr. Butler went on to say, "This untimely issue has modest total-return potential to 2008–2010. The company's comprehensive product base and wide geographic presence should permit the stock to increase in a relatively stable manner, albeit slowly."

## Reasons to Buy

■ *Standard & Poor's Stock Reports* gave Valspar a BUY rating on February 22, 2005. Its analyst, John F. Hingher, CFA, said, "The company historically posted return on equity (ROE) exceeding 20 percent, but ROE slipped below 20 percent in fiscal 2001, and has not returned to earlier levels. We attribute what we view as relatively lackluster recent ROE performance primarily to acquisitions that have not delivered sales growth commensurate with their book value. Although we remain concerned about ROE performance, our recommendation is BUY, in light of the continued positive economic environment."

■ The company has been very active on the acquisition front, particularly in the past decade. Since 1995, Valspar had made more than a score of acquisitions, including purchases of equity in joint ventures. VAL believes its most important acquisitions were Coates Company (in a series of four transactions, in 1996, 1997, 2000, and 2001); Dexter Packaging (1999); and Lilly Industries (2000).

The Coates acquisitions added to the company's packaging coatings businesses in a number of global locations. The Dexter move added to the company's packaging and industrial coatings businesses in Europe, the United States, and Asia. Lilly, previously one of the five largest industrial coatings and specialty chemical manufacturers in North America, greatly expanded the company's presence in wood, coil, and mirror coatings, as well as in nonindustrial automotive coatings.

More recently, in August 2004, Valspar completed the acquisition of the forest products business of Associated

Chemists, Inc. The acquired product line generated sales of about $28 million in 2003 and includes edge-sealers, surface primers, paints and stains, inks, and specialty chemicals for oriented strand board manufacturers and others in the forest products industry.

- Valspar has a solid record of earnings increases. In the past ten years (1994–2004) Earnings per share advanced from $1 to $2.71, a compound annual growth rate of 10.5 percent. However, there were two years when earnings declined. In 2001, EPS fell from $2.00 to $1.58, and in 2003, Earnings per share slid from $2.34 to $2.17. In this same ten-year span, Dividends per share increased from $0.26 to $0.63, a growth rate of 9.2 percent. What's more, dividends were boosted in each of those years.

Total assets: $2,634 million
Current ratio: 1.15
Common shares outstanding: 51 million
Return on 2004 shareholders' equity: 15.3%

| | 2004 | 2003 | 2002 | 2001 | 2000 | 1999 | 1998 | 1997 |
|---|---|---|---|---|---|---|---|---|
| Revenues (millions) | 2,441 | 2,248 | 2,127 | 1,921 | 1,483 | 1,388 | 1,155 | 1,017 |
| Net income (millions) | 142.8 | 112.5 | 120.1 | 51.5 | 86.5 | 82.1 | 72.1 | 65.9 |
| Earnings per share | 2.71 | 2.17 | 2.34 | 1.58 | 2.00 | 1.87 | 1.63 | 1.49 |
| Dividends per share | .63 | .59 | .56 | .54 | .52 | .46 | .42 | .36 |
| Price     high | 51.5 | 49.6 | 50.2 | 42.0 | 43.3 | 41.9 | 42.1 | 33.1 |
|     low | 44.7 | 37.6 | 34.8 | 26.5 | 19.8 | 29.3 | 25.8 | 26.8 |

Aggressive Growth

# Varian Medical Systems, Inc.

3100 Hansen Way ❑ Palo Alto, CA 94304–1030 ❑ (650) 424–5782 ❑ Dividend reinvestment plan not available ❑ Web site: *www.varian.com* ❑ Fiscal years end on Friday nearest September 30 ❑ Ticker symbol: VAR ❑ Listed: NYSE ❑ S&P rating: B+ ❑ Value Line financial strength rating: A

Varian Medical Systems had a solid year in fiscal 2004, with record earnings, revenues, net orders, and backlog. Net earnings for 2004 were up 28 percent, to $167 million ($1.18 per diluted share) versus net earnings of $131 million ($0.92 per diluted share) for fiscal 2003.

Fourth-quarter revenues were $345 million, up 14 percent from the year-ago quarter, bringing revenues for the year to $1.2 billion, 19 percent higher than total revenues for 2003. Total net orders for fiscal 2004 were $1.4 billion, up 21 percent from the prior year. The backlog at year-end stood at $970 million, 20 percent higher than at the end of fiscal year 2003.

"Our company had an outstanding quarter and fiscal year with growth in all of our segments," said CEO Richard M. Levy. "We saw strong demand for new products that support more precise image-guided and stereotactic cancer treatments as well as solid revenue growth in our emerging flat-panel, brachytherapy, and security and inspection products."

"Annual gross margin and operating margin increased to record levels," Levy added. "We generated operating cash flow of $63 million during the quarter and ended the fiscal year with $393 million in cash and marketable securities."

The company repurchased $82 million of its common stock during the quarter, leaving a balance of 1.5 million shares in the existing repurchase authorization.

## Company Profile

Varian Medical Systems is the world's leading manufacturer of integrated radiotherapy systems for treating cancer and other diseases; it is also a leading supplier of X-ray tubes for imaging in medical, scientific, and industrial applications. Established in 1948, the company has manufacturing sites in North America and Europe and in forty sales and support offices worldwide.

In 1999, the company (formerly Varian Associates, Inc.) reorganized itself into three separate publicly traded companies by spinning off two of its businesses to stockholders via a tax-free distribution.

Since then, the company has significantly broadened its product and business offerings, acquired new businesses, and set records for sales and net orders. More importantly, Varian put itself at the forefront of a radiotherapy revolution that is making a dramatic difference in the struggle against cancer.

About three out of every ten people will be afflicted with some form of cancer. The good news is that their chances of surviving, of beating cancer, have greatly improved, thanks to recent advances in radiation therapy—many of which have been led by Varian Medical Systems.

The company has three segments:

### Varian Oncology Systems

Varian Oncology Systems is the world's leading supplier of radiotherapy systems for treating cancer. Its integrated medical systems include linear accelerators and accessories, and a broad range of interconnected software tools for planning and delivering the sophisticated radiation treatments available to cancer patients. Thousands of patients all over the world are treated daily on Varian systems. Oncology Systems works closely with health-care professionals in community clinics, hospitals, and universities to improve cancer outcomes. The business unit also supplies linear accelerators for industrial inspection applications.

### Varian X-Ray Products

Varian X-Ray Products is the world's premier independent supplier of X-ray tubes, serving manufacturers of radiology equipment and industrial inspection equipment, as well as distributors of replacement tubes. This business provides the industry's broadest selection of X-ray tubes expressly designed for the most advanced diagnostic applications, including CT scanning, radiography, and mammography. These products meet evolving requirements for improved resolution, faster patient throughput, longer tube life, smaller dimensions, and greater cost efficiency. X-Ray Products also supplies a new line of amorphous silicon flat-panel X-ray detectors for medical and industrial applications.

## Ginzton Technology Center

The Ginzton Technology Center acts as Varian Medical Systems' research and development facility for breakthrough technologies and operates a growing brachytherapy business for the delivery of internal radiation to treat cancer and cardiovascular disease. In addition to brachytherapy, current efforts are focused on next-generation imaging systems and advanced targeting technologies for radiotherapy. The center is also investigating the combination of radiotherapy with other treatment modalities, such as bioengineered gene delivery systems.

## Shortcomings to Bear in Mind

■ *Standard & Poor's Stock Reports* had a mixed view of Varian on November 10, 2004, with a HOLD rating. In the words of Robert M. Gold, "We think revenue growth in coming quarters will continue to be bolstered by clinical adoption of IMRT in North America and Europe. However, we believe a decelerating pace of radiation equipment orders in North America largely reflects challenging year-to-year comparisons, a relatively mature North American market, and increased competition. As a result, we think there well be a protracted shift toward more volatile non-U.S. markets. We see future growth driven by sales of new image guided radiotherapy products and rising sales of linear accelerators for security purposes."

## Reasons to Buy

■ *Value Line Investment Survey* was more positive. On March 4, 2005, Lucien Virgile said, "The decision to buy Varian stock requires willingness to pay the premium that its powerful profit growth demands. A better-than-20 percent earnings advance is likely this year, and these shares offer substantial long-term appreciation potential, even though they are just an average choice for Timeliness."

■ According to recent studies, more than 6 million people worldwide succumb to cancer each year. Nearly twice as many others are diagnosed with the disease. In some countries, cancer is a leading cause of death among children. Mostly though, it is a disease primarily of aging, with people fifty or older—the "baby boomers"—now accounting for nearly 80 percent of diagnosed cases. In the United States, the chances that you'll eventually develop cancer are one in three if you are female, one in two if you are male. In a very real sense, cancer victimizes not only patients, but also their families and friends, colleagues and neighbors. Ultimately, the disease affects us all. The social and economic costs are staggering.

The fact is that half of U.S. patients receive radiotherapy as part of their treatment. Now, thanks to the new technology that Varian Medical Systems has helped to develop, radiotherapy is poised to play an even stronger role in cancer treatment, and many more patients could be cured by it. It's technology that is being implemented in all corners of the world.

■ With certain cancers, the odds of surviving are improving markedly, thanks to the growing use of a radiotherapy advance called intensity modulated radiation therapy, or IMRT. IMRT is being used to treat head and neck, breast, prostate, pancreatic, lung, liver, and central nervous system cancers. IMRT makes it possible for a larger and more effective dose of radiation to be delivered directly to the tumor, greatly sparing surrounding, healthy tissues. This is expected to result in a higher likelihood of cure with lower complication rates.

The clinical outcomes using IMRT are extremely promising. A study of early stage prostate cancer has shown that the higher radiation doses possible with IMRT have the potential to double the rate of tumor control to more than 95 percent. Using IMRT, clinicians were able to deliver high doses while reducing the rate of normal tissue complications from 10 percent to 2 percent. Similar results have been reported by doctors using IMRT to treat cancers of the head and neck.

Varian Medical Systems has joined forces with GE Medical Systems to combine the latest in diagnostic imaging results with advanced radiotherapy technologies in what are called See & Treat Cancer Care imaging and treatment tools. This approach enables physicians to see the distribution of malignant cells more clearly and treat them more effectively with precisely targeted radiation doses using IMRT.

■ Varian Medical Systems has long been the world's leading supplier of radiotherapy equipment. Now, the company's SmartBeam IMRT system, the culmination of twelve years and $300 million of development effort, is already making a difference for thousands of patients.

Today, a little more than 500 of the world's 5,700 radiotherapy centers for cancer treatment have acquired a set of integrated tools for SmartBeam IMRT from Varian Medical Systems. Almost one-fifth of them are now offering it to their patients, and many others are close behind.

In addition to promising outcomes and public demand for better care, new Medicare and Medicaid reimbursement rates are expected to help accelerate the rapid adoption of IMRT by both hospitals and free-standing cancer centers in the United States. In international markets, public health systems are under pressure to reduce patients' waiting periods by updating systems with more effective treatment technology that can treat more patients.

■ In 2003, Varian Medical System announced the acquisition of Zmed, Inc., a privately held supplier of radiation oncology software and accessories for ultrasound-based, image-guided radiotherapy, stereotactic radiation treatments, and image management. "We are pleased to add this growing business to our company," said Mr. Levy. "We expect it will contribute to our growth by adding several products that will enhance the versatility and capability of Varian's integrated radiation oncology networks."

**Total assets: $1,170 million**
**Current ratio: 1.92**
**Common shares outstanding: 136 million**
**Return on 2004 shareholders' equity: 28.4%**

|  |  | 2004 | 2003 | 2002 | 2001 | 2000 | 1999 | 1998 | 1997 |
|---|---|---|---|---|---|---|---|---|---|
| Revenues (millions) |  | 1,236 | 1,042 | 873 | 774 | 690 | 590 | 1,422 | 1426 |
| Net income (millions) |  | 167 | 131 | 94 | 68 | 53 | 8 | 74 | 82 |
| Earnings per share |  | 1.18 | .92 | .67 | .50 | .41 | .07 | .61 | .69 |
| Dividends per share |  | Nil | — | — | — | —tt | .03 | .10 | .09 |
| Price | high | 46.5 | 35.7 | 25.7 | 19.3 | 17.8 | 10.8 | 14.6 | 16.8 |
|  | low | 30.8 | 23.7 | 15.8 | 13.5 | 7.1 | 4.1 | 7.9 | 11.5 |

# Walgreen Company

200 Wilmot Road ❑ Deerfield, IL 60015 ❑ (847) 940–2500 ❑ Direct dividend reinvestment program is available: (888) 368–7346 ❑ Fiscal years end August 31 ❑ Web site: *www.walgreens.com* ❑ Ticker symbol: WAG ❑ S&P rating: A+ ❑ Value Line financial strength rating: A++

"We reiterate our BUY rating on Walgreen Company, based on the company's valuation and track record of using current earnings to finance future growth," said Christopher Graja, CFA, an analyst with Argus Research Company, on January 3, 2005.

"We think Walgreen's shares can return more than the Standard & Poor's Index, on a risk-adjusted basis, because of three factors that may not be fully reflected in the share price:

"1. Almost 30 percent of Walgreen's stores are less than three years old. These stores are likely to become more profitable as they become established.

"2. Walgreen launched Advantage90 last year, which allows customers to make in-store purchases of 90-day supplies of drugs used to treat long-term conditions such as high blood pressure. Advantage90 is a response to what some investors perceive to be a major threat to the drugstore industry—mandatory mail programs. In these programs, pharmacy benefit companies offer employers cost savings for giving their employees prescription plans requiring employees to buy certain drugs through mail-only pharmacies that are sometimes run by the pharmacy benefit company.

"3. Wall Street studies have shown that companies that sell 'staples' such as food and medicine often outperform the S&P 500, as the rate of profit growth slows. Argus expects S&P 500 profit growth to fall 7 percent in 2005, from 18 percent in 2004."

## Company Profile

Walgreens, one of the fastest-growing retailers in the United States, leads the chain drugstore industry in sales and profits. Sales for fiscal 2004 reached $37.5 billion, produced by 4,582 stores in forty-four states and Puerto Rico (up from 4,227 stores a year earlier).

Founded in 1901, Walgreens today has 130,000 employees The company's drugstores serve more than 3 million customers daily and average $6.8 million in annual sales per unit. That's $628 per square foot, among the highest in the industry. Walgreens has paid dividends in every quarter since 1933 and has raised the dividend in each of the past twenty-five years.

## Stand-Alone Stores

Competition from the supermarkets has convinced Walgreens that the best strategy is to build stand-alone stores. Since the rise of managed care, many pharmacy customers now make only minimal co-payments for prescriptions. That leaves convenience as the major factor in choosing a pharmacy. The free-standing format makes room for drive-thru windows, which provide a speedy way for drugstore customers to pick up or drop off prescriptions.

On the other hand, the company's stand-alone strategy is more expensive. Walgreen insists on building its units on corner lots near an intersection with a traffic light. Such leases normally cost more than a site in a strip mall.

## More than a Pharmacy

Home meal replacement has become a $100-billion business industry-wide. In the company's food section, Walgreens carries staples as well as frozen dinners, desserts, and pizzas. In some stores, expanded food sections carry such items as fruit, and ready-to-eat salads.

Walgreens experimented with one-hour photo service as early as 1982, but it was in the mid-1990s before, according to former CEO Dan Jorndt, "We really figured it out." Since 1998, one-hour processing has been available chain-wide, made profitable by "our high volume of business. We've introduced several digital photo products that are selling well and are evaluating the long-term impact of digital on the mass market."

## Shortcomings to Bear in Mind

- Although the company is still outperforming most of corporate America, there is some concern over its prescription departments, which contribute the bulk of company sales and profits. In several states, Medicaid health insurance programs for the poor are cutting what they pay pharmacists to dispense drugs. Private insurers as well are slashing what they pay pharmacists and drug-store chains as a way to cut rapidly rising health care costs. Walgreens executives, however, have a plan to deal with such pressures. "Our goal is to offset any margin declines by lowering selling, general and administration expenses at a faster rate," said Rick Hans, the company's finance director.

- The stock has performed so well in recent years that its P/E multiple is well above average, sometimes as high as forty times earnings.

## Reasons to Buy

- "In an aggressive bid for business in a new market, UnitedHealth Group, Inc. and Walgreen Company said they will team up to provide prescription-drug coverage to Medicare beneficiaries nationwide next year," said Vanessa Fuhrmans and Janet Adamy, writing for the *Wall Street Journal* on March 18, 2005. They went on to say, "The Medicare partnership marks a victory for Walgreen and its battle with mail-order pharmacies run by the pharmacy-benefit managers. To keep health-care costs down, those managers have encouraged employers to make their workers buy through their mail-order operations, rather than from pharmacies, the prescriptions they take regularly."

- Commenting on the Advantage90 program on September 27, 2004, CEO David Bernauer said, "Since January, we've doubled the number of insurance plans and employers offering Advantage90 and are now up to 75, including progressive and cost-conscious clients like Southwest Airlines. Not only do plans prefer offering their members a choice between mail and retail pharmacies, but we've found our average price of a 90-day prescription filled at retail is $20 less than our average price of a mail order prescription. Numbers like that get the attention of benefit managers."

- On September 27, 2004, Walgreen announced that it had completed thirty years of consecutive increases in sales and profits—only one of two companies among the *Fortune* 500 to achieve a current streak of that duration. What's more, it continued its aggressive expansion program, opening 436 new stores in fiscal 2004, including 208 in the fourth quarter alone.

- In fiscal 2004, Walgreens gained market share against all food, drug, and mass merchandise competitors in fifty-nine of its top sixty product categories, as measured by A.C. Nielsen. This represents more than 60 percent of Walgreens self-service sales. The gains, moreover, outpaced aggressive store expansion, reflecting growth in existing stores.

- Some investors are concerned that the company is diluting sales by putting stores so close together, thus cannibalizing itself. To that concern, Mr. Bernauer replied, "I haven't gone to a party in two years where that question hasn't come up. The answer is yes—when we open a store very near another one, the old store usually sees a drop in sales. But in virtually every case, it builds back to its original volume and beyond. Here's the scenario: as you add stores, overall sales in the market increase, while expenses are spread over a larger base. Bottom line, *profitability* increases. Our most profitable markets are the ones where we've built the strongest market share."

- Investors are also wondering about e-commerce. They ask, "Is there a long-term future?" To this concern, Mr. Bernauer said, "Though there's a lot of carnage on the early e-commerce road, we definitely see a future for *www.walgreens.com*. That's not, however, in "delivered-to-your-door" merchandise. Frankly, we never thought there would be a big demand for prescriptions by mail, and we were correct—well over 90 percent of prescription orders placed through our Web site are for store pickup. It's not convenient, when you need a prescription or a few drugstore items to wait three days for it to show up.

 "What *does* excite us is using the Internet to provide better service and information. We're already communicating by e-mail with nearly 20,000 prescription customers per day."

- Prescriptions, which accounted for sixty-three percent of sales in fiscal 2004, climbed 9.7 percent in the fourth quarter of 2004 and 10.9 percent of sales for the full year. Walgreens filled 443 million prescriptions in 2004, an increase of 10.8 percent over the previous year.

- The company's new pharmacy system, Intercom Plus, is now up and running in all Walgreen stores across the country. This system—costing over $150 million—has raised Walgreens service and productivity to a new level.

- A high number of drugs are coming off patent over the next few years, which means more generic drugs will come to market and will become a bigger percentage of prescriptions. To be sure, generics have a much lower price, but the drug store can add on a bigger profit.

- Recently, a major grocery chain cited drugstores as a reason behind disappointing sales gains: "Fill-in shopping needs," said the grocery CEO, "are increasingly being satisfied in convenience and drug stores." Walgreens, with highly convenient, on-the-way-home locations, is on the receiving end of this trend.

- With stores in forty-four states and Puerto Rico, Walgreens has a base of customers that covers more of the United States than any other drugstore chain. The company's national coverage is a major advantage in negotiations with managed-care pharmacy companies.

- Joseph Agnese, an analyst with *Standard & Poor's Stock Reports,* also had some kind words on January 4, 2005: "We have a STRONG BUY opinion on the shares. We see the valuation benefiting from a more favorable economic and competitive environment in 2005. We see continued improvement in the U.S. economy leading to improved store traffic conditions, as consumers take advantage of WAG's convenient locations and product offerings."

Total assets: $13,342 million,
Current ratio: 1.90
Common shares outstanding: 1022 million
Return on 2004 shareholders' equity: 17.6%

|  |  | 2004 | 2003 | 2002 | 2001 | 2000 | 1999 | 1998 | 1997 |
|---|---|---|---|---|---|---|---|---|---|
| Revenues (millions) | | 37,502 | 32,505 | 28,681 | 24,623 | 21,207 | 17,839 | 15,307 | 13,363 |
| Net income (millions) | | 1,360 | 1,176 | 1,019 | 886 | 756 | 624 | 514 | 436 |
| Earnings per share | | 1.32 | 1.14 | .99 | .86 | .74 | .62 | .51 | .44 |
| Dividends per share | | .18 | .15 | .15 | .14 | .14 | .13 | .13 | .12 |
| Price | high | 39.5 | 37.4 | 40.7 | 45.3 | 45.8 | 33.9 | 30.2 | 16.8 |
|  | low | 32.0 | 26.9 | 27.7 | 28.7 | 22.1 | 22.7 | 14.8 | 9.6 |

# Wal-Mart Stores, Inc.

702 Southwest Eighth Street ❏ P. O. Box 116 ❏ Bentonville, AR 72716–8611 ❏ (479) 273–8446 ❏ Direct dividend reinvestment plan available: (800) 438–6278 ❏ Web site: *www.walmartstores.com* ❏ Listed: NYSE ❏ Fiscal years end January 31st ❏ Ticker symbol: WMT ❏ S&P rating: A+ ❏ Value Line financial strength rating: A++

Wal-Mart did not appear to be a corporate colossus in 1962. That was the year that Sam Walton opened his first store in Rogers, Arkansas, with a sign saying "Wal-Mart Discount City. We sell for less." In the decades since, Wal-Mart has evolved into a $244-billion-a-year empire by selling—at a discount, of course—prodigious quantities of all manner of items, from clothing, food, hardware, and eye glasses to Kleenex, tooth brushes, pots and pans, and pharmaceuticals.

An essential key to Wal-Mart's success, says H. Lee Scott, the company's CEO, is "driving unnecessary costs out of businesses."

To keep prices at rock bottom, the company insists that its 65,000 suppliers become leaner machines that examine every farthing they spend. This ruthless drive to whittle away fat has clearly reshaped the practices of businesses that deal with Wal-Mart, as well as those that compete against them. Wal-Mart's strategies for holding costs in check—the use of cutting-edge technology, innovative logistics, reliance on imported goods, and a nonunion work force—are becoming industry standards.

## Company Profile

Wal-Mart is the world's number one retailer—larger than Sears, Kmart, and J.C. Penney combined. As of November 30, 2004, the company operated 1,363 Wal-Mart stores, 1,672 Supercenters, 550 Sam's Clubs, and seventy-six Neighborhood Markets in the United States. Internationally, the company operated units in the following countries: Mexico (687), Puerto Rico (54), Canada (246), Argentina (11),

Brazil (148), China (42), South Korea (16), Germany (92), and the United Kingdom (277). More than 100 million customers per week visit Wal-Mart Stores.

Wal-Mart operates four different retail concepts:

*Wal-Mart Discount Stores.* Since founder Sam Walton opened his first store in 1962, Wal-Mart has built more than 1,600 discount stores in the United States. The stores range in size from 40,000 to 125,000 square feet and carry 80,000 different items, including family apparel, automotive products, health and beauty aids, home furnishings, electronics, hardware, toys, sporting goods, lawn and garden items, pet supplies, jewelry, and housewares.

*Wal-Mart Supercenters.* Developed in 1988 to meet the growing demand for one-stop family shopping, Wal-Mart Supercenters today number more than 1,430 nationwide and are open twenty-four hours a day. Supercenters save customers time and money by combining full grocery lines and general merchandise under one roof. These units range in size from 109,000 to 230,000 square feet and carry 100,000 different items, 30,000 of which are grocery products.

*Wal-Mart Neighborhood Markets.* These stores offer groceries, pharmaceuticals, and general merchandise. Generally, these units are situated in markets with Wal-Mart Supercenters, supplementing a strong food distribution network and providing added convenience while maintaining Wal-Mart's everyday low prices. First opened in 1998, Neighborhood Markets range from 42,000 to 55,000 square feet and feature a wide variety of products, including fresh produce, deli foods, fresh meat and dairy items, health and beauty aids, one-hour photo, and drive-through pharmacies, to name a few.

*Sam's Clubs.* The nation's leading members-only warehouse club offers a broad selection of general merchandise and large-volume items at value prices. Since 1983, Sam's Club has been the preferred choice for small businesses, families, or anyone looking for great prices on name-brand products. Ranging in size from 110,000 to 130,000 square feet, the 533 Sam's Clubs nationwide offer merchandise for both office and personal use, bulk paper products, furniture, computer hardware, and software, groceries, television sets, and clothing. A nominal membership fee ($30 per year for businesses and $35 for individuals) helps defray operating costs and keeps prices exceptionally low.

## Shortcomings to Bear in Mind

- At 192,000 square feet, Wal-Mart Supercenters are about the size of four football fields. Wal-Mart quickly found that some customers have trouble navigating them. According to one shopper, "The stores are too big. It takes too long to get around." On the other hand, the store's "really good prices" keep them coming back, but warns, "We've just about decided we'll go somewhere else and pay more not to have to go through all the hassle."
- Unfortunately, there are a number of clouds hanging over the world's largest retailer, including its pending (as of late 2004) appeal of a sexual discrimination class-action lawsuit, as well as other litigation alleging problems related to its labor practices.

## Reasons to Buy

- Wal-Mart's success is no secret. The company was named "Retailer of the Century" by *Discount Store News;* made *Fortune* magazine's lists of the "Most Admired Companies in America" and the "100 Best Companies to Work For" and was ranked on *Financial Times* "Most Respected in the World" list.
- Wal-Mart makes a concerted effort to find out precisely what its customers want. To do this, the company relies on information technology. It does this by collecting and analyzing internally developed information, which it calls "data-mining." It has been doing this since 1990.

The result, by now, is an enormous database of purchasing information that enables management to place the right item in the right store at the right time. The company's computer system receives 8.4 million updates every minute on the items that customers take home—and the relationship between the items in each basket.

Many retailers talk a good game when it comes to mining data at cash registers as a way to build sales. Wal-Mart, since it has been doing this for the past dozen years, is sitting on an information trove so vast and detailed that it far exceeds what many manufacturers know about their own products. What's more, Wal-Mart's database is second in size only to that of the U.S. government, says one analyst. Wal-Mart also collects "market-basket data" from customer receipts at all of its stores, so it knows what products are likely to be purchased together. The company receives about 100,000 queries a week from suppliers and its own buyers looking for purchase patterns or checking a product.

Wal-Mart plans to use the data in its new Neighborhood Markets. Equipped with a drive-through pharmacy and selling both dry goods and perishables, the stores are a little smaller than typical suburban supermarkets. They are much smaller than Wal-Mart's Supercenters, the massive grocery-discount store combinations that Wal-Mart began opening in 1988.

This kind of information has significant value in and of itself. According to management, "Consider Wal-Mart's ability to keep the shelves stocked with exactly what customers want most, but still be able to keep inventories under tight control. Consider the common banana—so common, in fact, that the grocery carts of America contain bananas more often than any other single item. So why not make it easy for a shopper to remember bananas? In Wal-Mart grocery departments, bananas can be found not just in the produce section, but in the cereal and dairy aisles too."

- Wal-Mart has leaned some painful lessons about consumers, regulators, and suppliers around the world. Through trial and error, the company has quietly built a powerful force outside the United States. It's now the biggest retailer in Canada and Mexico.
- Argus Research Company had some favorable comments on February 17, 2005. Chris Graja, CFA, said "While it is clear that Wal-Mart faces challenges and risks, a major reason for our BUY recommendation is that other retailers must face Wal-Mart. The company's size, financial strength, and skill in managing expenses and logistics make it a formidable threat in almost any business it wants to enter. We also believe that these same attributes will help it to expand and gain market share around the world."
- "We have a STRONG BUY recommendation on the shares," said Joseph Agnese, writing for *Standard & Poor's Stock Reports* on February 25, 2005. "We view WMT as remaining well positioned

to increase its U.S. market share, due to continued low price leadership and an expanding merchandise assortment with improving quality. We concur with the company's view of a more favorable consumer spending outlook."

- On December 13, 2004, *Barron's* financial weekly had an upbeat appraisal of Wal-Mart, according to Jonathan R. Laing, who said "Wal-Mart is still increasing its store capacity by around 8 percent a year and has plenty of room to grow, in the Northeast and Western U.S., as well as overseas. The company estimates that it has some 2,700 'expansion opportunities' in the U.S. to add to its existing 3,600 domestic stores between replacing older discount stores with supercenters and building some 1,500 new stores. Wal-Mart is starting to achieve meaningful heft in Europe, South America, Japan, and China."

The Barron's article went on to say, "In addition, no retailer comes close to Wal-Mart's huge cost advantage as a result of its prodigious lead in sourcing, distribution, and other supply-side skills. The company hopes to double its share of U.S. retail sales in the years ahead from roughly 8 percent to 15 percent, while continuing to garner strong margins and returns on investments."

- "Wal-Mart—since it acquired the largest Mexican chain, Cifra, seven years ago—has efficiently seized 55 percent of Mexico's retail market (as measured among the four biggest publicly traded chains only)," according to an article in *Forbes* magazine on December 27, 2004, written by Richard C. Morais. "The former number two, Controladora Comercial Mexicana, a supermarket and restaurant chain, is down to a 15 percent share of the market, and the fast-falling number three, Grupo Gigante, is below 13 percent."

Total assets: $121 billion
Current ratio: 0.89
Common shares outstanding: 4,235 million
Return on 2004 shareholders' equity: 22.8%

|  |  | 2004 | 2003 | 2002 | 2001 | 2000 | 1999 | 1998 | 1997 |
|---|---|---|---|---|---|---|---|---|---|
| Revenues (millions) | | 288,189 | 258,681 | 244,524 | 217,799 | 191,329 | 165,013 | 137,634 | 117,958 |
| Net income (millions) | | 10,267 | 9,054 | 8,039 | 6,671 | 6,295 | 5,377 | 4,430 | 3,526 |
| Earnings per share | | 2.41 | 2.07 | 1.81 | 1.49 | 1.40 | 1.28 | .99 | .78 |
| Dividends per share | | .48 | .36 | .30 | .28 | .24 | .20 | .16 | .14 |
| Price | high | 61.3 | 60.2 | 63.9 | 58.8 | 68.9 | 70.3 | 41.4 | 21.0 |
|  | low | 51.1 | 46.2 | 43.7 | 41.5 | 41.4 | 38.7 | 18.8 | 11.0 |

Income

# Washington Real Estate Investment Trust

6110 Executive Boulevard ❏ Suite 800 ❏ Rockville, MD 20852 ❏ (301) 255–0761 ❏ Listed: NYSE ❏ Direct dividend reinvestment plan available: (877) 386–8123 ❏ Web site: *www.writ.com* ❏ Ticker symbol: WRE ❏ S&P rating: A- ❏ Value Line Financial Strength B++

"Real Estate Investment Trusts come in many flavors," said Brendan Coffey and Kurt Badenhausen, writing for *Forbes* magazine on December 13, 2004. "While REITs broadly track the economy, the various real estate sectors respond to different stimuli. Office REITs, the most numerous kind, are prey to the economic vicissitudes of the cities where they own property. The fortunes of health-care REITs are linked to Medicare reimbursement rates.

"Here, by category, we have assembled a list of REITs that are among the best over the past five years at increasing earnings—in REITland, called 'adjusted funds from operations.'

"Roughly speaking, AFFO is net income plus depreciation, minus upkeep costs, according to REIT analysts Green Street Advisors."

This is what the *Forbes* article had to say about Washington Real Estate Investment Trust:

"Diversified. These invest in a variety of properties, meaning they have had a decent

26 percent total return year to date. The standout here is Washington REIT, with a hand in everything from offices (at 46 percent, its largest holding) to apartments (15 percent). True to its name, this trust sticks to the Washington area, the fastest-growing region for two decades. One of its buildings houses offices of the International Monetary Fund and the World Bank."

## Company Profile

Washington Real Estate Investment Trust, founded in 1960, invests in a diversified range of income-producing properties. Management's purpose is to acquire and manage real estate investments in markets it knows well and to protect the company's assets from the risk of owning a single property-type, such as apartments, office buildings, industrial parks, or shopping centers.

WREIT achieves its objectives by owning properties in four different categories. The trust's properties are primarily situated within a two-hour radius of Washington, D.C. that stretches from Philadelphia in the north to Richmond, Virginia, in the south. At the end of 2004, its diversified portfolio consisted of sixty-nine properties: thirty-one office properties, eleven retail centers, nine multifamily properties, and eighteen industrial properties.

According to the company's 10-K report, "Our geographic focus is based on two principles:

"1. Real estate is a local business and is much more effectively selected and managed by owners located and with expertise in the region.

"2. Geographic markets deserving of focus must be among the nation's best markets with a strong primary industry foundation and be diversified enough to withstand downturns in their primary industry.

"We consider markets to be local if they can be reached from the Washington-centered market within two hours by car. Our Washington-centered market reaches north to Philadelphia, Pennsylvania and south to Richmond, Virginia. While we have historically focused most of our investments in the Greater Washington-Baltimore Region, in order to maximize acquisition opportunities, we will and have considered investments within the two-hour radius described above. We also will consider opportunities to duplicate our Washington-focused approach in other geographic markets which meet the criteria described above.

"All of our Trustees, officers, and employees live and work in the Greater Washington-Baltimore region, and our officers average more than twenty years experience in this region."

## Shortcomings to Bear in Mind

- Although WREIT is well diversified by type of property, it is not diversified geographically, since all of its holdings are within a two-hour radius of Washington, D.C. In the event of a serious disaster in that region, Washington Real Estate Investment Trust might have problems.

By contrast, many REITS have scores of properties across the United States, thus shielding them from hard times or natural disasters in any one location.

- *Value Line Investment Survey* doesn't share my enthusiasm for this stock. On January 21, 2005, Fritz R. Owens said, "This issue is ranked to lag the market in the year ahead. The stock also offers lackluster total-return potential out to 2007–2009. And although risk-averse, income-oriented investors may like WRE's record of 34 years of increasing dividends and its high Safety rank, they should be able to find better selections elsewhere."

## Reasons to Buy

- If you had invested $10,000 in Washington Real Estate at the end of 1971, your shares would have been worth $2,638,974 at the end of 2004.
- "Over the last few year, we have become more focused on adding modern medical office buildings to the portfolio," said CEO Edmund B. Cronin, Jr. in 2004. "Medical buildings, particularly new ones, located near growing, major hospital centers generally have very low volatility. In October 2003, we acquired a three-building medical office property, known as Prosperity Medical Park, located in Fairfax County, Virginia, near Inova Hospital. The buildings contain 255,000 square feet with on-side parking for staff and patients. At acquisition, the property was 98 percent leased, and is now 100 percent leased."
- Mr. Cronin is convinced that WREIT has lower risk than most investments. "One aspect of this lower risk profile is that the greater Washington-Baltimore technology sector achieves 38 percent of its sales to the federal government, as compared to 5 percent in Silicon Valley. That, along with the fact that federal government spending will continue to grow,

provides a platform for a soft landing in this region."

■ The Greater Washington, D.C. economy is a unique blend of "old economy" service companies and "new economy" high-technology growth companies, anchored by the very significant Federal government presence. On the growth side:

• Washington Dulles International Airport and Baltimore-Washington International Airport were ranked number one and two in passenger growth in 1999, the most recent year for which data are available.

• The Greater Washington region ranks first in the United States in high-tech and bio-tech employment.

• George Mason University Center for Regional Analysis (GMU) projects economic growth in the region of 4.1 percent in 2001, which is substantially higher than is projected for the nation as a whole.

• Federal spending in this region has increased every year for twenty-one consecutive years, even in years when federal spending has decreased nationally. GMU projects federal spending in the region will grow by 3 percent per year.

While growth is very important, from an investment perspective, economic stability is equally important. In this context, no other region in the country can compete with the Greater Washington region:

• Federal government spending accounts for 31 percent of the area's Gross Regional Product.

• The Greater Washington region is not exposed to new or old economy manufacturing fluctuations.

• Greater Washington is home to thirty-two colleges and universities, several of which have world-class reputations at both the undergraduate and graduate levels.

■ MAE East, situated in Tysons Corner, Virginia, is one of only two Internet convergence centers in the United States. The presence of MAE East and the thousands of high-tech firms in the area has spawned a concentration of data centers in the region where large Internet and other high-tech firms process tremendous amounts of data. As a result, it is estimated that up to 60 percent of the world's Internet traffic flows through Northern Virginia.

This concentration of high-tech companies has served to attract even more high-tech firms. Amazon.com, Cisco Systems, and Global Crossing have all set up shop in the Washington-Baltimore market.

The region's real estate markets are the beneficiary of this growth. Vacancies are extremely low, and rental rate growth is very strong.

■ Prior to acquiring a property, WREIT performs extensive inspections, tests, and financial analyzes to gain confidence about the property's future operating performance, as well as any required near-term improvements and long-term capital expenditures. Upon completion of this evaluation, the company develops well-informed operating projections for the property. Accordingly, when the company announces an acquisition and its anticipated return on investment, it is confident that the property will meet or exceed its projections.

■ Washington Real Estate Investment Trust has always recognized the value of capital improvements to remain competitive, increase revenues, reduce operating costs, and maintain and increase the value of its properties.

Total assets: $1,012 million
Current ratio: not relevant
Return on 2004 equity: 12.4%
Common shares outstanding: 42 million

| | 2004 | 2003 | 2002 | 2001 | 2000 | 1999 | 1998 | 1997 |
|---|---|---|---|---|---|---|---|---|
| Revenues (millions) | 172 | 164 | 153 | 148 | 135 | 119 | 104 | 79 |
| Net income (millions) | 46 | 45 | 52 | 52 | 45 | 44 | 41 | 30 |
| Funds from operations | 2.05 | 2.05 | 1.98 | 1.96 | 1.79 | 1.57 | 1.39 | 1.23 |
| Earnings per share | 1.09 | 1.13 | 1.32 | 1.38 | 1.16 | 1.02 | .96 | .90 |
| Dividends per share | 1.55 | 1.49 | 1.39 | 1.31 | 1.23 | 1.16 | 1.11 | 1.07 |
| Price high | 34.4 | 31.3 | 30.2 | 25.5 | 25.0 | 18.8 | 18.8 | 19.6 |
| low | 25.2 | 24.0 | 20.4 | 20.8 | 14.3 | 13.8 | 15.1 | 15.5 |

Growth and Income

# Wells Fargo & Company

420 Montgomery Street ❑ San Francisco, CA 94163 ❑ (415) 396–0523 ❑ Direct dividend reinvestment plan available: (800) 813–3324 ❑ Web site: *www.wellsfargo.com* ❑ Listed: NYSE ❑ Ticker symbol: WFC ❑ S&P rating: A ❑ Value Line financial strength rating: A+

On November 4, 2004, Wells Fargo said it was the first major U.S. bank to serve the $6-billion Philippine Remittance Market. "Wells Fargo has been a pioneer in providing remittance products and services that are safe, convenient and affordable," said Gene Gutierrez, product development manager, Wells Fargo Cross Border Payments Group. "Our Philippine Remittance product continues that tradition and offers our customers an important service that allows them to send money to family and friends in the Asia-Pacific region."

There are about 2 million U.S. residents of Filipino descent living in the United States, almost half of them in California. The domestic remittance market is a $50-billion business, and Filipino-bound remittances represent 8 percent of that total.

The International ATM Remittance Account to the Philippines is an account-to-ATM product. Wells Fargo customers in the United States can deposit funds into a dedicated consumer account, which are available the next business day for pick-up through a network of more than 4,000 ATMs

(MegaLink or ExpressNet) in the Philippines. Beneficiaries in the Philippines, using their pre-sent ATM cards, can access the account and withdraw up to $400 per day in cash.

This is the company's second international entry into the estimated $110-billion global remittance market. In 1995, Wells Fargo launched InterCuenta Express, the money-transfer product between the U.S. and Mexico, and in June 2004, with its partner banks, created the largest consumer remittance distribution network by a U.S. bank in Mexico.

## Company Profile

Wells Fargo & Company is a diversified financial services company, providing banking, insurance, investments, mortgages, and consumer finance from more than 5,900 stores, the Internet (*www.wellsfargo.com*) and other distribution channels across North America. Wells Fargo Bank, N.A. is the only "Aaa"-rated bank in the United States.

As of 2004, Wells Fargo had $397 billion in assets, was the fifth-largest among its domestic peers, and the market value of the stock ranked third among its peers.

In community banking, Wells Fargo has 3,076 stores in twenty-three states; 16.4 million customers, and is the nation's most extensive banking franchise. Its banking stores break down as follows:

| | | |
|---|---|---|
| Alaska (51) | Michigan (25) | Oregon (130) |
| Arizona (233) | Minnesota (179) | South Dakota (59) |
| California (831) | Montana (49) | Texas (510) |
| Colorado (130) | Nebraska (44) | Utah (141) |
| Idaho (95) | Nevada (104) | Washington (153) |
| Illinois (14) | New Mexico (104) | Wisconsin (58) |
| Indiana (39) | North Dakota (28) | Wyoming (18) |
| Iowa (80) | Ohio (1) | |

### Wells Fargo Card Services
In the realm of card services, WFC has:
- 6 million credit card accounts.
- $6.2 billion in average consumer credit cards outstanding.
- The nation's number two issuer of credit cards.
- 15.48 million debit card accounts.

Wells Fargo is the number one originator of home mortgages and the number two servicer of residential mortgages. Combined, the company's retail and wholesale lending operations fund about one of every eight homes financed annually in the United States.

Here is a summary of the company's home mortgage operations:
- Serving all fifty states through more than 1,900 mortgage and Wells Fargo banking stores, and the Internet.
- The nation's number one retail home mortgage lender.
- 4.9 million customers.
- Originations: $470 billion.
- Servicing: $753 billion.

### Credit Card Group
A leading provider of home equity and personal credit accounts with a combined portfolio of $64 billion. Sales channels include Retail Banking, Wells Fargo Home Mortgage, CCG Direct-to-Consumer (Internet/wellsfargo.com, telesales, and direct mail), wholesale and third-party mortgage brokers, finance companies, indirect dealer programs, and other third-party partners. In summary, this is how WFC stacks up:
- One of America's largest and fastest-growing providers of home equity and personal credit.
- Serving more than 2.1 million customer households.
- Largest lender of prime home equity (loans and lines of credit).
- First to introduce Home Asset Management Account, which combines a mortgage and home equity line of credit, enabling customers to finance a home in an all-in-one process.
- Number one in personal credit market share in Wells Fargo banking states.
- Largest provider of auto loans, excluding captive finance companies.

## Shortcomings to Bear in Mind
- In recent years, banks have been finding it increasingly difficult to expand revenues. Those with the broadest product mix are more likely to have an easier time registering top-line growth. In addition, savings from cost-cutting efforts, which have propelled earnings for many large banks in recent years, are becoming more difficult to come by, placing greater emphasis on top-line growth.
- *Standard & Poor's Stock Reports* had some disturbing comments on January 19, 2005, according to its analyst, Evan M. Momios, CFA, "The shares were up about 6 percent in 2004, compared to a 9 percent increase for the S&P 500. Based on the stock's valuation versus peers, and what we consider a mixed operating outlook, we expect the shares to be

average performers in the year ahead and we would remain on the sidelines."

## Reasons to Buy

- Highlights of 2004:
  - Record diluted Earnings per share of $4.09, up 12 percent from prior year's $3.65
  - Record net income of $7.0 billion, up 13 percent from prior year's $6.2 billion
  - Return on equity of 19.6 percent
  - Record revenue of $30.1 billion, up 6 percent from prior year; 11 percent revenue growth in businesses other than Wells Fargo Home Mortgage
  - Noninterest expense up 2 percent from prior year
- In 2004, CEO Richard M. Kovacevich said, "Businesses with annual revenues up to $20 million are the hub of job growth in our banking markets. We have an outstanding team of business bankers. We're now giving them more than central support—information systems, staffing models, and performance standards—so they can spend more time with customers and earn all their business, not just loans and deposits, but treasury management, 401(k)plans, trust services, merchant card, and their personal business, including investments."

  Mr. Kovacevich goes on to say, "A business banking customer of Wells Fargo can choose from among forty-seven products. Yet our average business banking customer has only 2.5 products with us. Half of them have only one product with us! Our goals in business banking are to double revenue in five years, get to five products per customer, be the primary provider for all their financial needs (business and personal) and be known as the best business bank in every single one of our markets."

- "Wells Fargo is well-positioned for growth over the pull to 2007–2009," said Randy Shrikishun, writing for *Value Line Investment Survey* on February 25, 2005. "Commercial loan activity will probably continue to rebound over this period, as the economic environment improves. Also, we believe the level of net charge-offs and nonperforming assets will decrease over the coming years."
- Wells Fargo's diversity of businesses makes the company much more than a bank. According to a WFC spokesman, "We're a diversified financial services company. Financial services is a highly fragmented and fast-growing industry. Our diversity helps us weather downturns that inevitably affect any one segment of our industry."

  Here's how diversified Wells Fargo is:

  Percentage of earnings
  - Community banking — 36%
  - Investments and insurance — 14%
  - Home mortgage and home equity — 19%
  - Specialized lending — 13%
  - Wholesale banking — 8%
  - Consumer finance — 6%
  - Commercial real estate — 4%

- Wells Fargo is a major player in the banking industry, as noted below:
  - No. 2 in total stores (5,900 stores)
  - No. 2 in banking (3,023 stores)
  - No. 1 in mortgages (1,009 stand-alone stores, 947 Wells Fargo banking stores with mortgage salespeople)
  - No. 1 in supermarkets (675 stores)
  - No. 4 consumer finance (1,241 stores)
  - No. 1 Internet bank (5.2 million active online customers)
  - A leading phone bank (20 million calls a month)
  - No. 3 ATM network (6,183 ATMs)

**Total assets: $322 billion**
**Return on average assets in 2004: 1.65%**
**Common shares outstanding: 1,692 million**
**Return on 2004 shareholders' equity: 19.6%**

|  | 2004 | 2003 | 2002 | 2001 | 2000 | 1999 | 1998 | 1997 |
|---|---|---|---|---|---|---|---|---|
| Loans (millions) | 269,600 | 249,182 | 192,772 | 168,738 | 157,405 | 116,294 | 104,860 | 41,288 |
| Total assets (millions) | 320,000 | 387,798 | 349,259 | 307,569 | 272,426 | 218,102 | 202,475 | 88,540 |
| Net income (millions) | 7,014 | 6,202 | 5,710 | 3,423 | 4,026 | 3,747 | 2,906 | 1,351 |
| Earnings per share | 4.09 | 3.65 | 3.32 | 1.97 | 2.33 | 2.23 | 1.75 | 1.75 |
| Dividends per share | 1.86 | 1.50 | 1.10 | 1.00 | .90 | .79 | .62 | .62 |
| Price    high | 64.0 | 59.2 | 54.8 | 54.8 | 56.4 | 49.9 | 43.9 | 39.5 |
| low | 54.3 | 43.3 | 38.1 | 38.3 | 31.4 | 32.2 | 27.5 | 21.4 |

# Index of Stocks by Category

# About the Author

John Slatter has a varied investment background and has served as a stock broker, securities analyst, and portfolio strategist. He is now a consultant with Klopp Investment Management, a firm in Cleveland, Ohio, that manages investment portfolios on a fee basis.

John Slatter has written hundreds of articles for such publications as *Barron's*, *Physician's Management*, *Ophthalmology Times*, and *Better Investing*, as well as for brokerage firms he has worked for, including Hugh Johnson & Company, and Wachovia Securities. His books include *Safe Investing*, *Straight Talk About Stock Investing*, and nine prior editions of *The 100 Best Stocks You Can Buy*.

John Slatter has been quoted in such periodicals as the *Cleveland Plain Dealer*, the *New York Times*, the *Gannett News Service*, the *Burlington Free Press*, the *Wall Street Journal*, the *Cincinnati Enquirer*, the *Toledo Blade*, the *Christian Science Monitor*, *Money Magazine*, the *Dayton Daily News*, and the *Buffalo News*. He has also been quoted in a number of books, including *The Dividend Investor* and *Stocks for the Long Run*, and he has also been interviewed on a number of radio stations, as well as by the CNBC daily television program *Today's Business*.

In August of 1988, John Slatter was featured in the *Wall Street Journal* concerning his innovative investment strategy that calls for investing in the ten highest-yielding stocks in the Dow Jones Industrial Average. This approach to stock selection is sometimes referred as "The Dogs of the Dow," a pejorative reference that Mr. Slatter does not believe is justified, since the stocks with high yields have, in the past, included such blue chips as Merck, IBM, 3M, General Electric, AT&T, Caterpillar, DuPont, ExxonMobil, J.P. Morgan Chase, and Altria.

John Slatter may be reached by calling (802) 879–4154 (during business hours only) or by writing him at 70 Beech Street, Essex Junction, Vermont 05452. His e-mail address is *john.slatter@verizon.net*.